P9-ARH-938

Brandnames: Who Owns What

(Revised)

Diane Waxer Frankenstein
in consultation with
George Frankenstein

Facts On File Publications
New York, New York • Oxford, England

Brandnames: Who Owns What (Revised)

Library of Congress Cataloging in Publication Data

Frankenstein, Diane.
Brandnames, who owns what.

Includes index.
1. United States—Manufactures—Directories.
2. Trade-marks—United States—Directories.
I. Frankenstein, George, joint author. II. Title.
T12.F72 602'.75 80-23592
ISBN 0-8160-1193-1

Printed in the United States of America
10 9 8 7 6 5 4 3 2 1

Contents

INTRODUCTION

The consumer sector of the U.S. economy has changed dramatically over the past 30 years. From hundreds of thousands of small, medium and even larger companies, the sector has consolidated into fewer, much larger diversified corporations.

Why this trend toward consolidation? Perhaps the most significant reason is the cost of capital. Consumer companies need capital to expand. The capital-rich large public corporations offer resources small companies cannot reasonably obtain. Selling out to a large corporation becomes the only way to gain needed capital. This trend has been important in the publishing industry. Publishers, traditionally cash poor, have sold out to conglomerates for access to capital to fund extensive projects and pay increasingly large advances. The trend was important in apparel as well.

Because of the cost of capital, large corporations are divesting themselves of divisions that either do not meet long-term strategic objectives or do not give an adequate return on investment. Such divisions are sold off so this capital can be redirected.

Still another reason for consolidation is the fact that smaller companies can no longer compete with large, well-capitalized corporations. Large corporations have resources that go beyond capital. These include depth and continuity of management; marketing expertise and greater advertising and distribution penetration from the same advertising dollar. For example, if you have 10 retail stores in the New York area and advertise in the *New York Times,* you get more extensive penetration than if you had two stores and must buy the same advertising space.

A third factor aiding consolidation is that smaller one product or one industry companies are more vulnerable to market changes and economic cycles. This has been most evident in such industries as recreational vehicles, housing and apparel. Many conglomerates have large participation in one industry, but because they are extremely diversified they can withstand economic swings without showing drastic cycles in earnings.

To stay in the forefront of the competition, research and development is very important. Again this is very expensive, and without sufficient resources smaller companies may have to compromise their goals. Technology has significantly changed almost every industry. If a company falls behind in technological development, it may not be able to compete. The computer and information processing industry is in the forefront of this change; General Motors now employs robots to improve efficiency; the apparel industry uses computer automated design and manufacturing; the computerized toy industry changes constantly; medical technology from lasers to pharmaceuticals is in perpetual forward motion.

Changing life styles and demographic changes have forced some companies to diversify as their markets change. This can be best illustrated by some examples:

-As the baby boom slowed, Gerber Products, known for baby food, went into life insurance for the elderly.

-Northwest Industries began as Chicago & Northwestern Railroad and, as the railroad industry changed, it used its assets to get into such businesses as leather boots and liquor.

-RCA saw the change in a mature TV market and diversified into consumer finance and bought Hertz Rent-A-Car.

Consolidation was not always by choice. Many mergers and acquisitions were public companies that were swallowed up by purchasing the stock on the open market or offering the shareholders substantial premiums for their stock. Efficient use of capital came into play—a company could buy another public company at far below the real asset value rather than start their own company.

**Fortune* (May 5, 1980), 92-93

The past 30 years has seen dramatic changes in entire industries. Foreign competition has changed many sources of our products. This is evident in the shoe, automobile and consumer electronic industries.

Brandnames: Who Owns What is designed to provide the consumer and businessperson with an easily accessible guide to the corporation that ultimately owns each product. Other reference works dealing with the structure of the modern corporation link the product with the subsidiary that produces it. This subsidiary in turn is owned by a larger parent corporation. By using *Brandnames,* the researcher can easily uncover the ultimate owner of the product and at the same time get an overview of the modern large corporation in its diversity.

Not all consumer products sold in the United States are listed in *Brandnames.* Given the number of businesses and the regional nature of many consumer companies, this would prove impossible. There were several criteria for inclusion. First, size. Second, that the company be listed on one of the major U.S. stock exchanges, i.e. the New York Stock Exchange, the American Stock Exchange or traded Over The Counter. This criteria excludes the vast majority of foreign corporations selling products in the United States. Only those such as Mitsubishi, which is listed on the New York Stock Exchange, are discussed. We have, however, included an appendix listing the brandnames associated with about 30 of the largest foreign corporations in terms of U.S. sales.

Brandnames also excludes companies dealing solely in customer services. Therefore the giant Bank of America is omitted, but Continental Corp., a giant in insurance and financial services is included because it owns Diners Club.

Brandnames includes entries on more than 700 major consumer corporations. Each contains the name, address and telephone number of the company as well as the name of the chief executive officer. Sales figures and number of shareholders are included to give the reader a measure of the size of the corporation and the pattern of holding. We have also given the exchange on which the stock is traded and company's symbol on the exchange.

Each entry contains a brief historical description of the company. This history is not a detailed analysis of corporation growth but a quick look at how a company has changed over time. In many cases this is done simply by citing changes in the company's name. For example, American Standard, Inc., now a diversified producer of building products and security equipment, traces its history back to the American Radiator Co., which produced only steam and hot water radiators. During the 1920's when it acquired Standard Sanitary, the leader in plumbing fixtures, it changed its name to American Radiator and Standard Sanitary Corp. The history also describes the types of activities in which the company is currently involved and, where important, what its future plans are.

The main portion of each entry is a listing and description of all consumer brands the company and its subsidiaries produce. Individual models are excluded. Therefore, in the Ford entry, you will find only "Ford—automobiles". The models are omitted. We have also left out franchises and distributorships.

The information was obtained from corporate annual reports and business periodicals, i.e. Standard & Poors, Moody's statistical services, etc. These sources are believed to be reliable, but their accuracy and completeness are not guaranteed. The book has been indexed to help the reader locate information either by the company's name or brand name product.

A great many people helped write this book. Papa Joe and Mama Bette sparked the idea for the book. Julian Bach had faith in the idea and backed me as an unknown author. Eleanora Schoenebaum was a delight to work with. Her expertise and good humor were always an inspiration. George initially gave me the interest in the business that motivated me to write this and kept me going with continued animated discussions on the dynamic world of business. Alyson Kuhn completed the typing between our many breakfasts and other breaks. Special thanks for their editorial assistance are extended to Katherine Bruce, Ellen Meltzer, and Donald Paneth.

Section I

Who Owns What
by
Category of Products

Section I

Who Owns What by Category of Products

Alcohol

Aalborg Akvait / *American Brands Inc.*
Adam's Antique Canadian Whiskies / *Seagram Co. Ltd.*
Adriatica / *National Distillers & Chemical Corp.*
Alberta Springs / *National Distillers & Chemical Corp.*
Almaden / *National Distillers & Chemical Corp.*
Altes / *G. Heileman Brewing Co. Inc.*
Amaretto di Saronno / *Glenmore Distilleries Co.*
Ambassador Deluxe / *Hiram Walker Resources Ltd.*
American / *Standard Brands Inc.*
Amigo Hermanos / *Safeway Stores Inc.*
Andeker / *Pabst Brewing Co.*
Anheuser-Busch / *Anheuser-Busch Companies Inc.*
Annie Green Springs Wine / *Heublein Inc.*
Arrow Cordials / *Heublein Inc.*
B & B / *Standard Brands Inc.*
Bacardi / *Bacardi Corp.*
Bahia Liqueur / *Heublein Inc.*
Balfour Cream / *Glenmore Distilleries Co.*
Ballantine / *Hiram Walker Resources Ltd.*
Barclay's Gold Label / *Hiram Walker Resources Ltd.*
Barclay's Rare Old Gin / *Hiram Walker Resources Ltd.*
Barossa Valley / *Safeway Stores Inc.*
Barton & Guestier (B & G) / *Seagram Co. Ltd.*
Beam's Black Label / *American Brands Inc.*
Beam's Choice Bourbon / *American Brands Inc.*
Bellows / *National Distillers & Chemical Corp.*
Bellows Partners / *National Distillers & Chemical Corp.*
Bellows reserve / *National Distillers & Chemical Corp.*
Benchmark / *Seagram Co. Ltd.*
Bersano / *Seagram Co. Ltd.*
Big Cat / *Pabst Brewing Co.*
Black & White Scotch / *Heublein Inc.*
Black Horse Ale / *Iroquois Brands Ltd.*
Black Label L.A. / *G. Heileman Brewing Co. Inc.*
Black Velvet / *Heublein Inc.*
Blatz / *G. Heileman Brewing Co. Inc.*
Blatz L.A. / *G. Heileman Brewing Co. Inc.*
Blatz Light / *G. Heileman Brewing Co. Inc.*
Blatz Light Cream Ale / *G. Heileman Brewing Co. Inc.*
Blitz / *G. Heileman Brewing Co. Inc.*
Boggs / *Heublein Inc.*
Boissiere / *National Distillers & Chemical Corp.*
Bols / *Brown Forman Distillers Corp.*
Bond & Lillard / *National Distillers & Chemical Corp.*
Boodles / *Seagram Co. Ltd.*
Bourbon de Luxe / *National Distillers & Chemical Corp.*
Bourbon Supreme / *Standard Brands Inc.*
Bowling Green / *Safeway Stores Inc.*
Brigadier / *National Distillers & Chemical Corp.*
Brown Derby / *Safeway Stores Inc.*
Buckhorn / *Olympia Brewing Co.*
Budlight / *Anheuser-Busch Companies Inc.*
Burgermeister / *G. Heileman Brewing Co. Inc.*
Burgermeister / *Pabst Brewing Co.*
Burnett's / *Seagram Co. Ltd.*
Burton's / *Standard Brands Inc.*
Busch / *Anheuser-Busch Companies Inc.*
Cacique / *Seagram Co. Ltd.*
Cafe Lolita / *Standard Brands Inc.*
Calvert Extra / *Seagram Co. Ltd.*
Canada House / *National Distillers & Chemical Corp.*
Canadian Hill / *Safeway Stores Inc.*
Canadian Ltd. / *Standard Brands Inc.*
Canadian Mist / *Brown Forman Distillers Corp.*
Canadian Silk Whiskey / *American Brands Inc.*
Cappela / *Heublein Inc.*
Captain Morgan / *Seagram Co. Ltd.*
Carling Black Label / *G. Heileman Brewing Co. Inc.*
Carling Black Label Light / *G. Heileman Brewing Co. Inc.*
Carling Red Cap / *G. Heileman Brewing Co. Inc.*
Carstairs / *Seagram Co. Ltd.*
Cella / *Brown Forman Distillers Corp.*
Century Club / *National Distillers & Chemical Corp.*
Champale Sparkling Wines / *Iroquois Brands Ltd.*
Charles Lefrance / *National Distillers & Chemical Corp.*
Chateau de La Chaize / *Seagram Co. Ltd.*

Chateau-Vallee / *Early California Industries, Inc.*
Chateaux / *American Brands Inc.*
Cherry Elsinore / *Standard Brands Inc.*
Chivas Regal / *Seagram Co. Ltd.*
Choice / *National Distillers & Chemical Corp.*
Christian Brothers / *Seagram Co. Ltd.*
Churchill / *Standard Brands Inc.*
Club / *Heublein Inc.*
CocoRibe / *National Distillers & Chemical Corp.*
Colony / *Heublein Inc.*
Colt 45, Malt Liquor / *G. Heileman Brewing Co. Inc.*
Comandon / *Standard Brands Inc.*
Commemorativo / *National Distillers & Chemical Corp.*
Coors / *Adolph Coors Co.*
Coors Extra Gold / *Adolph Coors Co.*
Coors Light / *Adolph Coors Co.*
Corbett Canyon Vineyard / *Glenmore Distilleries Co.*
Corby's Reserve / *Hiram Walker Resources Ltd.*
Courvoisier / *Hiram Walker Resources Ltd.*
Crab Orchard / *National Distillers & Chemical Corp.*
Crown Royal Canadian / *Seagram Co. Ltd.*
Crown Russe / *Seagram Co. Ltd.*
Dark Eyes / *American Brands Inc.*
DeKruper / *National Distillers & Chemical Corp.*
DeKruyper Geneva / *National Distillers & Chemical Corp.*
Desmond & Duff 12-year-old / *Glenmore Distilleries Co.*
Dom Brau / *Safeway Stores Inc.*
Don Q / *Heublein Inc.*
Drewrys / *G. Heileman Brewing Co. Inc.*
Duval / *Standard Brands Inc.*
Early Times / *Brown Forman Distillers Corp.*
Eastside / *Pabst Brewing Co.*
Ed. Phillips & Sons / *Alco Standard Corp.*
El Toro / *Standard Brands Inc.*
Erlanger / *Joseph Schlitz Brewing Co.*
Erza Brooks / *Standard Brands Inc.*
Expresso Coffee / *Glenmore Distilleries Co.*
Fall City / *G. Heileman Brewing Co. Inc.*
Felipe II Spanish / *Glenmore Distilleries Co.*
Fidelis / *Safeway Stores Inc.*
Fleischmann's / *Standard Brands Inc.*
Foster's / *Nabisco Brands Inc.*
Foster's Lager / *Standard Brands Inc.*
Four Roses / *Seagram Co. Ltd.*
Frank Schoonmaker / *Seagram Co. Ltd.*
Frydenlund / *Safeway Stores Inc.*
Gambarelli & Davito / *Heublein Inc.*
Garnier / *Standard Brands Inc.*
Gavilan / *Glenmore Distilleries Co.*
George Killian's Irish Red / *Adolph Coors Co.*
Geyser Peak / *Joseph Schlitz Brewing Co.*
Gilbey's / *National Distillers & Chemical Corp.*
Glen Grant Single Malt / *Seagram Co. Ltd.*
Glenlivet / *Seagram Co. Ltd.*
Glenmore / *Glenmore Distilleries Co.*
Gold Seal / *Seagram Co. Ltd.*
Gooderham Bonded Stock / *Hiram Walker Resources Ltd.*
Government House / *Hiram Walker Resources Ltd.*
Grain Belt / *G. Heileman Brewing Co. Inc.*
Grand MacNish / *Hiram Walker Resources Ltd.*
Grande Marque Red and Grande Marque White / *National Distillers & Chemical Corp.*
Grauado / *Seagram Co. Ltd.*
Guasti / *Beatrice Companies Inc.*
Guckenheimer / *Standard Brands Inc.*
Gunther / *F. & M. Schaefer Corp.*
Hamm's / *Olympia Brewing Co.*
Hartley / *Heublein Inc.*
Harwood Canadian / *Seagram Co. Ltd.*
Heidelberg / *G. Heileman Brewing Co. Inc.*
Henry Baron / *National Distillers & Chemical Corp.*
Henry Weinhard / *G. Heileman Brewing Co. Inc.*
Henry Weinhard Private Reserve / *Pabst Brewing Co.*
Hepok Mostar / *National Distillers & Chemical Corp.*
Herman Joseph's 1868 / *Adolph Coors Co.*
Hermitage / *National Distillers & Chemical Corp.*
Heublein / *Heublein Inc.*
Hill and Hill / *National Distillers & Chemical Corp.*
Hine / *Norton Simon Inc.*
Hiram Walker / *Hiram Walker Resources Ltd.*
Hiram Walker Crystal / *Hiram Walker Resources Ltd.*
Hiram Walker Crystal Gin / *Hiram Walker Resources Ltd.*
Hiram Walker Special Canadian / *Hiram Walker Resources Ltd.*
Hiram Walker Special Old Canadian / *Hiram Walker Resources Ltd.*
Hornitos / *National Distillers & Chemical Corp.*
Hungarian Tokay & Table Wines / *Heublein Inc.*
Imperial / *Hiram Walker Resources Ltd.*
India / *Bacardi Corp.*
Inglenook / *Heublein Inc.*
Inver House / *Standard Brands Inc.*
Irish Mist / *Heublein Inc.*
Italian Swiss Colony / *Heublein Inc.*
Jack Daniels / *Brown Forman Distillers Corp.*
Jacques Bonet / *Heublein Inc.*
James Fox / *Seagram Co. Ltd.*
Jameson / *Seagram Co. Ltd.*
Jim Beam / *American Brands Inc.*

Jose Cuervo Tequila / *Heublein Inc.*
Kahlua / *Hiram Walker Resources Ltd.*
Kaiser / *Seagram Co. Ltd.*
Kamchatka / *National Distillers & Chemical Corp.*
Kamora Coffee Liqueur / *American Brands Inc.*
Karl Manheim / *Safeway Stores Inc.*
Kavlana / *Safeway Stores Inc.*
Keller Geister / *National Distillers & Chemical Corp.*
Kentucky Colonel / *National Distillers & Chemical Corp.*
Kentucky Silk / *National Distillers & Chemical Corp.*
Kentucky Tavern / *Glenmore Distilleries Co.*
Kessler / *Seagram Co. Ltd.*
Kijafa / *Seagram Co. Ltd.*
Kiku Masamune / *Heublein Inc.*
King George IV / *National Distillers & Chemical Corp.*
King James / *Standard Brands Inc.*
Kingsbury / *G. Heileman Brewing Co. Inc.*
Korbel / *Brown Forman Distillers Corp.*
LA / *Anheuser-Busch Companies Inc.*
La Mesa / *Safeway Stores Inc.*
Laphroaig / *Standard Brands Inc.*
Lauder's / *Hiram Walker Resources Ltd.*
Le Domaine / *National Distillers & Chemical Corp.*
Ledo-Dionysus / *Alco Standard Corp.*
Lejon / *Heublein Inc.*
Leroux / *Seagram Co. Ltd.*
Lite / *Philip Morris Inc.*
Lochan Ora / *Seagram Co. Ltd.*
Logan Deluxe / *Seagram Co. Ltd.*
Lolita / *Standard Brands Inc.*
Lone Star / *Olympia Brewing Co.*
Lone Star / *G. Heileman Brewing Co. Inc.*
Lone Star Light / *G. Heileman Brewing Co. Inc.*
Lord Calvert / *Seagram Co. Ltd.*
Lowenbrau / *Philip Morris Inc.*
Maison Blanc / *Safeway Stores Inc.*
Malcolm Hereford's Cows / *Heublein Inc.*
Malt Duck, Apple & Grape / *G. Heileman Brewing Co. Inc.*
Mandarine Napoleon / *Glenmore Distilleries Co.*
Maraca / *Hiram Walker Resources Ltd.*
Martell / *Brown Forman Distillers Corp.*
Mattingly & Moore / *Seagram Co. Ltd.*
McNairs / *Safeway Stores Inc.*
Medalla / *Bacardi Corp.*
Meister Brau / *Philip Morris Inc.*
Metaxa 5-Star & 7-Star / *Standard Brands Inc.*
Michelob / *Anheuser-Busch Companies Inc.*
Michelob Light / *Anheuser-Busch Companies Inc.*
Mickey's Malt / *G. Heileman Brewing Co. Inc.*
Miller High Life / *Philip Morris Inc.*
Milshire / *Heublein Inc.*
Milwaukee's Best / *Philip Morris Inc.*
Mission Bell / *Heublein Inc.*
Moosehead / *Nabisco Brands Inc.*
Mount Vernon / *National Distillers & Chemical Corp.*
Mountain Castle / *Safeway Stores Inc.*
Mr. Boston / *Glenmore Distilleries Co.*
Mumm / *Seagram Co. Ltd.*
Myers / *Seagram Co. Ltd.*
National Bohemian / *G. Heileman Brewing Co. Inc.*
National Premium / *G. Heileman Brewing Co. Inc.*
Natural Light / *Anheuser-Busch Companies Inc.*
Navip / *National Distillers & Chemical Corp.*
Nectarose / *Seagram Co. Ltd.*
Nikolai / *Seagram Co. Ltd.*
Noilly Prat / *Brown Forman Distillers Corp.*
Old Calhoun / *Safeway Stores Inc.*
Old Crow / *National Distillers & Chemical Corp.*
Old Dover / *National Distillers & Chemical Corp.*
Old Forester / *Brown Forman Distillers Corp.*
Old Grand-Dad / *National Distillers & Chemical Corp.*
Old Log Cabin / *National Distillers & Chemical Corp.*
Old Milwaukee / *Joseph Schlitz Brewing Co.*
Old Overholt / *National Distillers & Chemical Corp.*
Old Smuggler / *Hiram Walker Resources Ltd.*
Old Style / *G. Heileman Brewing Co. Inc.*
Old Style L.A. / *G. Heileman Brewing Co. Inc.*
Old Style Light / *G. Heileman Brewing Co. Inc.*
Old Taylor / *National Distillers & Chemical Corp.*
Old Thompson / *Glenmore Distilleries Co.*
Olde English 800 / *Pabst Brewing Co.*
Olmeca / *Seagram Co. Ltd.*
Olympia / *Olympia Brewing Co.*
Olympia Gold / *Olympia Brewing Co.*
Ostrova / *Heublein Inc.*
Pabst Blue Ribbon / *Pabst Brewing Co.*
Pabst Extra Light East Side / *Pabst Brewing Co.*
Padre / *Safeway Stores Inc.*
Palo Viejo / *Seagram Co. Ltd.*
Party Tyme / *Seagram Co. Ltd.*
Pasha / *Seagram Co. Ltd.*
Paso Fino Rum Liqueur / *Standard Brands Inc.*
Passport / *Seagram Co. Ltd.*
Paul Masson / *Seagram Co. Ltd.*
Penedro Rose Wine / *Safeway Stores Inc.*
Peralta / *Safeway Stores Inc.*
Petri / *Heublein Inc.*
Pfeiffer / *G. Heileman Brewing Co. Inc.*
Piels / *F. & M. Schaefer Corp.*
PM / *National Distillers & Chemical Corp.*

Popov / *Heublein Inc.*
Premium / *Seagram Co. Ltd.*
Primo / *Joseph Schlitz Brewing Co.*
Queen Anne / *Seagram Co. Ltd.*
Rainier / *G. Heileman Brewing Co. Inc.*
Rainier Light / *G. Heileman Brewing Co. Inc.*
Rebel Yell / *Norton Simon Inc.*
Red, White & Blue / *G. Heileman Brewing Co. Inc.*
Red White & Blue Beer / *Pabst Brewing Co.*
Red, White & Blue Light / *G. Heileman Brewing Co. Inc.*
Relska / *Heublein Inc.*
Ricasoli / *Seagram Co. Ltd.*
Robertson's Oporto Port / *Standard Brands Inc.*
Rock Brook / *Safeway Stores Inc.*
Ron Merito / *National Distillers & Chemical Corp.*
Ronrico / *Seagram Co. Ltd.*
Rosegarden / *McKesson Corp.*
Royal Canadian / *Hiram Walker Resources Ltd.*
Royal Salute 21 / *Seagram Co. Ltd.*
Salignac / *Hiram Walker Resources Ltd.*
Sandeman Ports and Sherries / *Seagram Co. Ltd.*
Sangrole / *Heublein Inc.*
Sauza Silver and Sauza Gold / *National Distillers & Chemical Corp.*
Schaefer / *F. & M. Schaefer Corp.*
Schaefer Bock Beer / *F. & M. Schaefer Corp.*
Schaefer Cream Ale / *F. & M. Schaefer Corp.*
Schlitz / *Joseph Schlitz Brewing Co.*
Schlitz Light / *Joseph Schlitz Brewing Co.*
Schlitz Malt Liquor / *Joseph Schlitz Brewing Co.*
Schmidt / *G. Heileman Brewing Co. Inc.*
Schmidt Light / *G. Heileman Brewing Co. Inc.*
Seagram's V.O. / *Seagram Co. Ltd.*
Seagram's 7 Crown / *Seagram Co. Ltd.*
Select / *Pabst Brewing Co.*
Semkov / *Standard Brands Inc.*
Shadow Creek Sparkling / *Glenmore Distilleries Co.*
Skol / *Hiram Walker Resources Ltd.*
Smirnoff / *Heublein Inc.*
Something Special / *Seagram Co. Ltd.*
Sonoma Vineyards / *Sonoma Vineyards*
Southern Comfort / *Brown Forman Distillers Corp.*
Southern Host / *Standard Brands Inc.*
Southwest Distributors / *Alco Standard Corp.*
Souverain / *Standard Brands Inc.*
Special Export / *G. Heileman Brewing Co. Inc.*
Spey Royal / *American Brands Inc.*
St. Elmo / *Safeway Stores Inc.*
Stag / *G. Heileman Brewing Co. Inc.*
Stantons / *Safeway Stores Inc.*
Ste. Michelle / *United States Tobacco Co.*
Sterling / *G. Heileman Brewing Co. Inc.*
Stillbrook / *Standard Brands Inc.*
Sunny Brook / *National Distillers & Chemical Corp.*
Talisker 12 / *National Distillers & Chemical Corp.*
Tartan Royal / *Safeway Stores Inc.*
Ten High / *Hiram Walker Resources Ltd.*
Tipo / *Heublein Inc.*
T.J. Swann / *Heublein Inc.*
Torre Dei Conti Asti Spumante / *Glenmore Distilleries Co.*
Tres Generacianoes / *National Distillers & Chemical Corp.*
Tribute / *Joseph Schlitz Brewing Co.*
Tuborg / *G. Heileman Brewing Co. Inc.*
Tullamore Dew / *Heublein Inc.*
Tvarscki / *Standard Brands Inc.*
United Vintners / *Heublein Inc.*
United Wine & Spirits / *Alco Standard Corp.*
Vandermint / *Seagram Co. Ltd.*
Vat 69 Gold and Traditional / *National Distillers & Chemical Corp.*
Walker's Deluxe / *Hiram Walker Resources Ltd.*
Weibel / *Standard Brands Inc.*
White Horse / *Seagram Co. Ltd.*
Wiedemann / *G. Heileman Brewing Co. Inc.*
William Alsatian / *Standard Brands Inc.*
Williams & Humbert / *Standard Brands Inc.*
Windsor Supreme / *National Distillers & Chemical Corp.*
Windsor Vineyards / *Sonoma Vineyards*
Wolfschmidt / *Seagram Co. Ltd.*
Yamato / *Safeway Stores Inc.*
Yellowstone / *Glenmore Distilleries Co.*
Yukon Jack Canadian / *Heublein Inc.*
100 Pipers / *Seagram Co. Ltd.*

Amusement Parks & Recreation Areas

Brunswick / *Brunswick Corp.*
Budweiser / *Anheuser-Busch Companies Inc.*
Canada's Wonderland / *Taft Broadcasting Co.*
Cedar Point Park / *Cedar Point, Inc.*
Chicago Health Clubs / *Bally Manufacturing Corp.*
Circus Tower / *Wometco Enterprises Inc.*
Conch Tour Train / *Wometco Enterprises Inc.*
Coney Island / *Taft Broadcasting Co.*

The Dark Continent / *Anheuser-Busch Companies Inc.*
Epcot Center, Orlando, Florida / *Walt Disney Productions*
Fair Lanes Bowling Centers / *Fair Lanes Inc.*
Holiday / *Bally Manufacturing Corp.*
Holiday Spa / *Bally Manufacturing Corp.*
Jack LaLanne European / *Bally Manufacturing Corp.*
Magic Kingdom, Orlando, Florida / *Walt Disney Productions*
Malibu Grand Prix / *Warner Communications Inc.*
Miami Seaquarium / *Wometco Enterprises Inc.*
Michelob Classic Dark / *Anheuser-Busch Companies Inc.*
President's First Lady / *Bally Manufacturing Corp.*
Richard Simmons Anatomy Asylums / *Bally Manufacturing Corp.*
Royal Kaanapali / *Amfac Inc.*
Sack Theatre / *Cadence Industries Corp.*
Scandinavian / *Bally Manufacturing Corp.*
Sea World of Florida / *Harcourt Brace Jovanovich Inc.*
Silver Springs / *American Broadcasting Companies Inc.*
Silverado / *Amfac Inc.*
Six Flags / *Bally Manufacturing Corp.*
Valleyfair / *Cedar Point, Inc.*
VIC Tanney International / *Bally Manufacturing Corp.*
Weeki wache Spring / *American Broadcasting Companies Inc.*
Wild Waters / *American Broadcasting Companies Inc.*
Yosemite National Park & Curry Co. / *MCA Inc.*

Apparel

Abby Michael / *Bobbie Brooks Inc.*
Abe Schrader / *Abe Schrader Corp.*
Abe Schrader Corp / *Interco Inc.*
Act III / *United Merchants and Manufacturers Inc.*
Act III / *Jonathan Logan Inc.*
Action Casuals / *Levi Strauss & Co.*
ActionScene / *United Merchants and Manufacturers Inc.*
Active Support / *Consolidated Foods Corp.*
Adler / *Palm Beach Inc.*
Adorence / *Talley Industries Inc.*
Advantage / *Garan Inc.*
After Six / *After Six Inc.*
AJD / *Colgate-Palmolive Co.*
Alamac / *West Point-Pepperell Inc.*
Alan Flusser / *Phillips-Van Heusen Corp.*
Alaskanits / *Alba-Waldensian, Inc.*
Alatex / *Cluett, Peabody & Co. Inc.*
Alba / *Alba-Waldensian, Inc.*
Albert Nipon / *Warnaco Inc.*
Albert van Luit / *Gulf +* Western Industries Inc.
Alfie / *Kennington Ltd. Inc.*
Alias / *Levi Strauss & Co.*
Alice Stuart / *United Merchants and Manufacturers Inc.*
Alice Stuart / *Jonathan Logan Inc.*
Alive / *Consolidated Foods Corp.*
Allyn St. George / *Hartmarx Corp.*
Allyn St. George / *Phillips-Van Heusen Corp.*
Allyn St. George / *Interco Inc.*
Amanda / *Manhattan Industries Inc.*
American Miss / *Bodin Apparel, Inc.*
Amy Adams / *Jonathan Logan Inc.*
Anderson-Little / *F.W. Woolworth Co.*
Ando Giotto / *Edison Brothers Stores Inc.*
Andrea Gayle / *Leslie Fay Inc.*
Andrew St. John / *Talley Industries Inc.*
Andriano / *Talley Industries Inc.*
Angelo of Rome / *After Six Inc.*
Anne Klein / *Manhattan Industries Inc.*
Anne Klein / *Genesco Inc.*
Anne Klein for New Aspect / *Manhattan Industries Inc.*
Apparel Unlimited / *Nexus Industries Inc.*
Aris Isotoner / *Consolidated Foods Corp.*
Arrow / *Cluett, Peabody & Co. Inc.*
Artex / *Jostens Inc.*
Austin Hill / *Palm Beach Inc.*
Austin Reed for Women / *Hartmarx Corp.*
Austin Reed of Regent Street / *Hartmarx Corp.*
Austin Reed Sportswear / *Hartmarx Corp.*
Avon Fashions / *Avon Products Inc.*
Baby Comfort / *Riegel Textile Corp.*
Babycare / *Riegel Textile Corp.*
Backsiders / *Edison Brothers Stores Inc.*
Bali / *Consolidated Foods Corp.*
Banlon / *Munsingwear Inc.*
Ban-Lon / *Garan Inc.*
Banzai / *Edison Brothers Stores Inc.*
Baracuta / *Phillips-Van Heusen Corp.*
Bassett-Walker / *VF Corp.*
Bay Club / *Gulf +* Western Industries Inc.
Bay Trading Co. / *Talley Industries Inc.*
Bayard Sport / *Manhattan Industries Inc.*
Beach Babies / *Chesebrough-Pond's Inc.*
Bend Over Pants / *Levi Strauss & Co.*
Berkley Cravats / *Manhattan Industries Inc.*
Berman's / *W.R. Grace & Co.*

Bert Paley / *After Six Inc.*
Big Ben / *Blue Bell Inc.*
Big Mama / *J.P. Stevens & Co. Inc.*
Big Murph / *G.C. Murphy Co.*
Big Smith / *Colonial Commercial Corp.*
Big Yank / *Interco Inc.*
Bill Blass / *United Merchants and Manufacturers Inc.*
Bill Blass / *After Six Inc.*
Bill Blass / *Billy The Kid, Inc.*
Bill Blass / *Damon Creations Inc.*
Billy The Kid / *Billy The Kid, Inc.*
Biltwell / *Interco Inc.*
Black Diamond Mink / *Evans Inc.*
Blue Bell / *Blue Bell Inc.*
Bobbie Brooks / *Bobbie Brooks Inc.*
Bodin / *Bodin Apparel, Inc.*
Bodinit / *Bodin Apparel, Inc.*
Botany / *Talley Industries Inc.*
Botany 500 / *Talley Industries Inc.*
Breckenridge / *Leslie Fay Inc.*
Briarcreek / *VF Corp.*
Brights Creek / *Avon Products Inc.*
Brittania / *Chesebrough-Pond's Inc.*
Bronzini / *Manhattan Industries Inc.*
Brut / *Russ Togs Inc.*
Bryn Mawr / *Bobbie Brooks Inc.*
Burlington / *Burlington Industries Inc.*
Buster Brown / *Gerber Products Co.*
Butte Knit / *Jonathan Logan Inc.*
B.V.D. / *Northwest Industries Inc.*
BW / *VF Corp.*
Cacharel / *Phillips-Van Heusen Corp.*
Calamity Jane / *Billy The Kid, Inc.*
Calvin / *Palm Beach Inc.*
Calvin Klein / *Puritan Fashions Corp.*
Camp / *Genesco Inc.*
Campus / *Interco Inc.*
Campusport / *Interco Inc.*
Carnaby Street / *Edison Brothers Stores Inc.*
Carwood / *Stanwood Corp.*
Casey Jones / *Blue Bell Inc.*
Catalina / *Gulf* + Western Industries Inc.
Cavel / *Collins & Aikman*
Champion / *Gulf* + Western Industries Inc.
Chapelcord / *Beatrice Companies Inc.*
Chaps by Ralph Lauren / *Warnaco Inc.*
Chaps by Ralph Lauren / *Genesco Inc.*
Cheap Jeans / *Noel Industries Inc.*
Chemise by Kennington / *Kennington Ltd. Inc.*
Cherokee / *Interco Inc.*
Christian Dior / *Warnaco Inc.*
Christian Dior / *Genesco Inc.*
Christian Dior Grand Luxe / *Hartmarx Corp.*
Christian Dior Monsieur / *Hartmarx Corp.*
Christie Brinkley / *Russ Togs Inc.*
Cinderella / *Reeves Brothers Inc.*
Cine Star / *Movie Star Inc.*
Cinema Etoile / *Movie Star Inc.*
Classic Woman / *Palm Beach Inc.*
Cling Alon / *Sears, Roebuck & Co.*
Clipper Mist / *Interco Inc.*
Clothesworks / *Winter, Jack Inc.*
CMA / *Levi Strauss & Co.*
Cobbies by Cos Cob / *Oxford Industries Inc.*
Cole of California / *Gulf* + Western Industries Inc.
College Town / *Interco Inc.*
Coloralls / *Consolidated Foods Corp.*
Colore / *Kennington Ltd. Inc.*
Colours by Alexander Julian / *Genesco Inc.*
Composites / *Russ Togs Inc.*
Computa-Fit / *Edison Brothers Stores Inc.*
Cos Cob / *Oxford Industries Inc.*
Cosi L'Uomo / *Edison Brothers Stores Inc.*
Cotton Cooler / *Alba-Waldensian, Inc.*
Cotton 100 / *Phillips-Van Heusen Corp.*
Cotton-Aire / *Alba-Waldensian, Inc.*
Country Britches / *Phillips-Van Heusen Corp.*
Country Miss / *Hartmarx Corp.*
Country Set / *Palm Beach Inc.*
Country Suburbans / *Hartmarx Corp.*
Courchevel / *Damon Creations Inc.*
Cover Story / *Edison Brothers Stores Inc.*
Cowden / *Interco Inc.*
Craig Craely / *Palm Beach Inc.*
Crazy Horse / *Russ Togs Inc.*
Crazy Horse Girl / *Russ Togs Inc.*
Crazy Horse Teen / *Russ Togs Inc.*
Cricketeer / *Phillips-Van Heusen Corp.*
Cross Creek / *Quality Mills, Inc.*
Cross Your Heart / *Beatrice Companies Inc.*
Cut 'n Jump / *Medalist Industries Inc.*
Damon / *Damon Creations Inc.*
Daniel Hechter / *Marcade Group, Inc.*
Danskin / *Esmark Inc.*
Danskin / *Beatrice Companies Inc.*
David Hunter / *Levi Strauss & Co.*
Denise / *House of Ronnie Inc.*
Denver Jeans / *Kellwood Co.*
Derrieres / *Edison Brothers Stores Inc.*
Designer Depot / *K Mart Corp.*
Devon / *Interco Inc.*
Diane Von Furstenberg / *Puritan Fashions Corp.*
Diane Young / *Puritan Fashions Corp.*
Dione / *Palm Beach Inc.*
Dior / *Warnaco Inc.*
Discus / *Tultex Corp.*

Dobie Originals / *Cluett, Peabody & Co. Inc.*
Domani / *Puritan Fashions Corp.*
Don Robbie / *Interco Inc.*
Donald Brooks / *Genesco Inc.*
Donegal / *Interco Inc.*
Donmoor / *Cluett, Peabody & Co. Inc.*
D'Orsay / *Genesco Inc.*
Dottie Mann / *Development Corp. of America*
Duckster / *Pro Group Inc.*
Dudley Casuals / *Palm Beach Inc.*
Duofold / *Cluett, Peabody & Co. Inc.*
Duplexx / *West Point-Pepperell Inc.*
Duranude / *Collins & Aikman*
E. Joven / *Farah Manufacturing Co.*
Eagle Shirts / *Palm Beach Inc.*
Easy to Be Me / *Gulf* + Western Industries Inc.
EBS / *Edison Brothers Stores Inc.*
Endurables / *Sears, Roebuck & Co.*
ENRO / *Wilson Brothers*
Epic / *Palm Beach Inc.*
Erik Andrews / *United States Industries Inc.*
Ernesto W. / *Wolf, Howard B. Inc.*
Esprit by Campus / *Interco Inc.*
Esquire / *Gulf* + Western Industries Inc.
Etienne Aigner / *Phillips-Van Heusen Corp.*
Etro / *Manhattan Industries Inc.*
Evan Picone / *Palm Beach Inc.*
The Evans Collection / *Evans Inc.*
Excello / *Gulf* + Western Industries Inc.
Fairmont / *United States Industries Inc.*
Farah / *Farah Manufacturing Co.*
Fashion Conspiracy / *Edison Brothers Stores Inc.*
Fashion Jeans / *Levi Strauss & Co.*
Fashion Tree / *Development Corp. of America*
Fashion Tree for Men / *Development Corp. of America*
Fashionaire / *Hartmarx Corp.*
Fay's Closet / *Leslie Fay Inc.*
FC Ltd. / *Edison Brothers Stores Inc.*
FC Trotter / *Edison Brothers Stores Inc.*
Fergusson Atlantic / *Cluett, Peabody & Co. Inc.*
Ferrante / *Farah Manufacturing Co.*
Finesse / *J.P. Stevens & Co. Inc.*
Finesse / *Kellwood Co.*
Fitzgerald / *Palm Beach Inc.*
Five-O-One / *Levi Strauss & Co.*
Flirt / *Bodin Apparel, Inc.*
Flirt / *Stanwood Corp.*
Fog / *Interco Inc.*
Forever Young / *Puritan Fashions Corp.*
Forme' / *Alba-Waldensian, Inc.*
Fox Point / *Parker Pen Co.*
Foxcraft / *Wilson Brothers*
Frank Shorter Running Gear / *Levi Strauss & Co.*
French Cut / *Billy The Kid, Inc.*
Fruit of the Loom / *Northwest Industries Inc.*
Funny Girl / *Salant Corp.*
Gad-about / *VF Corp.*
Gale Gould / *Puritan Fashions Corp.*
Gant / *Palm Beach Inc.*
Garan / *Garan Inc.*
Garan by Marita / *Garan Inc.*
The Garan Man / *Garan Inc.*
Garanimals / *Garan Inc.*
Generra / *Farah Manufacturing Co.*
Gentlemen's Lady / *Edison Brothers Stores Inc.*
Geoffrey Beene / *Warnaco Inc.*
Geoffrey Beene / *Phillips-Van Heusen Corp.*
Giamo / *Bodin Apparel, Inc.*
Gil Truedsson / *Oxford Industries Inc.*
Givenchy / *Esmark Inc.*
Givenchy / *Beatrice Companies Inc.*
Givenchy Sport / *United States Industries Inc.*
Gladiator / *Medalist Industries Inc.*
Glen York / *Manhattan Industries Inc.*
Gleneagles / *Hartmarx Corp.*
Gloria Swanson / *Puritan Fashions Corp.*
Gloria Vanderbilt for Jonathan Logan / *Jonathan Logan Inc.*
Gold Toe / *Cluett, Peabody & Co. Inc.*
Gossard-Artemis / *Wayne-Gossard Corp.*
Graham & Gunn Ltd. / *Hartmarx Corp.*
Grand Slam / *Munsingwear Inc.*
Great American Factory / *Nexus Industries Inc.*
Great Western / *Hartmarx Corp.*
Green Apples / *Noel Industries Inc.*
Greif / *Genesco Inc.*
Guardian Angel / *Collins & Aikman*
Gurian / *Puritan Fashions Corp.*
Halston / *Phillips-Van Heusen Corp.*
Halston for Men / *Cluett, Peabody & Co. Inc.*
Halston V & VI / *Manhattan Industries Inc.*
Hampton Girl / *Hampton Industries Inc.*
Handmacher / *Hartmarx Corp.*
Hanes / *Consolidated Foods Corp.*
Happenstance / *Puritan Fashions Corp.*
Happy Legs / *Spencer Companies Inc.*
Harbor Master / *Jonathan Logan Inc.*
Hardwear / *Levi Strauss & Co.*
Harry Fischer / *After Six Inc.*
Hart Schaffner & Marx / *Hartmarx Corp.*
Haspel / *Palm Beach Inc.*
Hathaway / *Warnaco Inc.*
Health Knit / *Stanwood Corp.*
Health-tex / *Chesebrough-Pond's Inc.*
Heartbreak / *Edison Brothers Stores Inc.*

Hendel / *Pro Group Inc.*
Hennessey / *Phillips-Van Heusen Corp.*
Henry Grenthel / *Hartmarx Corp.*
Henry Grethel / *Manhattan Industries Inc.*
Her Majesty / *Gulf* + Western Industries Inc.
Heritage / *Wayne-Gossard Corp.*
Hickey Freeman / *Hartmarx Corp.*
Hilton Athletic Apparel / *Anthony Industries Inc.*
Holbrook / *Oxford Industries Inc.*
Hot Dogs / *Billy The Kid, Inc.*
House of Ronnie / *House of Ronnie Inc.*
Howard Wolf / *Wolf, Howard B. Inc.*
Hug-me-too / *Hartfield Zody's Inc.*
Hunter Haig / *Palm Beach Inc.*
Hunter Hill / *Wilson Brothers*
Ice Castles / *Edison Brothers Stores Inc.*
Imerman / *Jonathan Logan Inc.*
Impulse / *Kennington Ltd. Inc.*
Inspiration / *Edison Brothers Stores Inc.*
Interwoven / *Gulf* + Western Industries Inc.
Ironweve / *Collins & Aikman*
It's Pure Gould / *Interco Inc.*
Izod / *General Mills Inc.*
Jack Nicklaus / *Warnaco Inc.*
Jack Nicklaus / *Hartmarx Corp.*
Jack Winter / *Winter, Jack Inc.*
Jacksport / *Winter, Jack Inc.*
Jacques Berne' / *Edison Brothers Stores Inc.*
Jaeger / *Hartmarx Corp.*
James River Traders / *Avon Products Inc.*
Jantzen / *Blue Bell Inc.*
Janus / *Interco Inc.*
Jason Brooks / *Farah Manufacturing Co.*
Jason Gibbs / *After Six Inc.*
Jay Dubbs / *Edison Brothers Stores Inc.*
Jaymar / *Hartmarx Corp.*
Jaymar Sport / *Hartmarx Corp.*
"JBJ" / *Oxford Industries Inc.*
Jeans by Kasper / *Leslie Fay Inc.*
Jeans West & Des. / *Edison Brothers Stores Inc.*
Jeffrey Banks / *Oxford Industries Inc.*
Jhane Barnes / *Oxford Industries Inc.*
J.J. of Miami / *Development Corp. of America*
Joan Vass U.S.A. / *Wayne-Gossard Corp.*
Jodette / *Hartfield Zody's Inc.*
Jody / *Hartfield Zody's Inc.*
Jody of California / *Hartfield Zody's Inc.*
Jody-Tootique / *Hartfield Zody's Inc.*
Joe Namath / *Noel Industries Inc.*
John Alexander / *Interco Inc.*
John Henry / *Oxford Industries Inc.*
John Henry / *Manhattan Industries Inc.*
John Henry / *Farah Manufacturing Co.*
John Newcombe / *Gulf* + Western Industries Inc.
John Weitz / *Palm Beach Inc.*
John Weitz / *Gulf* + Western Industries Inc.
Johnny Carson / *Hartmarx Corp.*
Jonathan Logan / *Jonathan Logan Inc.*
Jordache / *Genesco Inc.*
Jordache / *Manhattan Industries Inc.*
Jordache Bigandtall Men's Sportswear / *National Service Industries Inc.*
Jordache Contemporary Mens' Sportswear / *National Service Industries Inc.*
Jordache Young Men's Sportswear / *National Service Industries Inc.*
Joseph Picone / *Palm Beach Inc.*
J.P. Allen / *Hartmarx Corp.*
Junior Bazaar / *Sears, Roebuck & Co.*
Just My Size / *Consolidated Foods Corp.*
Just Young / *Puritan Fashions Corp.*
JW & Des. / *Edison Brothers Stores Inc.*
JW & JW Jeans West / *Edison Brothers Stores Inc.*
Kantwet / *Questor Corp.*
Kasper for Joan Leslie / *Leslie Fay Inc.*
Kayser Roth / *Gulf* + Western Industries Inc.
Kelli Kaye / *Russ Togs Inc.*
Kellwood Fashions / *Kellwood Co.*
Kellwood Kasuals / *Kellwood Co.*
Kennington / *Kennington Ltd. Inc.*
Kennington for Boys / *Kennington Ltd. Inc.*
Kentfield / *Development Corp. of America*
Kicks / *Kellwood Co.*
Kid Stuff / *Farah Manufacturing Co.*
Kidproof / *Chesebrough-Pond's Inc.*
Kids "R" Us / *Toys "R" Us Inc.*
Kilgour, French & Stanbury / *Genesco Inc.*
Kingswell Kasuals / *Kellwood Co.*
Kleinerts / *Kleinerts Inc.*
Knit Knack / *Edison Brothers Stores Inc.*
Knitivo / *Leslie Fay Inc.*
Kollection / *Jonathan Logan Inc.*
Koret of North America / *Levi Strauss & Co.*
Koret-City Blues / *Levi Strauss & Co.*
Kover Alls / *Levi Strauss & Co.*
Kudos / *National Service Industries Inc.*
Lacoste / *General Mills Inc.*
Lady Arrow / *Cluett, Peabody & Co. Inc.*
Lady Devon / *Interco Inc.*
Lady Laura / *Russ Togs Inc.*
Lady Manhattan / *Manhattan Industries Inc.*
Lady Thomson / *Salant Corp.*
Lady Wrangler / *Blue Bell Inc.*
Lanier / *Oxford Industries Inc.*
Lanvin / *Damon Creations Inc.*

Lanvin / *Genesco Inc.*
Laradenois / *Consolidated Foods Corp.*
L'Avion & Biplane Des. / *Edison Brothers Stores Inc.*
L'Avion & Design / *Edison Brothers Stores Inc.*
LeBow / *After Six Inc.*
Lee / *VF Corp.*
Lee Riders / *VF Corp.*
Lee Wright / *Oxford Industries Inc.*
The Leg Works / *Edison Brothers Stores Inc.*
Leggs / *Consolidated Foods Corp.*
Leslie Fay / *Leslie Fay Inc.*
Leslie Fay Petite / *Leslie Fay Inc.*
Leslie J / *Leslie Fay Inc.*
Leslie Pomer / *Leslie Fay Inc.*
Levis / *Levi Strauss & Co.*
Life Span / *Alba-Waldensian, Inc.*
Lil' Wrangler / *Blue Bell Inc.*
Linnea Franco / *Edison Brothers Stores Inc.*
Liquidity by Alice Blaine / *Manhattan Industries Inc.*
Live Ins / *Noel Industries Inc.*
L'Mer / *Edison Brothers Stores Inc.*
Lollipop / *VF Corp.*
London Fog / *Interco Inc.*
Loro Piana / *Hartmarx Corp.*
Ltd. / *Leslie Fay Inc.*
Lucinda Rhodes / *Manhattan Industries Inc.*
Lustre-Skin / *Alba-Waldensian, Inc.*
M. Stitch Design / *Blue Bell Inc.*
Magda / *Bodin Apparel, Inc.*
Maincoats / *Interco Inc.*
Malcom Kenneth / *After Six Inc.*
Manchester / *Oxford Industries Inc.*
Manhattan / *Manhattan Industries Inc.*
Mann / *Billy The Kid, Inc.*
Marisa Christina / *Colgate-Palmolive Co.*
Marlene / *Marcade Group, Inc.*
Mar'v'lus / *Edison Brothers Stores Inc.*
Mason / *Riegel Textile Corp.*
Master Jac / *Kellwood Co.*
Maverick / *Blue Bell Inc.*
McGregor / *Oxford Industries Inc.*
McGregor / *Talley Industries Inc.*
McGregor / *Phillips-Van Heusen Corp.*
McGregor for Boys / *Hampton Industries Inc.*
Measure Up / *Talley Industries Inc.*
Medalist Ripon / *Medalist Industries Inc.*
Merona Sport / *Oxford Industries Inc.*
Mike Volbracht Sport / *Manhattan Industries Inc.*
Miss Austin / *Palm Beach Inc.*
Miss Ronnie / *House of Ronnie Inc.*
Misty Harbor / *United Merchants and Manufacturers Inc.*
Misty Harbor / *Jonathan Logan Inc.*
Modern Globe / *VF Corp.*
Modern Junior / *Jonathan Logan Inc.*
Mojud / *Gulf* + Western Industries Inc.
Monika Tilley for Christie Brinkley / *Russ Togs Inc.*
Mountain Grown / *Kellwood Co.*
Movie Star / *Movie Star Inc.*
Mr. Leggs / *Salant Corp.*
Mr. Wrangler / *Blue Bell Inc.*
Ms. Lee / *VF Corp.*
Ms. Russ / *Russ Togs Inc.*
Munsingwear / *Munsingwear Inc.*
Name Droppers / *Kellwood Co.*
Nat Nast / *Beatrice Companies Inc.*
Nazareth / *Gulf* + Western Industries Inc.
New Attitude / *Russ Togs Inc.*
New Expressions / *Bobbie Brooks Inc.*
New Friends / *Noel Industries Inc.*
NFL / *Kellwood Co.*
Nicholas by Niki Lu / *Development Corp. of America*
Niki-Lu / *Development Corp. of America*
Nino Cerruti / *Hartmarx Corp.*
Nino Cerruti / *Hartmarx Corp.*
Nitey Nite / *Riegel Textile Corp.*
No Fault / *Blue Bell Inc.*
No Nonsense / *Gulf* + Western Industries Inc.
Northfield / *Kellwood Co.*
Notorious / *Edison Brothers Stores Inc.*
N.P.W. / *Farah Manufacturing Co.*
Oak Tree / *Edison Brothers Stores Inc.*
Oleg Cassini / *Genesco Inc.*
Oleg Cassini / *Oxford Industries Inc.*
Olevia St / *Stanwood Corp.*
Olga / *Warnaco Inc.*
Olympian / *Beatrice Companies Inc.*
One To Nine / *Edison Brothers Stores Inc.*
Onesies / *Gerber Products Co.*
The Only Way / *Bodin Apparel, Inc.*
OSA / *Oxford Industries Inc.*
Oscar de la Renta / *Billy The Kid, Inc.*
Oscar de la Renta / *Oxford Industries Inc.*
Ot. Sport Plus Designs / *Edison Brothers Stores Inc.*
Our Gang / *Chesebrough-Pond's Inc.*
Our Girl / *Chesebrough-Pond's Inc.*
Outdoors Unlimited / *Interco Inc.*
Outlander / *Leslie Fay Inc.*
Palm Beach / *Palm Beach Inc.*
Pandora / *Gulf* + Western Industries Inc.
Panther / *Interco Inc.*
Par Avion / *Edison Brothers Stores Inc.*
Parallel Turn / *Edison Brothers Stores Inc.*
Pat Fashions / *Pat Fashions Industries Inc.*
Pelham / *G.C. Murphy Co.*
Pelican / *Manhattan Industries Inc.*

Penguin / *Munsingwear Inc.*
Penny Young / *Puritan Fashions Corp.*
Perry Ellis / *Genesco Inc.*
Perry Ellis / *Manhattan Industries Inc.*
Perry Ellis America / *Levi Strauss & Co.*
Personal / *Leslie Fay Inc.*
Personal Property / *Leslie Fay Inc.*
Petite - P.S. Street / *Edison Brothers Stores Inc.*
Petite Concept / *Interco Inc.*
Petite Street / *Edison Brothers Stores Inc.*
PGA Tour / *Phillips-Van Heusen Corp.*
Philip Gurian / *Puritan Fashions Corp.*
Phoenix / *Genesco Inc.*
Pierre Cardin / *Hartmarx Corp.*
Pierre Cardin / *Palm Beach Inc.*
Players / *Phillips-Van Heusen Corp.*
Playtex / *Beatrice Companies Inc.*
Playtops / *Esmark Inc.*
Polar Pairs / *Alba-Waldensian, Inc.*
Polo by Ralph Lauren / *Oxford Industries Inc.*
Polo for Boys by Ralph Lauren / *Palm Beach Inc.*
Polo University / *Genesco Inc.*
Poly Flinders / *United States Industries Inc.*
Pony / *Stanwood Corp.*
Portfolio by Perry Ellis / *Manhattan Industries Inc.*
Pour Les Hommes / *Development Corp. of America*
Premium / *Nexus Industries Inc.*
Present Co. / *Bobbie Brooks Inc.*
Pret-a-Porte / *Wolf, Howard B. Inc.*
Pride / *Medalist Industries Inc.*
Pringle of Scotland / *Warnaco Inc.*
Pro-Action by Campus / *Interco Inc.*
Proms & Promises / *Edison Brothers Stores Inc.*
Puritan / *Warnaco Inc.*
Puritan Dress / *Puritan Fashions Corp.*
Quail Hollow / *Stanwood Corp.*
Quality Mills / *Quality Mills, Inc.*
Queen Casuals / *Interco Inc.*
R & K Originals / *United Merchants and Manufacturers Inc.*
R & K Originals / *Jonathan Logan Inc.*
R & M Kaufman / *Russ Togs Inc.*
Racquet / *Hartmarx Corp.*
Rafael / *Genesco Inc.*
Ralph Lauren / *Oxford Industries Inc.*
Ramar / *Oxford Industries Inc.*
Rawlings / *Russ Togs Inc.*
Ready Set Go / *Chesebrough-Pond's Inc.*
Rear Gear / *Edison Brothers Stores Inc.*
Rejoice / *Interco Inc.*
Renee / *Giant Food Inc.*
Resistol Hats / *Levi Strauss & Co.*
Ridingate / *Hartmarx Corp.*
Ripon / *Medalist Industries Inc.*
Robert Stock / *Oxford Industries Inc.*
Ronnie Jana / *House of Ronnie Inc.*
Ronnie Togs / *House of Ronnie Inc.*
Rosanna / *Warnaco Inc.*
Rosario / *Bodin Apparel, Inc.*
Rosario / *Stanwood Corp.*
Rose Marie Reed / *United Merchants and Manufacturers Inc.*
Rose Marie Reid / *Jonathan Logan Inc.*
Round-the-Clock / *Esmark Inc.*
Round-the-Clock / *Beatrice Companies Inc.*
Royal Palm Beach / *Palm Beach Inc.*
RPM / *Cluett, Peabody & Co. Inc.*
Rugged Country / *Interco Inc.*
Russ / *Russ Togs Inc.*
Russ Girl / *Russ Togs Inc.*
Russ Petites / *Russ Togs Inc.*
Russ Teen / *Russ Togs Inc.*
Russ Togs / *Russ Togs Inc.*
Russell / *Russell Corp.*
Russie / *Russ Togs Inc.*
Rustler / *Blue Bell Inc.*
Sagamore Hotel / *New York*
Sand Knit / *Medalist Industries Inc.*
Sandcastle / *Gulf* + Western Industries Inc.
Sani Terry / *Alba-Waldensian, Inc.*
Sansabelt / *Hartmarx Corp.*
Sasson / *Hampton Industries Inc.*
Sasson's / *Leslie Fay Inc.*
Saturdays / *Cluett, Peabody & Co. Inc.*
SAV / *Manhattan Industries Inc.*
Savane / *Farah Manufacturing Co.*
Saybrook / *Puritan Fashions Corp.*
Schrader Sport / *Abe Schrader Corp.*
Scotchguard / *Minnesota Mining and Manufacturing Co. (3M)*
Sedgefield / *Blue Bell Inc.*
Seinsheimer / *Palm Beach Inc.*
Sheer Elegance / *Consolidated Foods Corp.*
Sheer Energy / *Consolidated Foods Corp.*
Shepler's / *W.R. Grace & Co.*
Ship 'n Shore / *General Mills Inc.*
Shirt Shed / *Nexus Industries Inc.*
Shirt Street / *Hampton Industries Inc.*
"Show-Me" / *Norton Simon Inc.*
Showtoon / *Consolidated Foods Corp.*
Signal / *Wayne-Gossard Corp.*
Sir Jac / *Kellwood Co.*
Skeets / *VF Corp.*
Ski Levis / *Levi Strauss & Co.*
Ski Skin / *Medalist Industries Inc.*
Slenderalls / *Consolidated Foods Corp.*

Small Stuff / *Edison Brothers Stores Inc.*
Snapdragon / *Edison Brothers Stores Inc.*
Sock Sense / *Gulf* + Western Industries Inc.
Solo / *Palm Beach Inc.*
Sound Waves / *Chesebrough-Pond's Inc.*
Spalding / *Warnaco Inc.*
Speedo / *Warnaco Inc.*
Spirit / *J.P. Stevens & Co. Inc.*
Sport / *Leslie Fay Inc.*
Sports Ralley / *Palm Beach Inc.*
Sportswear / *Russell Corp.*
Oxxford Clothes / *Levi Strauss & Co.*
Spring City / *Cluett, Peabody & Co. Inc.*
Stallion / *Stanwood Corp.*
Startown / *Interco Inc.*
Statler / *VF Corp.*
Stella Mae / *Edison Brothers Stores Inc.*
Stephen Casuals / *Abe Schrader Corp.*
Sterling & Hunt / *Hartmarx Corp.*
Studio One by Campus / *Interco Inc.*
Stuffed Shirt / *Interco Inc.*
Stunts / *Colonial Commercial Corp.*
Summer Sheer / *Consolidated Foods Corp.*
Sun Brite / *Kellwood Co.*
Super Silk / *Phillips-Van Heusen Corp.*
Support Can Be Beautiful / *Beatrice Companies Inc.*
Sutter Creek / *Levi Strauss & Co.*
Sutton / *Russ Togs Inc.*
Sweet Briar / *Development Corp. of America*
Sybil / *Spencer Companies Inc.*
Tailor's Bench / *Interco Inc.*
The Talbot's / *General Mills Inc.*
Talbott Knits / *United States Industries Inc.*
Taos / *Farah Manufacturing Co.*
Teddy Bear / *Kleinerts Inc.*
Temptease / *Alba-Waldensian, Inc.*
Thane / *Warnaco Inc.*
Thank Goodness It Fits / *Beatrice Companies Inc.*
Thank Heaven / *Edison Brothers Stores Inc.*
Thomson / *Salant Corp.*
Thumsup / *Sears, Roebuck & Co.*
Tijuca by Laura Pearson U.S.A. / *Wayne-Gossard Corp.*
Titus McDuff / *Phillips-Van Heusen Corp.*
Today's Girl / *Consolidated Foods Corp.*
Toddly Winks / *Quality Mills, Inc.*
Toni Petite / *Russ Togs Inc.*
Toni Todd / *Russ Togs Inc.*
Top Half / *Nexus Industries Inc.*
Top It Off / *Edison Brothers Stores Inc.*
Toughskins / *Sears, Roebuck & Co.*
Tour de France / *Interco Inc.*
Tourage SSE / *Levi Strauss & Co.*
Trebor / *Jonathan Logan Inc.*
Trigere Sport / *Abe Schrader Corp.*
Tropix Togs / *Nexus Industries Inc.*
Troutman / *VF Corp.*
True To You / *Edison Brothers Stores Inc.*
Tultex / *Tultex Corp.*
Turnbury / *Palm Beach Inc.*
TWCC / *Palm Beach Inc.*
Tweens / *Quality Mills, Inc.*
Two Horse Brand / *Levi Strauss & Co.*
Ultimates / *Alba-Waldensian, Inc.*
Ultra Image / *Spencer Companies Inc.*
Ultra-Stretch / *Farah Manufacturing Co.*
Underalls / *Consolidated Foods Corp.*
Union Underwear / *Northwest Industries Inc.*
Ursula Gogel / *Russ Togs Inc.*
Van Heusen / *Phillips-Van Heusen Corp.*
Van Raalte / *Cluett, Peabody & Co. Inc.*
Van Raalte / *Kellwood Co.*
Vanity Fair / *VF Corp.*
Varsity Town / *Palm Beach Inc.*
Vassarette / *Munsingwear Inc.*
Venice Industries / *Jonathan Logan Inc.*
Verona Knits / *Puritan Fashions Corp.*
VH / *Phillips-Van Heusen Corp.*
Vicky Ann / *Edison Brothers Stores Inc.*
Vicky Vaughn / *Russ Togs Inc.*
Villager / *United Merchants and Manufacturers Inc.*
The Villager / *Jonathan Logan Inc.*
Vino De Casa / *Edison Brothers Stores Inc.*
V-Line / *After Six Inc.*
Voll/Bracht / *Manhattan Industries Inc.*
W. Stitch Design / *Blue Bell Inc.*
Walter Holmes-Society Brand / *Hartmarx Corp.*
Warner's / *Warnaco Inc.*
Warren Knits / *Cluett, Peabody & Co. Inc.*
Wearabouts / *Consolidated Foods Corp.*
Weather Tamer / *Gerber Products Co.*
Weatherrogue / *Kellwood Co.*
Weathervane / *Hartmarx Corp.*
Webcraft / *Beatrice Companies Inc.*
W.F.F. / *Farah Manufacturing Co.*
White Stag / *Warnaco Inc.*
Windbreaker / *Phillips-Van Heusen Corp.*
Winnebago / *Winnebago Industries Inc.*
Winner Wear / *Kennington Ltd. Inc.*
Winnie-the-Pooh / *Sears, Roebuck & Co.*
Winning Edge / *Interco Inc.*
Valvoline / *Ashland Oil, Inc.*
Varsity / *Pep Boys - Manny, Moe & Jack*
Veritas / *Chevron Corp.*
Vistac / *Chevron Corp.*
Walker / *Tenneco Inc.*

Winteralls / *Consolidated Foods Corp.*
WOW (With-out-wire) / *Beatrice Companies Inc.*
Wrangler / *Blue Bell Inc.*
X-Span / *Alba-Waldensian, Inc.*
Young Squire / *United States Industries Inc.*
Yukon Trail / *National Service Industries Inc.*
417 / *Phillips-Van Heusen Corp.*
5-7-9 & Des / *Edison Brothers Stores Inc.*

Appliances

Acme Juicerator / *Dynamics Corp. of America*
ADI Appliances / *Mayflower Corp.*
Admiral / *Magic Chef Inc.*
Air Ease / *Magic Chef Inc.*
Airtemp / *Fedders Corp.*
Amana / *Raytheon Co.*
Armstrong / *Magic Chef Inc.*
Arvin / *Arvin Industries Inc.*
Auto Cup / *Ronco Teleproducts Inc.*
Auto-Flo / *Masco Corp.*
Bendix / *White Consolidated Industries Inc.*
Braun / *Gillette Co.*
Caloric / *Raytheon Co.*
Cedar Works / *Dibrel Brothers, Inc.*
Climatrol / *Fedders Corp.*
Cold Guard / *White Consolidated Industries Inc.*
Comfort Sensor / *McGraw Edison Co.*
Complexion Plus / *North American Philips Corp.*
Conair / *Conair Corp.*
Conaire / *Philips Industries Inc.*
Continental / *Conair Corp.*
Corona / *Rival Manufacturing Co.*
Crazy Curl / *Bristol Myers Co.*
Crosley / *White Consolidated Industries Inc.*
Curly 2 / *North American Philips Corp.*
Cushion Curl / *Conair Corp.*
Dial-A-Brew / *North American Philips Corp.*
Dixie / *Magic Chef Inc.*
Domestic / *White Consolidated Industries Inc.*
Dominion / *Scovill Inc.*
Edison / *Magic Chef Inc.*
Edison / *McGraw Edison Co.*
Electric Egg Scrambler / *Ronco Teleproducts Inc.*
Electric Works / *Mirro Corp.*
Elna / *White Consolidated Industries Inc.*
Farberware / *Kidde Inc.*
Fedders / *Fedders Corp.*
Filter Queen / *Health-Mor Inc.*
Food Dehydrator / *Ronco Teleproducts Inc.*
FreeStyle / *Dart & Kraft Inc.*
Frigidaire / *White Consolidated Industries Inc.*
Frost Queen / *Rangaire Corp.*
Gaffers & Sattler / *Magic Chef Inc.*
GE / *General Electric Co.*
Genie / *North American Philips Corp.*
Gibson / *White Consolidated Industries Inc.*
Glenwood / *Raytheon Co.*
Gotcha / *North American Philips Corp.*
Great Curl / *Helene Curtis Industries Inc.*
The Great One / *Helene Curtis Industries Inc.*
Hamilton Beach / *Scovill Inc.*
Hankscraft / *Gerber Products Co.*
Hardwick Stove Co. / *Maytag Co.*
Heil / *Whirlpool Corp.*
Hilton / *White Consolidated Industries Inc.*
Hobart / *Dart & Kraft Inc.*
Hoover / *Hoover Co.*
Hot Point / *General Electric Co.*
Inflate-All / *Coleman Company Inc.*
Ingraham / *McGraw Edison Co.*
Ingraham / *Magic Chef Inc.*
Jenn-Air / *Maytag Co.*
Johnson / *Magic Chef Inc.*
Kelvinator / *White Consolidated Industries Inc.*
Kenmore / *Sears, Roebuck & Co.*
Kenmore / *Roper Corp.*
Kirby / *Scott & Fetzer Co.*
Kitchen Aid / *Dart & Kraft Inc.*
Kwik Sweep / *Conair Corp.*
Ladybug / *North American Philips Corp.*
Lau & Conaire / *Philips Industries Inc.*
Le Chef / *Sunbeam Corp.*
Leonard / *White Consolidated Industries Inc.*
Magic Chef / *Magic Chef Inc.*
Magnawave™ / *Rangaire Corp.*
Markel / *Scovill Inc.*
Massage Works / *Conair Corp.*
Maytag / *Maytag Co.*
Miracle Broom / *Ronco Teleproducts Inc.*
Miracle Sander / *Ronco Teleproducts Inc.*
Mixmaster / *Sunbeam Corp.*
Modern Maid / *Raytheon Co.*
Modern Maid / *McGraw Edison Co.*
Mr. Dentist / *Ronco Teleproducts Inc.*
Nail Dazzler / *North American Philips Corp.*
National / *Dart & Kraft Inc.*
Norelco / *North American Philips Corp.*
Norge / *Magic Chef Inc.*
NuTone / *Scovill Inc.*
Oster / *Sunbeam Corp.*
P & B (Potter & Brumfield) / *AMF Inc.*

Paragon / *AMF Inc.*
Philco / *White Consolidated Industries Inc.*
Princess / *Health-Mor Inc.*
Radarange / *Raytheon Co.*
Rangaire / *Rangaire Corp.*
Ranger / *Rangaire Corp.*
Rexair Rainbow / *Kidde Inc.*
Rival / *Rival Manufacturing Co.*
Roy / *White Consolidated Industries Inc.*
Scotsman / *Household International, Inc.*
Shopmate / *McGraw Edison Co.*
Singer / *Singer Co.*
Son-Of-A-Gun / *Bristol Myers Co.*
Speed Queen / *Raytheon Co.*
Speed Queen / *McGraw Edison Co.*
"Steam" / *American Home Products Corp.*
Sunbeam / *Sunbeam Corp.*
T.H.E. / *Coleman Company Inc.*
Thermador / *Norris Industries Inc.*
Titan / *Rival Manufacturing Co.*
Toastmaster / *McGraw Edison Co.*
Toastmaster / *Magic Chef Inc.*
Trane / *American Standard Inc.*
True Reflection / *Conair Corp.*
Universal / *White Consolidated Industries Inc.*
Vesta / *White Consolidated Industries Inc.*
Waring / *Dynamics Corp. of America*
Waste King / *Norris Industries Inc.*
Water Fingers / *Conair Corp.*
Water Pik / *Teledyne Inc.*
West Bend / *Dart & Kraft Inc.*
Whirlpool / *Whirlpool Corp.*
White / *White Consolidated Industries Inc.*
White Westinghouse / *White Consolidated Industries Inc.*
Williams / *Magic Chef Inc.*
York / *Borg Warner Corp.*

Automotive Products & Services

ADAP Inc / *Rite Aid Corp.*
Amalie / *Witco Chemical Corp.*
Amoco / *Amoco Corp.*
Amoco Ultimate / *Amoco Corp.*
Anco / *Champion Spark Plug Co.*
APS / *Gulf* + Western Industries Inc.
ARCO Petro / *Atlantic Richfield Co.*
Armor All / *McKesson Corp.*
Armstrong / *Armstrong Rubber Co.*
Armstrong Brand / *Armstrong Rubber Co.*
Atlas / *Amoco Corp.*
Autolite / *Bendix Corp.*
Avis / *Beatrice Companies Inc.*
B. F. Goodrich / *B.F. Goodrich Co.*
Battery Tester / *Ronco Teleproducts Inc.*
BIG A / *Gulf* + Western Industries Inc.
Bitumuls / *Chevron Corp.*
Blazo / *Chevron Corp.*
Cadet / *Pep Boys - Manny, Moe & Jack*
Carcare / *Chevron Corp.*
Carleton / *Armstrong Rubber Co.*
Certicare / *Amoco Corp.*
Chain & Bar Lubricant / *Quaker State Oil Refining Corp.*
Champion / *Champion Spark Plug Co.*
Check / *Pep Boys - Manny, Moe & Jack*
Chevron / *Chevron Corp.*
Chevron & Chevron Design / *Chevron Corp.*
Clark / *Clark Oil & Refining Corp.*
Claylok / *Chevron Corp.*
COMP & Design / *Quaker State Oil Refining Corp.*
Concord / *Fuqua Industries Inc.*
Cordovan / *Grand Auto Inc.*
Cornell / *Pep Boys - Manny, Moe & Jack*
Cruisemaster / *Chevron Corp.*
Dekent / *Pep Boys - Manny, Moe & Jack*
Delo / *Chevron Corp.*
DeLuxe / *Quaker State Oil Refining Corp.*
Dichevrol / *Chevron Corp.*
Die Hard / *Sears, Roebuck & Co.*
Dieselect / *Chevron Corp.*
Direct / *Tenneco Inc.*
Du Bois / *Pep Boys - Manny, Moe & Jack*
Duplex / *Quaker State Oil Refining Corp.*
Dupli-Color / *American Home Products Corp.*
Energizer / *Union Carbide Corp.*
Esprit / *Fuqua Industries Inc.*
Exxon / *Exxon Corp.*
Firestone / *Firestone Tire & Rubber Co.*
Fisk / *Uniroyal Inc.*
Fleetmaster / *Uniroyal Inc.*
Ford / *Ford Motor Co.*
Ford Authorized Remanufactured / *Ford Motor Co.*
Ford Motor / *Ford Motor Co.*
Formula / *Armstrong Rubber Co.*
Fram Filters / *Bendix Corp.*
Frostemp / *Wynn's International, Inc.*
Gen Card / *GenCorp*
General Tire / *GenCorp*
Gold Seal / *Quaker State Oil Refining Corp.*
Goodyear / *Goodyear Tire & Rubber Co.*

Gould / *Gould Inc.*
Grand Champion / *Grand Auto Inc.*
Grand Custom / *Grand Auto Inc.*
Grand Prix / *Grand Auto Inc.*
Grand Security / *Grand Auto Inc.*
Gulf / *Chevron Corp.*
Gulf Lite / *Chevron Corp.*
Gulf Oil & Gas Products / *Gulf Oil Corp.*
Gulfpride / *Chevron Corp.*
Gulfwax / *Chevron Corp.*
Harmony / *Chevron Corp.*
Havoline / *Texaco Inc.*
Hudgins / *Southland Corp.*
Hurst / *Sunbeam Corp.*
Hyjet / *Chevron Corp.*
ICR / *Chevron Corp.*
Isocracking / *Chevron Corp.*
Kendall / *Witco Chemical Corp.*
Kent / *Pep Boys - Manny, Moe & Jack*
Kyso / *Chevron Corp.*
Laredo / *Uniroyal Inc.*
LDO / *Amoco Corp.*
Lend Lease / *Household International, Inc.*
Life / *Chevron Corp.*
Lincoln / *Ford Motor Co.*
Lloyd / *Pep Boys - Manny, Moe & Jack*
LubriMatic / *Witco Chemical Corp.*
M P & G / *Atlantic Richfield Co.*
Mac's / *Ashland Oil, Inc.*
Marson Auto-Body Repair Kits / *American Brands Inc.*
Medalist / *Grand Auto Inc.*
Mercury / *Ford Motor Co.*
Mobil / *Mobil Corp.*
Mobil Service Stations / *Mobil Corp.*
Mohawk / *Mohawk Rubber Co.*
Mohawk Rubber / *Danaher Corp.*
Monroe / *Tenneco Inc.*
Motorcraft / *Ford Motor Co.*
Muzzler / *Sears, Roebuck & Co.*
Mystee-Moly / *Pep Boys - Manny, Moe & Jack*
National Car Rental / *Household International, Inc.*
No-Nox / *Chevron Corp.*
Ora / *Chevron Corp.*
Oronite / *Chevron Corp.*
Oronite Alkane / *Chevron Corp.*
Owens / *Clark Oil & Refining Corp.*
Penn Seal / *Quaker State Oil Refining Corp.*
Pennzoil / *Pennzoil Co.*
Permatex / *Loctite Corp.*
Phillips / *Phillips Petroleum Co.*
Prestone II / *Union Carbide Corp.*
Q / *Quaker State Oil Refining Corp.*
Q/S / *Quaker State Oil Refining Corp.*
Quadrolube / *Quaker State Oil Refining Corp.*
Quaker Koat / *Quaker State Oil Refining Corp.*
Quaker State / *Quaker State Oil Refining Corp.*
Quaker State / *Quaker State Oil Refining Corp.*
Quaker State ATA / *Quaker State Oil Refining Corp.*
Quaker State ATF / *Quaker State Oil Refining Corp.*
Quaker State Carsaver Undercoating / *Quaker State Oil Refining Corp.*
Quaker State FLM / *Quaker State Oil Refining Corp.*
Quaker State Metal-Gard Undercoating / *Quaker State Oil Refining Corp.*
Quaker State Q / *Quaker State Oil Refining Corp.*
Quaker State SDA / *Quaker State Oil Refining Corp.*
Quaker State VCC / *Quaker State Oil Refining Corp.*
Quality / *Quaker State Oil Refining Corp.*
Rallye 340 & 280 / *Uniroyal Inc.*
Reese / *Masco Corp.*
Rheniforming / *Chevron Corp.*
Robertson's / *Fuqua Industries Inc.*
Rotunda / *Ford Motor Co.*
Royal Seal / *Uniroyal Inc.*
RPM / *Chevron Corp.*
Rubber Queen / *Lancaster Colony Corp.*
Seiberling / *Firestone Tire & Rubber Co.*
Senate / *Chevron Corp.*
Shawinigan / *Chevron Corp.*
Shell / *Shell Oil Co.*
Simoniz / *Union Carbide Corp.*
Speedy Muffler King - auto park / *Tenneco Inc.*
Standard / *Chevron Corp.*
Standard / *Amoco Corp.*
Starlite / *Wynn's International, Inc.*
Steeler / *Uniroyal Inc.*
Steelmaster / *Uniroyal Inc.*
Sterling / *Quaker State Oil Refining Corp.*
STP / *Esmark Inc.*
Super Blend / *Quaker State Oil Refining Corp.*
Superflex / *Quaker State Oil Refining Corp.*
Superior / *Witco Chemical Corp.*
Supreme / *Chevron Corp.*
Techron / *Chevron Corp.*
Tectyl / *Ashland Oil, Inc.*
Tenneco / *Tenneco Inc.*
Texaco / *Texaco Inc.*
Tiger Pan / *Uniroyal Inc.*
Tough Cat / *Kimberly-Clark Corp.*
Trop-Artic / *Phillips Petroleum Co.*
Tru-Pic (Service Mark) / *Chevron Corp.*
TSC / *Fuqua Industries Inc.*
U Fill'em / *Tenneco Inc.*
U Pump'em / *Victory Markets, Inc.*
Union 76 / *Unocal Corp.*
Uniroyal / *Uniroyal Inc.*

WD-40 / *WD-40 Co.*
Wheels / *Fay's Drug Co. Inc.*
Windsor / *Zimmer Corp.*
Wolf's Head / *Pennzoil Co.*
X-77 / *Chevron Corp.*
Zerol / *Chevron Corp.*
Zerolene / *Chevron Corp.*
Zimmer / *Zimmer Corp.*
Zimmer Cabriolet, Elegance Classic, Convertible / *Zimmer Corp.*

Beverages

Absopure / *Beatrice Companies Inc.*
Adams / *Royal Crown Companies Inc.*
Airway / *Safeway Stores Inc.*
Alhambra / *McKesson Corp.*
Aqua-Vend / *McKesson Corp.*
Arrow Head / *Beatrice Companies Inc.*
Aspen / *PepsiCo Inc.*
A&W / *Curtice-Burns Inc.*
Bama / *Borden Inc.*
Barcrest / *Beatrice Companies Inc.*
Barrelhead* / *Curtice-Burns Inc.*
Barrelhead Root Beer / *Norton Simon Inc.*
Belmont Springs / *The Coca-Cola Co.*
Bireley's / *Beatrice Companies Inc.*
Bright & Early / *The Coca-Cola Co.*
Brim / *General Foods Corp.*
Bubble Up / *I.C. Industries Inc.*
Butternut / *The Coca-Cola Co.*
caffeine-free Coca-Cola / *The Coca-Cola Co.*
caffeine-free diet Coke / *The Coca-Cola Co.*
caffeine-free TAB / *The Coca-Cola Co.*
California Products / *Beatrice Companies Inc.*
Canada Dry / *Norton Simon Inc.*
Canada Dry* / *Curtice-Burns Inc.*
Canterbury / *Safeway Stores Inc.*
Celestial Seasonings / *Dart & Kraft Inc.*
Chase & Sanborn / *Standard Brands Inc.*
Checkers / *Beatrice Companies Inc.*
cherry Coke / *The Coca-Cola Co.*
Choky / *Beatrice Companies Inc.*
Citro Crest / *Beatrice Companies Inc.*
Citrus Hill / *Procter & Gamble Co.*
Coca-Cola / *The Coca-Cola Co.*
Coolage / *Iroquois Brands Ltd.*
Country Time Lemonade / *General Foods Corp.*
Countrytime / *Curtice-Burns Inc.*
Cragmont / *Safeway Stores Inc.*
Crystal / *McKesson Corp.*
Crystal Light / *General Foods Corp.*
Dad's Root Beer / *I.C. Industries Inc.*
diet Coke / *The Coca-Cola Co.*
Diet Pepsi / *PepsiCo Inc.*
Diet Pepsi Free / *PepsiCo Inc.*
Diet Rite Cola / *Royal Crown Companies Inc.*
Diet Slice / *PepsiCo Inc.*
Dominade / *Amstar Corp.*
Douwe Egberts / *Consolidated Foods Corp.*
Dr. Pepper / *Dr. Pepper*
Dr. Pepper* / *Curtice-Burns Inc.*
Edwards / *Safeway Stores Inc.*
Fanta / *The Coca-Cola Co.*
Five Alive / *The Coca-Cola Co.*
Folger's / *Procter & Gamble Co.*
Fresca / *The Coca-Cola Co.*
Gatorade / *Quaker Oats Co.*
Gatorade Thirst Quencher / *Stokely-Van Camp Inc.*
General Foods International Coffees / *General Foods Corp.*
Gold Medal / *Beatrice Companies Inc.*
Great Bear / *Beatrice Companies Inc.*
Grove Crest / *Beatrice Companies Inc.*
Hawaiian Punch / *R.J. Reynolds*
Hawaii's Own / *Beatrice Companies Inc.*
Hi-C / *The Coca-Cola Co.*
High Point / *Procter & Gamble Co.*
Hires / *Procter & Gamble Co.*
Kava / *Borden Inc.*
Kingsbury Near Beer / *G. Heileman Brewing Co. Inc.*
Kool-Aid / *General Foods Corp.*
Lalani / *Safeway Stores Inc.*
Like / *Philip Morris Inc.*
Like* / *Curtice-Burns Inc.*
Magic Mountain Herb Tea / *Iroquois Brands Ltd.*
Malta India / *Bacardi Corp.*
Maryland Club / *The Coca-Cola Co.*
Maxim / *General Foods Corp.*
Maxwell House / *General Foods Corp.*
Mello Yello / *The Coca-Cola Co.*
Metbrau / *Iroquois Brands Ltd.*
Mi-Lem / *Iroquois Brands Ltd.*
Minute Maid / *The Coca-Cola Co.*
Mirinda / *PepsiCo Inc.*
Mountain Dew / *PepsiCo Inc.*

Mr. & Mrs. T. Cocktail Mix / *American Brands Inc.*
Mr. Pibb / *The Coca-Cola Co.*
Mug Old Fashioned Root Beer / *Beatrice Companies Inc.*
Natural Sun / *Orange-Co. Inc.*
Nehi / *Royal Crown Companies Inc.*
Nemasket Spring / *The Coca-Cola Co.*
Nob Hill / *Safeway Stores Inc.*
Old Judge / *Chock Full o' Nuts Corp.*
On-Tap / *PepsiCo Inc.*
Orange Crush / *Procter & Gamble Co.*
Orange Spot / *Norton Simon Inc.*
Ozarka / *Beatrice Companies Inc.*
Pan Free / *Beatrice Companies Inc.*
Par-T-Pak / *Royal Crown Companies Inc.*
Patio / *PepsiCo Inc.*
Patra / *Beatrice Companies Inc.*
Pepsi Cola / *PepsiCo Inc.*
Pepsi Free / *PepsiCo Inc.*
Pepsi Light / *PepsiCo Inc.*
Pepsi-Cola General Bottlers / *I.C. Industries Inc.*
Perrier / *Curtice-Burns Inc.*
Raffetto / *Iroquois Brands Ltd.*
RC Cola / *Royal Crown Companies Inc.*
RC-100 / *Royal Crown Companies Inc.*
Ritter Veg-Crest / *Curtice-Burns Inc.*
Sanka / *General Foods Corp.*
Seven Up / *Philip Morris Inc.*
Seven Up / *Curtice-Burns Inc.*
Shasta / *Safeway Stores Inc.*
Shasta / *Consolidated Foods Corp.*
Slice / *PepsiCo Inc.*
Slurpee / *Southland Corp.*
Snap-E-Tom / *Heublein Inc.*
Snow Crop / *The Coca-Cola Co.*
Snowy Peak / *Safeway Stores Inc.*
Sparklett's / *McKesson Corp.*
Sprite / *The Coca-Cola Co.*
Sturms / *Bacardi Corp.*
Sugar-Free Dr. Pepper / *Dr. Pepper*
Sunkist / *Curtice-Burns Inc.*
Superior Coffee / *Consolidated Foods Corp.*
Swing / *R.J. Reynolds*
Swiss Miss / *Beatrice Companies Inc.*
Tab / *The Coca-Cola Co.*
Tang / *General Foods Corp.*
Teem / *PepsiCo Inc.*
Tender Leaf Tea / *Standard Brands Inc.*
Texsun / *Royal Crown Companies Inc.*
Tropicana / *Beatrice Companies Inc.*
Veryfine / *Bacardi Corp.*
V-8 Juices / *Campbell Soup Co.*
Wagner / *A.E. Staley Manufacturing Co.*
Yoo-Hoo / *Iroquois Brands Ltd.*
Yuban / *General Foods Corp.*
Zing (Near Beer) / *G. Heileman Brewing Co. Inc.*

Broadcasting

Cablevision, TV / *Media General Inc.*
CATV / *Storer Broadcasting Co.*
CATV / *Westinghouse Electric Corp.*
CATV / *Acton Corp.*
CATV / *Wometco Enterprises Inc.*
CBS / *CBS Inc.*
Cinemax / *Time Inc.*
Cox Cable / *Cox Communications, Inc.*
Cruising World / *New York Times Co.*
Des Moines Register / *Gannett Co. Inc.*
Family Weekly / *Gannett Co. Inc.*
Gannett Media Sales / *Gannett Co. Inc.*
Gannett News Service / *Gannett Co. Inc.*
Gannett Outdoor / *Gannett Co. Inc.*
HBO / *Time Inc.*
KABC-TV & AM / *American Broadcasting Companies Inc.*
KAUM-FM / *American Broadcasting Companies Inc.*
KAYT-FM / *Harte-Hanks Communications Inc.*
KBHK-TV / *Chris Craft Industries, Inc.*
KBIZ-AM / *Post Corp.*
KCBS / *CBS Inc.*
KCBS-TV / *CBS Inc.*
KCCI-TV / *Cowles Communications*
KCEZ-FM / *Meredith Corp.*
KCMO-TV & AM / *Meredith Corp.*
KCNC-TV / *General Electric Co.*
KCOP-TV / *Chris Craft Industries, Inc.*
KCPX-AM/FM / *Columbia Picture Industries Inc.*
KCST-TV / *Storer Broadcasting Co.*
KDFW-TV / *Times Mirror Co.*
KDKA-TV & AM / *Westinghouse Electric Corp.*
KDNH-TV / *Cox Communications, Inc.*
KECC-TV / *Acton Corp.*
KEEL-AM / *Multimedia Inc.*
KERO-TV / *McGraw-Hill Inc.*
KEX-AM / *Taft Broadcasting Co.*
KFAB-AM / *Lee Enterprises Inc.*
KFI-AM / *Cox Communications, Inc.*
KFSM-TV / *New York Times Co.*
KFSN-TV / *Capital Cities Communications Inc.*
KFVS-TV / *American Family Corp.*
KFWB-AM / *Westinghouse Electric Corp.*

KFYE-FM / *Affiliated Publications Inc.*
KGMB-TV / *Lee Enterprises Inc.*
KGOR-FM / *Lee Enterprises Inc.*
KGO-TV & AM / *American Broadcasting Companies Inc.*
KGTV-TV / *McGraw-Hill Inc.*
KHEP-FM / *Affiliated Publications Inc.*
KHJ-TF / *GenCorp*
KHQA-TV / *Lee Enterprises Inc.*
KIAA-FM / *Outlet Co.*
KIIS-FM / *Gannett Co. Inc.*
KIKK-AM/FM / *Viacom International Inc.*
KILT-AM/FM / *LIN Broadcasting Corp.*
KIMN-AM / *Jefferson-Pilot Corp.*
KJQY-FM / *Westinghouse Electric Corp.*
KJR-AM / *Metromedia Inc.*
KKBQ-AM / *Gannett Co. Inc.*
KKBQ-FM / *Gannett Co. Inc.*
KLAC / *Metromedia Inc.*
KLAC-AM / *Capital Cities Communications Inc.*
KLOX-FM / *American Broadcasting Companies Inc.*
KMBC-TV / *Metromedia Inc.*
KMBQ-FM / *Multimedia Inc.*
KMET-FM / *Metromedia Inc.*
KMGH-TV / *McGraw-Hill Inc.*
KMOL-TV / *Chris Craft Industries, Inc.*
KMOX-TV & AM / *CBS Inc.*
KMPS-AM/FM / *Affiliated Publications Inc.*
KMSP-TV / *Chris Craft Industries, Inc.*
KNAI-FM / *RCA Corp.*
KNBC-TV / *RCA Corp.*
KNBR / *RCA Corp.*
KNX-AM / *CBS Inc.*
KOAX-FM / *Westinghouse Electric Corp.*
KOCO-TV / *Gannett Co. Inc.*
KODA-FM / *Westinghouse Electric Corp.*
KOIN-TV / *Lee Enterprises Inc.*
KOKH-TV / *John Blair & Co.*
KOSI-FM / *Westinghouse Electric Corp.*
KOST-FM / *Cox Communications, Inc.*
KOVR-TV / *Outlet Co.*
KPHO-TV / *Meredith Corp.*
KPIX-TV / *Westinghouse Electric Corp.*
KPNX-TV / *Gannett Co. Inc.*
KPOL-AM / *Capital Cities Communications Inc.*
KPTV-TV / *Chris Craft Industries, Inc.*
KQXT-FM / *Westinghouse Electric Corp.*
KRAK-AM/KSKK-FM / *Affiliated Publications Inc.*
KRIV-TV / *Metromedia Inc.*
KRLD-AM / *Metromedia Inc.*
KSAN-FM / *Metromedia Inc.*
KSAT-TV / *Outlet Co.*
KSBW-TV / *John Blair & Co.*
KSBY-TV / *John Blair & Co.*
KSCS-FM / *Capital Cities Communications Inc.*
KSDK-TV / *Multimedia Inc.*
KSDO/KSDO-FM / *Gannett Co. Inc.*
KSD-TV / *Gannett Co. Inc.*
KSFX-FM / *American Broadcasting Companies Inc.*
KSLA-TV / *Viacom International Inc.*
KSON AM&FM / *Jefferson-Pilot Corp.*
KTBC-TV / *Times Mirror Co.*
KTIV-TV / *American Family Corp.*
KTRK-TV / *Capital Cities Communications Inc.*
KTTV-TV / *Metromedia Inc.*
KTVI-TV / *Times Mirror Co.*
KTVO-TV / *Post Corp.*
KTVU-TV / *Cox Communications, Inc.*
KTVV-TV / *LIN Broadcasting Corp.*
KTVX-TV / *Chris Craft Industries, Inc.*
KUSA-AM / *Gannett Co. Inc.*
KUSA-TV / *Gannett Co. Inc.*
KVIL AM/FM / *John Blair & Co.*
KVOS-TV / *Wometco Enterprises Inc.*
KWWL-TV / *American Family Corp.*
KXAS-TV / *LIN Broadcasting Corp.*
KYGO-FM / *Jefferson-Pilot Corp.*
KYW-TV & AM / *Westinghouse Electric Corp.*
KYYS-FM / *Taft Broadcasting Co.*
KZLA-FM / *Capital Cities Communications Inc.*
Lake Valley Broadcasters / *Katy Industries, Inc.*
Lifetime / *Viacom International Inc.*
Louis Harris & Assoc. / *Gannett Co. Inc.*
Media General Cable-Cable TV / *Media General Inc.*
MSG / *Gulf* + Western Industries Inc.
Multimedia Cablevision / *Multimedia Inc.*
ON TV / *Oak Industries Inc.*
Showtime/The Movie Channel / *Viacom International Inc.*
Times Mirror Cable Television / *Times Mirror Co.*
WABC-TV & AM / *American Broadcasting Companies Inc.*
WAFF-TV / *American Family Corp.*
WAGA-TV / *Storer Broadcasting Co.*
WAIA-FM / *Cox Communications, Inc.*
WAKY-AM / *Multimedia Inc.*
WAND-TV / *LIN Broadcasting Corp.*
WANE-TV / *LIN Broadcasting Corp.*
WAVY-TV / *LIN Broadcasting Corp.*
WAXX-AM / *Post Corp.*
WBAP-AM/FM / *Capital Cities Communications Inc.*
WBBF-AM / *LIN Broadcasting Corp.*
WBBM-TV & AM / *CBS Inc.*
WBCY-FM / *Jefferson-Pilot Corp.*
WBIG-AM / *Jefferson-Pilot Corp.*
WBIR-TV / *Multimedia Inc.*

WBRC-TV / *Taft Broadcasting Co.*
WBT-AM / *Jefferson-Pilot Corp.*
WBTV-TV / *Jefferson-Pilot Corp.*
WBZ-TV, AM/FM / *Westinghouse Electric Corp.*
WCAU-TV & AM / *CBS Inc.*
WCBD-TV / *Media General Inc.*
WCBS-TV & AM / *CBS Inc.*
WCIX-TV / *Taft Broadcasting Co.*
WCKG-FM / *Cox Communications, Inc.*
WCMH-TV / *Outlet Co.*
WCPI-FM / *Columbia Picture Industries Inc.*
WCZY-AM/FM / *Gannett Co. Inc.*
WDAE-AM / *Gannett Co. Inc.*
WDAF-TV & AM / *Taft Broadcasting Co.*
WDAI-FM / *American Broadcasting Companies Inc.*
WDBO-TV and AM/FM / *Outlet Co.*
WDCA-TV / *Taft Broadcasting Co.*
WDIO-TV / *Harcourt Brace Jovanovich Inc.*
WDIV-TV / *Washington Post Co.*
WDOK-FM / *Gannett Co. Inc.*
WDVE-FM / *Taft Broadcasting Co.*
WEAU-TV / *Post Corp.*
WEMP-AM / *LIN Broadcasting Corp.*
WESH-TV / *Cowles Communications*
WETM-TV / *Times Mirror Co.*
WEZW-FM / *Multimedia Inc.*
WFAS-AM/FM / *Affiliated Publications Inc.*
WFBC-AM/FM / *Multimedia Inc.*
WFIL-AM / *LIN Broadcasting Corp.*
WFLA AM/FM / *John Blair & Co.*
WFOG-AM/FM / *Tech/Ops Inc.*
WFSB-TV / *Washington Post Co.*
WGBS-AM / *Jefferson-Pilot Corp.*
WGCI-AM / *Gannett Co. Inc.*
WGCI-FM / *Gannett Co. Inc.*
WGR-AM and FM / *Taft Broadcasting Co.*
WGR-FM / *Taft Broadcasting Co.*
WGRZ-TV / *General Cinema Corp.*
WHDH-AM / *John Blair & Co.*
WHEC-TV / *Viacom International Inc.*
WHIO-AM/FM / *Cox Communications, Inc.*
WHIO-TV / *Cox Communications, Inc.*
WHNT-TV / *New York Times Co.*
WHTM-TV / *Times Mirror Co.*
WHYT-FM / *Capital Cities Communications Inc.*
WIBC-AM / *John Blair & Co.*
WIL-AM/FM / *LIN Broadcasting Corp.*
WIND-AM / *Westinghouse Electric Corp.*
WINS-AM / *Westinghouse Electric Corp.*
WIOD-AM / *Cox Communications, Inc.*
WIOQ-FM / *Outlet Co.*
WIP-AM / *Metromedia Inc.*
WIQI-FM / *Gannett Co. Inc.*
WIRT-TV / *Harcourt Brace Jovanovich Inc.*
WISH-TV / *LIN Broadcasting Corp.*
WITI-TV / *Storer Broadcasting Co.*
WITN-TV / *American Family Corp.*
WJBK-TV / *Storer Broadcasting Co.*
WJIM-TV and AM/FM / *Gross Telecasting Inc.*
WJKS-TV / *Media General Inc.*
WJKW-TV / *Storer Broadcasting Co.*
WJR-AM/FM / *Capital Cities Communications Inc.*
WJRT-TV / *Knight-Ridder Newspapers Inc.*
WJXT-TV / *Washington Post Co.*
WJYE-FM / *Tech/Ops Inc.*
WJZ-TV / *Westinghouse Electric Corp.*
WKAQ-TV / *John Blair & Co.*
WKBD-TV / *Cox Communications, Inc.*
WKBT-TV / *Gross Telecasting Inc.*
WKBW-TV & AM / *Capital Cities Communications Inc.*
WKHX-FM / *Capital Cities Communications Inc.*
WKRC-TV & AM / *Taft Broadcasting Co.*
WKRN-TV / *Knight-Ridder Newspapers Inc.*
WKRQ-FM / *Taft Broadcasting Co.*
WKYC-TV / *RCA Corp.*
WKYS-FM / *RCA Corp.*
WLAK-FM / *Viacom International Inc.*
WLBZ-AM / *Acton Corp.*
WLCY-AM / *Harte-Hanks Communications Inc.*
WLKW-AM/FM / *Tech/Ops Inc.*
WLOS-TV & FM / *Wometco Enterprises Inc.*
WLQV-AM / *Gannett Co. Inc.*
WLS-TV & AM / *American Broadcasting Companies Inc.*
WLTW-FM / *Viacom International Inc.*
WLUC-TV / *Post Corp.*
WLUK-TV / *Post Corp.*
WLVI-TV / *Gannett Co. Inc.*
WLVQ-FM / *Taft Broadcasting Co.*
WLWT-TV / *Multimedia Inc.*
WLYF-FM / *Jefferson-Pilot Corp.*
WMAL-AM / *American Broadcasting Companies Inc.*
WMAZ-TV & AM / *Multimedia Inc.*
WMAZ-TV & AM / *RCA Corp.*
WMET-FM / *Metromedia Inc.*
WMJQ-FM / *LIN Broadcasting Corp.*
WMUR-TV / *Acton Corp.*
WMYD-TV / *Acton Corp.*
WMZQ-AM/FM / *Viacom International Inc.*
WNAP-FM / *John Blair & Co.*
WNBC-TV & AM / *RCA Corp.*
WNCN-FM / *GAF Corp.*
WNEW-AM/FM / *Metromedia Inc.*
WNEW-TV / *Metromedia Inc.*
WNIS-FM / *RCA Corp.*

WNWS-FM / *RCA Corp.*
WNYT-FM / *LIN Broadcasting Corp.*
WNYT-TV / *Viacom International Inc.*
WOKR-TV / *Post Corp.*
WOKV-AM/WAIV-FM / *Affiliated Publications Inc.*
Wometco / *Wometco Enterprises Inc.*
WOMO-FM / *Metromedia Inc.*
WOR-TV / *GenCorp*
WOTV-TV / *LIN Broadcasting Corp.*
WPAT-AM/FM / *Capital Cities Communications Inc.*
WPLG-TV / *Washington Post Co.*
WPLJ-FM / *American Broadcasting Companies Inc.*
WPRI-TV / *Knight-Ridder Newspapers Inc.*
WPRO-AM/FM / *Capital Cities Communications Inc.*
WPVI-TV / *Capital Cities Communications Inc.*
WPXI-TV / *Cox Communications, Inc.*
WQAD-TV / *New York Times Co.*
WQCY-FM / *Lee Enterprises Inc.*
WQRS-FM / *Outlet Co.*
WQXI-AM-FM / *Jefferson-Pilot Corp.*
WQXR-AM/FM / *New York Times Co.*
WRAX-FM / *American Broadcasting Companies Inc.*
WRBQ-FM / *Harte-Hanks Communications Inc.*
WRC-TV & AM / *RCA Corp.*
WREG-TV / *New York Times Co.*
WRIF-FM / *American Broadcasting Companies Inc.*
WRLM-FM / *Outlet Co.*
WROW AM/FM / *Capital Cities Communications Inc.*
WRTV-TV / *McGraw-Hill Inc.*
WRVA-AM / *Harte-Hanks Communications Inc.*
WRVQ-FM / *Harte-Hanks Communications Inc.*
WRVR-FM / *Viacom International Inc.*
WSAZ-TV / *Lee Enterprises Inc.*
WSB-AM / *Metromedia Inc.*
WSB-AM/FM / *Cox Communications, Inc.*
WSBK-TV / *Storer Broadcasting Co.*
WSB-TV / *Cox Communications, Inc.*
WSCV-TV / *John Blair & Co.*
WSGN-AM / *Harte-Hanks Communications Inc.*
WSNL-TV / *Wometco Enterprises Inc.*
WSOC-AM/FM / *Cox Communications, Inc.*
WSOC-TV / *Cox Communications, Inc.*
WSTM-TV / *Times Mirror Co.*
WSUN-AM / *Taft Broadcasting Co.*
WTAC-AM / *Fuqua Industries Inc.*
WTAD-AM / *Lee Enterprises Inc.*
WTAF-TV / *Taft Broadcasting Co.*
WTCN-TV / *Metromedia Inc.*
WTCN-TV / *Gannett Co. Inc.*
WTEN-TV / *Knight-Ridder Newspapers Inc.*
WTKR-TV / *Knight-Ridder Newspapers Inc.*
WTLV-TV / *Harte-Hanks Communications Inc.*
WTNH-TV / *Capital Cities Communications Inc.*
WTOC-TV / *American Family Corp.*
WTOM-TV / *United States Tobacco Co.*
WTOP-AM / *Outlet Co.*
WTTG-TV / *Metromedia Inc.*
WTVD-TV / *Capital Cities Communications Inc.*
WTVG-TV / *Storer Broadcasting Co.*
WTVH-TV / *Meredith Corp.*
WTVJ-TV / *Wometco Enterprises Inc.*
WTVN-TV & AM / *Taft Broadcasting Co.*
WUSL-FM / *LIN Broadcasting Corp.*
WVEZ-FM / *Multimedia Inc.*
WVIT-TV / *Viacom International Inc.*
WVTM-TV / *Times Mirror Co.*
WWBT-TV / *Jefferson-Pilot Corp.*
WWHT-TV / *Wometco Enterprises Inc.*
WWNC-AM / *Multimedia Inc.*
WWVA-AM / *Columbia Picture Industries Inc.*
WWWE-AM / *Gannett Co. Inc.*
WXFL-TV / *Media General Inc.*
WXIA-TV / *Gannett Co. Inc.*
WXIX-TV / *Metromedia Inc.*
WXYZ-TV & AM / *American Broadcasting Companies Inc.*
WYDE-AM / *Columbia Picture Industries Inc.*
WYNF-FM / *Taft Broadcasting Co.*
WZGO-FM / *Cox Communications, Inc.*
WZOU-FM / *John Blair & Co.*
WZTV / *Multimedia Inc.*
WZZM-TV / *Wometco Enterprises Inc.*
KKRZ-FM / *Kings Island Inn*

Building & Home Improvement Materials & Services

ABM Engineering Services / *American Building Maintenance Industries*
ABM Security Services / *American Building Maintenance Industries*
Accolade / *Pratt & Lambert, Inc.*
Acme / *Justin Industries Inc.*
Ajust-A-Rail / *Questor Corp.*
All-American / *Beatrice Companies Inc.*
Alumigrip / *Grow Group Inc.*
American Air Filter Amer-glas / *Allis-Chalmers Corp.*
American Building Maintenance Co. / *American Building Maintenance Industries*

American-Standard / *American Standard Inc.*
Ameritone / *Grow Group Inc.*
Ampco Parking Services / *American Building Maintenance Industries*
Amtech Elevator Services / *American Building Maintenance Industries*
Amtech Energy Services / *American Building Maintenance Industries*
Amtech Lighting Services / *American Building Maintenance Industries*
Aqua Chem / *Georgia-Pacific Corp.*
ARCO Solar / *Atlantic Richfield Co.*
Artistic / *Norris Industries Inc.*
Awlgrip / *Grow Group Inc.*
Baker / *Newell Companies Inc.*
Banner / *Beatrice Companies Inc.*
Benjamin / *Thomas Industries Inc.*
Best Jet / *Beatrice Companies Inc.*
Bilt Best / *Di Giorgio Corp.*
Body Shaper / *Beatrice Companies Inc.*
Boysen / *Grow Group Inc.*
BPS Paints / *Insilco Corp.*
Brite Bond / *GAF Corp.*
Bruce / *Triangle Pacific Corp.*
Bubble Stream / *Beatrice Companies Inc.*
Builders Brass / *Thomas Industries Inc.*
Builders Square / *K Mart Corp.*
C & M / *Thomas Industries Inc.*
Capri / *Thomas Industries Inc.*
Carver Tripp / *Clorox*
Celotex / *Jim Walter Corp.*
Centex Homes / *Centex Corp.*
Chicago Specialty / *Beatrice Companies Inc.*
Classic / *Questor Corp.*
Classic Bath / *Triangle Pacific Corp.*
Clean Stroke / *Newell Companies Inc.*
Clorox Pic-Wash / *Clorox*
Colony / *Valspar Corp.*
Color Key / *Grow Group Inc.*
Color Tile / *Color Tile Inc.*
Color Your World / *Color Tile Inc.*
Comm Air Mechanical Services / *American Building Maintenance Industries*
Corex / *American Cyanamid Company*
Culligan's Aqua Clear / *Beatrice Companies Inc.*
Dearborn / *Beatrice Companies Inc.*
Decora / *Beatrice Companies Inc.*
Del Mar / *Triangle Pacific Corp.*
Delta / *Masco Corp.*
Deltex / *Masco Corp.*
Deltique / *Masco Corp.*
Design-Tex / *Temtex Industries Inc.*
Devoe / *Grow Group Inc.*
Diamond / *Diamond International Corp.*
Diamond Lumber, Inc / *Michigan General Corp.*
Dura-Glide / *Stanley Works*
Easterday Supply Co. / *American Building Maintenance Industries*
"Easy Living" / *DeSoto, Inc.*
Easy Living / *Sears, Roebuck & Co.*
Edgemate / *Westvaco Corp.*
Elliott / *Valspar Corp.*
Enterprise Paints / *Insilco Corp.*
Epic / *Masco Corp.*
Ernst-Malmo / *Pay 'n Save Corp.*
Evans / *NVF Co.*
Excello / *Beatrice Companies Inc.*
EZ Paintr / *Newell Companies Inc.*
EZ Roller / *Newell Companies Inc.*
Featherlite / *Justin Industries Inc.*
Formica / *American Cyanamid Company*
Foster / *H.B. Fuller Co.*
Fox & Jacobs / *Centex Corp.*
GAF Star / *GAF Corp.*
Gardco / *Thomas Industries Inc.*
Georgia Pacific / *Georgia-Pacific Corp.*
Glidden / *SCM Corp.*
Grenadier / *Standard Brands Inc.*
Gro Master / *Rangaire Corp.*
Handee Ram Rod / *Beatrice Companies Inc.*
H.B. Fuller / *H.B. Fuller Co.*
Ideal Standard / *American Standard Inc.*
Imperial / *Collins & Aikman*
Instapure / *Teledyne Inc.*
Interstate Brick / *Questar Corp.*
IXL / *Triangle Pacific Corp.*
Jimco Stone Centers / *Jim Walter Corp.*
Kativo / *H.B. Fuller Co.*
Katzenbach & Warren / *Gulf* + Western Industries Inc.
Keller / *Keller Industries Inc.*
Kleen Stream / *Beatrice Companies Inc.*
Koro-Seal / *Grow Group Inc.*
Krestmark / *Michigan General Corp.*
Krylon / *Borden Inc.*
Lasco / *Philips Industries Inc.*
Lennon / *Thomas Industries Inc.*
Leslie-Locke / *Questor Corp.*
Leuen / *National Patent Development Corp.*
Liken / *Beatrice Companies Inc.*
Linear / *H.B. Fuller Co.*
Little Pete / *Beatrice Companies Inc.*
Lloyd Home & Building Centers Inc. / *American Maize Products Co.*
Lucite / *Clorox*
Magic Color Paint / *Insilco Corp.*

Magic-Door / *Stanley Works*
Majestic Fireplaces / *American Standard Inc.*
Malta / *Philips Industries Inc.*
Mary Carter Paint / *Insilco Corp.*
Masonite / *Masonite Corp.*
Master Shield / *Danaher Corp.*
Masury / *Valspar Corp.*
Max Bond / *H.B. Fuller Co.*
Minnesota / *Valspar Corp.*
Mirrolac / *Grow Group Inc.*
Modern Fold / *American Standard Inc.*
Monarch / *H.B. Fuller Co.*
Mountain Fuel / *Questar Corp.*
Mutschler / *Triangle Pacific Corp.*
M.W. Smith Lumber Co. / *SCM Corp.*
Naugahyde / *Uniroyal Inc.*
Oliver-MacLeod / *Thomas Industries Inc.*
Olympic / *Clorox*
Pan-O-Play / *Collins & Aikman*
Peerless / *Masco Corp.*
Perma-Door / *American Standard Inc.*
Pierce & Stevens / *Pratt & Lambert, Inc.*
Pipe Line / *Stanley Works*
Pitegoff / *Beatrice Companies Inc.*
Plasolux / *Grow Group Inc.*
Pratt & Lambert / *Pratt & Lambert, Inc.*
Price Pfister / *Norris Industries Inc.*
Protouch / *Newell Companies Inc.*
Rangaire / *Rangaire Corp.*
Red Devil Paints / *Insilco Corp.*
Redman / *Redman Industries Inc.*
Regency House / *Grow Group Inc.*
Riviera / *NVF Co.*
Rose Exterminator Co. / *American Building Maintenance Industries*
Sherwin-Williams / *Sherwin-Williams Co.*
Signal Landmark Properties / *Signal Companies Inc.*
Sinclair / *Insilco Corp.*
Speed Rex / *Grow Group Inc.*
Sprayit / *Thomas Industries Inc.*
Spred / *SCM Corp.*
Spred Satin / *SCM Corp.*
Standard / *American Standard Inc.*
Stan-Ray / *Stanley Works*
Style-A-Rail / *Questor Corp.*
Ten Year / *Pratt & Lambert, Inc.*
Tender Leaf / *Procter & Gamble Co.*
Texas Clay / *Temtex Industries Inc.*
Thermalite / *Justin Industries Inc.*
Thomas / *Thomas Industries Inc.*
Timberline / *GAF Corp.*
Tri Pac / *Triangle Pacific Corp.*
Tru-Glaze / *Grow Group Inc.*
U-install / *Stanley Works*
Ultima Wallcoverings / *Color Tile Inc.*
Valspar / *Valspar Corp.*
Vanguard / *GAF Corp.*
Versa / *Questor Corp.*
Vicracoustic/Vicratex / *Dayco Corp.*
Vistalite / *Rangaire Corp.*
Wall-Tex / *Borden Inc.*
Wayne / *Scott & Fetzer Co.*
"Weatherbeater" / *DeSoto, Inc.*
Weatherbeater / *Sears, Roebuck & Co.*
Wilsonart / *Dart & Kraft Inc.*
Wonder-Tones / *Grow Group Inc.*
Yorktowne / *Wickes Corp.*

Cosmetics

Adrien Arpel / *Seligman & Latz Inc.*
Advanced Formula / *Revlon Inc.*
Age Zone Controller / *Squibb Corp.*
Air Spun / *Pfizer Inc.*
Alexandra de Markoff / *Squibb Corp.*
Auraseva / *Squibb Corp.*
Aviance / *Chesebrough-Pond's Inc.*
Avon / *Avon Products Inc.*
Aziza / *Chesebrough-Pond's Inc.*
Beret / *Chesebrough-Pond's Inc.*
Blush-On / *Revlon Inc.*
Brush 'n Blush / *Schering-Plough Corp.*
Cachet / *Chesebrough-Pond's Inc.*
Charles of the Ritz / *Squibb Corp.*
Chimere / *Chesebrough-Pond's Inc.*
Colorsilk / *Revlon Inc.*
Corn Silk / *Chattem, Inc.*
Country Cordovans / *Squibb Corp.*
Cover Girl / *Noxell Corp.*
Custom Eyes / *Revlon Inc.*
Di Borghese / *Revlon Inc.*
Dorothy Gray / *Sterling Drug Inc.*
Ecco / *Revlon Inc.*
Equasion / *Pfizer Inc.*
Erno Laszlo / *Chesebrough-Pond's Inc.*
Eterna 27 / *Revlon Inc.*
Etherea / *Revlon Inc.*
Fiamma / *Revlon Inc.*
Flame Glo / *Del Laboratories Inc.*
Flex / *Revlon Inc.*
Formula 2 / *Revlon Inc.*
Fresh & Lovely / *Schering-Plough Corp.*

Geminesse / *Norton Simon Inc.*
Halston / *Norton Simon Inc.*
Intimate / *Revlon Inc.*
Jafra / *Gillette Co.*
Jean D'Albert / *Norton Simon Inc.*
Liqui Creame / *Squibb Corp.*
Love's Baby Soft / *Chattem, Inc.*
Love's Musky Jasmin / *Chattem, Inc.*
Lumina / *Revlon Inc.*
Mary Quant / *Norton Simon Inc.*
Matchabelli / *Chesebrough-Pond's Inc.*
Max Factor / *Norton Simon Inc.*
Maxi / *Norton Simon Inc.*
Maybelline / *Schering-Plough Corp.*
Milk Plus 6 / *Revlon Inc.*
Miners / *Norton Simon Inc.*
Miss Balmain / *Revlon Inc.*
Moisture Whip / *Schering-Plough Corp.*
Moon Drops / *Revlon Inc.*
Mudd / *Chattem, Inc.*
Nail Color / *Schering-Plough Corp.*
Natural Wonder / *Revlon Inc.*
Norell / *Revlon Inc.*
Orlane / *Norton Simon Inc.*
Outdoor Girl / *Norton Simon Inc.*
Polished Amber / *Revlon Inc.*
Power Glow / *Squibb Corp.*
Princess Marcella Borghese / *Revlon Inc.*
Pure Magic / *Norton Simon Inc.*
Revenescence / *Squibb Corp.*
Revlon / *Revlon Inc.*
Skin Balancing Makeup / *Revlon Inc.*
Soft Glow / *Squibb Corp.*
Tinkerbell / *MEM Co.*
Ultima II / *Revlon Inc.*
Ultra-Lucent / *Norton Simon Inc.*
Vanda / *Dart & Kraft Inc.*
Wind Song / *Chesebrough-Pond's Inc.*
Yves Saint Laurent / *Squibb Corp.*

Department, Discount, General Merchandise Stores & Mail Order Retailing

Abraham & Straus / *Federated Department Stores Inc.*
Alco / *Duckwall-Alco Stores, Inc.*
Alexander's / *Alexander's Inc.*
Allied Department Stores / *Michigan General Corp.*
Almy / *Almy Stores Inc.*
Almy's / *Stop & Shop Companies Inc.*
Ames / *Ames Department Stores Inc.*
Ann Taylor / *Allied Stores Corp.*
Associated Retail Stores / *Berkshire Hathaway Inc.*
Bacon's / *Mercantile Stores Co. Inc.*
Bamberger's / *R.H. Macy & Co. Inc.*
Bargain Center / *Kuhn's-Big K Stores Corp.*
Bargain World / *G.C. Murphy Co.*
Ben Franklin / *Household International, Inc.*
Bergdorf Goodman / *Carter Hawley Hale Stores, Inc.*
Best / *Best Products Co., Inc.*
Best Jewelry / *Best Products Co., Inc.*
Big K/Edwards / *Kuhn's-Big K Stores Corp.*
Block's / *Allied Stores Corp.*
Bloomingdale's / *Federated Department Stores Inc.*
Boatyard Village & Trail / *Specialty Restaurants Corp.*
Bon / *Allied Stores Corp.*
Bonwit Teller / *Allied Stores Corp.*
Bradlees / *Stop & Shop Companies Inc.*
Brights / *Wetterau, Inc.*
The Broadway / *Carter Hawley Hale Stores, Inc.*
Brooks Brothers / *Allied Stores Corp.*
Brookstone / *Quaker Oats Co.*
BryLane / *The Limited Inc.*
Bullock's/Bullock's Wilshire / *Federated Department Stores Inc.*
Burdine's / *Federated Department Stores Inc.*
Cain-Sloan / *Allied Stores Corp.*
Caldor / *Associated Dry Goods Corp.*
Caldor / *Caldor Inc.*
Carson, Pirie Scott / *Carson Pirie Scott & Company*
Castner-Knott / *Mercantile Stores Co. Inc.*
Catherine's Stout Shoppe / *Allied Stores Corp.*
The Children's Place / *Federated Department Stores Inc.*
Clarkin's / *Unishops Inc.*
Clark's / *Cook United Inc.*
Clover / *Strawbridge & Clothier*
Consolidated Sales Co. / *Cook United Inc.*
Cook's / *Cook United Inc.*
The Crescent / *Marshall Field & Co.*
Crowley's / *Crowley, Milner & Co.*
Davison's / *R.H. Macy & Co. Inc.*
Dayton Hudson / *Dayton Hudson Corp.*
Dayton's Department Stores / *Dayton Hudson Corp.*
de Lendrecie's / *Mercantile Stores Co. Inc.*
Denby's / *Outlet Co.*
Denver Dry Goods Co. / *Associated Dry Goods Corp.*
Dey Brothers / *Allied Stores Corp.*
Dolgin / *Modern Merchandising Inc.*
Dolgin's / *Best Products Co., Inc.*

Dollar / *Glosser Bros. Inc.*
Dollar General / *Dollar General Corp.*
Donaldson's / *Allied Stores Corp.*
Duckwall / *Duckwall-Alco Stores, Inc.*
Eagle Discount Centers / *Lucky Stores Inc.*
Edan Plaza / *Carson Pirie Scott & Company*
Edgar's / *Almy Stores Inc.*
Edward Malley / *Outlet Co.*
Edward Variety / *Kuhn's-Big K Stores Corp.*
Edwards / *Almy Stores Inc.*
El-Bee / *Elder-Beerman Stores Corp.*
Elder-Beerman / *Elder-Beerman Stores Corp.*
Emporium Capwell / *Carter Hawley Hale Stores, Inc.*
Family Department Stores / *A.J. Bayless Markets Inc.*
Famous-Barr Co. / *May Department Stores Co.*
Fashion Gallery / *Spencer Companies Inc.*
Fed-Mart / *The Fed Mart Corporation*
Filene's / *Federated Department Stores Inc.*
Filene's Basement / *Federated Department Stores Inc.*
Fingerhut / *American Can Co.*
Foley's / *Federated Department Stores Inc.*
Food Basket / *Lucky Stores Inc.*
Frank Lewis Grapefruit Club / *Standex International Corp.*
Frederick & Nelson / *Marshall Field & Co.*
Freeses / *Almy Stores Inc.*
Gamble Department Stores / *Wickes Corp.*
Garfinckel's / *Allied Stores Corp.*
Garfinkel's / *Garfinkle Brooks Brothers, Miller & Rhoads Inc.*
Gayfers / *Mercantile Stores Co. Inc.*
Gaylords / *Gaylords National Corp.*
Gee Bee Department Store / *Glosser Bros. Inc.*
Gem / *Hartfield Zody's Inc.*
Gemco / *Lucky Stores Inc.*
Giggletree / *United States Shoe Corp.*
Glass Block / *Mercantile Stores Co. Inc.*
Glosser Bros. / *Glosser Bros. Inc.*
Gold Circle / *Federated Department Stores Inc.*
Goldblatt's / *Goldblatt Brothers Inc.*
Golde's / *Interco Inc.*
Goldsmith's / *Federated Department Stores Inc.*
Goldwater's / *Associated Dry Goods Corp.*
Gorin's / *Almy Stores Inc.*
Grand Central / *Grand Central Inc.*
Great Western / *Modern Merchandising Inc.*
Great Western / *Best Products Co., Inc.*
Hahne & Co. / *Associated Dry Goods Corp.*
Halle's / *Marshall Field & Co.*
Hart / *Big Bear, Inc.*
Harzfeld's / *Garfinkle Brooks Brothers, Miller & Rhoads Inc.*
Heartland / *Supermarkets General Corp.*
Heaven / *Rite Aid Corp.*
Heck's / *Heck's Inc.*
Heer's / *Allied Stores Corp.*
Hennessy's / *Mercantile Stores Co. Inc.*
Hens & Kelly / *Twin Fair Inc.*
Herp's / *Allied Stores Corp.*
Herrschners / *Quaker Oats Co.*
Higbee / *Higbee Co.*
Hills / *SCOA Industries Inc.*
Hirsch Value Center / *Interco Inc.*
Hochschild-Kohn / *Supermarkets General Corp.*
House & Hale / *Almy Stores Inc.*
House of Almonds / *Tenneco Inc.*
Howard's Brandiscount / *Wickes Corp.*
Hudson's Department Stores / *Dayton Hudson Corp.*
I. Magnin / *Federated Department Stores Inc.*
Idaho / *Interco Inc.*
Interstate / *Toys "R" Us Inc.*
J. Brannam / *F.W. Woolworth Co.*
Jack London Village / *Specialty Restaurants Corp.*
Jafco / *Best Products Co., Inc.*
Jamesway / *Jamesway Corp.*
J.B. Ivey / *Marshall Field & Co.*
J.B. White's / *Mercantile Stores Co. Inc.*
J.C. Penney / *J.C. Penney Co., Inc.*
Jeans Galore / *Interco Inc.*
Jefferson Ward / *Mobil Corp.*
J.M. McDonald's / *Wickes Corp.*
Jofco / *Modern Merchandising Inc.*
John Wanamaker / *Carter Hawley Hale Stores, Inc.*
Jones Store / *Mercantile Stores Co. Inc.*
Jordan Marsh / *Allied Stores Corp.*
Jos. A. Bank / *Quaker Oats Co.*
Joseph Horne Co. / *Associated Dry Goods Corp.*
Joske's / *Allied Stores Corp.*
Joslins / *Mercantile Stores Co. Inc.*
JT General Stores / *American Stores Co.*
Jupiter / *K Mart Corp.*
Just for Kids / *United States Shoe Corp.*
J.W. Robinson Co. / *Associated Dry Goods Corp.*
K Mart / *K Mart Corp.*
Kash N' Karry / *Lucky Stores Inc.*
Kauai / *Amfac Inc.*
Kaufmann's / *May Department Stores Co.*
Kresge / *K Mart Corp.*
Kuhn's Variety / *Kuhn's-Big K Stores Corp.*
La Belle's / *Modern Merchandising Inc.*
LaBelle's / *Best Products Co., Inc.*
Lamonts / *Pay 'n Save Corp.*
Lane / *Laneco Inc.*
Lane / *Wetterau, Inc.*
Lane Bryant / *The Limited Inc.*

Laneco Stores & Discount Department Stores / *Laneco Inc.*
Lasalle's / *R.H. Macy & Co. Inc.*
Lawson's / *Consolidated Foods Corp.*
Lazarus / *Federated Department Stores Inc.*
Lechmere / *Dayton Hudson Corp.*
Leeds / *Modern Merchandising Inc.*
Leonard Krower & Son / *Gordon Jewelry Corp.*
Levy's / *Allied Stores Corp.*
Levy's / *Federated Department Stores Inc.*
Liberty House / *Amfac Inc.*
L'il Peach / *Supermarkets General Corp.*
Limited Express / *The Limited Inc.*
Limited Stores / *The Limited Inc.*
Lincoln Square / *Carson Pirie Scott & Company*
Linen Center / *Brown Group Inc.*
Lion / *Mercantile Stores Co. Inc.*
Loehmann's / *Associated Dry Goods Corp.*
Lord & Taylor / *Associated Dry Goods Corp.*
L.S. Ayres & Co., Inc. / *Associated Dry Goods Corp.*
Lucky / *Lucky Stores Inc.*
Maas Brothers / *Allied Stores Corp.*
Macy's / *R.H. Macy & Co. Inc.*
Magic Mart / *Sterling Stores Co. Inc.*
Main Street / *Federated Department Stores Inc.*
Margo's/Regan's / *Elder-Beerman Stores Corp.*
Marshall Field / *Marshall Field & Co.*
Mary's Gate Village / *Specialty Restaurants Corp.*
Masters / *Masters Inc.*
May Centers, Inc. / *May Department Stores Co.*
May Co., California / *May Department Stores Co.*
May Co., Cleveland / *May Department Stores Co.*
May D&F / *May Department Stores Co.*
May-Cohens / *May Department Stores Co.*
Mays / *J.W. Mays Inc.*
McAlpin's / *Mercantile Stores Co. Inc.*
Meier & Frank / *May Department Stores Co.*
Memco / *Lucky Stores Inc.*
Mervyn's / *Dayton Hudson Corp.*
Miller & Rhoads / *Garfinkle Brooks Brothers, Miller & Rhoads Inc.*
Miller & Rhoads / *Allied Stores Corp.*
Miller Sales / *Modern Merchandising Inc.*
Miller Sales / *Best Products Co., Inc.*
Miller's / *Garfinkle Brooks Brothers, Miller & Rhoads Inc.*
Miller's / *Allied Stores Corp.*
Money Management Institute / *Household International, Inc.*
Montgomery Ward / *Mobil Corp.*
Mount Vernon / *MCA Inc.*
Muller's / *Allied Stores Corp.*
Murphy's / *G.C. Murphy Co.*
Murphy's / *G.C. Murphy Co.*
Nancy's Choice / *The Limited Inc.*
Neiman-Marcus / *Carter Hawley Hale Stores, Inc.*
Nichols / *S.E. Nichols Inc.*
Nichols Discount City / *S.E. Nichols Inc.*
Odd Lot Trading / *Revco D.S. Inc.*
O.G. Wilson / *Zale Corp.*
O'Neil's / *May Department Stores Co.*
Ontario / *Cook United Inc.*
Outlet / *Outlet Co.*
Pathmark / *Supermarkets General Corp.*
Peavey Marts / *Peavey Co.*
Peck's Menswear / *Brown Group Inc.*
Pharmacity / *Supermarkets General Corp.*
Plymouth Shops / *Allied Stores Corp.*
P.N. Hirsch Store / *Interco Inc.*
Pomeroy's / *Allied Stores Corp.*
Powers Dry Goods Co. / *Associated Dry Goods Corp.*
Purity Supreme / *Supermarkets General Corp.*
PVH Outlet Stores / *Phillips-Van Heusen Corp.*
Rasco / *Wickes Corp.*
Read's / *Allied Stores Corp.*
Richman Brothers / *F.W. Woolworth Co.*
Rich's / *Federated Department Stores Inc.*
Richway / *Federated Department Stores Inc.*
Rickel Home Centers / *Supermarkets General Corp.*
Right House / *Mercantile Stores Co. Inc.*
Rink's / *Gray Drug Stores Inc.*
Ritter / *Curtice-Burns Inc.*
Roaman's / *The Limited Inc.*
Robinson's of Florida / *Associated Dry Goods Corp.*
Rogers / *Modern Merchandising Inc.*
Rogers / *Best Products Co., Inc.*
Roots / *Mercantile Stores Co. Inc.*
Roshek's Department Store / *Wickes Corp.*
S & S / *Peavey Co.*
Sanger-Harris / *Federated Department Stores Inc.*
Sarco / *Wickes Corp.*
Sears, Roebuck / *Sears, Roebuck & Co.*
Service Merchandise Catalog Showrooms / *Service Merchandise Co. Inc.*
Shillito Rikes / *Federated Department Stores Inc.*
ShopKo / *Super Valu Stores Inc.*
Sibley, Lindsay & Curr Co. / *Associated Dry Goods Corp.*
Sizes Unlimited / *The Limited Inc.*
Sky City Discount / *Interco Inc.*
Spare Change / *Elder-Beerman Stores Corp.*
Spencer Gifts / *MCA Inc.*
Standard Sales / *Modern Merchandising Inc.*
Star Store / *Almy Stores Inc.*
Steinbach / *Supermarkets General Corp.*
Sterling / *Sterling Stores Co. Inc.*

Stern's / *Allied Stores Corp.*
Stewart Dry Goods Co. / *Associated Dry Goods Corp.*
Store Company / *Dayton Hudson Corp.*
Stratford Jewelers / *Cook United Inc.*
Strawbridge & Clothier / *Strawbridge & Clothier*
Strouss / *May Department Stores Co.*
Sue Brett / *The Limited Inc.*
Sutton Place / *Vornado, Inc.*
Tall Collection / *The Limited Inc.*
Target / *Dayton Hudson Corp.*
TG & Y / *Household International, Inc.*
Thalhimer's / *Carter Hawley Hale Stores, Inc.*
"The Union" / *Marshall Field & Co.*
Towers / *Gaylords National Corp.*
Twin Fair / *Twin Fair Inc.*
Two Guys / *The Fed Mart Corporation*
Two Guys / *Vornado, Inc.*
Uncle Bill's / *Cook United Inc.*
United Jewelers & Distributors / *Gordon Jewelry Corp.*
Venture / *May Department Stores Co.*
Victoria's Secret / *The Limited Inc.*
Village Fashions / *Amfac Inc.*
Waiohai Hotel, Poipu Beach Hotel / *Amfac Inc.*
Wal-Mart / *Wal-Mart Stores Inc.*
Warehouse / *Glosser Bros. Inc.*
Weinstock's / *Carter Hawley Hale Stores, Inc.*
Wheelers / *Peavey Co.*
White Mart / *Farm House Foods Corp.*
Willoughby & Taylor / *Zale Corp.*
Witherill / *Almy Stores Inc.*
Woodward & Lothrop / *Woodward & Lothrop Inc.*
Woolco / *F.W. Woolworth Co.*
Woolworth / *F.W. Woolworth Co.*
Yellow Front / *Lucky Stores Inc.*
Zayre / *Zayre Corp.*
Zody's / *Hartfield Zody's Inc.*

Drugs & Healthcare Products

A & D / *Schering-Plough Corp.*
Ace / *Becton, Dickinson & Co.*
Acnomel / *SmithKline Beckman Corp.*
Advil / *American Home Products Corp.*
Afrin / *Schering-Plough Corp.*
Aftute / *Schering-Plough Corp.*
Agoral / *Warner-Lambert Co.*
Alfalfa Tabs / *Shaklee Corp.*
Allbee / *A.H. Robins Co. Inc*
Allerest / *Pennwalt Corp.*
Ambenyl-D / *Marion Laboratories Inc.*
Anacin / *American Home Products Corp.*
Anbesol / *American Home Products Corp.*
Answer / *Carter-Wallace Inc.*
Anusol / *Warner-Lambert Co.*
Aosoft / *Warner-Lambert Co.*
Arco / *Nature's Bounty, Inc.*
ARM / *SmithKline Beckman Corp.*
Arrest / *Uniroyal Inc.*
Arthritis Pain Formula / *American Home Products Corp.*
Artra / *Schering-Plough Corp.*
Ascriptin / *Rorer Group Inc.*
Ascription A/D / *Rorer Group Inc.*
Aspergum / *Schering-Plough Corp.*
Bacimycin / *Richardson-Vicks Inc.*
Barnes-Hind / *Revlon Inc.*
Basic Organics / *Iroquois Brands Ltd.*
Bauer & Black / *Colgate-Palmolive Co.*
Bauer & Black / *Becton, Dickinson & Co.*
Bausch & Lomb / *Bausch & Lomb Inc.*
Bayer / *Sterling Drug Inc.*
B-Complex / *Shaklee Corp.*
Becton-Dickinson / *Becton, Dickinson & Co.*
Begley Drug Stores / *Begley Co.*
Begley's Home Health Center / *Begley Co.*
Benylin / *Warner-Lambert Co.*
Benylin DM / *Warner-Lambert Co.*
Benzagel / *Rorer Group Inc.*
Benzedrex / *SmithKline Beckman Corp.*
Benzodent / *Richardson-Vicks Inc.*
Big 'B' Discount Drugs / *Big B, Inc.*
Big 'B' Home Health Care Center / *Big B, Inc.*
Bill Blass / *Sterndent Corp.*
Bisodol / *American Home Products Corp.*
Blink 'n Clean / *SmithKline Beckman Corp.*
Boil Ease / *Del Laboratories Inc.*
Brace / *Revlon Inc.*
Breacol / *Sterling Drug Inc.*
Bromo Seltzer / *Warner-Lambert Co.*
Broniton / *American Home Products Corp.*
Bronkaid / *Sterling Drug Inc.*
Brown Drug / *Alco Standard Corp.*
Bufferin / *Bristol Myers Co.*
Bushnell / *Bausch & Lomb Inc.*
Caladryl / *Warner-Lambert Co.*
Calcimax / *Revlon Inc.*
Calcium Magnesium / *Shaklee Corp.*
Caldecort / *Pennwalt Corp.*
Caltrate / *American Cyanamid Company*
Camalox / *Rorer Group Inc.*
Campho-Phenique / *Sterling Drug Inc.*

Carter's Pills / *Carter-Wallace Inc.*
Cefol / *Abbott Laboratories*
Centrum / *American Cyanamid Company*
Cepacol / *Richardson-Vicks Inc.*
Certified / *Fred Meyer*
Chewable Multivitamin and Multimineral Supplement / *Shaklee Corp.*
Chloraseptic / *Procter & Gamble Co.*
Chlor-Trimeton / *Schering-Plough Corp.*
Clean 'n Soak / *SmithKline Beckman Corp.*
Clear Eyes / *Abbott Laboratories*
Clearasil / *Richardson-Vicks Inc.*
Coburn / *Revlon Inc.*
Cod Liver Oil / *Schering-Plough Corp.*
Colace / *Bristol Myers Co.*
Cold Factor 12 / *Pennwalt Corp.*
Comfort Drops / *Revlon Inc.*
Comite / *Uniroyal Inc.*
Complete / *Richardson-Vicks Inc.*
Compound W. / *American Home Products Corp.*
Comtrex / *Bristol Myers Co.*
Congespirin / *Bristol Myers Co.*
Congestac / *SmithKline Beckman Corp.*
Contac / *SmithKline Beckman Corp.*
Contac Jr. / *SmithKline Beckman Corp.*
Continuous Curve / *Revlon Inc.*
Cool Ray / *Warner-Lambert Co.*
Correctol / *Schering-Plough Corp.*
Curad / *Colgate-Palmolive Co.*
Curity / *Colgate-Palmolive Co.*
Cushion Grip / *Schering-Plough Corp.*
Cutex / *Chesebrough-Pond's Inc.*
Cutex Perfect Color / *Chesebrough-Pond's Inc.*
Cyclent / *Abbott Laboratories*
Debrox / *Marion Laboratories Inc.*
Delfen / *Johnson & Johnson*
Demure / *Richardson-Vicks Inc.*
Denquil / *Richardson-Vicks Inc.*
Dermoplast / *American Home Products Corp.*
Desitin / *Pfizer Inc.*
Desquam-X / *Bristol Myers Co.*
Diatron Easytest / *Medivix Inc.*
Di-Gel / *Schering-Plough Corp.*
Dimacol / *A.H. Robins Co. Inc*
Dimatane / *A.H. Robins Co. Inc*
Dimetapp / *A.H. Robins Co. Inc*
Diovol / *Carter-Wallace Inc.*
Dista / *Eli Lilly & Co.*
Doan's Pills / *Purex Industries, Inc.*
Doctors' Pride / *Nature's Bounty, Inc.*
Dopram / *A.H. Robins Co. Inc*
Dramamine / *G.D. Searle & Co.*
Dristan / *American Home Products Corp.*
The Drug House / *Alco Standard Corp.*
Dry & Clear / *American Home Products Corp.*
Duff Brothers / *Alco Standard Corp.*
Duration / *Schering-Plough Corp.*
Ecotrin / *SmithKline Beckman Corp.*
Edmont / *Becton, Dickinson & Co.*
Elizabeth Arden / *Textron Inc.*
Emetrol / *Rorer Group Inc.*
Emko / *Schering-Plough Corp.*
Encaprin / *Procter & Gamble Co.*
Enrich / *Abbott Laboratories*
Ensure / *Abbott Laboratories*
Eppy / *Revlon Inc.*
e.p.t. / *Warner-Lambert Co.*
e.t.p. Plus / *Warner-Lambert Co.*
Excedrin / *Bristol Myers Co.*
Fast Aid / *SmithKline Beckman Corp.*
Faultless / *Abbott Laboratories*
Feasol / *SmithKline Beckman Corp.*
Fedahist / *Rorer Group Inc.*
Feen-A-Mint / *Schering-Plough Corp.*
Feosol Plus / *SmithKline Beckman Corp.*
Fergon / *Sterling Drug Inc.*
Fermalox / *Rorer Group Inc.*
Fixodent / *Richardson-Vicks Inc.*
Fomac Foam / *Rorer Group Inc.*
Formula 44 / *Richardson-Vicks Inc.*
Foster Medical / *Avon Products Inc.*
Fostex / *Bristol Myers Co.*
Freezone / *American Home Products Corp.*
Gaviscon / *Marion Laboratories Inc.*
Geer Drug / *Alco Standard Corp.*
Gelusil / *Warner-Lambert Co.*
Givenchy / *Sterndent Corp.*
Glacier Glass / *Bausch & Lomb Inc.*
Gly-Oxide / *Marion Laboratories Inc.*
Golden Bounty / *Squibb Corp.*
Good 'N Natural / *Nature's Bounty, Inc.*
Good Nature / *Carnation Company*
Groom & Clean / *Chesebrough-Pond's Inc.*
Haley's M-O / *Sterling Drug Inc.*
Halls / *Warner-Lambert Co.*
Head & Chest / *Procter & Gamble Co.*
Health Gard / *Chattem, Inc.*
Heet / *American Home Products Corp.*
Herb-Lax® Laxative / *Shaklee Corp.*
Hudson / *Cadence Industries Corp.*
Hydra-Mat / *Revlon Inc.*
Hydrocare Cleaning/Disinfecting Solution / *SmithKline Beckman Corp.*
Hydrocare Saline Solution / *SmithKline Beckman Corp.*
Hypotears / *Cooper Laboratories, Inc.*

Hytone / *Rorer Group Inc.*
Icy Hot / *G.D. Searle & Co.*
Infra-Rub / *American Home Products Corp.*
Insta-Focus / *Bausch & Lomb Inc.*
Iron plus Vitamin C / *Shaklee Corp.*
Ironized Yeast / *Sterling Drug Inc.*
Kaufman-Lattimer / *Alco Standard Corp.*
Kleenite / *Richardson-Vicks Inc.*
Kolantyl / *Richardson-Vicks Inc.*
Lacri-Lube / *SmithKline Beckman Corp.*
Lecithin / *Shaklee Corp.*
Lens Clear / *SmithKline Beckman Corp.*
Lens Mark / *Frigitronics Inc.*
Lens Plus / *SmithKline Beckman Corp.*
Lens Rins / *SmithKline Beckman Corp.*
Lens Wet / *SmithKline Beckman Corp.*
Lensine / *Cooper Laboratories, Inc.*
Lilly / *Eli Lilly & Co.*
Liquifilm Forte / *SmithKline Beckman Corp.*
Liquifilm Tears / *SmithKline Beckman Corp.*
Liquifilm Wetting Solution / *SmithKline Beckman Corp.*
Liqui-Lea® Multivitamin with Iron Supplement / *Shaklee Corp.*
Liquiprin / *Revlon Inc.*
Listerex / *Warner-Lambert Co.*
Listerine / *Warner-Lambert Co.*
Listermint / *Warner-Lambert Co.*
Lo-Dose / *Becton, Dickinson & Co.*
Lubriderm / *Warner-Lambert Co.*
Maalox / *Rorer Group Inc.*
Maalox Plus / *Rorer Group Inc.*
Maalox Theraputic Concentrate / *Rorer Group Inc.*
Mallinckrodt / *Avon Products Inc.*
Measurin / *Sterling Drug Inc.*
Mediquell / *Warner-Lambert Co.*
Medix Insulin Infusion Pump / *Medivix Inc.*
Metamucil / *G.D. Searle & Co.*
Mexsana / *Schering-Plough Corp.*
Micatin / *Johnson & Johnson*
Micro / *Becton, Dickinson & Co.*
Micro-K Extencaps / *A.H. Robins Co. Inc*
Midol / *Sterling Drug Inc.*
Miltown / *Carter-Wallace Inc.*
Mitchum / *Revlon Inc.*
Mucilose / *Sterling Drug Inc.*
Murine / *Abbott Laboratories*
Musterole / *Schering-Plough Corp.*
Myadec / *Warner-Lambert Co.*
Natalins / *Bristol Myers Co.*
Natura Brands / *Iroquois Brands Ltd.*
Natural Wealth / *Nature's Bounty, Inc.*
Nature's Bounty / *Nature's Bounty, Inc.*
Nature's Remedy / *Revlon Inc.*
Neo-Synephrine / *Sterling Drug Inc.*
Nitrol / *Rorer Group Inc.*
No Doz / *Bristol Myers Co.*
Norwich / *Procter & Gamble Co.*
NoSalt / *Revlon Inc.*
NTZ / *Sterling Drug Inc.*
NUK / *Gerber Products Co.*
Nuprin / *Bristol Myers Co.*
NyQuil / *Richardson-Vicks Inc.*
One Solution / *Revlon Inc.*
Optilets / *Abbott Laboratories*
Opus III Lens / *Frigitronics Inc.*
Oracin / *Richardson-Vicks Inc.*
Orafix / *Revlon Inc.*
Origin / *Iroquois Brands Ltd.*
Ornacol / *SmithKline Beckman Corp.*
Ornex / *SmithKline Beckman Corp.*
Ortho-Novum / *Johnson & Johnson*
Os-Cal / *Marion Laboratories Inc.*
Osco / *American Stores Co.*
Outgro / *American Home Products Corp.*
Ovral / *American Home Products Corp.*
Oxy / *Revlon Inc.*
Pamprin / *Chattem, Inc.*
Panadol / *Sterling Drug Inc.*
Parepectolin / *Rorer Group Inc.*
Pay Less Drug Stores / *K Mart Corp.*
Pepto Bismol / *Procter & Gamble Co.*
Percogesic / *Richardson-Vicks Inc.*
Perdiem / *Rorer Group Inc.*
Pernox / *Bristol Myers Co.*
Pertussin / *Chesebrough-Pond's Inc.*
Phenaphen / *A.H. Robins Co. Inc*
Phillips' Milk of Magnesia / *Sterling Drug Inc.*
PhisoAc Cream / *Sterling Drug Inc.*
Pine Bros. / *Squibb Corp.*
Pond's / *Chesebrough-Pond's Inc.*
Pond's Cream & Cocoa Butter / *Chesebrough-Pond's Inc.*
Pontocaine / *Sterling Drug Inc.*
Predictor / *American Home Products Corp.*
Prefrin / *SmithKline Beckman Corp.*
Premesyn PMS / *Chattem, Inc.*
Preparation H / *American Home Products Corp.*
Pretts / *Marion Laboratories Inc.*
Primatene Mist / *American Home Products Corp.*
Puritan's Pride / *Nature's Bounty, Inc.*
Q-tips / *Chesebrough-Pond's Inc.*
Quiet World / *American Home Products Corp.*
Radiance / *Iroquois Brands Ltd.*

Rave / *Chesebrough-Pond's Inc.*
Ray-Ban / *Bausch & Lomb Inc.*
Remgel / *Warner-Lambert Co.*
Retin A / *Johnson & Johnson*
Rigident / *Carter-Wallace Inc.*
Riopan / *American Home Products Corp.*
Rita-Ann Distributors / *Alco Standard Corp.*
Robaxin / *A.H. Robins Co. Inc*
Robitussin / *A.H. Robins Co. Inc*
Rocket / *Revlon Inc.*
Rolaids / *Warner-Lambert Co.*
Rondec II / *Abbott Laboratories*
Saraka / *Schering-Plough Corp.*
Saturn Lens / *Frigitronics Inc.*
Sav-on / *American Stores Co.*
Selectives / *Stanhome, Inc.*
Semicid / *American Home Products Corp.*
Semplice / *Stanhome, Inc.*
Sensitive Eyes / *Bausch & Lomb Inc.*
Shuron / *Textron Inc.*
Sight Savers / *Bausch & Lomb Inc.*
Silvadene / *Marion Laboratories Inc.*
Sinarest / *Pennwalt Corp.*
Sine Off / *SmithKline Beckman Corp.*
Sine-Aid / *Johnson & Johnson*
Sinutab / *Warner-Lambert Co.*
Skaggs / *American Stores Co.*
Sleep-Eze / *American Home Products Corp.*
Slo Phyllin / *Rorer Group Inc.*
Slo-bid / *Rorer Group Inc.*
Smith Higgins / *Alco Standard Corp.*
Soakare / *SmithKline Beckman Corp.*
Soflens / *Bausch & Lomb Inc.*
Soflens / *SmithKline Beckman Corp.*
Sofspin / *Bausch & Lomb Inc.*
Soft / *Warner-Lambert Co.*
Soft Mate / *Revlon Inc.*
Soma / *Carter-Wallace Inc.*
Soquette / *Revlon Inc.*
Sorbicare / *SmithKline Beckman Corp.*
Spec-T / *Squibb Corp.*
Spectrum / *Alco Standard Corp.*
Sportview / *Bausch & Lomb Inc.*
St. Joseph / *Schering-Plough Corp.*
Stresstabs / *American Cyanamid Company*
Stri-Dex / *Sterling Drug Inc.*
Strother Drug / *Alco Standard Corp.*
Style / *Del Laboratories Inc.*
Sufenta / *Johnson & Johnson*
Surbex / *Abbott Laboratories*
Sustagen / *Bristol Myers Co.*
Symptom / *Warner-Lambert Co.*
Tanac / *Del Laboratories Inc.*
Tears Plus / *SmithKline Beckman Corp.*
Teldrin / *SmithKline Beckman Corp.*
Telfa / *Colgate-Palmolive Co.*
Tempo / *Richardson-Vicks Inc.*
Tested / *Pay Less Drug Stores Northwest Inc.*
Theragran / *Squibb Corp.*
Throat Discs / *Marion Laboratories Inc.*
Titan / *Revlon Inc.*
Topex / *Richardson-Vicks Inc.*
Tortuga / *Bausch & Lomb Inc.*
Total / *SmithKline Beckman Corp.*
Tronolane / *Abbott Laboratories*
Troph-Iron / *SmithKline Beckman Corp.*
Trophite / *SmithKline Beckman Corp.*
Tums / *Revlon Inc.*
Tussy / *Sterling Drug Inc.*
Tylenol / *Johnson & Johnson*
Ultra Feminine / *Colgate-Palmolive Co.*
Unisol / *Cooper Laboratories, Inc.*
Universal / *Sterndent Corp.*
U3, U4 / *Bausch & Lomb Inc.*
Vanoxide / *Rorer Group Inc.*
Vanquish / *Sterling Drug Inc.*
Vaporub / *Richardson-Vicks Inc.*
Vaseline / *Chesebrough-Pond's Inc.*
Vaseline Dermatology Formula / *Chesebrough-Pond's Inc.*
Vaseline Intensive Care / *Chesebrough-Pond's Inc.*
Vasocon A / *Cooper Laboratories, Inc.*
Va-tra-nol / *Richardson-Vicks Inc.*
Vicks / *Richardson-Vicks Inc.*
ViDaylin / *Abbott Laboratories*
Vi-Flor / *Bristol Myers Co.*
Vigran / *Squibb Corp.*
Viro-Med Liquid / *American Home Products Corp.*
Visine / *Pfizer Inc.*
Vita-Cal® Vitamin and Mineral Supplement / *Shaklee Corp.*
Vita-C® Vitamin C Supplement / *Shaklee Corp.*
Vita-E® Vitamin E Supplement / *Shaklee Corp.*
Vital / *Abbott Laboratories*
Vita-Lea® for Children / *Shaklee Corp.*
Vita-Lea® Multivitamin and Multimineral Supplement / *Shaklee Corp.*
Vitamin World / *Nature's Bounty, Inc.*
Vitavax / *Uniroyal Inc.*
Wayfarer / *Bausch & Lomb Inc.*
Wet 'n' Soak / *SmithKline Beckman Corp.*
William T. Stover / *Alco Standard Corp.*

Wingel / *Sterling Drug Inc.*
Wings / *Bausch & Lomb Inc.*
Z-BEC / *A.H. Robins Co. Inc*
Zemo / *Schering-Plough Corp.*
Zinc / *Shaklee Corp.*
4-Way Cold Tablets / *Bristol Myers Co.*
4-Way Regular Spray / *Bristol Myers Co.*
6-12 Plus / *Sterling Drug Inc.*

Entertainment

ABC / *MCA Inc.*
ABC / *American Broadcasting Companies Inc.*
American International Pictures / *Filmways Inc.*
ARC/Columbia / *CBS Inc.*
Armour Handcrafts / *Greyhound Corp.*
Artista / *Binney & Smith Inc.*
Asylum / *Warner Communications Inc.*
Atco / *Warner Communications Inc.*
Avco Embassy Pictures Corp. / *Avco*
Bach / *North American Philips Corp.*
Baldwin / *Baldwin-United Corporation*
Bee / *Diamond International Corp.*
Benge / *Xcor International Inc.*
Bicycle / *Diamond International Corp.*
Bosendorfer / *Kimball International Inc.*
Boye / *Newell Companies Inc.*
"Break the Bank" / *John Blair & Co.*
Brut Productions / *Faberge Inc.*
Buena Vista Distribution Co. / *Walt Disney Productions*
Buescher / *North American Philips Corp.*
Bundy / *North American Philips Corp.*
Cagney & Lacey / *Orion Pictures Corp.*
Cleveland / *Xcor International Inc.*
Clinton / *Scovill Inc.*
Columbia / *Columbia Picture Industries Inc.*
Columbia Pictures / *The Coca-Cola Co.*
Columbia Pictures / *The Coca-Cola Co.*
Columbia Pictures Publications / *The Coca-Cola Co.*
Columbia Records / *CBS Inc.*
Congress / *Diamond International Corp.*
Conn / *Kimball International Inc.*
Coral / *MCA Inc.*
Corticelli / *Belding Heminway Co. Inc.*
Cotillion / *Warner Communications Inc.*
Country Music Television / *Telstar, Corp.*
Craft Master / *General Mills Inc.*
Crayola / *Binney & Smith Inc.*
Crochemaster / *Newell Companies Inc.*
Dallas / *Lorimar*
De Ford / *Xcor International Inc.*
Diana / *Newell Companies Inc.*
The Disney Channel / *Walt Disney Productions*
Disneyland Park, Anaheim, California / *Walt Disney Productions*
"Divorce Court" / *John Blair & Co.*
Dritz / *Scovill Inc.*
Eight is Enough / *Lorimar*
Elektra / *Warner Communications Inc.*
Epic Records / *CBS Inc.*
Epiphone / *Norlin Corporation*
ESPN / *Telstar, Corp.*
Excella / *Xcor International Inc.*
Falcon Crest / *Lorimar*
Filmways TV Productions / *Filmways Inc.*
Front Row / *Xcor International Inc.*
Gemeinhardt / *CBS Inc.*
General Cinemas / *General Cinema Corp.*
Gibson / *Norlin Corporation*
Glaesel / *North American Philips Corp.*
Gripper / *Scovill Inc.*
Guild / *Avnet Inc.*
Gulbransen / *CBS Inc.*
Heatter-Quigley TV / *Filmways Inc.*
Hero / *Scovill Inc.*
Hoop-De-Doo / *Newell Companies Inc.*
Ice Capades / *Metromedia Inc.*
Jet Records / *CBS Inc.*
Kimball / *Kimball International Inc.*
Knitmaster / *Newell Companies Inc.*
Knots Landing / *Lorimar*
Korg / *Gulf* + Western Industries Inc.
Krakauer / *Kimball International Inc.*
K-Tel / *K-Tel International*
La Mode / *Belding Heminway Co. Inc.*
Lassie / *Wrather Corp.*
Le Chic / *Belding Heminway Co. Inc.*
Lemaire / *Xcor International Inc.*
Lily / *Belding Heminway Co. Inc.*
Loews Theatres / *Loews Corp.*
Lone Ranger / *Wrather Corp.*
Lowrey / *Norlin Corporation*
Ludwig / *North American Philips Corp.*
Lyon-Healy / *CBS Inc.*
Madison Square Garden / *Gulf* + Western Industries Inc.
Malerne / *Xcor International Inc.*
Manhasset / *Xcor International Inc.*
Marigaux / *Xcor International Inc.*
MCA / *MCA Inc.*
MCA Home Video / *MCA Inc.*

MCA Records / *MCA Inc.*
McCall's / *Norton Simon Inc.*
Metro-Goldwyn-Mayer Productions / *Metro-Goldwyn-Mayer Film Co.*
MGM/UA / *MGM/UA Entertainment Co.*
Miles Do-It-Yourself Homebuilding / *Insilco Corp.*
Mirage / *Scovill Inc.*
Miss Universe-pageants / *Gulf* + Western Industries Inc.
Moog / *Norlin Corporation*
MTV: Music Television / *MTV Networks Inc.*
Multimedia Entertainment / *Multimedia Inc.*
National Broadcasting Co. / *RCA Corp.*
Needle Queen / *Quaker Oats Co.*
Needlemaster / *Newell Companies Inc.*
New York Knickerbockers / *Gulf* + Western Industries Inc.
New York Rangers / *Gulf* + Western Industries Inc.
Nickelodeon / *MTV Networks Inc.*
Nonesuch / *Warner Communications Inc.*
Nyguard / *Scovill Inc.*
Odyssey Records / *CBS Inc.*
Orion / *Orion Pictures Corp.*
Ovation / *Kaman Corp.*
Paramount Pictures & TV - entertainment / *Gulf* + Western Industries Inc.
Pearl / *Norlin Corporation*
Penn / *Belding Heminway Co. Inc.*
The Playboy Channel / *Playboy Enterprises Inc.*
Playboy Channel / *Telstar, Corp.*
Playboy Home Video / *Playboy Enterprises Inc.*
Portrait Records / *CBS Inc.*
Rastar / *Columbia Picture Industries Inc.*
RCA/Columbia Pictures / *The Coca-Cola Co.*
Rowan and Martin's Laugh-In / *Lorimar*
Ruby-Spears Productions / *Filmways Inc.*
Scovill / *Scovill Inc.*
Selmer / *North American Philips Corp.*
Sergeant Preston of the Yukon / *Wrather Corp.*
Showtime/The Movie Channel / *Telstar, Corp.*
Signet / *North American Philips Corp.*
Skippy, The Bush Kangroo / *Wrather Corp.*
Sportsmap / *Scovill Inc.*
Staylastic/Smith / *Scovill Inc.*
Story & Clark / *Norlin Corporation*
Strasser / *Xcor International Inc.*
Tempo / *Xcor International Inc.*
"The New York Experience" / *Trans-Lux Corp.*
"The South Street Venture" / *Trans-Lux Corp.*
Touchstone Films / *Walt Disney Productions*
Trans-Lux / *Trans-Lux Corp.*
Universal / *MCA Inc.*
VH-1/Video Hits One / *MTV Networks Inc.*
Walt Disney Pictures / *Walt Disney Productions*
Walt Disney World Complex, Orlando, Florida / *Walt Disney Productions*
The Waltons / *Lorimar*
Warner Bros. / *Warner Communications Inc.*
Waterford Park / *Ogden Corp.*
Wheeling Downs / *Ogden Corp.*
Whippersnap / *Scovill Inc.*
Whitmore / *Kimball International Inc.*
Whitney / *Kimball International Inc.*
Wonder Art / *Quaker Oats Co.*
Wonderland Music Co. / *Walt Disney Productions*
Wurlitzer / *Wurlitzer Co.*

Food

A & P / *Great Atlantic & Pacific Tea Co. Inc.*
Adams / *International Multifoods Corp.*
Adams / *Warner-Lambert Co.*
Adisa Snacks / *Beatrice Companies Inc.*
Adohr Farms / *Southland Corp.*
Adolph's / *Chesebrough-Pond's Inc.*
Adolphus / *Early California Industries, Inc.*
Ailiram / *Beatrice Companies Inc.*
Albers / *Carnation Company*
All American Gourmet Co. / *General Host Corp.*
All Natural / *Beatrice Companies Inc.*
Allsweet / *Esmark Inc.*
Almost Home / *Nabisco Brands Inc.*
Alpha-Bits / *General Foods Corp.*
American Beauty / *Hershey Foods Corp.*
American Hostess / *Beatrice Companies Inc.*
American Pickles / *Beatrice Companies Inc.*
Amfac Tropical Products / *Amfac Inc.*
Amore / *Universal Foods Corp.*
Anco / *Castle & Cooke Inc.*
Ann Page / *Great Atlantic & Pacific Tea Co. Inc.*
Antoine's / *Beatrice Companies Inc.*
Apollo / *Pillsbury Co.*
Appian Way / *Greyhound Corp.*
Argo / *CPC International Inc.*
Armour / *ConAgra Inc.*
Armour Star / *Greyhound Corp.*
Artic / *Beatrice Companies Inc.*
Aunt Fanny / *I.C. Industries Inc.*
Aunt Jemima / *Quaker Oats Co.*
Aunt Nellie's / *Beatrice Companies Inc.*
Austrian Alps / *United Brands Co.*
Autumn Grain / *American Bakeries Co.*

Avoset / *Anderson, Clayton & Co.*
Ayds / *Purex Industries, Inc.*
Azteca / *Pillsbury Co.*
B & G / *Consolidated Foods Corp.*
Baby Ruth / *Standard Brands Inc.*
Baby Ruth / *Nabisco Brands Inc.*
Bag'N Season Seasoning / *McCormick & Co. Inc.*
Baken-ets / *PepsiCo Inc.*
Baker's / *General Foods Corp.*
Baker's Joy / *Alberto Culver Co.*
Baker's Vanilla / *McCormick & Co. Inc.*
Baking Magic / *McCormick & Co. Inc.*
Ballard / *Pillsbury Co.*
Bancroft / *Southland Corp.*
Band Box / *Safeway Stores Inc.*
Banquet Foods / *ConAgra Inc.*
Banquet Tea / *McCormick & Co. Inc.*
Bar M / *TFI Companies Inc.*
Barbara Dee / *Beatrice Companies Inc.*
Bar-H / *Thorn Apple Valley, Inc.*
Barnum's Animals / *Nabisco Brands Inc.*
Baron's Table / *Beatrice Companies Inc.*
Bassetts / *Hershey Foods Corp.*
Batey / *Bacardi Corp.*
Bazooka / *Topps Chewing Gum Inc.*
Beanee Weenee / *Stokely-Van Camp Inc.*
Beatreme / *Beatrice Companies Inc.*
Beatrice / *Beatrice Companies Inc.*
Beatrice Olde Fashioned Recipe / *Beatrice Companies Inc.*
Becky Kay's / *Beatrice Companies Inc.*
Bee Gee Shrimp / *Katy Industries, Inc.*
Bee Hive / *Conwood Corp.*
Beebo / *Flowers Industries Inc.*
Beefbreak / *Beatrice Companies Inc.*
Beefeater / *Thorn Apple Valley, Inc.*
Beeforcan / *Beatrice Companies Inc.*
Beefsteak / *Ralston Purina Co.*
Beginner Flakes / *Gerber Products Co.*
Bel-Air / *Safeway Stores Inc.*
Bell / *Dean Foods Co.*
Bell Brand Snacks / *American Brands Inc.*
Belmont / *Jewel Companies Inc.*
Bernstein / *Curtice-Burns Inc.*
Best Buy / *Safeway Stores Inc.*
Best Foods / *CPC International Inc.*
Better Cheddars / *Nabisco Brands Inc.*
Betty Zane / *Stokely-Van Camp Inc.*
Bickford / *Beatrice Companies Inc.*
Biddles Rice Chips / *PepsiCo Inc.*
Big Block / *Hershey Foods Corp.*
Big Buddy / *Topps Chewing Gum Inc.*
Big Deal / *Southland Corp.*
Big Pete / *Beatrice Companies Inc.*
Big Pop / *Curtice-Burns Inc.*
Big Red / *William Wrigley Jr. Co.*
Big Stick / *Knudsen Corp.*
Big Top / *Weis Markets Inc.*
Big Town / *Lance Inc.*
Big Wheel / *Southland Corp.*
Bighorn / *Beatrice Companies Inc.*
Birds Eye / *General Foods Corp.*
Bisco / *Nabisco Brands Inc.*
Bisquick / *General Mills Inc.*
Bit-O-Honey / *Ward Foods Inc.*
Black Label / *George A. Hormel & Co.*
Block & Guggenheimer / *Consolidated Foods Corp.*
Blockbusters / *Topps Chewing Gum Inc.*
Blossom Time / *Safeway Stores Inc.*
Blue Bell Snacks / *American Brands Inc.*
Blue Bonnet / *Nabisco Brands Inc.*
Blue Bonnett / *Standard Brands Inc.*
Blue Boy / *Beatrice Companies Inc.*
Blue Boy / *Curtice-Burns Inc.*
Blue Ribbon / *Beatrice Companies Inc.*
Blue Valley / *Beatrice Companies Inc.*
Blue Water / *General Mills Inc.*
Bluebrook / *Jewel Companies Inc.*
B-Mart Food & Drugs / *Big B, Inc.*
Bob Evans / *Bob Evans Farms, Inc.*
Bob Ostrow / *United Brands Co.*
Body Buddies / *General Mills Inc.*
Boizet / *Beatrice Companies Inc.*
Bokar / *Great Atlantic & Pacific Tea Co. Inc.*
Bon Appetit / *McCormick & Co. Inc.*
Bonavita / *Universal Foods Corp.*
Bonkers! / *Nabisco Brands Inc.*
Bonnie / *Scot Lad Foods Inc.*
Bonnie Hubbard / *Fleming Companies Inc.*
Bonnie Maid / *Hannaford Bros. Co.*
Bonomo Turkish Taffy / *Tootsie Roll Industries Inc.*
Boo Berry / *General Mills Inc.*
Boquitas / *Beatrice Companies Inc.*
Borden / *Borden Inc.*
Borden Lite-Line / *Borden Inc.*
Bosco / *CPC International Inc.*
Bowers / *Beatrice Companies Inc.*
Brach / *American Home Products Corp.*
Bran & Raisin Instant Oatmeal / *Quaker Oats Co.*
Brander / *United Brands Co.*
Breads International / *Flowers Industries Inc.*
Breakstone / *Dart & Kraft Inc.*
Breath Savers / *Nabisco Brands Inc.*
Bredan / *Beatrice Companies Inc.*
Breeze / *Safeway Stores Inc.*
Brenner / *Beatrice Companies Inc.*

Brer Rabbit / *R.J. Reynolds*
Breyer's / *Dart & Kraft Inc.*
Briggs / *Southland Corp.*
Brooks / *Curtice-Burns Inc.*
Brown Miller / *Beatrice Companies Inc.*
Brown 'n Serve / *Esmark Inc.*
Brownberry Ovens / *Peavey Co.*
Brown'N Serve / *Beatrice Companies Inc.*
Bryan Foods / *Consolidated Foods Corp.*
Bubble Yum / *Nabisco Brands Inc.*
Bubblicious / *Warner-Lambert Co.*
Buc Wheats / *General Mills Inc.*
Buckeye / *Tasty Baking Co.*
Bud of California / *Castle & Cooke Inc.*
Bunny Pop / *Conwood Corp.*
Buring Foods / *Consolidated Foods Corp.*
Burny Bakers / *Beatrice Companies Inc.*
Burry's / *Quaker Oats Co.*
Burst O Lemon / *McCormick & Co. Inc.*
Busy Baker / *Safeway Stores Inc.*
Butcher Boy / *Central Soya Company Inc.*
Butter Maid / *Flowers Industries Inc.*
Butterball / *Beatrice Companies Inc.*
Butterball / *Esmark Inc.*
Butterchef Bakery / *Beatrice Companies Inc.*
Buttercrust / *Beatrice Companies Inc.*
Butterfinger / *Standard Brands Inc.*
Butterfingers / *Nabisco Brands Inc.*
Buttermaid / *Ward Foods Inc.*
C & H Sugar / *Amfac Inc.*
Cabell's / *Southland Corp.*
Cagle's / *Cagle's Inc.*
Cains Marcelle / *Culbro Corp.*
Cake-Mate / *McCormick & Co. Inc.*
Callard & Bowser / *Beatrice Companies Inc.*
Calumet Baking Powder / *General Foods Corp.*
Cameo / *Nabisco Brands Inc.*
Campbell's / *Campbell Soup Co.*
Campfire / *Borden Inc.*
Campofrio / *Beatrice Companies Inc.*
Candi Cane / *Safeway Stores Inc.*
Capitol Baking / *Capitol Food Industries Inc.*
Capitol Meats / *Capitol Food Industries Inc.*
Cap'n Crunch / *Quaker Oats Co.*
Capri / *Anderson, Clayton & Co.*
Captain Kids / *Beatrice Companies Inc.*
Captain's Choice / *Safeway Stores Inc.*
Cara Coa / *Iroquois Brands Ltd.*
Carando / *Di Giorgio Corp.*
Care*Free / *Nabisco Brands Inc.*
Caribe / *Central Soya Company Inc.*
Carmela / *Bacardi Corp.*
Carnation / *Carnation Company*
Carnation Country Foods / *Carnation Company*
Caroby / *Capitol Food Industries Inc.*
Carolina / *Colgate-Palmolive Co.*
Casera / *Campbell Soup Co.*
Casino / *Dart & Kraft Inc.*
Celeste / *Quaker Oats Co.*
Certo / *General Foods Corp.*
Certs / *Warner-Lambert Co.*
Champion / *Ward Foods Inc.*
Charleston Chew! / *Nabisco Brands Inc.*
CHB / *CHB Foods Inc.*
Cheerios / *General Mills Inc.*
Cheese Nips / *Nabisco Brands Inc.*
Chee-Tos / *PepsiCo Inc.*
Cheez Whiz / *Dart & Kraft Inc.*
Cheez-it / *American Brands Inc.*
Chef / *American Home Products Corp.*
Chef Boy-Ar-Dee / *American Home Products Corp.*
Chef Cut / *Jewel Companies Inc.*
Chef Kitchen / *Jewel Companies Inc.*
Chef Pierre / *Consolidated Foods Corp.*
Chef Ready / *Flowers Industries Inc.*
Chef-mate / *Carnation Company*
Cherry Valley / *Jewel Companies Inc.*
Chesty / *Culbro Corp.*
Chewels / *Warner-Lambert Co.*
Chex / *Ralston Purina Co.*
Chicken In A Biskit / *Nabisco Brands Inc.*
Chicken-of-the-Sea / *Ralston Purina Co.*
Chiclets / *Warner-Lambert Co.*
Chico / *United Brands Co.*
Chico-San / *H.J. Heinz Co.*
Chiffon / *Anderson, Clayton & Co.*
Chill Ripe / *Curtice-Burns Inc.*
Chip A Roos / *American Brands Inc.*
Chips Ahoy! / *Nabisco Brands Inc.*
Chipy / *Beatrice Companies Inc.*
Chiquita / *United Brands Co.*
Choco / *Maryland Cup Corp.*
Choco Crunch / *Knudsen Corp.*
Choc-o-Lunch / *Lance Inc.*
Chuckles / *Nabisco Brands Inc.*
Chun King / *R.J. Reynolds*
Chunky / *Ward Foods Inc.*
Church's Fried Chicken / *Church's Fried Chicken Inc.*
Churngold / *Beatrice Companies Inc.*
Cinch / *CHB Foods Inc.*
Cincinnati Fruit / *Beatrice Companies Inc.*
Cinnamon Life / *Quaker Oats Co.*
Cinnamon Toast Crunch / *General Mills Inc.*
Cisco's / *Central Soya Company Inc.*
Clamboat / *Hershey Foods Corp.*
Clark / *Beatrice Companies Inc.*

Clark / *Pillsbury Co.*
Claussen / *General Foods Corp.*
Clorets / *Warner-Lambert Co.*
Clover / *United Brands Co.*
Coco Supreme / *Carnation Company*
Cocoa Puffs / *General Mills Inc.*
Coconut Grove / *Standard Brands Inc.*
Coffee-Mate / *Carnation Company*
Coldbrook / *Safeway Stores Inc.*
College Inn / *R.J. Reynolds*
Colonial / *Anheuser-Busch Companies Inc.*
Colonial / *Curtice-Burns Inc.*
Colonial / *Campbell Taggart Inc.*
Colonial / *Beatrice Companies Inc.*
Comet Rice / *Early California Industries, Inc.*
Complete Pancake Mix / *General Mills Inc.*
Comstock / *Curtice-Burns Inc.*
Contadina / *Carnation Company*
Continental / *Federal Company*
Cook Book / *American Bakeries Co.*
Cookie Crisp / *Ralston Purina Co.*
Cool Whip / *General Foods Corp.*
Cooper Farms / *Southland Corp.*
Corn Bran / *Quaker Oats Co.*
Corn Total / *General Mills Inc.*
Corona / *United Brands Co.*
Coronation / *R.J. Reynolds*
Cortland Valley / *Curtice-Burns Inc.*
Cory-Lite / *Hershey Foods Corp.*
Costello's / *Beatrice Companies Inc.*
Cotillion / *Safeway Stores Inc.*
Cottage Fries / *Borden Inc.*
Cotton / *American Bakeries Co.*
Cotton's Holsum / *American Bakeries Co.*
Count Chocula / *General Mills Inc.*
Country Charm / *Dean Foods Co.*
Country Corn flakes / *General Mills Inc.*
Country Hearth / *Beatrice Companies Inc.*
Country Kitchen Syrup / *General Foods Corp.*
Country Meadow / *Borden Inc.*
Country Meal / *Campbell Taggart Inc.*
Country Pride / *ConAgra Inc.*
Country Pure peanut butter and condiments / *Safeway Stores Inc.*
Country Skillet / *ConAgra Inc.*
Country Stand / *Ralston Purina Co.*
Country Store / *Borden Inc.*
County Line / *Beatrice Companies Inc.*
Covered Wagon / *Safeway Stores Inc.*
Cow Boy Jo's / *Beatrice Companies Inc.*
Cracker Barrel / *Dart & Kraft Inc.*
Cracker Jack / *Ralston Purina Co.*
Cracker Jack / *Borden Inc.*
Crackin' Good / *Jewel Companies Inc.*
Crane / *Acton Corp.*
Cream / *A.E. Staley Manufacturing Co.*
Cream of Rice / *Nabisco Brands Inc.*
Cream of Wheat / *Nabisco Brands Inc.*
Creamettes / *Borden Inc.*
Creamies / *Tasty Baking Co.*
Creamland / *Dean Foods Co.*
Cremelado / *United Brands Co.*
Cremo / *Beatrice Companies Inc.*
Cremol Plus / *Esmark Inc.*
Cremora / *Borden Inc.*
Crescent / *Federal Company*
Crestwood Bakery / *Godfrey Co.*
Cris & Pitt's / *SCM Corp.*
Crisco / *Procter & Gamble Co.*
Crispy Oatmeal / *Ralston Purina Co.*
Crown Colony / *Safeway Stores Inc.*
Crunch N Munch / *American Home Products Corp.*
Crunchi-O's / *Curtice-Burns Inc.*
Crystal-Pak / *Cagle's Inc.*
Cudahy / *General Host Corp.*
Cure 81 / *George A. Hormel & Co.*
Curemaster / *George A. Hormel & Co.*
Curtiss / *Standard Brands Inc.*
Dainty Maid / *Ward Foods Inc.*
Dairy Glen / *Safeway Stores Inc.*
Dairy Kiss / *Giant Food Inc.*
Dairyland / *Safeway Stores Inc.*
Daitch / *Shopwell Inc.*
Dalewood / *Safeway Stores Inc.*
Danish Crown / *United Brands Co.*
Danish Delight / *Capitol Food Industries Inc.*
Dannon / *Beatrice Companies Inc.*
Dari Valley / *Knudsen Corp.*
David Lau / *Beatrice Companies Inc.*
Davis / *R.J. Reynolds*
Davy Jones / *Beatrice Companies Inc.*
Dean's / *Dean Foods Co.*
Dean's McCadam / *Dean Foods Co.*
Decker / *ConAgra Inc.*
Deep South / *Winn-Dixie Stores Inc.*
Del Monte / *R.J. Reynolds*
Delacre / *Campbell Soup Co.*
Deli Gourmet / *International Multifoods Corp.*
Delico / *Katy Industries, Inc.*
Dell / *Beatrice Companies Inc.*
Delmonico / *Hershey Foods Corp.*
Delmonico / *Conwood Corp.*
Delta Food / *Beatrice Companies Inc.*
Dennison's / *American Home Products Corp.*
Dentyne / *Warner-Lambert Co.*
Denyer-Dans / *Beatrice Companies Inc.*

Deran / *Borden Inc.*
Derby / *Beatrice Companies Inc.*
Detroit Pure Milk / *Borman's Inc.*
Devil Dogs / *Borden Inc.*
Dew Kist / *Jewel Companies Inc.*
Diet Chef / *Carnation Company*
DiLusso / *George A. Hormel & Co.*
Dinty Moore / *George A. Hormel & Co.*
D'Italiano / *American Bakeries Co.*
Dixie / *Stokely-Van Camp Inc.*
Dixie Crystals / *Savannah Foods & Industries Inc.*
Dixie Darling Bakers / *Winn-Dixie Stores Inc.*
Dixie Lily / *Beatrice Companies Inc.*
Dole / *Castle & Cooke Inc.*
Doll Brand / *Beatrice Companies Inc.*
Domino / *Amstar Corp.*
Domsea / *Campbell Soup Co.*
Doritos / *PepsiCo Inc.*
Dorothy Duncan / *Safeway Stores Inc.*
Doublemint / *William Wrigley Jr. Co.*
Doumak / *Beatrice Companies Inc.*
Downy Flake / *I.C. Industries Inc.*
Drake's / *Borden Inc.*
Dream Whip / *General Foods Corp.*
Dreamsicle / *Knudsen Corp.*
Dressel's / *American Bakeries Co.*
Dromedary / *Nabisco Brands Inc.*
Droste / *Standard Brands Inc.*
Drumstick / *Knudsen Corp.*
Dulany / *United Foods, Inc.*
Duncan Hines / *Procter & Gamble Co.*
Dunkin' Donuts / *Dunkin' Donuts Inc.*
Durkee / *SCM Corp.*
Duryea's / *CPC International Inc.*
Dutch Maid / *Kellogg Co.*
Dutch Valley / *Weis Markets Inc.*
Dynamints / *Warner-Lambert Co.*
D-Zerta / *General Foods Corp.*
Eagle / *Anheuser-Busch Companies Inc.*
Eagle Brand / *Borden Inc.*
Eagle Ice Cream / *Fisher Foods, Inc.*
Early California Favorites / *Early California Industries, Inc.*
Earth Bread / *Campbell Taggart Inc.*
Earth Grains / *Anheuser-Busch Companies Inc.*
Earth Grains / *Campbell Taggart Inc.*
Easy Cheese / *Nabisco Brands Inc.*
Eat-it-All / *Maryland Cup Corp.*
Eckrich / *Beatrice Companies Inc.*
Ege Kvist / *G. Heileman Brewing Co. Inc.*
Egg Beaters / *Standard Brands Inc.*
Eggo / *Kellogg Co.*
Eight O Clock / *Great Atlantic & Pacific Tea Co. Inc.*
El Charrito / *Anheuser-Busch Companies Inc.*
El Chico Frozen Mexican Dinner / *Campbell Taggart Inc.*
El Grande / *Safeway Stores Inc.*
El Molino Mills / *Iroquois Brands Ltd.*
El Pollo Loco / *Denny's Inc.*
Ellio's / *Purex Industries, Inc.*
Elsie / *Borden Inc.*
Embassy / *Southland Corp.*
Empress / *Safeway Stores Inc.*
Enchanted Isle / *Safeway Stores Inc.*
Energy Bars / *Shaklee Corp.*
Entenmann / *Warner-Lambert Co.*
Entenmann's / *General Foods Corp.*
EPA / *Shaklee Corp.*
Equal / *G.D. Searle & Co.*
Escoffier / *Heublein Inc.*
Escort / *Nabisco Brands Inc.*
Eskimo Pie / *Knudsen Corp.*
Euphrates / *Quaker Oats Co.*
Europe / *Beatrice Companies Inc.*
Everfresh / *United Foods, Inc.*
Everglades / *Savannah Foods & Industries Inc.*
Excel / *Medivix Inc.*
Extra / *William Wrigley Jr. Co.*
E-Z / *Borden Inc.*
E-Z Cut / *United Brands Co.*
Familiar / *Hershey Foods Corp.*
Family Pack/10 G's / *General Mills Inc.*
Fancifood / *Universal Foods Corp.*
Fanning's Bread & Butter / *CPC International Inc.*
Fantastix / *PepsiCo Inc.*
Farina / *Pillsbury Co.*
Farm Crest / *Ward Foods Inc.*
Farm Stand / *Jewel Companies Inc.*
Fashion Tone / *Jewel Companies Inc.*
fff (Fred's Frozen Foods) / *Central Soya Company Inc.*
Fiber Wafers / *Shaklee Corp.*
Fieldcrest / *Dean Foods Co.*
Fiesta / *Acton Corp.*
Fiestas / *Beatrice Companies Inc.*
Fig Newtons / *Nabisco Brands Inc.*
Figis / *American Can Co.*
Figurines / *Pillsbury Co.*
Fireside / *Beatrice Companies Inc.*
Fishamajig / *Hershey Foods Corp.*
Fisher / *Beatrice Companies Inc.*
Fisher Cheese / *Amfac Inc.*
Flako / *Quaker Oats Co.*
Flavor Ripe / *Beatrice Companies Inc.*
Fleischmann's / *Nabisco Brands Inc.*

Fleishmann's Egg Beaters / *Nabisco Brands Inc.*
Fleming's / *Fleming Companies Inc.*
Flora Danica / *Beatrice Companies Inc.*
Flowers / *Flowers Industries Inc.*
Fluf-Puft / *Safeway Stores Inc.*
Food Sticks / *Pillsbury Co.*
Fox Deluxe / *Pillsbury Co.*
FPI / *Beatrice Companies Inc.*
Franco American / *Campbell Soup Co.*
Frank N Stuff / *George A. Hormel & Co.*
Franken Berry / *General Mills Inc.*
Franklin / *American Home Products Corp.*
Frank's / *SCM Corp.*
Fred's / *Central Soya Company Inc.*
Freedent / *William Wrigley Jr. Co.*
Freezer Queen / *United Foods, Inc.*
Freshen-up / *Warner-Lambert Co.*
Fribble / *Hershey Foods Corp.*
Friendly / *Hershey Foods Corp.*
Friendly Frank / *Hershey Foods Corp.*
Friendly's Big Beef / *Hershey Foods Corp.*
Frito-Lay / *PepsiCo Inc.*
Fritos / *PepsiCo Inc.*
Frozen Novelties / *Carnation Company*
Fruit & Fibre / *General Foods Corp.*
Fruit Roll-Ups / *General Mills Inc.*
Fruitine / *Beatrice Companies Inc.*
Fudgesicle / *Knudsen Corp.*
Fudgetown / *Quaker Oats Co.*
Funyuns / *PepsiCo Inc.*
Fyffes / *United Brands Co.*
G & W / *Beatrice Companies Inc.*
Gail Borden Signature Quality / *Borden Inc.*
Gambills / *Beatrice Companies Inc.*
Gandy Quality Check / *Dean Foods Co.*
Garden Kiss / *Giant Food Inc.*
Gardenside / *Safeway Stores Inc.*
Gardner's / *G. Heileman Brewing Co. Inc.*
Gaucho / *Quaker Oats Co.*
Gaymont / *Conwood Corp.*
G.B. Raffetto / *Iroquois Brands Ltd.*
Gebhart / *Beatrice Companies Inc.*
Georgia / *Campbell Taggart Inc.*
Gerber / *Gerber Products Co.*
Germack / *Acton Corp.*
German Pumpernickel / *Flowers Industries Inc.*
GFI / *Beatrice Companies Inc.*
Gilroy Foods / *McCormick & Co. Inc.*
Girard's / *Early California Industries, Inc.*
Giroux / *Iroquois Brands Ltd.*
Gladiola / *Beatrice Companies Inc.*
Godiva / *Campbell Soup Co.*
Gold Cross / *Carnation Company*
Gold Medal Flour / *General Mills Inc.*
Gold Nugget / *Campbell Soup Co.*
Gold Rush / *Topps Chewing Gum Inc.*
Golden Almond / *Hershey Foods Corp.*
Golden Crisp / *Culbro Corp.*
Golden Flake / *Golden Enterprises Inc.*
Golden Grahams / *General Mills Inc.*
Golden Griddle / *CPC International Inc.*
Golden Image / *Dart & Kraft Inc.*
Golden Popcorn / *Culbro Corp.*
Golden Ridges / *Culbro Corp.*
Golden Smoked / *United Brands Co.*
Golden West / *McCormick & Co. Inc.*
Gold-n-Chees / *Lance Inc.*
Goobers / *Ward Foods Inc.*
Good Humor / *Beatrice Companies Inc.*
Good 'n Fruity / *Warner-Lambert Co.*
Good 'n Plenty / *Warner-Lambert Co.*
Good Seasonings / *General Foods Corp.*
Goodvalue / *Fleming Companies Inc.*
Gordon's / *Acton Corp.*
Gorton's / *General Mills Inc.*
Gourmet / *Beatrice Companies Inc.*
Grackin' Good Bakers / *Winn-Dixie Stores Inc.*
Gradu-Weight / *Stanhome, Inc.*
Gram Daddy / *Southland Corp.*
Grandma's / *PepsiCo Inc.*
Grandmother Joshua / *Beatrice Companies Inc.*
Granny Goose / *R.J. Reynolds*
Granny's / *Campbell Soup Co.*
Granola Dipps / *Quaker Oats Co.*
Grape-Nuts / *General Foods Corp.*
Great Beginnings / *George A. Hormel & Co.*
Green Giant / *Pillsbury Co.*
Green Tree / *United Brands Co.*
Greenwood / *Curtice-Burns Inc.*
Gregg's Gold-n-Soft / *A.E. Staley Manufacturing Co.*
Grey Poupon / *Heublein Inc.*
Grill Great / *Jewel Companies Inc.*
Guangmei / *Beatrice Companies Inc.*
Gulden's / *American Home Products Corp.*
Gum Dinger / *American Home Products Corp.*
Guys / *Borden Inc.*
Haagen-Dazs / *Pillsbury Co.*
Hain / *Ogden Corp.*
Haley's / *CHB Foods Inc.*
Halfsies / *Quaker Oats Co.*
Hamburger Helper / *General Mills Inc.*
Hancock's / *Lance Inc.*
Handschumacher Old World / *Curtice-Burns Inc.*
Harbison's / *Southland Corp.*
Harts Rolls / *Heublein Inc.*
Harvest / *Curtice-Burns Inc.*

Harvest Day / *Lucky Stores Inc.*
Health Bar / *Knudsen Corp.*
Healthy 'n Light Entrees / *Shaklee Corp.*
Heidi / *Giant Food Inc.*
Heifetz / *Dean Foods Co.*
Hellmann's and Best Foods / *CPC International Inc.*
Heritage Wholesalers / *Fisher Foods, Inc.*
Herrud / *Thorn Apple Valley, Inc.*
Hershey Baking Products / *Hershey Foods Corp.*
Hershey's Kisses / *Hershey Foods Corp.*
Het Luilekkerland BV / *Capitol Food Industries Inc.*
Heyday / *Nabisco Brands Inc.*
Hi Brand / *Consolidated Foods Corp.*
Hickory Host / *Thorn Apple Valley, Inc.*
Hidden Valley Ranch / *Clorox*
High Altitude Hungarian / *Peavey Co.*
Highway / *Safeway Stores Inc.*
Hi-Ho / *American Brands Inc.*
Hillbilly / *Campbell Taggart Inc.*
Hillshire Farms / *Consolidated Foods Corp.*
Hi-Pro / *Borden Inc.*
H-O / *CPC International Inc.*
Hoffman House / *Dean Foods Co.*
Hoffman's / *Anderson, Clayton & Co.*
Holanda / *Beatrice Companies Inc.*
Holland / *Beatrice Companies Inc.*
Holly / *Holly Sugar Corp.*
Holly Farms / *Federal Company*
Holly Ridge Farm / *Thorn Apple Valley, Inc.*
Hollywood / *Ogden Corp.*
Hollywood / *Campbell Taggart Inc.*
Holsum Bread / *G. Heileman Brewing Co. Inc.*
Home Brand / *ConAgra Inc.*
Home Brands / *Peavey Co.*
Home Hearth / *Nabisco Brands Inc.*
Home Pride / *Ralston Purina Co.*
Homefries / *Borden Inc.*
Hometown / *Flowers Industries Inc.*
Honey Crust / *Ward Foods Inc.*
Honey Grain / *Campbell Taggart Inc.*
Honey Maid / *Nabisco Brands Inc.*
Honeycomb / *General Foods Corp.*
Honey-Nut Cheerios / *General Mills Inc.*
Honey-Roll / *Maryland Cup Corp.*
Hormel / *George A. Hormel & Co.*
Horten's / *Southland Corp.*
Hostess / *Beatrice Companies Inc.*
Hostess / *Ralston Purina Co.*
Hostess / *Kellogg Co.*
Hot 'n' Fresh / *Campbell Taggart Inc.*
Hotel Bar / *Beatrice Companies Inc.*
Hubba Bubba Bubble Gum / *William Wrigley Jr. Co.*
Hula Chews / *American Home Products Corp.*
Humpty Dumpty / *American Brands Inc.*
Hungry Jack / *Pillsbury Co.*
Hunter / *United Brands Co.*
Hunt's / *Beatrice Companies Inc.*
Hunt-Wesson / *Norton Simon Inc.*
Hydrox / *American Brands Inc.*
I Screams / *Nabisco Brands Inc.*
Idle Wild Farm / *Idle Wild Foods Inc.*
Ile de France / *Universal Foods Corp.*
Illusions / *Medivix Inc.*
Imperial Kitchens / *Central Soya Company Inc.*
Indian Trail / *Dean Foods Co.*
Instant Maid / *Jewel Companies Inc.*
Instant Protein® Drink Mix / *Shaklee Corp.*
Ivory Club / *Ward Foods Inc.*
J. Hungerford Smith / *Norton Simon Inc.*
Jack's / *Beatrice Companies Inc.*
Jackson's / *Dillon Companies Inc.*
Jane Parker / *Great Atlantic & Pacific Tea Co. Inc.*
Janet Davis / *Valmac Industries Inc.*
Janet Lee / *Albertson's Inc.*
Javin / *Iroquois Brands Ltd.*
Jax Cheese Twists / *Culbro Corp.*
Jaxmor / *Anderson, Clayton & Co.*
JEB's / *Jewel Companies Inc.*
Jell-O / *General Foods Corp.*
Jell-O Pudding Pops / *General Foods Corp.*
Jell-Well / *Safeway Stores Inc.*
Jewel / *Topps Chewing Gum Inc.*
Jewel Maid / *Jewel Companies Inc.*
Jif / *Procter & Gamble Co.*
Jiffy / *American Home Products Corp.*
Jimmy Dean / *Consolidated Foods Corp.*
John Morrell / *United Brands Co.*
Johnston's / *Beatrice Companies Inc.*
Johnston's / *Ward Foods Inc.*
Jolly Rancher / *Beatrice Companies Inc.*
Joyett / *Safeway Stores Inc.*
Joyner's / *Esmark Inc.*
Jubilee / *Beatrice Companies Inc.*
Juice Bowl / *Campbell Soup Co.*
Juice Works / *Campbell Soup Co.*
Juicy Fruit / *William Wrigley Jr. Co.*
Jumbolina / *Ward Foods Inc.*
Junior Mints / *Nabisco Brands Inc.*
Juniors / *Tasty Baking Co.*
Junket / *Kellogg Co.*
Kaboom / *General Mills Inc.*
Kahn's Kitchens of Sara Lee / *Consolidated Foods Corp.*
Kalise / *Beatrice Companies Inc.*
Kandy Kakes / *Tasty Baking Co.*
Karo / *CPC International Inc.*

KAS / *Culbro Corp.*
Kaukauna Klub / *International Multifoods Corp.*
Keller's / *Beatrice Companies Inc.*
Kelling / *Acton Corp.*
Kellogg / *Kellogg Co.*
Kemps / *Acton Corp.*
KeyKo / *Beatrice Companies Inc.*
Kia-Ora / *Campbell Soup Co.*
Kilpatrick's / *Campbell Taggart Inc.*
King Colton / *Consolidated Foods Corp.*
King Midas / *Peavey Co.*
King's Choice / *Beatrice Companies Inc.*
Kingsford's / *CPC International Inc.*
Kingstaste / *Stokely-Van Camp Inc.*
Kiss / *Giant Food Inc.*
Kit Kat / *Hershey Foods Corp.*
Kitchen Bouquet / *Clorox*
Kitchens of the Oceans / *Ward Foods Inc.*
Kitty Clover / *Culbro Corp.*
Kix / *General Mills Inc.*
Kneip / *Beatrice Companies Inc.*
Knorr / *CPC International Inc.*
Knowltown / *Southland Corp.*
Knudsen / *Knudsen Corp.*
Kolb-Lena Cheese / *Katy Industries, Inc.*
Kounty Kist / *Pillsbury Co.*
Krackel / *Hershey Foods Corp.*
Kraft / *Dart & Kraft Inc.*
Kretschmer / *International Multifoods Corp.*
Krey / *United Brands Co.*
Krimpets / *Tasty Baking Co.*
Krispy / *American Brands Inc.*
Krispy Kreme / *Beatrice Companies Inc.*
Krun-cheez / *Acton Corp.*
Kuner's / *Stokely-Van Camp Inc.*
La Choy / *Beatrice Companies Inc.*
La Crosse / *Ward Foods Inc.*
La Crosta / *International Multifoods Corp.*
La Menorguina / *Beatrice Companies Inc.*
La Pina / *General Mills Inc.*
La Suprema Restaurant Style / *Curtice-Burns Inc.*
La Tolteca / *Standard Brands Inc.*
Lady Betty / *Beatrice Companies Inc.*
Lady Borden / *Borden Inc.*
Lady Lee / *Lucky Stores Inc.*
Lambrecht / *Beatrice Companies Inc.*
Lamb-Weston / *Amfac Inc.*
Lance / *Lance Inc.*
Lanchee / *Lance Inc.*
Landshire / *Southland Corp.*
Lane Country / *Laneco Inc.*
Lara Lynn / *Beatrice Companies Inc.*
Las Palmas / *Ogden Corp.*
Latums / *Beatrice Companies Inc.*
Lauderdale Farms / *Consolidated Foods Corp.*
Launder Maid / *Jewel Companies Inc.*
Lay's / *PepsiCo Inc.*
Lazzaroni / *Campbell Soup Co.*
Le Menu / *Campbell Soup Co.*
Le Sueur / *Pillsbury Co.*
Lecroy / *SCM Corp.*
LeGout / *Kellogg Co.*
Lewis / *CHB Foods Inc.*
Liberty / *Beatrice Companies Inc.*
Life / *Quaker Oats Co.*
Life Savers / *Nabisco Brands Inc.*
Light & Lean / *George A. Hormel & Co.*
Light 'N Fluffy / *Hershey Foods Corp.*
Light 'n' Fresh / *Beatrice Companies Inc.*
Light n' Lively / *Dart & Kraft Inc.*
Light Tasty Spread / *Standard Brands Inc.*
Lignoflex / *Beatrice Companies Inc.*
Li'l Sauces / *McCormick & Co. Inc.*
Lilly / *Southland Corp.*
Linden / *Curtice-Burns Inc.*
Lite / *American Bakeries Co.*
Lite-Line / *Borden Inc.*
Little Brownie / *Beatrice Companies Inc.*
Little Juan / *Central Soya Company Inc.*
Little Sizzlers / *George A. Hormel & Co.*
Lloyd J Harris / *Consolidated Foods Corp.*
Log Cabin / *Anderson, Clayton & Co.*
Log Cabin Syrup / *General Foods Corp.*
Long Life / *Beatrice Companies Inc.*
Longhorn / *Beatrice Companies Inc.*
Lords / *Beatrice Companies Inc.*
Lorna Doone / *Nabisco Brands Inc.*
Louis Rich / *General Foods Corp.*
Louis Sherry / *Beatrice Companies Inc.*
Lowrey's / *Beatrice Companies Inc.*
Lucca / *Curtice-Burns Inc.*
Lucerne / *Safeway Stores Inc.*
Luck's / *American Home Products Corp.*
Lucky Charms / *General Mills Inc.*
Lynden Farms / *Carnation Company*
Ma Brown / *Beatrice Companies Inc.*
Mackerel / *CHB Foods Inc.*
Mahatma / *Colgate-Palmolive Co.*
Major Grey's Chutney / *Iroquois Brands Ltd.*
Mallomars / *Nabisco Brands Inc.*
Malt Cup / *Knudsen Corp.*
Mann's / *Acton Corp.*
Manor / *Campbell Taggart Inc.*
Manwich / *Beatrice Companies Inc.*
Manwich Sandwich Sauce / *Norton Simon Inc.*
Marabou / *Hershey Foods Corp.*

Marionette / *Beatrice Companies Inc.*
Mario's / *Beatrice Companies Inc.*
Marquez / *Central Soya Company Inc.*
MarTenn / *Consolidated Foods Corp.*
Martha White / *Beatrice Companies Inc.*
Marvel / *Great Atlantic & Pacific Tea Co. Inc.*
Mary Dunbar / *Jewel Companies Inc.*
Mary Kitchen / *George A. Hormel & Co.*
Mason / *Tootsie Roll Industries Inc.*
Maybud / *Anderson, Clayton & Co.*
Mazola / *CPC International Inc.*
MBT / *Colgate-Palmolive Co.*
McCormick / *McCormick & Co. Inc.*
McKenzie's / *Curtice-Burns Inc.*
McKenzie's gold King / *Curtice-Burns Inc.*
Meadow Gold / *Beatrice Companies Inc.*
Melrose / *Safeway Stores Inc.*
Melville / *Standard Brands Inc.*
Menner / *Curtice-Burns Inc.*
Merckens / *Nabisco Brands Inc.*
Merico / *Campbell Taggart Inc.*
Merita / *American Bakeries Co.*
Metco / *Beatrice Companies Inc.*
Mexican Original / *Tyson Foods Inc.*
Mickelberry / *Mickelberry Corp.*
Mickey / *American Bakeries Co.*
Midwest Farms / *Southland Corp.*
Milk Duds / *Beatrice Companies Inc.*
Milk-Mate / *R.J. Reynolds*
Mini Chips / *Hershey Foods Corp.*
Minute Rice / *General Foods Corp.*
Minute Tapioca / *General Foods Corp.*
Miracle Whip / *Dart & Kraft Inc.*
Mister Mustard / *SCM Corp.*
Mister Salty / *Nabisco Brands Inc.*
M.J. Holloway's / *Beatrice Companies Inc.*
Molly Bushell / *Beatrice Companies Inc.*
Montco / *Fleming Companies Inc.*
Monterey Mushrooms / *Amfac Inc.*
Montini / *Ogden Corp.*
Moore's / *Clorox*
Morey's / *International Multifoods Corp.*
Morton / *Morton-Thiokol, Inc.*
Morton Lite Salt Mixture / *Morton-Thiokol, Inc.*
Morton Salt Substitute / *Morton-Thiokol, Inc.*
Mortons Nature's Seanonings / *Morton-Thiokol, Inc.*
Mother's Best / *Beatrice Companies Inc.*
Mountain Farm Pecan / *Flowers Industries Inc.*
Mountain High / *Beatrice Companies Inc.*
Mountain Man / *Campbell Taggart Inc.*
Mountain Top / *Lancaster Colony Corp.*
Mr. Big / *Ward Foods Inc.*
Mr. Continental / *Ward Foods Inc.*
Mr. Goodbar / *Hershey Foods Corp.*
Mr. Host / *Esmark Inc.*
Mr. T / *Quaker Oats Co.*
Mrs. Dash / *Alberto Culver Co.*
Mrs. Filberts / *Central Soya Company Inc.*
Mrs. Ihrie's / *Acton Corp.*
Mrs. Paul's Kitchens / *Campbell Soup Co.*
Mrs. Smith's Pies / *Kellogg Co.*
Mrs. Stover's / *Russell Stover Candies Inc.*
Mrs. Weaver's / *Dean Foods Co.*
Mrs. Wright's / *Safeway Stores Inc.*
M.S.B. / *Foodarama Supermarkets Inc.*
Mt. Ida / *Beatrice Companies Inc.*
Mueller's / *CPC International Inc.*
Munchos / *PepsiCo Inc.*
Murray's / *Beatrice Companies Inc.*
Mussleman's / *I.C. Industries Inc.*
My T Fine / *R.J. Reynolds*
My-Te-Fine / *Fred Meyer*
Nabisco / *Nabisco Brands Inc.*
Nagel / *Curtice-Burns Inc.*
Nalley / *Curtice-Burns Inc.*
Nathan Famous / *United Brands Co.*
National Food / *National Tea Co.*
Natural Harvest / *Jewel Companies Inc.*
Nature Valley Granola / *General Mills Inc.*
Nature's Own / *Flowers Industries Inc.*
Nekot / *Lance Inc.*
Nepco / *Curtice-Burns Inc.*
New Bac-o's / *General Mills Inc.*
New Trail / *Hershey Foods Corp.*
New York Frozen Foods / *Lancaster Colony Corp.*
Niblets / *Pillsbury Co.*
Nibs / *Hershey Foods Corp.*
Nice 'n' Lite / *Knudsen Corp.*
Nilla / *Nabisco Brands Inc.*
No stick / *CPC International Inc.*
No-Bake Cheese Cake / *Standard Brands Inc.*
Nonesuch / *Borden Inc.*
Nosy Club / *Ward Foods Inc.*
N-Rich / *Beatrice Companies Inc.*
Nucoa / *CPC International Inc.*
Nu-Made / *Safeway Stores Inc.*
Numar / *United Brands Co.*
Nutrament / *Bristol Myers Co.*
NutraSweet / *G.D. Searle & Co.*
Nuttall's / *Beatrice Companies Inc.*
Nutter Butter / *Nabisco Brands Inc.*
O & C / *SCM Corp.*
Occident / *Peavey Co.*
O'Grady's / *PepsiCo Inc.*
Oh Henry / *Ward Foods Inc.*

Old Bohemia / *Jewel Companies Inc.*
Old El Paso / *I.C. Industries Inc.*
Old London / *Borden Inc.*
Old Smokehouse / *George A. Hormel & Co.*
Old South Styles / *American Home Products Corp.*
Old Vienna / *Acton Corp.*
Olde Virginie / *Thorn Apple Valley, Inc.*
Olive Products / *Beatrice Companies Inc.*
Omega / *Beatrice Companies Inc.*
Open Pit Barbeque / *General Foods Corp.*
Orchard Kiss / *Giant Food Inc.*
Ore-Ida / *H.J. Heinz Co.*
Oreo / *Nabisco Brands Inc.*
Orleans / *I.C. Industries Inc.*
Oroweat / *General Foods Corp.*
Ortega / *Heublein Inc.*
Orville Redenbacher's Gourmet Popping Corn / *Beatrice Companies Inc.*
Orville Redenbacker's / *Norton Simon Inc.*
Oscar Mayer / *General Foods Corp.*
Oven Fry / *General Foods Corp.*
Ovenjoy / *Safeway Stores Inc.*
Oysterettes / *Nabisco Brands Inc.*
P & R / *Hershey Foods Corp.*
Pac Man / *American Home Products Corp.*
Pacific Club / *Ward Foods Inc.*
Pack Train / *Safeway Stores Inc.*
Palmeto / *Beatrice Companies Inc.*
Parafan / *United Brands Co.*
Parkay / *Dart & Kraft Inc.*
Partridge / *United Brands Co.*
Party Grahams / *Nabisco Brands Inc.*
Party Pride / *Safeway Stores Inc.*
Partytime / *Knudsen Corp.*
Patio / *R.J. Reynolds*
Pauly / *Beatrice Companies Inc.*
Pay Day / *Consolidated Foods Corp.*
Payco / *Beatrice Companies Inc.*
Pearson / *Nabisco Brands Inc.*
Pearson / *Standard Brands Inc.*
Pebbles / *General Foods Corp.*
Pepi's / *Beatrice Companies Inc.*
Pepperidge Farm / *Campbell Soup Co.*
Perky / *Penn Traffic Co.*
Pernigotti / *Beatrice Companies Inc.*
Pesta / *Dean Foods Co.*
Pet Inc. / *I.C. Industries Inc.*
Peter Eckrich / *Beatrice Companies Inc.*
Peter Pan / *Esmark Inc.*
Peter Pan / *Beatrice Companies Inc.*
Peter Piper / *Dean Foods Co.*
Pet-Ritz / *I.C. Industries Inc.*
Petybon / *Hershey Foods Corp.*
Peyton's / *United Brands Co.*
Pfeiffer / *Norton Simon Inc.*
Pfeiffer Foods / *Lancaster Colony Corp.*
Philadelphia / *Dart & Kraft Inc.*
Phoenix / *Beatrice Companies Inc.*
Pictsweet / *United Foods, Inc.*
PictSweet / *Stokely-Van Camp Inc.*
Piedmont / *Safeway Stores Inc.*
Pillsbury / *Pillsbury Co.*
Pillsbury Best / *Pillsbury Co.*
Pinata / *Standard Brands Inc.*
Pinwheels / *Nabisco Brands Inc.*
Piret's / *Vicorp Restaurants Inc.*
Pixie / *Federal Company*
Pizza Pal / *Universal Foods Corp.*
Planters / *Standard Brands Inc.*
Planters / *Nabisco Brands Inc.*
Plume De Veal / *Beatrice Companies Inc.*
Plus / *Richardson-Vicks Inc.*
Plymouth Rock / *Ward Foods Inc.*
Pomona Sunshine / *Stokely-Van Camp Inc.*
Pop Bottles / *Topps Chewing Gum Inc.*
Pop Tarts / *Kellogg Co.*
Pop the Juicy / *Topps Chewing Gum Inc.*
Popeye / *Stokely-Van Camp Inc.*
Poppin Fresh Doughboy / *Pillsbury Co.*
Popsicle / *Consolidated Foods Corp.*
Popsicle / *Knudsen Corp.*
Pops-Rite / *Conwood Corp.*
Posada / *Central Soya Company Inc.*
Poseidon / *Ward Foods Inc.*
Post / *General Foods Corp.*
Post Toasties / *General Foods Corp.*
Post 40% Bran / *General Foods Corp.*
Post-Tens / *General Foods Corp.*
Postum / *General Foods Corp.*
Potato Buds / *General Mills Inc.*
Poultry Specialties / *Consolidated Foods Corp.*
Praise / *Carnation Company*
Prego / *Campbell Soup Co.*
Premier Is / *Beatrice Companies Inc.*
Premium / *Nabisco Brands Inc.*
Prestige / *Fisher Foods, Inc.*
Presto Pop / *Conwood Corp.*
Price / *Dean Foods Co.*
Prima Salsa / *Norton Simon Inc.*
Prime Froz'n / *United Foods, Inc.*
Prince Paul / *Safeway Stores Inc.*
Pringle's / *Procter & Gamble Co.*
Progresso / *Ogden Corp.*
Pro-Lecin® Nibblers / *Shaklee Corp.*
ProLine / *Borden Inc.*
Proten / *Esmark Inc.*

P.S.-Personally Selected / *Fleming Companies Inc.*
Puffed Rice / *Quaker Oats Co.*
Puffed Wheat / *Quaker Oats Co.*
Puritan / *Procter & Gamble Co.*
Puritan / *Norton Simon Inc.*
Purity cheese products / *Anderson, Clayton & Co.*
Pushups / *Knudsen Corp.*
Putters / *American Home Products Corp.*
Quaker / *Quaker Oats Co.*
Quality / *Dean Foods Co.*
Quality / *Borden Inc.*
Que Bueno! / *Carnation Company*
Queen Kristina / *United Brands Co.*
Queen of Scot / *Scot Lad Foods Inc.*
Quik-Snak / *Acton Corp.*
Quinlan / *Ward Foods Inc.*
R. B. Rice / *Consolidated Foods Corp.*
Racing Wheels / *Hershey Foods Corp.*
Ragu Chunky Gardenstyle / *Chesebrough-Pond's Inc.*
Ragu Extra Thick and Zesty / *Chesebrough-Pond's Inc.*
Ragu Homestyle / *Chesebrough-Pond's Inc.*
Ragu Italian / *Chesebrough-Pond's Inc.*
Ragu Pizza Quick / *Chesebrough-Pond's Inc.*
Ragu traditional / *Chesebrough-Pond's Inc.*
Rainbo / *Anheuser-Busch Companies Inc.*
Rainbo / *Campbell Taggart Inc.*
Rainbo / *Beatrice Companies Inc.*
Rainbow / *Fleming Companies Inc.*
Rainbow Brite / *Ralston Purina Co.*
Raisinettes / *Ward Foods Inc.*
Ralston / *Ralston Purina Co.*
Ralston Purina / *Ralston Purina Co.*
Ramirez & Feraud / *Ogden Corp.*
Ranch Style / *American Home Products Corp.*
Ranchfries / *Borden Inc.*
Range Brand / *George A. Hormel & Co.*
Ready Crust / *Ward Foods Inc.*
ReaLemon / *Borden Inc.*
Reber / *Beatrice Companies Inc.*
Red & White / *S.M. Flickinger Co. Inc.*
Red & White / *Godfrey Co.*
Red Band / *General Mills Inc.*
Red Seal / *Universal Foods Corp.*
Red Star / *Universal Foods Corp.*
Red Tulip / *Beatrice Companies Inc.*
Reddi Whip / *Beatrice Companies Inc.*
Reddi-Whip / *Norton Simon Inc.*
Reddy Ice / *Southland Corp.*
Red's / *Curtice-Burns Inc.*
Reese's Peanut Butter Cups / *Hershey Foods Corp.*
Reese's Pieces / *Hershey Foods Corp.*
Reggie / *Standard Brands Inc.*
Regina Wine Vinegar / *Heublein Inc.*
Re-Mi Foods / *A.E. Staley Manufacturing Co.*
Reuben / *International Multifoods Corp.*
R.F. / *Beatrice Companies Inc.*
Rice Kringles / *General Foods Corp.*
Rich & Natural / *Knudsen Corp.*
Rich Grain / *Flowers Industries Inc.*
Richardson / *Beatrice Companies Inc.*
Rich'ning / *Carnation Company*
Rick / *Castle & Cooke Inc.*
Ridgie's / *Borden Inc.*
Ril-Sweet / *Schering-Plough Corp.*
Ring / *Topps Chewing Gum Inc.*
Ritz / *Nabisco Brands Inc.*
River / *Colgate-Palmolive Co.*
Riviana / *Early California Industries, Inc.*
Riviana Foods / *Colgate-Palmolive Co.*
Riviera / *Curtice-Burns Inc.*
Robert's / *Beatrice Companies Inc.*
Robin Hood / *International Multifoods Corp.*
Rodeo / *United Brands Co.*
Rold Gold / *PepsiCo Inc.*
Rolo / *Hershey Foods Corp.*
Roman Meal / *Flowers Industries Inc.*
Roman Meal / *Campbell Taggart Inc.*
Ron's Krispy Fried Chicken / *Church's Fried Chicken Inc.*
Ronzoni / *General Foods Corp.*
Rosarita / *Beatrice Companies Inc.*
Rothschilds / *Warner-Lambert Co.*
Royal / *Nabisco Brands Inc.*
Royal / *Standard Brands Inc.*
Royal Crest / *Beatrice Companies Inc.*
Royal Crown / *Thorn Apple Valley, Inc.*
Royal Dragon / *Standard Brands Inc.*
Royal Jewel / *Jewel Companies Inc.*
Royal Satin / *Safeway Stores Inc.*
Rudy's Farm / *Consolidated Foods Corp.*
Ruffles / *PepsiCo Inc.*
Rus-Ette / *Consolidated Foods Corp.*
Russell Stover / *Russell Stover Candies Inc.*
Rusto / *Federal Company*
Rye-Chee / *Lance Inc.*
RyKrisp / *Ralston Purina Co.*
Sable Soft / *Jewel Companies Inc.*
Sabritos / *PepsiCo Inc.*
Safari / *Campbell Taggart Inc.*
Safeway / *Safeway Stores Inc.*
Sahlman Seafoods / *Katy Industries, Inc.*
Salad Crispins / *Clorox*
Salad Supreme / *McCormick & Co. Inc.*
Salad Toppins / *McCormick & Co. Inc.*
Salada / *Kellogg Co.*
San Giorgio / *Hershey Foods Corp.*

Sani-Dairy / *Penn Traffic Co.*
Sanson / *Beatrice Companies Inc.*
Sara Lee / *Consolidated Foods Corp.*
Sauce Maison / *Iroquois Brands Ltd.*
Savorol / *Conwood Corp.*
Savoy / *Beatrice Companies Inc.*
Schiff Bro. / *Iroquois Brands Ltd.*
Schilling / *McCormick & Co. Inc.*
Scoopable / *Knudsen Corp.*
Scooter Pie / *Quaker Oats Co.*
Scot Farms / *Scot Lad Foods Inc.*
Scot Lad / *Scot Lad Foods Inc.*
Scotch Treat / *Safeway Stores Inc.*
Scott Petersen / *United Brands Co.*
Sea Trader / *Safeway Stores Inc.*
Sea-Alaska, Alaska Seas / *ConAgra Inc.*
Sealtest / *Dart & Kraft Inc.*
Seas-oleums / *McCormick & Co. Inc.*
Season-All / *McCormick & Co. Inc.*
Sedutto / *Pillsbury Co.*
See's Candies / *Berkshire Hathaway Inc.*
Sego / *I.C. Industries Inc.*
Sentry / *Godfrey Co.*
Serve / *Di Giorgio Corp.*
Seven Seas / *Anderson, Clayton & Co.*
Shady Lane / *Safeway Stores Inc.*
Shake 'N Bake / *General Foods Corp.*
Shaklee Slim Plan Cream of Chicken-Flavored Soup / *Shaklee Corp.*
Shaklee Slim Plan Drink Mix / *Shaklee Corp.*
Sidewalk Sundae / *Knudsen Corp.*
Silver Floss / *Curtice-Burns Inc.*
Simon Fischer / *Federal Company*
Simple Simon / *Ward Foods Inc.*
Sinex Tigers Milk / *Richardson-Vicks Inc.*
Singleton / *ConAgra Inc.*
Sippin' Pak / *Borden Inc.*
Sizzlean / *Beatrice Companies Inc.*
Sizzlean / *Esmark Inc.*
Skimline / *Borden Inc.*
Skinner Pasta / *Hershey Foods Corp.*
Skippy / *CPC International Inc.*
Skor / *Hershey Foods Corp.*
Skylark / *Safeway Stores Inc.*
Sleepy Hollow / *Safeway Stores Inc.*
Slender / *Carnation Company*
Smith Kendon / *Beatrice Companies Inc.*
Smith's / *General Mills Inc.*
Smok-A-Roma / *Safeway Stores Inc.*
Smoke Craft / *International Multifoods Corp.*
Smoky Hollow Foods / *Consolidated Foods Corp.*
Smooth n' Juicy / *Topps Chewing Gum Inc.*
Smucker's / *J.M. Smucker Co.*
Snack Pack / *Norton Simon Inc.*
Sno Caps / *Ward Foods Inc.*
Snoboy / *Pacific Gamble Robinson Co.*
Snow Crest / *SCM Corp.*
Snow Star / *Safeway Stores Inc.*
Snow's / *Borden Inc.*
Snyder's of Berlin / *Curtice-Burns Inc.*
Social Tea / *Nabisco Brands Inc.*
Soft / *Standard Brands Inc.*
Soup Ladle / *United Foods, Inc.*
Soup Starter / *Beatrice Companies Inc.*
Soup Starter / *Esmark Inc.*
Southern Bell / *Standard Brands Inc.*
Southern Farms / *Curtice-Burns Inc.*
Southern Queen / *Anderson, Clayton & Co.*
Spam / *George A. Hormel & Co.*
Special Dark / *Hershey Foods Corp.*
Specialty Foods / *Southland Corp.*
Spectracoat / *Universal Foods Corp.*
Spin Blend / *CPC International Inc.*
Spoon Size / *Nabisco Brands Inc.*
The Spreadables / *Carnation Company*
Spreckels / *Amstar Corp.*
Spring / *Warner-Lambert Co.*
Sprinkle Sweet / *Pillsbury Co.*
Sta Krisp / *Acton Corp.*
Staley / *A.E. Staley Manufacturing Co.*
Standard Meat / *Consolidated Foods Corp.*
Standby / *Pacific Gamble Robinson Co.*
Star / *Jewel Companies Inc.*
Star-Kist / *H.J. Heinz Co.*
Steakumm / *H.J. Heinz Co.*
Stella / *Universal Foods Corp.*
Sterling / *Safeway Stores Inc.*
Stew Starter / *Beatrice Companies Inc.*
Stilwell / *Flowers Industries Inc.*
Stir n' Frost / *General Mills Inc.*
Stokely's Finest / *Stokely-Van Camp Inc.*
Stokey / *United Foods, Inc.*
Stop & Shop / *Stop & Shop Companies Inc.*
Stove Top / *General Foods Corp.*
Stute / *Beatrice Companies Inc.*
Sucaryl / *Abbott Laboratories*
Sugar Crisp / *General Foods Corp.*
Sugar Daddy / *Nabisco Brands Inc.*
Sugar Plum / *Esmark Inc.*
SugarTwin / *Alberto Culver Co.*
Sun / *Godfrey Co.*
Sun Country / *International Multifoods Corp.*
Sun Dance / *Acton Corp.*
Sun Giant / *Tenneco Inc.*
Sunbeam / *Flowers Industries Inc.*
Sunbeam / *G. Heileman Brewing Co. Inc.*

Sunbelt / *Winn-Dixie Stores Inc.*
Sunkist / *R.J. Reynolds*
Sunlite / *Norton Simon Inc.*
Sunnybank / *Safeway Stores Inc.*
Sunrise / *Godfrey Co.*
Sunset Ridge / *American Home Products Corp.*
Sunshine / *Stokely-Van Camp Inc.*
Sunshine / *American Brands Inc.*
Sunshine Slender / *Nature's Sunshine Products, Inc.*
Super Bazooka / *Topps Chewing Gum Inc.*
Super Moist / *General Mills Inc.*
Super Pop / *Curtice-Burns Inc.*
Superbrano / *Winn-Dixie Stores Inc.*
Superior / *Ward Foods Inc.*
Supper Club / *Ward Foods Inc.*
Sure-Jell / *General Foods Corp.*
Swans Down Cake Flour / *General Foods Corp.*
Swanson / *Campbell Soup Co.*
Sweet 10 / *Pillsbury Co.*
Sweeta / *Squibb Corp.*
Swift / *Beatrice Companies Inc.*
Swiss Rose / *Beatrice Companies Inc.*
T. Mazetti / *Lancaster Colony Corp.*
Table Trim / *United Brands Co.*
Talmadge Farms / *Cagle's Inc.*
Taper / *Jewel Companies Inc.*
Tasty Bird / *Valmac Industries Inc.*
Tastykake / *Tasty Baking Co.*
Taystee / *American Bakeries Co.*
Tayto / *Beatrice Companies Inc.*
Tea House Tea / *McCormick & Co. Inc.*
Team / *Nabisco Brands Inc.*
Tempty / *Tasty Baking Co.*
Tender Mix / *Flowers Industries Inc.*
Tend'r Lean / *Esmark Inc.*
Tennessee / *United Foods, Inc.*
Thank You / *Curtice-Burns Inc.*
Thomas's / *CPC International Inc.*
Thorn Apple Valley / *Thorn Apple Valley, Inc.*
Three Minute / *Curtice-Burns Inc.*
Three Rivers / *Federal Company*
Tiffles / *PepsiCo Inc.*
Tiger's Milk / *Richardson-Vicks Inc.*
Tio Sancho / *McCormick & Co. Inc.*
Tip Top / *Ward Foods Inc.*
Toastchee / *Lance Inc.*
Toasted Wheat & Raisins / *Nabisco Brands Inc.*
Tobin's First Prize / *United Brands Co.*
Tom Sawyer / *United Brands Co.*
Tootsie / *Tootsie Roll Industries Inc.*
Tootsie Roll / *Tootsie Roll Industries Inc.*
Top / *Curtice-Burns Inc.*
Top Frost / *Victory Markets, Inc.*
Topco / *Victory Markets, Inc.*
Topic / *Carnation Company*
Toranto / *Safeway Stores Inc.*
Torteros / *Borden Inc.*
Tor-Ticos / *Culbro Corp.*
Tostitos / *PepsiCo Inc.*
Total / *General Mills Inc.*
Totino's / *Pillsbury Co.*
Town House / *Safeway Stores Inc.*
Town Pride / *Borman's Inc.*
Trail Blazer / *International Multifoods Corp.*
Treasure Cave / *Beatrice Companies Inc.*
Trident / *Warner-Lambert Co.*
Trio / *Carnation Company*
Triscuit / *Nabisco Brands Inc.*
Trophy / *Safeway Stores Inc.*
Trophy / *Esmark Inc.*
TV Time / *McCormick & Co. Inc.*
Twinkies / *Ralston Purina Co.*
Twizzlers / *Hershey Foods Corp.*
Tyson / *Tyson Foods Inc.*
Uneeda / *Nabisco Brands Inc.*
Uni-Chef / *Universal Foods Corp.*
Union Sugar / *Consolidated Foods Corp.*
Unique Loaf / *Anderson, Clayton & Co.*
University / *Jewel Companies Inc.*
Van Camps / *Ralston Purina Co.*
Van Camp's / *Stokely-Van Camp Inc.*
Van Camp's / *Quaker Oats Co.*
Van-o-Lunch / *Lance Inc.*
Velda Farms / *Southland Corp.*
Velkay / *Safeway Stores Inc.*
Velveeta / *Dart & Kraft Inc.*
Velvetouch / *Jewel Companies Inc.*
Verdi / *Safeway Stores Inc.*
Vermont Maid / *R.J. Reynolds*
Victor / *Curtice-Burns Inc.*
Vienna Finger Cookies / *American Brands Inc.*
Vista / *Lance Inc.*
Vita / *Dean Foods Co.*
Viva / *Beatrice Companies Inc.*
Viva / *Culbro Corp.*
Vlasic / *Campbell Soup Co.*
Von Comp / *Beatrice Companies Inc.*
Wanzer's / *Southland Corp.*
Ward Bros. / *Ward Foods Inc.*
Warsaw Rye-bread / *Flowers Industries Inc.*
Water Maid / *Colgate-Palmolive Co.*
Waverly / *Nabisco Brands Inc.*
Wayne Bun / *Standard Brands Inc.*
Weight Watchers / *United Brands Co.*
Weight Watchers / *H.J. Heinz Co.*
Wesley's Quaker Maid / *Borman's Inc.*

Wesson / *Beatrice Companies Inc.*
Wesson / *Norton Simon Inc.*
Westag / *Safeway Stores Inc.*
Whatchamacallit / *Hershey Foods Corp.*
Wheat Thins / *Nabisco Brands Inc.*
Wheaties / *General Mills Inc.*
Wheatsworth / *Nabisco Brands Inc.*
White Lily / *Federal Company*
White Rose / *Di Giorgio Corp.*
Whitman's / *I.C. Industries Inc.*
Whitney's / *Kellogg Co.*
Wick Fowler's Famous 2-Alarm Chili / *Noxell Corp.*
Willow Brook Farms / *Valmac Industries Inc.*
Wilson / *Beatrice Companies Inc.*
Windsor / *Morton-Thiokol, Inc.*
Windsor Coarse Pickling Salt / *Morton-Thiokol, Inc.*
Winter Garden / *United Foods, Inc.*
Wise's / *Borden Inc.*
Wolf Brand / *Quaker Oats Co.*
Wonder / *Early California Industries, Inc.*
Wonder / *Ralston Purina Co.*
Woody's / *Anderson, Clayton & Co.*
Wranglers / *George A. Hormel & Co.*
Wrigley's Spearmint / *William Wrigley Jr. Co.*
Wuppermann / *Iroquois Brands Ltd.*
Wyler / *Borden Inc.*
Y & S / *Hershey Foods Corp.*
Yankee / *Curtice-Burns Inc.*
Yodels / *Borden Inc.*
Yummy / *Jewel Companies Inc.*
Zero / *Consolidated Foods Corp.*
100% Natural / *Quaker Oats Co.*
5th Season / *McCormick & Co. Inc.*
50-50 Bar / *Knudsen Corp.*

Food Stores & Bakeries

A & P / *Great Atlantic & Pacific Tea Co. Inc.*
Acme Supermarkets / *American Stores Co.*
A.J. Bayless / *A.J. Bayless Markets Inc.*
Albertson's / *Albertson's Inc.*
Alpha Beta Supermarkets / *American Stores Co.*
am/pm / *Atlantic Richfield Co.*
Applebaum's / *National Tea Co.*
Aunt Nellie's / *Giant Food Inc.*
Barney's / *The Kroger Co.*
Barricini / *Southland Corp.*
Betty Crocker / *General Mills Inc.*
Big Bear / *Big Bear, Inc.*
Big Bear Bakeries / *Big Bear, Inc.*
Big E / *Jewel Companies Inc.*
Big T. / *Fleming Companies Inc.*
Bilo Stores / *The Kroger Co.*
Brigham's / *Jewel Companies Inc.*
Bruno's Food Store / *Bruno's Inc.*
Buddies / *Winn-Dixie Stores Inc.*
Buttrey / *American Stores Co.*
Buttrey / *Jewel Companies Inc.*
City Market / *Dillon Companies Inc.*
City Market / *The Kroger Co.*
Consumer Warehouse Foods / *Bruno's Inc.*
Convenient Food / *Conna Corp.*
Cooper-Martin / *Malone & Hyde Inc.*
Del Taco Mexican Cafe / *W.R. Grace & Co.*
Dillon Springfield / *Dillon Companies Inc.*
Dillon Stores / *Dillon Companies Inc.*
Dillons Food Stores / *The Kroger Co.*
Eisner / *American Stores Co.*
Eisner / *Jewel Companies Inc.*
Emma's Taco House / *Collins Foods International Inc.*
Erickson / *G. Heileman Brewing Co. Inc.*
Fairway / *Malone & Hyde Inc.*
Family Market / *Pacific Gamble Robinson Co.*
Farmer Jack / *Borman's Inc.*
Farmers' Market / *Marsh Supermarkets Inc.*
Fazio's / *Fisher Foods, Inc.*
First Stop / *Thorofare Markets Inc.*
Fisher / *Fisher Foods, Inc.*
Food Emporium / *Shopwell Inc.*
Food Fair Mini Mart / *Borman's Inc.*
Food for Less / *Fleming Companies Inc.*
Food King / *Victory Markets, Inc.*
Food Lane / *Laneco Inc.*
Food Lane / *Wetterau, Inc.*
Food Town / *Seaway Food Town Inc.*
Food World / *Bruno's Inc.*
Foodway / *Winn-Dixie Stores Inc.*
FranPris / *Beatrice Companies Inc.*
Fred Meyer Stores / *Fred Meyer*
Fry's Food Stores / *Dillon Companies Inc.*
Fry's Food Stores / *The Kroger Co.*
G & W Discount / *Borman's Inc.*
Gerbes Supermarkets / *The Kroger Co.*
Gerbs / *Dillon Companies Inc.*
Giant / *Giant Food Inc.*
Giant Foods / *Giant Food Inc.*
Giant Foods of America / *Malone & Hyde Inc.*
Gino's East of Chicago / *Collins Foods International Inc.*
Gooch Meats / *Cullum Companies Inc.*
Great American Food Stores / *Victory Markets, Inc.*
Gristede's / *Southland Corp.*

Grocery Warehouse / *Albertson's Inc.*
Hinky Dinky / *Cullum Companies Inc.*
Hoagy's Corner Deli / *Knudsen Corp.*
Hyde Park / *Malone & Hyde Inc.*
I.G.A. / *Fleming Companies Inc.*
Jewel / *American Stores Co.*
Jewel / *Jewel Companies Inc.*
Jewel T / *Jewel Companies Inc.*
Just Be Natural / *Wetterau, Inc.*
Kash 'n Karry / *Seaway Food Town Inc.*
Kentucky Fried Chicken / *Collins Foods International Inc.*
Kimball / *Winn-Dixie Stores Inc.*
King Scoopers / *Dillon Companies Inc.*
King Soopers / *The Kroger Co.*
Kohl's Food Stores / *Great Atlantic & Pacific Tea Co. Inc.*
Kroger Food Stores / *The Kroger Co.*
Kroger Sav-On / *The Kroger Co.*
Kwik Shop / *Dillon Companies Inc.*
Kwik Shop / *The Kroger Co.*
La Petite Boulangerie / *PepsiCo Inc.*
Lo-Buy / *The Kroger Co.*
Majik Market / *Munford Inc.*
Market Basket / *S.M. Flickinger Co. Inc.*
Marsh / *Marsh Supermarkets Inc.*
Martin's / *Hannaford Bros. Co.*
Michigan Markets / *Munford Inc.*
Migros / *Beatrice Companies Inc.*
Milgram / *Wetterau, Inc.*
Minimax / *Fleming Companies Inc.*
Mr. Quik / *Super Valu Stores Inc.*
National / *National Tea Co.*
Omar Bakeries / *Fisher Foods, Inc.*
Pantry / *Cullum Companies Inc.*
Pantry Pride / *Pantry Pride, Inc.*
Penny Fare / *Thorofare Markets Inc.*
Pic-Pac Supermarkets / *Malone & Hyde Inc.*
Piggly Wiggly / *Fleming Companies Inc.*
Plus Discount / *Great Atlantic & Pacific Tea Co. Inc.*
Prairie Market / *Pacific Gamble Robinson Co.*
Price Rite / *Mott's Supermarkets Inc.*
Quality / *Penn Traffic Co.*
Quik Stop / *Dillon Companies Inc.*
Quik Stop Markets / *The Kroger Co.*
Quik-Way Convenient Food Stores / *Hook Drugs Inc.*
Raleigh Foods / *Malone & Hyde Inc.*
Ralph's / *Federated Department Stores Inc.*
Record / *Beatrice Companies Inc.*
Red Owl / *Wickes Corp.*
Riverside / *Penn Traffic Co.*
Rylander / *Cullum Companies Inc.*
Sampson's / *Hannaford Bros. Co.*
Save Mart / *Wetterau, Inc.*
Sav-Mor / *The Kroger Co.*
Sav-Mor Store / *Dillon Companies Inc.*
Sentry Foods / *Godfrey Co.*
Shop N Save / *Hannaford Bros. Co.*
Shop Rite / *Foodarama Supermarkets Inc.*
Shop'N Save / *Wetterau, Inc.*
Shopwell / *Shopwell Inc.*
Southland / *Southland Corp.*
Star / *American Stores Co.*
Star / *Jewel Companies Inc.*
Stop & Shop / *Stop & Shop Companies Inc.*
Sun Foods / *Pantry Pride, Inc.*
Sun Foods / *Hannaford Bros. Co.*
Sunflower / *Super Valu Stores Inc.*
Super D. / *Malone & Hyde Inc.*
Super Duper / *S.M. Flickinger Co. Inc.*
Super Fresh Food Markets / *Great Atlantic & Pacific Tea Co. Inc.*
Super Plus Warehouse Stores / *Great Atlantic & Pacific Tea Co. Inc.*
Super Thrift / *S.M. Flickinger Co. Inc.*
Super Valu / *Super Valu Stores Inc.*
Sureway Food Stores / *Malone & Hyde Inc.*
Tex Super Duper Markets / *National Convenience Stores*
Thorofare / *Thorofare Markets Inc.*
Thriftway / *Fleming Companies Inc.*
Time Saver / *The Kroger Co.*
Times Savor / *Dillon Companies Inc.*
Tom Thumb / *Cullum Companies Inc.*
Tom Thumb Food Stores / *The Kroger Co.*
Tote 'N Save / *Marsh Supermarkets Inc.*
Tradewell / *Pacific Gamble Robinson Co.*
United Super / *Fleming Companies Inc.*
Value Center / *Shopwell Inc.*
Value King / *Fleming Companies Inc.*
Victory / *Victory Markets, Inc.*
Village Market / *Victory Markets, Inc.*
Village Pantry / *Marsh Supermarkets Inc.*
Von's / *Household International, Inc.*
Weis / *Weis Markets Inc.*
White Hen Pantry / *Jewel Companies Inc.*
Winn-Dixie / *Winn-Dixie Stores Inc.*
7-Eleven / *Southland Corp.*

Furniture

Action / *Lane Co. Inc.*

Action Office / *Herman Miller Inc.*
American Drew / *Baldwin-United Corporation*
American of Martinsville / *American Furniture Co.*
Athens / *Royal Crown Companies Inc.*
Autoglide / *Berkline Corp.*
Avon / *Mohasco Corp.*
Baby Line / *Questor Corp.*
Baker / *North American Philips Corp.*
Baker, Knapp & Tubbs / *North American Philips Corp.*
Barcalounger / *Mohasco Corp.*
Bassett / *Bassett Furniture Industries Inc.*
Bendix Products / *Bendix Corp.*
Berkline / *Berkline Corp.*
Bilt-Rite / *Gerber Products Co.*
Broyhill / *Interco Inc.*
CCA Furniture / *Beatrice Companies Inc.*
Century / *Gerber Products Co.*
Commonwealth / *Bassett Furniture Industries Inc.*
Corry Jamestown / *Hon Industries Inc.*
Co-Struc / *Herman Miller Inc.*
Daystroh / *Baldwin-United Corporation*
DeSoto / *DeSoto, Inc.*
Dresher / *Standex International Corp.*
Equa / *Herman Miller Inc.*
Ergon / *Herman Miller Inc.*
Ethan Allen / *Interco Inc.*
Ethospace / *Herman Miller Inc.*
Flotation / *Gulf* + Western Industries Inc.
Fortsmith Folding / *Beatrice Companies Inc.*
furniture rental / *Mohasco Corp.*
Futorian / *Mohasco Corp.*
Hekman / *Beatrice Companies Inc.*
Herman Miller / *Herman Miller Inc.*
Hickory / *Lane Co. Inc.*
Hide-a-Bed / *Gulf* + Western Industries Inc.
Home Crest / *Baldwin-United Corporation*
HTB / *Lane Co. Inc.*
Impact / *Bassett Furniture Industries Inc.*
Indiana / *Beatrice Companies Inc.*
James River Collection / *Lane Co. Inc.*
Jax / *Beatrice Companies Inc.*
John Hancock / *Beatrice Companies Inc.*
Kroehler / *Kroehler Manufacturing Co.*
Kroehler Citation / *Kroehler Manufacturing Co.*
Lane / *Lane Co. Inc.*
Lane Love Chests / *Lane Co. Inc.*
La-Z-Boy / *La-Z Boy Chair Co.*
La-Z-Lounger / *La-Z Boy Chair Co.*
La-Z-Rocker / *La-Z Boy Chair Co.*
Lea / *Baldwin-United Corporation*
Lullabye / *Questor Corp.*
Manor House / *Singer Co.*
Monarch / *Mohasco Corp.*
Montclair / *Bassett Furniture Industries Inc.*
National-Mt. Airy / *Bassett Furniture Industries Inc.*
Nebraska Furniture Mart / *Berkshire Hathaway Inc.*
Nod-A-Way / *Gerber Products Co.*
Nursery Originals / *Gerber Products Co.*
O'Sullivan / *Conroy Inc.*
Palladian Collection / *North American Philips Corp.*
Pennsylvania House / *General Mills Inc.*
Peters-Revington / *Mohasco Corp.*
Pilgrim House / *Standex International Corp.*
Reclina-Rocker / *La-Z Boy Chair Co.*
Reclina-Way / *La-Z Boy Chair Co.*
Rishel / *Hon Industries Inc.*
Riverside / *Arkansas Best Corp.*
Signature II / *La-Z Boy Chair Co.*
Simmons / *Gulf* + Western Industries Inc.
Sofette / *La-Z Boy Chair Co.*
Statley Homes Collection / *North American Philips Corp.*
Stratford / *Mohasco Corp.*
Stratolounger / *Mohasco Corp.*
Super Sagless / *Mohasco Corp.*
Thomas / *Thomas Industries Inc.*
Thomasville / *Armstrong World Industries Inc.*
Trend Line / *Mohasco Corp.*
U Rent Furniture / *Bekins Co.*
Venture / *Lane Co. Inc.*
Wallaway / *Berkline Corp.*
Weiman / *Bassett Furniture Industries Inc.*
Woodlor / *Kimball International Inc.*
Wooltex / *Gerber Products Co.*

Hardware, Tools & Garden Supplies

Acid-Gro / *Chevron Corp.*
Aircap / *Sunbeam Corp.*
Ajax / *Scovill Inc.*
Allis-Chalmers / *Allis-Chalmers Corp.*
Astro Turf / *Monsanto Co.*
Atkinson / *Vermont American Corp.*
Back to Nature / *Conwood Corp.*
Black & Decker / *The Black & Decker Corporation*
Bodyguard / *Hillenbrand Industries Inc.*
Boker Tree Brand / *Cooper Industries Inc.*
Bulldog / *Newell Companies Inc.*
Burpee / *ITT Corp.*

Case International / *Tenneco Inc.*
Contax / *Chevron Corp.*
Craftsman / *Roper Corp.*
Craftsman / *Singer Co.*
Craftsmen / *Sears, Roebuck & Co.*
Credo / *Blount Inc.*
Crescent / *Cooper Industries Inc.*
Dayco E-Z Lok / *Dayco Corp.*
Deco-Plants / *Ralston Purina Co.*
Delmo-Z / *Chevron Corp.*
Deluxe / *Vermont American Corp.*
Difolatan / *Chevron Corp.*
Dimilin / *Uniroyal Inc.*
Durabeam / *Dart & Kraft Inc.*
Dyanap / *Uniroyal Inc.*
Easco / *Easco Corp.*
Eastern / *Roper Corp.*
Econosize / *Chevron Corp.*
Elanco / *Eli Lilly & Co.*
Eldorado Tool / *Litton Industries Inc.*
Emhart / *Emhart Corp.*
Euroline / *Hillenbrand Industries Inc.*
Everain / *Beatrice Companies Inc.*
Ferry-Morse / *Purex Industries, Inc.*
Flea-B-Gon / *Chevron Corp.*
Flotox / *Chevron Corp.*
Gilmour / *Vermont American Corp.*
Gold Label / *Dayco Corp.*
Greenol / *Chevron Corp.*
Gug-Beta / *Chevron Corp.*
Handi-Man / *Newell Companies Inc.*
Handi-man / *HMW Industries, Inc.*
Handy Pro / *Edison Brothers Stores Inc.*
Handyman / *Edison Brothers Stores Inc.*
Harvest King / *Esmark Inc.*
Home Hardware / *Norris Industries Inc.*
Homelite / *Textron Inc.*
Hot Shot / *Stanley Works*
IBG / *Roper Corp.*
Isotox / *Chevron Corp.*
Jacobson / *Textron Inc.*
Jetline / *Thomas Industries Inc.*
Jetstream / *Beatrice Companies Inc.*
Jordan / *Newell Companies Inc.*
Kidde / *Kidde Inc.*
Kleenup / *Chevron Corp.*
Lawn-Boy / *Outboard Marine Corp.*
Life Span / *Stanley Works*
Light Water / *Minnesota Mining and Manufacturing Co. (3M)*
Lineberry / *Vermont American Corp.*
Lufkin / *Cooper Industries Inc.*
Magna / *Vermont American Corp.*
Marshall / *Vermont American Corp.*
Marvel Light Bulbs / *American Brands Inc.*
Master Lock / *American Brands Inc.*
McCrary / *Vermont American Corp.*
Medeco / *Hillenbrand Industries Inc.*
Melnor / *Beatrice Companies Inc.*
Michigan Bulb / *American Can Co.*
Monitor / *Chevron Corp.*
Multi-Lube / *Ronson Corp.*
Multi-Metals / *Vermont American Corp.*
Murray / *Murray Ohio Manufacturing Co.*
New Britain Tool / *Litton Industries Inc.*
New Holland / *Sperry Corp.*
Nicholson / *Cooper Industries Inc.*
Oregon Chain Saws / *Blount Inc.*
Oregon Firewood Center / *Blount Inc.*
Orthene / *Chevron Corp.*
Orthex / *Chevron Corp.*
Ortho / *Frank's Nursery and Crafts Inc.*
Ortho / *Chevron Corp.*
Orthocide / *Chevron Corp.*
Ortho-Gro / *Chevron Corp.*
Ortho-Guard / *Chevron Corp.*
Orthorix / *Chevron Corp.*
Outfox / *Chevron Corp.*
Panther / *Newell Companies Inc.*
Paraquat + Plus / *Chevron Corp.*
Phaltan / *Chevron Corp.*
Plant Helpers / *Corning Glass Works*
Poolflex / *Dayco Corp.*
Pop Rivet / *Emhart Corp.*
Powerlock / *Stanley Works*
Prime-Mover / *Hon Industries Inc.*
Pro Turf / *ITT Corp.*
Rainwave / *Beatrice Companies Inc.*
Ra-Pid-Gro / *Chevron Corp.*
Rat-B-Gon / *Chevron Corp.*
Roller-Measure / *Ronco Teleproducts Inc.*
Roper / *Roper Corp.*
Rotary / *Roper Corp.*
Rotor Tool / *Cooper Industries Inc.*
Ryan / *Outboard Marine Corp.*
Scotts / *ITT Corp.*
Scott's / *Frank's Nursery and Crafts Inc.*
Scram / *Chevron Corp.*
Slaymaker / *American Home Products Corp.*
Slug-Geta / *Chevron Corp.*
Snap-Cut / *Vermont American Corp.*
Snapper / *Fuqua Industries Inc.*
Snowbuster / *Allis-Chalmers Corp.*
Sprills / *Chevron Corp.*
Stanley / *Stanley Works*
Stormor / *Fuqua Industries Inc.*

Swivel-Lock / *Stanley Works*
Thorson / *Household International, Inc.*
Top-Cog / *Dayco Corp.*
Toro / *Frank's Nursery and Crafts Inc.*
Toro / *Toro Co.*
Triox / *Chevron Corp.*
Turf Builder / *ITT Corp.*
Unipel / *Chevron Corp.*
Uniphos / *Chevron Corp.*
Up-Start / *Chevron Corp.*
U.S. Brass / *Household International, Inc.*
Valued / *Vermont American Corp.*
Vermont American / *Vermont American Corp.*
Vermont Tap & Die / *Vermont American Corp.*
Vigoro / *Esmark Inc.*
Village Blacksmith / *McGraw Edison Co.*
Volck / *Chevron Corp.*
Weed-B-Gon / *Chevron Corp.*
Weiser / *Norris Industries Inc.*
Weller / *Cooper Industries Inc.*
Whirly / *Chevron Corp.*
Whirlybird / *Chevron Corp.*
Wiss / *Cooper Industries Inc.*
Workmate / *The Black & Decker Corporation*
Xcelite / *Cooper Industries Inc.*
Zincofol / *Chevron Corp.*

Homes, Mobile & Modular

The Addison, Boca Raton, Florida / *Walt Disney Productions*
Aliso Viejo / *Philip Morris Inc.*
All American / *Coachmen Industries Inc.*
Amherst / *De Rose Industries Inc.*
Aquarius / *Golden West Homes*
Arvida Corp. / *Walt Disney Productions*
Arvida Executive Center, Boca Raton, Florida / *Walt Disney Productions*
Arvida Park of Commerce, Boca Raton, Florida / *Walt Disney Productions*
Astron / *Zimmer Corp.*
Atlantic / *Champion Home Builders Co.*
Austen / *Skyline Corp.*
Avion / *Fleetwood Enterprises Inc.*
Beverly Manor / *De Rose Industries Inc.*
Boanza / *Redman Industries Inc.*
Boca West, Boca Raton, Florida / *Walt Disney Productions*
Brentwood / *De Rose Industries Inc.*
Broadway / *De Rose Industries Inc.*
BrooKwood / *Commodore Corp.*
Bryn Mawr Ocean Towers / *Dixon Ticonderoga Co.*
Buckingham / *Silvercrest Industries Inc.*
Calypso / *Golden West Homes*
Cambridge / *Commodore Corp.*
Cameo / *Commodore Corp.*
Cape Town / *Shelter Resources Corp.*
Cavalcade / *Commodore Corp.*
Champion / *Champion Home Builders Co.*
Chimney Lakes, Atlanta, Georgia / *Walt Disney Productions*
Chimney Springs, Atlanta Georgia / *Walt Disney Productions*
Citation / *Shelter Resources Corp.*
Citation / *Commodore Corp.*
Classic / *Commodore Corp.*
Coachmen / *Coachmen Industries Inc.*
Cocoplum, Coral Gables, Florida / *Walt Disney Productions*
Colonial / *Vintage Enterprises, Inc.*
Colony / *Shelter Resources Corp.*
Comet / *Commodore Corp.*
Commodore / *Commodore Corp.*
Concord / *Champion Home Builders Co.*
Coto de Caza, California / *Walt Disney Productions*
Cottage / *Silvercrest Industries Inc.*
Country Estate / *Golden West Homes*
Country Roads / *Shelter Resources Corp.*
Country Walk, Miami, Florida / *Walt Disney Productions*
Crimson / *Shelter Resources Corp.*
CrossCountry / *Coachmen Industries Inc.*
The Crossings, Miami, Florida / *Walt Disney Productions*
De Rose / *De Rose Industries Inc.*
Dearborn / *Coachmen Industries Inc.*
Duke / *Zimmer Corp.*
Eaton Park / *Redman Industries Inc.*
Edinborough / *Silvercrest Industries Inc.*
Endeavor Homes / *Di Giorgio Corp.*
English Squire / *Shelter Resources Corp.*
The Executive / *Executive Industries*
Fan / *Coachmen Industries Inc.*
Flagship / *Champion Home Builders Co.*
Flamenco / *Shelter Resources Corp.*
Flamingo / *Redman Industries Inc.*
Fleetwood / *Fleetwood Enterprises Inc.*
Frolic / *Coachmen Industries Inc.*
Frontier / *Commodore Corp.*
Fuqua Homes / *Fuqua Industries Inc.*
Futura / *De Rose Industries Inc.*

Gettysburgh / *Shelter Resources Corp.*
Glenwood / *Shelter Resources Corp.*
Golden Mansion / *Golden West Homes*
Golden West / *Golden West Homes*
Greenbriar / *Coachmen Industries Inc.*
Greenfield / *De Rose Industries Inc.*
Hermitage / *Shelter Resources Corp.*
Highlands Ranch / *Philip Morris Inc.*
Howard Manor / *Silvercrest Industries Inc.*
Huntington / *Champion Home Builders Co.*
Itasca / *Winnebago Industries Inc.*
Jamboree / *Fleetwood Enterprises Inc.*
Jamee / *Skyline Corp.*
Jimmy / *Coachmen Industries Inc.*
Kenco / *Coachmen Industries Inc.*
Key Biscayne / *Golden West Homes*
Key West / *Golden West Homes*
Kingsbrook / *Silvercrest Industries Inc.*
Kingston / *Golden West Homes*
Kirkwood / *Redman Industries Inc.*
Kozy / *Commodore Corp.*
La Palma / *Executive Industries*
Lakes of the Meadow, Florida / *Walt Disney Productions*
Lanchart / *LD Brinkman Corp.*
LaSalle (van-conversion) / *Champion Home Builders Co.*
Lindy / *Skyline Corp.*
Longboat Key Club, Florida / *Walt Disney Productions*
Lux / *Coachmen Industries Inc.*
Manatee / *Champion Home Builders Co.*
Marietta / *Shelter Resources Corp.*
Marlin / *Shelter Resources Corp.*
Mayfair / *De Rose Industries Inc.*
Meadow Creek / *Champion Home Builders Co.*
Metamora / *Champion Home Builders Co.*
Millpond, Boca Raton, Florida / *Walt Disney Productions*
Mission Viejo / *Philip Morris Inc.*
Monaco / *Shelter Resources Corp.*
Montego / *Shelter Resources Corp.*
Monterey / *Shelter Resources Corp.*
The Moors, Miami Lakes, Florida / *Walt Disney Productions*
MRV / *Coachmen Industries Inc.*
Nashua / *Zimmer Corp.*
Nation Wide Homes / *Insilco Corp.*
New Haven / *Champion Home Builders Co.*
New Moon / *Redman Industries Inc.*
Nova / *Commodore Corp.*
Oakwood / *Oakwood Homes Corp.*
Olympian / *Commodore Corp.*
Pace Arrow / *Fleetwood Enterprises Inc.*
Park River / *Champion Home Builders Co.*
Parkridge / *Champion Home Builders Co.*
Parkwood / *Shelter Resources Corp.*
Paseos, Boca Raton, Florida / *Walt Disney Productions*
Pathfinder / *Coachmen Industries Inc.*
Piedmont / *Champion Home Builders Co.*
Prestige / *Executive Industries*
Pronto / *Executive Industries*
Prowler / *Fleetwood Enterprises Inc.*
Regent / *Commodore Corp.*
Rembrandt / *De Rose Industries Inc.*
The Residential / *Shelter Resources Corp.*
Resort / *Fleetwood Enterprises Inc.*
Rich Craft / *Oakwood Homes Corp.*
Richfield / *Oakwood Homes Corp.*
Rosebrook / *De Rose Industries Inc.*
Rosemont / *De Rose Industries Inc.*
Rosewood / *De Rose Industries Inc.*
Royal Cambridge / *Shelter Resources Corp.*
Royal Chateau / *Shelter Resources Corp.*
Royal English / *Shelter Resources Corp.*
Royal Lancer / *Shelter Resources Corp.*
Royal Monarch / *Shelter Resources Corp.*
Sabal Chase, Miami, Florida / *Walt Disney Productions*
Salem / *Shelter Resources Corp.*
Sandpiper / *Executive Industries*
Santana / *Fleetwood Enterprises Inc.*
Sawgrass, Jacksonville, Florida / *Walt Disney Productions*
Sequoia / *Champion Home Builders Co.*
Shadow / *Coachmen Industries Inc.*
Shasta / *Coachmen Industries Inc.*
Sheraton / *Redman Industries Inc.*
Sheridan / *Shelter Resources Corp.*
Sherwood / *Shelter Resources Corp.*
Sherwood Manor / *Silvercrest Industries Inc.*
Shiloh / *Shelter Resources Corp.*
Silvercrest / *Silvercrest Industries Inc.*
Silverwood / *Silvercrest Industries Inc.*
Somerset / *Golden West Homes*
Southwind / *Fleetwood Enterprises Inc.*
Sportscoach / *Coachmen Industries Inc.*
Starcrest / *Silvercrest Industries Inc.*
Sunburst / *Shelter Resources Corp.*
Sunland / *Di Giorgio Corp.*
Sunnybrook / *Golden West Homes*
Sunridge / *Shelter Resources Corp.*
Sunview / *Champion Home Builders Co.*
Supreme / *De Rose Industries Inc.*
Supreme / *Silvercrest Industries Inc.*
Tamarack / *Champion Home Builders Co.*
Terry / *Fleetwood Enterprises Inc.*

Timber Creek, Boca Raton, Florida / *Walt Disney Productions*
Tioga / *Fleetwood Enterprises Inc.*
Titan / *Champion Home Builders Co.*
Town Center / *Walt Disney Productions*
Town Place, Boca Raton, Florida / *Walt Disney Productions*
TranStar / *Champion Home Builders Co.*
Trans-Van / *Champion Home Builders Co.*
Victor / *De Rose Industries Inc.*
Viking / *Coachmen Industries Inc.*
Villa West / *Golden West Homes*
Villager / *Shelter Resources Corp.*
Viscount / *Zimmer Corp.*
Walden / *Redman Industries Inc.*
Weston, Fort Lauderdale, Florida / *Walt Disney Productions*
Wilderness / *Fleetwood Enterprises Inc.*
Willow Springs, Atlanta, Georgia / *Walt Disney Productions*
Windsor / *Zimmer Corp.*
Winnebago / *Winnebago Industries Inc.*
Winston II / *Shelter Resources Corp.*
Wolverine / *Champion Home Builders Co.*
Woodlake / *Champion Home Builders Co.*
Woodridge / *Shelter Resources Corp.*
Yorkshire / *De Rose Industries Inc.*
Zimmer / *Zimmer Corp.*

Hotels, Motels, Resorts

Adventure Island / *Anheuser-Busch Companies Inc.*
Alameda Hotel / *UAL Inc.*
Alaska Prince Hotel / *UAL Inc.*
Amfac Hotels / *Amfac Inc.*
Anatole / *Loews Corp.*
The Arizona Biltmore Hotel - Phoenix / *UAL Inc.*
Atlantis Casino Hotel / *Elsinore Corp.*
Bayshore Inn / *UAL Inc.*
Bellevue Staford Hotel / *UAL Inc.*
Benson Hotel / *UAL Inc.*
Bonaventure Hotel / *UAL Inc.*
Bullfrog / *Del E. Webb Corp.*
Caesars Atlantic City / *Caesar's World, Inc.*
Caesars Brookdale / *Caesar's World, Inc.*
Caesars Cove Haven / *Caesar's World, Inc.*
Caesars Palace Hotel and Casino / *Caesar's World, Inc.*
Caesars Paradise Stream / *Caesar's World, Inc.*
Caesars Pocono Palace / *Caesar's World, Inc.*
Caesars Tahoe Hotel and Casino / *Caesar's World, Inc.*
Calgary Inn / *UAL Inc.*
Camino Real Hotel Cancun, Guadalajara, Mazatlan, Mexico City, Puerto Vallarta, Saltillo, San Salvador / *UAL Inc.*
Carlton Hotel / *UAL Inc.*
Carlton House Hotel / *UAL Inc.*
Carriage Inn / *Atlas Hotels Inc.*
Carson Inn Motel / *Carson Pirie Scott & Company*
Century Plaza Hotel / *UAL Inc.*
Cerromar Beach Hotel / *Eastern Air Lines Inc.*
Chosun / *UAL Inc.*
The Claridge Casino/Hotel / *Del E. Webb Corp.*
Coco-Palms Resort / *Amfac Inc.*
Continental Plaza Hotel / *UAL Inc.*
Copley Place / *UAL Inc.*
Courtyard by Marriott / *Marriott Corp.*
Crown Center Hotel / *UAL Inc.*
Dangling Rope Marina / *Del E. Webb Corp.*
Del Webb's High Sierra Casino/Hotel / *Del E. Webb Corp.*
Detroit Metropolitan Airport Hotel / *Host International Inc.*
Detroit Plaza Hotel / *UAL Inc.*
Disneyland Hotel & Convention Center / *Wrather Corp.*
Dorado Beach Hotel / *Eastern Air Lines Inc.*
Drake Hotel - Chicago / *Transworld Corp.*
Dusit Thani Hotel / *UAL Inc.*
Edmonton Plaza Hotel / *UAL Inc.*
Embassy Suites / *Holiday Inns Inc.*
Ethan Allen Inn / *Interco Inc.*
European Health Spas / *United States Industries Inc.*
Four Queens Hotel & Casino / *Elsinore Corp.*
Furnace Creek Inn / *Amfac Inc.*
Galleria / *UAL Inc.*
Galleria Plaza Hotel / *UAL Inc.*
Gentry Inn / *Jerrico Inc.*
Glenpointe / *Loews Corp.*
Golden Nugget Casino-Hotels / *Golden Nugget Inc.*
Grand Canyon National Park Lodges / *Amfac Inc.*
Hall's Crossing / *Del E. Webb Corp.*
Hampton Inns / *Holiday Inns Inc.*
Hanalei Hotel / *Atlas Hotels Inc.*
Harbour Cove / *Loews Corp.*
Harrah's / *Holiday Inns Inc.*
Hilton International Hotels / *Transworld Corp.*
Hite Marina / *Del E. Webb Corp.*
Holiday Inn Crowne Plaza / *Holiday Inns Inc.*
Holiday Inns - hotels / *Holiday Inns Inc.*

Horton Plaza Hotel / *Atlas Hotels Inc.*
Hotel Scandinavia / *UAL Inc.*
Hotel Toronto / *UAL Inc.*
Houston Oaks Hotel / *UAL Inc.*
Howard Johnson / *Loews Corp.*
Hyatt Lake Tahoe Hotel & Casino / *Elsinore Corp.*
Ilikai Hotel / *UAL Inc.*
Kaanapali Beach Hotel / *Amfac Inc.*
Keystone / *Ralston Purina Co.*
King Kamehameha Hotel / *Amfac Inc.*
Kings Inn / *Atlas Hotels Inc.*
La Napoule / *Loews Corp.*
Las Brisas / *UAL Inc.*
Las Brisas Hotel / *UAL Inc.*
Le Concorde / *Loews Corp.*
L'Enfant Plaza / *Loews Corp.*
Marriott Hotels & Resorts / *Marriott Corp.*
Mauna Kea Beach Hotel / *UAL Inc.*
Mayflower Hotel / *UAL Inc.*
MGM Grand Hotels / *MGM Grand Hotels, Inc.*
Michigan Inn Hotel / *UAL Inc.*
Mint Casino Hotel / *Del E. Webb Corp.*
Mission Valley Inn / *Atlas Hotels Inc.*
Miyako Hotel / *UAL Inc.*
Monarch at Sea Pines / *Marriott Corp.*
Monte Carlo Hotel / *Loews Corp.*
Monterey Plaza / *GenCorp*
Motel 6 / *City Investing Co.*
Nevada Club Casino/Hotel / *Del E. Webb Corp.*
Ocean Club / *Resorts International Inc.*
Oceanic Properties / *Castle & Cooke Inc.*
The Old Country / *Anheuser-Busch Companies Inc.*
Olympic Hotel / *UAL Inc.*
Pacifica Hotel / *Atlas Hotels Inc.*
Paradise Island Casino / *Resorts International Inc.*
Paradise Valley / *Loews Corp.*
Park Place / *Bally Manufacturing Corp.*
Peachtree Plaza Hotel / *UAL Inc.*
Philippine Plaza Hotel / *UAL Inc.*
The Pier House Inn & Beach Club / *Host International Inc.*
Playboy / *Playboy Enterprises Inc.*
Plaza Hotel / *UAL Inc.*
Quality Inn Motels / *Frisch's Restaurants Inc.*
Queen Mary/Spruce Goose / *Wrather Corp.*
Ramada Hotels / *Ramada Inns Inc.*
Ramada Inn / *Atlas Hotels Inc.*
Ramada Inn / *Loews Corp.*
Ramada Inns / *Ramada Inns Inc.*
Ramada Renaissance Hotels / *Ramada Inns Inc.*
Regency / *Loews Corp.*
Residence Inns / *Holiday Inns Inc.*
Resorts International Airlines (RIA) / *Resorts International Inc.*
Ritz, The / *Hardwicke Companies Inc.*
Royal Lahaina Hotel / *Amfac Inc.*
Sacramento Metropolitan Airport Hotel / *Host International Inc.*
Safety Harbor Spa / *Hardwicke Companies Inc.*
Shangri-La Hotel / *UAL Inc.*
Sheraton / *ITT Corp.*
South Coast Plaza Hotel / *UAL Inc.*
St. Francis Hotel / *UAL Inc.*
Summit Hotel / *Loews Corp.*
Sunburst Hotel / *Atlas Hotels Inc.*
Takanawa Prince Hotel / *UAL Inc.*
Tampa International Airport Hotel / *Host International Inc.*
Tokyo Prince Hotel / *UAL Inc.*
Town & Country Hotel / *Atlas Hotels Inc.*
Tropicana Hotel & Country Club / *Ramada Inns Inc.*
Tropicana Hotel and Casino / *Ramada Inns Inc.*
Utah / *UAL Inc.*
Ventana Canyon / *Loews Corp.*
Vista International / *Transworld Corp.*
Wahweap Lodge and Marina / *Del E. Webb Corp.*
Wailea Beach Hotel / *UAL Inc.*
Washington Plaza Hotel / *UAL Inc.*
Wentworth Hotel / *UAL Inc.*
Westbury Hotel / *Loews Corp.*
Westin Hotels / *UAL Inc.*
Westward Fools / *GenCorp*
William Penn / *UAL Inc.*
William Plaza Hotel / *UAL Inc.*

Household Furnishings

A Christmas Place / *Towle Manufacturing Co.*
Alexander Smith / *Mohasco Corp.*
Allibar / *C.H. Masland & Sons*
American Carpet Mills / *Keller Industries Inc.*
Amphora / *C.H. Masland & Sons*
Amphora Stripe 1 / *C.H. Masland & Sons*
Amphora Stripe 2 / *C.H. Masland & Sons*
Amphora Stripe 3 / *C.H. Masland & Sons*
Arabia / *Towle Manufacturing Co.*
Aristocraft / *Beatrice Companies Inc.*
Armstrong / *Armstrong World Industries Inc.*
Artolier / *Scovill Inc.*
Atmos / *Westinghouse Electric Corp.*
Auburn Brass / *Anchor Hocking Corporation*

Baker's Street / *American Home Products Corp.*
Barker Bros. / *Goldblatt Brothers Inc.*
Beauti-Blend / *J.P. Stevens & Co. Inc.*
Beauticale / *J.P. Stevens & Co. Inc.*
Beauty Queen / *Triangle Pacific Corp.*
Beautyrest / *Gulf* + Western Industries Inc.
Beneke / *Beatrice Companies Inc.*
Bennett-Ireland / *Sunbeam Corp.*
Bestpleat / *Springs Industries, Inc.*
Big Ben / *Talley Industries Inc.*
Bigelow-Stanford / *Baldwin-United Corporation*
Bloomcraft / *Gulf* + Western Industries Inc.
Blue Chip / *C.H. Masland & Sons*
Bogene / *Beatrice Companies Inc.*
Bombay Company / *Tandy Brands Inc.*
Borg / *Dart & Kraft Inc.*
Bouquet / *C.H. Masland & Sons*
Boutique / *General Housewares Corp.*
Brandon Street / *C.H. Masland & Sons*
Bravo / *Anchor Hocking Corporation*
Brearley / *Newell Companies Inc.*
Bremmer's Biscuits / *Ralston Purina Co.*
Brickworks / *Collins & Aikman*
Brigitte / *C.H. Masland & Sons*
Buffalo / *Oneida Ltd.*
Burlington / *Burlington Industries Inc.*
Cabin Craft / *West Point-Pepperell Inc.*
Canfield / *Anchor Hocking Corporation*
Cannon / *Cannon Mills Co.*
Cargo Express / *Fabri-Centers of America Inc.*
Carlin / *West Point-Pepperell Inc.*
Carlton / *Action Industries Inc.*
Carousel / *General Housewares Corp.*
Carte Blanche / *C.H. Masland & Sons*
Carvel Hall / *Towle Manufacturing Co.*
Catalyst / *C.H. Masland & Sons*
Celtic Classics / *C.H. Masland & Sons*
Chase / *United Merchants and Manufacturers Inc.*
Chateau / *General Housewares Corp.*
Chatham / *Chatham Manufacturing Company*
Chocolate Almond / *General Housewares Corp.*
Chromcraft / *Mohasco Corp.*
Classic / *General Housewares Corp.*
Classic American Foods / *General Housewares Corp.*
Classic Candles / *General Housewares Corp.*
Clear Elegance / *Corning Glass Works*
Cohama Riverdale / *United Merchants and Manufacturers Inc.*
Colby's / *Goldblatt Brothers Inc.*
Colonial candle of Cape Cod / *General Housewares Corp.*
Colonial Candles / *General Housewares Corp.*
Colonial Handipt / *General Housewares Corp.*
Colonnade / *Collins & Aikman*
Columbian / *General Housewares Corp.*
Comfortcale / *Cannon Mills Co.*
Comfy Home Furnishings / *Reeves Brothers Inc.*
Community / *Oneida Ltd.*
Con-Tact / *United Merchants and Manufacturers Inc.*
Contender / *J.P. Stevens & Co. Inc.*
Coppercraft Guild / *Dart & Kraft Inc.*
Cordless / *General Housewares Corp.*
Corelle / *Corning Glass Works*
Corning Ware / *Corning Glass Works*
Coronet / *RCA Corp.*
Cortley / *Decorator Industries Inc.*
Cory / *Hershey Foods Corp.*
Country Calico Mice / *Stanhome, Inc.*
Country Collection / *General Housewares Corp.*
Country Cousins / *Stanhome, Inc.*
Country Kitchens / *American Home Products Corp.*
Crossroads / *C.H. Masland & Sons*
Crown Corning / *Corning Glass Works*
Culinary Kits / *Corning Glass Works*
Custom Designs / *Springs Industries, Inc.*
Dear God Kids / *Stanhome, Inc.*
Decorama / *Decorator Industries Inc.*
The Decorator Collection / *General Housewares Corp.*
Del Mar / *Beatrice Companies Inc.*
Designer's Collection / *American Greetings Corporation*
Designers Guild / *Newell Companies Inc.*
Dorfile / *Newell Companies Inc.*
Drulane / *Towle Manufacturing Co.*
Dunharrow / *C.H. Masland & Sons*
Ecologizer / *Talley Industries Inc.*
Edgecraft / *Newell Companies Inc.*
Embracable / *J.P. Stevens & Co. Inc.*
Esmond / *Chatham Manufacturing Company*
Evans-Black / *Armstrong World Industries Inc.*
Everyday Gourmet / *Corning Glass Works*
Fabrique / *General Housewares Corp.*
Fancipans / *General Housewares Corp.*
F.B. Rogers / *National Silver Industries Inc.*
F.B. Rogers / *Towle Manufacturing Co.*
Feren Fruit Baskets / *Fisher Foods, Inc.*
Fieldcrest / *Fieldcrest Mills Inc.*
Figi's / *Metromedia Inc.*
Fine Arts / *J.P. Stevens & Co. Inc.*
Firth / *Mohasco Corp.*
Fortsmann / *J.P. Stevens & Co. Inc.*
Frederick Cooper / *Royal Crown Companies Inc.*
Frontier Campware / *General Housewares Corp.*
Gailstyn-Sulton / *Towle Manufacturing Co.*
Gallway Irish / *Towle Manufacturing Co.*
Garfield / *Stanhome, Inc.*

Georgian / *West Point-Pepperell Inc.*
Georgian House / *Towle Manufacturing Co.*
Gloria Vanderbilt / *Towle Manufacturing Co.*
Gloria Vanderbilt Collection / *J.P. Stevens & Co. Inc.*
Gold Label / *Cannon Mills Co.*
Gold Lance / *Towle Manufacturing Co.*
Good Cooking Equipment / *General Housewares Corp.*
Gorham / *Textron Inc.*
Graber / *Springs Industries, Inc.*
Graniteware / *General Housewares Corp.*
Grate Home and Fireplace Center / *Tandy Brands Inc.*
Greeff / *Gulf* + Western Industries Inc.
Grifftex / *West Point-Pepperell Inc.*
Growing Up / *Stanhome, Inc.*
Guestware / *Mobil Corp.*
Gulistan / *J.P. Stevens & Co. Inc.*
Hall Mack / *Scovill Inc.*
Handiform / *Beatrice Companies Inc.*
Hanson / *Sunbeam Corp.*
Harris & Mallow / *Thomas Industries Inc.*
Hawthorne / *C.H. Masland & Sons*
Heat Screen / *Sears, Roebuck & Co.*
Heatilator / *Hon Industries Inc.*
High Time / *C.H. Masland & Sons*
Hi-Heat / *Anchor Hocking Corporation*
Homart / *Sears, Roebuck & Co.*
Homecare / *Riegel Textile Corp.*
Homemade / *General Housewares Corp.*
Hopi / *C.H. Masland & Sons*
Houze / *Wilson Brothers*
Hoyne / *Royal Crown Companies Inc.*
Huffman-Koos / *Goldblatt Brothers Inc.*
International / *Katy Industries, Inc.*
Irvinware / *Towle Manufacturing Co.*
Irwinware / *Beatrice Companies Inc.*
Italia / *C.H. Masland & Sons*
Javit / *Towle Manufacturing Co.*
Jomon / *C.H. Masland & Sons*
Karastan / *Fieldcrest Mills Inc.*
Keller Carpets / *Keller Industries Inc.*
Keystone Ridgeway / *Wilson Brothers*
King Arthur / *C.H. Masland & Sons*
Kirsch / *Cooper Industries Inc.*
Kitchen Mates / *Riegel Textile Corp.*
Kitchen Pride / *Mirro Corp.*
Kwik-Kover / *United Merchants and Manufacturers Inc.*
La Parade / *C.H. Masland & Sons*
Lady Luck / *C.H. Masland & Sons*
Lady Pepperell / *West Point-Pepperell Inc.*
Lauffer / *Towle Manufacturing Co.*
Laura Ashley / *Burlington Industries Inc.*
L.E. Smith Glass / *Owens-Illinois, Inc.*
Lees / *Burlington Industries Inc.*
Leggacy / *Mirro Corp.*
Lenox / *Lenox Inc.*
Lenox / *Brown Forman Distillers Corp.*
Leonard / *Towle Manufacturing Co.*
Leyse Professional / *General Housewares Corp.*
Leyson / *General Housewares Corp.*
Libbey / *Owens-Illinois, Inc.*
Lightcraft / *Scovill Inc.*
Liz Claiborne / *Burlington Industries Inc.*
Lo Temp / *General Housewares Corp.*
Lochmoor / *C.H. Masland & Sons*
Long-Bell Cabinets / *International Paper Co.*
Loomcrafted / *Beatrice Companies Inc.*
Louver Drape / *Beatrice Companies Inc.*
Luxor / *West Point-Pepperell Inc.*
Magee / *Tandycrafts Inc.*
Magee / *Shaw Industries Inc.*
Magic Fit / *Newell Companies Inc.*
Magnalite / *General Housewares Corp.*
Magnalite Professional / *General Housewares Corp.*
Magnolia / *Beatrice Companies Inc.*
Mariarden / *C.H. Masland & Sons*
Maricopa / *C.H. Masland & Sons*
Martex / *West Point-Pepperell Inc.*
Max H. Kahn / *Beatrice Companies Inc.*
Merryweather / *J.P. Stevens & Co. Inc.*
Miracle Maid / *Dart & Kraft Inc.*
Mirro / *Mirro Corp.*
Miss Piggy / *Stanhome, Inc.*
Mohawk / *Mohasco Corp.*
Mojave Motif Collection / *C.H. Masland & Sons*
Moments / *Anchor Hocking Corporation*
Mom's / *General Housewares Corp.*
Monticello / *Burlington Industries Inc.*
Monticello / *Cannon Mills Co.*
Morgan Jones / *Springs Industries, Inc.*
Mr. Clemens Pottery / *Action Industries Inc.*
Muppet Babies / *Stanhome, Inc.*
Myriad / *C.H. Masland & Sons*
Nappe-Babcock / *Dart & Kraft Inc.*
National / *Royal Crown Companies Inc.*
National / *Towle Manufacturing Co.*
National Silver Company / *National Silver Industries Inc.*
Nelson-McCoy / *Lancaster Colony Corp.*
Newell / *Newell Companies Inc.*
North Star / *Chatham Manufacturing Company*
Northern / *Sunbeam Corp.*
Old Harbor / *Towle Manufacturing Co.*
Oleg Cassini / *Burlington Industries Inc.*

Oneida / *Oneida Ltd.*
Oriental / *General Housewares Corp.*
Ovenmates / *Beatrice Companies Inc.*
Oxford / *Lenox Inc.*
Oxford Hall / *Towle Manufacturing Co.*
Pacific / *M. Lowenstein Corp.*
Pacific Silver Care / *M. Lowenstein Corp.*
Pak-A-Potti / *Sears, Roebuck & Co.*
Palestra / *C.H. Masland & Sons*
PartyLine Gifts / *General Housewares Corp.*
Pastille / *C.H. Masland & Sons*
Paul-Marshal / *Unishops Inc.*
Pavonine / *C.H. Masland & Sons*
Pearson / *Lane Co. Inc.*
Pepperell / *West Point-Pepperell Inc.*
Pequot / *Springs Industries, Inc.*
Perfection In The Cup / *Hershey Foods Corp.*
Philadelphia / *Shaw Industries Inc.*
Pima / *C.H. Masland & Sons*
Pinehurst / *J.P. Stevens & Co. Inc.*
P.M.C. (Sheffield) / *Towle Manufacturing Co.*
Poole-Silversmiths / *Towle Manufacturing Co.*
Poppyseed Collection / *Stanhome, Inc.*
Portland Willamette / *Thomas Industries Inc.*
Pouliot / *Thomas Industries Inc.*
Precious Moments / *Stanhome, Inc.*
Presto / *National Presto Industries Inc.*
Princess House / *Beatrice Companies Inc.*
Priscilla Ware / *General Housewares Corp.*
Progress / *Kidde Inc.*
Puritan / *C.H. Masland & Sons*
Pyrex / *Corning Glass Works*
Pyroceram / *Corning Glass Works*
Pyroflam / *Corning Glass Works*
Radiance / *Springs Industries, Inc.*
Rainbow Kitchen Center / *Riegel Textile Corp.*
Rare Find / *C.H. Masland & Sons*
Ravenwood / *C.H. Masland & Sons*
Ready Brew / *Hershey Foods Corp.*
Ready Stick / *Sears, Roebuck & Co.*
Regal China / *American Brands Inc.*
Regalwood / *Newell Companies Inc.*
Renaissance Candles / *General Housewares Corp.*
Restwarmer / *Chatham Manufacturing Company*
Revere Ware / *Revere Copper & Brass Inc.*
Rhianna / *C.H. Masland & Sons*
Roomaker / *United Merchants and Manufacturers Inc.*
Royal Family / *Cannon Mills Co.*
Royal Velvet / *Fieldcrest Mills Inc.*
Sabre / *Shaw Industries Inc.*
Seiden / *Towle Manufacturing Co.*
Selig / *Gulf +* Western Industries Inc.
Seneca Textiles / *United Merchants and Manufacturers Inc.*
Sequence / *C.H. Masland & Sons*
Servables / *Corning Glass Works*
Seth Thomas / *Talley Industries Inc.*
Seurat / *C.H. Masland & Sons*
Shazam! / *C.H. Masland & Sons*
Shelton Ware / *Towle Manufacturing Co.*
Shenango China / *Anchor Hocking Corporation*
Sherbet / *C.H. Masland & Sons*
Shire Town / *C.H. Masland & Sons*
Silverstone / *Mirro Corp.*
Simtex / *J.P. Stevens & Co. Inc.*
Skinner / *Springs Industries, Inc.*
So Soft Pom Poms / *Springs Industries, Inc.*
So-Fro by Singer / *House of Fabrics Inc.*
Space Arranger / *Newell Companies Inc.*
Spartus / *Kidde Inc.*
Spectra / *General Housewares Corp.*
Springmaid / *Springs Industries, Inc.*
SpringsPerformance / *Springs Industries, Inc.*
St. Mary's / *Fieldcrest Mills Inc.*
Stanley U-Install / *Stanhome, Inc.*
Stanza 30 / *C.H. Masland & Sons*
Stanza 40 / *C.H. Masland & Sons*
Starlight / *Thomas Industries Inc.*
Sterling / *Scovill Inc.*
Steuben / *Corning Glass Works*
Stiffel / *Beatrice Companies Inc.*
Strawberry Shortcake / *Stanhome, Inc.*
Strips & Clips / *Newell Companies Inc.*
Sunsensor / *Corning Glass Works*
Sunshine Yellow / *General Housewares Corp.*
Supreme / *Towle Manufacturing Co.*
Syroco / *Dart & Kraft Inc.*
Tastemaker / *J.P. Stevens & Co. Inc.*
Telfair / *C.H. Masland & Sons*
Temper-Ware / *Lenox Inc.*
Teters / *United States Industries Inc.*
Textol / *General Housewares Corp.*
"The Bakery" / *Mirro Corp.*
Thermique / *Corning Glass Works*
Thermo-Serv / *Dart & Kraft Inc.*
Thomas / *Thomas Industries Inc.*
Thonet / *Gulf +* Western Industries Inc.
Tiffin / *Towle Manufacturing Co.*
Toroware / *General Housewares Corp.*
Towle / *Towle Manufacturing Co.*
Towne House / *C.H. Masland & Sons*
Treasured Memories / *Stanhome, Inc.*
Tupperware / *Dart & Kraft Inc.*
Tyndale / *Royal Crown Companies Inc.*
Ultrasuede Brand Fabric / *Springs Industries, Inc.*

Utica / *J.P. Stevens & Co. Inc.*
Val St Lambert / *Towle Manufacturing Co.*
Vellux / *West Point-Pepperell Inc.*
Ventaire / *Newell Companies Inc.*
Vera / *Burlington Industries Inc.*
Vera / *Manhattan Industries Inc.*
Visions / *Corning Glass Works*
Visions / *Kellwood Co.*
Wagner Ware / *General Housewares Corp.*
Wallace / *Katy Industries, Inc.*
Wallace Silversmiths / *HMW Industries, Inc.*
Walter / *West Point-Pepperell Inc.*
Waltham / *Kidde Inc.*
Wamsutta / *M. Lowenstein Corp.*
Weather Vane / *C.H. Masland & Sons*
Westclox / *Talley Industries Inc.*
Westfield Design / *Towle Manufacturing Co.*
William Adams / *Towle Manufacturing Co.*
Wilshire / *Newell Companies Inc.*
Woodridge / *C.H. Masland & Sons*
W.R. Case & Sons / *American Brands Inc.*
Yield House / *Standex International Corp.*

Household Products

Acryon / *Beatrice Companies Inc.*
Ajax soaps and detergents / *Colgate-Palmolive Co.*
American / *Scott Paper Co.*
Andrex / *Scott Paper Co.*
Antique / *Fort Howard Paper Co.*
Antrol / *American Home Products Corp.*
Aquilaun / *Stanhome, Inc.*
Argo / *CPC International Inc.*
Armour-Dial / *Greyhound Corp.*
At Ease® Scouring Cleaner / *Shaklee Corp.*
Aurora / *American Can Co.*
Baggies / *Colgate-Palmolive Co.*
Ball / *Ball Corp.*
Bartlett-Collins / *Lancaster Colony Corp.*
Basic-D® Automatic Dishwashing Concentrate / *Shaklee Corp.*
Basic-H® Concentrated Organic Cleaner / *Shaklee Corp.*
Basic-H® Concentrated Soil Conditioner / *Shaklee Corp.*
Basic-I® Industrial Cleaner / *Shaklee Corp.*
Basic-L® Laundry Concentrate / *Shaklee Corp.*
Beacon / *Sterling Drug Inc.*
Behold / *Bristol Myers Co.*
Belding Heminway / *Belding Heminway Co. Inc.*
Biz / *Procter & Gamble Co.*
Black Flag / *American Home Products Corp.*
Bo-Peep / *Purex Industries, Inc.*
Bounce / *Procter & Gamble Co.*
Bounty / *Procter & Gamble Co.*
Bowl Guard / *American Cyanamid Company*
Boyle Midway / *American Home Products Corp.*
Brawny / *American Can Co.*
Brillo / *Purex Industries, Inc.*
Brocade / *Safeway Stores Inc.*
Bruce / *Greyhound Corp.*
Cafe Duo / *North American Philips Corp.*
Calico Goose / *Papercraft Corp.*
Cameo / *Purex Industries, Inc.*
Candle-Lite / *Lancaster Colony Corp.*
Care Bears / *Papercraft Corp.*
Cascade / *Procter & Gamble Co.*
Cello / *Grow Group Inc.*
Charmin / *Procter & Gamble Co.*
Cheer / *Procter & Gamble Co.*
Chef de Cuisine / *Lancaster Colony Corp.*
Chief Kitchen Tools / *Newell Companies Inc.*
Classic Chiefware / *Newell Companies Inc.*
Clean & Smooth / *Economics Laboratory Inc.*
Clorox / *Clorox*
Clorox 2 / *Clorox*
Clout / *Kimberly-Clark Corp.*
Club Aluminum / *Standex International Corp.*
Cold Power / *Colgate-Palmolive Co.*
Colortex / *NVF Co.*
Combat / *American Cyanamid Company*
Comet / *Procter & Gamble Co.*
Comet / *Newell Companies Inc.*
Commander / *Grow Group Inc.*
Con-Tact / *Rubbermaid Inc.*
Cookables / *Rubbermaid Inc.*
Copley Square / *Maryland Cup Corp.*
Copper Glo / *American Cyanamid Company*
Cormatic / *Georgia-Pacific Corp.*
Coronet / *Georgia-Pacific Corp.*
Cottonelle / *Scott Paper Co.*
Counselor / *Newell Companies Inc.*
Couroc / *Royal Crown Companies Inc.*
Creative Bakeware / *Newell Companies Inc.*
Creative Cookware / *Newell Companies Inc.*
Crew / *Kimberly-Clark Corp.*
Culligan / *Beatrice Companies Inc.*
Cut Rite / *Scott Paper Co.*
Dash / *Procter & Gamble Co.*
Dawn / *Kimberly-Clark Corp.*
Dawn / *Procter & Gamble Co.*
d-Con / *Sterling Drug Inc.*

Debut / *Newell Companies Inc.*
Delsey / *Kimberly-Clark Corp.*
Delta / *Georgia-Pacific Corp.*
Depend-O / *American Home Products Corp.*
DeSoto / *DeSoto, Inc.*
Diamond Foil / *Reynolds Metals Co.*
Diaper Sweet / *A.E. Staley Manufacturing Co.*
Dip-it / *Economics Laboratory Inc.*
Dolly Madison / *Fort Howard Paper Co.*
Dome / *Ball Corp.*
Dow / *The Dow Chemical Company*
Downy / *Procter & Gamble Co.*
Drackett Co. / *Bristol Myers Co.*
Drano / *Bristol Myers Co.*
Dreft / *Procter & Gamble Co.*
Duracell / *Dart & Kraft Inc.*
Duro / *Loctite Corp.*
Dustbuster / *The Black & Decker Corporation*
Dynamo / *Colgate-Palmolive Co.*
Earth Grown / *Newell Companies Inc.*
Easy Off / *American Home Products Corp.*
Easy On / *American Home Products Corp.*
Easy Shelf / *Newell Companies Inc.*
Ebonware / *Newell Companies Inc.*
Ecko / *American Home Products Corp.*
Edon / *Fort Howard Paper Co.*
Electrasol / *Economics Laboratory Inc.*
Electrolux / *Consolidated Foods Corp.*
Endust / *Bristol Myers Co.*
Energine / *Sterling Drug Inc.*
Enterprise Aluminum / *Lancaster Colony Corp.*
Era / *Procter & Gamble Co.*
Erase / *Economics Laboratory Inc.*
Escort Kitchen Tools / *Newell Companies Inc.*
Esprit de Cuisine / *Newell Companies Inc.*
Esquire / *Papercraft Corp.*
Evergreen / *Safeway Stores Inc.*
Fab / *Colgate-Palmolive Co.*
Family Scott / *Scott Paper Co.*
Fashon/Beacon Hill / *GenCorp*
Fels-Naptha / *Purex Industries, Inc.*
Fiesta / *Scott Paper Co.*
Finesse / *Kellwood Co.*
Finish / *Economics Laboratory Inc.*
Fleecy / *Bristol Myers Co.*
Flex-Can Retortable Pouch / *Reynolds Metals Co.*
Flex-Straws / *Maryland Cup Corp.*
Florient / *Colgate-Palmolive Co.*
Foley Foodmill / *Newell Companies Inc.*
Foley VIII Cookware / *Newell Companies Inc.*
Fonda / *Saxon Industries Inc.*
Formby's / *Richardson-Vicks Inc.*
Formica Floor Shine / *American Cyanamid Company*
Formula 409 / *Clorox*
Fostoria Glass / *Lancaster Colony Corp.*
Free n' Soft / *Economics Laboratory Inc.*
Fresh Start / *Colgate-Palmolive Co.*
Fuller Brush / *Consolidated Foods Corp.*
Gain / *Procter & Gamble Co.*
Gala / *American Can Co.*
Galaxy / *Colgate-Palmolive Co.*
Gentle Fels / *Purex Industries, Inc.*
Glad / *Union Carbide Corp.*
Gladiator / *Grow Group Inc.*
Glass Magic / *Economics Laboratory Inc.*
Glass Shop / *Lancaster Colony Corp.*
Glit / *Katy Industries, Inc.*
Gold Label / *Grow Group Inc.*
Gourmet Gallery / *Papercraft Corp.*
The Great Cooks Collection / *Newell Companies Inc.*
Greenhouse / *Papercraft Corp.*
Griffin / *American Home Products Corp.*
Guildware / *Maryland Cup Corp.*
Handi-Wrap II / *The Dow Chemical Company*
Handle With Care / *Bristol Myers Co.*
Handy Wipes / *Colgate-Palmolive Co.*
Hawes / *American Home Products Corp.*
Heatables / *Rubbermaid Inc.*
Hefty / *Mobil Corp.*
Heirloom / *Lancaster Colony Corp.*
Hi-Dri / *Kimberly-Clark Corp.*
Hi-Lex-Liquid / *Purex Industries, Inc.*
Holdfast / *Woodstream Corp.*
Homemaker / *Beatrice Companies Inc.*
Homer Formby's / *Richardson-Vicks Inc.*
Hot Foot / *Beatrice Companies Inc.*
household product / *Shaklee Corp.*
HR2 / *American Home Products Corp.*
Hudson / *Georgia-Pacific Corp.*
Indiana Glass / *Lancaster Colony Corp.*
Ivory Liquid / *Procter & Gamble Co.*
Ivory Snow / *Procter & Gamble Co.*
Jason / *Scott & Fetzer Co.*
Javex / *Bristol Myers Co.*
Jet-Dry / *Economics Laboratory Inc.*
Job Squad / *Scott Paper Co.*
Joy / *Procter & Gamble Co.*
Kaydry / *Kimberly-Clark Corp.*
Kimtex / *Kimberly-Clark Corp.*
Kimtowels / *Kimberly-Clark Corp.*
Kimwipes / *Kimberly-Clark Corp.*
Kiss the Cook / *Papercraft Corp.*
Kitchen Craft / *Safeway Stores Inc.*
Kleen Guard / *Alberto Culver Co.*
Kleenex / *Kimberly-Clark Corp.*
Kleenups / *Kimberly-Clark Corp.*

Knomark / *Papercraft Corp.*
Kurly Kate / *Purex Industries, Inc.*
La France / *Purex Industries, Inc.*
Lady Scott / *Scott Paper Co.*
Lemon Sol / *American Cyanamid Company*
Lestoil / *Noxell Corp.*
Like Magic / *Grow Group Inc.*
Lime-A-Way / *Economics Laboratory Inc.*
Linens 'n Things / *Melville Corp.*
Linensoft / *Crown Zellerbach Corp.*
Liquid-L® Laundry Concentrate / *Shaklee Corp.*
Liquid-plumr / *Clorox*
Lite Saver / *Conair Corp.*
Lithowipe / *Kimberly-Clark Corp.*
Little Tikes / *Rubbermaid Inc.*
Loma-Rubber Queen / *Lancaster Colony Corp.*
Love My Carpet / *Sterling Drug Inc.*
Luau / *Crown Zellerbach Corp.*
Luxuria / *Beatrice Companies Inc.*
Lysol / *Sterling Drug Inc.*
Mardi Gras / *Fort Howard Paper Co.*
Marigold / *Safeway Stores Inc.*
Marina / *Crown Zellerbach Corp.*
Maryland / *Maryland Cup Corp.*
Masterbilt / *Newell Companies Inc.*
Masterset / *Newell Companies Inc.*
Match Light / *Clorox*
MD / *Georgia-Pacific Corp.*
MicroWare / *Anchor Hocking Corporation*
Minwax / *Sterling Drug Inc.*
Miracle White / *Bristol Myers Co.*
Mirro / *Newell Companies Inc.*
Moldan / *Katy Industries, Inc.*
Mop & Glow / *Sterling Drug Inc.*
Mr. Big / *Georgia-Pacific Corp.*
Mr. Clean / *Procter & Gamble Co.*
My Room / *GenCorp*
Nature-Bright Concentrated Laundry Brightener / *Shaklee Corp.*
Nature's Spring / *Nature's Sunshine Products, Inc.*
Niagara / *CPC International Inc.*
Nice 'n Soft / *Crown Zellerbach Corp.*
Northern Tissues / *Great Northern Nekoosa Corp.*
Nusoft / *CPC International Inc.*
O Cedar / *Bristol Myers Co.*
O-Cel-O / *General Mills Inc.*
Old Dutch / *Purex Industries, Inc.*
Old English / *American Home Products Corp.*
Orchid / *NVF Co.*
Oxydol / *Procter & Gamble Co.*
Paas / *Schering-Plough Corp.*
Page / *Fort Howard Paper Co.*
Pam / *American Home Products Corp.*
Pantaloon / *Grow Group Inc.*
Paper Fresh / *Scott Paper Co.*
Par / *Safeway Stores Inc.*
Par No Phosphate Detergent / *Safeway Stores Inc.*
Parade / *Safeway Stores Inc.*
Parson's / *Greyhound Corp.*
Pine Sol / *American Cyanamid Company*
Plastic Wood / *American Home Products Corp.*
Popee / *Kimberly-Clark Corp.*
Presto / *The Coca-Cola Co.*
Princess House / *Colgate-Palmolive Co.*
Purex / *Purex Industries, Inc.*
Purex / *Scott Paper Co.*
Quikcut / *Scott & Fetzer Co.*
Rain Drops / *A.E. Staley Manufacturing Co.*
Reed / *Westvaco Corp.*
Regio / *Kimberly-Clark Corp.*
Renuzit / *Bristol Myers Co.*
Reynolds Freezer Paper / *Reynolds Metals Co.*
Reynolds Oven Cooking Bags / *Reynolds Metals Co.*
Reynolds Plastic Wrap / *Reynolds Metals Co.*
Reynolds Redi-Pan Aluminum Foilware / *Reynolds Metals Co.*
Reynolds Wrap Household Aluminum Foil / *Reynolds Metals Co.*
Rid-X / *Sterling Drug Inc.*
Rit / *CPC International Inc.*
Royal Chef / *Lancaster Colony Corp.*
Royalcraft / *Saxon Industries Inc.*
Rubbermaid / *Rubbermaid Inc.*
Ruffies & Tuffies / *United States Industries Inc.*
Sani-Flush / *American Home Products Corp.*
Saran Wrap / *The Dow Chemical Company*
Satin Sheen® Dishwashing Liquid / *Shaklee Corp.*
Scotch-Brite / *Minnesota Mining and Manufacturing Co. (3M)*
Scott / *Scott Paper Co.*
Scott Family / *Scott Paper Co.*
Scotties / *Scott Paper Co.*
ScotTissue / *Scott Paper Co.*
ScotTowels / *Scott Paper Co.*
ScotTowels Junior / *Scott Paper Co.*
Scrub Free / *Economics Laboratory Inc.*
Servin' Saver / *Rubbermaid Inc.*
Shower Massage / *Teledyne Inc.*
Smokeless Ashtray / *Ronco Teleproducts Inc.*
Smooth 'n Easy / *Rubbermaid Inc.*
Sno-Bol / *A.E. Staley Manufacturing Co.*
So Dri / *Fort Howard Paper Co.*
Soft 'N Gentle / *Fort Howard Paper Co.*
Soft 'n Pretty / *Scott Paper Co.*
Soft Scrub / *Clorox*
Soft Weve / *Scott Paper Co.*

Softer Than Soft® Concentrated Fabric Conditioner / *Shaklee Corp.*
Soilax / *Economics Laboratory Inc.*
Solo / *Procter & Gamble Co.*
Spic & Span / *Procter & Gamble Co.*
Spill-Mate / *Crown Zellerbach Corp.*
Springfield / *Sunbeam Corp.*
Sta-Flo / *A.E. Staley Manufacturing Co.*
Stancraft / *Saxon Industries Inc.*
Stanley Hostess Party Plan / *Stanhome, Inc.*
Sta-Puf / *A.E. Staley Manufacturing Co.*
Static Guard / *Alberto Culver Co.*
Steamex / *Peavey Co.*
Sunshine Fresh / *Papercraft Corp.*
Super Saver / *Teledyne Inc.*
Su-Purb / *Safeway Stores Inc.*
Sweetheart / *Maryland Cup Corp.*
Sylvania / *GTE Corp.*
Ten-T / *Maryland Cup Corp.*
Teri / *Kimberly-Clark Corp.*
Thermos / *Household International, Inc.*
Thompson's Water Seal and Seal Stain / *Richardson-Vicks Inc.*
Tide / *Procter & Gamble Co.*
Tilex / *Clorox*
Tintex / *Papercraft Corp.*
Top Drawer / *American Home Products Corp.*
Top Job / *Procter & Gamble Co.*
Tough Act / *The Dow Chemical Company*
Trend / *Purex Industries, Inc.*
Trewax / *Grow Group Inc.*
Tri-Flow / *Richardson-Vicks Inc.*
Trophy / *Safeway Stores Inc.*
Truly Fine / *Safeway Stores Inc.*
Trump / *Woodstream Corp.*
Try-It / *Stanhome, Inc.*
Tucker / *Kidde Inc.*
Twice As Fresh / *Clorox*
Ty-D-Bol / *Papercraft Corp.*
Vanish / *Bristol Myers Co.*
Vanity Fair / *Diamond International Corp.*
Vera / *Crown Zellerbach Corp.*
Vi-Sol / *Bristol Myers Co.*
Viva / *Scott Paper Co.*
Waldorf / *Scott Paper Co.*
Washin 'n' Dry / *Colgate-Palmolive Co.*
White Cloud / *Procter & Gamble Co.*
White Magic / *Safeway Stores Inc.*
Windex / *Bristol Myers Co.*
Windsor Kitchen Tools / *Newell Companies Inc.*
Wizard / *American Home Products Corp.*
Wondersoft / *Kimberly-Clark Corp.*
Woolite / *American Home Products Corp.*
Worthmore / *Newell Companies Inc.*
X-14 / *American Home Products Corp.*
Zee / *Crown Zellerbach Corp.*
Ziploc / *The Dow Chemical Company*
Ziploc Microfreez / *The Dow Chemical Company*
Zud / *American Home Products Corp.*
3-in-One / *American Home Products Corp.*

Insurance

Alexander Hamilton / *Household International, Inc.*
Allstate / *Sears, Roebuck & Co.*
American Express Card / *American Express Co.*
American Express Gold Card / *American Express Co.*
American Express International Banking / *American Express Co.*
American Express Money Orders / *American Express Co.*
American Express Platinum Card / *American Express Co.*
American Express Travelers Cheques / *American Express Co.*
American Family Life Assurance Co. / *American Family Corp.*
American Founders / *Anderson, Clayton & Co.*
American Life Insurance Co. of New York / *Transamerica Corp.*
Arcadia Insurance Co. / *Borg Warner Corp.*
Arvida Financial Services / *Walt Disney Productions*
Arvida Realty Sales / *Walt Disney Productions*
Avco Financial Services Inc. / *Avco*
Best Insurors Insurance Agency / *Jim Walter Corp.*
Better Homes & Gardens Insurance Agency / *Meredith Corp.*
Caldwell Banker Real Estate Group / *Sears, Roebuck & Co.*
Capital Credit / *Union Corp.*
Cenguard / *Continental Corp.*
Cenguard Insurance / *Transworld Corp.*
CNA Financial Corp. / *Loews Corp.*
College/University Corp. Insurance Co. / *Baldwin-United Corporation*
Columbia Insurance / *Berkshire Hathaway Inc.*
Commercial Life / *Continental Corp.*
Consumer Financial Corp. / *ITT Corp.*
Continental Insurance / *Continental Corp.*
Countrywide Life Insurance Co. / *Transamerica Corp.*

CPI Group / *Continental Corp.*
Crown Valley Insurance / *Transamerica Corp.*
Dean Witter Financial Services Group / *Sears, Roebuck & Co.*
Disney Development Co. / *Walt Disney Productions*
Dun & Bradstreet / *Dun & Bradstreet Corp.*
Dunhill Personal / *Transworld Corp.*
Firemen's Fund Insurance / *American Express Co.*
Franklin Life Insurance / *American Brands Inc.*
Fred S. James & Co. Inc. / *Transamerica Corp.*
Gamble Alden Life Insurance Co. / *Wickes Corp.*
GEICO / *Berkshire Hathaway Inc.*
General Electric / *General Electric Co.*
Gentry Insurance / *Mayflower Corp.*
Gerber Life Insurance / *Gerber Products Co.*
Hartford Fire & Insurance Co. / *ITT Corp.*
Harvest Life / *Harcourt Brace Jovanovich Inc.*
HFC Income Tax Service / *Household International, Inc.*
HMI Credit Corp. / *Health-Mor Inc.*
The Home Group Inc / *City Investing Co.*
Household Bank / *Household International, Inc.*
IDS / *American Express Co.*
Indiana Insurance Company / *National Distillers & Chemical Corp.*
The Insurancenter / *Continental Corp.*
Joh M. Riehle & Co. Inc. / *Harcourt Brace Jovanovich Inc.*
John Alden Life Insurance Co. / *Wickes Corp.*
Knox, Lent & Tucker Inc. / *Harcourt Brace Jovanovich Inc.*
Loyalty Life / *Continental Corp.*
The Money Stores / *Transamerica Corp.*
Moody's / *Dun & Bradstreet Corp.*
Mutual Savings and Loan / *Berkshire Hathaway Inc.*
National Farmers Union Insurance / *Baldwin-United Corporation*
National Indemnity / *Berkshire Hathaway Inc.*
National Investors Life Insurance Co. / *Baldwin-United Corporation*
National Life of Canada / *Continental Corp.*
Occidental Life Insurance Co. / *Transamerica Corp.*
Paul Revere Life Insurance Co. & Equity Sales Co. & Realty Corp. / *Avco*
Philadelphia Life / *Tenneco Inc.*
Princeton / *Carnation Company*
Questar Development / *Questar Corp.*
Rover of Indiana / *Mayflower Corp.*
Shearson Lehman Brothers / *American Express Co.*
Signal Capitol / *Signal Companies Inc.*
Southland Life Insurance / *American Brands Inc.*
Southwestern General Life Ins. / *Tenneco Inc.*
Southwestern Life Insurance / *Tenneco Inc.*
Suburban Propane Gas Corp / *National Distillers & Chemical Corp.*
Toc (Stylized) / *Chevron Corp.*
Transamerica Accidental Life Insurance Co. / *Transamerica Corp.*
Transamerica Financial Corp. / *Transamerica Corp.*
Transamerica Insurance Co. / *Transamerica Corp.*
Transamerica Life Insurance & Annuity Co. / *Transamerica Corp.*
Transamerica Title Insurance Co. / *Transamerica Corp.*
Unicoa Corp. / *Teledyne Inc.*
United Consumer / *Scott & Fetzer Co.*
William Penn / *Continental Corp.*
Wolverine / *Transamerica Corp.*

Juvenile Products & Toys

Amtoy / *American Greetings Corporation*
Aviva / *Hasbro Bradley, Inc.*
Baby Fresh Wipes / *Scott Paper Co.*
Babygro / *Gerber Products Co.*
Beautyskin / *Nestle-LeMur Co.*
Cabbage Patch Kids / *Papercraft Corp.*
Cabbage Patch Kids / *Coleco Industries, Inc.*
Caldesene / *Pennwalt Corp.*
Care Bear Cousins / *American Greetings Corporation*
Care Bears / *General Mills Inc.*
Care Bears / *American Greetings Corporation*
Castle Rock / *K-Tel International*
Child Guidance / *CBS Inc.*
Circus World Toy Stores / *Rite Aid Corp.*
C.L.A.W. / *Tonka Corp.*
Clutch Poppers / *Tonka Corp.*
Comfortine / *Rorer Group Inc.*
C.R.A.B. / *Tonka Corp.*
Creative Playthings / *CBS Inc.*
Cuddly Crew / *American Greetings Corporation*
Diaparene / *Sterling Drug Inc.*
Diaper Pure / *American Home Products Corp.*
Emenee / *Ohio Art Co.*
Enfamil / *Bristol Myers Co.*
Erector Construction Sets / *CBS Inc.*
Ertl / *Kidde Inc.*
"Etch-A-Sketch" / *Ohio Art Co.*
Evenflo / *Questor Corp.*
Fast Traks / *Tonka Corp.*
Fisher Price Toys / *Quaker Oats Co.*
Fresh 'n Fancy / *Hasbro Bradley, Inc.*

Gabriel Toys / *CBS Inc.*
George A. Reach / *Lancaster Colony Corp.*
Gerber / *Gerber Products Co.*
Gerry / *Huffy Corp.*
GoBots / *Tonka Corp.*
Hasbro / *Hasbro Bradley, Inc.*
Heinz / *H.J. Heinz Co.*
He-Man and the Masters of the Universe / *Papercraft Corp.*
Huggies / *Kimberly-Clark Corp.*
Husky Hauler / *Coleco Industries, Inc.*
Ideal / *CBS Inc.*
Ideal / *Ideal Toy Corp.*
Infantseat / *Questor Corp.*
Isomil / *Abbott Laboratories*
Johnson & Johnson / *Johnson & Johnson*
Kay-Bee / *Melville Corp.*
Kenner / *General Mills Inc.*
Kleen Bebe / *Kimberly-Clark Corp.*
Knickerbocker / *Warner Communications Inc.*
Lil'Sport / *Ohio Art Co.*
Lionel Electric Trains / *General Mills Inc.*
Luvs / *Procter & Gamble Co.*
Mattel / *Mattel Inc.*
Mego / *Mego International Inc.*
Mighty Cycles / *Tonka Corp.*
Mighty Robots / *Tonka Corp.*
Mighty Tonka / *Tonka Corp.*
Mightys / *Tonka Corp.*
Milton Bradley Toys / *Milton Bradley Co.*
MPC Model Kits / *General Mills Inc.*
Nerf / *General Mills Inc.*
Ohio Art / *Ohio Art Co.*
Pampers / *Procter & Gamble Co.*
Parker Bros. / *General Mills Inc.*
Peanuts / *CBS Inc.*
Play & Learn / *Coleco Industries, Inc.*
Play Doh / *General Mills Inc.*
Playskool Educational Toys / *Milton Bradley Co.*
Power Cycle / *Coleco Industries, Inc.*
Powersuits / *Tonka Corp.*
ProSobee / *Bristol Myers Co.*
Puffs / *Procter & Gamble Co.*
Puzzler / *Tonka Corp.*
Regular Tonka / *Tonka Corp.*
Reliance / *Gerber Products Co.*
Romper Room / *Hasbro Bradley, Inc.*
Santa Claus, The Movie / *Papercraft Corp.*
Sectaurs / *Coleco Industries, Inc.*
Sesame St. / *CBS Inc.*
Silly Putty / *Binney & Smith Inc.*
Similac / *Abbott Laboratories*
Squeeze / *Lancaster Colony Corp.*
Star Fairies / *Tonka Corp.*
Star War I / *General Mills Inc.*
Strawberry Shortcake / *General Mills Inc.*
Teddy Time / *Riegel Textile Corp.*
Tinkertoy / *CBS Inc.*
Tiny Mightys / *Tonka Corp.*
Tiny Tonka / *Tonka Corp.*
T-N-T's / *Tonka Corp.*
Tonka / *Tonka Corp.*
Toss'ems / *Questor Corp.*
Vanity Fair / *Kidde Inc.*
Wash A-bye Baby / *Scott Paper Co.*
Wet Ones / *Sterling Drug Inc.*
Wonder Spring / *CBS Inc.*

Jewelry & Accessories

American / *Hillenbrand Industries Inc.*
American Tourister / *Hillenbrand Industries Inc.*
Argenzio Bros. / *Zale Corp.*
ArtCarved / *Brown Forman Distillers Corp.*
Associates / *Hillenbrand Industries Inc.*
Beautiful on the Outside, American Tourister on the Inside / *Hillenbrand Industries Inc.*
Biagi / *Swank Inc.*
Bohm-Allen / *Zale Corp.*
Bond Street Ltd. / *Richton Int'l Corp.*
Bonnie / *Jaclyn, Inc.*
Bulova / *Loews Corp.*
Business Equipment / *Hillenbrand Industries Inc.*
Business Equipment by American Tourister / *Hillenbrand Industries Inc.*
Buxton / *Beatrice Companies Inc.*
Canaveral / *Hillenbrand Industries Inc.*
Cartwheels / *Beatrice Companies Inc.*
Citation / *United Merchants and Manufacturers Inc.*
Classic / *Beatrice Companies Inc.*
Comfort Stride by No Nonsense / *Gulf* + Western Industries Inc.
Coro / *Richton Int'l Corp.*
Corocraft / *Richton Int'l Corp.*
Courier / *Sears, Roebuck & Co.*
Cowell & Hubbard / *Zale Corp.*
Cross Country / *Hillenbrand Industries Inc.*
D'Amigo / *Edison Brothers Stores Inc.*
Dependables / *Hillenbrand Industries Inc.*
Dicini / *Richton Int'l Corp.*
Dobbins / *Zale Corp.*
Dobbs / *Levi Strauss & Co.*

Don Loper / *Tandy Brands Inc.*
Dopp / *Beatrice Companies Inc.*
Ecru / *Katy Industries, Inc.*
Elgin / *Katy Industries, Inc.*
Empress / *Jaclyn, Inc.*
Encore / *United Merchants and Manufacturers Inc.*
Escort / *Hillenbrand Industries Inc.*
Etienne Aigner / *Jonathan Logan Inc.*
Fashionaire / *Beatrice Companies Inc.*
Flee Bags / *Beatrice Companies Inc.*
Forecast / *Sears, Roebuck & Co.*
Free Wheelers / *Hillenbrand Industries Inc.*
Frequent Flyer / *Hillenbrand Industries Inc.*
General Products / *Gordon Jewelry Corp.*
Givenchy / *United Merchants and Manufacturers Inc.*
Gorilla Bags / *Hillenbrand Industries Inc.*
Granat Brothers / *Zale Corp.*
Hallmark Jewelry / *Katy Industries, Inc.*
Harness House / *Manhattan Industries Inc.*
Hazel / *Jostens Inc.*
Hermann Loewenstein / *Katy Industries, Inc.*
Hi Lights / *McKesson Corp.*
Hickok / *Tandy Brands Inc.*
Hush Puppies / *Tandy Brands Inc.*
Jaclyn / *Jaclyn, Inc.*
J.B. Robinson / *W.R. Grace & Co.*
Joan Bari / *Edison Brothers Stores Inc.*
Jostens / *Jostens Inc.*
Jubilee / *Westinghouse Electric Corp.*
Keepsake / *Brown Forman Distillers Corp.*
Keepsake / *Lenox Inc.*
Le Mans / *Hillenbrand Industries Inc.*
Leg Looks / *Gulf* + Western Industries Inc.
Liberty of London / *Manhattan Industries Inc.*
Lisner / *United Merchants and Manufacturers Inc.*
London Fog / *Tandy Brands Inc.*
Longines-Wittnauer / *Westinghouse Electric Corp.*
Mark Force Vatco / *Beatrice Companies Inc.*
Marvella / *Richton Int'l Corp.*
Monet / *General Mills Inc.*
Monte Carlo / *Hillenbrand Industries Inc.*
Monterey / *Hillenbrand Industries Inc.*
New Dimensions / *Hillenbrand Industries Inc.*
Omega / *Beatrice Companies Inc.*
Oscar de la Renta / *Richton Int'l Corp.*
Pavanne / *Richton Int'l Corp.*
Peter Ashley / *Manhattan Industries Inc.*
Philippe / *Alberto Culver Co.*
Polara / *Westinghouse Electric Corp.*
Prince Gardner / *Swank Inc.*
Princess Gardner / *Swank Inc.*
Rally / *Hillenbrand Industries Inc.*
Reliables / *Hillenbrand Industries Inc.*
ResQ / *Hillenbrand Industries Inc.*
Richelieu / *United Merchants and Manufacturers Inc.*
Richton International Limited / *Richton Int'l Corp.*
Saronno / *Hillenbrand Industries Inc.*
Slavick / *Zale Corp.*
SLJ / *Seligman & Latz Inc.*
Soft Riders / *Hillenbrand Industries Inc.*
SoftTech / *Hillenbrand Industries Inc.*
Space Makers / *Hillenbrand Industries Inc.*
Spectrum / *Hillenbrand Industries Inc.*
Stifft's / *Zale Corp.*
Stowell / *Zale Corp.*
Styltex / *Hillenbrand Industries Inc.*
Supp-Hose / *Gulf* + Western Industries Inc.
Sureglide / *Hillenbrand Industries Inc.*
Swank / *Swank Inc.*
T.A.B. Accessories / *Tandy Brands Inc.*
Tammy Brooke / *Jaclyn, Inc.*
Tex Tan Western / *Tandy Brands Inc.*
Tourister / *Hillenbrand Industries Inc.*
Triumph / *Hillenbrand Industries Inc.*
Ultra Sense by No Nonsense / *Gulf* + Western Industries Inc.
Vendome / *Richton Int'l Corp.*
Verona / *Hillenbrand Industries Inc.*
Vilon / *Hillenbrand Industries Inc.*
Vytex / *Hillenbrand Industries Inc.*
Wagner's / *Zale Corp.*
Walking Wardrobe / *Hillenbrand Industries Inc.*
Wedgwood / *Swank Inc.*
Weisfield's Jewelry / *Weisfield's, Inc.*
Wiss & Lambert / *Zale Corp.*
Wittnauer / *Westinghouse Electric Corp.*
Wolf / *Zale Corp.*
Wright Kay / *Zale Corp.*
Yves Saint Laurent / *Manhattan Industries Inc.*
Zell Bros. / *Zale Corp.*

Motor Vehicles

Aljo Aries / *Skyline Corp.*
Aljo/Aly / *Skyline Corp.*
Aljo/Aly Alliance / *Skyline Corp.*
AMC Eagle / *American Motors Corp.*
Atlas/Condor (Cabstar) / *Nissan Motor Co., Ltd.*
Bluebird / *Nissan Motor Co., Ltd.*
Budget Rent-a-Car Corp. / *Transamerica Corp.*
Buick / *General Motors Corp.*
Cadillac / *General Motors Corp.*

Carolina Coach / *North American Philips Corp.*
Cedric / *Nissan Motor Co., Ltd.*
Chevrolet / *General Motors Corp.*
Chrysler / *Chrysler Corp.*
Crestwood / *Skyline Corp.*
Datson / *Nissan Motor Co., Ltd.*
Dodge / *Chrysler Corp.*
GMC / *General Motors Corp.*
Jeep / *American Motors Corp.*
K-cars / *Chrysler Corp.*
Kensington / *Skyline Corp.*
Key Largo / *Skyline Corp.*
Laurel / *Nissan Motor Co., Ltd.*
Layton / *Skyline Corp.*
Layton Celebrity / *Skyline Corp.*
Layton Funtime / *Skyline Corp.*
March (Micra) / *Nissan Motor Co., Ltd.*
Mobile Traveler / *Zimmer Corp.*
MT / *Zimmer Corp.*
Nomad Century / *Skyline Corp.*
Nomad Weekender / *Skyline Corp.*
Oldsmobile / *General Motors Corp.*
Plymouth / *Chrysler Corp.*
Pontiac / *General Motors Corp.*
President / *Nissan Motor Co., Ltd.*
Pulsar / *Nissan Motor Co., Ltd.*
Renault Alliance / *American Motors Corp.*
Renault Encore / *American Motors Corp.*
Saturn / *General Motors Corp.*
Scottsdale / *Skyline Corp.*
Skyline / *Nissan Motor Co., Ltd.*
Skyline Vans / *Skyline Corp.*
Sylvia / *Nissan Motor Co., Ltd.*
Tahoe / *Skyline Corp.*
Venture / *Bangor Punta Corp.*

Office Equipment & Supplies

Accu-point / *Gillette Co.*
Acme Visible Business Systems / *American Brands Inc.*
Adhes-A-Ply / *Dennison Manufacturing Co.*
Air Conditioned / *Dennison Manufacturing Co.*
Ambassador Shredders / *American Brands Inc.*
American Bride / *CBS Inc.*
American Greetings / *American Greetings Corporation*
American Seating / *Fuqua Industries Inc.*
Ansafone / *Pitney-Bowes Inc.*
Artec / *Kimball International Inc.*
At-A-Glance / *Textron Inc.*
Baldwin Paper / *Alco Standard Corp.*
Bar-Code / *Dennison Manufacturing Co.*
Baste & Sew / *Dennison Manufacturing Co.*
Baste & Sew Gluestik / *Dennison Manufacturing Co.*
Beckett Cover / *Hammermill Paper Co.*
Ben-Mont / *Avco*
Berkshire / *Textron Inc.*
Bic Pens / *Bic Corp.*
Boltiplast / *Dennison Manufacturing Co.*
Bondfax / *Dennison Manufacturing Co.*
Bostik / *Emhart Corp.*
Bostitch / *Textron Inc.*
Brunswick / *Dennison Manufacturing Co.*
Buccaneer* / *Dennison Manufacturing Co.*
Buckeye Cover / *Hammermill Paper Co.*
Buttoneer / *Dennison Manufacturing Co.*
Buzza / *RCA Corp.*
Cable-Post / *Dennison Manufacturing Co.*
Canon / *Canon, Inc.*
Caprice / *American Greetings Corporation*
Cardinal / *Jostens Inc.*
Carlton / *American Greetings Corporation*
Carpenter Paper / *Alco Standard Corp.*
Carter's & Design / *Dennison Manufacturing Co.*
CBS Software / *CBS Inc.*
Cedar King / *United States Tobacco Co.*
Central Paper / *Alco Standard Corp.*
Charley / *United States Tobacco Co.*
Cheshire / *Xerox Corp.*
CICO / *Dennison Manufacturing Co.*
Classic / *Kimberly-Clark Corp.*
Color Stik Kit / *Dennison Manufacturing Co.*
Copco Papers / *Alco Standard Corp.*
Copy Master / *Dennison Manufacturing Co.*
C.R. Gibson / *C. R. Gibson Co.*
Craft Originators / *Dennison Manufacturing Co.*
Cross / *A. T. Cross Company*
Crown & Shield / *Dennison Manufacturing Co.*
Crusader / *Jim Walter Corp.*
Data-Liter* / *Dennison Manufacturing Co.*
Day-Timers / *Beatrice Companies Inc.*
DCS / *Dennison Manufacturing Co.*
Decofast* / *Dennison Manufacturing Co.*
Deco-Rubs* / *Dennison Manufacturing Co.*
Dennison / *Dennison Manufacturing Co.*
Dennison & Design / *Dennison Manufacturing Co.*
Dict Alert / *Pitney-Bowes Inc.*
Dicta Mate / *Pitney-Bowes Inc.*
Dictaphone / *Pitney-Bowes Inc.*
Diplomat* / *Dennison Manufacturing Co.*
Director / *Dennison Manufacturing Co.*
Docu-Mate / *Barry Wright Corp.*
Domes / *Dennison Manufacturing Co.*

Doret / *Dennison Manufacturing Co.*
Drawing Board / *Pitney-Bowes Inc.*
Draws-A-Lot / *Dennison Manufacturing Co.*
Dry Ply / *Dennison Manufacturing Co.*
Dry Wipes / *Dennison Manufacturing Co.*
Dunn / *Dennison Manufacturing Co.*
Duo-Tang / *Textron Inc.*
Eagle / *Dennison Manufacturing Co.*
Easel-Y / *Dennison Manufacturing Co.*
Eastlight Filling / *American Brands Inc.*
Eastman / *Dennison Manufacturing Co.*
Easy-To-Use / *Dennison Manufacturing Co.*
Eaton / *Textron Inc.*
Econ-O-Fast / *Dennison Manufacturing Co.*
Electric / *Dennison Manufacturing Co.*
Elephant & Design* / *Dennison Manufacturing Co.*
Elmer's / *Borden Inc.*
Eversharp / *Parker Pen Co.*
Extra-Riter / *Dennison Manufacturing Co.*
Eye Ease / *Dennison Manufacturing Co.*
Fast/Break* / *Dennison Manufacturing Co.*
Fastonol / *Dennison Manufacturing Co.*
Firma-Grip / *Binney & Smith Inc.*
Flair / *Gillette Co.*
Forget-Me-Nots / *American Greetings Corporation*
Form-A-Label / *Standard Register Co.*
Garrett-Buchanan / *Alco Standard Corp.*
Geha / *Dennison Manufacturing Co.*
Gibson / *RCA Corp.*
Glocolor / *Dennison Manufacturing Co.*
Glue Stic* / *Dennison Manufacturing Co.*
Golden Arrow / *Dennison Manufacturing Co.*
Graphic Controls Corporation / *Times Mirror Co.*
Grayarc / *Pitney-Bowes Inc.*
Guardian / *Dennison Manufacturing Co.*
Hammermill Bond and Copier / *Hammermill Paper Co.*
Hammermill Paper Products / *Hammermill Paper Co.*
Heat Seal & Sign / *Dennison Manufacturing Co.*
Hi-Liter* / *Dennison Manufacturing Co.*
Holga / *Hon Industries Inc.*
Holly Hobby / *American Greetings Corporation*
Hon / *Hon Industries Inc.*
Honeywell / *Honeywell Inc.*
Honor Roll / *United States Tobacco Co.*
Hoyle / *Saxon Industries Inc.*
IBM / *International Business Machines Corp.*
Ideal / *Dennison Manufacturing Co.*
Ink Jet* / *Dennison Manufacturing Co.*
Kangaroo / *Dennison Manufacturing Co.*
Kleencote* / *Dennison Manufacturing Co.*
Kleenpac / *Dennison Manufacturing Co.*
Kodak / *Eastman Kodak Co.*
Kybe & Logo / *Dennison Manufacturing Co.*
Kybe Kleen / *Dennison Manufacturing Co.*
La Salle Messinger Paper / *Alco Standard Corp.*
Laurel / *American Greetings Corporation*
Le Page's / *Papercraft Corp.*
Lear Siegler / *Lear Siegler, Inc.*
Liquid Paper / *Gillette Co.*
Loctite / *Loctite Corp.*
Mail-Well Envelope / *Great Northern Nekoosa Corp.*
Mark Master* / *Dennison Manufacturing Co.*
Mark-A-Pen / *Dennison Manufacturing Co.*
Marks-A-Lot* / *Dennison Manufacturing Co.*
Marlboro / *Dennison Manufacturing Co.*
McDonald Designs / *Insilco Corp.*
Media Mates / *Dennison Manufacturing Co.*
Meritag / *Dennison Manufacturing Co.*
Micropor / *Dennison Manufacturing Co.*
Microsystem80 / *Jostens Inc.*
Mid-Continent Paper / *Alco Standard Corp.*
Midnight / *Dennison Manufacturing Co.*
Mini Label-Mate / *Dennison Manufacturing Co.*
Minidax / *Dennison Manufacturing Co.*
Miniwriter / *Pitney-Bowes Inc.*
Monarch Paper / *Alco Standard Corp.*
Mustang / *United States Tobacco Co.*
Nashua / *Nashua Corp.*
National / *Kimball International Inc.*
NCR / *NCR Corp.*
NCR Tower / *NCR Corp.*
NCR Worksaver / *NCR Corp.*
NCR 32 / *NCR Corp.*
Nekoosa Paper Products / *Great Northern Nekoosa Corp.*
Networkers / *Dennison Manufacturing Co.*
Never Forgets / *Dennison Manufacturing Co.*
Non-Blocking / *Dennison Manufacturing Co.*
Nu-Glue / *Dennison Manufacturing Co.*
NYIF—New York Institute of Finance / *Gulf +* Western Industries Inc.
Office Buddies / *Dennison Manufacturing Co.*
Office Spring / *Hershey Foods Corp.*
Ofrex Office Supplies / *American Brands Inc.*
Optimedia / *Barry Wright Corp.*
Oxynek / *Dennison Manufacturing Co.*
Paper Aid / *Dennison Manufacturing Co.*
Paper Corp. of U.S. / *Alco Standard Corp.*
Paper Mate / *Gillette Co.*
Parker / *Parker Pen Co.*
Pathfinder / *Pitney-Bowes Inc.*
PC Work Center / *Barry Wright Corp.*
Perma / *American Brands Inc.*
Perma-Flat / *Dennison Manufacturing Co.*
Pernaceran / *Dennison Manufacturing Co.*

Pitney-Bowes / *Pitney-Bowes Inc.*
Pleasant Thoughts / *RCA Corp.*
Plus Mark / *American Greetings Corporation*
Porelon / *Dennison Manufacturing Co.*
Post-It / *Minnesota Mining and Manufacturing Co. (3M)*
Post-Lite / *Dennison Manufacturing Co.*
Pres.A.Ply* / *Dennison Manufacturing Co.*
Presidax* / *Dennison Manufacturing Co.*
Prime Cut / *Dennison Manufacturing Co.*
Put Ons* / *Dennison Manufacturing Co.*
Quickie Letter / *Dennison Manufacturing Co.*
Razzle-Dazzle / *Dennison Manufacturing Co.*
Red Snapper / *Dennison Manufacturing Co.*
Reply / *Westvaco Corp.*
Rexel Office Products / *American Brands Inc.*
Ricoh / *Nashua Corp.*
Rite Ease / *Dennison Manufacturing Co.*
Ritoff / *Dennison Manufacturing Co.*
Rollex / *Dennison Manufacturing Co.*
Rollkleen / *Dennison Manufacturing Co.*
Rolodex / *Insilco Corp.*
Rotoflex / *Dennison Manufacturing Co.*
Rotronic / *Dennison Manufacturing Co.*
Rourke-Eno Paper / *Alco Standard Corp.*
Saxon / *Saxon Industries Inc.*
SCM / *SCM Corp.*
Scotch / *Minnesota Mining and Manufacturing Co. (3M)*
Scotchban / *Minnesota Mining and Manufacturing Co. (3M)*
SelecTone / *Westvaco Corp.*
Seneca Paper / *Alco Standard Corp.*
Sheaffer / *Textron Inc.*
Sign Master* / *Dennison Manufacturing Co.*
Site Ease / *Dennison Manufacturing Co.*
Skil/Chek / *Dennison Manufacturing Co.*
SLT / *Dennison Manufacturing Co.*
Smith-Corona / *SCM Corp.*
Soft Touch / *American Greetings Corporation*
Special Occasion / *Dennison Manufacturing Co.*
Sperry / *Sperry Corp.*
Spin-Print / *Dennison Manufacturing Co.*
Stanbond / *Standard Register Co.*
Standard Register / *Standard Register Co.*
Stanset / *Standard Register Co.*
Stanwid / *Standard Register Co.*
Statrol / *Dennison Manufacturing Co.*
Stenocraft / *Jim Walter Corp.*
Stenso / *Dennison Manufacturing Co.*
Sterling / *Borden Inc.*
Stickless / *Dennison Manufacturing Co.*
Stix-All / *Borden Inc.*
Stix-A-Lot / *Dennison Manufacturing Co.*
Strathmore Bond / *Hammermill Paper Co.*
Stripflex / *Dennison Manufacturing Co.*
Style-Riter / *Dennison Manufacturing Co.*
Success / *RCA Corp.*
Super Kleen Cote / *Dennison Manufacturing Co.*
Super Quink / *Parker Pen Co.*
Supreme / *Jim Walter Corp.*
Swingline Stapler / *American Brands Inc.*
Tabulink / *Dennison Manufacturing Co.*
Ticonderoga / *Dixon Ticonderoga Co.*
Trans-Liter / *Dennison Manufacturing Co.*
Trim-Tip / *Dennison Manufacturing Co.*
Ufonic / *Jostens Inc.*
Univac / *Sperry Corp.*
Universal Paper / *Alco Standard Corp.*
Urchins / *American Greetings Corporation*
Valentine Sands / *Textron Inc.*
Veritrac / *Pitney-Bowes Inc.*
Vinylbond / *Dennison Manufacturing Co.*
Voracryl / *Dennison Manufacturing Co.*
Wedge-Lok* / *Dennison Manufacturing Co.*
Weircliff / *Dennison Manufacturing Co.*
White Glove / *Dennison Manufacturing Co.*
Wilson Jones / *American Brands Inc.*
Wisco / *Great Northern Nekoosa Corp.*
Woman to Woman / *American Greetings Corporation*
Wonder Bond / *Borden Inc.*
Wordsworth / *Dennison Manufacturing Co.*
Write Bros. / *Gillette Co.*
Wyomissing / *Alco Standard Corp.*
X-Pert / *Dennison Manufacturing Co.*
X-Tra-Liter / *Dennison Manufacturing Co.*
Ziggy / *American Greetings Corporation*
Zilog / *Exxon Corp.*
Zipset / *Standard Register Co.*
5 O'clock / *Dennison Manufacturing Co.*

Perfumes & Toiletries

Acqua di Selva / *MEM Co.*
Alexandra / *Squibb Corp.*
Andiamo / *Revlon Inc.*
Aphrodisia / *Faberge Inc.*
Aromance / *Squibb Corp.*
Aromance 2001 Disk Player / *Squibb Corp.*
Aston / *Squibb Corp.*
Babe / *Faberge Inc.*
Bill Blass for Women / *Revlon Inc.*

Blue Jeans / *American Cyanamid Company*
Blue Stratos / *American Cyanamid Company*
Braggi / *Revlon Inc.*
British Sterling / *Textron Inc.*
Brut 33 / *Faberge Inc.*
Cabriole / *Eli Lilly & Co.*
Calvin Klein / *Minnetonka Inc.*
Caring / *MEM Co.*
Caron / *A.H. Robins Co. Inc*
Carven / *American Cyanamid Company*
Cavale / *Faberge Inc.*
Cerissa / *Revlon Inc.*
Chaps / *Warner Communications Inc.*
Charivari / *Squibb Corp.*
Charlie / *Revlon Inc.*
Chaz / *Revlon Inc.*
Check Up / *Minnetonka Inc.*
Chloe / *Eli Lilly & Co.*
Ciara / *Revlon Inc.*
CIE / *American Cyanamid Company*
Colourscents / *Revlon Inc.*
Coty / *Pfizer Inc.*
Countess Isserlyn / *Squibb Corp.*
Country Diary / *Minnetonka Inc.*
Crepe de Chine / *Sterling Drug Inc.*
Dayfresh / *Kimberly-Clark Corp.*
Derma Scrub / *Minnetonka Inc.*
Djerkiss / *Nestle-LeMur Co.*
Elizabeth Arden / *Eli Lilly & Co.*
Embracing / *MEM Co.*
English Leather / *MEM Co.*
Enjoli / *Squibb Corp.*
Enjoli Midnight / *Squibb Corp.*
Faberge / *Faberge Inc.*
Fenjala / *Johnson & Johnson*
Fleurs de Jontue / *Revlon Inc.*
Flora Danica / *Swank Inc.*
Forever Krystle / *Squibb Corp.*
Fresh Music / *Squibb Corp.*
Geoffrey Beene / *American Cyanamid Company*
Gianni Versace / *Squibb Corp.*
Gianni Versace Pour L'Homme / *Squibb Corp.*
Grey Flannel / *American Cyanamid Company*
Hai-Karate / *Pfizer Inc.*
Halston/Orlane / *Beatrice Companies Inc.*
Institute Swiss / *Minnetonka Inc.*
Jade East / *Swank Inc.*
John Weitz / *MEM Co.*
Jontue / *Revlon Inc.*
Khara / *Norton Simon Inc.*
Kouros / *Squibb Corp.*
Lagerfeld / *Eli Lilly & Co.*
L'Air du Temps / *American Cyanamid Company*
L'Homme / *Minnetonka Inc.*
Lov'me / *Nestle-LeMur Co.*
Lucien Lelong / *Nestle-LeMur Co.*
Macho / *Faberge Inc.*
Manpower / *Greyhound Corp.*
Marchand / *Nestle-LeMur Co.*
Mavis / *Nestle-LeMur Co.*
Max Factor / *Beatrice Companies Inc.*
Moisture Quotient (M2) / *Helene Curtis Industries Inc.*
Monsieur Balmain / *Revlon Inc.*
Musk / *MEM Co.*
Nina Ricci / *American Cyanamid Company*
Obsession / *Minnetonka Inc.*
Old Spice / *American Cyanamid Company*
Opium / *Squibb Corp.*
Parfumes Corday / *Norton Simon Inc.*
Parfums Pierre Cardin / *American Cyanamid Company*
Perfumatics 2000 / *Revlon Inc.*
Pierre Cardin / *Swank Inc.*
Pierre Cardin / *American Cyanamid Company*
Pinaud / *Nestle-LeMur Co.*
Pique / *Redken Laboratories Inc.*
Polo / *Warner Communications Inc.*
Pour Homme / *Squibb Corp.*
Racquet Club / *MEM Co.*
Rive Gauche / *Squibb Corp.*
Roger & Gallet / *Minnetonka Inc.*
Roman Brio / *Pfizer Inc.*
Royal Copenhagen / *Swank Inc.*
Scoundrel / *Revlon Inc.*
Seaforth / *Nestle-LeMur Co.*
Sean / *Jhirmack Enterprises Inc.*
Sharing / *MEM Co.*
Speidel / *Textron Inc.*
Stan-Homme / *Stanhome, Inc.*
Stephen Burrows / *Norton Simon Inc.*
Tabac / *American Cyanamid Company*
Tender Touch / *Helene Curtis Industries Inc.*
Tigress / *Faberge Inc.*
Timberline / *MEM Co.*
Tuxedo / *Warner Communications Inc.*
Village / *Minnetonka Inc.*
Wind Drift / *MEM Co.*
Woodhue / *Faberge Inc.*
Y / *Squibb Corp.*
YSL / *Squibb Corp.*
Yu / *Nestle-LeMur Co.*
Zizanie / *Faberge Inc.*

Personal Care Products

Acnaveen / *Cooper Laboratories, Inc.*
Adorn / *Gillette Co.*
Advent / *Conair Corp.*
Aeroshave / *American Home Products Corp.*
Afro Sheen / *Johnson Products Co. Inc.*
Alberto Balsam / *Alberto Culver Co.*
Alberto Jojoba / *Alberto Culver Co.*
Alberto Mousse / *Alberto Culver Co.*
Alberto VO5 / *Alberto Culver Co.*
Algele / *Jhirmack Enterprises Inc.*
Almay / *Beatrice Companies Inc.*
Alpha Keri / *Bristol Myers Co.*
Always / *Procter & Gamble Co.*
Ammens Powder / *Bristol Myers Co.*
Anchor Brush / *North American Philips Corp.*
Anyday / *Kimberly-Clark Corp.*
Apple Pectin / *La Maur Inc.*
Apricot Hand & Body Lotion / *Shaklee Corp.*
Aquamarine / *Revlon Inc.*
Aquanet / *Faberge Inc.*
Arrange® Hair Spray / *Shaklee Corp.*
Arrid / *Carter-Wallace Inc.*
Assure / *Johnson & Johnson*
Atra / *Gillette Co.*
Atra Plus / *Gillette Co.*
Attends / *Procter & Gamble Co.*
Atune / *Helene Curtis Industries Inc.*
Aveeno / *Cooper Laboratories, Inc.*
Avert / *Kimberly-Clark Corp.*
Bain de Soleil / *Squibb Corp.*
Ballet / *Kimberly-Clark Corp.*
Ban / *Bristol Myers Co.*
Band-Aid / *Johnson & Johnson*
Bantu / *Johnson Products Co. Inc.*
Barbasol / *Pfizer Inc.*
Basic Skin Care Trios / *Shaklee Corp.*
Bath Essence Bubble Bath / *Shaklee Corp.*
BDB / *Del Laboratories Inc.*
Beautifax / *La Maur Inc.*
Ben Gay / *Pfizer Inc.*
Bic Lady Shaver / *Bic Corp.*
Bic Lighter / *Bic Corp.*
Bic Shaver / *Bic Corp.*
Bic Shaver for Sensitive Skin / *Bic Corp.*
Bit-o-wax / *John O. Butler Co.*
Blazer / *Colgate-Palmolive Co.*
Blondit / *MEM Co.*
Body On Tap / *Bristol Myers Co.*
Body Plus / *La Maur Inc.*
Born Blonde / *Bristol Myers Co.*
Boutique / *Kimberly-Clark Corp.*
Breck / *American Cyanamid Company*
Brevia / *Kimberly-Clark Corp.*
Brush Plus / *Gillette Co.*
Buf-Puf / *Minnesota Mining and Manufacturing Co. (3M)*
Butler / *John O. Butler Co.*
Cabbage Patch Kids / *Riegel Textile Corp.*
Camay / *Procter & Gamble Co.*
Carefree / *Johnson & Johnson*
Caryl Richards / *Faberge Inc.*
Cashmere Bouquet / *Colgate-Palmolive Co.*
Casuals / *Kimberly-Clark Corp.*
Cellucotton / *Kimberly-Clark Corp.*
Cellutrol / *Ronco Teleproducts Inc.*
Ceramic Glaze / *Faberge Inc.*
ChapStick / *A.H. Robins Co. Inc*
Claire Burke / *Minnetonka Inc.*
Clairesse / *Bristol Myers Co.*
Clairmist / *Bristol Myers Co.*
Clairol / *Bristol Myers Co.*
Classy Curl / *Johnson Products Co. Inc.*
Clean & Clear / *Revlon Inc.*
Clear-Dip / *John O. Butler Co.*
Clinical Response / *Redken Laboratories Inc.*
Coast / *Procter & Gamble Co.*
CoEts / *Johnson & Johnson*
Colgate / *Colgate-Palmolive Co.*
Collegev Complex / *Revlon Inc.*
Conair Perm / *Conair Corp.*
Conair Thermal Protection / *Conair Corp.*
Condition / *Bristol Myers Co.*
Confidents / *Scott Paper Co.*
Consort / *Alberto Culver Co.*
Coppertone / *Schering-Plough Corp.*
Courant / *Colgate-Palmolive Co.*
Cream of Nature / *Revlon Inc.*
Crest / *Procter & Gamble Co.*
Cruex / *Pennwalt Corp.*
Cuticura / *Purex Industries, Inc.*
Daisy / *Gillette Co.*
Danex / *SmithKline Beckman Corp.*
Denalen / *American Home Products Corp.*
Denorex / *American Home Products Corp.*
Deodorant Cream / *Shaklee Corp.*
Depend / *Kimberly-Clark Corp.*
Dermassage / *Colgate-Palmolive Co.*
Desenex / *Pennwalt Corp.*
Desert Flower / *American Cyanamid Company*
Desert Wind® Roll-On Deodorant / *Shaklee Corp.*
Directories / *Seligman & Latz Inc.*
Dr. Wild & Design / *Edison Brothers Stores Inc.*

Drixoral / *Schering-Plough Corp.*
Dry Idea / *Gillette Co.*
Dry Look / *Gillette Co.*
EarthBorn / *Gillette Co.*
Eez-Thru / *John O. Butler Co.*
EFA / *Jhirmack Enterprises Inc.*
Efferdent / *Warner-Lambert Co.*
Effergrip / *Warner-Lambert Co.*
Egyptian Henna / *Nestle-LeMur Co.*
Emulave / *Cooper Laboratories, Inc.*
Enden / *Helene Curtis Industries Inc.*
Esoterica / *Revlon Inc.*
Everynight / *Helene Curtis Industries Inc.*
Existence / *Colgate-Palmolive Co.*
Fanci-Full / *Revlon Inc.*
Farrah-Fawcett / *Faberge Inc.*
FDS / *Alberto Culver Co.*
Felicity / *Esmark Inc.*
Fem Mist / *La Maur Inc.*
Fems / *Kimberly-Clark Corp.*
Final Finish / *Edison Brothers Stores Inc.*
Final Net / *Bristol Myers Co.*
Finesse / *Helene Curtis Industries Inc.*
Flossmate / *John O. Butler Co.*
Foamy / *Gillette Co.*
Foamy Gel / *Gillette Co.*
Foot Cream / *Shaklee Corp.*
Foot Fixer / *Bristol Myers Co.*
Fresh / *Pennwalt Corp.*
Futura / *Kimberly-Clark Corp.*
Gee Your Hair Smells Terrific / *American Brands Inc.*
Gelave / *Jhirmack Enterprises Inc.*
Gentle Touch / *American Brands Inc.*
Gentle Treatment / *Johnson Products Co. Inc.*
Get Set / *Alberto Culver Co.*
Gillette / *Gillette Co.*
Gleem / *Procter & Gamble Co.*
Gloss-8 / *Schering-Plough Corp.*
Good News / *Gillette Co.*
G.U.M. / *John O. Butler Co.*
Hair's Daily Requirement / *Revlon Inc.*
Hard As Nails / *Del Laboratories Inc.*
Head & Shoulders / *Procter & Gamble Co.*
Heaven Scent / *Colgate-Palmolive Co.*
Hi & Dri / *Revlon Inc.*
Hydro-Minerali / *Revlon Inc.*
Hydron / *National Patent Development Corp.*
Iolab / *Johnson & Johnson*
Ion / *La Maur Inc.*
Irish Spring / *Colgate-Palmolive Co.*
Ivory / *Procter & Gamble Co.*
Jean Nate / *Squibb Corp.*
Jergens / *American Brands Inc.*
Jeri / *Rorer Group Inc.*
Jheri Redding milk 'n honee / *Conair Corp.*
Jheri Redding mousse / *Conair Corp.*
Jhirmack / *Jhirmack Enterprises Inc.*
Jhirmack / *Beatrice Companies Inc.*
Johnson's Dental Floss / *Johnson & Johnson*
Just Wonderful / *Faberge Inc.*
Kimbies / *Kimberly-Clark Corp.*
Kindness / *Bristol Myers Co.*
Kleenguard / *Kimberly-Clark Corp.*
Kotex / *Kimberly-Clark Corp.*
La Cross / *Del Laboratories Inc.*
La Maur / *La Maur Inc.*
La Prairie / *American Cyanamid Company*
Lady Schick / *North American Philips Corp.*
Lady Shaklee Body Creme / *Shaklee Corp.*
Lady's Choice / *American Cyanamid Company*
Lava / *Procter & Gamble Co.*
Lavocol / *Warner-Lambert Co.*
Le Mur / *Nestle-LeMur Co.*
Leather Lotion / *Edison Brothers Stores Inc.*
Leather Raincoat / *Edison Brothers Stores Inc.*
Leeming/Pacquin / *Pfizer Inc.*
Liberte / *Kimberly-Clark Corp.*
Lightdays / *Kimberly-Clark Corp.*
Lilt / *Procter & Gamble Co.*
Little Travelers / *Kimberly-Clark Corp.*
Loving Care / *Bristol Myers Co.*
Lys / *Kimberly-Clark Corp.*
Man Care Collection / *North American Philips Corp.*
Man Size / *Kimberly-Clark Corp.*
Maxithins / *Tambrands Inc.*
Meadow Blend® Soap-Free Cleansing Bar / *Shaklee Corp.*
Meadow Blend® Soap-Free Liquid Cleanser / *Shaklee Corp.*
Melanex® Topical Solution / *Neutrogena Corporation*
Mersene / *Colgate-Palmolive Co.*
Mill Creek / *Richardson-Vicks Inc.*
Modern Ortho / *Papercraft Corp.*
Modess / *Johnson & Johnson*
Moisture Formula / *Johnson Products Co. Inc.*
Moisture Renewal / *Redken Laboratories Inc.*
Moisturphlex / *Jhirmack Enterprises Inc.*
Moroline / *Schering-Plough Corp.*
Musk Dusk / *La Maur Inc.*
Nair / *Carter-Wallace Inc.*
Namel Dry / *La Maur Inc.*
Natural Honey / *Revlon Inc.*
Natural Man / *La Maur Inc.*
Natural Wonder Super Nails / *Revlon Inc.*
Naturally Blonde / *Bristol Myers Co.*

Nature's Sunshine / *Nature's Sunshine Products, Inc.*
NCA / *Jhirmack Enterprises Inc.*
Neet / *American Home Products Corp.*
Nestle / *Nestle-LeMur Co.*
Neutrogena / *Neutrogena Corporation*
Neutrogena Origine Suisse System™ / *Neutrogena Corporation*
New Concept® Organic Dentifrice / *Shaklee Corp.*
New Dawn II / *Alberto Culver Co.*
New Era / *La Maur Inc.*
New Freedom / *Kimberly-Clark Corp.*
New Lengths / *Del Laboratories Inc.*
Nice 'n Easy / *Bristol Myers Co.*
Norwegian Formula Hand Cream / *Neutrogena Corporation*
Noxzema / *Noxell Corp.*
Nucleic A / *La Maur Inc.*
Nutri-Pak / *Jhirmack Enterprises Inc.*
Nutri-Tonic / *Del Laboratories Inc.*
O.B. / *Johnson & Johnson*
Ogilvie / *Sterling Drug Inc.*
Oil of Olay / *Richardson-Vicks Inc.*
OP / *Schering-Plough Corp.*
Orajel / *Del Laboratories Inc.*
Oral B / *Cooper Laboratories, Inc.*
PAAS / *Schering-Plough Corp.*
Pacquin / *Pfizer Inc.*
Palmolive Gold / *Colgate-Palmolive Co.*
Paula Kent / *Redken Laboratories Inc.*
Payless / *Pay Less Drug Stores Northwest Inc.*
Pearl Drops / *Carter-Wallace Inc.*
Perio-pic / *John O. Butler Co.*
Perma Soft / *La Maur Inc.*
Personal Touch / *Warner-Lambert Co.*
Pert / *Procter & Gamble Co.*
Petal Soft / *Tambrands Inc.*
PH Plus / *Redken Laboratories Inc.*
PHinale / *Jhirmack Enterprises Inc.*
PhisoDan / *Sterling Drug Inc.*
PhisoDerm / *Sterling Drug Inc.*
Piz Buin / *Bristol Myers Co.*
Plakfinder / *John O. Butler Co.*
Playtex / *Esmark Inc.*
Plus Platinum / *Warner-Lambert Co.*
Prell / *Procter & Gamble Co.*
PreSun / *Bristol Myers Co.*
Pretty Feet & Hands / *Revlon Inc.*
Protect / *Marion Laboratories Inc.*
Protect / *John O. Butler Co.*
Proteinized Shampoo / *Shaklee Corp.*
Proxabrush / *John O. Butler Co.*
Purpose / *Johnson & Johnson*
Quantum / *Helene Curtis Industries Inc.*
Quick Tan (Q.T.) / *Schering-Plough Corp.*
Rain Coat / *Edison Brothers Stores Inc.*
Rainbath / *Neutrogena Corporation*
Rainsilk™ Hair Care Products / *Shaklee Corp.*
Rain-Tree / *Noxell Corp.*
Rapid Shave / *Colgate-Palmolive Co.*
Rayette / *Faberge Inc.*
Reach / *Johnson & Johnson*
Realistic / *Revlon Inc.*
Red Cote / *John O. Butler Co.*
Redken / *Redken Laboratories Inc.*
Redken/Lapinal / *Redken Laboratories Inc.*
Rejuvia / *Del Laboratories Inc.*
Respond / *Colgate-Palmolive Co.*
Revco / *Revco D.S. Inc.*
Rheaban / *Pfizer Inc.*
Right Guard / *Gillette Co.*
Right-Kind/Sub-G / *John O. Butler Co.*
Rise / *Carter-Wallace Inc.*
Rite Aid / *Rite Aid Corp.*
RK for Men / *Redken Laboratories Inc.*
Roux / *Revlon Inc.*
Royal Persian Henna / *Conair Corp.*
Safeguard / *Procter & Gamble Co.*
Saf-Tip / *Warner-Lambert Co.*
Sally Hansen / *Del Laboratories Inc.*
Sardo / *Schering-Plough Corp.*
Sardoettes / *Schering-Plough Corp.*
Satin Collection / *North American Philips Corp.*
Saxon / *Richardson-Vicks Inc.*
Schick / *Warner-Lambert Co.*
Schick / *North American Philips Corp.*
Schick-Super II / *Warner-Lambert Co.*
Scholl / *Schering-Plough Corp.*
Scope / *Procter & Gamble Co.*
Sea & Ski / *Carter-Wallace Inc.*
Secret / *Procter & Gamble Co.*
Security / *Kimberly-Clark Corp.*
Selsun Blue / *Abbott Laboratories*
Shade / *Schering-Plough Corp.*
Shaklee Classics Beauty Products / *Shaklee Corp.*
Shaklee Naturals Skin Care and Hair Care Products / *Shaklee Corp.*
Shape Ups / *Conair Corp.*
Sheeld / *Edison Brothers Stores Inc.*
Shepard's / *Rorer Group Inc.*
Shower-to-Shower / *Johnson & Johnson*
Showtime / *Schering-Plough Corp.*
Silkience / *Gillette Co.*
Skin Dew / *Colgate-Palmolive Co.*
Skin Life / *Colgate-Palmolive Co.*
Smile Factory / *John O. Butler Co.*
Smooth Touch / *Schering-Plough Corp.*

Snuggems / *Kimberly-Clark Corp.*
So Dry / *American Cyanamid Company*
Soft & Dri / *Gillette Co.*
Softique / *Kimberly-Clark Corp.*
SoftSoap / *Minnetonka Inc.*
Solarcaine / *Schering-Plough Corp.*
Special Skin Care Products / *Shaklee Corp.*
Speed Shine / *Edison Brothers Stores Inc.*
Spray Net / *Helene Curtis Industries Inc.*
Stayfree / *Johnson & Johnson*
Steri-Pad / *Johnson & Johnson*
Style / *La Maur Inc.*
Styling Research / *Redken Laboratories Inc.*
Suave / *Helene Curtis Industries Inc.*
Sudden Beauty Facial / *American Home Products Corp.*
Sudden Tan / *Schering-Plough Corp.*
Sulfur-8 / *Schering-Plough Corp.*
Sundown / *Johnson & Johnson*
Sun-In / *Chattem, Inc.*
Super Chromium / *Warner-Lambert Co.*
Sure / *Procter & Gamble Co.*
Sure & Natural Maxishields / *Johnson & Johnson*
Sweet-Heart / *Purex Industries, Inc.*
Tame / *Gillette Co.*
Tampax / *Tambrands Inc.*
Taper-Line / *John O. Butler Co.*
TCB / *Alberto Culver Co.*
T/Derm® Tar Emollient / *Neutrogena Corporation*
Techmatic / *Gillette Co.*
Terme de Montecatini / *Revlon Inc.*
T/Gel® Therapeutic Shampoo / *Neutrogena Corporation*
Thin-Line / *John O. Butler Co.*
Tiarra / *Nature's Sunshine Products, Inc.*
Tickle / *Bristol Myers Co.*
Tinactin / *Schering-Plough Corp.*
Ting / *Pennwalt Corp.*
Tioga® Men's Cologne / *Shaklee Corp.*
Tioga® Men's Skin Conditioner / *Shaklee Corp.*
Tip Top / *Faberge Inc.*
Tiss / *Kimberly-Clark Corp.*
Tone / *Greyhound Corp.*
Toni Home Permanents / *Gillette Co.*
Trac II / *Gillette Co.*
Travel Care Collection / *North American Philips Corp.*
Trav-Ler / *John O. Butler Co.*
TRESemme / *Alberto Culver Co.*
Tropical Blend / *Schering-Plough Corp.*
Tucks / *Warner-Lambert Co.*
Tuff-Spun / *John O. Butler Co.*
Ultra Brite / *Colgate-Palmolive Co.*
Ultra Sheen / *Johnson Products Co. Inc.*
Ultra Sheen's Precise / *Johnson Products Co. Inc.*
Ultra Star / *Johnson Products Co. Inc.*
Ultra Wave / *Johnson Products Co. Inc.*
Ultraswim / *American Cyanamid Company*
Ultrex / *Warner-Lambert Co.*
Uniperm / *Helene Curtis Industries Inc.*
Vanseb / *SmithKline Beckman Corp.*
Velvet Tip / *John O. Butler Co.*
Vetar / *Rorer Group Inc.*
Vidal Sassoon / *Richardson-Vicks Inc.*
Vintage Bubble Bath / *MEM Co.*
Vita E / *La Maur Inc.*
Vitalis / *Bristol Myers Co.*
Vogue / *Kimberly-Clark Corp.*
White Bright / *Edison Brothers Stores Inc.*
White Rain / *Gillette Co.*
Wilkinson / *Colgate-Palmolive Co.*
Wondra / *Procter & Gamble Co.*
Woodbury / *American Brands Inc.*
Zero / *National Patent Development Corp.*
Zest / *Procter & Gamble Co.*
24 Hour / *La Maur Inc.*

Pet Products & Animal Foods

Alley Cat / *Ralston Purina Co.*
Amore / *H.J. Heinz Co.*
Avitron / *Carter-Wallace Inc.*
Bonkers / *Beatrice Companies Inc.*
Bonnie / *Savannah Foods & Industries Inc.*
Bonz / *Ralston Purina Co.*
Bright Eyes / *Carnation Company*
Buffet / *Carnation Company*
Butcher Bones / *Nabisco Brands Inc.*
Butcher's Blend / *Ralston Purina Co.*
Cadillac / *United States Tobacco Co.*
Chef's Blend / *Carnation Company*
Chow / *Ralston Purina Co.*
Chuck Wagon / *Ralston Purina Co.*
Classic / *Carnation Company*
Come 'n' Get It / *Carnation Company*
Come 'N Get It Puppy Formula / *Carnation Company*
Country Cousin / *Carnation Company*
Cycle / *Anderson, Clayton & Co.*
Dry Kitten Chow / *Ralston Purina Co.*
Fancy Feast / *Carnation Company*
Field 'n Farm / *Ralston Purina Co.*
Fish Ahoy / *Carnation Company*

Fit & Trim / *Ralston Purina Co.*
Fresh 'n' Clean / *Carter-Wallace Inc.*
Fresh Step / *Clorox*
Friskies / *Carnation Company*
Friskies Buffet / *Carnation Company*
Friskies Dinners / *Carnation Company*
Gaines Burgers / *Anderson, Clayton & Co.*
Geisler / *ConAgra Inc.*
Glamor Puss / *CHB Foods Inc.*
Golden Choice / *Savannah Foods & Industries Inc.*
Good Mews / *Ralston Purina Co.*
Gravy Train / *Anderson, Clayton & Co.*
Happy Cat / *Ralston Purina Co.*
Hearty / *Carnation Company*
Hero / *Ralston Purina Co.*
Hills / *Colgate-Palmolive Co.*
Jerky / *H.J. Heinz Co.*
Kat Nip / *Safeway Stores Inc.*
Ken-L Ration / *Quaker Oats Co.*
Kibbles 'n Bits / *Quaker Oats Co.*
Lassie / *Carter-Wallace Inc.*
Linatone / *Carter-Wallace Inc.*
Litter Green / *Clorox*
Lovin Spoonfuls / *Ralston Purina Co.*
Meaty Bone / *H.J. Heinz Co.*
Meow Mix / *Ralston Purina Co.*
Mighty Dog / *Carnation Company*
Milk-Bone / *Nabisco Brands Inc.*
Moist & Chunky / *Ralston Purina Co.*
Pard / *Savannah Foods & Industries Inc.*
Perk / *CHB Foods Inc.*
Petuna / *CHB Foods Inc.*
Pooch / *Safeway Stores Inc.*
Purina / *Ralston Purina Co.*
Puss 'n Boots / *Quaker Oats Co.*
Recipe / *Campbell Soup Co.*
Sea Dog / *Ralston Purina Co.*
Sergeant's / *A.H. Robins Co. Inc*
Sherwood Forest / *International Multifoods Corp.*
Skippy / *CHB Foods Inc.*
Snausages / *Quaker Oats Co.*
Splash / *Savannah Foods & Industries Inc.*
Sportmix / *Savannah Foods & Industries Inc.*
Strong Heart / *Esmark Inc.*
Sturdy / *CHB Foods Inc.*
Teltra / *Warner-Lambert Co.*
Tender Chunks / *Quaker Oats Co.*
Theralin / *Carter-Wallace Inc.*
Top Choice / *Anderson, Clayton & Co.*
Twinco / *Carter-Wallace Inc.*
Vets / *CHB Foods Inc.*
Victory / *Carter-Wallace Inc.*
Wells / *Savannah Foods & Industries Inc.*
Whisker Lickins / *Ralston Purina Co.*
"Woodstocks" / *ConAgra Inc.*
9 Lives / *H.J. Heinz Co.*

Photographic Products

Agfa / *GAF Corp.*
Ascor / *Berkey Photo, Inc.*
Bell & Howell / *Bell & Howell Co.*
Berkey / *Berkey Photo, Inc.*
Camera Art / *Carnation Company*
Canon / *Canon, Inc.*
Colorcraft / *Fuqua Industries Inc.*
Direct Photo / *Berkey Photo, Inc.*
Eastman / *Eastman Kodak Co.*
GAF / *GAF Corp.*
Gossen / *Berkey Photo, Inc.*
Kelly Film / *Berkey Photo, Inc.*
Ladd / *Warner Communications Inc.*
Omega / *Berkey Photo, Inc.*
Pana-Vue / *GAF Corp.*
Photo Decals / *Berkey Photo, Inc.*
Photo Gallery / *Berkey Photo, Inc.*
Polaroid / *Polaroid Corp.*
Portrait World / *Fotomat Corp.*
Rodenstock / *Berkey Photo, Inc.*
Rollei / *Berkey Photo, Inc.*
System80 / *Jostens Inc.*
Technicolor / *Technicolor Inc.*
Viewmaster / *GAF Corp.*
Viking / *Fuqua Industries Inc.*
Zero Halliburton / *Berkey Photo, Inc.*
3M / *Minnesota Mining and Manufacturing Co. (3M)*

Publishing and Printers

A Spectrum Book / *Gulf* + Western Industries Inc.
Aardvark / *McGraw-Hill Inc.*
Academic Press / *Harcourt Brace Jovanovich Inc.*
ACC / *Gulf* + Western Industries Inc.
Ace Books / *Filmways Inc.*
Advertiser / *Multimedia Inc.*
The Advocate / *Times Mirror Co.*
Agnew Tech-Tran / *Macmillan Inc.*
Alabama Journal / *Multimedia Inc.*

Alex / *Gulf* + Western Industries Inc.
American / *Gannett Co. Inc.*
American Demographics / *Dow Jones & Company Inc.*
American Machinist / *McGraw-Hill Inc.*
American Photographer / *CBS Inc.*
American-News / *Knight-Ridder Newspapers Inc.*
The Answer / *Houghton Mifflin Co.*
Apartment Life / *Meredith Corp.*
Appleton-Century-Crofts / *Gulf* + Western Industries Inc.
Architectural Record / *McGraw-Hill Inc.*
Archway / *Gulf* + Western Industries Inc.
Arco / *Prentice-Hall Inc.*
Arco / *Gulf* + Western Industries Inc.
Argus Leader / *Gannett Co. Inc.*
Argus / *Gannett Co. Inc.*
The Ashland City Times / *Multimedia Inc.*
Asian Wall St. Journal / *Dow Jones & Company Inc.*
The Asian Wall Street Journal Weekly / *Dow Jones & Company Inc.*
Associated Music Publisher / *Macmillan Inc.*
Audio / *CBS Inc.*
Automotive Retailer Publishing / *Harcourt Brace Jovanovich Inc.*
Aviation Week / *McGraw-Hill Inc.*
Backpacker / *CBS Inc.*
Ballinger / *Harper & Row Publishers Inc.*
Bank Street Writer / *Scholastic Inc.*
Banner-Independent / *New York Times Co.*
Barnes & Noble / *Harper & Row Publishers Inc.*
Barrington Publications / *Gulf* + Western Industries Inc.
Barron's / *Dow Jones & Company Inc.*
Basic Books / *Harper & Row Publishers Inc.*
Basin Week / *Harte-Hanks Communications Inc.*
Baxter Bulletin / *Multimedia Inc.*
BBP / *Gulf* + Western Industries Inc.
Beacon Journal / *Knight-Ridder Newspapers Inc.*
Beacon Press / *Media General Inc.*
Bennett Publishing / *Macmillan Inc.*
Benziger / *Macmillan Inc.*
Berkeley / *MCA Inc.*
Berlitz / *Macmillan Inc.*
Bert's Bargain Bonanza / *Harte-Hanks Communications Inc.*
Better Homes & Gardens / *Meredith Corp.*
BJ / *MCA Inc.*
Blair Inserts / *John Blair & Co.*
Blue Book of Pension Funds / *Gulf* + Western Industries Inc.
Blue Ribbon / *Scholastic Inc.*
Boating / *CBS Inc.*
Book of the Month Club / *Time Inc.*
Bookhill / *Harcourt Brace Jovanovich Inc.*
Bookthrift / *Gulf* + Western Industries Inc.
Bookware / *Gulf* + Western Industries Inc.
The Boston *Globe* / *Affiliated Publications Inc.*
BPC Design / *Gulf* + Western Industries Inc.
Bradbury Press / *Macmillan Inc.*
Brady / *Gulf* + Western Industries Inc.
Branzo's Valley Review / *Harte-Hanks Communications Inc.*
Brentwood Publishing Corp. / *Gulf* + Western Industries Inc.
BRS/Saunders / *CBS Inc.*
Buffalo Evening News / *Berkshire Hathaway Inc.*
Bureau of Business Practice / *Gulf* + Western Industries Inc.
Business Mailers / *Macmillan Inc.*
Business Week / *McGraw-Hill Inc.*
Bystream / *Harcourt Brace Jovanovich Inc.*
Byte / *McGraw-Hill Inc.*
Californian / *Gannett Co. Inc.*
Caller / *Harte-Hanks Communications Inc.*
Campbell Press / *Meredith Corp.*
Cape Cod Standard Times newspaper, Hyannis, Mass. / *Dow Jones & Company Inc.*
Car & Driver / *CBS Inc.*
Career Placement Registry, Inc. / *Plenum Publishing Corp.*
Cassell / *Macmillan Inc.*
Charles E. Merrill / *Bell & Howell Co.*
Chemical Engineering / *McGraw-Hill Inc.*
Chemical Week / *McGraw-Hill Inc.*
Childcraft / *Scott & Fetzer Co.*
Chilton Co. / *American Broadcasting Companies Inc.*
Chronicle Tribune / *Gannett Co. Inc.*
Citizen Register / *Gannett Co. Inc.*
Citizen / *Multimedia Inc.*
Citizen / *Gannett Co. Inc.*
Citizens Journal / *Capital Cities Communications Inc.*
Citizen-Times / *Multimedia Inc.*
City Press / *Meredith Corp.*
Clairborne Progress / *New York Times Co.*
Clarion Books / *Houghton Mifflin Co.*
Clarion-Ledger / *Gannett Co. Inc.*
The Classroom Answer / *Houghton Mifflin Co.*
Cliggott Publishing Co. / *Media General Inc.*
Coach / *Scholastic Inc.*
Coal Age / *McGraw-Hill Inc.*
Cole / *Metromedia Inc.*
Collamore Press / *Macmillan Inc.*
Collier Macmillan / *Macmillan Inc.*
Coloradoan / *Gannett Co. Inc.*
Comet / *New York Times Co.*

Commercial-News / *Gannett Co. Inc.*
Commercial / *New York Times Co.*
Companion Guides / *Gulf* + Western Industries Inc.
Consultants Bureau / *Plenum Publishing Corp.*
Co-Op Mailings / *Macmillan Inc.*
Cornerstone Library / *Gulf* + Western Industries Inc.
Coronado / *Harcourt Brace Jovanovich Inc.*
Coronado Journal / *Harte-Hanks Communications Inc.*
Courier-Democrat / *Harte-Hanks Communications Inc.*
Courier-News / *Gannett Co. Inc.*
Courier-Post / *Gannett Co. Inc.*
Courier / *Lee Enterprises Inc.*
Coward-McCann & Geoghegan Inc. / *MCA Inc.*
Cupertino Courier / *Meredith Corp.*
C.V. Mosby / *Times Mirror Co.*
Cycle World / *CBS Inc.*
Cycle / *CBS Inc.*
DaCapo Press / *Plenum Publishing Corp.*
Daily Camera / *Knight-Ridder Newspapers Inc.*
Daily Citizen / *Harte-Hanks Communications Inc.*
Daily Corinthian / *New York Times Co.*
Daily Courier / *New York Times Co.*
Daily Enterprise / *New York Times Co.*
Daily Leader / *Harte-Hanks Communications Inc.*
Daily Mail / *Harte-Hanks Communications Inc.*
Daily News Record / *Capital Cities Communications Inc.*
Daily News / *Knight-Ridder Newspapers Inc.*
Daily News / *Gannett Co. Inc.*
Daily News / *New York Times Co.*
Daily Olympian / *Gannett Co. Inc.*
Daily Record & Advertiser / *Harte-Hanks Communications Inc.*
Daily Register / *Capital Cities Communications Inc.*
Daily Tidings / *Capital Cities Communications Inc.*
Daily Times / *Knight-Ridder Newspapers Inc.*
Daily Transcript / *Post Corp.*
Daily World / *New York Times Co.*
Dansville Press / *Harcourt Brace Jovanovich Inc.*
Data Communications / *McGraw-Hill Inc.*
Data Resources / *McGraw-Hill Inc.*
Davidson Printing Co. / *Harcourt Brace Jovanovich Inc.*
DC / *Warner Communications Inc.*
D.C. Heath & Co. / *Raytheon Co.*
Dellen Publishing / *Macmillan Inc.*
Delmar / *Litton Industries Inc.*
Deltak / *Gulf* + Western Industries Inc.
Democrat & Advertiser / *Harte-Hanks Communications Inc.*
Democrat & Chronicle / *Gannett Co. Inc.*
Democrat-Herald / *Capital Cities Communications Inc.*
Democrat / *Knight-Ridder Newspapers Inc.*
Dickson Herald / *Multimedia Inc.*
Discover / *Time Inc.*
Dispatch / *Knight-Ridder Newspapers Inc.*
Dispatch / *New York Times Co.*
Dolphin Curricula / *Houghton Mifflin Co.*
Donnelley Directories / *Dun & Bradstreet Corp.*
Dow Jones / *Dow Jones & Company Inc.*
Dow Jones Books / *Dow Jones & Company Inc.*
Dow Jones News/Retrieval / *Dow Jones & Company Inc.*
Dow Jones Software Publishing / *Dow Jones & Company Inc.*
Dow Phone / *Dow Jones & Company Inc.*
Dryden Press / *CBS Inc.*
Eagle-Beacon / *Knight-Ridder Newspapers Inc.*
Eagle / *Harte-Hanks Communications Inc.*
Eagle / *Knight-Ridder Newspapers Inc.*
East San Jose Sun / *Meredith Corp.*
Echo / *Harte-Hanks Communications Inc.*
EEE - Eastern Economy Editions / *Gulf* + Western Industries Inc.
Electrical Construction & Maintenance / *McGraw-Hill Inc.*
Electronic Learning / *Scholastic Inc.*
Electronics Week / *McGraw-Hill Inc.*
EMIS / *McGraw-Hill Inc.*
Engineering News Record / *McGraw-Hill Inc.*
Enquirer & News / *Gannett Co. Inc.*
Enquirer / *Knight-Ridder Newspapers Inc.*
Enquirer / *Gannett Co. Inc.*
ERC - Executive Reports / *Gulf* + Western Industries Inc.
Erisa Benefit Funds / *Gulf* + Western Industries Inc.
Evening News / *Blue Chip Stamps*
Express Progress / *Harte-Hanks Communications Inc.*
Express / *Capital Cities Communications Inc.*
Express / *Harte-Hanks Communications Inc.*
F.A. Owen / *Harcourt Brace Jovanovich Inc.*
Family Circle / *New York Times Co.*
Family Computing / *Scholastic Inc.*
Famous Music Corp. / *Gulf* + Western Industries Inc.
Far Eastern Economic Review / *Dow Jones & Company Inc.*
Fashion Showcase / *Harte-Hanks Communications Inc.*
Field & Stream / *CBS Inc.*
Fireside / *Gulf* + Western Industries Inc.
Fleming H. Revell / *SFN Co.*
Flying / *CBS Inc.*

Food & Wine / *American Express Co.*
Forecast / *Scholastic Inc.*
Fortune / Time Inc.
Four Winds Press / *Macmillan Inc.*
The Free Press / *Macmillan Inc.*
Free Press / Dow Jones & Company Inc.
Free Press / Gannett Co. Inc.
Free Press / Knight-Ridder Newspapers Inc.
Frommer-Pasmantier / *Gulf +* Western Industries Inc.
Frye Copysystems / *Signal Companies Inc.*
Fryemaric / *Signal Companies Inc.*
Gallatin Examiner-News / Multimedia Inc.
Games / Playboy Enterprises Inc.
Gatlinburg Press / Harte-Hanks Communications Inc.
Gazette / Lee Enterprises Inc.
Gazette / Gannett Co. Inc.
Gazette-Times / Lee Enterprises Inc.
Get Along Gang / *Scholastic Inc.*
Ginn / *Xerox Corp.*
GIS / *Houghton Mifflin Co.*
Glencoe / *Macmillan Inc.*
Globe Corner Bookstore / *Affiliated Publications Inc.*
Globe Pequot Press / *Affiliated Publications Inc.*
Globe-Gazette / Lee Enterprises Inc.
Globe / Dow Jones & Company Inc.
Golden West Publishing / *Media General Inc.*
Golf Digest / New York Times Co.
Golf World / New York Times Co.
Golf / Times Mirror Co.
Graduating Engineer / McGraw-Hill Inc.
Great American Magazines / *Avon Products Inc.*
Greenwave / *Harte-Hanks Communications Inc.*
Grosset & Dunlap / *Filmways Inc.*
Grune & Stratton / *Harcourt Brace Jovanovich Inc.*
GuestInformant / *LIN Broadcasting Corp.*
Harper & Row / *Harper & Row Publishers Inc.*
Harper & Row School Division / *Macmillan Inc.*
Harry N. Abrams Co. / *Times Mirror Co.*
The Hartford Courant / Times Mirror Co.
Harvest/HBJ / *Harcourt Brace Jovanovich Inc.*
Health Care Services / *National Education Corp.*
Heavy Metal / *National Lampoon Inc.*
Herald Banner / Harte-Hanks Communications Inc.
Herald Dispatch / Gannett Co. Inc.
Herald Republic / Harte-Hanks Communications Inc.
Herald Statesmen / Gannett Co. Inc.
Herald-Journal / New York Times Co.
Herald-Review / Lee Enterprises Inc.
Herald / Washington Post Co.
Herald / Harte-Hanks Communications Inc.
Herald / Post Corp.
Herald / Knight-Ridder Newspapers Inc.
Herald / Gannett Co. Inc.
Herald / Knight-Ridder Newspapers Inc.
Herald-Tribune / New York Times Co.
High Fidelity / *American Broadcasting Companies Inc.*
Highlander Publications / *Media General Inc.*
History Book Club / *Harcourt Brace Jovanovich Inc.*
Hitchock Publishing Co. / *American Broadcasting Companies Inc.*
The H.M. Gousha Company / *Times Mirror Co.*
Holt, Rinehart & Winston / *CBS Inc.*
Home Buyers Guide / Harte-Hanks Communications Inc.
Home Mechanix / CBS Inc.
Homeowner / Harte-Hanks Communications Inc.
Houghton Mifflin Software / *Houghton Mifflin Co.*
HP Books / *Knight-Ridder Newspapers Inc.*
Hudson / *Litton Industries Inc.*
IBD - International Book Distributors / *Gulf +* Western Industries Inc.
IBP - Institute for Business Planning / *Gulf +* Western Industries Inc.
Idaho Statesmen / Gannett Co. Inc.
Ideal Publishing Corp. / *Filmways Inc.*
IFI/Plenum Data / *Plenum Publishing Corp.*
Impact / *Signal Companies Inc.*
Independent Record / Lee Enterprises Inc.
Independent / Dow Jones & Company Inc.
Independent / Harte-Hanks Communications Inc.
Independent / Meredith Corp.
Indiana Prairie Farmer / American Broadcasting Companies Inc.
Inquirer / Knight-Ridder Newspapers Inc.
Insight Guides / *Gulf +* Western Industries Inc.
Instructor Book Club / *Harcourt Brace Jovanovich Inc.*
International Management / McGraw-Hill Inc.
Item & Advertiser / Harte-Hanks Communications Inc.
Item / Gannett Co. Inc.
Item / Dow Jones & Company Inc.
Jackson *Daily News / Gannett Co. Inc.*
Jeppesen Sanderson / *Times Mirror Co.*
J.K. Lasser / *Gulf +* Western Industries Inc.
John Wiley / *John Wiley & Sons, Inc.*
Johnson Reprint / *Harcourt Brace Jovanovich Inc.*
Journal & Advertiser / Harte-Hanks Communications Inc.
Journal & Courier / Gannett Co. Inc.
Journal News / Harte-Hanks Communications Inc.

Journal of Commerce / *Knight-Ridder Newspapers Inc.*
Journal-News / *Gannett Co. Inc.*
Journal / *Lee Enterprises Inc.*
Journal / *Gannett Co. Inc.*
Journal-Times / *Lee Enterprises Inc.*
Jove / *MCA Inc.*
Julian Messner / *Gulf* + Western Industries Inc.
Kleenol / *Ronson Corp.*
K-Power / *Scholastic Inc.*
Kurt & Helen Wolff Books / *Harcourt Brace Jovanovich Inc.*
La Jolla Light / *Harte-Hanks Communications Inc.*
Law & Business Inc. / *Harcourt Brace Jovanovich Inc.*
Leader & Press / *Gannett Co. Inc.*
Leader Publishing Co. / *Harte-Hanks Communications Inc.*
Leaf Chronicle / *Multimedia Inc.*
Ledger / *Knight-Ridder Newspapers Inc.*
Ledger / *New York Times Co.*
Legal Times of Washington / *Harcourt Brace Jovanovich Inc.*
Leisureguides / *LIN Broadcasting Corp.*
Lexington Herald-Leader / *Knight-Ridder Newspapers Inc.*
Life News Publishing / *Harte-Hanks Communications Inc.*
Life / *Time Inc.*
Linden Press / *Gulf* + Western Industries Inc.
Lippincott / *Harper & Row Publishers Inc.*
Little Brown & Co. / *Time Inc.*
Little Nickel Want Ads / *Capital Cities Communications Inc.*
Little Simon / *Gulf* + Western Industries Inc.
Litton / *Litton Industries Inc.*
Long Shadow Books / *Gulf* + Western Industries Inc.
Los Angeles Times / *Times Mirror Co.*
Los Feliz Hills News / *Meredith Corp.*
Lothrop, Lee & Shepard / *SFN Co.*
Maclean Hunter / *Macmillan Inc.*
Macmillan / *Macmillan Inc.*
Macmillan Prof. Journals / *Macmillan Inc.*
Mad / *Warner Communications Inc.*
Mail Tribune / *Dow Jones & Company Inc.*
Marriage Mail™ / *John Blair & Co.*
Marshall Publishing / *Harte-Hanks Communications Inc.*
Marvel / *Cadence Industries Corp.*
Matthew Bender / *Times Mirror Co.*
McCormick-Mathers / *Litton Industries Inc.*
McGraw Hill / *McGraw-Hill Inc.*
McKnight Publishing / *Macmillan Inc.*
Media Journal / *Harte-Hanks Communications Inc.*
Mercury News / *Knight-Ridder Newspapers Inc.*
Messenger / *New York Times Co.*
Metals Week / *McGraw-Hill Inc.*
Microzine / *Scholastic Inc.*
Miller Publishing Co. / *American Broadcasting Companies Inc.*
Milpitas Post / *Meredith Corp.*
Missoulian / *Lee Enterprises Inc.*
Modern Bride / *CBS Inc.*
Modern Photography / *American Broadcasting Companies Inc.*
Modern Plastics / *McGraw-Hill Inc.*
Monarch / *Gulf* + Western Industries Inc.
Money / *Time Inc.*
Montana Standard / *Lee Enterprises Inc.*
Moultrie Weekly Observer / *Multimedia Inc.*
Mountain States Publishing Co. / *Harte-Hanks Communications Inc.*
Mountain View Sun / *Meredith Corp.*
Mountain Visitor / *Harte-Hanks Communications Inc.*
Multi-Fill / *Ronson Corp.*
Music City News / *Multimedia Inc.*
National Business & Employment Weekly / *Dow Jones & Company Inc.*
National Lampoon / *National Lampoon Inc.*
National Register Publishing / *Macmillan Inc.*
Nebraska Farmer Co. / *Harcourt Brace Jovanovich Inc.*
Network Mail / *John Blair & Co.*
New Mexican / *Gannett Co. Inc.*
New World Dictionaries / *Gulf* + Western Industries Inc.
New York Graphic Society / *Time Inc.*
New York Times Index / *New York Times Co.*
New York Times News Service / *New York Times Co.*
New York Times / *New York Times Co.*
News Democrat / *Capital Cities Communications Inc.*
News Herald / *Harte-Hanks Communications Inc.*
News Herald / *Gannett Co. Inc.*
News Messenger / *Harte-Hanks Communications Inc.*
News Messenger / *Gannett Co. Inc.*
News Sentinel / *Knight-Ridder Newspapers Inc.*
News Star / *Gannett Co. Inc.*
News-Banner / *Post Corp.*
News-Chief / *Multimedia Inc.*
Newsday / *Times Mirror Co.*
News-Leader / *New York Times Co.*
News-Leader / *Capital Cities Communications Inc.*
Piedmont Publishing / *Media General Inc.*
News-Press / *Gannett Co. Inc.*
News / *Dow Jones & Company Inc.*

News / *Harte-Hanks Communications Inc.*
News / *Capital Cities Communications Inc.*
News / *Knight-Ridder Newspapers Inc.*
News / *Multimedia Inc.*
News / *Post Corp.*
News / *New York Times Co.*
News / *Gannett Co. Inc.*
News-Times / *Dow Jones & Company Inc.*
News-Times / *Capital Cities Communications Inc.*
News-Topic / *New York Times Co.*
News-Tribune / *Post Corp.*
News-Tribune / *Knight-Ridder Newspapers Inc.*
Newsweek / *Washington Post Co.*
Next / *Litton Industries Inc.*
North Sun / *Meredith Corp.*
North Texas Publishing Co. / *Harte-Hanks Communications Inc.*
Northland Press / *Justin Industries Inc.*
Northwest Leader / *Meredith Corp.*
Norwich *Bulletin* / *Gannett Co. Inc.*
Nucleonics Week / *McGraw-Hill Inc.*
Oakland Press / *Capital Cities Communications Inc.*
Observer Dispatch / *Gannett Co. Inc.*
Observer / *Knight-Ridder Newspapers Inc.*
Ocean County Reporter / *Capital Cities Communications Inc.*
Official Airline Guides / *Dun & Bradstreet Corp.*
Oregon Statesman / *Gannett Co. Inc.*
Osborne Books / *McGraw-Hill Inc.*
Outdoor Life / *Times Mirror Co.*
Outlook / *Capital Cities Communications Inc.*
Oxford Shopping News / *Harte-Hanks Communications Inc.*
Oxmoor House / *Time Inc.*
Pacific Daily News / *Gannett Co. Inc.*
Palladium-Item / *Gannett Co. Inc.*
Paris News / *Harte-Hanks Communications Inc.*
Parker / *Gulf* + Western Industries Inc.
Parkside Journal / *Meredith Corp.*
PC Apprentice / *Gulf* + Western Industries Inc.
PennWell Publishing Co. / *Macmillan Inc.*
Pennysaver / *Capital Cities Communications Inc.*
Pennysaver Plus / *Harte-Hanks Communications Inc.*
Pennysaver Shopping News / *Capital Cities Communications Inc.*
People / *Time Inc.*
People's Press / *Dow Jones & Company Inc.*
Perennial / *Harper & Row Publishers Inc.*
P-H Information Services Division / *Gulf* + Western Industries Inc.
PHA - Prentice-Hall of America / *Gulf* + Western Industries Inc.
PHalarope Books / *Gulf* + Western Industries Inc.
PHB - Editora Prentice-Hall do Brasil / *Gulf* + Western Industries Inc.
PHH - Prentice-Hall Hispanoamericana / *Gulf* + Western Industries Inc.
PHI - Prentice-Hall International / *Gulf* + Western Industries Inc.
PHINet / *Gulf* + Western Industries Inc.
Phoenix / *Gannett Co. Inc.*
The Physician & Sports Medicine / *McGraw-Hill Inc.*
Piedmont / *Multimedia Inc.*
Pioneer Press / *Knight-Ridder Newspapers Inc.*
Pitman Learning / *Macmillan Inc.*
Platt & Munk / *Filmways Inc.*
Playboy / *Playboy Enterprises Inc.*
Plenum Press / *Plenum Publishing Corp.*
Pocket Books / *Gulf* + Western Industries Inc.
Pocono Record / *Dow Jones & Company Inc.*
Point Pleasant Register / *Multimedia Inc.*
Popular Computing / *McGraw-Hill Inc.*
Popular Photography / *CBS Inc.*
Popular Science / *Times Mirror Co.*
Poseidon / *Gulf* + Western Industries Inc.
Post Newspapers / *Post Corp.*
Post Productions / *Post Corp.*
Post-Crescent / *Post Corp.*
Postgraduate Medicine / *McGraw-Hill Inc.*
Post / *Capital Cities Communications Inc.*
Post / *Times Mirror Co.*
Post-Tribune / *Knight-Ridder Newspapers Inc.*
Power / *McGraw-Hill Inc.*
Praeger Publishing / *CBS Inc.*
Prairie Farmer / *American Broadcasting Companies Inc.*
Prentice-Hall / *Gulf* + Western Industries Inc.
Prentice-Hall / *Prentice-Hall Inc.*
Prentice-Hall Media / *Gulf* + Western Industries Inc.
Press Citizen / *Gannett Co. Inc.*
Press-Democrat / *New York Times Co.*
Press-Gazette / *Gannett Co. Inc.*
Press-Record / *Post Corp.*
Press-Republican / *Dow Jones & Company Inc.*
Press / *Harte-Hanks Communications Inc.*
Press / *Gannett Co. Inc.*

Press-Telegram / Knight-Ridder Newspapers Inc.
Progress / Multimedia Inc.
Public Opinion / Gannett Co. Inc.
Publishers Paper Co. / *Times Mirror Co.*
Pulse Journal / Harte-Hanks Communications Inc.
Pyramid / *Harcourt Brace Jovanovich Inc.*
Quad-City Times / Lee Enterprises Inc.
Reader's Choice Catalog / *Scholastic Inc.*
Record Eagle / Dow Jones & Company Inc.
Record News / Harte-Hanks Communications Inc.
Record Publishing Co. / *Harte-Hanks Communications Inc.*
Record Times / Harte-Hanks Communications Inc.
Record / Multimedia Inc.
Record / Gannett Co. Inc.
Red River Valley Bargain Bulletin / Harte-Hanks Communications Inc.
Register Star / Gannett Co. Inc.
Reminder Publishing / *Harte-Hanks Communications Inc.*
Reporter Dispatch / Gannett Co. Inc.
Reporter News / Harte-Hanks Communications Inc.
Reporter / New York Times Co.
The Reporter / Gannett Co. Inc.
Reprise / *Warner Communications Inc.*
Reston / *Gulf* + Western Industries Inc.
Review / Harte-Hanks Communications Inc.
Reward Books / *Gulf* + Western Industries Inc.
Richmond Newspapers / *Media General Inc.*
Road & Track / CBS Inc.
Ronsonol / *Ronson Corp.*
RSI Logo - Resource Systems International / *Gulf* + Western Industries Inc.
The Runner / *MCA Inc.*
The Runner / CBS Inc.
Sail / Meredith Corp.
San Diego (Calif.) Sentinel Publishing Co. / *Harte-Hanks Communications Inc.*
San Francisco Progress / Harte-Hanks Communications Inc.
Santa Cruz Sentinel / Dow Jones & Company Inc.
Saratoga News / Meredith Corp.
Saratogian / Gannett Co. Inc.
Schaum / *McGraw-Hill Inc.*
Schirmer / *Macmillan Inc.*
Schwann / *American Broadcasting Companies Inc.*
Science Year / *Scott & Fetzer Co.*
Scribe / Meredith Corp.
Scribner Book Company / *Macmillan Inc.*
Sentinel Publishers / *Harte-Hanks Communications Inc.*
Sentinel / Capital Cities Communications Inc.
Sentinel / Multimedia Inc.
Sevier County News Record / Harte-Hanks Communications Inc.
Sharon Herald / Dow Jones & Company Inc.
Shopping Guide / Harte-Hanks Communications Inc.
Shoreline / Capital Cities Communications Inc.
Simon & Schuster / *Gulf* + Western Industries Inc.
Skiing Trade News / CBS Inc.
Skiing / CBS Inc.
Ski / Times Mirror Co.
Software Tenforty / *Gulf* + Western Industries Inc.
South China Morning Post / Dow Jones & Company Inc.
South Middlesex Daily / Harte-Hanks Communications Inc.
South San Jose Sun / Meredith Corp.
Southern Illinoisan / Lee Enterprises Inc.
Southwestern / *SFN Co.*
Spectrum Books / *Prentice-Hall Inc.*
Sporting Goods Dealer / Times Mirror Co.
Sporting News / Times Mirror Co.
Sports Illustrated / Time Inc.
Springfield Leader & Press / Gannett Co. Inc.
Standard / *Standex International Corp.*
Standard & Poors / McGraw-Hill Inc.
Standard Rate and Data Service / *Macmillan Inc.*
Standard Star / Gannett Co. Inc.
Standard / Harte-Hanks Communications Inc.
Standard-Times / Dow Jones & Company Inc.
Star Gazette / Gannett Co. Inc.
Star News / Harte-Hanks Communications Inc.
Star-Banner / New York Times Co.
Star-Bulletin / Gannett Co. Inc.
Star-Courier / Lee Enterprises Inc.
Star-News / Multimedia Inc.
Star-News / New York Times Co.
Star-News / Knight-Ridder Newspapers Inc.
Star / Dow Jones & Company Inc.
Star / Multimedia Inc.
Star / Lee Enterprises Inc.
Star-Telegram / Capital Cities Communications Inc.
Star/Times / Capital Cities Communications Inc.
State Gazette / New York Times Co.
State Journal / Gannett Co. Inc.
The Staunton Leader / Multimedia Inc.
Steck-Vaughn / *National Education Corp.*
Steeple Books / *Gulf* + Western Industries Inc.
Stereo Review / CBS Inc.
Stewart-Houston Times / Multimedia Inc.
The Stone School / *Macmillan Inc.*
Sturgis *Journal / Gannett Co. Inc.*
Successful Farming / Meredith Corp.
Summit / *Gulf* + Western Industries Inc.

Sun Bulletin / *Gannett Co. Inc.*
Sun City News-Sun / *Dow Jones & Company Inc.*
Sun Newspapers / *Post Corp.*
Sunlight Shopper / *Harte-Hanks Communications Inc.*
Sun / *Meredith Corp.*
Sun / *Gannett Co. Inc.*
Sun / *New York Times Co.*
Taylor Publishing / *Insilco Corp.*
Teaching and Computers / *Scholastic Inc.*
Technical Information / *Media General Inc.*
Telegraph and News / *Knight-Ridder Newspapers Inc.*
Telesaver Publishers / *Harte-Hanks Communications Inc.*
Tempo Books / *Filmways Inc.*
Tennessean / *Gannett Co. Inc.*
Tennis Magazine / *New York Times Co.*
Textile World / *McGraw-Hill Inc.*
Time-Life / *Time Inc.*
Time / *Times Mirror Co.*
Time / *Time Inc.*
Times Daily / *New York Times Co.*
Times Delta / *Gannett Co. Inc.*
Times Democrat / *Gannett Co. Inc.*
Times Herald / *Gannett Co. Inc.*
Times Leader / *Capital Cities Communications Inc.*
Times Mirror Press / *Times Mirror Co.*
Times Observer / *Meredith Corp.*
Times-Herald Record / *Dow Jones & Company Inc.*
Times-Herald / *Times Mirror Co.*
Times-News / *New York Times Co.*
Times / *Dow Jones & Company Inc.*
Times / *Multimedia Inc.*
Times / *Knight-Ridder Newspapers Inc.*
Times / *Harte-Hanks Communications Inc.*
The Times / *Gannett Co. Inc.*
Times / *New York Times Co.*
Times-Sentinel / *Multimedia Inc.*
Times-Union / *Gannett Co. Inc.*
Today / *Gannett Co. Inc.*
Today / *Gannett Co. Inc.*
Torchbook / *Harper & Row Publishers Inc.*
Touchstone / *Gulf* + Western Industries Inc.
Town Crier / *Meredith Corp.*
Transcript / *Post Corp.*
TransMedica / *CBS Inc.*
Travel & Leisure / *American Express Co.*
Treehouse Press / *Gulf* + Western Industries Inc.
The Tribune / *Media General Inc.*
Tribune / *Lee Enterprises Inc.*
Tribune / *Multimedia Inc.*
Tribune / *New York Times Co.*
Tribune / *Gannett Co. Inc.*
TV Crosswords / *CBS Inc.*
Twin City News-Record / *Post Corp.*
Union Bulletin / *Knight-Ridder Newspapers Inc.*
Union-Gazette / *Dow Jones & Company Inc.*
Union-Recorder / *Knight-Ridder Newspapers Inc.*
United Electronics Institute / *Macmillan Inc.*
University Park Press / *SFN Co.*
USA TODAY / *Gannett Co. Inc.*
Valley News Dispatch / *Gannett Co. Inc.*
Valley Scene / *Harte-Hanks Communications Inc.*
Valley View / *Harte-Hanks Communications Inc.*
Van Nostrand Reinhold / *Litton Industries Inc.*
Van/De Publishing Co. / *Harte-Hanks Communications Inc.*
Vest Pocket Guides / *Gulf* + Western Industries Inc.
Virgin Islander / *Gannett Co. Inc.*
Voyager/HBJ / *Harcourt Brace Jovanovich Inc.*
The Wall Street Journal/Europe / *Dow Jones & Company Inc.*
Wall Street Journal / *Dow Jones & Company Inc.*
Wallaby / *Gulf* + Western Industries Inc.
Wallaces Farmer / *American Broadcasting Companies Inc.*
Walton Tribune / *Harte-Hanks Communications Inc.*
Wanderer Books / *Gulf* + Western Industries Inc.
Warner Books / *Warner Communications Inc.*
Washington Business School / *Macmillan Inc.*
The Washington Post National Weekly Edition / *Washington Post Co.*
Washington Post / *Washington Post Co.*
Washington Square Press / *Gulf* + Western Industries Inc.
Wausau *Daily Herald* / *Gannett Co. Inc.*
Weekly Light / *Harte-Hanks Communications Inc.*
Weekly Reader / *Xerox Corp.*
Westlake Post / *Meredith Corp.*
White County Citizen / *Harte-Hanks Communications Inc.*
Wiley Learning Technologies / *John Wiley & Sons, Inc.*
William Morrow & Co. / *SFN Co.*
Wilshire Independent / *Meredith Corp.*
Wilshire Press / *Meredith Corp.*

Wilson Learning Corp. / *John Wiley & Sons, Inc.*
Winona Daily News / *Lee Enterprises Inc.*
Winston/Seabury Press / *CBS Inc.*
Wisconsin Agriculturist / *American Broadcasting Companies Inc.*
Wisconsin State Journal / *Lee Enterprises Inc.*
Woman's Day / *CBS Inc.*
Women's Wear Daily / *Capital Cities Communications Inc.*
Word Incorporated Reference Material / *American Broadcasting Companies Inc.*
World Book / *Scott & Fetzer Co.*
World / *Gannett Co. Inc.*
W / *Capital Cities Communications Inc.*
Yachting / *CBS Inc.*
Year Book / *Scott & Fetzer Co.*
Year Book Medical / *Times Mirror Co.*
York County Coast Star / *New York Times Co.*
York Steak Houses / *General Mills Inc.*
Young Parent Book Club / *Harcourt Brace Jovanovich Inc.*
The Zehring Company / *Macmillan Inc.*

Restaurants

Adam & Eve / *Restaurant Associates Industries, Inc.*
Amity House / *Weis Markets Inc.*
Arby's Roast Beef / *Royal Crown Companies Inc.*
Baby Doe's Matchless Mine / *Specialty Restaurants Corp.*
Bakers Square / *Vicorp Restaurants Inc.*
Barley Mow / *Host International Inc.*
Baxter's / *W.R. Grace & Co.*
Bennigan's / *Pillsbury Co.*
Bickford Family Fare / *Dorsey Corp.*
Bickford's Family Fare / *Bickford Corp.*
Big Boy / *Frisch's Restaurants Inc.*
Big Boy Jrs. / *Marriott Corp.*
Big Boy Restaurants / *Marriott Corp.*
Big Daddy's Lounges / *Flanigan's Enterprises Inc.*
Big T / *TFI Companies Inc.*
Bishop Buffets / *K Mart Corp.*
Blackbeard's Galley & Grog / *Atlas Hotels Inc.*
Bob Evans / *Bob Evans Farms, Inc.*
Bombay Bicycle Club / *Associated Hosts, Inc.*
Boston Sea Party / *International Multifoods Corp.*
Boundary Oak / *Specialty Restaurants Corp.*
Brasserie / *Restaurant Associates Industries, Inc.*
Briar Gate / *Walgreen Co.*
Bristol Bar & Grill / *W.R. Grace & Co.*
Burger King / *Diversifoods Inc.*
Burger King / *Pillsbury Co.*
Canteen / *Transworld Corp.*
Captain Cook's Galley / *Atlas Hotels Inc.*
Captain D's / *Shoney's South Inc.*
Carlos Murphy's / *Vicorp Restaurants Inc.*
Carrows / *W.R. Grace & Co.*
Casa Gallardo / *General Mills Inc.*
Casa Maria / *Host International Inc.*
Castaway / *Specialty Restaurants Corp.*
Charlie Brown's / *Restaurant Associates Industries, Inc.*
Charlie Brown's / *Host International Inc.*
Chart House / *Chart House Inc.*
The Chart House / *Diversifoods Inc.*
Chick 'N Steak Houses / *Fair Lanes Inc.*
Chili Pepper / *Specialty Restaurants Corp.*
Chock Full o' Nuts / *Chock Full o' Nuts Corp.*
Coco's / *W.R. Grace & Co.*
Coffee Cafe / *Restaurant Associates Industries, Inc.*
Crabcooker / *Specialty Restaurants Corp.*
Crafts Inn / *Restaurant Associates Industries, Inc.*
Crawdaddy's / *Specialty Restaurants Corp.*
Crystal T's Emporium / *Atlas Hotels Inc.*
Danvers / *Shoney's South Inc.*
Darryl's / *General Mills Inc.*
Denny's / *Denny's Inc.*
Dockside Terrace / *Restaurant Associates Industries, Inc.*
El Chico Mexican Restaurants / *Campbell Taggart Inc.*
El Torito / *W.R. Grace & Co.*
Elbys / *American Stores Co.*
Emil Villa Barbecues / *Clorox*
Engine House Pizza / *Quaker Oats Co.*
English / *Fair Lanes Inc.*
Everglades Park Motel / *Restaurant Associates Industries, Inc.*
Farrell's / *Marriott Corp.*
Foxfires / *Marsh Supermarkets Inc.*
Franklin Stove / *Host International Inc.*
Fred Gang's / *Lucky Stores Inc.*
Fred Harvey / *Amfac Inc.*
Friendly / *Hershey Foods Corp.*
Furr's / *K Mart Corp.*
Garden Spot / *Wendy's International Inc.*
Gatti's / *LD Brinkman Corp.*
Gino's / *Gino's Inc.*
Gladstone's / *W.R. Grace & Co.*
Godfather's Pizza / *Diversifoods Inc.*
The Good Earth / *General Mills Inc.*
Grandy's / *Saga Corp.*
H. Salt Esq. / *Heublein Inc.*

Hanover Trail / *Campbell Soup Co.*
Hardee's / *Transworld Corp.*
Hardwicke Pubs / *Hardwicke Companies Inc.*
Harvest House / *F.W. Woolworth Co.*
His Lordship's / *Specialty Restaurants Corp.*
Holly Farms / *Federal Company*
Houlihan's Old Place / *W.R. Grace & Co.*
Humpty Dumpty's / *Walgreen Co.*
Hungry Charlie's / *Restaurant Associates Industries, Inc.*
Hungry Fisherman / *Shoney's South Inc.*
Jack-in-the-Box / *Ralston Purina Co.*
Jake's / *Restaurant Associates Industries, Inc.*
Jamoke Landing / *Specialty Restaurants Corp.*
Jerry's / *Jerrico Inc.*
John Peel / *Restaurant Associates Industries, Inc.*
Jolly Trolley / *Restaurant Associates Industries, Inc.*
Joshua Tree / *Host International Inc.*
J.P. Seafield's / *Shoney's South Inc.*
Julie's Place / *Associated Hosts, Inc.*
Kapok Tree Restaurants / *Kapok Corp.*
Kentucky Fried Chicken / *Heublein Inc.*
Kip's / *Frisch's Restaurants Inc.*
La Fiesta / *W.R. Grace & Co.*
La Petite Boulangerie / *Calny, Inc.*
L&N Seafood Grills / *Morrison Inc.*
Long John Silver's Sea Food Shoppes / *Jerrico Inc.*
Luby's / *Luby's Cafeterias, Inc.*
Luminarias / *Specialty Restaurants Corp.*
Lums / *Colgate-Palmolive Co.*
Luther's Bar-B-Q / *Diversifoods Inc.*
Lyon's / *Consolidated Foods Corp.*
Magic Pan Creperies / *Quaker Oats Co.*
Mamma Leone's / *Restaurant Associates Industries, Inc.*
Maxwell's Plum / *Hardwicke Companies Inc.*
McDonald's / *McDonald's Corp.*
Mister Donut / *International Multifoods Corp.*
Monterey Whaling Co. / *Vicorp Restaurants Inc.*
Morrison's / *Morrison Inc.*
Moshulu / *Specialty Restaurants Corp.*
Moxie's Deluxe Grille and Bar / *Diversifoods Inc.*
Mrs. Winner's Fried Chicken / *Volunteer Capital Corp.*
Nassau Inn / *Restaurant Associates Industries, Inc.*
Normandy Beach / *Specialty Restaurants Corp.*
Odyssey / *Specialty Restaurants Corp.*
Ole Frijole / *Calny, Inc.*
Orange Hill / *Specialty Restaurants Corp.*
Palmer Square / *Restaurant Associates Industries, Inc.*
Perkins Restaurant / *Holiday Inns Inc.*
Perry's Smorgy / *Calny, Inc.*
Peter Pan Restaurant / *Kapok Corp.*
Phineas / *Host International Inc.*
Piccadilly / *Piccadilly Cafeterias, Inc.*
Picnic 'n Chicken / *Atlas Hotels Inc.*
Pieces of Eight / *Specialty Restaurants Corp.*
Pietro's / *Campbell Soup Co.*
Pizza Hut / *PepsiCo Inc.*
P.J. Barnum's / *Restaurant Associates Industries, Inc.*
Plankhouse / *W.R. Grace & Co.*
Ponderosa Steak House / *Ponderosa Inc.*
Ports O' Call / *Specialty Restaurants Corp.*
Prime 'n Wine / *Frisch's Restaurants Inc.*
Promenade Cafe / *Restaurant Associates Industries, Inc.*
Proud Bird / *Specialty Restaurants Corp.*
The Proud Popover / *Quaker Oats Co.*
Publick House / *Restaurant Associates Industries, Inc.*
P.V. Martin's / *Dixon Ticonderoga Co.*
Que Pasa / *W.R. Grace & Co.*
Queen Mary / *Specialty Restaurants Corp.*
Quincy's Family Steak House / *Transworld Corp.*
Quinn's Mill / *Victoria Station Inc.*
Ranch House / *Colgate-Palmolive Co.*
Rax / *Restec Systems, Inc.*
Red Barn / *City Investing Co.*
Red Lobster Inns / *General Mills Inc.*
Reef / *Specialty Restaurants Corp.*
Reflections on the Bay / *Restaurant Associates Industries, Inc.*
Reuben's / *W.R. Grace & Co.*
Robin Hood / *Walgreen Co.*
Roy Rogers / *Frisch's Restaurants Inc.*
Roy Rogers / *Marriott Corp.*
Ruby Tuesday's / *Morrison Inc.*
Rustler Steak Houses / *Gino's Inc.*
Rusty Pelican / *Specialty Restaurants Corp.*
Rusty Pelican Restaurants / *Rusty Pelican Restaurants, Inc.*
Samurai / *Hardwicke Companies Inc.*
Savoy Restaurant / *Kapok Corp.*
Scoops / *Gray Drug Stores Inc.*
Seymour's / *Restaurant Associates Industries, Inc.*
Shanghai Red's / *Specialty Restaurants Corp.*
Shoney's / *Shoney's South Inc.*
Silver Spoon / *Morrison Inc.*
Sirloin Stockade / *Lucky Stores Inc.*
Sizzler Family Steak House / *Collins Foods International Inc.*
Smuggler's Inn / *Associated Hosts, Inc.*
Sophie's / *Specialty Restaurants Corp.*
Soup 'r Scoops / *Gray Drug Stores Inc.*
Space Needle / *UAL Inc.*
Spoons / *Saga Corp.*

Steak & Ale / *Pillsbury Co.*
Steak & Salad / *Ponderosa Inc.*
Steak 'n' Egg / *Carson Pirie Scott & Company*
Straw Hat Pizza / *Saga Corp.*
Stroller / *Frisch's Restaurants Inc.*
Stuart Anderson's Black Angus/Cattle Company / *Saga Corp.*
Sunbird / *Specialty Restaurants Corp.*
Taco Bell / *Calny, Inc.*
Taco Bell / *PepsiCo Inc.*
Taco Plaza / *ConAgra Inc.*
Tavern-on-the-Green / *Hardwicke Companies Inc.*
TJ Applebee's / *W.R. Grace & Co.*
Toddle House / *Carson Pirie Scott & Company*
Trattoria / *Restaurant Associates Industries, Inc.*
The Velvet Turtle / *Saga Corp.*
Victoria Station / *Victoria Station Inc.*
Village Inn / *Vicorp Restaurants Inc.*
Wag's / *Walgreen Co.*
Wendy's Old-Fashioned Hamburgers / *Wendy's International Inc.*
What's Your Beefs / *Restaurant Associates Industries, Inc.*
Willie Moffatt's / *Shoney's South Inc.*
Winchell's / *Denny's Inc.*
Yankee Whaler / *Specialty Restaurants Corp.*
Zantigo Mexican American Restaurants / *Heublein Inc.*
Zum Zum / *Restaurant Associates Industries, Inc.*
91st Bomb Group / *Specialty Restaurants Corp.*
94th Aero Squadron / *Specialty Restaurants Corp.*

Recreational Products & Sporting Goods

Ajay / *Fuqua Industries Inc.*
Aladdin's Castle / *Bally Manufacturing Corp.*
Alcort / *AMF Inc.*
Amberlight / *Temtex Industries Inc.*
American Athletic / *AMF Inc.*
American Camper / *Fuqua Industries Inc.*
AMFLite / *AMF Inc.*
Anthony Swimming Pools / *Anthony Industries Inc.*
Arnold Palmer / *Pro Group Inc.*
Ash Flash / *Fuqua Industries Inc.*
August Barr / *Lancaster Colony Corp.*
Bally / *Bally Manufacturing Corp.*
Bally/Midway / *Bally Manufacturing Corp.*
Bally/Sente / *Bally Manufacturing Corp.*
Barr / *Lancaster Colony Corp.*
Beachport Spas / *Katy Industries, Inc.*
Bear / *Kidde Inc.*
Ben Hogan / *AMF Inc.*
Bertram / *Whittaker Corp.*
Bic Sport Rack System / *Bic Corp.*
Black Fin / *Zimmer Corp.*
Bosman / *Beatrice Companies Inc.*
Brunswick / *Brunswick Corp.*
Bulls Eye / *American Brands Inc.*
Byrons / *Beatrice Companies Inc.*
Caber / *Questor Corp.*
Cal / *Lear Siegler, Inc.*
Cal / *Bangor Punta Corp.*
California Cooperage / *Coleman Company Inc.*
Californian / *Minstar Inc.*
Canadian Camper / *Fuqua Industries Inc.*
Carlson / *Conroy Inc.*
CCI Ammunition / *Blount Inc.*
Charmglow / *Beatrice Companies Inc.*
Coleco / *Coleco Industries, Inc.*
Coleco-Vision / *Coleco Industries, Inc.*
Coleman / *Coleman Company Inc.*
Coleman Flotation Products / *Coleman Company Inc.*
Collins Dynamics / *Coleman Company Inc.*
Comet / *Fuqua Industries Inc.*
Conibear / *Woodstream Corp.*
Contempra / *Thomas Industries Inc.*
Cook 'n Cajun / *Beatrice Companies Inc.*
Crosman / *Coleman Company Inc.*
Cruisers / *Mirro Corp.*
Cushman / *Outboard Marine Corp.*
Cypress Gardens / *ERO Industries Inc.*
D. Gottleib & Co. / *Columbia Picture Industries Inc.*
Discount / *American Can Co.*
Dorcy / *Fuqua Industries Inc.*
Double X / *Olin Corp.*
Dufour Bic Sailboard / *Bic Corp.*
En. R. Gizer / *Nature's Sunshine Products, Inc.*
Evinrude / *Outboard Marine Corp.*
E-Z-Go / *Textron Inc.*
Fenwick / *Woodstream Corp.*
Fiberform / *United States Industries Inc.*
First Flight / *Pro Group Inc.*
Flipper / *Bally Manufacturing Corp.*
Flygon / *Beatrice Companies Inc.*
Free Spirit / *Sears, Roebuck & Co.*
Fulton / *Masco Corp.*
Glastron / *Conroy Inc.*
Golden Eagle Archery / *Coleman Company Inc.*
Grumman / *Grumman Corp.*
Gym Dandy / *CBS Inc.*
Hampshire / *Morton Shoe Companies Inc.*
Harmony Hut / *American Can Co.*

Hart / *Beatrice Companies Inc.*
Hatteras / *AMF Inc.*
Havahart / *Woodstream Corp.*
Head / *AMF Inc.*
Highlander / *Fuqua Industries Inc.*
Hillary / *Sears, Roebuck & Co.*
Hobie Cat / *Coleman Company Inc.*
Hotze / *Pro Group Inc.*
Huffy / *Huffy Corp.*
Huffy Bicycle / *Huffy Corp.*
Hutch / *Fuqua Industries Inc.*
Igloo / *Anderson, Clayton & Co.*
Jacuzzi / *Kidde Inc.*
James H. McClory / *Pro Group Inc.*
Jeanneau / *Bangor Punta Corp.*
Jeanneau / *Lear Siegler, Inc.*
Jimmy McClory's Golf Shop / *Pro Group Inc.*
Johnson / *Outboard Marine Corp.*
Keds & Pro Keds / *Fuqua Industries Inc.*
Kelty Pack / *Kellwood Co.*
Kicks / *Beatrice Companies Inc.*
Kingsford / *Clorox*
Lark / *Beatrice Companies Inc.*
Larson / *Minstar Inc.*
Looney-Tunes / *Fuqua Industries Inc.*
Lund / *Minstar Inc.*
MacGregor / *Wickes Corp.*
Major League Baseball / *Fuqua Industries Inc.*
Mares / *AMF Inc.*
Mariner / *Brunswick Corp.*
Master Craft Boats/Skis / *Coleman Company Inc.*
MerCruiser / *Brunswick Corp.*
Mercury / *Brunswick Corp.*
Midway / *Bally Manufacturing Corp.*
Mirro-Craft / *Mirro Corp.*
Mitre / *Genesco Inc.*
Musicland / *American Can Co.*
My Buddy / *ERO Industries Inc.*
National Football League / *Fuqua Industries Inc.*
Nemrod / *ERO Industries Inc.*
Neosho / *Sunbeam Corp.*
Nesco / *Fuqua Industries Inc.*
Newhouse / *Woodstream Corp.*
Nissen / *Kidde Inc.*
Northwoods / *Woodstream Corp.*
O'Brien / *Coleman Company Inc.*
O'Day / *Bangor Punta Corp.*
O'Day / *Lear Siegler, Inc.*
Oklahoma Trailer / *Fuqua Industries Inc.*
Old Pal / *Woodstream Corp.*
Olin / *Olin Corp.*
Omega / *Brunswick Corp.*
Oneida / *Woodstream Corp.*
Oscar & Lil' Oscar / *Coleman Company Inc.*
Peak 1 / *Coleman Company Inc.*
Peerless / *Pro Group Inc.*
Penn / *GenCorp*
Pflueger / *Anthony Industries Inc.*
P.G.A. / *Kidde Inc.*
Pinnacle Golf Products / *American Brands Inc.*
Piper / *Lear Siegler, Inc.*
Playmate Pro Classic / *Fuqua Industries Inc.*
Poly-Lite / *Coleman Company Inc.*
Precor / *Dart & Kraft Inc.*
President / *Anthony Industries Inc.*
Prince / *Chesebrough-Pond's Inc.*
Prindle / *Lear Siegler, Inc.*
Private Call / *Coleco Industries, Inc.*
Pro-Comfort / *Schering-Plough Corp.*
Purdy Stik / *Anthony Industries Inc.*
Quantum / *Brunswick Corp.*
Quicksilver / *Brunswick Corp.*
R C Sunlight / *Medalist Industries Inc.*
Raleigh / *Huffy Corp.*
Rally / *Mirro Corp.*
RAM-X / *Coleman Company Inc.*
Ranger / *Bangor Punta Corp.*
Ranging, Inc. / *Coleman Company Inc.*
RCBS Ammunition Accessories / *Blount Inc.*
Rid-O-Ray / *Beatrice Companies Inc.*
Riva / *Whittaker Corp.*
Rupert / *Masco Corp.*
Samsonite / *Beatrice Companies Inc.*
Seamco / *Dart & Kraft Inc.*
Seaway / *United States Industries Inc.*
Shakespeare Electronics & Fiberglas / *Anthony Industries Inc.*
Shakespeare Fishing Tackle / *Anthony Industries Inc.*
Shoreline / *Fuqua Industries Inc.*
Sigma / *Anthony Industries Inc.*
Silvertip / *Olin Corp.*
Skeeter Products, Inc. / *Coleman Company Inc.*
Slumber Tents / *ERO Industries Inc.*
Smith & Wesson / *Lear Siegler, Inc.*
Smith & Wesson / *Bangor Punta Corp.*
Snauwaert / *Questor Corp.*
Soniform, Inc. / *Coleman Company Inc.*
Spalding / *Questor Corp.*
Speer Ammunition / *Blount Inc.*
Spirit Yachts / *Conroy Inc.*
St. Louis Cardinals / *Anheuser-Busch Companies Inc.*
Standard / *Pro Group Inc.*
Starcraft / *Lear Siegler, Inc.*
Starcraft / *Bangor Punta Corp.*
Structo / *Household International, Inc.*
Super-Max-22 / *Olin Corp.*

Sylvan / *KDI Corp.*
Telestar / *Coleco Industries, Inc.*
Titleist / *American Brands Inc.*
Tony Trabert / *Pro Group Inc.*
Total Gym / *Dart & Kraft Inc.*
Trailmate / *ERO Industries Inc.*
Trojan / *Whittaker Corp.*
Tyler / *Bangor Punta Corp.*
Tyrolia / *AMF Inc.*
Ugly stik / *Anthony Industries Inc.*
Universal / *Kidde Inc.*
Valley / *Kidde Inc.*
Victor / *Woodstream Corp.*
Weather-Rite / *Fuqua Industries Inc.*
Weaver / *Olin Corp.*
Wellcraft / *Minstar Inc.*
Wellcraft / *Aegis Corp.*
Wenzel / *Kellwood Co.*
West Bend / *Dart & Kraft Inc.*
Western Cutlery Company, Inc / *Coleman Company Inc.*
Wheelmaster / *Fuqua Industries Inc.*
Whispertouch / *Anthony Industries Inc.*
Wilson / *PepsiCo Inc.*
Winchester / *Olin Corp.*
Winnebago / *Winnebago Industries Inc.*
Wonderline / *Anthony Industries Inc.*
Zebco / *Brunswick Corp.*

Shoes

AAU / *International Seaway Trading Corp.*
Acme / *Northwest Industries Inc.*
Adores / *Lehigh Valley Industries Inc.*
Aerodyne / *Converse Inc.*
Air Step / *Brown Group Inc.*
Albert Durelle / *Edison Brothers Stores Inc.*
All Star / *Converse Inc.*
All-Abouts / *Edison Brothers Stores Inc.*
Ambassador / *Interco Inc.*
American Gentleman / *Craddock-Terry Shoe Corp.*
Andiamo / *Craddock-Terry Shoe Corp.*
Angel Treads / *R.G. Barry Corporation*
Anne Welles / *Edison Brothers Stores Inc.*
Athena / *Converse Inc.*
Auditions / *Craddock-Terry Shoe Corp.*
Aventura / *Brown Group Inc.*
Bare Traps / *Chesebrough-Pond's Inc.*
Bass / *Chesebrough-Pond's Inc.*
Bass / *Chesebrough-Pond's Inc.*
Bass Sunjuns / *Chesebrough-Pond's Inc.*
Bass Weejuns / *Chesebrough-Pond's Inc.*
Bates Floataways / *Wolverine World Wide Inc.*
Bates Floaters / *Wolverine World Wide Inc.*
Belle Amie / *Morse Shoe Inc.*
Bernardo / *R.G. Barry Corporation*
Big Val / *Genesco Inc.*
Bill Blass / *United States Shoe Corp.*
Bona Allen / *Tandy Brands Inc.*
Brooks / *Wolverine World Wide Inc.*
Buskens / *Brown Group Inc.*
Buster Brown / *Brown Group Inc.*
California Sun-Kicks / *Edison Brothers Stores Inc.*
Capezio / *Goldblatt Brothers Inc.*
Capezio/Q / *United States Shoe Corp.*
Captivators / *Edison Brothers Stores Inc.*
Caressa / *Caressa, Inc.*
Carina / *Caressa, Inc.*
Casualets / *Edison Brothers Stores Inc.*
Cedar Crest / *Genesco Inc.*
Celebres / *Morton Shoe Companies Inc.*
Chandlers / *Edison Brothers Stores Inc.*
Charm Step / *Genesco Inc.*
Chippewa / *Justin Industries Inc.*
Chris Evert Calypso / *Converse Inc.*
Cimaron / *Converse Inc.*
Clicks / *Edison Brothers Stores Inc.*
Clover / *Caressa, Inc.*
Cobbies / *United States Shoe Corp.*
Coleman / *Wolverine World Wide Inc.*
Coles / *Edison Brothers Stores Inc.*
Connie / *Brown Group Inc.*
Contempos / *Craddock-Terry Shoe Corp.*
Converse / *Converse Inc.*
Country Boots / *Morse Shoe Inc.*
Crawdad's / *Interco Inc.*
Dan Post / *Northwest Industries Inc.*
David Eving / *United States Shoe Corp.*
De Liso / *Brown Group Inc.*
Dearfoams / *R.G. Barry Corporation*
Dearfoams for Kids / *R.G. Barry Corporation*
Dearfoams for Men / *R.G. Barry Corporation*
Delinda / *Edison Brothers Stores Inc.*

Di Vina / *Interco Inc.*
Dingo / *Northwest Industries Inc.*
Dominion / *Genesco Inc.*
Dori / *Lehigh Valley Industries Inc.*
Durango / *United States Industries Inc.*
Easy Street / *Genesco Inc.*
El Dorado / *United States Shoe Corp.*
Eleganza / *Caressa, Inc.*
Etienne Aigner / *United Merchants and Manufacturers Inc.*
Etonic / *Colgate-Palmolive Co.*
Evan-Picone for Women / *United States Shoe Corp.*
Fanfares / *Brown Group Inc.*
Fantasy / *Genesco Inc.*
Field Star / *Converse Inc.*
Flites / *Morton Shoe Companies Inc.*
Florsheim / *Goldblatt Brothers Inc.*
Florsheim / *Interco Inc.*
Foamtread / *Wellco Enterprises Inc.*
Foot Joy / *General Mills Inc.*
Footworks / *Brown Group Inc.*
Force-5 / *Converse Inc.*
Fortune / *Genesco Inc.*
Fortune / *Genesco Inc.*
Fred West / *Edison Brothers Stores Inc.*
Freeman / *Goldblatt Brothers Inc.*
Freeman / *United States Shoe Corp.*
French Room / *Edison Brothers Stores Inc.*
French Shriner for Men / *United States Shoe Corp.*
Frye / *Alberto Culver Co.*
Fun Kicks / *Edison Brothers Stores Inc.*
Garolini / *United States Shoe Corp.*
Gazelle / *Converse Inc.*
Geppetto / *Lehigh Valley Industries Inc.*
Goldtred / *Spencer Companies Inc.*
Grasshoppers / *Stride Rite Corp.*
Grizzlies / *Interco Inc.*
Gussini / *Edison Brothers Stores Inc.*
Happy Timers / *Edison Brothers Stores Inc.*
Harbor Town by Hush Puppies / *Wolverine World Wide Inc.*
Herman / *Stride Rite Corp.*
Herman Survivors / *Stride Rite Corp.*
Hi-Pals / *Wellco Enterprises Inc.*
Hush Puppies / *Wolverine World Wide Inc.*
Hy-Test / *Interco Inc.*
Idlers / *Interco Inc.*
Incredible / *Caressa, Inc.*
Intaglio / *Edison Brothers Stores Inc.*
Intimates / *Edison Brothers Stores Inc.*
J Chigholm / *United States Shoe Corp.*
Jacqueline / *Brown Group Inc.*
Jarman / *Genesco Inc.*
Jewel Box / *Edison Brothers Stores Inc.*
Jiffies / *Gulf* + Western Industries Inc.
Jimmy Connors Commodore / *Converse Inc.*
John Malloy / *Edison Brothers Stores Inc.*
"John Muir Collection" / *Stride Rite Corp.*
John Ritchie / *Genesco Inc.*
Johnston & Murphy / *Genesco Inc.*
Joyce / *United States Shoe Corp.*
Julius Marlow / *Interco Inc.*
Junior Parade / *Edison Brothers Stores Inc.*
Justin Boots / *Justin Industries Inc.*
Kaepa / *Wolverine World Wide Inc.*
Keds / *Stride Rite Corp.*
Kenny Rogers / *United States Shoe Corp.*
Knockarounds / *Stride Rite Corp.*
Lady Wellco Magic Band / *Wellco Enterprises Inc.*
Laredo / *Genesco Inc.*
Lasco / *International Seaway Trading Corp.*
Laser / *Converse Inc.*
Lauren Evan / *Simco Stores, Inc.*
Left Bankers / *Edison Brothers Stores Inc.*
Levis for Feet / *Levi Strauss & Co.*
Levis Shoes and Boots / *Brown Group Inc.*
Life Stride / *Brown Group Inc.*
Liz Claiborne / *United States Shoe Corp.*
Lucchese / *Blue Bell Inc.*
Lucchese / *Northwest Industries Inc.*
Lydiard Equinox / *Converse Inc.*
Madye's / *R.G. Barry Corporation*
Marquise / *Brown Group Inc.*
Marrantino / *Spencer Companies Inc.*
Maserati / *Brown Group Inc.*
Maverick / *Converse Inc.*
Melo-Tred / *Edison Brothers Stores Inc.*
Melville / *Melville Corp.*
Members Only / *United States Shoe Corp.*
Miss Qualicraft / *Edison Brothers Stores Inc.*
Miss Wonderful / *Interco Inc.*
Mr. Seymour/Martinique / *Caressa, Inc.*
Mushrooms / *United States Shoe Corp.*
Naturalizer / *Goldblatt Brothers Inc.*
Naturalizer / *Brown Group Inc.*
Neolite Soles / *Goodyear Tire & Rubber Co.*
Nocona / *Justin Industries Inc.*
Nolan Miller's Dynasty Collection / *Lehigh Valley Industries Inc.*
Nurse-Mates / *Morse Shoe Inc.*
Odessa / *Converse Inc.*
Old Maine Trotters / *Penobscot Shoe Co.*
Olympian / *Morse Shoe Inc.*
Oomphies / *United States Industries Inc.*
Outdoor Boots / *Morse Shoe Inc.*

Pacers / *Gulf +* Western Industries Inc.
Pathfinder / *Justin Industries Inc.*
Pedwin / *Brown Group Inc.*
Perry's / *Unishops Inc.*
Personality / *Interco Inc.*
Philippe / *Caressa, Inc.*
Pim Poms / *R.G. Barry Corporation*
Playgoers / *Edison Brothers Stores Inc.*
Polly Preston / *Craddock-Terry Shoe Corp.*
Polo / *Northwest Industries Inc.*
Polykins / *R.G. Barry Corporation*
Precedent / *Converse Inc.*
Predictions / *Edison Brothers Stores Inc.*
Presentations / *Edison Brothers Stores Inc.*
Pro Keds / *Stride Rite Corp.*
Pro-Champs / *Morse Shoe Inc.*
Qualicraft / *Edison Brothers Stores Inc.*
Qualicraft Juniors / *Edison Brothers Stores Inc.*
Quoddy / *Wolverine World Wide Inc.*
Ralph Lauren / *Northwest Industries Inc.*
Rand / *Interco Inc.*
Red Cross / *Goldblatt Brothers Inc.*
Reed St. James / *Wolverine World Wide Inc.*
Revenge / *Converse Inc.*
Ridge Runners / *Edison Brothers Stores Inc.*
Risque / *Brown Group Inc.*
Roblee / *Brown Group Inc.*
Romorini / *Edison Brothers Stores Inc.*
Royal Imperial / *Interco Inc.*
Royal Red Ball / *Stride Rite Corp.*
Scats / *SCOA Industries Inc.*
Screen Star / *Northwest Industries Inc.*
Shoe World / *Edison Brothers Stores Inc.*
Simco / *Simco Stores, Inc.*
Sioux Mox / *Wolverine World Wide Inc.*
Snug Treads / *R.G. Barry Corporation*
Socialites / *United States Shoe Corp.*
Sod Hoppers / *Edison Brothers Stores Inc.*
Soft Spot / *Morse Shoe Inc.*
Sperry Topsider / *Stride Rite Corp.*
Sportstar / *Converse Inc.*
S.R.O. / *Caressa, Inc.*
Stage 1 / *Craddock-Terry Shoe Corp.*
Starion / *Converse Inc.*
Startech / *Converse Inc.*
Stormers / *Morse Shoe Inc.*
Street Fighter / *Colgate-Palmolive Co.*
Streetcars / *Morton Shoe Companies Inc.*
Stride Rite / *Stride Rite Corp.*
Stride Rite Booteries / *Stride Rite Corp.*
Suede Stick / *Edison Brothers Stores Inc.*
Sundowners / *R.G. Barry Corporation*
Super Sole / *Spencer Companies Inc.*
Surfboards / *International Seaway Trading Corp.*
Sweet Steps / *Edison Brothers Stores Inc.*
Sweets / *Edison Brothers Stores Inc.*
S-111 / *Converse Inc.*
Texas Boots / *United States Shoe Corp.*
Thomas Wallace / *Interco Inc.*
Three Cheers / *R.G. Barry Corporation*
Thunderbolt / *Converse Inc.*
Topicals / *Edison Brothers Stores Inc.*
Topnicks / *Spencer Companies Inc.*
Town & Country / *Edison Brothers Stores Inc.*
Town & Country / *Wolverine World Wide Inc.*
Tretorn / *Colgate-Palmolive Co.*
Tribute / *Converse Inc.*
Tru-Stitch / *Wolverine World Wide Inc.*
Umberto Bellini / *Lehigh Valley Industries Inc.*
Viner / *Wolverine World Wide Inc.*
Vogue / *Genesco Inc.*
Warwick Shoe Company / *Outlet Co.*
Weber / *Stride Rite Corp.*
Weeds / *Interco Inc.*
Wellco / *Wellco Enterprises Inc.*
The Wild Pair / *Edison Brothers Stores Inc.*
Wildcats / *Brown Group Inc.*
Wildwoods / *Morton Shoe Companies Inc.*
Wimzees / *Wolverine World Wide Inc.*
Windy Hill / *International Seaway Trading Corp.*
Winthrop / *Interco Inc.*
Wolverine / *Wolverine World Wide Inc.*
Worthmore / *Interco Inc.*
Wrangler / *Genesco Inc.*
Zips / *Stride Rite Corp.*

Specialty Retailing

Aaron Rose / *Zale Corp.*

Aaronson's Brothers Stores / *Volume Merchandising Inc.*
Abercrombie & Fitch / *Oshman's Sporting Goods Inc.*
Action Associated Hardware / *Action Industries Inc.*
Action Home Center / *Action Industries Inc.*
Activeworld / *F.W. Woolworth Co.*
Adams Drug / *Adams Drug Co., Inc.*
Adler Shoe Shops / *Weyenberg Shoe Manufacturing Co.*
Aggies / *Genesco Inc.*
Agnew / *Genesco Inc.*
Albertson's / *Albertson's Inc.*
Allegany Mall / *Volume Merchandising Inc.*
Amalfi / *United States Shoe Corp.*
Ameritex / *United Merchants and Manufacturers Inc.*
Ammex / *Hardwicke Companies Inc.*
Angels / *W.R. Grace & Co.*
Ann Taylor / *Garfinkle Brooks Brothers, Miller & Rhoads Inc.*
Arnold / *Borman's Inc.*
Arnold's / *Unimax Group Inc.*
Arpeggios / *United States Shoe Corp.*
Ashby's, Ltd. / *Best Products Co., Inc.*
Asley's Retail Outlets / *Kellwood Co.*
Athletic Shoe Factory / *F.W. Woolworth Co.*
August Max / *United States Shoe Corp.*
Auto Shack / *Malone & Hyde Inc.*
B. Dalton / *Dayton Hudson Corp.*
Bailey, Banks & Biddle / *Zale Corp.*
Baker / *Outlet Co.*
Bandolino / *United States Shoe Corp.*
The Banister Shoe Co / *United States Shoe Corp.*
Barry's / *Unimax Group Inc.*
Bell Bros. / *Genesco Inc.*
Berean / *Standex International Corp.*
Betty Gay / *Gaylords National Corp.*
Betty Gay / *Volume Merchandising Inc.*
Beverly Shop / *Volume Merchandising Inc.*
Big B / *Begley Co.*
Big Bear / *Fuqua Industries Inc.*
Big Bens / *Integrity Entertainment Corp.*
Big Daddy's Liquors / *Flanigan's Enterprises Inc.*
Bi-Mart / *Pay 'n Save Corp.*
BJ's Wholesale Club / *Zayre Corp.*
Black, Starr & Frost / *Kay Corp.*
Blake's / *Phillips-Van Heusen Corp.*
Blends 'n Trends / *Kenwin Shops Inc.*
Blue Chip Stamps / *Berkshire Hathaway Inc.*
Boswells' of Vandevers / *Zale Corp.*
Brandstand / *United States Shoe Corp.*
Breuners / *Marshall Field & Co.*
Brittain's / *Genesco Inc.*
Brodnax Jewelers / *Zale Corp.*
Brooks / *Brooks Fashion Stores Inc.*
Brooks / *Adams Drug Co., Inc.*
Brooks Brothers / *Garfinkle Brooks Brothers, Miller & Rhoads Inc.*
Builder's Emporium / *Wickes Corp.*
By-Way Shoe Stores / *SCOA Industries Inc.*
Cal-Fed / *Volume Merchandising Inc.*
Candy Stores / *Southland Corp.*
Career Image / *United States Shoe Corp.*
Caren Charles / *United States Shoe Corp.*
Carriage Drugs / *Wetterau, Inc.*
Cashways/Allwoods Building Centers / *W.R. Grace & Co.*
Casual Corner / *United States Shoe Corp.*
Catherine's Stout Shoppe / *Garfinkle Brooks Brothers, Miller & Rhoads Inc.*
Central Hardware Home Improvement Stores / *Interco Inc.*
Certified Leasing / *National Service Industries Inc.*
Chadwick's of Boston / *Zayre Corp.*
Channel / *W.R. Grace & Co.*
Chaps / *Unishops Inc.*
Charles / *Volume Merchandising Inc.*
Charles & Co. / *Southland Corp.*
Charles B. Perkins / *Stop & Shop Companies Inc.*
Charm Shops / *Volume Merchandising Inc.*
Charming Shoppes / *Charming Shoppes Inc.*
Chas. A. Stevens / *Hartmarx Corp.*
Checker Auto Parts Stores / *Lucky Stores Inc.*
Cherry & Webb / *Outlet Co.*
Chess King / *Melville Corp.*
Chief Auto Parts / *Southland Corp.*
Children's Palace / *Cole National Corp.*
Child's World / *Cole National Corp.*
Churchill Audio Centers / *Friendly Frost Inc.*
Cincinnati Shoe Co / *United States Shoe Corp.*
Circle K / *Circle K Corp.*
Circuit City / *Circuit City Stores, Inc.*
Circuit City Superstore / *Circuit City Stores, Inc.*
Citizens / *Gordon Jewelry Corp.*
Cloth World / *Brown Group Inc.*
Coast-to-Coast / *Household International, Inc.*
Cobbie Cuddlers / *United States Shoe Corp.*
Consumer Value Stores / *Melville Corp.*
Consumer's Pharmacy / *Malone & Hyde Inc.*
Contempo Casuals / *Carter Hawley Hale Stores, Inc.*
The Continental / *Host International Inc.*
Corrigan / *Zale Corp.*
Cosco / *Cluett, Peabody & Co. Inc.*
Cover Girl / *Genesco Inc.*
Coward / *Lane Bryant Inc.*
Crackers / *United States Shoe Corp.*
Craft Bazaar / *Munford Inc.*

Craft Showcase / *Cole National Corp.*
Craft Showcase / *House of Fabrics Inc.*
Crown Books / *Dart Drug Corp.*
Cub Foods / *Super Valu Stores Inc.*
Curious Cargo / *Munford Inc.*
Daniel's / *Gordon Jewelry Corp.*
Dart / *Dart Drug Corp.*
David's / *Petrie Stores Corp.*
Debbie Howell Cosmetics / *Johnson Products Co. Inc.*
deJongs / *Hartmarx Corp.*
Devon / *Pantry Pride, Inc.*
Dexter / *Genesco Inc.*
D.G. Calhoun / *Dillon Companies Inc.*
Diana Marco / *Petrie Stores Corp.*
Discount Fabrics / *Discount Fabrics Inc.*
Dixie / *Kenwin Shops Inc.*
Dolland & Aitchison / *American Brands Inc.*
Dollar Fair Stores / *Action Industries Inc.*
Dorman's Auto Centers / *Lucky Stores Inc.*
Double Up / *Wickes Corp.*
D.P. Paul / *Gordon Jewelry Corp.*
Drug Fair / *Gray Drug Stores Inc.*
Dry Goods / *SCOA Industries Inc.*
Duane's / *Interco Inc.*
Duling Optical / *Dentsply International Inc.*
Ebeling & Reuss / *Alco Standard Corp.*
Eckerd / *Jack Eckerd Corp.*
Eckerd / *Jack Eckerd Corp.*
Eckerd Drug / *Adams Drug Co., Inc.*
Eddie Bauer / *General Mills Inc.*
Entertainment / *Entertainment Publications Inc.*
Entertel / *Entertainment Publications Inc.*
Extra Special / *Lane Bryant Inc.*
Eyelab / *Quaker Oats Co.*
Fabric Gallery / *Discount Fabrics Inc.*
Fabs Fashion Fabrics / *Wickes Corp.*
Factory Fallout / *Billy The Kid, Inc.*
Factory to You / *Genesco Inc.*
Family Mart / *Great Atlantic & Pacific Tea Co. Inc.*
Farr's / *Lane Bryant Inc.*
Fashion Bug / *Charming Shoppes Inc.*
Fashion Bug Plus / *Charming Shoppes Inc.*
Fashion Complex / *Volume Merchandising Inc.*
Fashionfair / *Gray Drug Stores Inc.*
Fay's / *Fay's Drug Co. Inc.*
Fayva / *Morse Shoe Inc.*
Feder's Jewelers / *Gordon Jewelry Corp.*
Field Brothers / *Hartmarx Corp.*
Fine's / *Interco Inc.*
Fish / *Peavey Co.*
Fixler Brothers / *Quaker Oats Co.*
Flagg Bros. / *Genesco Inc.*
Flair / *Outlet Co.*
Flanigan's / *Flanigan's Enterprises Inc.*
Florsheim Thayer McNeil / *Interco Inc.*
Flower Time / *General Host Corp.*
Foot Locker / *F.W. Woolworth Co.*
Foot Scene / *Genesco Inc.*
Fotomat / *Fotomat Corp.*
Fox Stanley Photo / *Fox-Stanley Photo Products Inc.*
Foxmoor / *Melville Corp.*
F.R. Tripler & Co. / *Hartmarx Corp.*
Franciscan Gift Shop / *Host International Inc.*
Frank Bros. / *Genesco Inc.*
Franklins / *Petrie Stores Corp.*
Frank's Nursery & Crafts / *General Host Corp.*
Frank's Nursery and Crafts Stores / *Frank's Nursery and Crafts Inc.*
Fredelle / *F.W. Woolworth Co.*
Friendly Frost Appliance Stores / *Friendly Frost Inc.*
Friendly Frost Garden Centers / *Friendly Frost Inc.*
Front Row / *United States Shoe Corp.*
Frost Bros. / *Manhattan Industries Inc.*
Frugal Frank's / *F.W. Woolworth Co.*
Fun City / *Lionel Corp.*
Furrow / *Payless Cashways Inc.*
G & G Shops / *Petrie Stores Corp.*
G. Fox & Co. / *May Department Stores Co.*
GallenKamp / *SCOA Industries Inc.*
Garlind / *Volume Merchandising Inc.*
Gasen / *The Kroger Co.*
Gerber Children's Centers / *Gerber Products Co.*
Gold Art Creations / *Unimax Group Inc.*
Gordon's / *Gordon Jewelry Corp.*
Grand Auto / *Grand Auto Inc.*
Granson / *Volume Merchandising Inc.*
Gray Drug / *Gray Drug Stores Inc.*
Gray's / *Volume Merchandising Inc.*
Guarantee / *Genesco Inc.*
Gumps / *Macmillan Inc.*
Haag / *Peoples Drug Stores Inc.*
Hahn / *United States Shoe Corp.*
Hamburger's / *Phillips-Van Heusen Corp.*
Hancock / *Lucky Stores Inc.*
Handy City / *W.R. Grace & Co.*
Handy Dan / *W.R. Grace & Co.*
Harcourt Brace Jovanovich / *Harcourt Brace Jovanovich Inc.*
Hardy / *Genesco Inc.*
Harris & Frank / *Phillips-Van Heusen Corp.*
Hartfield / *Hartfield Zody's Inc.*
Hartfields / *Petrie Stores Corp.*
Hastings / *Hartmarx Corp.*
Hausmann / *Zale Corp.*
Health Mart / *Peoples Drug Stores Inc.*
Hecht's / *May Department Stores Co.*

Helen's / *Wal-Mart Stores Inc.*
Henry's / *Zale Corp.*
Herman's World of Sporting Goods / *W.R. Grace & Co.*
Hershberg's / *Zale Corp.*
Hertzberg / *Zale Corp.*
Hess & Culbertson / *Zale Corp.*
Hickory Farms of Ohio / *General Host Corp.*
High Brows / *American Greetings Corporation*
Hilliary Jaymes / *United States Shoe Corp.*
Himself the Elf / *American Greetings Corporation*
Hirsch & Son / *Unimax Group Inc.*
Hit or Miss / *Zayre Corp.*
Holt, Renfrew / *Carter Hawley Hale Stores, Inc.*
Home Centers / *Goldblatt Brothers Inc.*
Home Entertainment / *Teledyne Inc.*
Home Front / *United States Shoe Corp.*
Honey Bear Farm / *Carson Pirie Scott & Company*
Hook Drugstores / *Hook Drugs Inc.*
Hot Sam Stores / *General Host Corp.*
House of Fabrics / *House of Fabrics Inc.*
House of Fine Fabrics / *Fabri-Centers of America Inc.*
House of Value / *Pay Less Drug Stores Northwest Inc.*
House of Vision / *House of Vision Inc.*
House Works! / *W.R. Grace & Co.*
Howland / *Supermarkets General Corp.*
The Hub / *Manhattan Industries Inc.*
Hugh M Woods / *Payless Cashways Inc.*
Hughes & Hatcher / *Outlet Co.*
IBM Product Centers / *International Business Machines Corp.*
Innes Shoe Stores / *Genesco Inc.*
Its-A-Dilly / *Lucky Stores Inc.*
J. Byrons / *Jack Eckerd Corp.*
J. Herbert Hall / *Gordon Jewelry Corp.*
J. Riggings / *United States Shoe Corp.*
Jaccard's / *Zale Corp.*
Jack Henry Stores / *Hartmarx Corp.*
Jacob Reed & Sons / *Outlet Co.*
Jacobs / *Zale Corp.*
Jaison's / *Charming Shoppes Inc.*
Jas K. Wilson/Washer Bros. / *Hartmarx Corp.*
Jax / *Fisher Foods, Inc.*
Jaymar / *Hartmarx Corp.*
Jaymar/Sansabelt Shops / *Hartmarx Corp.*
Jay's / *National Convenience Stores*
Jay's / *Godfrey Co.*
Jean Nicole / *Petrie Stores Corp.*
Jean Nicole / *Miller-Wohl Co. Inc.*
Jim Handy / *Godfrey Co.*
Jo Ann Fabrics / *Fabri-Centers of America Inc.*
J.O. Jones / *Hartmarx Corp.*
Jobe-Rose / *Zale Corp.*
Joy Shop / *Volume Merchandising Inc.*
Juster's / *Phillips-Van Heusen Corp.*
Karl's / *Hartfield Zody's Inc.*
Kay Jewelers / *Kay Corp.*
Kelly's Corner / *Volume Merchandising Inc.*
Kennedy's / *Phillips-Van Heusen Corp.*
Kent Drugs / *Adams Drug Co., Inc.*
Kenwin / *Kenwin Shops Inc.*
Key / *Begley Co.*
The Key Shop / *Cole National Corp.*
Kids Mart / *F.W. Woolworth Co.*
Kindy Optical / *Dentsply International Inc.*
Kinney / *F.W. Woolworth Co.*
Kleinhans / *Hartmarx Corp.*
Klopfenstein's / *Hartmarx Corp.*
K-Mart / *Melville Corp.*
Knit Studios / *Jonathan Logan Inc.*
Koerber & Baber / *Zale Corp.*
Kragen Auto Supply Store / *Lucky Stores Inc.*
Krone Mode / *F.W. Woolworth Co.*
Kucharo's / *Hartmarx Corp.*
Kuppenheimer / *Hartmarx Corp.*
L & G Sporting Goods / *Lucky Stores Inc.*
La Moda / *Volume Merchandising Inc.*
Lady Foot Locker / *F.W. Woolworth Co.*
Lady Rose / *Masters Inc.*
Lafayette/Circuit City / *Circuit City Stores, Inc.*
Lane / *Peoples Drug Stores Inc.*
Lane Bryant / *Lane Bryant Inc.*
Laneco / *Wetterau, Inc.*
Lang Vicary / *Hartmarx Corp.*
Lauriat's / *Chadwick-Miller Inc.*
Lawton Jewelers / *Gordon Jewelry Corp.*
Le Roys / *Unimax Group Inc.*
Leath / *Wickes Corp.*
Lee / *Peoples Drug Stores Inc.*
Lee Ward's Creative Crafts / *General Mills Inc.*
Leopold, Price & Rolle / *Hartmarx Corp.*
Levitts / *Zale Corp.*
Levy Wolf / *Hartmarx Corp.*
Lewis / *F.W. Woolworth Co.*
LFD / *Michigan General Corp.*
Liemandt / *Hartmarx Corp.*
Life Uniform & Shoe Shops / *Angelica Corp.*
The Linen Locker / *Wolverine World Wide Inc.*
Linz Bros. / *Gordon Jewelry Corp.*
Lionel Kiddie City / *Lionel Corp.*
Lionel Playworld / *Lionel Corp.*
Lionel Toy Warehouse / *Lionel Corp.*
Little Folk Shop / *F.W. Woolworth Co.*
Little Red Shoe House / *Wolverine World Wide Inc.*
Littler / *Hartmarx Corp.*
Litwin / *Zale Corp.*

Live Wire / *F.W. Woolworth Co.*
Lizzie B / *Miller-Wohl Co. Inc.*
London Towne / *Interco Inc.*
Lorch Jewelry Stores / *Jim Walter Corp.*
Lumberjack / *Payless Cashways Inc.*
Man Store / *Hartmarx Corp.*
Manhattan Factory Outlet / *Manhattan Industries Inc.*
Marianne / *Petrie Stores Corp.*
Marine Tobacco Co. / *Host International Inc.*
Mark Cross Inc / *A. T. Cross Company*
Marshalls / *Melville Corp.*
Max Davis / *Zale Corp.*
Maxwell / *Wickes Corp.*
Mays / *Lucky Stores Inc.*
McNeel's / *Zale Corp.*
Medi Mart / *Stop & Shop Companies Inc.*
Meis / *Brown Group Inc.*
Mermod, Jaccard & King / *Gordon Jewelry Corp.*
Merritt Schaefer & Brown / *Hartmarx Corp.*
Midas Muffler Shop / *I.C. Industries Inc.*
Miller Taylor / *Interco Inc.*
Miller-Wohl / *Miller-Wohl Co. Inc.*
Mindlin / *Zale Corp.*
Mission / *Zale Corp.*
Monfried Optical / *Dentsply International Inc.*
Morgan / *Zale Corp.*
Morgan-Hayes of Houston / *Weyenberg Shoe Manufacturing Co.*
Morris Levy / *Hartmarx Corp.*
Morse / *Morse Shoe Inc.*
Morville / *After Six Inc.*
Nescott Drug / *Adams Drug Co., Inc.*
Newman Benton / *Lane Bryant Inc.*
Nordstrom's / *Nordstrom Inc.*
Northwest Fabrics / *Peavey Co.*
Nunn-Bush / *Weyenberg Shoe Manufacturing Co.*
Old Mill / *Hartmarx Corp.*
Ole's / *W.R. Grace & Co.*
Open Country / *Melville Corp.*
Orchard Supply Hardware / *W.R. Grace & Co.*
Original Cookie / *Cole National Corp.*
Osco / *Jewel Companies Inc.*
Oshman's / *Oshman's Sporting Goods Inc.*
Outrigger / *United States Shoe Corp.*
Page Drug Stores / *Cullum Companies Inc.*
The Paint Place / *Pratt & Lambert, Inc.*
Pam's for Fashion / *Volume Merchandising Inc.*
Pants Corral / *Giant Food Inc.*
The Paper Cutter / *Fay's Drug Co. Inc.*
Pappagallo / *United States Shoe Corp.*
Pay Less Drug / *Pay Less Drug Stores Northwest Inc.*
Pay 'n Save / *Pay 'n Save Corp.*
Payless Cashways / *Payless Cashways Inc.*
Payless Shoe Source (Volume Shoe Corp.) / *May Department Stores Co.*
Payrite / *Malone & Hyde Inc.*
Peavey/Thunderbird / *Peavey Co.*
Peer Gordon / *Hartmarx Corp.*
Peoples / *Peoples Drug Stores Inc.*
Pep Boys / *Pep Boys - Manny, Moe & Jack*
Petite Sophisticate / *United States Shoe Corp.*
Petrie Stores / *Petrie Stores Corp.*
Petty's / *Malone & Hyde Inc.*
Peyton / *Kenwin Shops Inc.*
Philipsborn / *Outlet Co.*
Pic 'N' Save / *Pic 'N' Save Corp.*
Pic-A-Dilly / *Lucky Stores Inc.*
Pickwick / *Dayton Hudson Corp.*
Picture Plaza / *Gray Drug Stores Inc.*
Pidgeon's / *Zale Corp.*
Pilgrim / *Standex International Corp.*
Place Two / *Nordstrom Inc.*
Playland / *Greenman Bros. Inc.*
Playtown / *Lionel Corp.*
Playworld / *Greenman Bros. Inc.*
Porter's Stevens / *Hartmarx Corp.*
Precision Lenscrafters / *United States Shoe Corp.*
Primera / *Volume Merchandising Inc.*
Proving Ground / *United States Shoe Corp.*
Radio Shack / *Tandy Corp.*
Radio Shack Computer Centers / *Tandy Corp.*
Randy River / *F.W. Woolworth Co.*
Rave / *Petrie Stores Corp.*
Ray Beers / *Hartmarx Corp.*
RB Furniture / *RB Industries Inc.*
Reach / *Fuqua Industries Inc.*
Red Cross / *United States Shoe Corp.*
Red Cross Shoes / *Higbee Co.*
Reed / *Peoples Drug Stores Inc.*
Regal Shoe Shops / *Brown Group Inc.*
Revco / *Revco D.S. Inc.*
Reward/Dexter / *Genesco Inc.*
R.G. Branden's / *Dayton Hudson Corp.*
Rider's / *Zale Corp.*
Ringmakers / *Unimax Group Inc.*
Rogers / *Zale Corp.*
Roots / *Hartmarx Corp.*
Rosenfield / *Zale Corp.*
Rosenzweig's / *Zale Corp.*
Rost Jewelers / *Gordon Jewelry Corp.*
Sacaldi / *F.W. Woolworth Co.*
Sam Goody / *American Can Co.*
Sam's Wholesale Clubs / *Wal-Mart Stores Inc.*
Sanborns / *Volume Merchandising Inc.*
Saving Spree / *Entertainment Publications Inc.*
Schirmer / *Macmillan Inc.*

Scott / *Scot Lad Foods Inc.*
See's Candy / *Blue Chip Stamps*
Selby / *United States Shoe Corp.*
Selco / *Zale Corp.*
Ships Bell / *Unimax Group Inc.*
Shoe Stop / *Hartfield Zody's Inc.*
Shop-n-Go / *National Convenience Stores*
Shop-Rite / *Mott's Supermarkets Inc.*
Showcase of Fine Fabrics / *Fabri-Centers of America Inc.*
Sigma Gifthouse / *Towle Manufacturing Co.*
Silverwoods / *Hartmarx Corp.*
Small's / *Outlet Co.*
Smart & Thrifty / *Kenwin Shops Inc.*
Smart Size / *Lane Bryant Inc.*
Snyder / *Wickes Corp.*
So-Fro Fabrics / *House of Fabrics Inc.*
Somerville Lumber / *Payless Cashways Inc.*
Something Else / *American Greetings Corporation*
Something New / *American Greetings Corporation*
Sommer & Kaufman / *Genesco Inc.*
Sommers / *Malone & Hyde Inc.*
Sparky's Virgin Island / *Host International Inc.*
Sportwest / *Pay 'n Save Corp.*
Stacy / *Lucky Stores Inc.*
Stacy Adams / *Weyenberg Shoe Manufacturing Co.*
Standard Shoes / *Weyenberg Shoe Manufacturing Co.*
Standard Sportswear / *Interco Inc.*
Star Trek / *Gulf* + Western Industries Inc.
Stelens / *Volume Merchandising Inc.*
Stop-n-Go / *National Convenience Stores*
Strawberry Shortcake / *American Greetings Corporation*
Stuart Brooks / *United States Shoe Corp.*
Stuarts / *Petrie Stores Corp.*
Sudamatex / *United Merchants and Manufacturers Inc.*
Sumit Stores / *American Greetings Corporation*
Sun Drug / *Adams Drug Co., Inc.*
Sun Foods / *Godfrey Co.*
Sunset Sport Center / *Malone & Hyde Inc.*
Super Drug / *National Convenience Stores*
Super Quik / *National Convenience Stores*
Superior / *Begley Co.*
SupeRx / *The Kroger Co.*
Susan Terry / *Masters Inc.*
Susie's / *F.W. Woolworth Co.*
Suzanne / *Kenwin Shops Inc.*
Sweeny & Co. Jewelers / *Gordon Jewelry Corp.*
Sycamore Specialty Stores / *Associated Dry Goods Corp.*
Tagway / *Morton Shoe Companies Inc.*
Tandy Leather Stores / *Tandycrafts Inc.*
Tandy Tool Stores / *Tandycrafts Inc.*
T.H. Mandy / *United States Shoe Corp.*
Thal's / *Winkelman Stores Inc.*
Thayer McNeil / *Interco Inc.*
Things Remembered / *Cole National Corp.*
Thom McAn / *Melville Corp.*
Thompson Boland & Lee / *Interco Inc.*
Three Sisters / *Petrie Stores Corp.*
Three Sisters / *Miller-Wohl Co. Inc.*
Thrift Drugstores / *J.C. Penney Co., Inc.*
Thrifty Shop / *Volume Merchandising Inc.*
T.J. Maxx / *Zayre Corp.*
Today / *Winkelman Stores Inc.*
Tony Lama / *Tony Lama Co. Inc.*
Tops / *Volume Merchandising Inc.*
Total Sports / *W.R. Grace & Co.*
Touraine / *Outlet Co.*
Toy City / *Wetterau, Inc.*
Toy World / *Wickes Corp.*
Toys "R" Us / *Toys "R" Us Inc.*
Toytown / *Lionel Corp.*
Trak Auto / *Dart Drug Corp.*
Travel America at Half-Price / *Entertainment Publications Inc.*
Tuscany Imports / *Alco Standard Corp.*
Ultra Precise Beauty Boutique / *Johnson Products Co. Inc.*
United Shirt Store / *Interco Inc.*
Upstage / *Morse Shoe Inc.*
Urdang's / *Masters Inc.*
Valmart / *Genesco Inc.*
Value Giant / *Pay Less Drug Stores Northwest Inc.*
Valu-Rite / *McKesson Corp.*
Video Concepts / *Jack Eckerd Corp.*
Village Casuals / *Masters Inc.*
Vitamin Quota / *Cadence Industries Corp.*
Volume Shoe Corp. / *May Department Stores Co.*
Von Tobel's / *Pay 'n Save Corp.*
VPS'N Downs / *United States Shoe Corp.*
V.S. Kids / *United States Shoe Corp.*
W & J Sloane / *RB Industries Inc.*
Walden Book Company / *K Mart Corp.*
Walgreen / *Walgreen Co.*
Walkers / *Hartmarx Corp.*
Wallachs / *Hartmarx Corp.*
Wallpapers to Go / *General Mills Inc.*
Walter Morton / *Hartmarx Corp.*
Warehouse Club / *W.R. Grace & Co.*
We Are Sportswear / *General Mills Inc.*
Wellby Super Drugstores / *Hannaford Bros. Co.*
Weyenberg / *Weyenberg Shoe Manufacturing Co.*
Weyenberg Massagic / *Weyenberg Shoe Manufacturing Co.*

Whelan Drug / *Adams Drug Co., Inc.*
Wherehouse / *Integrity Entertainment Corp.*
Wherehouse Entertainment / *Wherehouse Entertainment, Inc.*
White Drug / *Farm House Foods Corp.*
Whitney / *Petrie Stores Corp.*
Wickes / *Wickes Corp.*
Wicks & Greenman / *Hartmarx Corp.*
Willoughbys / *Berkey Photo, Inc.*
Wilsons / *Melville Corp.*
Winkelman / *Winkelman Stores Inc.*
Winkelman's / *Petrie Stores Corp.*
Wise Fashion / *Volume Merchandising Inc.*
Wolf Bros. / *Hartmarx Corp.*
Wolff's / *Hartmarx Corp.*
Woman's World / *Wickes Corp.*
World Bazaar / *Munford Inc.*
World Tobacco Co. / *Host International Inc.*
Wright Line Direct / *Barry Wright Corp.*
Xerox / *Xerox Corp.*
Yard Birds / *Pay 'n Save Corp.*
Youth Centre / *Unishops Inc.*
Zachry / *Hartmarx Corp.*
Zodeems / *Hartfield Zody's Inc.*

Television, Radios & Audiovisual Equipment

Acoustic Dynamics / *Soundesign Corp.*
Action Code / *National Education Corp.*
Ampex / *Signal Companies Inc.*
Apple / *Apple Computer Inc.*
Apple II / *Apple Computer Inc.*
AR / *Teledyne Inc.*
Archer / *Tandy Corp.*
Atlantic / *Warner Communications Inc.*
Benson Optical Co. / *Frigitronics Inc.*
Betamax / *Sony Corp.*
B&K-Precision / *Dynascan Corp.*
Brain / *John Blair & Co.*
Caramate / *Singer Co.*
Channel Master Satellite Systems / *Avnet Inc.*
Channel Masters / *Avnet Inc.*
Cobra / *Dynascan Corp.*
Conairphone / *Conair Corp.*
Conairphone Call Keeper / *Conair Corp.*
Crystal / *Litton Industries Inc.*
Currentron / *Sony Corp.*
Dashmate / *Sears, Roebuck & Co.*
Data General/One / *Data General Corp.*
Desktop Generation / *Data General Corp.*
Diablo / *Xerox Corp.*
Dynamicron / *Sony Corp.*
The Entertainment Station / *Mayflower Corp.*
Express Commander / *Sony Corp.*
General Electric / *General Electric Co.*
Goldengate / *Cullinet Software Inc.*
GTE / *GTE Corp.*
Harmon Kardon / *Beatrice Companies Inc.*
Heath / *Zenith Electronics Corp.*
Hitachi / *Hitachi Ltd.*
House of Vision / *Frigitronics Inc.*
Infinity / *Electro Audio Dynamics Inc.*
International Bureau of Software Test / *Gulf +* Western Industries Inc.
Jenkel Davidson / *Frigitronics Inc.*
Jensen / *Esmark Inc.*
JVC / *Matsushita Electric Industrial Co. Ltd.*
KLH / *Electro Audio Dynamics Inc.*
Lab Series / *Norlin Corporation*
LaserWriter / *Apple Computer Inc.*
Lloyd's / *Lloyd's Electronics Inc.*
Lloyd's Electronics / *Bacardi Corp.*
Macintosh / *Apple Computer Inc.*
Magnavision / *North American Philips Corp.*
Magnavox / *North American Philips Corp.*
Magnecord / *Telex Corp.*
Marantz / *Marantz Inc.*
Matsushita / *Matsushita Electric Industrial Co. Ltd.*
Micronta / *Tandy Corp.*
Monteverdi / *Lloyd's Electronics Inc.*
National / *Matsushita Electric Industrial Co. Ltd.*
Networx / *North American Philips Corp.*
Olson / *Teledyne Inc.*
Ostertag Optical Service / *Frigitronics Inc.*
Panasonic / *Matsushita Electric Industrial Co. Ltd.*
Patrolman / *Tandy Corp.*
Peerless / *Electro Audio Dynamics Inc.*
Philco / *North American Philips Corp.*
Philips Lamps / *North American Philips Corp.*
Philips PL / *North American Philips Corp.*
Philips-MCA / *North American Philips Corp.*
Pianocorder / *Marantz Inc.*
Qualitone / *Xcor International Inc.*
Quasar / *Matsushita Electric Industrial Co. Ltd.*
Quik-Comm / *General Electric Co.*
RCA / *RCA Corp.*
Realistic / *Tandy Corp.*
Realtone / *Soundesign Corp.*
Record Vacuum / *Ronco Teleproducts Inc.*
Rembrandt / *Electro Audio Dynamics Inc.*
Rentabeta / *Marantz Inc.*

Resco Electronics Stores / *Astrex Inc.*
Science Fair / *Tandy Corp.*
Sony / *Sony Corp.*
Soundesign / *Soundesign Corp.*
Spacenet / *GTE Corp.*
Sprint / *GTE Corp.*
Sunray de Puerto Rico / *Bacardi Corp.*
Superscope / *Marantz Inc.*
Sylvania / *North American Philips Corp.*
Tanglewood / *Soundesign Corp.*
Technics / *Matsushita Electric Industrial Co. Ltd.*
Tel Avail / *John Blair & Co.*
Telecopier / *Xerox Corp.*
Teledyne / *Teledyne Inc.*
Telemotive / *Dynascan Corp.*
Telenet / *GTE Corp.*
Telex / *Telex Corp.*
Tenna-Rotor / *North American Philips Corp.*
Texas Instruments / *Texas Instruments Inc.*
Trend-Spotter / *Cullinet Software Inc.*
Trinitron / *Sony Corp.*
Victor / *Matsushita Electric Industrial Co. Ltd.*
Video Arcade / *Sears, Roebuck & Co.*
Viking / *Telex Corp.*
Walkman / *Sony Corp.*
Westinghouse Lamps / *North American Philips Corp.*
Wire Tree Plus / *North American Philips Corp.*
Zenith / *Zenith Electronics Corp.*
3M / *Minnesota Mining and Manufacturing Co. (3M)*

Tobacco, Tobacco Products & Accessories

Amphora / *United States Tobacco Co.*
Antonio y Cleopatra / *American Brands Inc.*
Apple / *R.J. Reynolds*
Apple Sun Cured / *R.J. Reynolds*
Argosy Black / *United States Tobacco Co.*
Bagpipe / *Loews Corp.*
Beech-Nut / *Loews Corp.*
Benson & Hedges / *Philip Morris Inc.*
Berekley Cigaretts / *American Brands Inc.*
Between-the-Acts / *Loews Corp.*
B.G. Twist / *Conwood Corp.*
Big Red / *Loews Corp.*
Black Maria / *Conwood Corp.*
Blackstone / *Universal Cigar Corp.*
Blend Eleven / *United States Tobacco Co.*
Bourbon Blend / *American Brands Inc.*
Brandee / *Culbro Corp.*
Bravura / *Bayuk Cigars Inc.*
Brown's Mule / *R.J. Reynolds*
Bull of the Woods / *Conwood Corp.*
Bulls Eye / *Conwood Corp.*
Buttercup / *Culbro Corp.*
Caesar / *Bayuk Cigars Inc.*
Cambridge / *Philip Morris Inc.*
Camel / *R.J. Reynolds*
Cannon Ball / *Conwood Corp.*
Carlton / *American Brands Inc.*
Carter Hall / *R.J. Reynolds*
Cheroot / *Bayuk Cigars Inc.*
Chico / *Bayuk Cigars Inc.*
Churchill / *Bayuk Cigars Inc.*
Cigarillo / *Bayuk Cigars Inc.*
Clover Bloom / *Conwood Corp.*
Condor / *American Brands Inc.*
Conwood / *Conwood Corp.*
Corina / *Culbro Corp.*
Corona / *Bayuk Cigars Inc.*
Days Work / *R.J. Reynolds*
Dental / *Conwood Corp.*
Devoe / *United States Tobacco Co.*
Dexter / *Universal Cigar Corp.*
Doral / *R.J. Reynolds*
Drum / *United States Tobacco Co.*
Dupont / *Gillette Co.*
El Trelles / *Universal Cigar Corp.*
Elegante / *Bayuk Cigars Inc.*
English Corona / *Bayuk Cigars Inc.*
Epicure / *Bayuk Cigars Inc.*
Erik / *Loews Corp.*
Fancy Tale / *Bayuk Cigars Inc.*
Favorite / *Conwood Corp.*
Fiesta / *Bayuk Cigars Inc.*
Frieder / *United States Tobacco Co.*
Gallante / *Bayuk Cigars Inc.*
Garcia y Vega / *Bayuk Cigars Inc.*
Garrett / *Conwood Corp.*
George Washington / *R.J. Reynolds*
Gold Label / *Culbro Corp.*
Gold River / *Culbro Corp.*
Gold Wedding / *Bayuk Cigars Inc.*
Golden Lights / *Loews Corp.*
Gran Corona / *Bayuk Cigars Inc.*
Gran Premio / *Bayuk Cigars Inc.*
Granada / *Bayuk Cigars Inc.*
Greenbrier / *Culbro Corp.*
Haddon Hall / *Universal Cigar Corp.*
Half & Half / *American Brands Inc.*
Hamlet / *American Brands Inc.*
Havana Blossom / *Loews Corp.*

Haw Ken / *Conwood Corp.*
Honest / *Conwood Corp.*
Java Tip / *Bayuk Cigars Inc.*
Kent / *Loews Corp.*
Kentucky Club / *Culbro Corp.*
Kentucky King / *Conwood Corp.*
Kentucky Twist / *Conwood Corp.*
King Edward / *American Maize Products Co.*
La Corona / *American Brands Inc.*
La Primadora / *Universal Cigar Corp.*
Lancaster / *Culbro Corp.*
London Dock / *Culbro Corp.*
Lucky Joe / *Conwood Corp.*
Lucky Strike / *American Brands Inc.*
Lucky 100's / *American Brands Inc.*
Macanudo / *Culbro Corp.*
Madeira / *R.J. Reynolds*
Madison / *Loews Corp.*
Maestro / *Bayuk Cigars Inc.*
Mammoth Cave / *Conwood Corp.*
Marlboro / *Philip Morris Inc.*
Max / *Loews Corp.*
Merit / *Philip Morris Inc.*
Meriweather's Pig Tail / *Conwood Corp.*
Mexican Blunt / *Bayuk Cigars Inc.*
Model / *United States Tobacco Co.*
Montclair / *American Brands Inc.*
Moore's Red Leaf / *Conwood Corp.*
More / *R.J. Reynolds*
Napoleon / *Bayuk Cigars Inc.*
Navy Sweet / *Culbro Corp.*
Newport / *Loews Corp.*
Now / *R.J. Reynolds*
Old Gold / *Loews Corp.*
Old Holborn / *American Brands Inc.*
Old Joe / *Conwood Corp.*
Old Taylor / *Conwood Corp.*
Omega / *Loews Corp.*
Optimo / *Universal Cigar Corp.*
Our Advertiser / *R.J. Reynolds*
Paladin Blackcherry / *American Brands Inc.*
Pall Mall / *American Brands Inc.*
Pan Deluxe / *Bayuk Cigars Inc.*
Panatella / *Bayuk Cigars Inc.*
Parliament / *Philip Morris Inc.*
Partagas / *Culbro Corp.*
Peach / *Conwood Corp.*
Peach & Honey / *Conwood Corp.*
Penn's Natural Leaf / *Conwood Corp.*
Perfecs Garcia / *United States Tobacco Co.*
Perfecto / *Bayuk Cigars Inc.*
Philip Morris / *Philip Morris Inc.*
Phillips / *Bayuk Cigars Inc.*
Players / *Philip Morris Inc.*
Prince Albert / *R.J. Reynolds*
Railroad Mills Sweet / *Culbro Corp.*
Rainbow / *Conwood Corp.*
Ramon Allones / *Culbro Corp.*
Ram's Horn / *Conwood Corp.*
Real / *R.J. Reynolds*
Red Bud / *Conwood Corp.*
Red Coon / *Conwood Corp.*
Red Fox / *Conwood Corp.*
Redwood / *Culbro Corp.*
Regalo / *Bayuk Cigars Inc.*
Reynolds' Natural Leaf / *R.J. Reynolds*
Rice's Best / *Conwood Corp.*
Ripe Peaches / *Conwood Corp.*
Robert Burns / *Culbro Corp.*
Roi Tan / *American Brands Inc.*
Romero / *Bayuk Cigars Inc.*
Rose Bud / *Conwood Corp.*
Rough Country / *Conwood Corp.*
Royal Danish / *Culbro Corp.*
R.T. Junior / *Conwood Corp.*
Sail Pipe / *American Brands Inc.*
Salem / *R.J. Reynolds*
Samson's Big 4 / *Conwood Corp.*
Santa Fe / *Universal Cigar Corp.*
Saratoga / *Philip Morris Inc.*
Seal / *United States Tobacco Co.*
Senator / *Bayuk Cigars Inc.*
Shakespeare / *Culbro Corp.*
Silk Cut / *American Brands Inc.*
Silva Thins / *American Brands Inc.*
Silver Creek / *Culbro Corp.*
Skandinavik / *Culbro Corp.*
Snuffettes / *Conwood Corp.*
Sobraine / *American Brands Inc.*
Spanish Tip / *Bayuk Cigars Inc.*
Sport / *Bayuk Cigars Inc.*
Spring / *Loews Corp.*
Square / *Culbro Corp.*
Superior / *Culbro Corp.*
Swisher Sweet / *American Maize Products Co.*
Tareyton / *American Brands Inc.*
Taylor Made / *Conwood Corp.*
Taylor's Pride / *Conwood Corp.*
Tempo / *R.J. Reynolds*
Tijuana Smalls / *Culbro Corp.*
Tiparillos / *Culbro Corp.*
Titan / *Bayuk Cigars Inc.*
Top / *R.J. Reynolds*
Tops Sweet / *Culbro Corp.*
Triumph cigarettes / *Loews Corp.*
True cigarettes / *Loews Corp.*

Twist Lemon Menthol / *American Brands Inc.*
Van Dyck / *Culbro Corp.*
Vantage / *R.J. Reynolds*
Viking / *Culbro Corp.*
Virginia Slims / *Philip Morris Inc.*
Warren / *Conwood Corp.*
Washington / *Bayuk Cigars Inc.*
Webster / *Bayuk Cigars Inc.*
White Owl / *Culbro Corp.*
Whitehall / *Culbro Corp.*
Wildcat / *Conwood Corp.*
William Penn / *Culbro Corp.*
Winchester / *R.J. Reynolds*
Winston / *R.J. Reynolds*
Work Horse / *R.J. Reynolds*
Workmate / *Culbro Corp.*
WPBN-TV / *United States Tobacco Co.*
Yellow Tag / *Conwood Corp.*
"160" / *Bayuk Cigars Inc.*
7-20-4 / *Universal Cigar Corp.*

Travel & Travel Agencies

American Airlines / *American Airlines Inc.*
American Airlines / *AMR Corp.*
Beech / *Raytheon Co.*
Brewster Transportation / *Greyhound Corp.*
California Parlor Car Tours Co. / *Greyhound Corp.*
Cartan / *Avco*
Chalk's International Airline / *Resorts International Inc.*
Condo Rentalbank / *Entertainment Publications Inc.*
Eastern Airlines / *Eastern Air Lines Inc.*
Entertainment Travel Services, Inc. / *Entertainment Publications Inc.*
Frontier / *GenCorp*
Frontier Horizon / *GenCorp*
Garden State Coachways / *Dixon Ticonderoga Co.*
Golden Nugget / *Golden Nugget Inc.*
Greyhound Bus Service / *Greyhound Corp.*
Greyhound Group Travel / *Greyhound Corp.*
Hartmann / *Brown Forman Distillers Corp.*
Landmark Services / *MCA Inc.*
Missouri-Kansas-Texas Railroad / *Katy Industries, Inc.*
Pan American Airlines / *Pan Am Corp.*
Piper / *Bangor Punta Corp.*
Sea World / *Harcourt Brace Jovanovich Inc.*
Sky Chefs / *AMR Corp.*
Sun Line Cruise Ships / *Marriott Corp.*
Trans International Airlines / *Transamerica Corp.*
Transamerica Airlines / *Transamerica Corp.*
TWA / *Trans World Airlines Inc.*
United Airlines / *UAL Inc.*
Universal Studio Tours / *MCA Inc.*
US Air / *U.S. Air Group Inc.*
Walt Disney Travel Co. / *Walt Disney Productions*

Section II

Consumer Goods Companies

Section II

Consumer Goods Companies

Abbott Laboratories

Abbott Park
North Chicago, IL 60064
(312) 937-6100

Chief Executive Officer: R.A. Schoellhorn
1984 Annual Sales Volume: 3,100M
1984 Shares Outstanding: 120,234,000
Shareholders: 34,963
Exchange: NY
Symbol: ABT

Corporate History: Abbott Laboratories was incorporated in 1900 as the Abbott Alkaloidal Company and has operated under its present name since 1914. Dr. Wallace C. Abbott founded the company in Chicago in 1888 to make drug products for his patients and then for use by other physicians. Today Abbott is a worldwide company devoted to the discovery, development, manufacture, and sale of a broad and diversified line of human health-care products and services. Abbott has two major business segments: pharmaceutical and nutritional products—include a broad line of adult and pediatric pharmaceuticals, nutritionals, vitamins, and hematinics. Also included are personal care products, agricultural and chemical products, and bulk pharmaceuticals, hospital and laboratory products—include a broad line of intravenous and irrigating fluids and related administration equipment, venipuncture products, anesthetics, diagnostic instruments and tests, critical care and suctioning equipment, and other specialty products for hospitals, clinical laboratories and home health care.

Brandnames of Products and Services:

Cefol	*filmtab vitamin*
Clear Eyes	*eye care preparation*
Cyclent	*vitamins*
Enrich	*food supplement*
Ensure	*nutritional liquid*
Faultless	*hot water bottles*
Isomil	*sucrose-free soy protein formula*
Murine	*eye and ear care preparations*
Optilets	*vitamins*
Rondec II	*vitamins*
Selsun Blue	*anti-dandruff shampoo*
Similac	*infant formula*
Sucaryl	*noncaloric sweeteners*
Surbex	*vitamins*
Tronolane	*hemorrhoidal cream*
ViDaylin	*children's vitamins*
Vital	*nutritional powder*

Action Industries Inc.

460 Nixon Rd.
Cheswick, PA 15024
(412) 782-4800

Chief Executive Officer: Ernest S. Berez
1984 Annual Sales Volume: 167,359,400
1984 Shares Outstanding: 6,358,570
Shareholders: 1,400
Exchange: AMEX

Corporate History: Action Industries was incorporated in 1946 as the F&B Woodenware Co. Its name was changed to Associated Hardware Supply Co. in 1952 and to its present title in 1968. The company makes plastic housewares and markets housewares and hardware items manufactured by others in the United States and abroad. In 1983 the company purchased Sabin Industrial a maker of dinnerware and glassware.

Brandnames of Products and Services:

Action Associated Hardware	*specialty stores*
Action Home Center	*specialty stores*
Carlton	*glassware*
Dollar Fair Stores	*specialty stores*
Mr. Clemens Pottery	*dinnerware*

Acton Corp.

411 Massachusetts Ave.
P.O. Box 407
Acton, Mass. 01720
(617) 263-7711

Chief Executive Officer: S.J. Phillips
Exchange: AM
Symbol: ATN
Corporate History: Acton Corp. originally incorporated in 1960 as Rego Insulated Wire Corp. Its present name was adopted in 1976. Acton operates radio and TV stations; it owns and operates 50 community antenna television (CATV) systems. Because the stations are primarily in mature television markets, future growth is limited and Acton recently has branched out into snack foods in order to increase earnings and maximize the return to shareholders.
Brandnames of Products and Services:

CATV	*cable television*
Crane	*potato chips*
Fiesta	*tortilla chips*
Germack	*pistachio nuts*
Gordon's	*potato chips*
KECC-TV	*station, El Centro, Calif.*
Kelling	*nuts*
Kemps	*nuts*
Krun-cheez	*snack foods*
Mann's	*potato chips*
Mrs. Ihrie's	*potato chips*
Old Vienna	*potato chips and pretzels*
Quik-Snak	*snack foods*
Sta Krisp	*snack foods*
Sun Dance	*corn chips*
WLBZ-AM	*radio station, Bangor, Maine*
WMUR-TV	*station, Manchester, N.H.*
WMYD-TV	*station, R.I.*

Adams Drug Co., Inc.

75 Sabin St.
Pawtucket, R.I. 02860
(401) 724-9500

Chief Executive Officer: Donald Salmanson
Exchange: NY
Symbol: ADG
Corporate History: The company, incorporated in 1972, operates approximately 360 retail drug stores in the Northeast. It acquired the Whelan Drug chain in 1973 and the following year gained control of the Nescott and Eckerd drugstore chains.
Brandnames of Products and Services:

Adams Drug	*drugstores*
Brooks	*drugstores*
Eckerd Drug	*drugstores*
Kent Drugs	*drugstores*
Nescott Drug	*drugstores*
Sun Drug	*drugstores*
Whelan Drug	*drugstores*

Aegis Corp.

250 Catalonia Ave.
Coral Gables, Fla. 33134
(305) 445-9686

Chief Executive Officer: C.W. Jordan
Exchange: AM
Symbol: AO
Corporate History: Aegis incorporated in 1949 as TransTex Transmission Co. Its present title was adopted in 1974. The company makes tread rubber, which accounted for 32.5% of revenues in 1979 and fiberglass pleasure boats which comprised 35.9% of revenues. It is also involved in heavy industry and in supplying services and products to the oil and natural gas industry.
Brandnames of Products and Services:

Wellcraft	*pleasure boats*

Affiliated Publications Inc.

135 Morrissey Blvd.
Boston, MA 02107
(617) 929-2000

Chief Executive Officer: William O. Taylor
1984 Annual Sales Volume: 344M
1984 Shares Outstanding: 12,237,963
Shareholders: 3,438
Exchange: AM
Symbol: AFP
Corporate History: The company, incorporated in 1973, has business interests, through various subsidiaries, which include publication of the Boston *Globe*, radio broadcasting, cable-television and radio common carrier systems, and book publishing.
Brandnames of Products and Services:

The Boston *Globe*	*newspaper, Boston, MA*

Globe Corner Bookstore	*bookstore*
Globe Pequot Press	*book publisher*
KFYE-FM	*radio station, Fresno, CA*
KHEP-FM	*radio station, Phoenix, AZ*
KMPS-AM/FM	*radio station, Seattle, WA*
KRAK-AM/KSKK-FM	*radio stations, Sacramento, CA*
WFAS-AM/FM	*radio station, White Plains, N.Y.*
WOKV-AM/ WAIV-FM	*radio stations, Jacksonville, FL*

After Six Inc.

2137 Market St.
Philadelphia, Pa. 19103
(215) 561-6666

Chief Executive Officer:	R.C. Rudofker
Exchange:	AM
Symbol:	TUX

Corporate History: The company was established in 1903 and incorporated in 1946 as S. Rudofker's Sons Inc. In 1967 it adopted its present title. After Six designs, makes and markets men's wear. The nation's largest manufacturer of men's formal wear, it also operates as small retail chain in the Philadelphia area. In fiscal 1980 apparel provided 86% of sales and retailing 14%.

Brandnames of Products and Services:

After Six	*men's formal wear*
Angelo of Rome	*men's sportcoats*
Bert Paley	*men's leather wear*
Bill Blass	*men's formal wear*
Harry Fischer	*men's outer wear*
Jason Gibbs	*men's outer wear*
LeBow	*men's suits*
Malcom Kenneth	*men's overcoats*
Morville	*men's apparel stores*
V-Line	*men's clothes*

Alba-Waldensian, Inc.

P.O. Box 100
Valdese, NC 28690
(704) 874-2191

Chief Executive Officer:	W.D. Schubert
1984 Annual Sales Volume:	48M
1984 Shares Outstanding:	1,858,605
Shareholders:	849
Exchange:	AM
Symbol:	AWS

Corporate History: The company incorporated in 1928 as Pilot Full Fashion Mills Inc. In 1955 its name was changed to Alba Hosiery Mills, Inc. and in 1961 to Alba-Waldensian, Inc. The firm makes women's intimate apparel, dance and exercise apparel, women's and men's hosiery products and men's underwear. It also produces medical accessories including antiembolism hosiery, heel and elbow products, nonslip patient slippers, knitted stockinette, extensible net tubing, incontinent pants, and lymphedema sleeves.

Brandnames of Products and Services:

Alaskanits	*ladies' & men's hosiery & tights*
Alba Cotton-Aire	*men's & women's hosiery* *intimate apparel & hosiery*
Cotton Cooler	*women's, girls' and children's panties*
Forme'	*intimate apparel*
Life Span	*heel, knee & elbow pads, protectors & braces*
Lustre-Skin	*women's, girls' and children's panties*
Polar Pairs	*women's hosiery*
Sani Terry	*intimate apparel*
Temptease	*women's, girls' & children's leotards, tights, panties, trunks & slipper socks*
Ultimates	*women's hosiery*
X-Span	*medical dressing retainers*

Alberto Culver Co.

2525 W. Artmitage Ave.
Melrose Park, Ill. 60160
(312) 450-3000

Chief Executive Officer:	L.H. Lavin
1984 Annual Sales Volume:	349M
1984 Shares Outstanding:	3,851,784
Shareholders:	2,032

Exchange: NY
Symbol: ACV
Corporate History: The principal business of Alberto-Culver is manufacturing and marketing products for personal use or use in the home. It has manufacturing facilities in eight countries, and its products are sold in more than 100 countries. Incorporated in 1961, the company offers a wide variety of product lines which include hair preparations, feminine hygiene products and household and grocery items. The company was founded in 1955 with the Alberto VO5 line of products and expanded in the area of household cleaning items and specialty foods. It grew out of three joint ventures operating under the trade names Alberto Culver Co., Leonard H. Lavin & Co. and American Cosmetics Corp., through the issuance of 950,000 common shares (including 427,500 to L.H. Lavin) and assumption of certain liabilities. In July 1969, it bought the West Berlin maker of skin care products, Firma Ludwig Scherk, for about $1.5 million. In 1977 all the shares of John A. Frye Shoe Co. were acquired for $8.5 million in cash and notes. In 1983, it acquired Indola Cosmetics B.V., a Netherlands based company that markets hair care products.
Brandnames of Products and Services:

Alberto Balsam	*hair conditioner*
Alberto Jojoba	*hair conditioner*
Alberto Mousse	*styling foam*
Alberto VO5	*hair care products*
Baker's Joy	*baking spray*
Consort	*hair care products*
FDS	*feminine deodorant spray*
Frye	*leather boots*
Get Set	*hair care products*
Kleen Guard	*furniture polish*
Mrs. Dash	*low-sodium food products*
New Dawn II	*hair color*
Philippe	*ladies' handbags*
Static Guard	*anti-static spray*
SugarTwin	*sugar substitute*
TCB	*hair care products*
TRESemme	*hair care products*

Albertson's Inc.

250 Parkcenter Blvd.
P.O. Box 20
Boise, ID 83726
(208) 344-7441

Chief Executive Officer: Warren E. McCain
1984 Annual Sales Volume: 4,736M
1984 Shares Outstanding: 33,107,024
Shareholders: 6,347
Exchange: NY
Symbol: ABS
Corporate History: The company was founded in 1939. In 1969 it was incorporated as AFS Inc. and later the same year adopted its current name. Albertson's, Inc. is the seventh largest supermarket chain in the U.S. Its 434 stores in 17 western and southern states include 90 combination food-drug units, 81 super-stores and 263 conventional supermarkets. The company also operates distribution and manufacturing facilities to support the retail operations.
Brandnames of Products and Services:

Albertson's	*pharmacies*
Albertson's	*supermarkets*
Grocery Warehouse	*supermarkets*
Janet Lee	*canned food products*

Alco Standard Corp.

P.O. Box 834
Valley Forge, PA 19482
(215) 296-8000

Chief Executive Officer: Ray B. Mundt
1984 Annual Sales Volume: 3,392M
1984 Shares Outstanding: 21,255,203
Shareholders: 11,538
Exchange: NY
Symbol: ASN
Corporate History: The company, originally incorporated in 1928, was incorporated under the name Alco Standard Corp. in 1952. During 1984 Alco reorganized its operations into the following seven groups of products and services: communications products (paper products, office products); health services; industrial distribution (metal products, container products); Consumer distribution (wine and spirits, gift and glassware); foodservice equipment, aerospace, and other businesses.
Brandnames of Products and Services:

Baldwin Paper	*paper products*
Brown Drug	*drug stores, health care products*
Carpenter Paper	*paper products*
Central Paper	*paper products*
Copco Papers	*paper products*
The Drug House	*drug stores, health care products*
Duff Brothers	*drug stores, health care products*

Ebeling & Reuss	*gifts, glassware*
Ed. Phillips & Sons	*wines and spirits*
Garrett-Buchanan	*paper products*
Geer Drug	*drug store, health care products*
Kaufman-Lattimer	*drug store, health care products*
La Salle Messinger Paper	*paper products*
Ledo-Dionysus	*wines and spirits*
Mid-Continent Paper	*paper products*
Monarch Paper	*paper products*
Paper Corp. of U.S.	*paper products*
Rita-Ann Distributors	*health care products*
Rourke-Eno Paper	*paper products*
Seneca Paper	*paper products*
Smith Higgins	*drug stores, health care services*
Southwest Distributors	*wines and spirits*
Spectrum	*drug stores, health care services*
Strother Drug	*drug stores, health care services*
Tuscany Imports	*gifts, glassware*
United Wine & Spirits	*wines, spirits*
Universal Paper	*paper products*
William T. Stover	*drug stores, health care products*
Wyomissing	*paper products*

Alexander's Inc.

500 Seventh Ave.
New York, NY 10018
(212) 560-2121

Chief Executive Officer: Robin L. Farkas
1984 Annual Sales Volume: 517M
1984 Shares Outstanding: 4,519,168
Shareholders: 4,280
Exchange: NY
Symbol: ALX

Corporate History: Alexander's was founded in 1928 and incorporated in 1955 as Farbro Corp.; the present title was adopted in 1968. It consists of a retailing organization of 15 department stores serving New York City and surrounding areas. Ready-to-wear apparel and accessories account for about 77 % of sales.

Brandnames of Products and Services:

Alexander's	*department stores*

Allied Stores Corp.

1114 Avenue of the Americas
New York, NY 10036
(212) 764-2000

Chief Executive Officer: Thomas M. Macioce
1984 Annual Sales Volume: 3,970,469,000
1984 Shares Outstanding: 20,970,000
Shareholders: 19,000
Exchange: NY
Symbol: ALS

Corporate History: Allied Stores, one of the nation's largest retailing organizations, operates 597 department stores and specialty stores in 45 states, the District of Columbia, and Japan. The company was incorporated in 1928 as Hahn Department Stores, and the present title was adopted in 1935. The department stores are divided into semi-autonomous operating divisions, each with its own management and merchandising staffs, in order to serve the fashion needs of the local markets. Allied Stores is also a significant factor in specialty store retailing, a field the company entered in April 1979 with the acquisition of the Bonwit Teller and Plymouth Shops divisions from Genesco, Inc. Its position in specialty store retailing was significantly expanded in 1981 with the acquisition of Garfinckel, Brooks Brothers, Miller & Rhoads. The company now operates six specialty store divisions — Brooks Brothers, Bonwit Teller, Garfinckel, Ann Taylor, Catherine's Stout Shoppe, and Plymouth Shops — which in 1984 represented about 18% of sales.

Brandnames of Products and Services:

Ann Taylor	*specialty stores*
Block's	*department stores*
Bon	*department stores*
Bonwit Teller	*specialty stores*
Brooks Brothers	*specialty stores*
Cain-Sloan	*department stores*
Catherine's Stout Shoppe	*specialty stores*
Dey Brothers	*department stores*
Donaldson's	*department stores*
Garfinckel's	*specialty stores*
Heer's	*department stores*
Herp's	*department stores*
Jordan Marsh	*department stores*

Joske's	*department stores*
Levy's	*department stores*
Maas Brothers	*department stores*
Miller & Rhoads	*department stores*
Miller's	*department stores*
Muller's	*department stores*
Plymouth Shops	*specialty stores*
Pomeroy's	*department stores*
Read's	*department stores*
Stern's	*department stores*

Allis-Chalmers Corp.

1205 70th St.
West Allis, Wisc. 53201-0512
(414) 475-2000

Chief Executive Officer: D.C. Scott
1984 Annual Sales Volume: 1.3B
1984 Shares Outstanding: 14,272,485
Shareholders: 22,829
Exchange: NY
Symbol: AH
Corporate History: Allis-Chalmers Corp. maintains offices in many of the world's major cities and operates manufacturing plants in 13 countries. It is a specialized technology company which develops, designs, manufactures and markets products, processes, systems and services on a worldwide scale for improving the quality of air; processing fluids and solids; agriculture; and material handling. Consumer products represent only a small portion of its business. Allis-Chalmers was incorportated as Allis Chalmers Manufacturing Co. in 1913. It acquired the assets of Allis Chalmers Co. which had been formed in New Jersey in 1909 as a consolidation of four long-established manufacturing concerns: Edward P. Allis Co. of Milwaukee; Fraser & Chalmers Co. of Chicago; Gates Iron Works of Chicago and Dickson Manufacturing Co. of Scranton, Penn. The present title was adopted in 1917.
Brandnames of Products and Services:

Allis-Chalmers	*lawn and garden implements*
American Air Filter Amer-glas	*home furnace filter*
Snowbuster	*snowthrower*

Almy Stores Inc.

1440 Soldiers Field Rd.
Boston, Mass 02135
(617) 782-5100

Chief Executive Officer: R. Gorin
Exchange: AM
Symbol: ALY
Corporate History: The company incorporated in 1968 as Gorin's Inc. and adopted its present name in 1978. It operates 32 department stores in the Eastern part of the United States.
Brandnames of Products and Services:

Almy	*department stores*
Edgar's	*department stores*
Edwards	*department stores*
Freeses	*department stores*
Gorin's	*department stores*
House & Hale	*department stores*
Star Store	*department stores*
Witherill	*department stores*

American Airlines Inc.

P.O. Box 61616
Dallas-Ft. Worth Airport, Texas 75261
(214) 355-1234

Chief Executive Officer: A.V. Casey
Exchange: NY
Symbol: AMR
Corporate History: American Airlines was founded in 1930 as a consolidation of more than 85 small companies. Under the direction of C.R. Smith, American eventually became a profitable and innovative company. It was the first airline to emphasize passenger rather than freight service, the first to use stewardesses and the first to have planes built to its specifications. In 1959 it introduced jet planes to commercial flight. Until the 1960s American was the largest airline in the U.S. Since then it has been surpassed by United.
Brandnames of Products and Services:

American Airlines

American Bakeries Co.

100 Park Avenue
New York, NY 10017
(212) 687-7225

Chief Executive Officer:	E. Garrett Bewkes, Jr.
1984 Annual Sales Volume:	499M
1984 Shares Outstanding:	2,636,591
Shareholders:	6,000
Exchange:	NY
Symbol:	ABA

Corporate History: American Bakeries incorporated in 1924 as Purity Bakeries Corp. and adopted its present title in 1953. The company operates 18 bakeries producing a variety of baked goods including bread, buns, rolls, doughnuts, cakes, muffins, and pastries. Prior to 1984, the company disposed of all businesses other than bakery products. In 1985, it acquired Cotton Brothers, Inc., a Louisiana baked-goods company. Also, in early 1985, it acquired Camp Coast to Coast, Inc., a travel and leisure services company.

Brandnames of Products and Services:

Autumn Grain	*breads*
Cook Book	*breads*
Cotton	*bread*
Cotton's Holsum	*bread*
D'Italiano	*bread*
Dressel's	*frozen baked goods and desserts*
Lite	*diet bread*
Merita	*breads*
Mickey	*cakes*
Taystee	*breads*

American Brands Inc.

245 Park Ave.
New York, NY 10167
(212) 880-4200

Chief Executive Officer:	E.W. Whittemore
1984 Annual Sales Volume:	$7 billion
1984 Shares Outstanding:	55,084,731
Shareholders:	101,303
Exchange:	NY
Symbol:	AMB

Corporate History: American Brands which grew out of The American Tobacco Company, has evolved from a company with a single product line, tobacco, into an organization with two core businesses — packaged consumer goods and financial services — and a growing stake in office products. Since the Company began diversifying in 1966, $2.6 billion has been invested in acquiring new businesses. In addition to domestic tobacco products, major lines now include international tobacco, financial services, hardware and security, distilled beverages, office, food and golf products, optical goods and services and personal care products. In 1984, acquired companies contributed 56% of operating income. American Brands is the only U.S. tobacco producer with more cigarette sales outside the country than within, based on its ownership of Britain's second largest tobacco firm, Gallaher. In 1980 tobacco accounted for 63% of sales.

Brandnames of Products and Services:

Aalborg Akvait	
Acme Visible Business Systems	
Ambassador Shredders	
Antonio y Cleopatra	*cigars*
Beam's Black Label	*bourbon*
Beam's Choice Bourbon	
Bell Brand Snacks	
Berekley Cigaretts	
Blue Bell Snacks	
Bourbon Blend	*tobacco products*
Bulls Eye	*athletic products*
Canadian Silk Whiskey	
Carlton	*cigarettes*
Chateaux	*cordials*
Cheez-it	*crackers*
Chip A Roos	*cookies*
Condor	*tobacco products*
Dark Eyes	*vodka*
Dolland & Aitchison	*spectacles, contact lenses*
Eastlight Filling	*filling and storage products*
Franklin Life Insurance	
Gee Your Hair Smells Terrific	*shampoo*
Gentle Touch	*skin products*
Half & Half	*pipe tobacco*
Hamlet	*tobacco products*
Hi-Ho	*crackers*
Humpty Dumpty	*snack foods*
Hydrox	*cookies*
Jergens	*skin care products*
Jim Beam	*whiskey*
Kamora Coffee Liqueur	

Krispy	*crackers*
La Corona	*cigars*
Lucky Strike	*cigarettes*
Lucky 100's	*cigarettes*
Marson Auto-Body Repair Kits	
Marvel Light Bulbs	
Master Lock	
Montclair	*cigarettes and tobacco*
Mr. & Mrs. T. Cocktail Mix	
Ofrex Office Supplies	
Old Holborn	*tobacco products*
Paladin Blackcherry	*pipe tobacco*
Pall Mall	*cigarettes*
Perma	*filling and storage supplies*
Pinnacle Golf Products	
Regal China	
Rexel Office Products	
Roi Tan	*cigars*
Sail Pipe	*tobacco*
Silk Cut	*cigarettes*
Silva Thins	*cigarettes*
Sobraine	*cigarettes*
Southland Life Insurance	
Spey Royal	*Scotch*
Sunshine	*biscuits*
Swingline Stapler	
Tareyton	*cigarettes*
Titleist	*athletic equipment*
Twist Lemon Menthol	*cigarettes*
Vienna Finger Cookies	
Wilson Jones	*office products*
Woodbury	*soap*
W.R. Case & Sons	*cutlery*

American Broadcasting Companies Inc.

1330 Avenue of the Americas
New York, N.Y. 10019
(212) 887-7777

Chief Executive Officer: L.H. Goldenson
Exchange: NY
Symbol: ABC
Corporate History: ABC incorporated in 1949 as United Paramount Theatres Inc. In 1953, the name was changed to American Broadcasting-Paramount Theatres, and in 1965 the present name was adopted. ABC operates in the areas of broadcasting, publishing and leisure attractions. The television group licenses, produces and acquires programs for its network of 200 affiliated stations, of which five are company-owned. The radio division includes 1,596 radio stations. Broadcasting has provided the majority of the company's revenues and earnings. ABC is expanding into the production of motion pictures, cable TV programming and home video software.

Brandnames of Products and Services:

ABC	*entertainment center, Century City, Los Angeles, Calif.*
Chilton Co.	*publishing house*
High Fidelity	*publishing*
Hitchock Publishing Co.	
Indiana Prairie Farmer	*periodical*
KABC-TV & AM	*radio station, Los Angeles, Calif.*
KAUM-FM	*radio station, Houston, Texas*
KGO-TV & AM	*radio station, San Francisco, Calif.*
KLOX-FM	*radio station, Los Angeles, Calif.*
KSFX-FM	*radio station, Los Angeles, Calif.*
Miller Publishing Co.	
Modern Photography	*periodical*
Prairie Farmer	*periodical*
Schwann	*publications*
Silver Springs	*recreational facilities, Fla.*
WABC-TV & AM	*radio station, New York, N.Y.*
Wallaces Farmer	*agricultural publications*
WDAI-FM	*radio station, Chicago, Ill.*
Weeki wache Spring	*recreational facilities, Fla.*
Wild Waters	*recreational facilities, Calif.*
Wisconsin Agriculturist	*periodical*
WLS-TV & AM	*radio station, Chicago, Ill.*
WMAL-AM	*radio station, Wash. DC*
Word Incorporated Reference Material	*periodical*

WPLJ-FM	*radio station, New York, N.Y.*
WRAX-FM	*radio station, Wash., D.C.*
WRIF-FM	*radio station, Detroit, Mich.*
WXYZ-TV & AM	*radio station, Detroit, Mich.*

American Building Maintenance Industries

333 Fell St.
San Francisco, CA 94102
(415) 864-5150

Chief Executive Officer: R. David Anacker
1984 Annual Sales Volume: 374M
1984 Shares Outstanding: 3,541,000
Shareholders: 3,070
Exchange: NY
Symbol: ABM

Corporate History: American Building Maintenance Industries provides services for the operation of thousands of buildings in the United States and Canada. Through its three functionally-oriented groups, the company provides fully integrated services for building owners and managers. The Janitorial Services Group provides all aspects of basic housekeeping to a wide range of businesses. The AMTECH Group, through its various divisions, provides services aimed at running the electro-mechanical aspects of a building or office complex. Services include elevator repair and refurbishment, air conditioning installation and maintenance, and lighting maintenance. The Public Services Group includes parking facility management, all aspects of business security, wholesale distribution of janitorial supplies and equipment, and pest control services to residential and commercial customers.

Brandnames of Products and Services:

ABM Engineering Services
ABM Security Services
American Building Maintenance Co.
Ampco Parking Services
Amtech Elevator Services
Amtech Energy Services
Amtech Lighting Services
Comm Air Mechanical Services
Easterday Supply Co.
Rose Exterminator Co.

American Can Co.

American Lane
P.O. Box 3610
Greenwich, CT 06836-3610
(203) 552-2000

Chief Executive Officer: William S. Woodside
1984 Annual Sales Volume: 4,213M
1984 Shares Outstanding: 25,161,131
Shareholders: 77,400
Exchange: NY
Symbol: AC

Corporate History: Since 1981, American Can Co. has become virtually a new firm. Following a decision to restructure the company in that year, it has engaged in a series of divestitures, acquisitions, and repositionings. In all, American Can has divested approximately 25 operations for total proceeds worth more than $900 million; the bulk of these funds has financed key acquisitions in higher-growth areas linked by common strategic characteristics: strong competitive market positions serving specialty market niches; lower fixed capital requirements; and with expertise in information-based marketing and distribution channels. American Can Co. was incorporated in 1901, consolidating more than 60 companies engaged in the manufacture of tin cans and other types of containers and packages. Today, the firm operates in three principal industry segments: financial services, specialty retailing, and packaging.

Brandnames of Products and Services:

Aurora	*bathroom tissue*
Brawny	*paper towels*
Discount	*music stores*
Figis	*delicacies*
Fingerhut	*mail order house*
Gala	*paper towels*
Harmony Hut	*music stores*
Michigan Bulb	*garden and nursery products*
Musicland	*music stores*
Sam Goody	*music stores*

American Cyanamid Company

One Cyanamid Plaza
Wayne, NJ 07470
(201) 831-2000

Chief Executive Officer:	George J. Sella, Jr.
1984 Annual Sales Volume:	3,857M
1984 Shares Outstanding:	48,664,372
Shareholders:	60,968
Exchange:	NY
Symbol:	ACY

Corporate History: The company incorporated in 1907 as a manufacturer of fertilizers. During the 1920s it acquired a number of chemical companies and bought Lederle Laboratories, a leading drug producer and Cyanamid's major profit center until the 1970s. Over the past 30 years American Cyanamid has diversified into fragrances, personal care products, optics, home care products and insurance. In 1984 agricultural products accounted for 23% of sales, specialty chemicals 26%, medical products 27%, consumer goods 14% and Formica, 10%. Its foreign operations accounted for 30% of its sales in 1984.

Brandnames of Products and Services:

Blue Jeans	*women's toiletries*
Blue Stratos	*men's fragrance*
Bowl Guard	*toilet bowl cleaner*
Breck	*hair care products*
Caltrate	*vitamin supplement*
Carven	*fragrance*
Centrum	*vitamins*
CIE	*fragrance*
Combat	*roach killer*
Copper Glo	*copper cleaner*
Corex	*laminate*
Desert Flower	*hand and body lotion*
Formica	*decorative laminates*
Formica Floor Shine	*floor wax*
Geoffrey Beene	*fragrances*
Grey Flannel	*fragrances*
Lady's Choice	*deodorant*
L'Air du Temps	*fragrances*
La Prairie	*skin care products*
Lemon Sol	*disinfectant cleaner*
Nina Ricci	*fragrance*
Old Spice	*men's fragrance and toiletries*
Parfums Pierre Cardin	*fragrances*
Pierre Cardin	*men's toiletries*
Pine Sol	*disinfectant*
So Dry	*deodorant*
Stresstabs	*vitamins*
Tabac	*fragrance*
Ultraswim	*hair care products*

American Express Co.

American Express Plaza
New York, NY 10004
(212) 323-2000

Chief Executive Officer:	J.D. Robinson III
1984 Annual Sales Volume:	12,895M
1984 Shares Outstanding:	217,410,678
Shareholders:	51,211
Exchange:	NY
Symbol:	AXP

Corporate History: American Express has evolved from the roots of many individual companies: The company's travel-related and banking services sprang from three companies that combined in 1850 to meet an exploding demand for freight forwarding—the transport of small packages and packets of money—through rugged North American frontier country. Robberies and holdups were common, and American Express employees were expected to foil masked bandits with the same efficiency that they used to verify invoices. The company's banking services first became a separate entity in 1919, when they were grouped together in The American Express Company, Incorporated. The "Inc. Company," as it was known, was charged primarily with helping American Express expand internationally in the post-World War I period to meet the demand of a travel-hungry American people. Its name was changed to American Express International Banking Corporation in 1968. Shearson Lehman started in 1960 as Carter, Berlind, Potoma & Weill, a small, entrepreneurial firm that recognized the impact technological and economic changes would have on the securities industry. It built a highly cost-effective operations and back-office processing capability that helped it to absorb other firms, such as Shearson, Hammill & Co. Incorporated. One of its oldest components is Lehman Brothers, which started out in 1850 as a general store in Montgomery Alabama, and subsequently became a major investment banking power. IDS started business in 1894 in response to financial panics that wiped out the savings of many small investors in the American Midwest. John E. Tappan, a 25-year-old law student, began a firm called Investors Syndicate that helped people save part of their income on a systematic basis. Fireman's Fund Insurance was born in San Francisco in 1863 during the rough-and-tumble days that followed the Gold Rush. It was organized to provide protection against the fires that frequently ravaged the city, and 10 percent of its annual net income was donated to volunteer fire companies, a practice from which it took its name.

Brandnames of Products and Services:

American Express Card	
American Express Gold Card	
American Express International Banking	
American Express Money Orders	
American Express Platinum Card	
American Express Travelers Cheques	
Firemen's Fund Insurance	
Food & Wine	*publication*
IDS	*financial services*
Shearson Lehman Brothers	*financial services*
Travel & Leisure	*periodical*

American Family Corp.

1932 Wynnton Rd.
Columbus, GA 31999
(404) 323-3431

Chief Executive Officer: John B. Amos
1984 Annual Sales Volume: 823.6M
1984 Shares Outstanding: 19,898,909
Shareholders: 12,284
Exchange: NY
Symbol: AFL

Corporate History: American Family Corp. incorporated in 1973, acquiring all shares of American Family Life Assurance Co., which had been established in 1955. American Family Corp. emphasizes the sale of insurance policies to cover the expenses of cancer. Offers a variety of life insurance plans. It also operates broadcasting stations.

Brandnames of Products and Services:

American Family Life Assurance Co.	
KFVS-TV	*Cape Girardeau, Mo.*
KTIV-TV	*Sioux City, Iowa*
KWWL-TV	*Cedar Rapids, Iowa*
WAFF-TV	*Huntsville, Ala.*
WITN-TV	*Greenville, N.C.*
WTOC-TV	*Savannah, Ga.*

American Furniture Co.

Hairston St.
Martinsville, VA 24112
(703) 632-2061

Chief Executive Officer: R.M. Simmons, Jr.
1984 Annual Sales Volume: 94M
1984 Shares Outstanding: 2,459,216
Shareholders: 2,659
Exchange: OTC
Symbol: AFUR

Corporate History: The company, incorporated in 1906, manufactures both wood and upholstered furniture for living room, bedroom and dining room as well as for hotels and motels. It makes all parts except the face veneers and hardware.

Brandnames of Products and Services:

American of Martinsville	*furniture*

American Greetings Corporation

10500 American Road.
Cleveland, OH 44144
(216) 252-7300

Chief Executive Officer: Irving I. Stone
1984 Annual Sales Volume: 946M
1984 Shares Outstanding: 31,495,197
Shareholders: 8,608
Exchange: OTC
Symbol: AGREA

Corporate History: American Greetings Corp. was founded in 1906 and last incorporated in 1944 as American Greeting Publishers Inc. Its present title was adopted in 1952. The company designs and makes greeting cards, gift wrapping, paper party goods and stationery. In recent years it also has expanded into custom-made gifts, stuffed animals, calendars and other materials based on its greeting card business. The company's products are sold in about 80,000 retail outlets throughout the world.

Brandnames of Products and Services:

American Greetings	*greeting cards*

Amtoy	*toys*
Caprice	*greeting cards*
Care Bear Cousins	*stuffed animals*
Care Bears	*stuffed animals*
Carlton	*greeting cards*
Cuddly Crew	*stuffed animals*
Designer's Collection	*small giftware and novelty items*
Forget-Me-Nots	*greeting cards*
High Brows	*greeting cards*
Himself the Elf	*card and gift stores*
Holly Hobby	*greeting cards, giftwrap, party goods*
Laurel	*greeting cards*
Plus Mark	*giftwrap and greeting cards*
Soft Touch	*greeting cards*
Something Else	*greeting cards*
Something New	*greeting cards*
Strawberry Shortcake	*specialty item*
Sumit Stores	*card and gift stores*
Urchins	*greeting cards and party goods*
Woman to Woman	*series cards*
Ziggy	*greeting cards and party goods*

American Home Products Corp.

685 Third Ave.
New York, N.Y. 10017
(212) 878-5000

Chief Executive Officer: J.W. Culligan
1984 Annual Sales Volume: 4,485M
1984 Shares Outstanding: 152,614,295
Shareholders: 79,500
Exchange: NY
Symbol: AHP

Corporate History: American Home Products Corp. was incorporated in 1926 as a consolidation of several manufacturers of proprietary drug products. Throughout its history it has relied upon a strategy of acquiring rather than developing drug, food and home care products. Today the company is a well diversified producer of consumer goods.

Brandnames of Products and Services:

3-in-One	*oil*
Advil	*analgesic*
Aeroshave	*shaving cream*
Anacin	*analgesic*
Anbesol	*antiseptic*
Antrol	*household product*
Arthritis Pain Formula	*analgesic*
Baker's Street	*bakeware*
Bisodol	*antacid*
Black Flag	*insecticide*
Boyle Midway	*household products*
Brach	*candy*
Broniton	*asthma product*
Chef	*frozen foods*
Chef Boy-Ar-Dee	*Italian food*
Compound W.	*wart remover*
Country Kitchens	*housewares*
Crunch N Munch	*popcorn*
Denalen	*denture cleaner*
Dennison's	*food products*
Denorex	*medicated shampoo*
Depend-O	*bowl cleaner*
Dermoplast	*sunburn relief spray*
Diaper Pure	*diaper cleaner*
Dristan	*analgesic*
Dry & Clear	*medicated cleanser*
Dupli-Color	*auto spray paint*
Easy Off	*oven cleaner*
Easy On	*starch*
Ecko	*cooking utensils*
Franklin	*nuts*
Freezone	*corn remover*
Griffin	*shoe polish*
Gulden's	*mustard*
Gum Dinger	*bubble gum*
Hawes	*furniture polish*
Heet	*muscle ointment*
HR2	*rug shampoo*
Hula Chews	*chocolate*
Infra-Rub	*muscle ointment*
Jiffy	*popcorn*
Luck's	*canned chili*
Neet	*depilatories*
Old English	*furniture polish*
Old South Styles	*beans*
Outgro	*corn remover*
Ovral	*oral contraceptive*
Pac Man	*foods*
Pam	*cooking spray*
Plastic Wood	
Predictor	*pregnancy test kit*
Preparation H	*hemorrhoid remedy*
Primatene Mist	*asthma treatment*
Putters	*peanut butter*
Quiet World	*personal hygiene products*
Ranch Style	*beans*

Riopan	*liquid antacid*
Sani-Flush	*toilet bowl cleaner*
Semicid	*contraceptive*
Slaymaker	*combination locks*
Sleep-Eze	*sleep inducer*
"Steam"	*rug-cleaning machine*
Sudden Beauty Facial	
Sunset Ridge	*chocolates*
Top Drawer	*kitchen tools*
Viro-Med Liquid	*packaged medicine*
Wizard	*aerosols*
Wizard	*charcoal lighter; air freshener*
Woolite	*cold water wash*
X-14	*mildew remover spray*
Zud	*cleanser*

American Maize Products Co.

41 Harbor Plaza Drive
P.O. Box 10128
Stamford, CT 06904
(203) 356-9000

Chief Executive Officer: William Ziegler III
1984 Annual Sales Volume: 414 M
1984 Shares Outstanding: 5,253,541
Shareholders: 1,617
Exchange: AM
Symbol: AZEA

Corporate History: American Maize Products incorporated in 1906 as Western Glucose Co.; its present title was adopted in 1908. The company's corn-processing division makes food and industrial corn starches and syrups. Subsidiaries make and distribute cigars, and operate retail home & building centers by the name of Lloyd Home & Building Centers, Inc. American Fructose Corporation, a majority owned subsidiary (67.8%), produces high-fructose corn syrup, a nutritive sweetener used for baking, beverages, and a variety of other products.

Brandnames of Products and Services:

King Edward	*cigars*
Lloyd Home & Building Centers Inc.	*home improvement centers*
Lundy Briggs	*lumber yard*
Swisher Sweet	*cigars*

American Motors Corp.

27777 Franklin Rd.
Southfield, MI 48034
(313) 827-1000

Chief Executive Officer: J.J. Dedeurwaerder
1984 Annual Sales Volume: 4,200M
1984 Shares Outstanding: 110,000,000
Shareholders: 103,000
Exchange: NY
Symbol: AMO

Corporate History: The company incorporated in 1916 as Nash Motors Co. Its name was changed to Nash-Kelvinator Corp. in 1937 on merger with Kelvinator Corp., a refrigerator manufacturer. Its present name was adopted in 1954 following merger with Hudson Motor Car Co. AMC sold Kelvinator to White Consolidated in 1968. The company produced the first American compact car, the Rambler. In an effort to maintain viability AMC concluded an arrangement with Renault, the large French auto maker in 1979. Renault has provided AMC with some $500 million to build Renault cars in the United States in exchange for a 46.1% equity interest in American Motors.

Brandnames of Products and Services:

AMC Eagle	*automobile*
Jeep	*sports vehicle*
Renault Alliance	*automobile*
Renault Encore	*automobile*

American Standard Inc.

40 W. 40th St.
New York, N.Y. 10018
(212) 703-5100

Chief Executive Officer: W.A. Marquard
1984 Annual Sales Volume: 3,214M
1984 Shares Outstanding: 39,106,655
Shareholders: 36,500
Exchange: NY
Symbol: AST

Corporate History: In 1881 American Radiator Co. was founded as a manufacturer of steam and hot water radiators. In 1929 it combined with Standard Sanitary, the leader in plumbing fixtures, to form the American Radiator and Standard Sanitary Corp. The company became the leading manufacturer of bathroom fixtures in the U.S. During the 1960s American Standard diversified into a variety of home products and security equipment. It also has expanded into the foreign market and now does over half its business outside of the

United States. In 1984, American Standard acquired the Trane Co., the world's second largest manufacturer of air conditioning equipment.

Brandnames of Products and Services:

American-Standard	*bathroom and plumbing fixtures*
Ideal Standard	*bathroom and plumbing fixtures*
Majestic Fireplaces	
Modern Fold	*movable walls and partitions*
Mosler	*safes and security systems*
Perma-Door	*residential steel doors*
Standard	*building products*
Trane	*air conditioning products*

American Stores Co.

709 East South Temple
P.O. Box 27447
Salt Lake City, UT 84127
(801) 539-0112

Chief Executive Officer:	L.S. Skaggs
1984 Annual Sales Volume:	12,118M
1984 Shares Outstanding:	30,076,000
Shareholders:	14,824
Exchange:	NY
Symbol:	ASC

Corporate History: American Stores Co. is engaged primarily in the operation of retail stores, selling drug and food merchandise through 1,486 retail food, drug and combination drug/food stores in 40 states. The company was formed in 1979 through the acquisition of American Stores (a supermarket operator) by Skaggs Companies (an operator of drug and combination food-drug stores). It was one of the largest mergers in U.S. retailing history and resulted in a huge company spanning the continent. The company has grown rapidly through acquisition.

Brandnames of Products and Services:

Acme Supermarkets	
Alpha Beta Supermarkets	
Buttrey	*food stores*
Eisner	*food stores*
Elbys	*restaurants*
Jewel	*food stores*
JT General Stores	
Osco	*drugstores*
Sav-on	*drugstores*
Skaggs	*drugstores*
Star	*markets*

Ames Department Stores Inc.

2418 Main St.
Rocky Hill, Conn. 06067
(203) 563-8234

Chief Executive Officer:	H. Gilman
1984 Annual Sales Volume:	822,000,000
1984 Shares Outstanding:	13,583,000
Shareholders:	2,500
Exchange:	NY
Symbol:	ADD

Corporate History: The company, incorporated in 1962, operates a chain of 180 discount department stores in eleven northeastern states from Maine to Virginia, all operating under the name, "Ames".

Brandnames of Products and Services:

Ames	*discount department stores*

Amfac Inc.

44 Montgomery Street
P.O. Box 7813
San Francisco, CA 94120
(415) 772-3300

Chief Executive Officer:	Myron Du Bain
1984 Annual Sales Volume:	2.4 billion
1984 Shares Outstanding:	16,634,301
Shareholders:	10,000
Exchange:	NY
Symbol:	AMA

Corporate History: Amfac is a diversified services company with principal lines of business in wholesale distribution, food processing, hotels and resorts, retail, agriculture and property. The company was incorporated in Hawaii in 1918 and is the successor to a business founded in 1849. Prior to 1968, substantially all of Amfac's revenues were derived from operations within Hawaii. Since that time, Amfac has expanded its operations and by 1979 nearly three-quarters of its revenues were derived from operations in the continental U.S. Amfac today includes nearly 21,000 people working in operations located throughout 47 states, Guam and Australia. Its diverse operations include: one of the nation's largest wholesale distribution networks; the largest aboveground mushroom-growing facility on the West Coast; a major supplier of frozen, french-fried potatoes for the nation's fast-food industry; prominent regional retail chains; and leading resort and property developments.

Brandnames of Products and Services:

Amfac Hotels	
Amfac Tropical Products	*papayas*
C & H Sugar	
Coco-Palms Resort	*Hawaii*
Fisher Cheese	
Fred Harvey	*restaurants and resorts*
Furnace Creek Inn	*Calif.*
Grand Canyon National Park Lodges	
Kaanapali Beach Hotel	*Hawaii*
Kauai	*department stores*
King Kamehameha Hotel	*Hawaii*
Lamb-Weston	*frozen potatoes*
Liberty House	*department store*
Monterey Mushrooms	
Royal Kaanapali	*golf course*
Royal Lahaina Hotel	*Hawaii*
Silverado	*golf and country club*
Village Fashions	*off-price stores*
Waiohai Hotel, Poipu Beach Hotel	*Hawaii*

AMF Inc.

777 Westchester Ave.
White Plains, NY 10604
(914) 694-9000

Chief Executive Officer:	W.T. York
1984 Annual Sales Volume:	1,061M
1984 Shares Outstanding:	26,127,622
Shareholders:	55,976
Exchange:	NY
Symbol:	AMF

Corporate History: Incorporated in 1900 as a maker of automatic cigarette and cigar machinery, today AMF is a major producer of leisure time products including boats, recreational vehicles, sporting goods, and ski products. In 1968 it purchased Harley-Davidson, a motorcycle manufacturer for more than $3 million. The following year it bought Slickcraft Boat Co. During 1970-1971 it acquired Head Ski Co. and Wiener Metallwarenfabrick Smolka & Co. for a total of $28.5 million. It purchased Atlas Recreation Vehicles and the Marine Division of North American Rockwell Corp. in 1972. In trying to reduce its dependence on leisure goods, AMF shed its Harley-Davidson subsidiary in 1981. As a result AMF will reduce leisure to about half of its sales. Harley has 31% of the market for heavy-weight cycles but only 5% of the total market now dominated by the Japanese.

Brandnames of Products and Services:

Alcort	*marine recreational products*
American Athletic	*gymnasium equipment*
AMFLite	*bowling products*
Ben Hogan	*golf equipment and accessories*
Hatteras	*marine recreational products*
Head	*sporting goods (tennis and skis)*
Mares	*recreational products*
P & B (Potter & Brumfield)	*electrical products*
Paragon	*electrical products*
Tyrolia	*ski products*

Amoco Corp.

200 E. Randolph Dr.
Chicago, IL 60601
(312) 856-3800

Chief Executive Officer:	R.M. Morrow
1984 Annual Sales Volume:	26,949M
1984 Shares Outstanding:	283,571,000
Shareholders:	182,571
Exchange:	NY
Symbol:	AN

Corporate History: Amoco Corp. was incorporated as Standard Oil Company (Indiana)in 1889 to refine petroleum for the Midwest. In 1984, it ranked seventh among U.S. producers of crude oil, supplying about 4% of the nation's total. Historically Amoco has concentrated heavily on domestic oil sources and was not as severely hit by the Arab oil embargoes of the 1970s as the other oil giants. Nevertheless it gets more than 50% of its crude supply from overseas. Today the company has oil, mineral and chemical operations in 38 countries. Amoco is the nation's leading retail marketer of gasoline, which it sells in 33 states.

Brandnames of Products and Services:

Amoco	*oil-related products*
Amoco Ultimate	*motor oil (synthetic)*

Atlas	*automotive products*
Certicare	*auto servicing*
LDO	*automotive products*
Standard	*automotive products*

AMR Corp.

4200 American Blvd.
Fort Worth, TX 76155
(817) 355-1234

Chief Executive Officer: Robert L. Crandall
1984 Annual Sales Volume: 5.4 billion
1984 Shares Outstanding: 53,436,704
Shareholders: 35,276
Exchange: NY
Symbol: AMR

Corporate History: American Airlines Inc. is the principal subsidiary of AMR Corp., accounting for about 95 percent of its business in 1984. American serves 114 airports in 33 states, the District of Columbia, Bermuda, Canada, the Caribbean, Great Britain, Mexico and Puerto Rico. American Airlines was founded in 1930 as a consolidation of more than 85 small companies. Under the direction of C.R. Smith, American eventually became a profitable and innovative company. It was the first airline to emphasize passenger rather than freight service, the first to use stewardesses and the first to have planes built to its specifications. In 1959 it introduced jet planes to commercial flight. AMR Corp. was formed in 1982.

Brandnames of Products and Services:

American Airlines	
Sky Chefs	*airport concessions*

Amstar Corp.

1251 Avenue of the Americas
New York, NY 10020
(212) 489-9000

Chief Executive Officer: Howard B. Wentz, Jr.
1984 Annual Sales Volume: 1,298M
1984 Shares Outstanding: 8,040,162
Shareholders: All shares owned by Amstar Holdings Inc.
Exchange: OTC
Symbol: ASR

Corporate History: Amstar incorporated in 1966 under the name Domino Sugar Co. Amstar is the nation's largest manufacturer and distributor of nutritive sweeteners as well as an important supplier of industrial and technical products. It is a cane sugar refiner, a beet sugar processor and a corn sweetener manufacturer. Its sugar output is sold in bulk and liquid forms, and marketed principally under the Domino name in the East and under the Spreckels name in the West. Amstar also makes starch, paper bags and cartons, and laminated packaging structures. Its industrial and technical products companies manufacture a wide range of tools, equipment and materials for a variety of industrial markets, as well as sophisticated electronic and other equipment for defense markets.

Brandnames of Products and Services:

Dominade	*dry mix for noncarbonated drinks*
Domino	*cane sugar*
Spreckels	*beet sugar*

Anchor Hocking Corporation

109 N. Broad St.
Lancaster, OH 43132
(614) 687-2111

Chief Executive Officer: J. Ray Topper
1984 Annual Sales Volume: 713M
1984 Shares Outstanding: 10,545,854
Shareholders: 6,246
Exchange: NY
Symbol: ARH

Corporate History: Anchor Hocking, incorporated in 1928, is a diversified manufacturer of household, consumer and industrial products, including glass, plastic and china ovenware and tableware, glass and plastic industrial components, and cabinet and decorative hardware. Packaging products include plastic and metal closures and specialty glass containers for the toiletries, cosmetic and pharmaceutical industries.

Brandnames of Products and Services:

Auburn Brass	*brass hardware*
Bravo	*glassware*
Canfield	*glassware & servingware*
glassware	
glassware & dinnerware	
Hi-Heat	*microwave accessories*
MicroWare	*microwave accessories*
Moments	*glassware & servingware*
ovenware	
Shenango China	*china*

Anderson, Clayton & Co.

1100 Louisiana
P.O. Box 2538
Houston, TX 77002
(713) 651-0641

Chief Executive Officer: T.J. Barlow
1984 Annual Sales Volume: 1,524M
1984 Shares Outstanding: 12,050,301
Shareholders: 4,674
Exchange: NY
Symbol: AYL

Corporate History: Anderson, Clayton & Co. was founded in 1904 as a cotton merchandising partnership. It was incorporated in 1929. For many years it was the largest cotton company in the world. But in the 1960s the market for cotton declined as synthetic fabrics became popular. The company began diversifying and phasing out its cotton business. Today, Anderson Clayton is a diversified foods producer with operations in the United States, Mexico and Brazil. The company processes and markets consumer and institutional foods, oilseed products, and animal and poultry feeds. Its non-food operations include property/casualty insurance, life insurance, general merchandise warehousing and distribution services, materials handling equipment and a consumer line of thermoplastic ice chests and beverage coolers.

Brandnames of Products and Services:

American Founders	*life insurance*
Avoset	*non-dairy creamer*
Capri	*salad dressings and shortenings*
Chiffon	*margarine*
Cycle	*pet foods*
Gaines Burgers	*pet foods*
Gravy Train	*pet foods*
Hoffman's	*specialty cheese products*
Igloo	*plastic ice chests*
Jaxmor	*shortening and salad dressings*
Log Cabin	*syrup*
Maybud	*cheese products*
Purity cheese products	
Seven Seas	*salad dressings*
Southern Queen	*salad dressings and shortening*
Top Choice	*pet foods*
Unique Loaf	*cheese products*
Woody's	*cheese products*

Angelica Corp.

10176 Corporate Square Dr.
St. Louis, MO 63132
(314) 991-4150

Chief Executive Officer: Leslie F. Loewe
1984 Annual Sales Volume: 246.4 Million
1984 Shares Outstanding: 9,268,901
Shareholders: 2,962
Exchange: NY
Symbol: AGL

Corporate History: The company, incorporated in 1904, provides rental and laundry services of textiles and garments primarily to health care institutions; manufactures and markets uniforms and career apparel for institutions and businesses; and operates a national chain of retail uniform and shoe stores. Its retail operations consist of 129 uniform specialty shops throughout the United States.

Brandnames of Products and Services:

Life Uniform & Shoe Shops

Anheuser-Busch Companies Inc.

One Busch Place
St. Louis, Mo. 63118
(314) 577-3314

Chief Executive Officer: August A. Busch III
1984 Annual Sales Volume: 6,501M
1984 Shares Outstanding: 47,035,268
Shareholders: 30,007
Exchange: NY
Symbol: ABUD

Corporate History: Anheuser-Busch Companies, Inc. (incorporated in 1979), is a diversified corporation whose subsidiaries include the world's larest brewing organization, Anheuser-Busch, Inc. (which began operations in 1852), and the country's second largest producer of fresh baked goods, Campbell-Taggart, Inc. Other subsidiaries operate in the fields of container manufacturing and recycling, malt and rice production, international beer marketing, wine, snack foods, baker's yeast, family entertainment, real estate development, major league baseball, stadium ownership, creative services, rail car repair and transportation services.

Brandnames of Products and Services:

Adventure Island	*water recreation park, Tampa, FL*
Anheuser-Busch	*beer*

Budlight	*beer*
Budweiser	*beer*
Busch	*beer*
Colonial	*bakery products*
The Dark Continent	*theme park, Florida*
Eagle	*snack food*
Earth Grains	*bakery products*
El Charrito	*Mexican foods*
LA	*beer*
Michelob	*beer*
Michelob Classic Dark	*beer*
Michelob Light	*beer*
Natural Light	*beer*
The Old Country	*theme park, Williamsburg, VA*
Rainbo	*bakery products*
St. Louis Cardinals	*baseball team*

Anthony Industries Inc.

4900 Triggs St.
City of Commerce
Los Angeles, CA 90022
(213) 268-4877

Chief Executive Officer: Bernard I. Forester
1984 Annual Sales Volume: 214M
1984 Shares Outstanding: 3,248,795
Shareholders: 1,926
Exchange: NY
Symbol: ANT

Corporate History: The company, incorporated in 1959, manufactures both recreational products and industrial products. The recreational products group consists of Shakespeare Fishing Tackle, Anthony Swimming Pools, and Hilton Athletic Apparel. The industrial products group consists of Shakespeare Monofilament, Shakespeare Electronics and Fiberglass (antennas and light poles) and Simplex (insulative sheathing and laminated, coated paper products).

Brandnames of Products and Services:

Anthony Swimming Pools	*pools*
Hilton Athletic Apparel	*athletic apparel*
Pflueger	*fishing tackle*
President	*fishing rods, outboard motors*
Purdy Stik	*fishing rod*
Shakespeare Electronics & Fiberglas	*mobile antennas, fiberglass light poles*
Shakespeare Fishing Tackle	*fishing tackle, outboard motors*
Sigma	*fishing line*
Ugly stik	*fishing rod*
Whispertouch	*nylon thread*
Wonderline	*fishing equipment*

Apple Computer Inc.

20525 Mariani Avenue
Cupertino, CA 95014
(408) 966-1010

Chief Executive Officer: John Sculley
1984 Annual Sales Volume: 1,516M
1984 Shares Outstanding: 60,535,146
Shareholders: 45,000
Exchange: OTC
Symbol: AAPL

Corporate History: Apple Computer, Inc. develops, manufactures, and markets personal computer systems for business, education, science, industry, and the home.

Brandnames of Products and Services:

Apple	*home computer*
Apple II	*home computer*
LaserWriter	*computer printer*
Macintosh	*home computer*

Arkansas Best Corp.

1000 S. 21st St.
Fort Smith, AR 72902
(501) 785-6000

Chief Executive Officer: H.L. Hembree
1984 Annual Sales Volume: 530M
1984 Shares Outstanding: 4,995,059
Shareholders: 1,839
Exchange: NY
Symbol: ABZ

Corporate History: The company, incorporated in 1966, is engaged in trucking, furniture manufacturing, and truck-tire recapping. Under its Riverside brand, it produces a full line of medium-priced furniture that sells in all 50 states.

Brandnames of Products and Services:

Riverside	*furniture*

Armstrong Rubber Co.

500 Sargent Dr.
New Haven, CT 06536-0201
(203) 784-2200

Chief Executive Officer:	James A. Walsh
1984 Annual Sales Volume:	666M
1984 Shares Outstanding:	9,641,571
Shareholders:	2,821
Exchange:	NY
Symbol:	ArmsR

Corporate History: The Armstrong Rubber Company is the manufacturer of a wide variety of tires and inner tubes sold primarily in the replacement market through a network of independent dealers and distributors. The company also ranks among the the top three U.S. tire manufacturers in the production of agricultural and industrial/small implement tires for the original equipment market and produces synthetic rubber and related products through its subsidiary, Copolymer Rubber & Chemical Corporation. In March 1985, Armstrong acquired Blackstone Corporation, an international manufacturer of vehicular heat exchangers. Armstrong Rubber is a major supplier of tires to Sears, Roebuck and Co., and has been since 1936. The company has 12 manufacturing locations in ten states in addition to the Blackstone facilities.

Brandnames of Products and Services:

Armstrong	*automotive tires, rubber products*
Armstrong Brand	*tires & inner tubes*
Carleton	*tires*
Formula	*tires*

Armstrong World Industries Inc.

P.O. Box 3001
Lancaster, PA 17604
(717) 397-0611

Chief Executive Officer:	Joseph L. Jones
1984 Annual Sales Volume:	1,569M
1984 Shares Outstanding:	23,879,000
Shareholders:	11,324
Exchange:	NY
Symbol:	ACK

Corporate History: The company was founded in 1860 and incorporated in 1891. In 1980, its name was changed from Armstrong Cork Company to Armstrong World Industries, Inc. Armstrong today is primarily a manufacturer and marketer of interior furnishings. Its products include floor coverings (resilient flooring and carpets), ceiling systems, and furniture. Armstrong also makes and markets a variety of specialty products for the building, automotive, textile and other industries. The company's activities extend worldwide. Armstrong and its affiliated companies operate more than 50 plants in the United States and seven countries.

Brandnames of Products and Services:

Armstrong	*carpets, ceilings, flooring, furniture and industrial products*
Evans-Black	*carpets*
Thomasville	*furniture*

Arvin Industries Inc.

1531 Thirteenth St.
Columbus, Ind. 47201
(812) 378-3441

Chief Executive Officer:	James K. Baker
1984 Annual Sales Volume:	781,986,000
1984 Shares Outstanding:	11,343,108
Shareholders:	8,027
Exchange:	NY
Symbol:	ARV

Corporate History: Arvin Industries incorporated in 1921 as Indianapolis Pump & Tube Co.; its name was changed to Noblitt-Sparks Industries in 1927. The present name was adopted in 1950. The company is a major producer of automotive exhaust systems, portable electric heaters and compact stereos. In 1978 Arvin's engineering and research capabilities were strengthened by the acquisition of Calspan Corp., a company specializing in many areas of scientific study.

Brandnames of Products and Services:

Arvin	*home appliances*

Ashland Oil, Inc.

1401 Winchester Ave.
Ashland, KY 41101
(606) 329-3333

Chief Executive Officer:	John R. Hall
1984 Annual Sales Volume:	8,544M
1984 Shares Outstanding:	28,020,854
Shareholders:	42,400

Exchange: NYSE
Symbol: ASH
Corporate History: Ashland Oil, Inc. was founded in 1924 in Ashland, Ky., as a regional refiner and marketer of petroleum products. Today, Ashland is one of the 45 largest industrial corporations in America. In addition to its traditional refining, transportation and marketing business, Ashland has operations for oil and gas exploration and production, chemical manufacturing, marketing and distribution, coal mining and marketing, highway construction, and engineering services. The company is active in all 50 states as well as internationally and employs nearly 34,000 people worldwide. Ashland is the nation's largest independent petroleum refiner and a leading supplier of petroleum products to independent marketers. It owns three refineries with a combined capacity of 357,000 barrels per day and has a growing presence in retail gasoline marketing through its SuperAmerica combination gasoline and retail stores. Ashland is the parent corporation of Valvoline Oil Company, the nation's no. 3 marketer of branded, packaged motor oil. The nation's largest distributor of industrial chemical products, Ashland also has a strong position in a number of specialty chemical markets. In addition, Ashland is a leading coal producer.
Brandnames of Products and Services:

Mac's	*automotive chemicals*
Tectyl	*rust preventive and metal protectant*
Valvoline	*motor oil*

Associated Dry Goods Corp.

417 Fifth Ave.
New York, N.Y. 10016
(212) 679-8700

Chief Executive Officer: Joseph H. Johnson
1984 Annual Sales Volume: 4,107M
1984 Shares Outstanding: 15,424,829
Shareholders: 6,493
Exchange: NY
Symbol: DG
Corporate History: Associated Dry Goods Corp. was incorporated in 1916 out of a combination of Lord & Taylor and several other stores. Today, it is one of the larger retailing organizations in the United States, conducting its business in 31 states and the District of Columbia through 11 quality department store divisions, one women's specialty shop division and two upscale discount store subsidiaries.
Brandnames of Products and Services:

Caldor	*discount stores*
Denver Dry Goods Co.	*department stores*
Goldwater's	*department stores*
Hahne & Co.	*department stores*
Joseph Horne Co.	*department stores*
J.W. Robinson Co.	*department stores*
Loehmann's	*discount stores*
Lord & Taylor	*department stores*
L.S. Ayres & Co., Inc.	*department stores*
Powers Dry Goods Co.	*department stores*
Robinson's of Florida	*department stores*
Sibley, Lindsay & Curr Co.	*department stores*
Stewart Dry Goods Co.	*department stores*
Sycamore Specialty Stores	*department stores*

Associated Hosts, Inc.

8447 Wilshire Blvd.
Beverly Hills, CA 90211
(213) 653-6010

Chief Executive Officer: Joseph Bulasky
1984 Annual Sales Volume: 94M
1984 Shares Outstanding: 4,425,443
Shareholders: 775
Exchange: OTC
Symbol: AHST
Corporate History: The company, incorporated in 1964, operates 75 restaurants in 26 states under a number of names and formats. All of the firm's restaurants offer sit down service and alcoholic beverages, but provide a variety of menus and price ranges as well as decors. It also owns the Beverly Hillcrest Hotel in Los Angeles, leases another hotel in Westlake, California, and manages one other in Beverly Hills.
Brandnames of Products and Services:

Bombay Bicycle Club	*restaurants*
Julie's Place	*restaurants*
Smuggler's Inn	*restaurants*

Astrex Inc.

150 Fifth Ave.
New York, NY 10011
(212) 989-5000

Chief Executive Officer: Morris Kass
1984 Annual Sales Volume: 24M
1984 Shares Outstanding: 1,600,014
Shareholders: 800
Exchange: AM
Symbol: ASI

Corporate History: Astrex Inc., incorporated in 1960, is engaged in the distribution of electronic parts and components manufactured by others. The company's operations are located in the northeastern part of the United States. The company maintains an inventory of more than 25,000 different electronic parts and components at its various locations.

Brandnames of Products and Services:

Resco Electronics Stores	*component parts*

Atlantic Richfield Co.

515 So. Flower St.
Los Angeles, CA 90071
(213) 486-3511

Chief Executive Officer: R.O. Anderson
1984 Annual Sales Volume: 24,654M
1984 Shares Outstanding: 235,852,837
Shareholders: 197,000
Exchange: NY
Symbol: ARC

Corporate History: Atlantic Richfield Co. was incorporated in 1870 in Pennsylvania as the Atlantic Refining Co. Atlantic Richfield's present name was adopted following the merger of Richfield Oil Corp. into Atlantic Refining in 1966. Three years later, Atlantic Richfield acquired Sinclair Oil Corp. In 1977, it acquired Anaconda Co., one of the largest copper, aluminum, and uranium producers in the world. Atlantic Richfield's energy sources are primarily in the United States, including Alaska's Prudhoe Bay and Beaufort Sea. However, the company also produces petroleum liquids from its interests in Indonesia and Dubai. In addition, the company sells certain refined petroleum products in Brazil and elsewhere in the world markets. It also manufactures and markets petrochemicals. Other business interests include the mining of coal and various minerals.

Brandnames of Products and Services:

am/pm	*convenience food stores*
ARCO Petro	*automotive products*
ARCO Solar	*home photovaltaic products*
M P & G	*tune up centers*

Atlas Hotels Inc.

500 Hotel Circle
P.O. Box 80098
San Diego, Calif. 92138
(714) 291-2232

Chief Executive Officer: C.T. Brown
Exchange: OTC
Symbol: AHTL

Corporate History: The company incorporated in 1958 as King Hotel Corp. and adopted its present title in 1959. It owns and operates motor hotels and convention facilities in Arizona, California and Hawaii.

Brandnames of Products and Services:

Blackbeard's Galley & Grog	*restaurants Newport Beach and Maui*
Captain Cook's Galley	*restaurant Maui*
Carriage Inn	*Los Angeles, Calif.*
Crystal T's Emporium	*restaurant San Diego, Calif.*
Hanalei Hotel	*San Diego, Calif.*
Horton Plaza Hotel	*San Diego, Calif.*
Kings Inn	*San Diego, Calif.*
Mission Valley Inn	*San Diego, Calif.*
Pacifica Hotel	*Los Angeles, Calif.*
Picnic 'n Chicken	*fast-food restaurant*
Ramada Inn	*San Diego, Calif.*
Sunburst Hotel	*Scottsdale, Ariz.*
Town & Country Hotel	*San Diego, Calif.*

Avco

1275 King St.
Greenwich, Conn. 06830
(203) 552-1800

Chief Executive Officer: J.R. Kerr
Exchange: NY
Symbol: AV

Corporate History: Avco was founded in 1929 as a holding company for some of the country's earliest airlines. Today, it is a diversified corporation that offers consumer finance, insurance and management services; manufactures transportation structures, farm equipment and other products; and has interests in motion picture distribution and land development. In 1980, finance and insurance provided 55% of sales and products and services 45%.

Brandnames of Products and Services:

Avco Embassy Pictures Corp.	
Avco Financial Services Inc.	*insurance; consumer finance*
Ben-Mont	*giftwrap products*
Cartan	*travel bureaus*
Laguna Niguel	*planned community, Calif.*
Paul Revere Life Insurance Co. & Equity Sales Co. & Realty Corp.	
Rancho Bernardo	*planned community, San Diego, Calif.*
Ridgegate	*planned community, La Jolla, Calif.*
Village Park	*planned community, Encinitas, Calif.*

Avnet Inc.

767 Fifth Ave.
New York, N.Y. 10153
(212) 644-1050

Chief Executive Officer: Anthony Hamilton
1984 Annual Sales Volume: 1.6 billion
1984 Shares Outstanding: 36,810,000
Shareholders: 14,000
Exchange: NY
Symbol: AVT

Corporate History: Avnet was incorporated in 1955. Today it is the world's largest distributor of electronic components and computer products for industrial and military customers. Components are shipped either as received from its suppliers or with assembly or other value added. It also produces or distributes other electronic, electrical, electro-automotive and video communications products.

Brandnames of Products and Services:

Channel Masters	*television antennas*
Channel Master Satellite Systems	*micro-beam earth stations*
Guild	*musical instruments and accessories*

Avon Products Inc.

9 West 57th St.
New York, NY 10019
(212) 593-4017

Chief Executive Officer: Hicks B. Waldron
1984 Annual Sales Volume: 3,140,000,000
1984 Shares Outstanding: 83.84 million
Shareholders: 95,000
Exchange: NY
Symbol: AVP

Corporate History: The company was founded in 1886 and incorporated in 1916 as the California Perfume Co. The present name, Avon Products, Inc., was first used in 1930. It was adopted as the corporate name in 1950. Avon Products, Inc. includes four divisions: Beauty Products markets fragrance, make-up, skin care, jewelry and gift-and-decorative products for women, men and children. The products are sold to customers primarily in their homes by almost 1.4 million independent sales representatives in some 40 countries. Mallinckrodt develops, manufactures and markets a wide range of health care products, which account for about two-thirds of its sales. The division also markets specialty chemicals and flavor, fragrance and cosmetic chemicals. Foster Medical is a leader in the home health care field and participates in the medical supply business. Direct Response includes four direct-mail operations: Avon Fashions-women's apparel; James River Traders (men's and women's apparel); Brights Creek (children's apparel); and Great American Magazines subscription service.

Brandnames of Products and Services:

Avon	*fragrance, make-up, skin care, jewelry and gift-and-decorative products*
Avon Fashions	*women's apparel*
Brights Creek	*children's apparel*
Foster Medical	*home health care and medical supply services and products*
Great American Magazines	*subscription service*
James River Traders	*men's and women's apparel*
Mallinckrodt	*health care, specialty chemical, and flavor, fragrance and cosmetic chemical products*

Bacardi Corp.

G.P.O. Box 3549
San Juan, PR 00936
(809) 795-1560

Chief Executive Officer: Manuel L. del Valle
1984 Annual Sales Volume: 271M
1984 Shares Outstanding: 19,967,280
Shareholders: 788
Exchange: OTC
Symbol: BACA
Corporate History: The original Bacardi rum business was founded in Cuba in 1862 and was incorporated in Cuba as Compania Ron Bacardi in 1919. In 1958 the Cuban corporation granted to Bacardi International the rights to manufacture and sell Bacardi products worldwide with the exception of Cuba, Bermuda, the Bahamas and the United Kingdom. The company's Cuban properties were confiscated by the Castro government in 1960. In 1983 the company acquired 60% of Willmark Electronics, Inc. and Sunray de Puerto Rico, distributors of electronic consumer products in Puerto Rico. In 1984 the company acquired the remaining 40% of these companies. In 1983 the company acquired Lloyd's Electronics, Inc. a designer, importer and marketer of electronic consumer products.
Brandnames of Products and Services:

Bacardi	*rum & other alcoholic beverages*
Batey	*seasonings*
Carmela	*sausages*
India	*beer*
Lloyd's Electronics	*home electronics*
Malta India	*non-alcoholic beer*
Medalla	*beer*
Sturms	*mixed drinks, powdered milk*
Sunray de Puerto Rico	*home electronics*
Veryfine	*fruit juices*

Baldwin-United Corporation

1801 Gilbert Ave.
Cincinnati, Ohio 45002
(513) 852-7821

Chief Executive Officer: M.P. Thompson
Exchange: NY
Symbol: BDW
Corporate History: Baldwin was founded in 1898 as a maker of musical instruments. It was one of the first corporations to become involved in selling on the installment plan. The company last incorporated in 1977 as D.H. Baldwin Co. and adopted its current name in 1978 upon merger with United Corp. Today it is a diversified financial services holding company with interests in insurance, banking and savings and loan operations as well as musical instrument manufacturing. In January 1981 it agreed in principle to acquire Sperry Hutchinson Co. the nation's leading trading stamp and promotional services company. In fiscal 1979 insurance operations accounted for 39.6% of sales, savings and loan activities 15.6% musical instruments 19.3% and other financial services 25.5%.
Brandnames of Products and Services:

American Drew	*furniture*
Baldwin	*musical instruments*
Bigelow-Stanford	*carpets*
College/University Corp. Insurance Co.	
Daystroh	*furniture*
Empire Savings and Loan Association	
Home Crest	*furniture*
Lea	*furniture*
National Farmers Union Insurance	
National Investors Life Insurance Co.	
S & H Green Stamps	*trading stamps*
Top Value Enterprise	*trading stamps*

Ball Corp.

345 South High St.
Muncie, IN 47302
(317) 747-6100

Chief Executive Officer: R.M. Ringoen
1984 Annual Sales Volume: 1,050 million
1984 Shares Outstanding: 11,340
Shareholders: 5,761
Exchange: NY
Symbol: BLL
Corporate History: Ball was founded in 1880 as a container manufacturer, first of kerosene and paint cans and, shortly thereafter, glass jars and closures. It was last incorporated in 1922 and was called Ball Brothers Company Incorporated until the name was changed to Ball Corporation in 1969. Ball is primarily a packaging com-

pany with 70% of its sales coming from glass, metal and plastic containers. In addition, Ball manufactures industrial products, including industrial plastic products, decorated metal and such zinc products as penny blanks for the U.S. Treasury. The company develops and manufactures systems for NASA, the military, and international space programs within its technical products activity.

Brandnames of Products and Services:

Ball	*glass, metal, and plastic containers*
Dome	*seal closures for glass containers*

Bally Manufacturing Corp.

8700 West Bryn Mawr Avenue
Chicago, IL 60631
(312) 399-1300

Chief Executive Officer: Robert E. Mullane
1984 Annual Sales Volume: 1,349 M
1984 Shares Outstanding: 26,941,739
Shareholders: 17,353
Exchange: NY
Symbol: BLY

Corporate History: Bally was founded in 1931 as Lion Manufacturing. It produced a wooden slot machine called the Ballyhoo. Today it is primarily engaged in the design, manufacture, leasing and operation of coin-operated amusement and gaming equipment. The company also makes amusement equipment for the home consumer market. In 1978, it purchased the Park Place Hotel and Casino in Atlantic City, N.J. Bally's Health & Tennis Corporation of America (HTCA) subsidiary operates 323 health and fitness centers. The company's Six Flags Corporation operates seven theme parks and two water recreation parks.

Brandnames of Products and Services:

Aladdin's Castle	*pinball machines and arcade games*
Bally	*slot machines*
Bally/Midway	*video games*
Bally/Sente	*video games*
Chicago Health Clubs	*health clubs*
Flipper	*pinball machines*
Holiday	*health clubs*
Holiday Spa	*health clubs*
Jack LaLanne European	*health clubs*
Midway	*arcade games*
Park Place	*hotel in Atlantic City, N.J.*
President's First Lady	
Richard Simmons Anatomy Asylums	*health clubs*
Scandinavian	*health clubs*
Six Flags	*amusement parks*
VIC Tanney International	*health clubs*

Bangor Punta Corp.

1 Greenwich Plaza
Greenwich, Conn. 06830
(203) 622-8100

Chief Executive Officer: D.W. Wallace
Exchange: NY
Symbol: BNK

Corporate History: The company incorporated in 1932 as Punta Alegre Sugar Corp. Its name was changed to B.P. Alegre Sugar Corp. in 1964 and Bangor Punta Corp. in 1967. It is a diversified holding company with subsidiaries in aviation, handguns, law enforcement and sporting goods, and recreational and leisure time products.

Brandnames of Products and Services:

Cal	*boats and campers*
Jeanneau	*boats*
O'Day	*boats*
Piper	*aircraft*
Ranger	*recreational products*
Smith & Wesson	*law enforcement and sporting goods*
Starcraft	*recreational products*
Tyler	*recreational products*
Venture	*motor coaches*

R.G. Barry Corporation

13405 Yarmouth Road N.W.
Pickerington, OH 43147
(614) 864-6400

Chief Executive Officer: Gordon Zacks
1984 Annual Sales Volume: 120M
1984 Shares Outstanding: 3,646,875
Shareholders: 2,700
Exchange: AM
Symbol: RGB

Corporate History: The company, last incorporated in 1975, chiefly makes leisure time comfort footwear. The parent corporation was founded in 1945. The company operates seven manufacturing plants in the U.S. and Mexico. During 1982 the company terminated production and marketing of its Mushroom brand line and sold these rights to U.S. Shoe Corp. In 1983 the company ceased production and marketing of its Quoddy brand line and sold these rights to Wolverine Worldwide, Inc.

Brandnames of Products and Services:

Angel Treads	*slippers*
Bernardo	*women's footwear*
Dearfoams	*slippers for women*
Dearfoams for Kids	*slippers for children*
Dearfoams for Men	*slippers for men*
Madye's	*slippers*
Pim Poms	*slippers*
Polykins	*slippers*
Snug Treads	*slippers*
Sundowners	*men's slippers*
Three Cheers	*slippers*

Bassett Furniture Industries Inc.

P.O. Box 626
Main St.
Bassett, VA 24055
(703) 629-7511

Chief Executive Officer: R.H. Spilman
1984 Annual Sales Volume: 398M
1984 Shares Outstanding: 8,307,794
Shareholders: 3,700
Exchange: OTC
Symbol: BSET

Corporate History: The company, founded in 1902 and incorporated in 1930, makes bedroom, dining and living room furniture, plus occasional tables, wall units, entertainment centers, computer furniture, and contract office furniture.

Brandnames of Products and Services:

Bassett	*bedroom & dining room furn., occasional tables, juvenile furn. wall units*
Bassett	*living room furniture, bedding*
Commonwealth	*furniture*
Impact	*bedroom and occasional furniture*
Montclair	*chairs & living room furniture*
National-Mt. Airy	*bedroom and dining room furniture*
Weiman	*living room furniture*

Bausch & Lomb Inc.

One Lincoln First Square
Rochester, NY 14604
(716) 338-6000

Chief Executive Officer: D.E. Gill
1984 Annual Sales Volume: 534M
1984 Shares Outstanding: 29,716,000
Shareholders: 6,700
Exchange: NY
Symbol: BOL

Corporate History: Bausch & Lomb incorporated in 1908; its products are used throughout the world by eye-care professionals and consumers for the care, correction, and enhancement of vision. The company produces and sells specialized biomedical products and services, and precision optical devices, such as microscopes, for scientific use. Professional eye care products consist of contact lenses, ophthalmic instruments, and computerized management systems for eye-care professionals. Health care and consumer products comprise contact lens solutions, and such optical products for the extension of vision and eye protection as binoculars, riflescopes, telescopes, and sunglasses. Biomedical products include specialized biotechnical products and services, and this division of the company is the world's leading producer of laboratory animals.

Brandnames of Products and Services:

Bausch & Lomb	*contact lens care accessories and solution*
Bushnell	*binoculars, telescopes, riflescopes*
Glacier Glass	*sunglasses*
Insta-Focus	*binoculars*
Ray-Ban	*sunglasses*
Sensitive Eyes	*contact lens solutions*
Sight Savers	*lens cleaners*
Soflens	*contact lens care accessories and solutions*
Sofspin	*contact lens*
Sportview	*binoculars*
Tortuga	*sunglasses*
U3, U4	*contact lens*
Wayfarer	*sunglasses*
Wings	*sunglasses*

A.J. Bayless Markets Inc.

111 E. Buckeye Rd.
Phoenix, Ariz. 85004
(602) 262-0311

Chief Executive Officer: R.S. Hagel
Exchange: OTC
Symbol: BAYM
Corporate History: The company, incorporated in 1930, operates supermarkets and department stores in Arizona.
Brandnames of Products and Services:

Family Department Stores	*Ariz.*
A.J. Bayless	*supermarkets Ariz.*

Bayuk Cigars Inc.

2150 S. Andrews Ave.
Ft. Lauderdale, Fla. 33310
(305) 525-8433

Chief Executive Officer: E.A. Mishkin
Exchange: NY
Symbol: BYK
Corporate History: The company, incorporated in 1920, manufactures low- and medium-priced cigars. It is the fifth largest cigar company in the United States, with an estimated 8% of the market.
Brandnames of Products and Services:

Bravura	*cigars*
Caesar	*cigars*
Cheroot	*cigars*
Chico	*cigars*
Churchill	*cigars*
Cigarillo	*cigars*
Corona	*cigars*
Elegante	*cigars*
English Corona	*cigars*
Epicure	*cigars*
Fancy Tale	*cigars*
Fiesta	*cigars*
Gallante	*cigars*
Garcia y Vega	*cigars*
Gold Wedding	*cigars*
Granada	*cigars*
Gran Corona	*cigars*
Gran Premio	*cigars*
Java Tip	*cigars*
Maestro	*cigars*
Mexican Blunt	*cigars*
Napoleon	*cigars*
Panatella	*cigars*
Pan Deluxe	*cigars*
Perfecto	*cigars*
Phillips	*cigars*
Regalo	*cigars*
Romero	*cigars*
Senator	*cigars*
Spanish Tip	*cigars*
Sport	*cigars*
Titan	*cigars*
Washington	*cigars*
Webster	*cigars*
"160"	*cigars*

Beatrice Companies Inc.

2 North LaSalle St.
Chicago, IL 60602
(312) 782-3820

Chief Executive Officer: James L. Dutt
1984 Annual Sales Volume: 9,327M
1984 Shares Outstanding: 91,806,480
Shareholders: 51,380
Exchange: NY
Symbol: BRY
Corporate History: Beatrice, the nation's largest food company, was founded in 1894 in Beatrice, Nebraska, as a butter business. It developed Meadow Gold, the first butter to be advertised in a national magazine, in 1912. Historically Beatrice has had an aggressive acquisition strategy. Since 1943 it has bought more than 400 companies. The company began as a manufacturer of dairy products and in 1943 expanded into non-dairy foods. Beatrice has operations in more than 30 countries and markets products and services in more than 100 countries. The company is organized into four business segments—U.S. food, consumer products, international food and Avis/other operations. In 1984 Beatrice acquired Esmark, Inc.
Brandnames of Products and Services:

Absopure	*distilled and spring water*
Acryon	*leisure and household products*
Adisa Snacks	*snack foods*
Ailiram	*biscuits, confections*
All-American	*tools, health care products*
All Natural	*barbecue sauce*
Almay	*cosmetics, skin care products*
American Hostess	*ice cream*

American Pickles	
Antoine's	*food products*
Aristocraft	*cabinets*
Arrow Head	*bottled drinking water*
Artic	*ice cream*
Aunt Nellie's	*food products*
Avis	*rental cars*
Banner	*painting equipment*
Barbara Dee	*cookies*
Barcrest	*beverage mixes*
Baron's Table	*specialty meats*
Beatreme	*dairy products and flavorings*
Beatrice	*food products*
Beatrice Olde Fashioned Recipe	*ice cream*
Becky Kay's	*cookies*
Beefbreak	*meat specialties*
Beeforcan	*meat specialties*
Beneke	*bathroom accessories*
Best Jet	*painting equipment*
Bickford	*food products*
Bighorn	*specialty meats*
Big Pete	*specialty meats*
Bireley's	*orange drink*
Blue Boy	*ice cream*
Blue Ribbon	*condiments*
Blue Valley	*dairy products*
Body Shaper	*plumbing supplies*
Bogene	*closet accessories*
Boizet	*specialty food products*
Bonkers	*cat treats*
Boquitas	*snack foods*
Bosman	*barbecue equipment*
Bowers	*candies*
Bredan	*butter*
Brenner	*candy*
Brown Miller	*condiments*
Brown'N Serve	*breakfast meats*
Bubble Stream	*plumbing equipment*
Burny Bakers	*food products*
Butterball	*poultry products*
Butterchef Bakery	*products*
Buttercrust	*baked goods*
Buxton	*leather accessories*
Byrons	*barbecue equipment*
California Products	*beverage mixes*
Callard & Bowser	*confections*
Campofrio	*sausage, specialty meats*
Captain Kids	*food products*
Cartwheels	*travel bags*
CCA Furniture	*accessories*
Chapelcord	*school and religious apparel*
Charmglow	*barbecue grills and outdoor products*
Checkers	*beverages*
Chicago Specialty	*plumbing repair, remodeling prods*
Chipy	*snack foods*
Choky	*hot chocolate*
Churngold	*condiments*
Cincinnati Fruit	*condiments and fountain syrups*
Citro Crest	*beverage mixes*
Clark	*candy*
Classic	*travel bags*
Colonial	*cookies*
Cook 'n Cajun	*barbecue equipment*
Costello's	*food products*
Country Hearth	*baked goods*
County Line	*cheeses & cheese spreads*
Cow Boy Jo's	*meat specialties*
Cremo	*milk, ice cream*
Cross Your Heart	*bras*
Culligan	*water purifiers*
Culligan's Aqua Clear	*drinking water system*
Dannon	*yogurt*
Danskin	*bodywear, leotards, tights*
David Lau	*food products*
Davy Jones	*candy*
Day-Timers	*diaries, time planners*
Dearborn	*brass home improvement equipment*
Decora	*cabinets*
Dell	*condiments*
Del Mar	*window coverings*
Delta Food	*products*
Denyer-Dans	*specialty meats*
Derby	*tamales*
Dixie Lily	*food products*
Doll Brand	*oriental foods*
Dopp	*travel bags*
Doumak	*marshmallows*
Eckrich	*specialty meats*
Europe	*food bars*
Everain	*garden equipment*
Excello	*painting supplies and equipment*
Fashionaire	*travel bags*
Fiestas	*snack foods*
Fireside	*marshmallows*
Fisher	*nuts*
Flavor Ripe	*specialty food products*
Flee Bags	*travel bags*
Flora Danica	*cheese*

Flygon	*electrical barbecue equipment*
Fortsmith Folding	*tables and chairs*
FPI	*specialty foods*
FranPris	*food distribution*
Fruitine	*specialty foods*
Gambills	*food products*
G & W	*pizzas*
Gebhart	*Mexican foods*
GFI	*specialty meats*
Givenchy	*hosiery*
Gladiola	*food products*
Gold Medal	*beverages*
Good Humor	*ice cream*
Gourmet	*ice cream*
Grandmother Joshua	*specialty products*
Great Bear	*bottling drinking water*
Grove Crest	*beverage mixes*
Guangmei	*snack foods*
Guasti	*wine products*
Halston/Orlane	*fragrances and skin care products*
Handee Ram Rod	*plumbing supplies*
Handiform	*closet accessories*
Harmon Kardon	*high-fidelity components*
Hart	*skis*
Hawaii's Own	*fruit drinks*
Hekman	*furniture*
Holanda	*ice cream, ice cream stores*
Holland	*dairy products*
Homemaker	*leisure and household products*
Hostess	*hams*
Hotel Bar	*butter*
Hot Foot	*leisure and household products*
Hunt's	*canned tomato products*
Indiana	*moulding and frame furniture*
Irwinware	*bar accessories*
Jack's	*snack foods*
Jax	*furniture accessories*
Jetstream	*garden equipment*
Jhirmack	*hair care products*
John Hancock	*outdoor furniture*
Johnston's	*yogurt*
Jolly Rancher	*candy*
Jubilee	*specialty food products*
Kalise	*ice cream*
Keller's	*butter and eggs*
KeyKo	*condiments*
Kicks	*luggage*

King's Choice	*cheese*
Kleen Stream	*plumbing products*
Kneip	*specialty meats*
Krispy Kreme	*baked goods*
La Choy	*Oriental foods*
Lady Betty	*condiments*
Lambrecht	*pizza*
La Menorguina	*ice cream*
Lara Lynn	*food products*
Lark	*luggage*
Latums	*baked goods*
Liberty	*condiments*
Light 'n' Fresh	*baked goods*
Lignoflex	*food products*
Liken	*interior design*
Little Brownie	*cookies and baked goods*
Little Pete	*plumbing supplies*
Longhorn	*food products*
Long Life	*aseptic dairy products*
Loomcrafted	*interior design products*
Lords	*candy*
Louis Sherry	*ice cream, frozen desserts*
Louver Drape	*window coverings*
Lowrey's	*specialty meats*
Luxuria	*leisure and household products*
Ma Brown	*food products*
Magnolia	*bathroom accessories*
Manwich	*sloppy joe sauce*
Marionette	*condiments*
Mario's	*condiments*
Mark Force Vatco	*travel accessories*
Martha White	*bakery products*
Max Factor	*cosmetics & fragrances*
Max H. Kahn	*curtains*
Meadow Gold	*dairy products*
Melnor	*garden equipment*
Metco	*cheese*
Migros	*food distribution*
Milk Duds	*candy*
M.J. Holloway's	*candy*
Molly Bushell	*confections*
Mother's Best	*food products*
Mountain High	*yogurt*
Mt. Ida	*olives*
Mug Old Fashioned Root Beer	
Murray's	*food products*
Nat Nast	*sportswear*
N-Rich	*non-dairy creamer*
Nuttall's	*confections*
Olive Products	*condiments*

Olympian	*sportswear*
Omega	*travel bags*
Omega	*food products*
Orville Redenbacher's Gourmet Popping Corn	*popping corn*
Ovenmates	*household goods*
Ozarka	*bottled drinking water*
Palmeto	*baked goods*
Pan Free	*beverage mixes*
Patra	*fruit juices and drinks*
Pauly	*natural cheeses*
Payco	*ice cream, novelties*
Pepi's	*meat specialty products*
Pernigotti	*confections, snack foods*
Peter Eckrich	*specialty products*
Peter Pan	*peanut butter products*
Phoenix	*candy*
Pitegoff	*painting supplies*
Playtex	*intimate apparel, rubber gloves*
Plume De Veal	*veal products*
Premier Is	*ice cream*
Princess House	*closet accessories*
Rainbo	*food products*
Rainwave	*garden equipment*
Reber	*food products*
Record	*food distribution*
Reddi Whip	*whipped cream*
Red Tulip	*candy*
R.F.	*specialty meats*
Richardson	*candy*
Rid-O-Ray	*electrical barbecue equipment*
Robert's	*cookies*
Rosarita	*mexican foods*
Round-the-Clock	*hoisery*
Royal Crest	*yogurt*
Samsonite	*luggage, furniture*
Sanson	*ice cream*
Savoy	*confections and biscuits*
Sizzlean	*variety meats*
Smith Kendon	*confections*
Soup Starter	*food product*
Stew Starter	*food product*
Stiffel	*lamps*
Stute	*jams & juices*
Support Can Be Beautiful	*bras*
Swift	*meat products*
Swiss Miss	*cocoa products*
Swiss Rose	*cheeses*
Tayto	*snack foods*
Thank Goodness It Fits	*bras*
Treasure Cave	*blue cheese*
Tropicana	*fruit juice, fruit juice drinks*
Viva	*milk & cottage cheese*
Von Comp	*confections*
Webcraft	*printing, paper products*
Wesson	*vegetable oils*
Wilson	*specialty meats*
WOW (With-out-wire)	*bras*

Becton, Dickinson & Co.

Mack Centre Dr.
Paramus, NJ 07652
(201) 967-3700

Chief Executive Officer: W.J. Howe
1984 Annual Sales Volume: 1,127M
1984 Shares Outstanding: 21,227,000
Shareholders: 8,375
Exchange: NY
Symbol: BDX
Corporate History: Becton, Dickinson & Co., incorporated in 1906, manufactures and sells health care products. The company also produces industrial safety equipment, including protective clothing.
Brandnames of Products and Services:

Ace	*bandages*
Bauer & Black	*support bandages*
Becton-Dickinson	*health care products*
Edmont	*dipped latex and vinyl plastic gloves*
Lo-Dose	*disposable syringes*
Micro	*fine insulin needles*

Begley Co.

P.O. Box 1000
Richmond, KY 40475
(606) 623-2550

Chief Executive Officer: Robert J. Begley
1984 Annual Sales Volume: 66M
1984 Shares Outstanding: 552,052
Shareholders: 660
Exchange: OTC
Symbol: BGLY
Corporate History: Founded in 1921, the company presently operates 42 drugstores in Kentucky, 125 dry

cleaning stores in nine southern and midwestern states and five home health care centers in Kentucky.

Brandnames of Products and Services:

Begley Drug Stores	*drugstores*
Begley's Home Health Center	*health equipment store*
Big B	*dry-cleaning stores*
Key	*dry-cleaning stores*
Superior	*dry-cleaning stores*

Bekins Co.

777 Flower St.
Glendale, Calif 91201
(213) 240-6400

Chief Executive Officer: A.L. Labinger
Exchange: OTC
Symbol: BEKN

Corporate History: The company, incorporated in 1923, is a holding company for Bekins Moving & Storage, the largest moving and storage firm in the United States. Bekins Van Lines is the fifth largest long-distance van line in the country. The company also owns termite control, building maintenance and guard services.

Brandnames of Products and Services:

Ace Pest Control	
Ace Termite Control	
Bekins Van Lines	*moving and storage*
U Rent Furniture	

Belding Heminway Co. Inc.

1430 Broadway
New York, NY 10018
(212) 944-6040

Chief Executive Officer: Richard Hausman
1984 Annual Sales Volume: 124M
1984 Shares Outstanding: 2,793,074
Shareholders: 2,144
Exchange: NY
Symbol: BHY

Corporate History: Belding Heminway Company, Inc., incorporated in 1947, manufactures and markets industrial thread and specialty fabrics used by manufacturers in a wide range of consumer and industrial products. Belding is also a leading distributor in the United States of a diversified line of home sewing products, including buttons, threads and notions. Belding Heminway has two major divisions - industrial and home sewing.

Brandnames of Products and Services:

Belding Heminway	*sewing notions*
Corticelli	*notions*
La Mode	*buttons*
Le Chic	*buttons*
Lily	*threads and lap-craft materials*
Penn	*notions*

Bell & Howell Co.

5215 Old Orchard Road
Skokie, IL 60077-1076
(312) 470-7100

Chief Executive Officer: Donald N. Frey
1984 Annual Sales Volume: 714M
1984 Shares Outstanding: 7,923,321
Shareholders: 5,866
Exchange: NY
Symbol: BHW

Corporate History: Bell & Howell was incorporated in 1907 as a manufacturer of high-quality still and motion picture cameras and related equipment. Since then, it has diversified into business equipment and electronic instruments and the operation of training and educational institutes. The company sold its consumer camera division in 1979 to J. Osawa & Co.; currently these cameras are sold under the Bell & Howell Mamiya label. In 1984 the company acquired the computer output on microfilm business of the 3M Company.

Brandnames of Products and Services:

Bell & Howell	*audio-visual equipment, document/mail processing equipment, visual communications systems*
Charles E. Merrill	*textbook publisher*
De Vry Institute of Technology	*Chicago, Dallas, New York*
Missouri Institute of Technology	*Kansas City, Mo.*
Ohio Institute of Technology	*Columbus, Ohio*

Bendix Corp.

Bendix Center
Southfield, Mich. 48076
(313) 352-5000

Chief Executive Officer: W.M. Agee
Exchange: NY
Symbol: BX
Corporate History: Bendix was founded in 1924 as a supplier of automotive parts, particularly starters and braking systems. Today its automotive division still accounts for about one-half of its sales, with Ford its largest customer. It incorporated in 1929 as Bendix Aviation Corp. and grew tremendously during World War II when the military increased its orders dramatically. Its present title was adopted in 1960. Bendix is a worldwide manufacturer engaged in four lines of business: automotive, aerospace-electronics, forest products and industrial energy. The company's major markets have been the automakers and the military. It is strong in the automobile equipment replacement market, which does well when car sales slip. Bendix has attempted to diversify in an effort to limit its dependence on its two major markets. It sold off 2 of its natural resource companies in 1980. Following the 1980 acquisition of Warner & Swasey, Bendix became the nation's second largest machine tool manufacturer, behind Cincinnati's Milacron.
Brandnames of Products and Services:

Autolite	*spark plugs*
Bendix Products	*self-assembly furniture*
Fram Filters	*automotive product*

Berkey Photo, Inc.

One Water Street
White Plains, NY 10601
(914) 997-9700

Chief Executive Officer: Jerry J. Burgdoerfer
1984 Annual Sales Volume: 216M
1984 Shares Outstanding: 4,566,000
Shareholders: 4,507
Exchange: NY
Symbol: BKY
Corporate History: The company, incorporated in 1960, manufactures and distributes photography equipment. The Company's businesses include color and black-and-white film processing for the amateur photographer, photo services for the professional photographer, and the marketing and distribution of more than 100 products in the fields of photographic and video equipment and supplies. In 1984 the company acquired Marden-Kane, Inc. a promotional services company.
Brandnames of Products and Services:

Ascor	*lighting equipment*
Berkey	*photofinishing*
Direct Photo	*photofinishing*
Gossen	*photographic equipment*
Kelly Film	*photofinishing*
Omega	*enlargers, photography equipment*
Photo Decals	*film accessory*
Photo Gallery	*film accessory*
Rodenstock	*lenses*
Rollei	*photographic products*
Willoughbys	*camera store, New York, N.Y.*
Zero Halliburton	*camera and video cases*

Berkline Corp.

One Berkline Drive
Morristown, TN 37814
(615) 586-1461

Chief Executive Officer: Lawrence W. Whalen, Jr.
1984 Annual Sales Volume: 83M
1984 Shares Outstanding: 1,538,000
Shareholders: 801
Exchange: OTC
Symbol: BERK
Corporate History: The company, incorporated in 1970, makes upholstered furniture which it markets throughout the U.S. and Canada.
Brandnames of Products and Services:

Autoglide	*reclining chair*
Berkline	*furniture*
Wallaway	*reclining chair (close-to-the-wall)*

Berkshire Hathaway Inc.

1440 Kiewit Plaza
Omaha, NE 68131
(402) 346-1400

Chief Executive Officer: Warren E. Buffett
1984 Annual Sales Volume: 201M
1984 Shares Outstanding: 1,146,909
Shareholders: 3,125
Exchange: OTC

Symbol: BKHT

Corporate History: Founded in 1899, Berkshire Hathaway's four major businesses are as follows: underwriting of property and casualty insurance, candy production and sale, newspaper publishing, and retailing of home furnishings.

Brandnames of Products and Services:

Associated Retail Stores	*apparel stores*
Blue Chip Stamps	*trading stamps*
Buffalo Evening News	*newspaper*
Columbia Insurance	*reinsurance*
GEICO	*insurance*
Mutual Savings and Loan	*savings & loan bank*
National Indemnity	*reinsurance*
Nebraska Furniture Mart	*furniture*
See's Candies	*confections*

Best Products Co., Inc.

Parham Road
Richmond, VA 23227
(804) 261-2000

Chief Executive Officer: A. Lewis
1984 Annual Sales Volume: 2,300M
1984 Shares Outstanding: 27,000,000
Shareholders: 9,600
Exchange: NY
Symbol: BES

Corporate History: Best Products Co., Inc., one of the nation's largest discount retailers, was founded in 1957 in Richmond, Va. The company is principally engaged in selling jewelry and nationally advertised brand-name merchandise through a yearly catalog and the nation's largest chain of catalog showrooms. The company's merchandising philosophy is based upon low-margin, high-volume principles. In the fall of 1984, Best printed more than 11 million catalogs containing approximately 8,500 items of merchandise in the following categories: jewelry, housewares, sporting goods, toys, cameras and electronics, giftware, and seasonal. The company's showrooms offer catalog merchandise plus nearly 5,000 additional items.

Brandnames of Products and Services:

Ashby's, Ltd.	*specialty retailing*
Best	*catalog showrooms*
Best Jewelry	*retail store*
Dolgin's	*catalog showrooms*
Great Western	*catalog showrooms*
Jafco	*catalog showrooms*
LaBelle's	*catalog showrooms*
Miller Sales	*catalog showrooms*
Rogers	*catalog showrooms*

Bickford Corp.

1330 Soldiers Field Rd.
Brighton, Mass. 02135
(617) 782-4010

Chief Executive Officer: J.C. Harding II
Exchange: AM
Symbol: BIK

Corporate History: The company incorporated in 1970 as la Touraine Foods. It adopted its present title in 1978. The firm operates coffee shops and pancake houses in the Eastern part of the United States. In 1976, attempting to diversify, Bickford acquired the jewelry manufacturing business, Vargas Manufacturing.

Brandnames of Products and Services:

Bickford's Family Fare	*coffee shops*

Bic Corp.

Wiley St.
Milford, CT 06460
(203) 783-2000

Chief Executive Officer: Bruno Bich
1984 Annual Sales Volume: 246M
1984 Shares Outstanding: 6,060,000
Shareholders: 2,000
Exchange: AM
Symbol: BIC

Corporate History: Bic Corp. was founded in 1958 as Waterman Bic Pen Corp.; the present title was adopted in 1982. Bic is a diversified company primarily engaged in the manufacture and sale of low-cost disposable plastic consumer products. It is the largest manufacturer in North America of ball pen writing instruments, and butane lighters. In 1976, the company introduced BIC Shaver, a disposable shaver, which today enjoys an 18% share of the blade market. In 1985, it introduced the BIC Shaver for Sensitive Skin, the first shaver to address this need. BIC leisure products, subsidiary of BIC, markets Dufour BIC Sailboards and the BIC Sport Rack System in the U.S.

Brandnames of Products and Services:

Bic Lady Shaver	
Bic Lighter	
Bic Pens	
Bic Shaver	
Bic Shaver for Sensitive Skin	
Bic Sport Rack System	*modular car-top carrier system*
Dufour Bic Sailboard	

Big B, Inc.

201 8th Street West
Birmingham, AL 35202
(205) 785-0335

Chief Executive Officer: Joseph S. Bruno
1984 Annual Sales Volume: 148M
1984 Shares Outstanding: 6,589,328
Shareholders: 3,518
Exchange: OTC
Symbol: NMS

Corporate History: Big B Inc. opened its first Big B Discount Drug Store in 1968. Organized as a corporation in Alabama in 1972, it was operated as a drug store division of Bruno's Inc. until the latter was transferred to Big B in 1977. Big B operates a chain of 109 drug stores in Alabama, Mississippi, Florida, Georgia and Tennessee. It also operates five grocery and drug combination stores in Alabama and three home health care stores in Alabama and Georgia.

Brandnames of Products and Services:

Big 'B' Discount Drugs	*drug stores*
Big 'B' Home Health Care Center	*convalescent aids*
B-Mart Food & Drugs	*combination stores*

Big Bear, Inc.

770 West Goodale Ave.
Columbus, OH 43212
(614) 464-6500

Chief Executive Officer: Michael J. Knilans
1984 Annual Sales Volume: 747M
1984 Shares Outstanding: 6,284,125
Shareholders: 563
Exchange: OTC
Symbol: BGBR

Corporate History: Big Bear, Inc., founded in 1934, is composed of two major business segments: Big Bear Inc., a chain of 61 retail food stores in Ohio and West Virginia, and Hart Stores Inc., a chain of 27 discount department stores in Ohio, West Virginia and Kentucky.

Brandnames of Products and Services:

Big Bear	*supermarkets*
Big Bear Bakeries	*bakeries*
Hart	*discount department stores*

Billy The Kid, Inc.

4171 N. Mesa Building D
PO Box 9817
El Paso, Texas 79988
(915) 545-4000

Chief Executive Officer: T.A. Pendergast
Exchange: AM
Symbol: BTK

Corporate History: The company incorporated in 1971 as Hortex Inc. and adopted its present title in 1972. It began as a manufacturer of boys' wear which constituted 75% of its sales as of the late 1970s. Faced with a shrinking market because of the decline in the birth rate, it added a girls' line and a designer line.

Brandnames of Products and Services:

Bill Blass	*women's jeans*
Billy The Kid	*children's clothing*
Calamity Jane	*children's clothing*
Factory Fallout	*apparel stores*
French Cut	*designer jeans*
Hot Dogs	*children's clothing*
Mann	*children's clothing*
Oscar de la Renta	*jeans*

Binney & Smith Inc.

1100 Church Lane
Easton, Pa. 18042
(215) 253-6271

Chief Executive Officer: R.J. McChesney
Exchange: NY
Symbol: BYS

Corporate History: The company, originally incorporated in 1902, is a leading manufacturer of children's art materials and educational games.

Brandnames of Products and Services:

Artista	*paints*
Crayola	*crayons and chalk*
Firma-Grip	*glue*
Silly Putty	*toy*

The Black & Decker Corporation

701 East Joppa Rd.
Towson, MD 21204
(301) 583-3900

Chief Executive Officer:	Laurence J. Farley
1984 Annual Sales Volume:	1,533M
1984 Shares Outstanding:	50,338,773
Shareholders:	18,697
Exchange:	NY
Symbol:	BDK

Corporate History: Black & Decker is a manufacturer and marketer of products for use in and around the home and for professional applications. With manufacturing facilities in twelve countries and products sold in over fifty, the company is the world's leading producer of power tools and has recently become one of the world's largest suppliers of household products. Black & Decker was incorporated in 1910 as a manufacturer of industrial machinery. In 1946, the company entered the consumer market with electric drills, and in 1979 entered the household products business with the introduction of its cordless, rechargeable vacuum, the Dustbuster. In 1983, the company accelerated its expansion into this market by acquiring General Electric's Housewares division, becoming one of the world's three largest producers of housewares. The official name of the company, previously The Black and Decker Manufacturing Company, was changed in January 1985 to The Black & Decker Corporation. Its emphasis on internal product development has resulted in a significant number of new products; in fact, in 1984 one-third of the company's sales came from products that did not exist five years ago.

Brandnames of Products and Services:

Black & Decker	*tools & household products*
Dustbuster	*cordless vacuum*
Workmate	*hobby-crafter vise*

John Blair & Co.

1290 Avenue of the Americas
New York, NY 10104
(212) 603-5000

Chief Executive Officer:	Jack W. Fritz
1984 Annual Sales Volume:	842M
1984 Shares Outstanding:	7,993
Shareholders:	2,757
Exchange:	NY
Symbol:	BJ

Corporate History: Incorporated in 1935, John Blair & Company is a diversified marketing and communications company whose business comprises marketing services, broadcasting station ownership, station representation, and printing and television programming. The company's ADVO-System subsidiary is the nation's largest processor of carrier-route-sorted third-class mail. Another subsidiary, John Blair Marketing, is a leading producer of couponing and other promotional programs. Through its Blair Television, Blair Radio and Blair/RAR divisions, the company represents broadcasting stations in the sale of advertising time. Its Blair Entertainment division has a growing business in the development and distribution of television programming, and the division's RPR Productions unit is a producer of special television sports programming material for networks and stations. Another unit, Blair-Span, produces and distributes Spanish-language television programming. In graphics, the company is a major printer of catalogs and other advertising and promotional material through its three printing subsidiaries, Alden Press, American Printers & Lithographers, and Meehan-Tooker.

Brandnames of Products and Services:

Blair Inserts	*newspaper coupon inserts*
Brain	*radio computer system for sales and research*
"Break the Bank"	*syndicated tv series*
"Divorce Court"	*syndicated tv series*
KOKH-TV	*Oklahoma City, Okla.*
KSBW-TV	*Salinas/Monterey/San Jose, Calif.*
KSBY-TV	*San Luis Obispo/Santa Barbara, Calif.*
KVIL AM/FM	*radio station, Dallas, TX*
Marriage Mail™	*targeted shared-mail distribution*
Network Mail	*direct mail coupon/ promotion programs*
Tel Avail	*tv computer system for sales and research*

WFLA AM/FM	*radio station, Tampa FL*
WHDH-AM	*Boston, Mass.*
WIBC-AM	*Indianapolis, IN*
WKAQ-TV	*San Juan, Puerto Rico*
WNAP-FM	*Indianapolis, IN*
WSCV-TV	*Miami-Ft. Lauderdale, FL*
WZOU-FM	*Boston, Mass.*

Blount Inc.

4520 Executive Park Dr. P.O. Box 949
Montgomery, AL 36192-1201
(205) 272-8020

Chief Executive Officer: Winton M. Blount
1984 Annual Sales Volume: 847M
1984 Shares Outstanding: 11,845,954
Shareholders: 8,000
Exchange: AM
Symbol: BLT
Corporate History: The company is the successor to a business organized in 1946; it has been publicly owned since 1972. Blount is an international company with construction and manufacturing operations in three primary business segments: construction and engineering, specialty steel, and machinery and equipment. Blount is a leader in the construction, construction management, engineering and design of non-residential and industrial buildings and of heavy construction projects in both the public and private sectors worldwide. It ranks among the largest construction companies in the world. The company is also in the business of developing and operating waste-to-energy, cogeneration, hydro-power, water and sewage treatment projects for municipalities and industry. Blount is a fully integrated producer of specialty steels, principally stainless and high alloy steels. The company's Washington Steel subsidiary is regarded as one of the low-cost and most efficient producers of stainless in the United States. Blount's Omark subsidiary is the world's leading manufacturer of cutting chain for woodcutters and a maker of cutting tools and garden cutlery for professional and home craftsmen. It is a leading manufacturer of hydraulic materials handling equipment for use in pulpwood and timber harvesting in North America, and the largest domestic manufacturer of powerloads for powder-actuated tools, and the leading manufacturer of gun care equipment.
Brandnames of Products and Services:

CCI Ammunition	
Credo	*blades, bits, hand tools*
Oregon Chain Saws	
Oregon Firewood Center	*firewood accessories*
RCBS Ammunition Accessories	
Speer Ammunition	

Blue Bell Inc.

335 Church Court
Greensboro, N.C. 27401
(919) 373-3400

Chief Executive Officer: L.K. Mann
Exchange: NY
Symbol: BBL
Corporate History: Blue Bell began in 1916 as Jellico Manufacturing Co. By 1930, as the Blue Bell Overall Co., it was the largest producer of work clothes in the world. It changed its name to Blue Bell in 1943. Today the company is second only to Levi Strauss in western wear for the entire family. It also makes utility clothing, uniforms for rental and sportswear. In 1979 it acquired Jantzen, the swimwear manufacturer for $51.7 million. Foreign sales provided 55% of its operating profits in 1979.
Brandnames of Products and Services:

Big Ben	*utility clothing*
Blue Bell	*apparel*
Casey Jones	*apparel*
Jantzen	*sportswear*
Lady Wrangler	*apparel*
Lil' Wrangler	*apparel*
Lucchese	*Western boots*
Maverick	*apparel*
Mr. Wrangler	*apparel*
M. Stitch Design	*apparel*
No Fault	*apparel*
Rustler	*apparel*
Sedgefield	*apparel*
Wrangler	*apparel*
W. Stitch Design	*apparel*

Blue Chip Stamps

5801 South Eastern Ave.
Los Angeles, Calif. 90040
(213) 685-8615

Chief Executive Officer: D.A. Koeppel
Exchange: OTC
Symbol: BLUE
Corporate History: The Blue Chip Stamps Co. began in 1956 and was incorporated in 1968. This diversified company is involved in candy, newspaper and trading stamp businesses, as well as the savings and loan business. See's Candy makes candy and sells it through retail stores in 12 Midwestern and Western states. Blue Chip acquired the Buffalo Evening News in 1977. Wesco Financial Corp. (80.1% owned) wholly owns the Mutual Savings & Loan Assoc.
Brandnames of Products and Services:

Blue Chip Stamps	
Evening News	*newspaper, Buffalo, N.Y.*
Mutual Savings & Loan Assoc.	
Pinkerton's Inc.	*security and investigation service company*
See's Candy	*specialty store*
Wesco Financial Corporation	*Pasadena, Calif.*

Bobbie Brooks Inc.

3830 Kelley Ave.
Cleveland, OH 44114
(216) 881-5300

Chief Executive Officer: M. Saltzman
1984 Annual Sales Volume: 67M
1984 Shares Outstanding: 5,334,863
Shareholders: 7,385
Exchange: NY
Symbol: BBK
Corporate History: The company, founded in 1939 and last incorporated in 1946, is primarily a designer and manufacturer of women's apparel.
Brandnames of Products and Services:

Abby Michael	*women's sportswear*
Bobbie Brooks	*women's sportswear*
Bryn Mawr	*sportswear*
New Expressions	*junior apparel*
Present Co.	*junior apparel*

Bob Evans Farms, Inc.

3776 S. High St.
PO Box 07863, Station G.
Columbus, Ohio 43207
(614) 491-2225

Chief Executive Officer: R.L. Evans
Exchange: OTC
Symbol: BOBE
Corporate History: The company began in Ohio shortly after World War II and incorporated in 1957. It makes pork products, which it sells to more than 7,000 retail outlets, and operates 55 family-type restaurants. Its reputation for quality, spread by word of mouth, has enabled it to expand its restaurants without a large advertising budget.
Brandnames of Products and Services:

Bob Evans	*family-style restaurants*
Bob Evans	*pork products*

Bodin Apparel, Inc.

3500 NW 79th St.
Miami, Fla. 33147
(305) 836-9500

Chief Executive Officer: B.L. Feldman
Exchange: AM
Symbol: BDN
Corporate History: The company incorporated in 1962 as Universal Knitting Mills Inc. and adopted its present title in 1971. It designs and makes sportswear.
Brandnames of Products and Services:

American Miss	*women's sportswear*
Bodin	*women's sportswear*
Bodinit	*women's sportswear*
Flirt	*jeans*
Giamo	*women's sportswear*
Magda	*women's sportswear*
The Only Way	*women's sportswear*
Rosario	*jeans*

Borden Inc.

277 Park Avenue
New York, NY 10172
(212) 573-4000

Chief Executive Officer: E.J. Sullivan
1984 Annual Sales Volume: 4,568M

1984 Shares Outstanding: 26,008,000
Shareholders: 43,400
Exchange: NY
Symbol: BN

Corporate History: Borden was founded in 1857 as a producer of condensed milk. It expanded throughout the century in the dairy business and by 1929 was among the largest food companies in the United States. That year it began acquiring chemical concerns and since has become a major producer of basic chemicals. After years of acquisitions, Borden is now selling off various subsidiaries. It has approximately 10% of the U.S. cheese market. However, the company plans to eliminate its bulk cheese operation while continuing to make processed low fat and substitute cheeses. The sell-offs will mean that Borden will be split 50-50 between food and chemicals. Borden, which produces Lady Borden ice cream is also the nation's largest producer of formaldehyde.

Brandnames of Products and Services:

Bama	*glass-packed fruit drinks and condiments*
Borden	*food products*
Borden Lite-Line	*low calorie dairy products*
Campfire	*marshmallows*
Cottage Fries	*potato chips*
Country Meadow	*imitation cheese*
Country Store	*dehydrated potatoes*
Cracker Jack	*candy*
Creamettes	*pasta*
Cremora	*non-dairy creamer*
Deran	*confections*
Devil Dogs	*food product*
Drake's	*bakery goods*
Eagle Brand	*sweetened condensed milk*
Elmer's	*glue home products*
Elsie	*ice cream*
E-Z	*cake mix*
Gail Borden Signature Quality	*fortified milk*
Guys	*foods*
Hi-Pro	*milk*
Homefries	*snacks*
Kava	*instant coffee*
Krylon	*spray paints*
Lady Borden	*ice cream*
Lite-Line	*low calorie snacks & dairy products*
Nonesuch	*mince meat*
Old London	*melba toast*
ProLine	*milk*
Quality	*fortified milk*
Ranchfries	*snacks*
ReaLemon	*lemon juice*
Ridgie's	*potato chips*
Sippin' Pak	*fruit juices*
Skimline	*milk*
Snow's	*seafood*
Sterling	*plastic office accessories*
Stix-All	*adhesives*
Torteros	*snacks*
Wall-Tex	*vinyl wall coverings*
Wise's	*snacks*
Wonder Bond	*adhesive*
Wyler	*bouillon and drink mixes*
Yodels	*snack food product*

Borg Warner Corp.

200 South Michigan Ave.
Chicago, IL 60604
(312) 322-8500

Chief Executive Officer: J.F. Bere
1984 Annual Sales Volume: 3,915M
1984 Shares Outstanding: 90,538,000
Shareholders: 43,100
Exchange: NY
Symbol: BOR

Corporate History: Borg-Warner Corp. was founded in 1928 as a consolidation of four auto-parts manufacturers. It primarily produces durable goods, including air conditioning and refrigeration units, chemicals and plastics, industrial machinery and automotive parts. Ford is its largest customer. Borg-Warner is attempting to enter the service industry and hopes to make half its profits from that sector. Its service components include inventory and retail financing, leasing and special insurances, and fire and theft protection services.

Brandnames of Products and Services:

Arcadia Insurance Co.	
Guardian	*smoke detectors*
Pyr-A-Lon	*fire extinguishers*
Wells Fargo	*smoke and fire detectors*
York	*air conditioning*

Borman's Inc.

18718 Borman Ave.
Detroit, MI 48228
(313) 270-1000

Chief Executive Officer: Paul Borman
1984 Annual Sales Volume: 996M
1984 Shares Outstanding: 2,803,404
Shareholders: 2,753
Exchange: NY
Symbol: BRF
Corporate History: Founded in 1928 and incorporated in 1950, Borman's operates 85 supermarkets, 16 convenience stores, one drugstore and one wholesale outlet in the Detroit metropolitan area.
Brandnames of Products and Services:

Arnold	*drugstore*
Detroit Pure Milk	*milk processing, dairy foods*
Farmer Jack	*supermarkets*
Food Fair Mini Mart	*convenience food stores*
G & W Discount	*grocery outlet*
Town Pride	*food products*
Wesley's Quaker Maid	*ice cream*

Bristol Myers Co.

345 Park Ave.
New York, NY 10022
(212) 546-4000

Chief Executive Officer: Richard L. Gelb
1984 Annual Sales Volume: 4,189M
1984 Shares Outstanding: 137,365,414
Shareholders: 40,147
Exchange: NY
Symbol: BMY
Corporate History: Bristol Myers Co. was founded in 1887 as the Clinton Pharmaceutical Co., a manufacturer of drugs for physicians. Its present name was adopted in 1900. During the 1950s the company expanded into consumer health and beauty products with the acquisition of Clairol hair products. In the next decade it acquired home care products. Bristol Myers ranks second (only to American Home Products) among eight major proprietary drug companies in the U.S. and is third behind International Flavors and Fragrances in toiletries and cosmetics. Clairol has 65% of U.S. hair coloring market and contributes 21% of Bristol Myers profits.

Brandnames of Products and Services:

4-Way Cold Tablets	
4-Way Regular Spray	
Alpha Keri	*body products*
Ammens Powder	
Ban	*antiperspirants*
Behold	*furniture care product*
Body On Tap	*beer-enriched shampoo*
Born Blonde	*hair colorings*
Bufferin	*analgesic*
Clairesse	*hair colorings*
Clairmist	*pump hair spray*
Clairol	*hair products*
Colace	*anti-constipants*
Comtrex	*cold reliever*
Condition	*shampoo*
Congespirin	*cold liquid*
Crazy Curl	*styling wand*
Desquam-X	*acne product*
Drackett Co.	*cleaning products*
Drano	*drain opener*
Endust	*furniture care product*
Enfamil	*infant formula*
Excedrin	*analgesics*
Final Net	*hairspray*
Fleecy	*fabric softener*
Foot Fixer	*foot care product*
Fostex	*acne product*
Handle With Care	*fabric detergent*
Javex	*laundry bleaches (only in Canada)*
Kindness	*hair products*
Loving Care	*hair colorings*
Miracle White	*laundry products*
Natalins	*vitamins*
Naturally Blonde	*hair colorings*
Nice 'n Easy	*hair coloring product*
No Doz	*tablets*
Nuprin	*analgesic*
Nutrament	*energy food*
O Cedar	*brooms and mops*
Pernox	*acne products*
Piz Buin	*sunscreen*
PreSun	*sunscreen*
ProSobee	*milk-free formula*
Renuzit	*air freshener*
Son-Of-A-Gun	*hair dryer*
Sustagen	*nutritional supplement*
Tickle	*deodorant*
Vanish	*bowl freshener*
Vanish	*bowl cleaner*

Vi-Flor	*children's vitamins*
Vi-Sol	*children's vitamins*
Vitalis	*hair preparation*
Windex	*window cleaner*

Brooks Fashion Stores Inc.

370 7th Avenue
New York, N.Y. 10001
(212) 860-7700

Chief Executive Officer: A.M. Saul
Exchange: OTC
Symbol: BKFS
Corporate History: Brooks, incorporated in 1923, operates a chain of women's junior apparel specialty stores in over 30 Eastern, Southern and Midwestern states. The stores carry medium priced sportswear. In recent years the company has followed a policy of expansion through acquisitions. In 1980 it acquired Specialty Stores, previously a unit of Zayre Corp. In the same year Brooks announced an agreement in principle to acquire I. Edwards Company, a small Southern-based retailer of young women's moderate to higher priced apparel.
Brandnames of Products and Services:

Brooks	*women's apparel stores*

Brown Forman Distillers Corp.

850 Dixie Highway
Louisville, KY 40210
(502) 585-1100

Chief Executive Officer: W.L.L. Brown, Jr.
1984 Annual Sales Volume: 1,208M
1984 Shares Outstanding: 7,466,839
Shareholders: 6,881
Exchange: AM
Symbol: BFDB
Corporate History: Brown Forman Distillers is one of the country's leading producers and distributors of high-quality alcoholic beverages. Founded in 1870, Brown Forman is the largest Kentucky-based distiller and incorporated in 1933 as Brown Forman Distillery Co. In 1979, it acquired for $94,613,000 cash all shares of Southern Comfort Corp. Through Lenox Inc., Brown Forman also manufactures Lenox china, crystal and giftware, Hartmann luggage, Keepsake and Art-Carved jewelry.
Brandnames of Products and Services:

ArtCarved	*jewelry*
Bols	*liquers and brandies*
Canadian Mist	*whiskey*
Cella	*wines*
Early Times	*bourbon whiskey*
Hartmann	*luggage*
Jack Daniels	*whiskey*
Keepsake	*jewelry*
Korbel	*California champagnes and brandy*
Lenox	*china*
Martell	*coqnacs*
Noilly Prat	*vermouth*
Old Forester	*bourbon whiskey*
Southern Comfort	

Brown Group Inc.

8400 Maryland Ave.
St. Louis, MO 63105
(314) 854-4000

Chief Executive Officer: B.A. Bridgewater, Jr.
1984 Annual Sales Volume: 1,572M
1984 Shares Outstanding: 20,038,712
Shareholders: 9,883
Exchange: NY
Symbol: BG
Corporate History: Brown Group Inc. was founded in 1878 and incorporated in 1913. It is the largest American manufacturer of brand-name footwear. It is the leading national operator of leased retail shoe departments and of women's specialty footwear stores. It also owns and operates the chain of retail fabric stores, Cloth World. The latter, acquired in 1970, operates more than 300 retail stores, mainly in the southern part of the United States.
Brandnames of Products and Services:

Air Step	*shoes*
Aventura	*shoes*
Buskens	*shoes*
Buster Brown	*children's shoes*
Cloth World	*fabric stores*
Connie	*shoes*
De Liso	*shoes*
Fanfares	*shoes*
Footworks	*shoes*
Jacqueline	*shoes*
Levis Shoes and Boots	
Life Stride	*shoes*
Linen Center	*linen, bathroom items stores*

Marquise	*shoes*
Maserati	*shoes*
Meis	*family fashion stores*
Naturalizer	*shoes*
Peck's Menswear	*men's clothing stores*
Pedwin	*shoes*
Regal Shoe Shops	
Risque	*shoes*
Roblee	*shoes*
Wildcats	*children's shoes*

Bruno's Inc.

2620 W. 13th St.
Birmingham, AL 35218
(205) 785-9400

Chief Executive Officer: Angelo Bruno
1984 Annual Sales Volume: 716M
1984 Shares Outstanding: 18,400,152
Shareholders: 4,661
Exchange: OTC
Symbol: BRNO
Corporate History: The company, incorporated in 1959, operates supermarkets and discount drug stores in northern and central Alabama.
Brandnames of Products and Services:

Bruno's Food Store	
Consumer Warehouse Foods	*food stores*
Food World	*food stores*

Brunswick Corp.

One Brunswick Plaza
Skokie, IL 60076
(312) 470-4700

Chief Executive Officer: J.F. Reichert
1984 Annual Sales Volume: 1,470M
1984 Shares Outstanding: 21.4M
Shareholders: 29,000
Exchange: NY
Symbol: BC
Corporate History: Brunswick was founded in 1845 by John Brunswick who built the first made-in-America billiard table. It was incorporated as Brunswick-Balke-Collender Co. in 1907 and the present name was adopted in 1960. It is a diversified company operating in three business areas: marine power, recreation, and technical. The marine power business consists of the Mercury Marine Division which manufactures outboard motors, stern drives and marine parts and accessories used primarily for pleasure boating and to a lesser extent for commercial applications. The recreation businesses are: Brunswick, which manufactures bowling capital equipment and supplies; Brunswick Recreation Centers, which operates a chain of approximately 180 retail bowling centers in the United States, Canada, Central America and Europe; and Zebco, which produces fishing reels, reel/rod combinations and electric trolling motors. The technical businesses are: Defense, which produces radomes, mobile shelters and camouflage for the U.S. military; Technetics, which manufactures filters and filtration systems, specialty materials and golf club shafts; Vapor, which manufactures components for the rapid-transit and railroad industries; and Valve & Control, which manufactures valves, controls and pumps for the energy and aerospace/military markets. In 1984, the marine power business accounted for 53% of revenues; the recreation businesses, 19%, and the technical businesses, 27%.
Brandnames of Products and Services:

Briarwood	*games*
Brunswick	*sporting goods*
Brunswick	*recreation centers*
Mariner	*outboard motors*
MerCruiser	*marine powered boats*
Mercury	*outboard motors*
Omega	*fishing reels*
Quantum	*fishing reels & rods*
Quicksilver	*marine accessories*
Zebco	*fishing reels*

Burlington Industries Inc.

3330 W. Friendly Ave.
Greensboro, NC 27420
(919) 379-2000

Chief Executive Officer: W.A. Klopman
1984 Annual Sales Volume: 3,169M
1984 Shares Outstanding: 28,531,102
Shareholders: 24,182
Exchange: NY
Symbol: BUR
Corporate History: Burlington Industries was founded in 1923 and incorporated 14 years later as Burlington Mills. The name was changed to its present title in 1955. The company began as a basic textile producer but diversified into home furnishings in the 1960s. Today it is the largest and most diversified manufacturer of textiles and related products for the apparel and home industries.

Brandnames of Products and Services:

Burlington	*home furnishings*
Burlington	*hosiery and socks*
Laura Ashley	*home furnishings*
Lees	*carpets*
Liz Claiborne	*home furnishings*
Monticello	*carpets*
Oleg Cassini	*home furnishings*
Vera	*home furnishings*

John O. Butler Co.

4635 West Foster Ave.
Chicago, IL 60630
(312) 777-4000

Chief Executive Officer: Emanuel B. Tarrson
1984 Annual Sales Volume: 29M
1984 Shares Outstanding: 3,207,060
Shareholders: 260
Exchange: OTC
Symbol: BUTC

Corporate History: The company, founded in 1923 by Dr. John O. Butler and last incorporated in 1973, is primarily engaged in the design, manufacture and sale of oral hygiene products designed to be useful in the prevention of tooth decay, the prevention and treatment of periodontal (gum) disease and the maintenance of oral health. The company's principal products are "professional" toothbrushes, dental floss and flossing aids, interproximal brushes and other preventive aids. The company sells to the dental professional market, which consists primarily of dentists and dental hygienists who dispense dental products to their patients. Sales to the consumer retail market are made primarily through chain drug stores and drug wholesalers distributing to independent drug stores and, to a lesser extent, to mass merchandisers and chain food stores. In 1984, sales outside the United States, principally in Canada, Sweden and Japan, accounted for approximately 27.1% of the company's total sales.

Brandnames of Products and Services:

Bit-o-wax	*tooth care products*
Butler	*tooth care products*
Clear-Dip	*tooth care products*
Eez-Thru	*tooth care products*
Flossmate	*tooth care products*
G.U.M.	*tooth care products*
Perio-pic	*tooth care products*
Plakfinder	*tooth care products*
Protect	*tooth care products*
Proxabrush	*tooth care products*
Red Cote	*tooth care products*
Right-Kind/Sub-G	*tooth care products*
Smile Factory	*tooth care products*
Taper-Line	*tooth care products*
Thin-Line	*tooth care products*
Trav-Ler	*tooth care products*
Tuff-Spun	*tooth care products*
Velvet Tip	*tooth care products*

Cadence Industries Corp.

21 Henderson Dr.
West Caldwell, N.J. 07006
(201) 227-5100

Chief Executive Officer: S. Feinberg
Exchange: NY
Symbol: CDE

Corporate History: Cadence incorporated in 1937 as United Cigar-Whelan Stores Corp. In 1957 the name was changed to United Whelan Corp. and in 1967 to Perfect Film and Chemical Corp. It adopted its current name in 1970. The company is primarily engaged in magazine and comic book publishing, the manufacutre of business products and the marketing of drugs and pharmaceuticals. It also operates a chain of 47 movie theaters in eastern Massachusetts.

Brandnames of Products and Services:

Hudson	*vitamins*
Marvel	*comics*
Sack Theatre	*movie theaters*
Vitamin Quota	*health stores*

Caesar's World, Inc.

1801 Century Park East
Los Angeles, CA 90067
(213) 552-2711

Chief Executive Officer: Henry Gluck
1984 Annual Sales Volume: 621M
1984 Shares Outstanding: 29,717,000
Shareholders: 35,000
Exchange: NY
Symbol: CAW

Corporate History: The company was incorporated in 1958 as a successor to a business founded in 1936. In 1961 the name changed from Lum's Bar, Inc. to Lum's Inc. It adopted its present title in 1971. As of that date the company disposed of its Lum's restaurants. It is now involved in the operation of hotels and casinos.

Brandnames of Products and Services:

Caesars Atlantic City	*hotel and casino Atlantic City, NJ*
Caesars Brookdale	*resort, Lakeville, PA*
Caesars Cove Haven	*resort, Lakeville, PA*
Caesars Palace Hotel and Casino	*Las Vegas, NV*
Caesars Paradise Stream	*resort, Lakeville, PA*
Caesars Pocono Palace	*resort, Lakeville, PA*
Caesars Tahoe Hotel and Casino	*Stateline, NV*

Cagle's Inc.

1155 Hammond Drive N.E.
Atlanta, GA 30328
(404) 394-8223

Chief Executive Officer: J. Douglas Cagle
1984 Annual Sales Volume: 148M
1984 Shares Outstanding: 2,326,038
Shareholders: 789
Exchange: AM
Symbol: CGL
Corporate History: Cagle's Inc. was founded in 1945 and today is one of the nation's largest poultry processing companies. The company also produces smoked ham, bacon, sausage and other ham products.
Brandnames of Products and Services:

Cagle's	*chicken*
Crystal-Pak	*chicken products*
Talmadge Farms	*processed meats*

Caldor Inc.

20 Glover Ave.
Norwalk, Conn. 06852
(203) 846-1641

Chief Executive Officer: C. Bennett
Exchange: AM
Symbol: CA
Corporate History: The company, incorporated in 1961, operates approximately 60 discount stores.
Brandnames of Products and Services:

Caldor	*general merchandise discount*

Calny, Inc.

1650 Borel Place ▪101
San Mateo, CA 94402
(415) 574-2455

Chief Executive Officer: Robert Larive
1984 Annual Sales Volume: 44M
1984 Shares Outstanding: 4,520,824
Shareholders: 725
Exchange: OTC
Symbol: CLNY
Corporate History: Calny, Inc. was organized in 1969 and is the largest franchisee of Taco Bell Mexican fast-food restaurants and the only Taco Bell franchisee in the United States which is publicly held. Calny presently operates a total of 88 Taco Bell restaurants in the Western United States, together with two La Petite Boulangerie bakeries in the greater Seattle, Washington area and a chain of five buffet-style restaurants in California.
Brandnames of Products and Services:

La Petite Boulangerie	*bakery*
Ole Frijole	*fast-food restaurants*
Perry's Smorgy	*fast-food restaurants*
Taco Bell	*fast-food restaurant*

Campbell Soup Co.

Campbell Place
Camden, NJ 09101
(609) 342-4800

Chief Executive Officer: R. Gordon McGovern
1984 Annual Sales Volume: 3,657M
1984 Shares Outstanding: 32,257,249
Shareholders: 49,400
Exchange: NY
Symbol: CPB
Corporate History: Campbell Soup Co. was founded in 1869. In 1897 it began manufacturing condensed soup and, by 1904, was selling 60 million cans per year. Forty-five percent of the company's products are soup. Because children under 12 are the primary consumers of soup and this segment of the population has been declining, the company has been looking for new product development. During the 1950s Campbell began diversifying into other food products. Today Campbell produces more than 1,000 products.

Brandnames of Products and Services:

Campbell's	*soups and other food products*
Casera	*foods*
Delacre	*cookies and pastries*
Domsea	*seafood*
Franco American	*food products*
Godiva	*chocolates*
Gold Nugget	*poultry*
Granny's	*soups*
Hanover Trail	*restaurants*
Juice Bowl	*juices*
Juice Works	*juices*
Kia-Ora	*soups and condiments*
Lazzaroni	*cookies*
Le Menu	*frozen dinners*
Mrs. Paul's Kitchens	*frozen fish*
Pepperidge Farm	*food products*
Pietro's	*Gold Coast pizza restaurants*
Prego	*spaghetti sauce*
Recipe	*pet food*
Swanson	*food products*
Vlasic	*specialty food items*
V-8 Juices	

Campbell Taggart Inc.

6211 Lemmon Ave.
Dallas, Tex. 75221
(214) 358-9211

Chief Executive Officer: B.O. Mead
Exchange: NY
Symbol: CTI
Corporate History: The company incorporated in 1927 under the name of Campbell Taggart Assoc. Bakeries Inc. the present title was adopted in 1971. It is the nation's second largest wholesale baker, operating 63 bakeries and five refrigerated dough plants throughout the U.S.
Brandnames of Products and Services:

Colonial	*bread*
Country Meal	*variety breads and pastries*
Earth Bread	*variety breads and pastries*
Earth Grains	*breads, pastries, croutons*
El Chico Frozen Mexican Dinner	
El Chico Mexican Restaurants	
Georgia	*cookies and wafers*
Hillbilly	*variety breads and pastries*
Hollywood	*variety breads and pastries*
Honey Grain	*variety breads and pastries*
Hot 'n' Fresh	*refrigerated dough*
Kilpatrick's	*bread*
Manor	*bread*
Merico	*English muffins, snack cakes and pies*
Mountain Man	*biscuits*
Rainbo	*breads, sweet cakes, cookies*
Roman Meal	*variety breads and pastries*
Safari	*crackers*

Cannon Mills Co.

Kannapolis, N.C. 28081
(704) 933-1221

Chief Executive Officer: O.G. Stolz
Exchange: NY
Symbol: CAN
Corporate History: The company, founded in 1887, was incorporated in 1928 as a consolidation of nine businesses. It is engaged in the development, manufacture and sale of textile products, with the major emphasis on household textile goods. The operation is a fully integrated business, from the spinning of raw cotton to direct distribution of the finished products.
Brandnames of Products and Services:

Cannon	*towels, sheets, bedspreads*
Comfortcale	*towels, sheets, bedspreads*
Gold Label	*towels, sheets, bedspreads*
Monticello	*towels, sheets, bedspreads*
Royal Family	*towels, sheets, bedspreads*

Canon, Inc.

7-1, Nishi-Shinjuku 2-chome, Shinjuku-ku
Tokyo 160 Japan
003-246-6111

Chief Executive Officer: Ryuzaburo Kaku
1984 Annual Sales Volume: 3,308M
1984 Shares Outstanding: 613,776,000
Exchange: OTC
Symbol: CANX
Corporate History: In 1935 the company developed Japan's first 35-mm focal-plane shutter camera, the Kwanon. In the 1950's the company expanded into movie cameras, TV broadcast lenses, x-ray cameras and lenses. In the 60's & 70's, the company entered the field of office equipment with electronic typewriters, calculators

and copy machines. The Canon group employs worldwide over 30,000 people. In 1984 63.8% of sales were from business machines, 26.9% cameras, and 9.3% optical and other products.

Brandnames of Products and Services:

Canon	*cameras, optical equipment*
Canon	*business machines typewriters, calculators, copy machines, printers*

Capital Cities Communications Inc.

24 East 51 Street
New York, NY 10022
(212) 421-9595

Chief Executive Officer: Thomas S. Murphy
1984 Annual Sales Volume: 940M
1984 Shares Outstanding: 12,890,053
Shareholders: 4,850
Exchange: NY
Symbol: CCB

Corporate History: The company was incorporated in 1946 as Hudson Valley Broadcasting Co. Its name was changed to Capital Cities Television Corp. in 1957, to Capital Cities Broadcasting Corp. in 1959 and to its present title in 1973. The company and its subsidiaries operate television and radio broadcasting stations and cable television systems and publish newspapers and magazines.

Brandnames of Products and Services:

Citizens Journal	*weekly newspaper, Arlington, TX*
Daily News Record	*newspaper, New York, N.Y.*
Daily Register	*newspaper Red Bank, NJ*
Daily Tidings	*newspaper Ashland, OR*
Democrat-Herald	*newspaper Albany, OR*
Express	*weekly newspaper Lebanon, OR*
KFSN-TV	*Fresno, Calif.*
KLAC-AM	*radio station Los Angeles, CA*
KPOL-AM	*radio station, Los Angeles, Calif.*
KSCS-FM	*radio station, Fort Worth, Texas*
KTRK-TV	*Houston, Texas*
KZLA-FM	*radio station, Los Angeles, Calif.*
Little Nickel Want Ads	*shopping guide Seattle-Tacoma, WA*
News Democrat	*newspaper, Belleville, Ill.*
News-Leader	*weekly newspaper Highland, IL*
News	*weekly newspaper Springfield, OR*
News-Times	*weekly newspaper Newport, OR*
Oakland Press	*newspaper, Pontiac, Mich.*
Ocean County Reporter	*weekly newspaper Toms River, NJ*
Outlook	*weekly newspaper Gresham, OR*
Pennysaver	*shopping guide Sacramento and Stockton, CA*
Pennysaver Shopping News	*Wichita and Topeka, KS, and Springfield, MO*
Post	*weekly newspaper Sandy, OR*
Sentinel	*weekly newspaper Cottage Grove, OR*
Shoreline	*weekly newspapers Guilford, CT*
Star-Telegram	*newspaper, Fort Worth, Texas*
Star/Times	*newspaper, Kansas City, Mo.*
Times Leader	*newspaper Wilkes-Barre, PA*
WBAP-AM/FM	*radio station, Fort Worth, Texas*
WHYT-FM	*radio station Detroit, MI*
WJR-AM/FM	*radio station Detroit, Mich.*
WKBW-TV & AM	*radio station, Buffalo, N.Y.*
WKHX-FM	*radio station Marietta-Atlanta, GA*
Women's Wear Daily	*newspaper New York, NY*
WPAT-AM/FM	*radio station, Patterson, N.Y.*
WPRO-AM/FM	*radio station, Providence, R.I.*
WPVI-TV	*Philadelphia, Pa.*
W	*biweekly version of Women's Wear Daily*
WROW AM/FM	*radio station, Albany, N.Y.*
WTNH-TV	*New Haven, Conn.*
WTVD-TV	*Durham-Raleigh, N.C.*

Capitol Food Industries Inc.

105 West Adams St.
Chicago, Ill. 60603
(312) 782-1838

Chief Executive Officer: B.J. Vincent
Exchange: AM
Symbol: CFS
Corporate History: The company, incorporated in 1963, is a diversified specialty food concern. Consumer food products accounted for 71% of the sales in 1979 and foreign operations accounted for 15% of total sales.
Brandnames of Products and Services:

Capitol Baking	*cookies and crackers*
Capitol Meats	*tamales and chili products*
Caroby	*carob-flavored low-fat milk*
Danish Delight	*cookies and crackers*
Het Luilekkerland BV	*liver pate and sausages*

Caressa, Inc.

3601 NW 54th St.
Miami, Fla. 33142
(305) 633-8605

Chief Executive Officer: Robert Taicher
Exchange: AM
Symbol: CSA
Corporate History: Caressa incorporated in 1959 as Taicher Shoe Corp. and adopted its present title in 1961. The company wholesales women's shoes which are made primarily in Spain. It recently acquired a 40% interest in Don Sophisticates, a designer, manufacturer and importer of women's apparel.
Brandnames of Products and Services:

Caressa	*women's shoes*
Carina	*women's shoes*
Clover	*women's shoes*
Eleganza	*women's shoes*
Incredible	*women's shoes*
Mr. Seymour/ Martinique	*women's shoes*
Philippe	*women's shoes*
S.R.O.	*women's shoes*

Carnation Company

5045 Wilshire Blvd.
Los Angeles, CA 90036
(213) 932-6000

Chief Executive Officer: H. E. Olson
1984 Annual Sales Volume: 3,365M
1984 Shares Outstanding: 34,718,366
Shareholders: 10,428
Exchange: NY
Symbol: CMK
Corporate History: Carnation was founded in 1899 and last incorporated in 1920 as Carnation Milk Products Co. Its present title was adopted in 1929. The company began in the dairy business and gradually expanded first into the processing of dairy products and then into non-dairy food items, including animal feeds, containers and products for the scholastic market. Carnation's products are marketed in over 130 countries.
Brandnames of Products and Services:

Albers	*food products*
Bale	*school pins and awards*
Bright Eyes	*pet foods*
Buffet	*pet food*
Camera Art	*photography*
Carnation	*food products*
Carnation Country Foods	*food products*
Chef-mate	*food products*
Chef's Blend	*pet food*
Classic	*pet foods*
Coco Supreme	*food products*
Coffee-Mate	*non-dairy creamer*
Collegiate Cap & Gown	*academic, choral, pulpit apparel*
Come 'n' Get It	*pet food*
Come 'N Get It Puppy Formula	*pet foods*
Contadina	*food products*
Country Cousin	*pet foods*
Diet Chef	*diet foods*
Fancy Feast	*pet foods*
Fish Ahoy	*pet foods*
Friskies	*pet food*
Friskies Buffet	*pet foods*
Friskies Dinners	*pet foods*
Frozen Novelties	*food products*
Gold Cross	*evaported milk*
Good Nature	*vitamins, food supplements*
Hearty	*pet foods*
Herff Jones	*achievement awards*

Lynden Farms	*frozen potato products*
Mighty Dog	*pet food*
Nystrom and Eye Gate	*multimedia learning systems*
Praise	*non-dairy creamer*
Princeton	*products for fund raising*
Que Bueno!	*mexican foods*
Rich'ning	*non-dairy creamer*
Slender	*diet foods*
The Spreadables	*sandwich spreads*
Topic	*non-dairy creamer*
Trio	*dehydrated potatoes and sauces*

Carson Pirie Scott & Company

One South State Street
Chicago, IL. 60603
(312) 245-8000

Chief Executive Officer: Peter S. Willmott
1984 Annual Sales Volume: 1,177M
1984 Shares Outstanding: 4,941,947
Shareholders: 2,836
Exchange: NY
Symbol: CRN

Corporate History: The company was founded in 1854 and last incorporated in 1969 as CPS Inc. Later that same year it adopted its current name. Carson Pirie Scott & Co. operates retail department stores, food services, and lodging and resort facilities. It also makes floor coverings for the wholesale market. As of 1984, it operated 23 department stores and specialty shops in Illinois and Indiana under the name Carson Pirie Scott. In 1984, the company acquired County Seat Stores, a chain of approximately 275 retail specialty stores in 32 states.

Brandnames of Products and Services:

Carson, Pirie Scott	*department stores*
Carson Inn Motel	*Rennselaer, Ind.*
Dobbs Houses	*restaurants*
Edan Plaza	*shopping center, Chicago, Ill.*
Honey Bear Farm	*highway rest stops*
Lincoln Square	*shopping center, Urbana, Ill.*
Steak 'n' Egg	*specialty restaurants*
Toddle House	*restaurants*

Carter Hawley Hale Stores, Inc.

550 South Flower St.
Los Angeles, CA 90071
(213) 620-0150

Chief Executive Officer: P.M. Hawley
1984 Annual Sales Volume: 3,900M
1984 Shares Outstanding: 19,066,885
Shareholders: 11,700
Exchange: NY
Symbol: CHH

Corporate History: Carter Hawley Hale Stores, Inc., is a major North American retailer operating six department and four specialty store divisions, and two divisions providing information and market services. The company was incorporated in 1897 as The Emporium and Golden Rule Bazaar. Its present title was adopted in 1974. It is the largest department chain in the West. In an effort to upgrade its image, Carter-Hawley Hale acquired a number of very fashionable stores in the 1960s and 1970s. These included Neiman Marcus, Bergdorf Goodman, and John Wanamaker. One of its major holdings, Walden Books, sells books through 504 retail stores and 23 leased departments. Sunset House, a gift store chain, sells through 38 retail shops and by mail order.

Brandnames of Products and Services:

Bergdorf Goodman	*high-fashion specialty store*
The Broadway	*department stores*
Contempo Casuals	*women's apparel stores*
Emporium Capwell	*department stores*
Holt, Renfrew	*high-fashion specialty stores*
John Wanamaker	*department stores*
Neiman-Marcus	*high-fashion specialty stores*
Thalhimer's	*department stores*
Weinstock's	*department stores*

Carter-Wallace Inc.

767 Fifth Ave.
New York, NY 10153
(212) 758-4500

Chief Executive Officer: H.H. Hoyt, Jr.
1984 Annual Sales Volume: 323M
1984 Shares Outstanding: 7,789,000
Shareholders: 4,376
Exchange: NY
Symbol: CAR

Corporate History: Carter-Wallace, last incorporated in 1968, markets toiletries, pharmaceuticals, diagnostic specialties, proprietary drugs, and pet products. The original company was incorporated in 1937 as Carter Products Inc., successor to Carter Medicine Co., a business chartered in 1880. The current name was adopted in 1965.

Brandnames of Products and Services:

Answer	*at-home pregnancy test kit*
Arrid	*deodorant and anti-perspirant*
Avitron	*vitamin supplements for birds*
Carter's Pills	*laxative*
Diovol	*antacid product*
Fresh 'n' Clean	*dog shampoo*
Lassie	*pet products*
Linatone	*pet food supplements*
Miltown	*tranquilizer*
Nair	*depilatory*
Pearl Drops	*tooth polish and smoker's tooth polish*
Rigident	*denture adhesive*
Rise	*shaving cream*
Sea & Ski	*sun care products*
Soma	*muscle relaxant*
Theralin	*pet vitamin supplements*
Twinco	*pet grooming aids*
Victory	*pet insecticides*

Castle & Cooke Inc.

Financial Plaza of Pacific
P.O. Box 2990
Honolulu, HI 96802
(808) 548-6611

Chief Executive Officer: R.D. Cook
1984 Annual Sales Volume: 1,500M
1984 Shares Outstanding: 27,600,000
Shareholders: 23,000
Exchange: NY
Symbol: CKE

Corporate History: Castle & Cooke Inc. was founded in 1851 by missionaries to Hawaii and incorporated in 1894. It is engaged in the worldwide production, processing, distribution and marketing of food products, which account for approximately 85% of its revenues. The company is the fourth largest landowner in Hawaii, with 150,000 acres including virtually all of the island of Lanai.

Brandnames of Products and Services:

Anco	*produce*
Bud of California	*producc*
Dole	*produce & processed products*
Oceanic Properties	*land development Hawaii*
Rick	*produce*

CBS Inc.

51 W. 52nd St.
New York, NY 10019
(212) 975-4321

Chief Executive Officer: Thomas H. Wyman
1984 Annual Sales Volume: 4,925M
1984 Shares Outstanding: 29,717,639
Shareholders: 23,455
Exchange: NY
Symbol: CBS

Corporate History: CBS is a diversified entertainment and information company in the principal businesses of broadcasting, recorded music and publishing. The company's broadcast operations include one of the nation's three commercial broadcast television networks, two nationwide radio networks, five television stations and six AM and seven FM radio stations, and a unit for production and distribution of programming for selected markets. The company is the world's largest producer, manufacturer and marketer of recorded music, a leading music publisher and a producer of music video programs. CBS's publishing operations comprise magazines, books, home computer software, and online data bases for consumer, educational and professional markets. CBS also has interests in toy manufacturing and marketing, and is involved through joint ventures in videocassette manufacturing, marketing and distribution; motion picture production and distribution; cable television programming; and the development of videotex services.

Brandnames of Products and Services:

American Bride	*periodical*
American Photographer	*periodical*
ARC/Columbia	*records*
Audio	*periodical*
Backpacker	*periodical*
Boating	*periodical*
BRS/Saunders	*publishing*
Car & Driver	*periodical*
CBS	*radio and television*
CBS Software	
Child Guidance	*toys*
Columbia Records	
Creative Playthings	*toys*

Cycle	*periodical*
Cycle World	*periodical*
Dryden Press	*publishing*
Epic Records	
Erector Construction Sets	
Field & Stream	*periodical*
Flying	*periodical*
Gabriel Toys	
Gemeinhardt	*musical instruments*
Gulbransen	*musical instruments*
Gym Dandy	*home playground equipment*
Holt, Rinehart & Winston	*publishing house*
Home Mechanix	*periodical*
Ideal	*toys, games & dolls*
Jet Records	
KCBS	*San Francisco, Calif.*
KCBS-TV	*Los Angeles, Calif.*
KMOX-TV & AM	*St. Louis, MO.*
KNX-AM	*Los Angeles, Calif.*
Lyon-Healy	*musical instruments*
Modern Bride	*periodical*
Odyssey Records	
Peanuts	*toys*
Popular Photography	*periodical*
Portrait Records	
Praeger Publishing	
Road & Track	*periodical*
The Runner	*periodical*
Sesame St.	*toys*
Skiing	*periodical*
Skiing Trade News	*periodical*
Stereo Review	*periodical*
Tinkertoy	*construction sets*
TransMedica	*publishing*
TV Crosswords	*periodical*
WBBM-TV & AM	*Chicago, Ill.*
WCAU-TV & AM	*Philadelphia, Pa.*
WCBS-TV & AM	*New York, N.Y.*
Winston/Seabury Press	*publishing*
Woman's Day	*periodical*
Wonder Spring	*hobby horses*
Yachting	*periodical*

Cedar Point, Inc.

P.O. Box 759
Sandusky, Ohio 44870
(419) 626-0830

Chief Executive Officer: R.L. Munger
Exchange: OTC
Symbol: CEDR

Corporate History: The company, incorporated in 1905, owns and operates amusement parks. Cedar Point Park is mid-America's largest family amusement park. It covers 364 acres and includes an amusement park, a 400-room hotel, a 725-boat marina and a 600-vehicle camper village.

Brandnames of Products and Services:

Cedar Point Park	*family amusement park, Sandusky, Ohio*
Valleyfair	*amusement park, Shakopee, Minn.*

CenCor Inc.

12th & Baltimore, City Center Square
P.O. Box 26610
Kansas City, MO 64196
(816) 474-4750

Chief Executive Officer: Robert F. Brozman
1984 Annual Sales Volume: 47M
1984 Shares Outstanding: 1,411,000
Shareholders: 340
Exchange: OTC
Symbol: CNCR

Corporate History: CenCor Inc. incorporated in 1968. The company is engaged in personal service businesses in 34 states. Its operations include 62 consumer finance offices, 14 career colleges, 80 review course locations, and 10 temporary help offices.

Brandnames of Products and Services:

Century Acceptance	*consumer finance offices*
Colleges of Medical & Dental Assistance	
La Petite Academy	*preschool daycare centers*
Mr. Tax of America	*tax preparation service*
Sunny Girls	*temporary help agencies*
Timely Talent	*temporary help agencies*

Centex Corp.

4600 Republic Bank Tower
Dallas, TX 75201
(214) 748-7901

Chief Executive Officer: Frank M. Crossen
1984 Annual Sales Volume: 1,183M
1984 Shares Outstanding: 19,949,861
Shareholders: 1,625
Exchange: NY
Symbol: CTX

Corporate History: Since its founding in 1950 as a Dallas-based residential and commercial construction company, Centex Corp. has evolved into a multi-industry company. Centex, through its subsidiaries, currently operates in four business segments: home building, general construction, cement and oil and gas.

Brandnames of Products and Services:

Centex Homes	*home building*
Fox & Jacobs	*home building*

Central Soya Company Inc.

1300 Ft. Wayne National Bank Bldg.
Ft. Wayne, IN 46802
(219) 425-5100

Chief Executive Officer: D.P. Eckrich
1984 Annual Sales Volume: 1,831M
1984 Shares Outstanding: 14,100,000
Shareholders: 11,601
Exchange: NY
Symbol: CSY

Corporate History: Central Soya, founded and incorporated in 1934, is an international agribusiness and food processing company, marketing products to customers in more than 50 countries. The company's major businesses include food processing, feed manufacturing, soybean processing, and grain merchandising. The company operates more than 75 plants and facilities worldwide.

Brandnames of Products and Services:

Butcher Boy	*prepared, frozen convenience foods*
Caribe	*food products*
Cisco's	*prepared, frozen convenience foods*
fff (Fred's Frozen Foods)	*prepared, frozen convenience foods*
Fred's	*frozen foods*
Imperial Kitchens	*prepared, frozen convenience foods*
Little Juan	*prepared, frozen convenience foods*
Marquez	*prepared, frozen convenience foods*
Mrs. Filberts	*margarines and salad products*
Mrs. Filbert's	*food products*
Posada	*prepared, frozen convenience foods*

Chadwick-Miller Inc.

10 Pequot Industrial Park
300 Turnpike St.
Canton, Mass. 02021
(617) 828-8300

Chief Executive Officer: Oscar Miller
Exchange: AM
Symbol: CWK

Corporate History: The company, incorporated in 1967, distributes more than 1,000 articles of stationery, notions and giftwares. In 1980 retailing accounted for 39% of sales with the remaining coming from the import division.

Brandnames of Products and Services:

Lauriat's	*retail books and stationery*

Champion Home Builders Co.

5573 E. North St.
Dryden, MI 48428
(313) 796-2211

Chief Executive Officer: Joseph J. Morris
1984 Annual Sales Volume: 353M
1984 Shares Outstanding: 35,487,194
Shareholders: 35,000
Exchange: AM
Symbol: CHB

Corporate History: Champion, incorporated in 1953 makes manufactured homes and motor homes It also produces related component parts used in its products. In fiscal 1984 manufactured homes provided approximately 85% of sales and vehicles approximately 14%. Products are sold by about 20 independent dealers throughout the United States.

Brandnames of Products and Services:

Atlantic	*manufactured homes*

Champion	*manufactured homes*
Champion	*motor homes*
Concord	*manufactured homes*
Flagship	*motor homes*
Huntington	*manufactured homes*
LaSalle (van-conversion)	
Manatee	*manufactured homes*
Meadow Creek	*manufactured homes*
Metamora	*manufactured homes*
New Haven	*manufactured homes*
Parkridge	*manufactured homes*
Park River	*manufactured homes*
Piedmont	*manufactured homes*
Sequoia	*manufactured homes*
Sunview	*manufactured homes*
Tamarack	*manufactured homes*
Titan	*manufactured homes*
Titan	*motor homes*
TranStar	*motor homes*
Trans-Van	*motor homes*
Wolverine	*manufactured homes*
Woodlake	*manufactured homes*

Champion Spark Plug Co.

900 Upton Ave.
Toledo, OH 43661
(419) 535-2567

Chief Executive Officer: R.A. Stranahan, Jr.
1984 Annual Sales Volume: 816M
1984 Shares Outstanding: 38,381,000
Shareholders: 13,200
Exchange: NY
Symbol: CHM
Corporate History: The company, incorporated in 1938, makes spark plugs, jet igniters and other ignition devices. It also manufactures windshield wiper blades, arms and refills, and steering locks.
Brandnames of Products and Services:

Anco	*windshield wipers*
Champion	*automotive equipment*

Charming Shoppes Inc.

450 Winks Lane
Bensalem, PA 19020
(215) 245-9100

Chief Executive Officer: Morris Sidewater
1984 Annual Sales Volume: 297M
1984 Shares Outstanding: 21,657,310
Shareholders: 3,855
Exchange: OTC
Symbol: CHRS
Corporate History: The company, incorporated in 1969 as Fashion Bug Inc., operates 444 women's specialty apparel shops, in twenty-two states throughout the East, South, and Midwest.
Brandnames of Products and Services:

Charming Shoppes	*women's apparel stores*
Fashion Bug	*women's apparel stores*
Fashion Bug Plus	*women's apparel stores*
Jaison's	*women's apparel stores*

Chart House Inc.

666 Jefferson St.
Suite 1000
Lafayette, La. 70501
(318) 233-6400

Chief Executive Officer: R.K. Luckey
Exchange: OTC
Symbol: CHHO
Corporate History: Chart House incorporated in 1968 as National Food Services Inc. It adopted its present name in 1974. It owns two chains of steak houses and operates as a franchised licensee of Burger King restaurants under agreement with Burger King Corp., owned by Pillsbury Co. It is the largest franchiser of Burger King restaurants in the nation. Chart House also sublicenses others to operate Burger King units. The hamburger division accounted for 68% of sales in 1979, steak houses the remainder.
Brandnames of Products and Services:

Chart House	*restaurants*
Cork 'n Cleaver	*restaurants*

Chatham Manufacturing Company

East Main Street
Elkin, NC 28621
(919) 835-2211

Chief Executive Officer: P.W. Glidewell, III
1984 Annual Sales Volume: 124M
1984 Shares Outstanding: 1,800,000
Shareholders: 1,010
Exchange: OTC
Symbol: CHAT
Corporate History: The company, incorporated in 1894, is a diversified textile company which manufactures yarns, blankets, furniture and automobile upholstery and markets them worldwide. In 1985 65% of total sales were from furniture fabrics and upholstery, 28% from bedding products, and 7% from yarn and other products.
Brandnames of Products and Services:

Chatham	*blankets*
Esmond	*blankets*
North Star	*blankets*
Restwarmer	*automatic mattress pad*

Chattem, Inc.

1715 West 38th Street
Chattanooga, TN 37409
(615) 821-4571

Chief Executive Officer: Alex Guerry
1984 Annual Sales Volume: 64M
1984 Shares Outstanding: 1,846,229
Shareholders: 1500
Exchange: OTC
Symbol: CHTT
Corporate History: The company, incorporated in 1909, makes proprietary drugs, cosmetics and hygiene products, as well as specialty chemicals. It makes a key ingredient used in the manufacture of Di-Gel, Rolaids and Bufferin. Historically the company has not emphasized research and is more concerned with marketing products developed by others. However, the company's largest selling product is Pamprin which it developed in the late 1950s. In 1984, 78 per cent of total sales came from health and beauty aids, 22 per cent from special chemicals.
Brandnames of Products and Services:

Corn Silk	*cosmetics*
Health Gard	*vitamins*
Love's Baby Soft	*fragrance*
Love's Musky Jasmin	*fragrance*
Mudd	*skin care products*
Pamprin	*pre-menstrual tablet*
Premesyn PMS	*pre-menstrual tablet*
Sun-In	*hair lightener*

CHB Foods Inc.

772 Tuna St.
P.O. Box 3510
Terminal Isl., Calif. 90731
(213) 831-8941

Chief Executive Officer: R.J. Pasarow
Exchange: AM
Symbol: CBF
Corporate History: The company, incorporated in 1932, processes and cans a variety of food products. Through acquisitions it has become a national branded pet food manufacturer. Products are sold in both institutional and consumer sizes.
Brandnames of Products and Services:

CHB	*(Californian Home Brand) foods*
Cinch	*cake mixes*
Glamor Puss	*cat foods*
Haley's	*canned foods*
Lewis	*foods*
Mackerel	*foods*
Perk	*pet foods*
Petuna	*cat foods*
Skippy	*pet foods*
Sturdy	*pet foods*
Vets	*pet foods*

Chesebrough-Pond's Inc.

33 Benedict Place
Greenwich, CT 06830
(203) 661-2000

Chief Executive Officer: R.E. Ward
1984 Annual Sales Volume: 1,857M
1984 Shares Outstanding: 35,132,000
Shareholders: 15,712
Exchange: NY
Symbol: CBM
Corporate History: The company incorporated in 1880 as Chesebrough Mfg. Co. Its first product was Vaseline Petroleum Jelly. Its present title was adopted in 1955 upon merger with Pond's Extract Co., a cosmetic manu-

facturer. Today it makes cosmetics, specialty products, toiletries, specialty foods and children's apparel in 25 countries and sells them in more than 140 countries. Health and beauty aids, cosmetics, and fragrances now make up less than one-half of the company's sales.

Brandnames of Products and Services:

Adolph's	*food specialties*
Aviance	*fragrances*
Aziza	*cosmetics*
Bare Traps	*women's footwear*
Bass	*pre-teen footwear*
Bass	*men's and women's footwear*
Bass Sunjuns	*footwear*
Bass Weejuns	*footwear*
Beach Babies	*swim wear*
Beret	*fragrance*
Brittania	*children's wear*
Cachet	*fragrances*
Chimere	*fragrance*
Cutex	*polish remover*
Cutex Perfect Color	*cosmetics*
Erno Laszlo	*skin-care preparations*
Groom & Clean	*hair dressing*
Health-tex	*children's clothing*
Kidproof	*jeans*
Matchabelli	*aftershave and cologne*
Our Gang	*boys' wear*
Our Girl	*girls wear*
Pertussin	*cough and cold products*
Pond's	*beauty creams and lotions*
Pond's Cream & Cocoa Butter	*lotion*
Pond's Cream & Cocoa Butter	*bath beads*
Prince	*tennis apparel, equipment, and racquets*
Q-tips	*cotton swabs and cotton balls*
Ragu Chunky Gardenstyle	*spaghetti sauces*
Ragu Extra Thick and Zesty	*spaghetti sauces*
Ragu Homestyle	*spaghetti sauce*
Ragu Italian	*cooking sauces*
Ragu Pizza Quick	*sauces, crust mix and kit*
Ragu traditional	*spaghetti sauces*
Rave	*hair care products*
Ready Set Go	*active wear*
Sound Waves	*children's clothing*
Vaseline	*petroleum jelly*
Vaseline	*lip balm*
Vaseline	*hair tonic*
Vaseline Dermatology Formula	*cream and lotion*
Vaseline Intensive Care	*baby products*
Vaseline Intensive Care	*lotions*
Vaseline Intensive Care	*bath beads*
Wind Song	*fragrance*

Chevron Corp.

225 Bush St.
San Francisco, CA 94104
(415) 894-7700

Chief Executive Officer:	George M. Keller
1984 Annual Sales Volume:	1,534M
1984 Shares Outstanding:	342,109,258
Shareholders:	231,000
Exchange:	NY
Symbol:	CHV

Corporate History: Headquartered in San Francisco, the business was incorporated in 1879 as the Pacific Coast Oil Co. Merged with the Standard Oil group of companies in 1900, it became independent 11 years later, as Standard Oil Co. (California). In 1984, Gulf Corp. was acquired by Chevron. In the same year, the name Chevron Corp. was adopted to give the company a distinct and unified identity. Chevron Corp. is a major international oil company which has activities in more than 80 countries. The company engages in worldwide, integrated petroleum operations which consist of exploring for and producing crude oil and natural gas; transporting crude oil, natural gas and petroleum products by pipelines, marine vessels and motor equipment; operating large refinery complexes for converting crude oil to finished products; and marketing crude oil, natural gas and the many products derived from petroleum. The company and its affiliates own and have interests in operations located throughout the world which manufacture and market a wide range of chemicals and fertilizers for industrial, agricultural and residential uses. The company also engages in real estate development and is involved in non-petroleum minerals exploration and production and projects related to alternate energy resources, primarily geothermal.

Brandnames of Products and Services:

Acid-Gro	*fertilizer*
Bitumuls	*asphalt paving material*

Blazo	*pressure appliance fuel*
Carcare	*auto repair services*
Chevron	*petroleum products, petrochemicals, industrial and agricultural chemicals*
Chevron & Chevron Design	*petroleum products, petrochemicals, industrial and agricultural chemicals*
Claylok	*oil well chemicals and services*
Contax	*herbicide*
Cruisemaster	*tires and automotive parts*
Delmo-Z	*nutrient spray*
Delo	*motor oils*
Dichevrol	*dielectric fluid*
Dieselect	*fuel oil*
Difolatan	*fungicide*
Econosize	*sizing chemical*
Flea-B-Gon	*insecticide*
Flotox	*garden chemical*
Greenol	*plant nutrient*
Gug-Beta	*snail bait*
Gulf	*resin, petroleum products, petrochemicals, and industrial chemicals*
Gulf Lite	*charcoal lighter, torch fuel and fire starter sticks*
Gulfpride	*motor oil*
Gulfwax	*wax*
Harmony	*lube oil*
Hyjet	*hydraulic fluid*
ICR	*catalysts*
Isocracking	*catalysts*
Isotox	*insecticides*
Kleenup	*herbicide*
Kyso	*petroleum products*
Life	*oil analysis services*
Monitor	*insecticides*
No-Nox	*gasoline, fuel additives, gasoline additives, oil additives*
Ora	*refinery additives*
Oronite	*petrochemicals and industrial chemicals*
Oronite Alkane	*detergent intermediates*
Orthene	*insecticides*
Orthex	*fungicides*
Ortho	*agricultural and consumer chemical products*
Orthocide	*fungicides*
Ortho-Gro	*fertilizer*
Ortho-Guard	*plant protectant*
Orthorix	*fungicides*
Outfox	*herbicide*
Paraquat + Plus	*herbicide*
Phaltan	*fungicide*
Ra-Pid-Gro	*fertilizers*
Rat-B-Gon	*rat bait*
Rheniforming	*catalysts*
RPM	*motor oil*
Scram	*dog repellant*
Senate	*lube oil*
Shawinigan	*carbon black*
Slug-Geta	*slug bait*
Sprills	*fungicide*
Standard	*petroleum products*
Supreme	*gasoline*
Techron	*gasoline additive*
Toc (Stylized)	*real estate development services*
Triox	*herbicide*
Tru-Pic (Service Mark)	*oil well services*
Unipel	*fertilizers*
Uniphos	*fertilizers*
Up-Start	*plant starter chemicals*
Veritas	*lube oil*
Vistac	*oil*
Volck	*plant spray*
Weed-B-Gon	*herbicide*
Whirly	*fertilizer spreader*
Whirlybird	*fertilizer spreader*
X-77	*spray adjuvant*
Zerol	*refrigeration fluid*
Zerolene	*motor oil*
Zincofol	*fungicide*

Chock Full o' Nuts Corp.

370 Lexington Ave.
New York, NY 10017
(212) 532-0300

Chief Executive Officer:	Leon Pordy
1984 Annual Sales Volume:	117M
1984 Shares Outstanding:	4,746,000
Shareholders:	12,000
Exchange:	NY
Symbol:	CHF

Corporate History: The company was incorporated in 1932. It is the successor to a single store that sold nut meats, founded by William Black in 1922. In the 1920s Black's business expanded into a chain of 18 nut stores. Beginning in 1933, the stores were converted into restaurants. The coffee business was added in 1953. The corporation today produces and markets coffee, principally under its famous "Chock Full o'Nuts" trademark.

Brandnames of Products and Services:

Chock Full o' Nuts	*coffee*
Old Judge	*coffee*

Chris Craft Industries, Inc.

600 Madison Ave.
New York, N.Y. 10022
(212) 421-0200

Chief Executive Officer:	Herbert J. Siegel
1984 Annual Sales Volume:	166M
1984 Shares Outstanding:	6,206,990
Shareholders:	3,825
Exchange:	NY
Symbol:	CCN

Corporate History: The company incorporated in 1928 as National Automotive Fibres, Inc., a consolidation of two companies that manufactured cotton padding used for automobile upholstery. In 1959 the name changed to NAFI Corp. It adopted its present title in 1962. Traditionally, the company has been known in the consumer market as a manufacturer of pleasure boats. But in 1980 it discontinued that division. The Company's principal business is now television broadcasting. The operations of Chris-Craft's television broadcasting subsidiary, BHC are conducted through BHC's wholly owned subsidiary Chris-Craft Television, Inc., and BHC's 50.3%-owned subsidiary, UTV. In 1984 the Company became the largest shareholder in Warner Communications, Inc. with 28.7% of the voting power of WCI. The Company's industrial division manufactures continuous-web specialty films, rubber and plastic foams, and fiber materials which are made into a variety of products for industry.

Brandnames of Products and Services:

KBHK-TV	*UHF-Ind. station - San Francisco*
KCOP-TV	*station, Los Angeles*
KMOL-TV	*VHF-NBC station - San Antonio*
KMSP-TV	*VHF-Ind. station - Minn./St. Paul*
KPTV-TV	*station, Portland*
KTVX-TV	*VHF-ABC station - Salt Lake City*

Chrysler Corp.

12000 Lynn Townsend Dr.
Highland Park, Mich. 48203
(313) 956-5252

Chief Executive Officer:	L.A. Iacocca
1984 Annual Sales Volume:	19,717M
1984 Shares Outstanding:	121,051,978
Shareholders:	151,298
Exchange:	NY
Symbol:	C

Corporate History: Chrysler traces its history back to Maxwell Motor Car in the 1920s. During the early part of the decade Walter Chrysler, president of Maxwell, developed a moderately priced high-speed car, a combination thought impossible by other auto makers. He called it the Chrysler 50. In 1925 he changed the name of the company to his own. Under Chrysler's direction the company introduced several new cars—the DeSoto and Plymouth—and acquired several more companies, principally Dodge. The company was extremely profitable and remained so even during the depression, but after Walter Chrysler's death in 1940 it began to decline. It proved unable to keep abreast of consumer demands, emphasizing engineering rather than styling. During the 1970s its losses mounted until they reached $205,000,000 in 1978. In 1979 its share of the American car market plunged from 16% to 9%. The following year Chrysler received a $1.5 billion loan guarantee from the federal government.Depressed levels of automobile sales occurred during the 1980-82 period. Sales of vehicles manufactured in the United States were adversely affected by increased competition from foreign automotive manufacturers. Chrysler was particularly affected by its limited ability to produce smaller, more fuel-efficient lines of cars and consumer concern about the viability of Chrysler. The improvement in Chrysler's retail car market share from the 1980 level was largely attributed to the successful introduction of a range of new front-wheel-drive products. The improvement in Chrysler's retail truck market share in 1984 was attributable to the introduction of Chrysler's new front-wheel-drive miniwagons.

Brandnames of Products and Services:

Chrysler	*automobiles*
Dodge	*automobiles*
K-cars	*automobiles*
Plymouth	*automobiles*

Church's Fried Chicken Inc.

Post Office Box BH001
San Antonio, TX 78284
(512) 735-9392

Chief Executive Officer: J. David Bamberger
1984 Annual Sales Volume: 634M
1984 Shares Outstanding: 37,666,802
Shareholders: 3,490
Exchange: NY
Symbol: CHU
Corporate History: Church's, incorporated in 1965, operates through company-owned and franchised fast-food chicken stores. At the end of 1984, there were 1,155 stores in 30 states, all under the name "Church's Fried Chicken," except for 39 stores mostly in the Houston area operated under the name "Ron's Krispy Fried Chicken."
Brandnames of Products and Services:

Church's Fried Chicken	*fast-food stores*
Ron's Krispy Fried Chicken	*fast-food stores*

Circle K Corp.

4500 S. 40th St.
Phoenix, Ariz 85040
(602) 268-1351

Chief Executive Officer: F.T. Hervey
Exchange: AM
Symbol: CKP
Corporate History: The company, incorporated in 1951, operates a chain of convenience food stores in the West and Southwest.
Brandnames of Products and Services:

Circle K	*convenience stores*

Circuit City Stores, Inc.

2040 Thalbro St.
Richmond, VA 23230
(804) 257-4265

Chief Executive Officer: A.L. Wurtzel
1984 Annual Sales Volume: 520M
1984 Shares Outstanding: 10.4 million
Shareholders: 3,000
Exchange: NY
Symbol: CC
Corporate History: Incorporated in 1949, Circuit City Stores is a retailer of television sets, appliances and audio equipment. It changed its name from Wards Co., Inc. in June 1984.
Brandnames of Products and Services:

Circuit City	*video, audio, and consumer electronics*
Circuit City Superstore	*video, audio, consumer electronics and appliances*
Lafayette/Circuit City	*video, audio, consumer electronics*

City Investing Co.

59 Maiden Lane
New York, N.Y. 10038
(212) 759-5300

Chief Executive Officer: G.T. Scharffenberger
Exchange: NY
Symbol: CNV
Corporate History: The company was incorporated in 1904 as a property investment business. During the 1940s it gained ownership of several Broadway theaters as well as the Hotel Carlyle and Parke-Bernet auction house. In the 1960s it diversified and today is a holding company whose subsidiaries are engaged in surance, manufacturing, housing and other operations.
Brandnames of Products and Services:

The Home Group Inc	*insurance*
Motel 6	*budget motel chain*
Red Barn	*restaurants*

Clark Oil & Refining Corp.

8530 West National Ave.
Milwaukee, Wis. 53277
(414) 321-5100

Chief Executive Officer: R.G. Reed III
Exchange: NY
Symbol: CKO
Corporate History: The company was incorporated in 1934. The corporate name was Petco Corp. until 1954, when it assumed its present title. It operates two petroleum refineries and service station chains.

Brandnames of Products and Services:

Clark	*service stations*
Owens	*service stations*

Clorox

1221 Broadway
Oakland, CA 94612
(415) 271-7000

Chief Executive Officer:	C.S. Hatch
1984 Annual Sales Volume:	975M
1984 Shares Outstanding:	25,821,000
Exchange:	NY
Symbol:	CLX

Corporate History: The Clorox Company was founded in Oakland, CA in 1913 and takes its name from *Clorox* liquid bleach, its only product until 1969, when the first steps were taken to diversify. Clorox today is a broadly based company which is diversifying its product line both through acquisitions and through its own internal research and development. One company manufactures and markets a line of household consumer products sold through grocery stores and other retail outlets. In addition, products are marketed to food service customers, including restaurants, hotels, schools, and others. The company manufactures and markets a full line of oil- and latex-based architectural coatings sold through paint and building supply centers and other retail outlets. The company also operates a small restaurant chain.

Brandnames of Products and Services:

Carver Tripp	*interior stains and finishes*
Clorox	*liquid bleach*
Clorox Pic-Wash	*soil and stain remover*
Clorox 2	*bleach*
Emil Villa Barbecues	*restaurants*
Formula 409	*all-purpose spray cleaner*
Fresh Step	*cat box filler*
Hidden Valley Ranch	*dressing mixes*
Kingsford	*charcoal briquets*
Kitchen Bouquet	*cooking sauces*
Liquid-plumr	*drain opener*
Litter Green	*cat box filler*
Lucite	*latex interior wall paint & extension base paint*
Match Light	*instant lighting charcoal briquets*
Moore's	*frozen foods*
Olympic	*oil and latex stains, wood preservative, exterior paints*
Salad Crispins	*salad toppings*
Soft Scrub	*liquid cleanser*
Tilex	*mildew stain remover*
Twice As Fresh	*air freshener*

Cluett, Peabody & Co. Inc.

510 Fifth Ave.
New York, N.Y. 10036
(212) 930-3000

Chief Executive Officer:	H.H. Henley, Jr.
1984 Annual Sales Volume:	949M
1984 Shares Outstanding:	8,389,528
Shareholders:	10,402
Exchange:	NY
Symbol:	CLU

Corporate History: Cluett Peabody was founded in 1851 and incorporated in 1913. For more than 70 years it had made only one product: starched collars. Today it is a leading producer of men's, women's, children's, and young men's apparel. It is the world's largest shirt maker.

Brandnames of Products and Services:

Alatex	*men's sportswear*
Arrow	*men's shirts, sportswear, hosiery, underwear*
Cosco	*factory outlet stores*
Dobie Originals	*young girls' sportswear*
Donmoor	*boys' sportswear*
Duofold	*men's underwear*
Fergusson Atlantic	*men's underwear*
Gold Toe	*men's hosiery*
Halston for Men	*apparel*
Lady Arrow	*women's blouses and sportswear*
RPM	*men's sportswear and furnishings*
Saturdays	*men's sportswear*
Spring City	*men's underwear*
Van Raalte	*gloves and intimate apparel*
Warren Knits	*menswear*

Coachmen Industries Inc.

601 E. Beardsley, P.O. Box 3300
Elkhart, IN 46514
(219) 262-0123

Chief Executive Officer: T.H. Corson
1984 Annual Sales Volume: 528M
1984 Shares Outstanding: 8,673,138
Shareholders: 2,705
Exchange: NY
Symbol: COA
Corporate History: Coachmen Industries, Inc., founded in 1964, is a diversified corporation divided into three operating entities: the Recreatioinal Vehicle, Parts and Supply, and Housing Groups.
Brandnames of Products and Services:

All American	*modular homes*
Coachmen	*recreational vehicles, vans, manufactured housing*
CrossCountry	*motorhomes*
Dearborn	*vans*
Fan	*recreational vehicles*
Frolic	*recreational vehicles*
Greenbriar	*vans*
Jimmy	*vans*
Kenco	*parts for recreational vehicles, vans, pickup trucks*
Lux	*recreational vehicle/van seating*
MRV	*recreational vehicles*
Pathfinder	*motorhomes*
Shadow	*recreational vehicle curtains, draperies, mini-blinds, window shades*
Shasta	*recreational vehicles*
Sportscoach	*motorhomes*
Viking	*recreational vehicles, van tops*

The Coca-Cola Co.

310 North Avenue N.W.
Atlanta, GA 30313
(404) 676-2121

Chief Executive Officer: Roberto Goizueta
1984 Annual Sales Volume: 7,364M
1984 Shares Outstanding: 130 MILLION
Shareholders: 75,862
Exchange: NY
Symbol: KO
Corporate History: The Coca-Cola, Company incorporated in 1919 is the world's largest manufacturer and distributor of soft drink concentrates and syrups. "Coke," invented in 1886 as a "cure-all," accounts for 70% of the company's soft drink sales both in the United States and abroad. It is currently sold in more than 155 countries. Coke has become a symbol of America and the American lifestyle. Coco Coca-Cola not sell "Coke," but sells the syrup to 1,450 bottlers which are often big businesses in their own right. Coca-Cola is no longer a one product company. It currently produces other soft drink beverages, teas, coffees, and citrus products. The Coca-Cola Company is also a major producer and distributor of motion pictures and television programs. In 1984 the company's entertainment business released such films as "Ghostbusters," "The Karate Kid," "A Soldier's Story"; "A Passage to India," produced "T. J. Hooker" and other television series, and released for syndication such programs as "Hart to Hart."
Brandnames of Products and Services:

Belmont Springs	*spring water*
Belmont Springs	*distilled water*
Bright & Early	*concentrated breakfast beverage*
Butternut	*coffee*
caffeine-free Coca-Cola	*beverage*
caffeine-free diet Coke	*beverage*
caffeine-free TAB	*beverage*
cherry Coke	*beverage*
Coca-Cola	*beverages*
Columbia Pictures	*television and cinema*
Columbia Pictures	*Pay Television*
Columbia Pictures Publications	*sheet music*
diet Coke	*beverage*
Fanta	*beverages*
Five Alive	*concentrated beverages*
Fresca	*beverages*
Hi-C	*fruit drinks*
Maryland Club	*coffee and tea*
Mello Yello	*beverages*
Minute Maid	*frozen concentrated juices*
Mr. Pibb	*beverages*
Nemasket Spring	*spring water*
Presto	*plastic wraps, bags, cutlery, cotton swabs, air fresheners, moist towelettes*

RCA/Columbia Pictures	*home video, cassettes and discs*
Snow Crop	*frozen concentrated juices*
Sprite	*beverages*
Tab	*beverages*

Coleco Industries, Inc.

999 Quaker Lane South
West Hartford, CT 06110
(203) 725-6000

Chief Executive Officer: Arnold C. Greenberg
1984 Annual Sales Volume: 775M
1984 Shares Outstanding: 16,140,000
Shareholders: 10,487
Exchange: NY
Symbol: CLO

Corporate History: Founded in 1932, Coleco Industries makes a variety of toys and entertainment products for the family. These include ride-on vehicles for children, plastic wading pools, children's backyard play and furniture products, and electronic entertainment products. Coleco markets Cabbage Patch Kids dolls and accessories and Sectaurs action figures.

Brandnames of Products and Services:

Cabbage Patch Kids	*dolls*
Coleco	*toys and swimming pools*
Coleco-Vision	*video game*
Husky Hauler	*toys*
Play & Learn	*children's games and toys*
Power Cycle	*toys*
Private Call	*phone*
Sectaurs	*toys*
Telestar	*video games*

Coleman Company Inc.

250 N. St. Francis Ave.
Wichita, KS 67202
(316) 261-3211

Chief Executive Officer: Sheldon Coleman
1984 Annual Sales Volume: 454M
1984 Shares Outstanding: 6,853,682
Shareholders: 5,118
Exchange: NY
Symbol: CLN

Corporate History: The company makes and markets outdoor recreational products, including camping products, sleeping bags, and tents. It incorporated in 1928 as the Coleman Lamp & Stove Co., which was founded in 1901. The present name was adopted in 1945.

Brandnames of Products and Services:

California Cooperage	*hot tubs, spas*
Coleman	*camping equipment and trailers*
Coleman Flotation Products	*life wests*
Collins Dynamics	*12-volt intensity electric lanterns, fixed-lighting systems*
Crosman	*air guns*
Golden Eagle Archery	*bows & accessories*
Hobie Cat	*sailboats, canoes*
Inflate-All	*air conditioning*
Master Craft Boats/Skis	*fiberglass water ski boats, water skis*
O'Brien	*water skis*
Oscar & Lil' Oscar	*coolers*
Peak 1	*backpack equipment*
Poly-Lite	*coolers*
RAM-X	*canoes*
Ranging, Inc.	*optical rangefinders*
Skeeter Products, Inc.	*high performance fiberglass fishing boats*
Soniform, Inc.	*underwater safety & survival equipment*
T.H.E.	*heat pump*
Western Cutlery Company, Inc	*outdoor, camping & sports cutlery*

Cole National Corp.

29001 Cedar Rd.
Cleveland, Ohio 44124
(216) 449-4100

Chief Executive Officer: J.E. Cole
Exchange: NY
Symbol: CLE

Corporate History: The company incorporated in 1949 as Jeco Supplies Inc. The name changed shortly after to National Key Shops Inc. and to its present title in 1960. It operates 430 retail optical departments and 706 key duplicating departments, mainly in Sears Robuck and Montgomery Ward Stores. It also owns 302 gift and engraving stores, 11 arts and crafts stores and 54 stores offering baked-on-the-premises cookies. In January 1981 it acquired Child World Inc. which operates toy stores in the Northeast and Midwest.

Brandnames of Products and Services:

Children's Palace	*toy stores*
Child's World	*toy stores*
Craft Showcase	*arts and crafts stores*
The Key Shop	*key stores*
Original Cookie	*cookie stores*
Things Remembered	*gift stores*

Colgate-Palmolive Co.

300 Park Ave.
New York, N.Y. 10022
(212) 310-2000

Chief Executive Officer: Reuben Mark
1984 Annual Sales Volume: 4,910M
1984 Shares Outstanding: 83,032,524
Shareholders: 45,300
Exchange: NY
Symbol: CL

Corporate History: Colgate-Palmolive incorporated in 1923 as Eastern Operating Co. Shortly thereafter the name was changed to Palmolive Co. In 1953 the current name was adopted. The company is a worldwide producer and distributor of household and personal care products. More than half of its business is outside the United States; three-quarters of the company's profits are generated from foreign sales. During the early 1970s the company expanded out of household products and bought over 21 companies with sales of over $1 billion. Colgate-Palmolive today sells more than 3,000 products in 135 countries

Brandnames of Products and Services:

Ajax soaps and detergents	
AJD	*sport caps*
Baggies	*household products*
Bauer & Black	*first aid products*
Blazer	*personal care products*
Carolina	*food products*
Cashmere Bouquet	*soap*
Cold Power	*soaps and detergents*
Colgate	*toothpaste*
Courant	*personal care products*
Curad	*bandages*
Curity	*first aid products*
Dermassage	*soap and personal care products*
Dynamo	*detergent*
Etonic	*golf and running shoes*
Existence	*personal care products*
Fab	*soaps and detergents*
Florient	*air freshener*
Fresh Start	*laundry detergents*
Galaxy	*floor cleaners*
Handy Wipes	*household products*
Heaven Scent	*personal care products*
Hills	*pet foods*
Irish Spring	*soap*
Lums	*restaurant*
Mahatma	*food products*
Marisa Christina	*apparel*
MBT	*broth*
Mersene	*denture cleaner*
Palmolive Gold	*soap*
Princess House	*gift products*
Ranch House	*restaurants*
Rapid Shave	*shaving cream*
Respond	*shampoo*
River	*food products*
Riviana Foods	
Skin Dew	*personal care products*
Skin Life	*personal care products*
Street Fighter	*jogging shoes*
Telfa	*first aid products*
Tretorn	*shoes*
Ultra Brite	*toothpaste*
Ultra Feminine	*personal care products*
Washin 'n' Dry	*household product*
Water Maid	*food products*
Wilkinson	*personal care products*

Collins & Aikman

210 Madison Ave.
New York, NY 10016
(212) 587-1200

Chief Executive Officer: Donald F. McCullough
1984 Annual Sales Volume: 931M
1984 Shares Outstanding: 12,612,151
Shareholders: 10,750
Exchange: NY
Symbol: CK

Corporate History: Collins & Aikman is a producer of specialty products in three segments: non-fabricated textiles (requiring further processing before use), fabricated textiles, and wall coverings. Bathroom curtains and accessories, yarns, and automobile upholstery are some of the company's products, as well as neckwear interlinings and flag bunting

Brandnames of Products and Services:

Brickworks	*fabric*
Cavel	*apparel*
Colonnade	*carpets*
Duranude	*pantyhouse*
Guardian Angel	*sleepwear*
Imperial	*wallcoverings*
Ironweve	*hosiery*
Pan-O-Play	*recreational floor surfacing*

Collins Foods International Inc.

5400 Alla Road
Los Angeles, Calif. 90066
(213) 827-2300

Chief Executive Officer: J.A. Collins
1984 Annual Sales Volume: 499M
1984 Shares Outstanding: 8,723,412
Shareholders: 2,546
Exchange: NY
Symbol: CF

Corporate History: The company, incorporated in 1968, is the largest franchiser of Kentucky Fried Chicken and also operates and licenses others to operate 451 Sizzler Family Steak Houses.

Brandnames of Products and Services:

Emma's Taco House	*restaurant*
Gino's East of Chicago	*restaurant*
Kentucky Fried Chicken	*stores*
Sizzler Family Steak House	*restaurants*

Colonial Commercial Corp.

181 S. Franklin Ave.
Valley Stream, NY 11581
(516) 791-2000

Chief Executive Officer: Bernard Korn
1984 Annual Sales Volume: 14M
1984 Shares Outstanding: 3,604,306
Shareholders: 1,574
Exchange: OTC
Symbol: COL

Corporate History: The company, incorporated in 1964, makes work wear and Western clothes. It also engages in mortgage banking activities and the construction material business.

Brandnames of Products and Services:

Big Smith	*work wear and Western wear*
Stunts	*Western wear*

Color Tile Inc.

515 Houston St
Fort Worth, TX 76102
(817) 870-9400

Chief Executive Officer: J.A. Wilson
1984 Annual Sales Volume: 283M
1984 Shares Outstanding: 9,120,000
Shareholders: 8,000
Exchange: OTC
Symbol: TILE

Corporate History: Color Tile, formerly a wholly owned subsidiary of Tandycrafts Inc., was incorporated in 1978. It operates a nationwide chain of 630 stores featuring a broad selection of floor and wall tiles aimed at the do-it-yourself home decorating and remodeling market. The stores carry nationally advertised brands, but approximately 60% of their product line is private-labeled under the Color Tile name. An additional 152 stores were acquired in October 1984 with the acquisition of Color Your World in Canada.

Brandnames of Products and Services:

Color Tile	*floor and wall tile*
Color Your World	*Paints*
Ultima Wallcoverings	*wallcoverings*

Columbia Picture Industries Inc.

711 Fifth Ave.
New York, N.Y. 10022
(212) 751-4400

Chief Executive Officer: F.T. Vincent, Jr.
Exchange: NY
Symbol: CPS

Corporate History: Columbia was founded in 1924 by Harry and John Cohn. Under their direction the company made such films as *On The Waterfront* and *The Caine Mutiny.* More recently it has had such successes as *The Deep* and *Close Encounters of the Third Kind.* Today Columbia and its subsidiaries produce and distribute motion pictures and television series, design and manufacture amusement games and print sheet music. The company also operates several radio stations.

Brandnames of Products and Services:

Columbia	*pictures, publications, home entertainment and video discs*
D. Gottleib & Co.	*pinball machines*
KCPX-AM/FM	*radio station, Salt Lake City, Utah*
Rastar	*film productions*
WCPI-FM	*radio station, Wheeling, W. Va.*
WWVA-AM	*radio station, Wheeling, W. Va.*
WYDE-AM	*radio station, Birmingham, Ala.*

Commodore Corp.

P.O. Box 295
Syracuse, IN 46567
(219) 457-4431

Chief Executive Officer:	R.J. Gans
1984 Annual Sales Volume:	215M
1984 Shares Outstanding:	12,000,000
Shareholders:	4,000
Exchange:	AM
Symbol:	CCT

Corporate History: Commodore Corp., incorporated in 1968, makes and sells mobile homes.

Brandnames of Products and Services:

BrooKwood	*mobile homes*
Cambridge	*mobile homes*
Cameo	*mobile homes*
Cavalcade	*mobile homes*
Citation	*mobile homes*
Classic	*mobile homes*
Comet	*mobile homes*
Commodore	*mobile homes*
Frontier	*mobile homes*
Kozy	*mobile homes*
Nova	*mobile homes*
Olympian	*mobile homes*
Regent	*mobile homes*

ConAgra Inc.

One Central Park Plaza
Omaha, NB 68102
(402) 978-4000

Chief Executive Officer:	C.M. Harper
1984 Annual Sales Volume:	3,302M
1984 Shares Outstanding:	33,152,000
Shareholders:	12,000
Exchange:	NY
Symbol:	CAG

Corporate History: The company was incorporated in 1919. It is a diversified producer of basic food products and of formula feeds, fertilizers, animal health products and other farm supply products and services. In fiscal 1984, prepared foods accounted for 44% of sales, grain processing and merchandising 25% and agricultural products 31%.

Brandnames of Products and Services:

AgriBasics, NutriBasics	*feeds, feed additives*
Armour	*processed meats, frozen foods, cheese*
Banquet Foods	*frozen foods*
Country Pride	*poultry products*
Country Skillet	*fish and poultry*
Decker	*processed meats*
Geisler	*pet accessories*
Home Brand	*preserves, jellies, peanut butter, syrup*
Sea-Alaska, Alaska Seas	*frozen seafood*
Singleton	*seafood (frozen)*
Taco Plaza	*Mexican restaurants*
"Woodstocks"	*wildlife products, wild birdseed*

Conair Corp.

11 Executive Ave.
Edison, NJ 08817
(201) 287-4800

Chief Executive Officer: Leandro P. Rizzuto
1984 Annual Sales Volume: 260M
1984 Shares Outstanding: 9,648,042
Shareholders: 1,600
Exchange: NY
Symbol: CAA

Corporate History: The company incorporated in 1972 as Continental Hair Products and adopted its current name in 1976. The company designs and makes hair care appliances and products. In 1983 Conair acquired Zotos International, Inc. A developer and manufacturer of professional-use-only hair care products

Brandnames of Products and Services:

Advent	*hair care products*
Conair	*hair care appliances*
Conair Perm	*Home Permanent*
Conairphone	*consumer telephone*
Conairphone Call Keeper	*telephone answering machine*
Conair Thermal Protection	*hair care products*
Continental	*hair dryer*
Cushion Curl	*hairsetter*
Jheri Redding milk 'n honee	*hair care products*
Jheri Redding mousse	*hair care products*
Kwik Sweep	*vacuum*
Lite Saver	*flashlight*
Massage Works	*body massagers*
Royal Persian Henna	*shampoo and conditioner*
Shape Ups	*personal care products*
True Reflection	*mirror*
Water Fingers	*shower massage*

Conna Corp.

981 South Third St.
P.O. Box 660
Louisville, KY 40203
(502) 584-1281

Chief Executive Officer: Joe P. Peden
1984 Annual Sales Volume: 414M
1984 Shares Outstanding: 11,912,000
Shareholders: 1,200
Exchange: OTC
Symbol: CONA

Corporate History: The company incorporated as Convenient Food Mart of Louisville Inc. in 1959. The name was changed to Convenient Industries in 1968 and to the present title in 1979. The company is one of the largest food store operators and franchisers in the United States, operating 391 stores mainly in the East and Midwest.

Brandnames of Products and Services:

Convenient Food	*supermarkets*

Conroy Inc.

3355 Cherry Ridge Dr.
San Antonio, Tex. 78230
(512) 341-7792

Chief Executive Officer: K.M. Orme
Exchange: AM
Symbol: CRY

Corporate History: The company incorporated in 1966 by the merger of Consolidated Royalty Oil Co. and Western Exploration Co. It makes fiberglass pleasure boats and during the past decade has been expanding its ready-to-assemble furniture line. In 1980 furniture accounted for 62% of sales and marine products 38%.

Brandnames of Products and Services:

Carlson	*pleasure boats*
Glastron	*pleasure boats*
O'Sullivan	*ready-to-assemble furniture lines*
Spirit Yachts	*pleasure boats*

Consolidated Foods Corp.

Three First National Plaza
Chicago, IL 60602-4260
(312) 726-2600

Chief Executive Officer:	John H. Bryan, Jr.
1984 Annual Sales Volume:	7,000M
1984 Shares Outstanding:	54,932,300
Shareholders:	40,500
Exchange:	NY
Symbol:	CFD

Corporate History: The company was founded in 1939. Today Consolidated Foods is an international company whose major businesses are the manufacturing and marketing of consumer products, principally packaged goods; the manufacturing and distribution of products for the foodservice industry; and the manufacturing and marketing of products sold directly to the consumer. The corporation's products include many well-known brands which compete primarily in the North American and European markets. In 1984 consumer foods accounted for 27% of sales, beverages 20%, consumer personal products 20%, food distribution 19% and direct sales 14%.

Brandnames of Products and Services:

Active Support	*hosiery*
Alive	*hosiery*
Aris Isotoner	*knitwear*
B & G	*pickles & relishes*
Bali	*intimate apparel*
Block & Guggenheimer	*food*
Bryan Foods	*processed and fresh meats*
Buring Foods	*(food)*
Chef Pierre	*pies*
Coloralls	*hosiery*
Douwe Egberts	*beverages*
Electrolux	*vacuum cleaners*
Fuller Brush	*household products*
Hanes	*women's hosiery and men's underwear*
Hi Brand	*food*
Hillshire Farms	*smoked meats*
Jimmy Dean	*sausage*
Just My Size	*hosiery*
Kahn's Kitchens of Sara Lee	*frozen bakery products and fresh meats*
King Colton	*sausage*
Laradenois	*apparel*
Lauderdale Farms	*food*
Lawson's	*convenience stores*
Leggs	*hosiery*
Lloyd J Harris	*frozen bakery products*
Lyon's	*restaurant*
MarTenn	*sausage*
Pay Day	*candy bar*
Popsicle	*frozen dessert*
Poultry Specialties	*food*
R. B. Rice	*sausage*
Rudy's Farm	*sausage*
Rus-Ette	*frozen potato products*
Sara Lee	*frozen bakery products*
Shasta	*beverages*
Sheer Elegance	*hosiery*
Sheer Energy	*hosiery*
Showtoon	*boy's underwear*
Slenderalls	*hosiery*
Smoky Hollow Foods Standard Meat	*processed and fresh meats*
Summer Sheer	*hosiery*
Superior Coffee	*beverage*
Today's Girl	*hosiery*
Underalls	*hosiery*
Union Sugar	*(food)*
Wearabouts	*leisure apparel*
Winteralls	*hosiery*
Zero	*candy bar*

Continental Corp.

180 Maiden Lane
New York, N.Y. 10038
(212) 440-3980

Chief Executive Officer:	John P. Mascotte
1984 Annual Sales Volume:	4,641M
1984 Shares Outstanding:	49,643,538
Shareholders:	29,843
Exchange:	NY
Symbol:	CIC

Corporate History: Founded in 1853, Continental is one of the largest insurance organizations in the world, with more than $4 billion in revenues and nearly $10 billon in assets. The company has property/ casualty and life/health operations throughout the U.S. and in more than 60 countries around the world. Continental markets its insurance products and services primarily through three distribution networks. Independent agents, national brokers and non-traditional distributors.

Brandnames of Products and Services:

Cenguard	*insurance services*

Commercial Life	*insurance services*
Continental Insurance	*insurance services*
CPI Group	*insurance services*
Fireman's Insurance Co. of Newark, NJ	
The Insurancenter	*insurance services*
Loyalty Life	*insurance services*
National Life of Canada	*insurance services*
William Penn	*insurance services*

Converse Inc.

55 Fordham Road
Wilmington, MA 01887
(617) 657-5500

Chief Executive Officer: Richard B. Loynd
1984 Annual Sales Volume: 266M
1984 Shares Outstanding: 5,477,600
Shareholders: 960
Exchange: OTC
Symbol: CURS

Corporate History: Converse, Inc., incorporated in 1982, is a leading manufacturer and supplier of athletic shoes, marketing a wide variety of models designed for basketball, running, racquet sports and field sports. The company also designs and markets athletic apparel. In 1984, 66.2% of sales were from basketball shoes, 15.6% from running shoes, 10.9% from shoes for racquet sports, 3.3% from shoes for field sports, and 4.0% other (which includes apparel).

Brandnames of Products and Services:

Aerodyne	*aerobic shoes*
All Star	*basketball shoes*
Athena	*women's running shoes*
Chris Evert Calypso	*tennis shoes*
Cimaron	*basketball shoes*
Converse	*athletic shoes and apparel*
Field Star	*multi-use cleated shoes*
Force-5	*running shoes*
Gazelle	*running shoes*
Jimmy Connors Commodore	*tennis shoes*
Laser	*running shoes*
Lydiard Equinox	*running shoes*
Maverick	*basketball shoes*
Odessa	*running shoes*
Precedent	*basketball shoes*
Revenge	*running shoe*
Sportstar	*football shoes*
Starion	*basketball shoes*
Startech	*basketball shoes*
S-111	*cleated shoes*
Thunderbolt	*running shoes*
Tribute	*women's basketball shoes*

Conwood Corp.

813 Ridge Lake Blvd.
Memphis, TN 38119
(901) 761-2050

Chief Executive Officer: W.M. W.M. Rosson
1984 Annual Sales Volume: 198M
1984 Shares Outstanding: 11,149,865
Shareholders: 5,300
Exchange: NY
Symbol: CWD

Corporate History: Conwood Corp., incorporated in 1966, is a major producer of snuff and chewing tobacco. It has diversified into such fields as popcorn, for grocery outlets and theater and concession operators and equipment for theaters and concessionaires.

Brandnames of Products and Services:

Back to Nature	*plant spray*
Bee Hive	*popcorn*
B.G. Twist	*tobacco*
Black Maria	*chewing tobacco*
Bull of the Woods	*chewing tobacco*
Bulls Eye	*chewing tobacco*
Bunny Pop	*popcorn*
Cannon Ball	*chewing tobacco*
Clover Bloom	*tobacco*
Conwood	*tobacco*
Delmonico	*popcorn*
Dental	*tobacco snuff*
Favorite	*tobacco*
Garrett	*tobacco snuff*
Gaymont	*yogurt and other food products*
Haw Ken	*tobacco*
Honest	*tobacco snuff*
Kentucky King	*tobacco*
Kentucky Twist	*tobacco*
Lucky Joe	*tobacco*
Mammoth Cave	*tobacco*
Meriweather's Pig Tail	*tobacco*
Moore's Red Leaf	*tobacco*
Old Joe	*tobacco*

Old Taylor	*tobacco*
Peach	*snuff*
Peach & Honey	*snuff*
Penn's Natural Leaf	*tobacco*
Pops-Rite	*popcorn and seasoning*
Presto Pop	*popcorn and seasoning*
Rainbow	*snuff*
Ram's Horn	*tobacco*
Red Bud	*tobacco*
Red Coon	*chewing tobacco*
Red Fox	*tobacco*
Rice's Best	*tobacco*
Ripe Peaches	*tobacco*
Rose Bud	*tobacco*
Rough Country	*tobacco*
R.T. Junior	*tobacco*
Samson's Big 4	*tobacco*
Savorol	*seasoning salt*
Snuffettes	*tobacco and snuff*
Taylor Made	*tobacco*
Taylor's Pride	*tobacco*
Warren	*tobacco*
Wildcat	*tobacco*
Yellow Tag	*tobacco*

Cook United Inc.

16501 Rockside Rd.
Maple Heights, Ohio 44137
(216) 475-1000

Chief Executive Officer: M.M. Lewis
Exchange: NY
Symbol: CCF

Corporate History: The comapany was incorporated in 1925 as Cook Coffee Co. and adopted its present title in 1969. It operates specialty retail outlets and discount department stores.

Brandnames of Products and Services:

Clark's	*discount department stores and gasoline stations*
Consolidated Sales Co.	*discount department stores and gasoline stations*
Cook's	*discount department stores and gasoline stations*
Ontario	*discount department stores and gasoline stations*
Stratford Jewelers	*catalog and showroom, Cleveland, Ohio*
Uncle Bill's	*discount department stores and gasoline stations*

Cooper Industries Inc.

1001 Fannin, Suite 4000 (P.O. Box 4446)
Houston, TX 77210
(713) 739-5400

Chief Executive Officer: Robert Cizik
1984 Annual Sales Volume: 2,030M
1984 Shares Outstanding: 42,185,000
Shareholders: 30,949
Exchange: NY
Symbol: CBE

Corporate History: Cooper Industries was incorporated in 1929 as Cooper-Bessemer Corp., a combination of C & G Cooper Co., founded in Mt. Vernon, Ohio in 1833, and the Bessemer Gas Engine Co., established in 1900. Its present title was adopted in 1965. The company operates in three major business segments: tools and hardware, compression and drilling equipment, and electrical and electronic products. In 1984, tools and hardware accounted for 29% of sales, compression and drilling equipment for 32%, and electrical and electrical products for 39%. In 1979, Cooper acquired Gardner-Denver Company, a maker of oilfield drilling equipment and mining and construction machinery. In 1981, Crouse-Hinds Company—a leading manufacturer of electrical equipment was acquired. The deal included Belden Corporation, a wire and cable producer. Presently, in 1985, the company is in the process of finalizing a merger with McGraw-Edison Company, a leading manufacturer and supplier of products and services to industrial, utility, commercial and automotive markets worldwide.

Brandnames of Products and Services:

Boker Tree Brand	*hand tools*
Crescent	*hand tools*
Kirsch	*drapery hardware*
Lufkin	*hand tools*
Nicholson	*hand tools*
Rotor Tool	*pneumatic tools*
Weller	*hand tools*
Wiss	*hand tools*
Xcelite	*hand tools*

Cooper Laboratories, Inc.

755 Page Mill Rd.
Palo Alto, Calif. 94304
(415) 494-8181

Chief Executive Officer: P.G. Montgomery
Exchange: NY

Symbol: COO

Corporate History: The company, incorporated in 1961, develops, manufactures and sells prescription and over-the-counter pharmaceuticals, skin care products, therapeutic products and services for ocular diseases, and contact lens care products.

Brandnames of Products and Services:

Acnaveen	*skin cleansers*
Aveeno	*skin cleanser*
Emulave	*skin cleanser*
Hypotears	*moisturizing eye drops*
Lensine	*solution for hard contact lenses*
Oral B	*toothbrushes and dental floss*
Unisol	*solution for soft contact lenses*
Vasocon A	*antihistamine*

Adolph Coors Co.

Golden, CO 80401
(303) 279-6565

Chief Executive Officer: W.K. Coors
1984 Annual Sales Volume: 1,133MM
1984 Shares Outstanding: 35,012,000
Shareholders: 8,667
Exchange: OTC
Symbol: ACCOB

Corporate History: The company was founded in 1873 by Adolph Coors, a German immigrant. The world's largest brewery has remained on its present site and to this day, all Coors beer is produced on this one location. During Prohibition, when many brewers were forced to close, Coors survived by producing milk, "near beer," and ceramics. Following repeal of Prohibition, beer was distributed to 11 western states, and in 1976 began a market expansion that has now brought Coors beer to 44 states plus Washington, D.C. The company will be a national brewery by 1990. In addition to beer, the company also has subsidiary operations in industrial ceramics, food products, hearing conservation, energy development, can manufacturing, transportation, packaging, aluminum recycling, and its newest operation, Coor BioTech Products.

Brandnames of Products and Services:

Coors	*beer*
Coors Extra Gold	*beer*
Coors Light	*beer*
George Killian's Irish Red	*ale*
Herman Joseph's 1868	*beer*

Corning Glass Works

Houghton Park
Corning, NY 14831
(607) 974-9000

Chief Executive Officer: James R. Houghton
1984 Annual Sales Volume: 1,733M
1984 Shares Outstanding: 42,378,056
Shareholders: 13,900
Exchange: NY
Symbol: GLW

Corporate History: Corning Glass Works traces its origin to a glass business established by the Houghton family in 1851. The present corporation was incorporated in 1936. Corning is engaged principally in the manufacuture and sale of products made from specialty glasses and related inorganic materials having special properties of chemical stability, electrical resistance, heat resistance, light transmission and mechanical strength. In addition, Corning produces medical instruments, electronic devices, and markets clinical laboratory services. In 1984 products (housewares and tableware) accounted for approximately 24% of sales; consumer durable components (components used in the manufacture of consumer goods such as automobiles and television sets) 22%; capital goods components (components for products linked to capital investment by industry) 24%; and health and science products (products and services related to clinical and general laboratory sciences and ophthalmic lenses) 30%. In 1982 Corning acquired Met Path Laboratories, a leading blood testing service.

Brandnames of Products and Services:

Clear Elegance	*casseroles*
Corelle	*dinnerware*
Corning Ware	*cookware*
Crown Corning	*glassware, stemware*
Culinary Kits	*housewares*
Everyday Gourmet	*housewares*
Plant Helpers	*plant care products*
Pyrex	*ovenware and food storage containers*
Pyroceram	*housewares*
Pyroflam	*housewares*
Servables	*bakeware*
Steuben	*crystal*
Sunsensor	*sunglasses, lenses*
Thermique	*heat-resistant carafes*

Visions	*carafes*

Cowles Communications

444 Seabreeze Blvd.
Daytona Beach, Fla. 32018
(904) 258-1800

Chief Executive Officer: M.C. Whatmore
Exchange: NY
Symbol: CWL

Corporate History: The company incorporated in 1936 as Look, Inc.; the name was changed to Cowles Magazine Inc. in 1944 and to Cowles Magazine & Broadcasting Inc. in 1961. Its current title was adopted in 1965. In 1971 it sold *Family Circle* and other properties to the *New York Times.* Today its principal asset is $2.6 million of *New York Times* Class A shares which it received in the exchange. This represents a 22% interest in the *Times* combined Class A and B shares. Because of its large stockholdings it is considered a closed-end non-diversified management investment company. Its major product *Look* magazine folded in 1967. Today Cowles operates two television stations.

Brandnames of Products and Services:

KCCI-TV	*Des Moines, Iowa*
WESH-TV	*Daytona*

Cox Communications, Inc.

1400 Lake Hearn Drive
Atlanta, GA 30319
(404) 843-5000

Chief Executive Officer: William A. Schwartz
1984 Annual Sales Volume: 743M
1984 Shares Outstanding: 28,328,216
Shareholders: 3,200
Exchange: NY
Symbol: COX

Corporate History: The company, incorporated in 1964 as Cox Broadcasting Corporation, is involved in broadcasting, cable television, automobile auctions, and the radio common-carrier business. In 1984 broadcasting interests accounted for 37.6% of sales and cable operations 54.5%. Automobile auctions made up 7.2%. In 1982 the company changed its name to Cox Communications.

Brandnames of Products and Services:

Cox Cable	*cable television*
KDNH-TV	*St. Louis, Mo.*
KFI-AM	*Los Angeles, Calif.*
KOST-FM	*Los Angeles, Calif.*
KTVU-TV	*San Francisco/Oakland, Calif.*
WAIA-FM	*Miami, Fla.*
WCKG-FM	*Chicago*
WHIO-AM/FM	*Dayton, Ohio*
WHIO-TV	*Dayton, Ohio*
WIOD-AM	*Miami, Fla.*
WKBD-TV	*Detroit*
WPXI-TV	*Pittsburgh, Pa.*
WSB-AM/FM	*Atlanta, Ga.*
WSB-TV	*Atlanta, Ga.*
WSOC-AM/FM	*Charlotte, N.C.*
WSOC-TV	*Charlotte, N.C.*
WZGO-FM	*Philadelphia, Pa.*

CPC International Inc.

International Plaza
Englewood Cliffs, NJ 07632
(201) 894-4000

Chief Executive Officer: James R. Eiszner
1984 Annual Sales Volume: 4,373M
1984 Shares Outstanding: 48,586,553
Shareholders: 48,000
Exchange: NY
Symbol: CPC

Corporate History: The company, founded in 1906, incorporated in 1959 as Corn Products Co. Ten years later the name was changed to CPC International Inc. it initially concentrated on supplying corn to industry, but in the past 25 years has expanded into the consumer foods market. It acquired Best Foods in 1958. In 1970 it acquired Thomas's Inc. Despite its dominance in the U.S. market, its international operations are the most important component of its business, they account for 58% of its sales. CPC is the world's largest corn wet miller, producing a wide range of products used by more than 70 different industries. These products include corn starches, corn syrups, high fructose corn syrups, and dextrose, as well as corn and animal feed ingredients.

Brandnames of Products and Services:

Argo	*Cornstarch*
Argo	*Laundry starches*
Best Foods	*food products*
Bosco	*milk supplement*
Duryea's	*cornstarch*
Fanning's Bread & Butter	*pickles*

Golden Griddle	*pancake syrup*
Hellmann's and Best Foods	*mayonnaise and salad dressing*
H-O	*cereals*
Karo	*corn syrup*
Kingsford's	*cornstarch*
Knorr	*soups and mixes*
Mazola	*corn oil and margarine*
Mueller's	*spaghetti, macaroni and pasta products*
Niagara	*spray starch*
No stick	*shortening*
Nucoa	*margarines*
Nusoft	*fabric softener*
Rit	*fabric tints and dyes*
Skippy	*peanut butter*
Spin Blend	*salad dressing*
Thomas's	*English muffins and baked-goods*

Craddock-Terry Shoe Corp.

3100 Albert Lankford Dr.
Lynchburg Expressway
Lynchburg, VA 24506
(804) 845-3411

Chief Executive Officer: G. Bruce Miller
1984 Annual Sales Volume: 83M
1984 Shares Outstanding: 1,549,592
Shareholders: 1,549
Exchange: OTC
Symbol: CDCK

Corporate History: The company, incorporated in 1938, manufactures shoes. As of 1984 it operated 93 retail shoe stores. The company also sells footwear through a mail-order footwear business.

Brandnames of Products and Services:

American Gentleman	*shoes*
Andiamo	*women's shoes*
Auditions	*women's shoes*
Contempos	*women's shoes*
Polly Preston	*shoes*
Stage 1	*shoes*

A. T. Cross Company

One Albion Road
Lincoln, RI 02865
(401) 333-1200

Chief Executive Officer: Bradford R. Boss
1984 Annual Sales Volume: 133M
1984 Shares Outstanding: 8,240,807
Shareholders: 1,860
Exchange: AM
Symbol: ATXA

Corporate History: The company was incorporated in 1916 as a successor to a business founded in 1846. The company makes fine writing instruments including chrome ball point pens, mechanical pencils, porous point pens, fountain pens and desk sets. In 1983 the Company acquired Mark Cross Inc. This wholly-owned subsidiary markets luggage, leather goods and specialty gift items.

Brandnames of Products and Services:

Cross	*writing instruments and desk sets*
Mark Cross Inc	*luggage, leather goods, gift items*

Crowley, Milner & Co.

2301 West Lafayette Blvd.
Detroit, MI 48126
(313) 962-2400

Chief Executive Officer: Robert B. Carlson
1984 Annual Sales Volume: 93M
1984 Shares Outstanding: 509,067
Shareholders: 221
Exchange: AM
Symbol: COM

Corporate History: The company, incorporated in 1914, operates 10 department stores primarily in the Detroit metropolitan area. The stores sell middle to middle-better price lines in men's, women's and children's apparel, accessories and decorative home furnishings.

Brandnames of Products and Services:

Crowley's	*department stores*

Crown Zellerbach Corp.

1 Bush St.
San Francisco, CA 94104
(415) 951-5000

Chief Executive Officer: W.T. Creson
1984 Annual Sales Volume: 3,094M
1984 Shares Outstanding: 27.2 Million
Shareholders: 23,368
Exchange: NY
Symbol: ZB
Corporate History: The company can trace its origins back to the California gold rush when Anthony Zellerbach began providing desperately needed paper to the region. It was founded in 1870 and incorporated in 1924 as Zellerbach Corp. to act as a holding company. Its present title was adopted in 1928. It is one of the largest paper concerns in the country, although its brandname products are not well-known outside of the West. During the 1960s the company expanded into the Eastern United States and into such nations as Holland and Chile. In 1982, it sold Crown Zellerbach Canada, Ltd and interests in Holland and Chile.
Brandnames of Products and Services:

Linensoft	*bathroom tissue*
Luau	*paper napkins*
Marina	*bathroom tissue*
Nice 'n Soft	*bathroom tissue*
Spill-Mate	*paper products*
Vera	*facial tissue*
Zee	*earthtones paper napkins, paper towels, and lunch bags*

Culbro Corp.

387 Park Ave. South
New York, NY 10016-8899
(212) 561-8700

Chief Executive Officer: E.M. Cullman
1984 Annual Sales Volume: 1,094M
1984 Shares Outstanding: 4,212,575
Shareholders: 1,716
Exchange: NY
Symbol: CUC
Corporate History: The company was incorporated in 1906 as the United Cigar Manufacturers Co. The name was changed in 1917 to General Cigar Co., and in 1916 the present title was adopted. The company makes food products, health and beauty care items, and tobacco products.
Brandnames of Products and Services:

Brandee	*tobacco products*
Buttercup	*tobacco products*
Cains Marcelle	*potato chips*
Chesty	*potato chips*
Corina	*cigars*
Golden Crisp	*potato chips*
Golden Popcorn	
Golden Ridges	*potato chips*
Gold Label	*cigars*
Gold River	*tobacco products*
Greenbrier	*tobacco products*
Jax Cheese Twists	*snack food*
KAS	*potato chips*
Kentucky Club	*tobacco products*
Kitty Clover	*potato chips*
Lancaster	*tobacco products*
London Dock	*tobacco*
Macanudo	*cigars*
Navy Sweet	*tobacco products*
Partagas	*cigars*
Railroad Mills Sweet	*tobacco products*
Ramon Allones	*cigars*
Redwood	*tobacco products*
Robert Burns	*cigars*
Royal Danish	*tobacco products*
Shakespeare	*cigars*
Silver Creek	*tobacco products*
Skandinavik	*tobacco products*
Square	*tobacco*
Superior	*tobacco*
Tijuana Smalls	*cigars*
Tiparillos	*cigars*
Tops Sweet	*tobacco product*
Tor-Ticos	*tortilla chips*
Van Dyck	*cigars*
Viking	*tobacco product*
Viva	*corn chips*
Whitehall	*tobacco product*
White Owl	*cigars*
William Penn	*cigars*
Workmate	*tobacco product*

Cullinet Software Inc.

400 Blue Hill Drive
Westwood, MA 02090
(617) 329-7700

Chief Executive Officer: John J. Cullinane
1984 Annual Sales Volume: 120M

1984 Shares Outstanding: 14,873,925
Shareholders: 3,100
Exchange: NY
Symbol: CUL

Corporate History: Cullinet was founded in 1968. The company changed its name from Cullinane Database Systems Inc. to Cullinet Software Inc. in 1983. It develops, markets, and supports software products for IBM and IBM-compatible hardware users. These products fall into three broad categories — database management, applications, and decision systems, including personal computer software.

Brandnames of Products and Services:

Goldengate	*computer products*
Trend-Spotter	*computer products*

Cullum Companies Inc.

14303 Inwood Road
Dallas, TX 75234
(214) 661-9700

Chief Executive Officer: Charles G. Cullum
1984 Annual Sales Volume: 1,228M
1984 Shares Outstanding: 8,190,736
Shareholders: 2,230
Exchange: OTC
Symbol: CULL

Corporate History: Cullum Companies Inc. was incorporated in 1953 as A.W. Cullum & Co. Inc. and changed its name to its present title in 1969. The company engages in retail merchandising. It operates 101 supermarkets in Dallas, Texas, Los Angeles California, and various cities in Nebraska, Iowa and North and South Dakota, some in combination with drug stores. It also operates seven warehouse markets in Missouri, Arkansas, Kansas, Oklahoma, and Tennessee and and a meat packing business.

Brandnames of Products and Services:

Gooch Meats	
Hinky Dinky	*supermarkets*
Page Drug Stores	
Pantry	*supermarkets*
Rylander	*supermarkets*
Tom Thumb	*supermarkets*

Curtice-Burns Inc.

One Lincoln First Sq.
P.O. Box 681
Rochester, NY 14603
(716) 325-1020

Chief Executive Officer: Robert L. Hutchinson
1984 Annual Sales Volume: 612M
1984 Shares Outstanding: 3,647,965
Shareholders: 2,300
Exchange: AM
Symbol: CBI

Corporate History: The company was incorporated in 1961 for the purpose of acquiring the two businesses formerly operated as Curtice Brothers Co. and Burns-Alton Corp. The company's business is principally conducted in one industry segment, the processing and sale of various food products. Through its ten operating divisions, the company produces and markets a variety of processed food products, including canned vegetables, frozen vegetables and fruits, canned desserts, canned fruits and juices, condiments and salad dressings, snack foods, pickles, canned meat dishes and salads, soft drinks, processed meats, and cereal products.

Brandnames of Products and Services:

A&W	*beverages*
Barrelhead*	*beverages*
Bernstein	*salad dressings*
Big Pop	*snack food*
Blue Boy	*canned vegetables*
Brooks	*condiments, canned foods*
Canada Dry*	*beverages*
Chill Ripe	*canned and frozen vegetables*
Colonial	*meats, meat products*
Comstock	*canned foods*
Cortland Valley	*sauerkraut*
Countrytime	*lemonade*
Crunchi-O's	*snack food*
Dr. Pepper*	*beverages*
Fenway	*frankfurters*
Greenwood	*beets*
Handschumacher Old World	*meats, meat products*
Harvest	*oat cereals*
La Suprema Restaurant Style	*tortilla chips*
Like*	*beverages*
Linden	*chicken dinners*
Lucca	*specialty foods*
McKenzie's	*vegetable products*

McKenzie's gold King	*vegetable products*
Menner	*rice products*
Nagel	*meats, meat products*
Nalley	*snack food, canned foods*
Nepco	*frankfurters*
Perrier	*beverages*
Red's	*Mexican foods*
Ritter	*vegetable products*
Ritter Veg-Crest	*vegetable juices*
Riviera	*Specialty food products*
Seven Up	*beverage*
Silver Floss	*sauerkraut*
Snyder's of Berlin	*snack food*
Southern Farms	*vegetable products*
Sunkist	*beverages*
Super Pop	*snack food*
Thank You	*canned foods*
Three Minute	*cereals, grits*
Top	*meats, meat products*
Victor	*sauerkraut*
Yankee	*frankfurters*

Damon Creations Inc.

16 E. 34th St
New York, N.Y. 10016
(212) 683-2465

Chief Executive Officer: Michael Rappaport
1984 Annual Sales Volume: 45M
1984 Shares Outstanding: 1,099,926
Shareholders: 466
Exchange: AM
Symbol: DNI

Corporate History: The company was founded in 1935 and incorporated in 1946. It makes and sells higher-priced men's apparel. In 1984, its products were sold to about 2,700 department stores and specialty shops throughout the United States.

Brandnames of Products and Services:

Bill Blass	*men's apparel*
Courchevel	*men's apparel*
Damon	*men's apparel*
Lanvin	*men's apparel*

Danaher Corp.

1645 Palm Beach Lakes Blvd.
West Palm Beach, FL 33401
(305) 471-2700

Chief Executive Officer: Steven M. Rales
1984 Annual Sales Volume: 91M
1984 Shares Outstanding: 10,191,904
Shareholders: 6,775
Exchange: NY
Symbol: DHR

Corporate History: Founded in 1969 and reorganized in 1978 as diversified mortgage investors, Danaher Corp. adopted its present name in 1984. Prior to 1984 the company was solely engaged in real estate. In 1984 the company acquired Mohawk Rubber Co. and Master Shield, Inc. Because of these acquisitions, in 1984 13% of sales were from real estate, 77% from rubber and related automotive products, and 10% from vinyl/plastic consumer goods.

Brandnames of Products and Services:

Master Shield	*household sliding window, profiles*
Mohawk Rubber	*tires, automotive products*

Dart Drug Corp.

3301 Pennsy Dr.
Landover, Md. 20785
(301) 772-6000

Chief Executive Officer: H.H. Haft
Exchange: OTC
Symbol: DRUGA

Corporate History: Dart Drug was established in 1954 and incorporated in 1960. It operates 56 discount drugstores in the Washington D.C. area. Dart also owns drug store-home centers for the do-it-yourself market, 14 Crown book stores and seven Trak Auto parts stores.

Brandnames of Products and Services:

Crown Books	*stores*
Dart	*drugstores*
Trak Auto	*discount auto parts stores*

Dart & Kraft Inc.

2211 Sanders Road
Northbrook, IL 60062
(312) 498-8000

Chief Executive Officer:	John M. Richman
1984 Annual Sales Volume:	9,759M
1984 Shares Outstanding:	47,901,094
Shareholders:	70,200
Exchange:	NY
Symbol:	DKI

Corporate History: The present company was formed in 1980 upon the merger of Dart Industries and Kraft Inc. The merger made it one of the 30 largest industrial companies in the United States. Dart is a major producer of household products such as Tupperware, West Bend cookware and Duracell batteries. Kraft, which invented processed cheese in 1916, is the largest maker of dairy products in the United States. Its products are distributed in 30 countries. Recent company acquisitions include Celestial Seasonings herb teas, Lender's bagels, Precor exercise equipment and Borg bathroom scales.

Brandnames of Products and Services:

Borg	*bathroom scales*
Breakstone	*dairy products*
Breyer's	*dairy products*
Casino	*food products*
Celestial Seasonings	*herb teas*
Cheez Whiz	*cheese products*
Coppercraft Guild	*copper giftware*
Cracker Barrel	*cheese*
Durabeam	*flashlights*
Duracell	*batteries*
FreeStyle	*cordless iron*
Golden Image	*imitation cheese*
Hobart	*kitchen appliances*
Kitchen Aid	*kitchen appliances*
Kraft	*dairy products*
Lender's	*bagels*
Light n' Lively	*dairy products*
Miracle Maid	*cookware*
Miracle Whip	*salad dressing*
Nappe-Babcock	*cushions, pillows, insulated bags*
National	*garbage disposals*
Parkay	*margarine*
Philadelphia	*cream cheese*
Precor	*exercise equipment*
Sealtest	*ice cream products*
Seamco	*sporting goods*
Syroco	*home decorative accessories and furniture*
Thermo-Serv	*serving ware*
Total Gym	*exercise equipment*
Tupperware	*food containers and household products*
Vanda	*cosmetics*
Velveeta	*cheese products*
West Bend	*appliances*
West Bend	*exercise equipment*
Wilsonart	*decorative laminates*

Data General Corp.

4400 Computer Dr.
Westboro, MA 01580
(617) 366-8911

Chief Executive Officer:	Edson D. de Castro
1984 Annual Sales Volume:	1,161M
1984 Shares Outstanding:	24,566,218
Shareholders:	8,000
Exchange:	NY
Symbol:	DGN

Corporate History: Incorporated in 1968, Data General designs, makes, sells and services general-purpose computers, including peripheral equipment and software, and provides related products and services, including training and maintenance.

Brandnames of Products and Services:

Data General/One	*computers*
Desktop Generation	*computers*

Dayco Corp.

333 West First St.
Dayton, OH 45402
(513) 226-7000

Chief Executive Officer:	R.J. Jacob
1984 Annual Sales Volume:	901M
1984 Shares Outstanding:	7.137,781
Shareholders:	11,595
Exchange:	NY
Symbol:	DAY

Corporate History: The company, incorporated May 17, 1905, is a manufacturer of rubber, plastic, chemical and automotive products. It also makes consumer products including wall coverings & garden hoses. In 1984 consumer products accounted for 14% of sales with the remainder coming from industrial and transportation products.

Brandnames of Products and Services:

Dayco E-Z Lok	*hose couplings*
Gold Label	*V-Belts*
Poolflex	*swimming pool vacuum hose*
Top-Cog	*power transmission belts*
Vicracoustic/ Vicratex	*wall coverings*

Dayton Hudson Corp.

777 Nicollet Mall
Minneapolis, MN 55402
(612) 370-6948

Chief Executive Officer: Kenneth A. Macke
1984 Annual Sales Volume: 8,000M
1984 Shares Outstanding: 97,000,000
Shareholders: 15,000
Exchange: NY
Symbol: DH

Corporate History: The company was formed in 1969 from a merger of Dayton's, a Minneapolis department store company, and Hudson's, a Detroit department store company. Today it is a diversified retailer which operates stores in 48 states. During the past decade it has expanded into low-margin and specialty stores. One of its chains, B. Dalton, operates bookstores in 48 states; it is the largest book seller in the nation. The company also owns Target, a discount chain, and Mervyn's, a popular-priced softgoods chain. In 1980 the company acquired the Ayr-Way discount chain which it merged into the Target chain. In fiscal 1984, department stores provided 19.3% of sales, Target 44.3%, speciality stores 9.7% and Mervyn's 26.7%.

Brandnames of Products and Services:

B. Dalton	*bookstores*
Dayton Hudson	*department stores*
Dayton's Department Stores	
Hudson's Department Stores	
Lechmere	*discount stores*
Mervyn's	*department stores*
Pickwick	*bookstores*
R.G. Branden's	*housewares stores*
Store Company	*department stores*
Target	*discount store*

Dean Foods Co.

3600 N. River Rd.
Franklin Park, Ill. 60131
(312) 625-6200

Chief Executive Officer: Kenneth Douglas
Exchange: OTC
Symbol: DEAN

Corporate History: The company was incorporated in 1968 as Delaware Dean Foods. The present title was adopted in 1963. It processes and distributes dairy and specialty food products. In the 1970s, when other food companies diversified, Dean concentrated on perfecting cost control to improve the profitability of its dairies.

Brandnames of Products and Services:

Bell	*dairy products*
Country Charm	*ice cream*
Creamland	*dairy products*
Dean's	*dairy products*
Dean's McCadam	*cheese products*
Fieldcrest	*dairy products*
Gandy Quality Check	*dairy products*
Heifetz	*pickles*
Hoffman House	*sauces*
Indian Trail	*cranberry food products*
Mrs. Weaver's	*food spreads*
Pesta	*pickles*
Peter Piper	*relish, mustard, pickles*
Price	*ice cream*
Quality	*ice cream*
Vita	*herring*

Decorator Industries Inc.

8675 NW 53rd St
Miami, Fla. 33166
(305) 591-9550

Chief Executive Officer: W. Bassett
Exchange: AM
Symbol: DII

Corporate History: The company, incorporated in 1953, makes both made-to-measure and ready-made draperies, bedspreads and other decorative products.

Brandnames of Products and Services:

Cortley	*draperies*
Decorama	*draperies*

Del Laboratories Inc.

565 Broad Hollow Road
Farmingdale, NY 11735
(516) 293-7070

Chief Executive Officer: Dan K. Wassong
1984 Annual Sales Volume: 87M
1984 Shares Outstanding: 1,079,979
Shareholders: 967
Exchange: AM
Symbol: DLI

Corporate History: Del Laboratories incorporated in 1961 as Maradel Products Inc. and adopted its present title in 1966. It is a manufacturer and distributor of cosmetics and proprietary drugs. In the cosmetics field, its principal products are nail care, color cosmetics, beauty implements, bleach and depilatories, and hair care products. In the drug field, products range from oral analgesics to acne treatment products and ear drop medications.

Brandnames of Products and Services:

BDB	*wart remover*
Boil Ease	*pain relief for boils*
Flame Glo	*cosmetics*
Hard As Nails	*nail care products*
La Cross	*manicure implements*
New Lengths	*nail care products*
Nutri-Tonic	*hair care products*
Orajel	*oral pain killer*
Rejuvia	*skin care products*
Sally Hansen	*nail care products and cosmetics*
Style	*opthalmic ointment*
Tanac	*cold sore remedy*

Dennison Manufacturing Co.

300 Howard street
Framingham, MA 01701
(617) 879-0511

Chief Executive Officer: Nelson S. Gifford
1984 Annual Sales Volume: 684M
1984 Shares Outstanding: 14,521,465
Shareholders: 10,500
Exchange: NY
Symbol: DSN

Corporate History: Dennison was established in Maine in 1844 by Andrew Dennison and moved to Boston where it was incorporated in 1878. Classified primarily as a manufacturer of paper products and related items, and of machinery, Dennison concentrates in these market segments: stationery and computer supplies, retails systems, packaging, fasteners, identification systems, and the manufacture or conversion of technical papers for business and industry.

Brandnames of Products and Services:

5 O'clock	*paper products*
Adhes-A-Ply	*adhesives*
Air Conditioned	*gummed paper*
Bar-Code	*labels*
Baste & Sew	*fabric adhesive stick*
Baste & Sew Gluestik	*fabric adhesive stick*
Boltiplast	*adhesives*
Bondfax	*copying paper*
Brunswick	*crepe paper, reenforcements*
Buccaneer*	*carbon paper, typing ribbons*
Buttoneer	*fasteners*
Cable-Post	*loose leaf binders*
Carter's & Design	*Carter ink company products*
CICO	*liquid paste (Carter's)*
Color Stik Kit	*colored pencils*
Copy Master	*labels*
Craft Originators	*plastic products*
Crown & Shield	*ink eradicator*
Data-Liter*	*markers*
DCS	*computer supplies*
Decofast*	*flexible cloth labels*
Deco-Rubs*	*artistic design transfers*
Dennison	*stationery products*
Dennison & Design	*wraps, crepe paper labels, tags, fasteners, etc.*
Diplomat*	*loose leaf notebook*
Director	*computer accessories*
Domes	*decorative emblems*
Doret	*stationery supplies*
Draws-A-Lot	*markers*
Dry Ply	*decals*
Dry Wipes	*markers*
Dunn	*paper products*
Eagle	*blank books, binders*
Easel-Y	*loose leaf binders*
Eastman	*stationery supplies*
Easy-To-Use	*paper products*
Econ-O-Fast	*plastic fasteners for tags*
Electric	*carbon paper*
Elephant & Design*	*memory system discs*
Extra-Riter	*ball point pens*
Eye Ease	*record keeping products*

Fast/Break*	*pressure sensitive label paper*
Fastonol	*pressure sensitive label paper*
Geha	*stationery*
Glocolor	*rub on glue (stick)*
Glue Stic*	*adhesive in stick form*
Golden Arrow	*paper product*
Guardian	*paper product*
Heat Seal & Sign	*stationery*
Hi-Liter*	*marking pens*
Ideal	*typewriter ribbons*
Ink Jet*	*printing apparatus*
Kangaroo	*padded mailing envelopes*
Kleencote*	*carbon paper*
Kleenpac	*typewriter ribbons*
Kybe & Logo	*computer system*
Kybe Kleen	*computer system*
Mark-A-Pen	*fiber point markers*
Mark Master*	*permanent ink & pens*
Marks-A-Lot*	*felt tip marking pens*
Marlboro	*crepe paper, reenforcements, labels*
Media Mates	*plastic hangers*
Meritag	*tags/tickets magnet coated*
Micropor	*stamp pads*
Midnight	*writing ink/carbon paper*
Minidax	*ministrip embossing tape*
Mini Label-Mate	*miniature tape embosser*
Networkers	*loose leaf binders*
Never Forgets	*computer peripheral equipment*
Non-Blocking	*sheet formed gummed paper*
Nu-Glue	*adhesive*
Office Buddies	*small pressure sens. labels*
Oxynek	*paper product*
Paper Aid	*stationery product*
Perma-Flat	*gummed paper*
Pernaceran	*stationery product*
Porelon	*stationery product*
Post-Lite	*protective mailing envelopes*
Pres.A.Ply*	*labels*
Presidax*	*printed bar-code labels*
Prime Cut	*pressure sensitive label with liner*
Put Ons*	*labels*
Quickie Letter	*correspondence forms*
Razzle-Dazzle	*decorative glitter*
Red Snapper	*stationery supplies*
Rite Ease	*analysis pad - national*
Ritoff	*stationery supplies*
Rollex	*stationery supplies*
Rollkleen	*stationery supplies*
Rotoflex	*stationery supplies*
Rotronic	*machinery*
Sign Master*	*watercolor ink pens*
Site Ease	*record keeping products*
Skil/Chek	*educational training kits*
SLT	*stationery supplies*
Special Occasion	*stationery supplies*
Spin-Print	*adhesive labels*
Statrol	*antistatic chair mats*
Stenso	*self-adhesive & transfer letters and numbers*
Stickless	*carbon paper*
Stix-A-Lot	*adhesive cement & dispenser*
Stripflex	*adhesive*
Style-Riter	*marking device*
Super Kleen Cote	*office supplies*
Tabulink	*office supplies*
Trans-Liter	*marking pencils*
Trim-Tip	*pen-type markers*
Vinylbond	*loose leaf binders*
Voracryl	*solvent for printing ink*
Wedge-Lok*	*fasteners*
Weircliff	*stationery product*
White Glove	*duplicating carbon paper*
Wordsworth	*magnetic diskettes*
X-Pert	*porous point pens*
X-Tra-Liter	*markers*

Denny's Inc.

16700 Valley View Ave.
La Mirada, CA 90637
(714) 739-8100

Chief Executive Officer:	Vern O. Curtis
1984 Annual Sales Volume:	1,216M
1984 Shares Outstanding:	15,523,869
Shareholders:	3,800
Exchange:	NY
Symbol:	DEN

Corporate History: Incorporated in 1959, Denny's Inc. operates restaurants, donut houses and quick service char-broiled chicken units. The company's 1,038 restaurants were operated primarily as "Denny's" in 43 states and Canada. Its 836 donut houses were known as Winchell's in 17 states. In 1983, the company purchased El Pollo Loco, a 19-unit chain in Southern California; the acquisition included the rights to expand the concept worldwide except in Mexico.

Brandnames of Products and Services:

Denny's	*restaurants*
El Pollo Loco	*char-broiled chicken*
Winchell's	*donut houses*

Dentsply International Inc.

570 W. College Ave.
York, Pa. 17404
(717) 845-7511

Chief Executive Officer: H.M. Thornton
Exchange: NY
Symbol: DSP
Corporate History: The company, incorporated in 1899, produces dental supplies and in recent years has expanded its operations into optical products.
Brandnames of Products and Services:

Duling Optical	*specialty stores*
Kindy Optical	*specialty stores*
Monfried Optical	*specialty stores*

De Rose Industries Inc.

4002 Meadows Dr.
Indianapolis, Ind. 46205
(317) 545-6145

Chief Executive Officer: R.A. De Rose
Exchange: AM
Symbol: DRI
Corporate History: The company, incorporated in 1964, makes mobile homes. Units are sold completely furnished and equipped to 220 dealers, mostly East of the Rocky Mountains.
Brandnames of Products and Services:

Amherst	*mobile homes*
Beverly Manor	*mobile homes*
Brentwood	*mobile homes*
Broadway	*mobile homes*
De Rose	*mobile homes*
Futura	*mobile homes*
Greenfield	*mobile homes*
Mayfair	*mobile homes*
Rembrandt	*mobile homes*
Rosebrook	*mobile homes*
Rosemont	*mobile homes*
Rosewood	*mobile homes*
Supreme	*mobile homes*
Victor	*mobile homes*
Yorkshire	*mobile homes*

DeSoto, Inc.

1700 So. Mt. Prospect Rd.
Des Plaines, IL 60018
(312) 391-9000

Chief Executive Officer: Richard R. Missar
1984 Annual Sales Volume: 407M
1984 Shares Outstanding: 4,764,830
Shareholders: 3,356
Exchange: NY
Symbol: DSO
Corporate History: The company was incorporated in 1927 as United Wall Paper Factories Inc., consolidating four wallpaper manufacturers. It makes chemical coatings (consumer paints and industrial coatings) and specialty products (detergents and other household cleaning products, surfactants, emulsifiers, speciality chemicals and fireplace furnishings). Approximately 64% of the company's 1984 net sales were to Sears, Roebuck and Co. The company supplies consumer paints, household detergents, household cleaning products and fireplace furnishings to Sears. In 1984 DeSoto acquired Petrochemicals Co. Inc.; Southland Paint Co. Inc.; Detergents, Inc.; Plex Chemical Corp.; and the agricultural chemicals business of Magna Corp.
Brandnames of Products and Services:

DeSoto	*fireplace equipment*
DeSoto	*laundry detergents*
"Easy Living"	*paints*
"Weatherbeater"	*paints*

Development Corp. of America

2514 Hollywood Blvd.
Hollywood, Fla. 33020
(305) 920-6600

Chief Executive Officer: Alvin Sherman
Exchange: AM
Symbol: DCA
Corporate History: The company incorporated in 1975. The parent company was incorporated in 1970 as DCA of Delaware Inc. Development Corp. makes ladies' sportswear. It also builds condominium apartments and single-family homes, which made up 65% of sales in 1979.
Brandnames of Products and Services:

Dottie Mann	*ladies' sportswear*
Fashion Tree	*ladies' sportswear*
Fashion Tree for Men	*apparel*

J.J. of Miami	*ladies' apparel*
Kentfield	*men's apparel*
Nicholas by Niki Lu	*men's apparel*
Niki-Lu	*ladies' apparel*
Pour Les Hommes	*men's apparel*
Sweet Briar	*men's apparel*

Diamond International Corp.

733 Third Ave.
New York, N.Y. 10017
(212) 697-1700

Chief Executive Officer: W.J. Koslo
Exchange: NY
Symbol: DN
Corporate History: The company, founded in 1881, incorporated in 1930 as Diamond Match Co. As the market for matches declined, Diamond branched out into a variety of wood products—tissues, paper, lumber and ice cream sticks. Diamond is the country's largest manufacturer of playing cards. It also operates gambling casinos in Nevada and Atlantic City. Its fastest growing business is its retail home supply centers, Diamond Building Supply Home Centers, which sell hardware, tools and lumber. There are over 116 stores in 17 states.
Brandnames of Products and Services:

Bee	*playing cards*
Bicycle	*playing cards*
Congress	*playing cards*
Diamond	*building materials and home supply centers*
Vanity Fair	*household paper products*

Dibrel Brothers, Inc.

512 Bridge St.
Danville, VA 24541
(804) 792-7511

Chief Executive Officer: Richard B. Bridgforth, Jr.
1984 Annual Sales Volume: 382M
1984 Shares Outstanding: 4,373,043
Shareholders: 1,092
Exchange: OTC
Symbol: DNIC
Corporate History: The company incorporated in 1904 as a leaf tobacco dealer engaged in the purchasing, redrying, packing, storing and sale of leaf tobacco. It also manufactures home ice cream freezers and decorative woodenware. In fiscal 1984 tobacco products made up more than 90% of sales.
Brandnames of Products and Services:

Cedar Works	*home ice cream freezers*

Di Giorgio Corp.

1 Maritime Plaza
San Francisco, Calif. 94111
(415) 765-0100

Chief Executive Officer: Peter F. Scott
1984 Annual Sales Volume: 1,036M
1984 Shares Outstanding: 5,939,000
Shareholders: 7,000
Exchange: NY
Symbol: DIG
Corporate History: The company incorporated in 1920 as Di Giorgio Fruit Corp. and adopted its present name in 1965. It has interests in food processing, wholesale distribution of groceries and drugs, and building materials and land development.
Brandnames of Products and Services:

Bilt Best	*windows*
Carando	*Italian specialty meats*
Endeavor Homes	*prefabricated houses*
Serve	*single-serving condiments*
Sunland	*juices and citrus beverages*
White Rose	*food products*

Dillon Companies Inc.

700 E. 30th St.
Hutchinson, Kan. 67501
(316) 663-6801

Chief Executive Officer: R.E. Dillon, Jr.
Exchange: NY
Symbol: DLK
Corporate History: The company incorporated in 1921 as J.S. Dillon & Sons Stores Co. and adopted its present title in 1968. Dillon operates more than 480 supermarkets, convenience food stores and junior department stores in the Midwest and West. It is one of the most profitable supermarket chains in the nation. In total it operates over 480 stores.
Brandnames of Products and Services:

City Market	*supermarkets*
D.G. Calhoun	*junior apparel stores*
Dillon Springfield	*supermarkets*
Dillon Stores	*supermarkets*

Fry's Food Stores	
Gerbs	*food stores*
Jackson's	*ice cream products*
King Scoopers	*supermarkets*
Kwik Shop	*convenience food stores*
Quik Stop	*convenience food stores*
Sav-Mor Store	*supermarkets*
Times Savor	*convenience food stores*

Discount Fabrics Inc.

4370 NE Halsey St.
Portland, Ore. 97213
(503) 288-9343

Chief Executive Officer: B.I. Galitzki
Exchange: AM
Symbol: DFI
Corporate History: The company, incorporated in 1965, sells fashion fabric and sewing notions through retail stores in the Western United States.
Brandnames of Products and Services:

Discount Fabrics	*fabric stores*
Fabric Gallery	*fabric stores*

Diversifoods Inc.

500 Park Blvd.
Itasca, IL 60143
(312) 773-9500

Chief Executive Officer: William E. Trotter, II
1984 Annual Sales Volume: 554M
1984 Shares Outstanding: 33,563,191
Shareholders: 3,500
Exchange: OTC
Symbol: DFDI
Corporate History: Diversifoods, the restaurant company, is a restaurant operator and franchisor of more than 1,400 restaurants in 48 states, Canada, Puerto Rico and the U.S. Virgin Islands. As of 1984 the company operated 378 Burger King restaurants (Diversifoods is the largest franchisee in the Burger King chain); 895 Godfather's pizza restaurants; 55 Chart House restaurants; 68 Luther's Bar-B-Q restaurants; and nine Moxie's Deluxe Grille and Bar restaurants.
Brandnames of Products and Services:

Burger King	*restaurants*
The Chart House	*restaurants*
Godfather's Pizza	*restaurants*
Luther's Bar-B-Q	*restaurants*
Moxie's Deluxe Grille and Bar	*restaurants*

Dixon Ticonderoga Co.

756 Beachland Blvd.
Vero Beach, FL 32964
(305) 231-3190

Chief Executive Officer: David K. Brewster
1984 Annual Sales Volume: 66M
1984 Shares Outstanding: 1,110,290
Shareholders: 621
Exchange: OTC
Symbol: DIXY
Corporate History: In 1983, Bryn Mawr Corp. acquired The Joseph Dixon Crucible Co. and the new entity was named the Dixon Ticonderoga Co. The company operates in five business segments: consumer, refractory, graphite and lubricant products, real estate, and transportation.
Brandnames of Products and Services:

Bryn Mawr Ocean Towers	*real estate*
Garden State Coachways	*bus line*
Prang	*art supplies*
P.V. Martin's	*restaurant*
Ticonderoga	*writing, and maching materials*

Dollar General Corp.

427 Beech St.
Scottsville, KY 42164
(502) 237-5444

Chief Executive Officer: C. Turner, Jr.
1984 Annual Sales Volume: 480.5M
1984 Shares Outstanding: 15,654,000
Shareholders: 3,500
Exchange: OTC
Symbol: DOLR
Corporate History: The company, incorporated in 1955, specializes in merchandising irregular and close-out goods at bargain prices through retail stores.
Brandnames of Products and Services:

Dollar General	*discount stores*

Dorsey Corp.

One Central Plaza
Chattanooga, TN 37402
(615) 267-2973

Chief Executive Officer: John T. Pollock
1984 Annual Sales Volume: 521M
1984 Shares Outstanding: 2,668,914
Shareholders: 2,043
Exchange: NY
Symbol: DSY
Corporate History: The Dorsey Corp. founded in 1959, is a manufacturer of plastic containers, cargo trailers and utility vehicles. In 1984 the company acquired Bickford's Family Fare, Inc. a chain of 28 restaurants located in New England. The company's other two operating subsidiaries are Sewell Plastics and Dorsey Trailers Inc.
Brandnames of Products and Services:

Bickford Family Fare	*restaurants*

The Dow Chemical Company

2030 Dow Center
Midland, MI 48640
(517) 636-1000

Chief Executive Officer: P.F. Oreffice
1984 Annual Sales Volume: 11,418M
1984 Shares Outstanding: 194,000,000
Shareholders: 133,700
Exchange: NY
Symbol: DOW
Corporate History: The Dow Chemical Company, founded in 1897 and incorporated in 1947, makes chemicals, metals, plastics, packaging materials, pharmaceuticals, and consumer products. Slightly more than fifty percent of its sales come from supplying chemicals to other industrial and chemical companies. In 1960 the company began a dramatic program of expansion into foreign markets. In recent years Dow has developed a program to make it energy independent. It now produces three-quarters of its own electricity and steam, and has rapidly expanded its role in specialty products for industry and consumers.
Brandnames of Products and Services:

Dow	*bathroom cleaner, oven cleaner*
Handi-Wrap II	*brand plastic film*
Saran Wrap	*brand plastic film*
Tough Act	*brand heavy duty bathroom cleaner*
Ziploc	*plastic bags*
Ziploc Microfreez	*brand microwave cooking bags*

Dow Jones & Company Inc.

22 Cortlandt St.
New York, N.Y. 10007
(212) 285-5000

Chief Executive Officer: Warren H. Phillips
1984 Annual Sales Volume: 966M
1984 Shares Outstanding: 64,323,662
Shareholders: 16,000
Exchange: NY
Symbol: DJ
Corporate History: Dow Jones, founded in 1882 and last incorporated in 1949, is one of the nation's leading publishing firms, specializing in business and financial news reporting. Its *Wall Street Journal,* established in 1889, is the nation's largest-selling daily newspaper. The company has a computerized news retrieval service for homes and offices which gives it a solid footing in the emerging data base industry. In recent years technology has helped to lower the information seller's cost while broadening the demand for its services.
Brandnames of Products and Services:

American Demographics	*magazine, Ithaca, NY*
Asian Wall St. Journal	*newpaper*
The Asian Wall Street Journal Weekly	*newspaper*
Barron's	*financial weekly*
Cape Cod Standard Times newspaper, Hyannis, Mass.	
Dow Jones	*news services*
Dow Jones Books	*publishing*
Dow Jones News/ Retrieval	*database publishing*
Dow Jones Software Publishing	*software*
Dow Phone	*telephone-based info. service*
Far Eastern Economic Review	*periodical*

Free Press	*newspaper, Mankato, Minn.*
Globe	*newspaper, Joplin, Mo.*
Independent	*newspaper, Ashland, Ky.*
Item	*newspaper, Sunbury, Pa.*
Mail Tribune	*newspaper, Medford, Ore.*
National Business & Employment Weekly	*periodical*
News	*newspaper, Newburyport, Mass.*
News-Times	*newspaper, Danbury, Conn.*
People's Press	*newspaper, Owatonna, Minn.*
Pocono Record	*newspaper, Stroudsbury, Pa.*
Press-Republican	*newspaper, Plattsburgh, N.Y.*
Record Eagle	*newspaper, Traverse City, Mich.*
Santa Cruz Sentinel	*newspaper, Santa Cruz, CA*
Sharon Herald	*newspaper, Sharon, Pa.*
South China Morning Post	*newspaper, Hong Kong*
Standard-Times	*newspaper, New Bedford, Mass.*
Star	*newspaper, Oneonta, N.Y.*
Sun City News-Sun	*newpaper, Sun City, AZ*
Times-Herald Record	*newspaper, Middletown, N.Y.*
Times	*newspaper, Beverly, Mass.*
Union-Gazette	*newspaper, Port Jervis, N.Y.*
The Wall Street Journal/Europe	*newspaper, Brussels, Belgium*
Wall Street Journal	*newspaper, New York, N.Y.*

Dr. Pepper

5523 E. Mockingbird Lane
Box 225086
Dallas, Texas 75265
(214) 824-0331

Chief Executive Officer: W.W. Clements
Exchange: NY
Symbol: DOC
Corporate History: Incorporated in 1923, Dr. Pepper makes soft drink syrup and concentrate for bottled and canned beverages. It is the fourth-largest company in the soft drink industry, with almost 6% of the nation's soft drink market.

Brandnames of Products and Services:

Dr. Pepper	*beverages*
Sugar-Free Dr. Pepper	*beverages*

Duckwall-Alco Stores, Inc.

401 Cottage
Abilene, KS 67410
(913) 263-3350

Chief Executive Officer: Robert R. Soelter
1984 Annual Sales Volume: 317M
1984 Shares Outstanding: 4,979,821
Shareholders: 2,091
Exchange: OTC
Symbol: DUCK
Corporate History: Alco-Duckwall Stores Inc., which originated in 1965, operates 126 discount stores and 32 variety stores in 14 states: Arkansas, Colorado, Iowa, Kansas, Louisiana, Minnesota, Mississippi, Missouri, Nebraska, New Mexico, South Dakota, Tennessee, Texas, and Wyoming. Many stores are located in smaller communities that range from 5,000 to 20,000 in population.

Brandnames of Products and Services:

Alco	*discount stores*
Duckwall	*variety stores*

Dun & Bradstreet Corp.

299 Park Ave.
New York, N.Y. 10017
(212) 593-6800

Chief Executive Officer: Charles W. Moritz
1984 Annual Sales Volume: 2,397M
1984 Shares Outstanding: 76,065,000
Shareholders: 12,615
Exchange: NY
Symbol: DNB
Corporate History: New York City silk merchant Louis Tappan established The Mercantile Agency in 1841 in response to an economic slump that was affecting the conduct of business in the port city of New York. The Mercantile Agency gathered information regarding the financial worth of individuals doing business there. The Mercantile Agency eventually was absorbed by Robert G. Dun and the firm became known as the R.G. Dun Corportion in 1859. Dun utilized the first typewriters purchased for commercial use, and also sent his reports across the nation via the Pony Express prior to yielding

to the superior U.S. Postal Service. In 1933, R.G. Dun merged with John M. Bradstreet of Cincinnati, Ohio, to form Dun & Bradstreet. In 1984, the Dun & Bradstreet Corporation is the world's leading provider and disseminator of business information and related services, with worldwide operating revenues of nearly $2.4 billion in 1984. D&B serves its customers with services in three general areas: business information services, publishing and marketing services.

Brandnames of Products and Services:

Donnelley Directories	*publishing*
Dun & Bradstreet	*credit services*
Moody's	*investor services*
Official Airline Guides	*guides*

Dunkin' Donuts Inc.

P.O. Box 317
Randolph, MA 02368
(617) 961-4000

Chief Executive Officer:	R.M. Rosenberg
1984 Annual Sales Volume:	90M
1984 Shares Outstanding:	4,761,418
Shareholders:	2,704
Exchange:	OTC
Symbol:	DUNK

Corporate History: Incorporated in 1960, Dunkin' Donuts operates and franchises the largest chain of coffee and donut shops in the world, with operations in 35 states, Puerto Rico, Canada and 12 foreign countries.

Brandnames of Products and Services:

Dunkin' Donuts	*fast-food shops and donuts*

Dynamics Corp. of America

475 Steamboat Rd.
Greenwich, CT 06830
(203) 869-3211

Chief Executive Officer:	Andrew Lozyniak
1984 Annual Sales Volume:	140M
1984 Shares Outstanding:	4,268,127
Shareholders:	8,307
Exchange:	NY
Symbol:	DYA

Corporate History: The company incorporated in 1924 as Claude Neon Light Inc. In 1946 its name was changed to Claude Neon Inc. and in 1955 to its present title. It makes electrical appliances, and electronic devices, metal products and equipment, and power and controlled environmental systems.

Brandnames of Products and Services:

Acme Juicerator	*Kitchen Appliances*
Waring	*kitchen appliances*

Dynascan Corp.

6460 W. Cortland Ave.
Chicago, IL 60635
(312) 889-8870

Chief Executive Officer:	C. Korn
1984 Annual Sales Volume:	125M
1984 Shares Outstanding:	4,645,188
Exchange:	OTC
Symbol:	DYNA

Corporate History: Incorporated in 1961, Dynascan imports CB radios, corded and cordless telephones, answering machines, and automatic telephone dialers. Dynascan also imports and manufactures a line of electronic testing equipment and industrial radio remote control systems for material handling.

Brandnames of Products and Services:

B&K-Precision	*electronic testing equipment*
Cobra	*CB, telephones, answering machines & dialers*
Telemotive	*radio remote-control systems*

Early California Industries, Inc.

10960 Wilshire Blvd.
Los Angeles, CA 90024
(213) 879-1480

Chief Executive Officer:	Gerald D. Murphy
1984 Annual Sales Volume:	240M
1984 Shares Outstanding:	2,643,498
Shareholders:	1,621
Exchange:	OTC
Symbol:	ERLY

Corporate History: Early California Industries incorporated in 1964 upon the merger of B.E. Glick & Sons, the Pacific Olive Co. and Sunland Olive Co. The company is engaged primarily in the food processing business, with rice, olives, and bulk wine its principal food product lines. the company is also involved in the production and sale of fire retardants, the distribution of laboratory chemicals and international agribusiness consulting.

Brandnames of Products and Services:

Adolphus	*rice*
Chateau-Vallee	*Wine*
Comet Rice	*rice*
Early California Favorites	*olives and specialty food products*
Girard's	*dressings and condiments*
Riviana	*olives and peppers*
Wonder	*rice*

Easco Corp.

201 N. Charles St.
Baltimore, MD 21201
(301) 837-9550

Chief Executive Officer: R.P. Sullivan
1984 Annual Sales Volume: 571M
1984 Shares Outstanding: 7,137,166
Shareholders: 4,779
Exchange: NY
Symbol: ES

Corporate History: The company was incorporated in 1919 as Eastern Rolling Mill Co. Its name was changed to Eastern Stainless Steel Corp. in 1944, and to its present title in 1969. It makes hand tools, aluminum products, and industrial grating.

Brandnames of Products and Services:

Easco	*hand tools*

Eastern Air Lines Inc.

Miami International Airport
Miami, FL 33148
(305) 873-2211

Chief Executive Officer: Frank Borman
1984 Annual Sales Volume: 4,364M
1984 Shares Outstanding: 47,730,137
Shareholders: 80,892
Exchange: NY
Symbol: EAL

Corporate History: Eastern Air Lines was founded in the late 1920s. During the 1930s the company was headed by Eddie Rickenbacker, who transformed it from a money loser to a winner. Rickenbacker's emphasis on economy created dissatisfied customers who switched to other airlines when the Civil Aeronautics Board permitted competition on Eastern routes in the 1950s. Profits declined in the 1960s and 1970s. But under the direction of Frank Borman, the former astronaut, the company has turned around. Although Eastern's route system is mainly north-south, it also serves major cities in the West and has expanded its east-west route system. Among the major domestic cities served by Eastern are Albany, Albuquerque, Atlanta, Austin, Baltimore, Birmingham, Boston, Buffalo, Charlotte, Chicago, Cleveland, Columbus, Dallas/Ft. Worth, Denver, Detroit, El Paso, Ft. Lauderdale, Hartford-Springfield, Houston, Indianpolis, Jacksonville, Kansas City, Las Vegas, Los Angeles, Louisville, Miami, Milwaukee, Minneapolis-St. Paul, Nashville, Newark, New Orleans, New York, Omaha, Oklahoma City, Orlando, Philadelphia, Phoenix, Pittsburgh, Portland (Oregon), Providence, San Antonio, San Francisco, San Juan, Salt Lake City, St. Louis, Seattle, Tampa, Tucson and Washington, D.C. In addition, Eastern provides air service between points in the United States and Argentina, the Bahamas, Bermuda, Bolivia, Canada, the Caribbean, Chile, Colombia, Costa Rica, Ecuador, Mexico, Panama, Paraguay, Peru (currently suspended pending negotiations between the U.S. government and Peru), Puerto Rico and the Virgin Islands. Eastern's regularly scheduled passenger services include no-reservation, assured-space service known as the Air-Shuttle, which currently operates between Boston and New York and Washington, D.C. The company also transports mail and air freight over portions of its routes.

Brandnames of Products and Services:

Cerromar Beach Hotel	*Puerto Rico*
Dorado Beach Hotel	*Puerto Rico*
Eastern Airlines	

Eastman Kodak Co.

343 State St.
Rochester, N.Y. 14650
(716) 724-4000

Chief Executive Officer: Colby H. Chandler
1984 Annual Sales Volume: 10,600M
1984 Shares Outstanding: 155,600,000
Shareholders: 190,000
Exchange: NY
Symbol: EK

Corporate History: Eastman Kodak was founded in 1880 and incorporated in 1901. It introduced film on rolls in 1884 and a light, portable camera in 1888. Today it is the world's largest producer of photographic equipment and supplies as well as an important manufacturer of synthetic fibers, plastics, and chemicals.

Kodak has traditionally catered to the amateur photography market but has expanded in recent years into a number of new markets such as copiers, blood analyzers, and electronic products. Photography and photo-related equipment accounted for 80% of its sales in 1979 and chemicals 20%. Almost 40% of Kodak's sales are outside the United States.

Brandnames of Products and Services:

Eastman	*chemicals, plastics, fibers*
Kodak	*photographic and information management products*

Jack Eckerd Corp.

8333 Bryan Dairy Road
PO Box 4689
Clearwater, FL 33518
(813) 397-7461

Chief Executive Officer:	Stewart Turley
1984 Annual Sales Volume:	2,622M
1984 Shares Outstanding:	37,687,000
Shareholders:	21,000
Exchange:	NY
Symbol:	ECK

Corporate History: Eckerd incorporated in 1961 as Eckerd Drugs of Florida, and adopted its present title in 1969. It operates 1,510 stores in 15 states: 60 retail department stores in Florida; and 158 optical centers in the South, as well as 207 video home entertainment states in 29 states.

Brandnames of Products and Services:

Eckerd	*optical stores*
Eckerd	*drugstores*
J. Byrons	*junior department stores*
Video Concepts	*video stores*

Economics Laboratory Inc.

Osborn Building
St. Paul, MN 55102
(612) 224-4678

Chief Executive Officer:	F.T. Lanners, Jr.
1984 Annual Sales Volume:	704M
1984 Shares Outstanding:	13,570,000
Shareholders:	5,100,000
Exchange:	OTC
Symbol:	ECON

Corporate History: The company, incorporated in 1924, develops, makes, and sells cleaning products and equipment.

Brandnames of Products and Services:

Clean & Smooth	*liquid hand soap*
Dip-it	*stain remover*
Electrasol	*dishwasher detergent*
Erase	*air freshener*
Finish	*Dishwasher detergent*
Free n' Soft	*antistatic clothes softener*
Glass Magic	*spot remover for dishwasher*
Jet-Dry	*rinse additive for dishwasher*
Lime-A-Way	*lime and rust deposit remover*
Scrub Free	*spray bathroom and kitchen cleaners*
Soilax	*wall and floor washing product*

Edison Brothers Stores Inc.

501 N. Broadway (P.O. Box 14020)
St. Louis, MO 63178
(314) 331-6000

Chief Executive Officer:	B.A. Edison
1984 Annual Sales Volume:	1,055M
1984 Shares Outstanding:	10,305,000
Shareholders:	6,000
Exchange:	NY
Symbol:	EBS

Corporate History: The company was founded in 1922 and incorporated in 1929. It primarily sells women's shoes and handbags through approximately 1,234 stores. In 1969, it moved into the do-it-yourself home improvement center market with the acquisition of Handyman. It entered the apparel field in 1970 with the acquisition of the Size 5-7-9 Shops; Jeans West was acquired in 1971 and Fashion Conspiracy in 1977. The Gussini shoe stores were acquired in 1984. The company operates a total of approximately 2,355 retail stores. In 1984, footwear accounted for 49% of sales, home improvement centers 25%, and apparel 26%.

Brandnames of Products and Services:

5-7-9 & Des	*apparel*
Albert Durelle	*shoes*
All-Abouts	*shoes*
Ando Giotto	*apparel*
Anne Welles	*shoes*
Backsiders	*apparel*

Banzai	*apparel*
California Sun-Kicks	*shoes*
Captivators	*shoes*
Carnaby Street	*apparel*
Casualets	*shoes*
Chandlers	*shoes*
Clicks	*shoes*
Coles	*shoes*
Computa-Fit	*hosiery*
Cosi L'Uomo	*apparel*
Cover Story	*apparel*
D'Amigo	*handbags & wallets*
Delinda	*shoes*
Derrieres	*apparel*
Dr. Wild & Design	*shoe polish*
EBS	*handbags & shoes*
Fashion Conspiracy	*apparel*
FC Ltd.	*apparel*
FC Trotter	*apparel*
Final Finish	*dry cleaner treatment*
Fred West	*shoes*
French Room	*shoes*
Fun Kicks	*slippers & shoes*
Gentlemen's Lady	*apparel*
Gussini	*shoes*
Handyman	*hardware*
Handy Pro	*hardware*
Happy Timers	*children's shoes*
Heartbreak	*apparel*
Ice Castles	*apparel*
Inspiration	*apparel*
Intaglio	*shoes*
Intimates	*slippers*
Jacques Berne'	*apparel*
Jay Dubbs	*apparel*
Jeans West & Des.	*apparel*
Jewel Box	*shoes*
Joan Bari	*jewelry, handbags*
John Malloy	*shoes*
Junior Parade	*children's shoes*
JW & Des.	*apparel*
JW & JW Jeans West	*apparel*
Knit Knack	*apparel*
L'Avion & Biplane Des.	*apparel*
L'Avion & Design	*apparel*
Leather Lotion	*cleaner & conditioner for leather/vinyl*
Leather Raincoat	*water repellent for vinyl/leather*
Left Bankers	*shoes*
The Leg Works	*hosiery*
Linnea Franco	*apparel*
L'Mer	*apparel*
Mar'v'lus	*hosiery*
Melo-Tred	*shoes*
Miss Qualicraft	*shoes*
Notorious	*apparel*
Oak Tree	*clothing*
One To Nine	*apparel*
Ot. Sport Plus Designs	*apparel*
Parallel Turn	*apparel*
Par Avion	*apparel*
Petite - P.S. Street	*apparel*
Petite Street	*apparel*
Playgoers	*shoes*
Predictions	*shoes*
Presentations	*shoes*
Proms & Promises	*apparel*
Qualicraft	*shoes*
Qualicraft Juniors	*shoes*
Rain Coat	*water repellent treatment*
Rear Gear	*apparel*
Ridge Runners	*shoes*
Romorini	*shoes*
Sheeld	*shoe heels protective cover*
Shoe World	*shoes*
Small Stuff	*apparel*
Snapdragon	*apparel*
Sod Hoppers	*shoes*
Speed Shine	*polishing goods*
Stella Mae	*apparel*
Suede Stick	*shoes*
Sweets	*shoes*
Sweet Steps	*shoes*
Thank Heaven	*apparel*
Topicals	*shoes*
Top It Off	*apparel*
Town & Country	*shoes*
True To You	*apparel*
Vicky Ann	*apparel*
Vino De Casa	*apparel*
White Bright	*cleaner for leather/vinyl*
The Wild Pair	*shoes*

Elder-Beerman Stores Corp.

3155 Elbee Road
Dayton, OH 45439
(513) 296-2700

Chief Executive Officer: Max Gutmann
1984 Annual Sales Volume: 287M
1984 Shares Outstanding: 3,155,016
Shareholders: 1,555
Exchange: OTC
Symbol: ELDR

Corporate History: The Elder-Beerman Stores Corp. is a corporation resulting from the merger in 1962 of the Elder & Johnston Co., incorporated in 1905, and Beerman Stores, organized in 1945. The principal business of the company is retail sales and the distribution of consumer-oriented goods. In 1984 the company operated 21 Elder-Beerman department stores in Ohio and Indiana, 103 El-Bee shoe store outlets in ten midwestern and southern states, 80 Margo's/Regan's stores in five southern states and 26 Spare Change stores in five states.

Brandnames of Products and Services:

El-Bee	*discount shoe stores*
Elder-Beerman	*department stores*
Margo's/Regan's	*women's apparel and accessories*
Spare Change	*junior sportswear stores*

Electro Audio Dynamics Inc.

98 Cutter Mill Road
Great Neck, NY 11021
(516) 466-5100

Chief Executive Officer: Martin Bader
1984 Annual Sales Volume: 36M
1984 Shares Outstanding: 2,746,305
Shareholders: 2,240
Exchange: AM
Symbol: EAD

Corporate History: The company was founded in 1942 and reincorporated in 1954 as Airflow Products Inc. In 1959 the name changed to Eastern Air Devices. The present title was adopted in 1974. Electro Audio Dynamics makes high-fidelity products and antennas for the consumer markets. A subsidiary, Technodyne Inc., manufactures high density printed circuit boards, circuit connecting devices, and medical electronic equipment.

Brandnames of Products and Services:

Infinity	*high-fidelity speakers and systems*
KLH	*high-fidelity speakers and systems*
Peerless	*high-fidelity speakers and headphones*
Rembrandt	*TV and FM antennas*

Eli Lilly & Co.

Lilly Corporate Center
Indianapolis, IN 46285
(317) 261-2000

Chief Executive Officer: R.D. Wood
1984 Annual Sales Volume: 3,109M
1984 Shares Outstanding: 72,855,000
Shareholders: 29,000
Exchange: NY
Symbol: LLY

Corporate History: Eli Lilly, one of the largest drug companies in the United States, was founded in 1876. It became prominent in 1923 when it first produced insulin commercially. During the next four decades, it developed more than 1,000 drugs, including Darvon, DES, Seconal and methadone. It was important in producing the Salk polio vaccine, introduced in 1954. Lilly is principally an ethical drug manufacturer. Its massive, and effective, advertising campaigns are directed solely toward the medical profession. Yet it also produces more than $350 million worth of agricultural chemicals a year.

Brandnames of Products and Services:

Cabriole	*fragrance*
Chloe	*fragrance and products*
Dista	*pharmaceutical*
Elanco	*agricultural products*
Elizabeth Arden	*cosmetics*
Lagerfeld	*perfumes*
Lilly	*pharmaceutical products*

Elsinore Corp.

300 S. Fourth Street, Suite ▪501
Las Vegas, NV 89101
(702) 382-2385

Chief Executive Officer: Robert R. Maxey
1984 Annual Sales Volume: 200M
1984 Shares Outstanding: 9,777,830

Shareholders: 7,155
Exchange: AM
Symbol: ELS
Corporate History: The company incorporated in 1972 as a wholly owned subsidiary of Hyatt Corp. It owns two hotel-casinos in Nevada, and, 91.5% of a casino hotel in Atlantic City, N.J.
Brandnames of Products and Services:

Atlantis Casino Hotel	*Atlantic City, New Jersey*
Four Queens Hotel & Casino	*Las Vegas, Nev.*
Hyatt Lake Tahoe Hotel & Casino	*Nev.*

Emhart Corp.

426 Colt Highway
Farmington, Conn. 06032
(203) 678-3000

Chief Executive Officer: T.M. Ford
1984 Annual Sales Volume: 1,795M
1984 Shares Outstanding: 27,581,835
Shareholders: 20,976
Exchange: NY
Symbol: EMH
Corporate History: Emhart, incorporated in 1902, manufactures builders' machinery, hardware, fasteners, industrial components and store equipment and security systems. It is the nation's largest manufacturer of machinery for the production of footwear. Foreign operations account for more than half of its profits; the company did business in more than 130 countries.
Brandnames of Products and Services:

Bostik	*glue products and adhesives*
Emhart	*hardware*
Kwikset	*door locks*
Notifier	*burglar and smoke alarms*
Pop Rivet	*molly bolts*
Sesamee	*padlocks*

Entertainment Publications Inc.

1400 N. Woodward Ave.
Birmingham, MI 48011
(313) 642-8300

Chief Executive Officer: Hughes L. Potiker
1984 Annual Sales Volume: 26M
1984 Shares Outstanding: 3,960,000
Shareholders: 529
Exchange: OTC
Symbol: EPUB
Corporate History: Entertainment Publications, Inc., founded in 1962, publishes and markets discount coupon books. The coupon books contain discount offers for restaurants, lodging, theatre, sports events, concerts, shows, and in some areas, retail merchandise and services.
Brandnames of Products and Services:

Condo Rentalbank	*reservation rental service*
Entertainment	*coupon books*
Entertainment Travel Services, Inc.	*travel agency*
Entertel	*telephone marketing firm*
Saving Spree	*coupon books*
Travel America at Half-Price	*coupon books*

ERO Industries Inc.

5940 W. Touhy Ave.
Chicago, IL 60648
(312) 647-0700

Chief Executive Officer: Martin N. Sandler
1984 Annual Sales Volume: 30M
1984 Shares Outstanding: 1,400,000
Shareholders: 1,200
Exchange: AM
Symbol: ERO
Corporate History: Chicago-based Ero Industries, last incorporated in 1975, manufactures and distributes leisure products, including slumber and sleeping bags, other slumber products and personal flotation devices and water skis from the Cypress Gardens Ski Division. In addition, the company imports water sports products, masks, fins, and goggles. The newly acquired Surprise! Division imports and markets products for infants and children, including bags, totes, headwear and novelty gift products.
Brandnames of Products and Services:

Cypress Gardens	*water skis & life jackets*
My Buddy	*swim-training device*
Nemrod	*swim & dive equipment*
Slumber Tents	*outdoor play accessories*
Trailmate	*sleeping bags & camping equipment*

Esmark Inc.

55 E. Monroe St.
Chicago, Ill. 60603
(312) 431-3600

Chief Executive Officer: D.P. Kelly
Exchange: NY
Symbol: ESM
Corporate History: Esmark was originally formed in 1885 as Swift Brothers, a meat packer. In 1969 it adopted its present names. Today it is a holding company operating in five areas: food, chemical and industrial products, personal products, high fidelity materials and automotive products. In 1975 it acquired International Playtex, the largest maker of women's undergarments in the nation; in 1980 it acquired Danskin, which holds well over half the market for women's dance costumes and has recently diversified into swimwear and sportswear. Esmark attempted to sell off the fresh meat portion of Swift's in 1979 while keeping the subsidiary's dry grocieries.
Brandnames of Products and Services:

Allsweet	*margarine*
Brown 'n Serve	*precooked sausages*
Butterball	*turkeys*
Cremol Plus	*shortening*
Danskin	*ladies' swimwear and dancewear*
Felicity	*glycerine soap*
Givenchy	*intimate apparel*
Harvest King	*lawn care*
Jensen	*audio and high-fidelity equipment*
Joyner's	*hams*
Mr. Host	*hams*
Peter Pan	*peanut butter*
Playtex	*personal hygiene products, garments, household products*
Playtops	*sport bras*
Proten	*food products*
Round-the-Clock	*hosiery*
Sizzlean	*food products*
Soup Starter	*food products*
STP	*automotive products*
Strong Heart	*dog food*
Sugar Plum	*hams*
Tend'r Lean	*food products*
Trophy	*margarine*
Vigoro	*garden care products*

Evans Inc.

36 South State St.
Chicago, IL 60603
(312) 855-2000

Chief Executive Officer: David B. Meltzer
1984 Annual Sales Volume: 136M
1984 Shares Outstanding: 524,750
Shareholders: 350
Exchange: OTC
Symbol: EVAN
Corporate History: Founded in 1930, Evans Inc. was incorporated under Delaware law in 1963. Evans is a retailer of fur apparel, cloth coats and suits, dresses, sportswear and related items in 18 stores in Chicago, Washington, D.C., Dallas-Fort Worth, Las Vegas, Oklahoma City and New Orleans areas. It operates leased departments in 120 locations in 18 major department store chains in metropolitan centers throughout the United States. In 1984, the company acquired assets from The House of Black Diamond, Inc., including the trademark Black Diamond Mink.
Brandnames of Products and Services:

Black Diamond Mink	*furs*
The Evans Collection	*furs*

Evans Products Co.

1121 SW Salmon St.
Portland, Ore. 97208
(503) 222-5592

Chief Executive Officer: M.A. Orloff
Exchange: NY
Symbol: EVY
Corporate History: The company, incorporated in 1923, makes and sells building materials, custom homes and transportation equipment, and operates building materials stores.
Brandnames of Products and Services:

Alamo Enterprises	*home improvement stores-retail*
Capp's	*custom homes*
Comfort Zone	*interior paint*
Creative	*cabinets*
Grossman's	*home improvement stores-retail*
Hubbard	*home improvement stores*

Johnson & Lindsley	*retail home improvement*
Moore's	*home improvement stores*
"Paintable/ Stainable"	*moldings*
Ridge's	*custom homes*
Riviera	*cabinets*

Executive Industries

550 E. La Palma Ave.
Anaheim, Calif. 92806
(714) 524-8640

Chief Executive Officer: T.E. Frank
Exchange: AM
Symbol: EII
Corporate History: The company, incorporated in 1969, makes mobile homes at its plant facilities in California.
Brandnames of Products and Services:

The Executive	*motor homes*
La Palma	*motor homes*
Prestige	*motor homes*
Pronto	*motor homes*
Sandpiper	*motor homes*

Exxon Corp.

1251 Ave. of the Americas
New York, NY 10020-1198
(212) 333-6900

Chief Executive Officer: C.C. Garvin, Jr.
1984 Annual Sales Volume: 90,854M
1984 Shares Outstanding: 816,169,000
Shareholders: 839,000
Exchange: NY
Symbol: XON
Corporate History: Standard Oil was founded in 1870 by John D. Rockefeller. Under his direction it became a giant, controlling 95% of the nation's refining in 1880. Having gained control of the domestic market, Rockefeller moved quickly into the foreign market. By 1885 almost three-fourths of the company's sales were being made outside the United States. In 1911 the Supreme Court declared the company in violation of antitrust laws and ordered it broken up. It was divided into 34 separate companies. Standard Oil of New Jersey was one of them; it adopted the title Exxon in 1972. During the first half of the century the company expanded its drilling activities into South America and the Middle East and in recent years into Alaska and the North Sea. Today it controls a vast amount of oil through its own reserves and through agreements with various nations and governments. Exxon ranks number one in natural gas production and gasoline sales. It is the largest company in the world, with sales larger than the GNP's of many nations. One writer has estimated that it sells $10 million in products each hour.
Brandnames of Products and Services:

Exxon	*gasoline and automotive products*
Zilog	*microcomputers*

Faberge Inc.

1345 Avenue of the Americas
New York, N.Y. 10019
(212) 581-3500

Chief Executive Officer: G. Barrie
Exchange: NY
Symbol: FBG
Corporate History: Faberge was incorporated in 1939 as Raymond Laboratories Inc. Its name was changed to Rayette Inc. in 1951; to Rayette Faberge in 1965; and to the present name in 1969. The company ranks seventh in the United States in the manufacture and distribution of frangrances, toiletries and cosmetics. In addition, the company produces television films.
Brandnames of Products and Services:

Aphrodisia	*fragrance*
Aquanet	*hairsprays*
Babe	*fragrance*
Brut Productions	*films, television films*
Brut 33	*toiletries*
Caryl Richards	*hair care*
Cavale	*fragrance*
Ceramic Glaze	*nail product*
Faberge	*toiletries*
Farrah-Fawcett	*hair care products*
Just Wonderful	*hairspray*
Macho	*men's fragrance*
Rayette	*hair care products*
Tigress	*fragrance*
Tip Top	*hair care accessories*
Woodhue	*fragrance*
Zizanie	*men's fragrance*

Fabri-Centers of America Inc.

23550 Commerce Park Rd.
Beachwood, OH 44122
(216) 464-2500

Chief Executive Officer: M. Rosskamm
1984 Annual Sales Volume: 209M
1984 Shares Outstanding: 5,050,111
Shareholders: 1,463
Exchange: NY
Symbol: FCA
Corporate History: The company incorporated in 1951 as Cleveland Fabric Shops Inc. and adopted its present title in 1968. It operates approximately 628 retail outlets in 34 states, principally in the East.
Brandnames of Products and Services:

Cargo Express	*tableware division*
House of Fine Fabrics	*fabric stores*
Jo Ann Fabrics	*fabric stores*
Showcase of Fine Fabrics	*boutique-style fabric stores*

Fair Lanes Inc.

1112 North Rolling Rd.
Baltimore, MD 21228
(301) 788-6300

Chief Executive Officer: Walter J. Hall
1984 Annual Sales Volume: 84M
1984 Shares Outstanding: 13,028,441
Shareholders: 2,100
Exchange: OTC
Symbol: FAIR
Corporate History: Fair Lanes, Inc., a Maryland corporation, was incorporated in 1948 and is the successor to a business that commenced in 1923. Fair Lanes is the largest independent operator of bowling centers in the United States. It currently operates 105 centers with 3,936 lanes in 18 states and Puerto Rico. The company also owns The English Company, which operates 15 restaurants in Maryland and Delaware, and has a 47% interest in BTR Realty, Inc., a publicly held real estate development company.
Brandnames of Products and Services:

Chick 'N Steak Houses	*restaurants*
English	*restaurants*
Fair Lanes Bowling Centers	

Farah Manufacturing Co.

8889 Gateway West
El Paso, TX 79925
(915) 593-4444

Chief Executive Officer: William F. Farah
1984 Annual Sales Volume: 251M
1984 Shares Outstanding: 5,814,198
Shareholders: 4,415
Exchange: NY
Symbol: FRA
Corporate History: Incorporated in 1947, Farah manufactures apparel for men, women and boys. The business was begun in 1920. In the 1960s Farah became one of the fastest-growing wearing apparel makers in the nation when it developed inexpensive, durable, permanently pressed slacks, but declined during the 1970s. It revived in the latter part of the decade with the addition of a new line of women's wear. During 1984, the company purchased Generra Sportswear Co. and certain of its affiliates.
Brandnames of Products and Services:

E. Joven	*young men's apparel*
Farah	*men's and women's sportswear*
Ferrante	*young men's apparel*
Generra	*apparel*
Jason Brooks	*boys' apparel*
John Henry	*men's apparel*
Kid Stuff	*boy's apparel*
N.P.W.	*young men's apparel*
Savane	*men's apparel*
Taos	*men's apparel*
Ultra-Stretch	*men's jeans*
W.F.F.	*designer men's apparel*

Farm House Foods Corp.

773 N. Van Buren
Milwaukee, Wisc. 53202
(414) 271-5050

Chief Executive Officer: .D.E. Runge
Exchange: OTC
Symbol: FHFC
Corporate History: Farm House incorporated in 1966 as Bankers Credit Cards Inc. and adopted its present title in 1971. It engages in wholesale distribution of food and operates retail drug stores primarily in the Midwest. During 1978-80 Farm House acquired over 50% interest in Scot Lad Foods, a wholesale distributor of foods to supermarkets, primarily in the Midwest. In fiscal

1980 wholesale food accounted for 90.3% of sales and drugs 9.7%.

Brandnames of Products and Services:

White Drug	*drugstores*
White Mart	*variety stores*

Fay's Drug Co. Inc.

7245 Henry Clay Blvd.
Liverpool, NY 13088
(315) 457-5970

Chief Executive Officer: H.A. Panasci
1984 Annual Sales Volume: 366M
1984 Shares Outstanding: 14,000,000
Shareholders: 8,000
Exchange: NY
Symbol: FAY

Corporate History: The company, incorporated in 1966, operates 119 drug stores, primarily in upstate New York, Massachusetts and Pennsylvania, and also operates Wheels Discount Auto Parts & Supplies Stores, and The Paper Cutter Stores, which retail office supplies, books, greeting cards, & party supplies at discount prices.

Brandnames of Products and Services:

Fay's	*drugstores*
The Paper Cutter	*discount office supplies, books, greeting cards & party supplies*
Wheels	*discount auto parts & supplies*

Fedders Corp.

158 Highway 206
Peapack, NJ 07977
(201) 234-2100

Chief Executive Officer: Salvatore Giordano
1984 Annual Sales Volume: 120M
1984 Shares Outstanding: 12,714,932
Shareholders: 8,929
Exchange: NY
Symbol: FJQ

Corporate History: The company, founded in 1896 and incorporated in 1913, makes air conditioners and other heat transfer products. It manufactures under private label for Montgomery Ward, J.C. Penney and others. During 1984, stockholders approved a reorganization plan under which Fedders Corp., a New York corporation that is primarily an operating corporation, became a wholly owned subsidiary of Fedders Corp., a Delaware holding company. The New York corporation's name was changed to Fedders USA Inc.

Brandnames of Products and Services:

Airtemp	*air conditioners*
Climatrol	*air conditioners*
Fedders	*air conditioners*

Federal Company

1755-D Lynnfield Road
Memphis, TN 38119-7244
(901) 761-3610

Chief Executive Officer: R. Lee Taylor II
1984 Annual Sales Volume: 1,304M
1984 Shares Outstanding: 8,239,000
Shareholders: 5,011
Exchange: NY
Symbol: FFF

Corporate History: Federal Co. was incorporated in 1925 as the Federal Compress and Warehouse Co., a consolidation of 28 food businesses. It produces flour and baking supplies—primarily to commercial bakeries—animal feed and condiments. Under its Holly Farm brand it is the nation's largest supplier of broiler chickens. The company maintains plants, mills and other facilities in 21 states.

Brandnames of Products and Services:

Continental	*specialty food products*
Crescent	*specialty food products*
Holly Farms	*fried chicken restaurants*
Holly Farms	*poultry products*
Pixie	*specialty food products*
Rusto	*food products*
Simon Fischer	*specialty food products*
Three Rivers	*flour and bakery products*
White Lily	*flour and bakery products*

Federal Express Corp.

2990 Airways Blvd., Memphis International Airport
Memphis, TN 38131
(901) 369-3600

Chief Executive Officer: Fredrick W. Smith
1984 Annual Sales Volume: 1,436M
1984 Shares Outstanding: 46,403,577
Shareholders: 7,477
Exchange: NY
Symbol: FDX

Corporate History: Federal Express was incorporated in 1971 and commenced operations in 1972. The company provides an overnight, door-to-door express delivery service for high priority packages and documents Monday through Saturday between 145 airports in the United States, certain points in Canada and Puerto Rico and on a limited basis to Europe and the Far East. Local offices are maintained in approximately 300 cities. This service, which serves approximately 90% of the United States' population, is provided through an integrated air-ground transportation system utilizing company personnel and equipment. In addition to the overnight services, a one-to-two hour electronic document transmission service was introduced in 1984.

Brandnames of Products and Services:

Courier Pak	*overnight delivery service*
Overnight Letter	*overnight delivery service*
Priority One	*overnight delivery service*
ZapMail	*same day electronic delivery service*

Federated Department Stores Inc.

7 W. Seventh St.
Cincinnati, OH 45202
(513) 579-7000

Chief Executive Officer: Howard Goldfeder
1984 Annual Sales Volume: 9,672M
1984 Shares Outstanding: 48,725,223
Shareholders: 22,500
Exchange: NY
Symbol: FDS

Corporate History: The company incorporated in 1929 as an alliance of retailers such as S.F. Rothchild, who owned Abraham & Straus and Louis Kirstein, who ran Filene's. The merger was headed by Fred Lazarus of Ohio. The corporation in 1984 included 19 operating divisions with 589 stores in major retail markets in 34 states.

Brandnames of Products and Services:

Abraham & Straus	*department stores*
Bloomingdale's	*department stores*
Bullock's/Bullock's Wilshire	*department stores*
Burdine's	*department stores*
The Children's Place	*department stores*
Filene's	*department stores*
Filene's Basement	*department stores*
Foley's	*department stores*
Gold Circle	*general merchandise*
Goldsmith's	*department stores*
I. Magnin	*department stores*
Lazarus	*department stores*
Levy's	*department stores*
Main Street	*department stores*
Ralph's	*supermarkets*
Rich's	*department stores*
Richway	*department stores*
Sanger-Harris	*department stores*
Shillito Rikes	*department stores*

The Fed Mart Corporation

3851 Rosecrans St.
San Diego, Calif. 92110
(714) 574-7111

Chief Executive Officer: Jan Heydorn
Exchange: AM
Symbol: FMI

Corporate History: The company incorporated in 1954 as Loma Supply Co. and adopted its present name in 1959. It operates a chain of low-margin retail stores and recently acquired the discount department store chain, Two Guys. Hugo Mann, a German company, owns 88% of Fed-Mart.

Brandnames of Products and Services:

Fed-Mart	*discount department stores*
Two Guys	*discount department stores*

Fieldcrest Mills Inc.

326 E. Stadium Dr.
Eden, NC 27288
(919) 627-3000

Chief Executive Officer: F.X. Larkin
1984 Annual Sales Volume: 573M
1984 Shares Outstanding: 3,867,500
Shareholders: 2,615
Exchange: NY
Symbol: FLD

Corporate History: Fieldcrest Mills, Inc., incorporated in 1953, manufactures and markets bedroom and bathroom textile products as well as rugs and carpets. The company operates 24 manufacturing facilities in the Southeast.

Brandnames of Products and Services:

Fieldcrest	*bed and bath products*
Karastan	*rugs and carpets*

Royal Velvet	*bed and bath products, carpets and rugs*
St. Mary's	*bed and bath products*

Filmways Inc.

2049 Century Park East
Los Angeles, Calif. 90067
(213) 557-8700

Chief Executive Officer: R.L. Bloch
Exchange: NY
Symbol: FWY
Corporate History: The company, incorporated in 1968, is engaged in television and motion picture production and distribution, publishing, insurance and data processing. In fiscal 1979-80 entertainment accounted for 63% of sales, publishing 22%, manufacturing 5% and data processing 10%.
Brandnames of Products and Services:

Ace Books	*publishing house*
American International Pictures	
Filmways TV Productions	*motion picture and TV production*
Grosset & Dunlap	*publishing house*
Heatter-Quigley TV	
Ideal Publishing Corp.	
Platt & Munk	*publishing house*
Ruby-Spears Productions	*television*
Tempo Books	*publishing house*

Firestone Tire & Rubber Co.

1200 Firestone Parkway
Akron, OH 44317
(216) 379-7000

Chief Executive Officer: J.J. Nevin
1984 Annual Sales Volume: 4,161M
1984 Shares Outstanding: 43,392,273
Shareholders: 33,583
Exchange: NY
Symbol: FIR
Corporate History: Founded in 1900. Firestone Tire & Rubber Company is one of the world's largest manufacturers of tires for automobiles, trucks, and agricultural and construction equipment. The company's principal business is the development, manufacture, and sale of a broad line of tires for the original equipment and replacement markets throughout the world. Firestone is also a major supplier of automotive maintenance and repair services with thousands of independent dealers and approximately 1,500 company-operated tire and automotive service centers in the United States. In addition, the company produces and sells truck wheels and rims, molded rubber products, single-ply rubber roofing systems, air springs, and synthetic and natural rubber and latex. The company employs approximately 60,000 people throughout the world.
Brandnames of Products and Services:

Firestone	*automotive accessories and stores*
Seiberling	*tires*

Fisher Foods, Inc.

5300 Richmond Rd.
Bedford Heights, OH 44146
(216) 292-7000

Chief Executive Officer: Carl H. Linder
1984 Annual Sales Volume: 503M
1984 Shares Outstanding: 4,988,808
Shareholders: 4,055
Exchange: NY
Symbol: FHR
Corporate History: The company incorporated in 1908 as Fisher Bros. Co and adopted its present name in 1961. The company is engaged principally in the distribution of food at both the retail and wholesale level. As of 1984 the company operated 47 supermarkets in Ohio, a food wholesaling business in Ohio and Pennsylvania, two discount drug and variety stores in the Cleveland area, an ice cream plant and a bakery.
Brandnames of Products and Services:

Eagle Ice Cream	
Fazio's	*supermarket*
Feren Fruit Baskets	*gift items*
Fisher	*food warehouse stores*
Heritage Wholesalers	*foods*
Jax	*discount drug stores*
Omar Bakeries	
Prestige	*donuts*

Flanigan's Enterprises Inc.

16565 N.W. 15th Ave.
Miami, FL 33169
(305) 624-9681

Chief Executive Officer: Joseph G. Flanigan
1984 Annual Sales Volume: 59M
1984 Shares Outstanding: 930,935
Shareholders: 1,065
Exchange: AM
Symbol: BDL

Corporate History: The company was incorporated in 1959 and originally operated in South Florida as a chain of small cocktail lounges and package stores. By 1970 the company had established a chain of "Big Daddy's" lounges and package stores between Vero Beach, Florida and Homestead, Florida. From 1970 to 1979 the company expanded its lounges and package stores throughout Florida and opened lounges (but not package stores) in five other "sun-belt" states. In 1975, the company discontinued most of its package store operations in Florida, except in the four Southeastern Florida counties (Key West to Palm Beach) and expanded its lounges into the former package store space. Over the past 6 years, the company has sold some of its older units and certain marginal units in Florida and units in other marketing areas. As of 1984, the company operated a total of 60 units-retail package storesm cocktail lounges and combination units.

Brandnames of Products and Services:

Big Daddy's Liquors	*liquor stores*
Big Daddy's Lounges	
Flanigan's	*liquor stores*

Fleetwood Enterprises Inc.

3125 Myers St.
Riverside, Calif. 92523
(714) 785-3500

Chief Executive Officer: J.C. Crean
1984 Annual Sales Volume: 1,420M
1984 Shares Outstanding: 23,582,402
Shareholders: 5,400
Exchange: NY
Symbol: FLE

Corporate History: The company, incorporated in 1957, designs and produces prefabricated housing, travel trailers and motor homes. Products are sold through 3,800 independent dealers in 49 states and Canada. The company operates 43 manufacturing plants in 17 states and Canada.

Brandnames of Products and Services:

Avion	*trailer trailers*
Fleetwood	*motor homes and recreational vehicles*
Jamboree	*motor homes*
Pace Arrow	*motor homes*
Prowler	*travel trailers*
Resort	*travel trailers*
Santana	*vans*
Southwind	*motor homes*
Terry	*travel trailers*
Tioga	*motor homes*
Wilderness	*travel trailers*

Fleming Companies Inc.

6301 Waterford Blvd.
Box 26647
Oklahoma City, OK 73126
(405) 840-7200

Chief Executive Officer: R.D. Harrison
1984 Annual Sales Volume: 5,511M
1984 Shares Outstanding: 19,861,614
Shareholders: 7,178
Exchange: NY
Symbol: FLM

Corporate History: The company was incorporated in Kansas in 1915 as Lux Mercantile Co., and its name changed to Fleming-Wilson Mercantile in 1918 and to Fleming Companies in 1972. In 1981, the company was reincorporated as an Oklahoma Corporation. Fleming Companies is engaged primarily in the wholesale distribution of food and related products. It currently serves about 4,520 retail food stores in 31 states. Fleming also is a major foodservice supplier to more than 21,000 restaurants, institutions and eating establishments.

Brandnames of Products and Services:

Big T.	*supermarkets*
Bonnie Hubbard	*foods*
Fleming's	*foods*
Food for Less	*supermarkets*
Goodvalue	*foods*
I.G.A.	*supermarkets*
Minimax	*supermarkets*
Montco	*foods*
Piggly Wiggly	*supermarkets*
P.S.-Personally Selected	*foods*
Rainbow	*foods*

Thriftway	*supermarkets*
United Super	*supermarkets*
Value King	*supermarkets*

S.M. Flickinger Co. Inc.

45 Azalea Dr.
P.O. Box 1086
Buffalo, N.Y. 14240
(716) 668-7200

Chief Executive Officer: J.D. Metcalf
Exchange: OTC
Symbol: FLIC
Corporate History: Incorporated in 1921, Flickinger sells food and health and beauty aids. It also operates supermarkets in the Eastern United States.
Brandnames of Products and Services:

Market Basket	*supermarkets*
Red & White	*food products*
Super Duper	*super markets*
Super Thrift	*supermarkets*

Flowers Industries Inc.

U.S. Highway 19 South
P.O. Box 1338
Thomasville, Ga. 31799-1338
(912) 226-9110

Chief Executive Officer: Amos McMullian
1984 Annual Sales Volume: 603M
1984 Shares Outstanding: 15,600,000
Shareholders: 3,000
Exchange: NY
Symbol: FLO
Corporate History: Flowers, incorporated in 1968, is a diversified food company, producing baked foods, snack products, frozen and convenience foods which are marketed primarily in the southeast. The company operates 30 food plants in 13 states.
Brandnames of Products and Services:

Beebo	*snack foods*
Breads International	*baked foods*
Butter Maid	*bread*
Chef Ready	*food products*
Flowers	*snack foods, bread, cake, rolls*
German Pumpernickel	*bread*
Hometown	*baked foods*
Mountain Farm Pecan	*snack items*
Nature's Own	*baked foods*
Rich Grain	*baked foods*
Roman Meal	*bread*
Stilwell	*convenience foods*
Sunbeam	*breads, buns, rolls*
Tender Mix	*baked foods*
Warsaw Rye-bread	

Foodarama Supermarkets Inc.

303 W. Main St.
Freehold, NJ 07728
(201) 462-4700

Chief Executive Officer: Joseph J. Saker
1984 Annual Sales Volume: 451M
1984 Shares Outstanding: 1,341,059
Shareholders: 1,700
Exchange: AM
Symbol: FSM
Corporate History: The company, a New Jersey corporation formed in 1958, operates a chain of 29 Shop-Rite supermarkets in four states—New Jersey, New York, Pennsylvania and Connecticut. Its operating policy is based on the sale of merchandise at lowmark-ups with a view to achieving a high sales volume per store and a rapid inventory turnover.
Brandnames of Products and Services:

M.S.B.	*(Money Saving Brand) food products*
Shop Rite	*supermarkets*

Ford Motor Co.

The American Road
Dearborn, MI 48121
(313) 322-3000

Chief Executive Officer: D.E. Petersen
1984 Annual Sales Volume: 52,366M
1984 Shares Outstanding: 184,100,000
Shareholders: 285,000
Exchange: NY
Symbol: Ford M
Corporate History: Ford was founded in 1903 by Henry Ford, a leader in the development of the automobile. The key to Ford's success was turning out inexpensive cars for the mass market. He introduced the Model T in 1908. Over the next 20 years more than 16 million

were sold. An innovative manager, Ford transformed modern industry by developing the mass assembly line. He also paid his workers twice the going wage under the assumption that a highly paid worker could afford his cars. During the 1920s Ford was the nation's leading car manufacturer but by the 1930s, in part because of Henry Ford's failure to keep abreast of poor management, it had fallen to second place where it still stands today. After World War II, Henry Ford, with the help of such "whiz kids" as Robert MacNamara, brought the ailing company back to life. Ford had a well-publicized failure with the Edsel in the 1950s but came on again strong with the Mustang in the 1960s.

Brandnames of Products and Services:

Ford	*automobiles and trucks*
Ford Authorized Remanufactured	*parts*
Ford Motor	*parts and accessories*
Lincoln	*automobiles*
Mercury	*automobiles*
Motorcraft	*parts & accessories*
Rotunda	*tools & equipment*

Fort Howard Paper Co.

P.O. Box 19130
Green Bay, WI 54307-9130
(414) 435-8821

Chief Executive Officer: P.J. Schierl
1984 Annual Sales Volume: 1,339M
1984 Shares Outstanding: 31,545,000
Shareholders: 9,300
Exchange: NY
Symbol: FHP

Corporate History: The company makes paper towels, toilet tissue, paper napkins, and other paper goods. It was incorporated in 1967 as a successor to a Wisconsin concern formed in 1919.

Brandnames of Products and Services:

Antique	*household paper products*
Dolly Madison	*household paper products*
Edon	*household paper products*
Mardi Gras	*household paper products*
Page	*household paper products*
So Dri	*household paper products*
Soft 'N Gentle	*household paper products*

Fotomat Corp.

205 9th Street North
St. Petersburg, FL 33701
(813) 823-2027

Chief Executive Officer: Ross E. Roeder
1984 Annual Sales Volume: 181M
1984 Shares Outstanding: 24,689,286
Shareholders: 6,300
Exchange: AM
Symbol: FOT

Corporate History: The company, incorporated in 1971, is a major factor in the photofinishing industry with 2,262 retail stores which also sell film and accessories. IN 1983, the company acquired Portrait World Inc., which processes film into portraits for independent photographers.

Brandnames of Products and Services:

film, accessories, videotape products	
Fotomat	*photofinishing stores*
Portrait World	*film development services*

Fox-Stanley Photo Products Inc.

8750 Tesoro Dr.
San Antonio, Texas 78286
(512) 828-9111

Chief Executive Officer: Carl D. Newton, Jr.
1984 Annual Sales Volume: 152M
1984 Shares Outstanding: 3,146,415
Shareholders: 1,724
Exchange: NY
Symbol: FSP

Corporate History: The company, incorporated in 1936, is one of the largest photo finishers in the United States. It does business in 34 states. It is competing with Berkey Photo and Photomat for the number two spot in photo finishing. (Eastman Kodak Co. is number one.) The company is accelerating its expansion in one-hour retail photofinishing labs.

Brandnames of Products and Services:

Fox Stanley Photo	*photofinishing stores*

Frank's Nursery and Crafts Inc.

6399 East Nevada
Detroit, Mich. 48234
(313) 366-8400

Chief Executive Officer: I. William Sherr
Exchange: AM
Symbol: FKS
Corporate History: The company, incorporated in 1957, operates a chain of 78 retail garden centers and craft stores, mostly in the Midwest. In 1979 lawn and garden supplies accounted for 52% of sales and craft merchandise 23%. The remaining 25% came from Christmas merchandise, artificial flowers, and tools and equipment.
Brandnames of Products and Services:

Frank's Nursery and Crafts Stores	
Ortho	*fertilizer*
Scott's	*fertilizer*
Toro	*lawn mowers*

Fred Meyer

3800 Southeast 22nd Ave.
Portland, Ore. 97202
(503) 235-8844

Chief Executive Officer: O.B. Robertson
Exchange: OTC
Symbol: MEYR
Corporate History: The company, incorporated in 1927, operates 65 retail centers located primarily in the Pacific Northwest. It is one of the leading general merchandisers and food retailers in the area. In 1979 retail food and non-food accounted for 79.3% of sales, and wholesale 20.7%.
Brandnames of Products and Services:

Certified	*pharmaceutical products*
Fred Meyer Stores	*food, general merchandise and apparel stores*
My-Te-Fine	*dairy and baking products*

Friendly Frost Inc.

123 Frost St.
Westbury, N.Y. 11590
(516) 334-8100

Chief Executive Officer: Daniel Schmier
Exchange: AM
Symbol: FF
Corporate History: The company, incorporated in 1943, operates home appliance and radio centers. Subject to FCC approval, an agreement has been reached to sell its WTFM radio station.
Brandnames of Products and Services:

Churchill Audio Centers	*specialty stores*
Friendly Frost Appliance Stores	*specialty stores*
Friendly Frost Garden Centers	*specialty stores*

Frigitronics Inc.

770 River Rd.
Shelton, CT 06484
(203) 929-6321

Chief Executive Officer: Ralph E. Crump
1984 Annual Sales Volume: 124M
1984 Shares Outstanding: 3,194,270
Shareholders: 3,384
Exchange: NY
Symbol: FRG
Corporate History: The company was organized in Delaware in 1967 as a successor to Frigitronics of Conn. Inc., which was incorporated in 1963. The company, through a group of subsidiaries, is engaged in the development, manufacture and sale of eye care products and medically oriented surgical and diagnostic instruments. Its operations are divided among three divisions. 1) Optical manufacturing and distribution division; develops, manufactures and sells intraocular lenses for the restoration of vision following cataract extraction, soft and hard contact lenses and eyeglass frames. 2) Eye care services division; owns and operates a nationwide chain of 385 retail stores for the sale of prescription eyewear which is processed in 20 company-owned laboratories; the division also processes eyeglass prescriptions wholesale. 3) Instrument manufacturing division; is developing, manufacturing and selling cryosurgical instruments and related equipment.

Brandnames of Products and Services:

Benson Optical Co.	*eyecare store*
House of Vision	*eyecare store*
Jenkel Davidson	*eyecare store*
Lens Mark	*lens dispenser*
Opus III Lens	*hard contact (eye)*
Ostertag Optical Service	*eyecare store*
Saturn Lens	*soft contact (eye)*

Frisch's Restaurants Inc.

2800 Gilbert Ave.
Cincinnati, OH 45206
(513) 961-2660

Chief Executive Officer: J.C. Maier
1984 Annual Sales Volume: 126M
1984 Shares Outstanding: 4,385,544
Shareholders: 2,688
Exchange: AM
Symbol: FRS

Corporate History: Frisch's Restaurant, Inc. operates and franchises coffee shop and carry-out restaurants. These operations are located in Ohio, Indiana, Kentucky, Florida, Oklahoma, Texas and Kansas. Additionally, the company operates two motor inns and three specialty restaurants in metropolitan Cincinnati.

Brandnames of Products and Services:

Big Boy	*restaurants*
Kip's	*restaurant*
Prime 'n Wine	*restaurants*
Quality Inn Motels	*in Cincinnati area*
Roy Rogers	*restaurants*
Stroller	*restaurant*

H.B. Fuller Co.

3530 North Lexington Ave.
St. Paul, MN 55112
(612) 481-1588

Chief Executive Officer: A.L. Andersen
1984 Annual Sales Volume: 450M
1984 Shares Outstanding: 9,188,776
Shareholders: 3,157
Exchange: OTC
Symbol: FULL

Corporate History: Founded in 1887, H.B. Fuller Company is a manufacturerof adhesives, sealants, coatings, paints, and specialty waxes, as well as sanitation chemicals. The company has plants and technical service centers in 41 U.S. cities and 30 countries worldwide. The company was incorporated in 1915 and employs approximately 4,000 people.

Brandnames of Products and Services:

Foster	*adhesive materials/coatings*
H.B. Fuller	*adhesives*
Kativo	*paints*
Linear	*reinforcing tape*
Max Bond	*panel and construction adhesive*
Monarch	*chemical products/ detergents*

Fuqua Industries Inc.

4900 Georgia Pacific Center
Atlanta, GA 30303
(404) 658-9000

Chief Executive Officer: J.B. Fuqua
1984 Annual Sales Volume: 855M
1984 Shares Outstanding: 9,510,817
Shareholders: 9,927
Exchange: NY
Symbol: FQA

Corporate History: Fuqua Industries is a diversified manufacturing, distribution and service company with four principle areas of business: lawn and garden (Snapper Power Equipment), photofinishing (Colorcraft Corp.), sporting goods (Fuqua's), and seating (Fuqua's). In 1984, lawn and garden accounted for 57% of Fuqua's operating profit, photofinishing 14%, sporting goods 28% and the seating and other segment reported 1% of the operating profit. In 1984 net income from operations was $37,000,000.

Brandnames of Products and Services:

Ajay	*golf accessories & physical fitness equipment*
American Camper	*sporting good equipment*
American Seating	*office systems, theater & stadium seats*
Ash Flash	*bicycle accessories*
Big Bear	*farm and auto stores*
Canadian Camper	*sporting goods equipment*
Colorcraft	*photo finishing*
Comet	*boat trailers*
Concord	*boat trailers*
Dorcy	*flashlight & lantern*
Esprit	*motorcycle accessories*
Fuqua Homes	*mobile homes*
Highlander	*boat trailers*

Hutch	*team sports equipment*
Keds & Pro Keds	*athletic hosiery*
Looney-Tunes	*athletic hosiery*
Major League Baseball	*athletic hosiery*
National Football League	*athletic hosiery*
Nesco	*sporting goods equipment*
Oklahoma Trailer	*boat trailers*
Playmate Pro Classic	*golf accessories*
Reach	*team sports equipment*
Robertson's	*farm and auto stores*
Shoreline	*boat trailers*
Snapper	*lawn and garden equipment*
Stormor	*grain bins*
TSC	*farm and auto supply stores*
Viking	*mail-order photo finishing*
Weather-Rite	*sport equipment*
Wheelmaster	*bicycle accessories*
WTAC-AM	*radio station, Flint, Mich.*

GAF Corp.

140 W. 51st St.
New York, N.Y. 10020
(212) 582-7600

Chief Executive Officer: Dr. J. Werner
Exchange: NY
Symbol: GAF

Corporate History: The company incorporated in 1929 as American I.G. Chemical Corp. and merged with the wholly-owned General Aniline Works in 1939, taking the name of General Aniline & Film Corp. It adopted its current title in 1968. The formation of the company was overseen by I.G. Farben Industries of Germany, the leading German producer of chemical and allied products. The company makes chemical, photographic and reprographic products. In 1979 building materials accounted for 49% of sales, photo and reproduction products 26% and chemicals 25%.

Brandnames of Products and Services:

Agfa	*photo products*
Brite Bond	*floor tile*
GAF	*photo products*
GAF Star	*flooring*
Pana-Vue	*photographic slides*
Timberline	*shingles*
Vanguard	*siding*
Viewmaster	*photo viewers*
WNCN-FM	*radio station, N.Y.C.*

Gannett Co. Inc.

Lincoln Tower
Rochester, NY 14604
(716) 546-8600

Chief Executive Officer: A.H. Neuharth
1984 Annual Sales Volume: 1,960M
1984 Shares Outstanding: 80,159,729
Shareholders: 10,688
Exchange: NY
Symbol: Gannett

Corporate History: Gannett was formed in 1906 with the merger of three upstate New York papers. Today, Gannett is a nationwide information company that publishes 85 daily newspapers, including USA TODAY, and 35 non-daily newspapers; operates six television and 16 radio stations and the largest outdoor advertising company in North America; as well as marketing, news television production, research, satellite information systems and a national group of commercial printing facilities. Gannett has operations in 36 states, Guam, the Virgin Islands, and Canada.

Brandnames of Products and Services:

American	*newspaper, Hattiesburg, MS*
Argus Leader	*newspaper, Sioux Falls, S.D.*
Argus	*newspaper, Mount Vernon, N.Y.*
Californian	*newspaper, Salinas, Calif.*
Chronicle Tribune	*newspaper, Marion, Ind.*
Citizen Register	*newspaper, Ossining, N.Y*
Citizen	*newspaper, Tuscon, Ariz.*
Clarion-Ledger	*newspaper, Jackson, MS, MS*
Coloradoan	*newspaper, Ft. Collins, Colo.*
Commercial-News	*newspaper, Danville, Ill.*
Courier-News	*newspaper, Bridgewater, N.J.*
Courier-Post	*newspaper, Camden, N.J.*
Daily News	*newspaper St. Thomas, VI*
Daily News	*newspaper, Tarryton, N.Y.*
Daily Olympian	*newspaper, Olympia, Wash.*
Democrat & Chronicle	*newspaper, Rochester, N.Y.*
Des Moines Register	*Newspaper Des Moines, Iowa*
Enquirer & News	*newspaper, Battle Creek, Mich.*
Enquirer	*newspaper, Cincinnati, Ohio*

Family Weekly	*magazine*
Free Press	*newspaper, Burlington, Vt.*
Gannett Media Sales	*New York, NY*
Gannett News Service	*Washington, DC*
Gannett Outdoor	*advertising New York, NY*
Gazette	*newspaper, Chillicothe, Ohio*
Gazette	*newspaper, Niagara Falls, N.Y.*
Gazette	*newspaper, Reno, Nev.*
Herald Dispatch	*newspaper, Huntington, W.V.*
Herald	*newspaper, Bellingham, Wash.*
Herald Statesmen	*newspaper, Yonkers, N.Y.*
Idaho Statesmen	*newspaper, Boise, Idaho*
	newspaper, San Rafael, Cal.
Item	*newspaper, Port Chester, N.Y.*
Jackson *Daily News*	*newspaper, Jackson, MS*
Journal & Courier	*newspaper, Lafayette, Ind.*
Journal-News	*newspaper, Nyack, N.Y.*
Journal	*newspaper, Poughkeepsie, N.Y.*
Journal	*newspaper, Coffeyville, Kan.*
Journal	*newspaper, Pensacola, Fla.*
Journal	*newspaper, Wilmington, Del.*
Journal	*newspaper, Ithaca, N.Y.*
KIIS-FM	*Los Angeles, Calif.*
KKBQ-AM	*Houston, TX*
KKBQ-FM	*Houston, TX*
KOCO-TV	*Oklahoma City, Okla.*
KPNX-TV	*Phoenix, Ariz.*
KSDO/KSDO-FM	*San Diego, CA*
KSD-TV	*St. Louis, Mo.*
KUSA-AM	*St. Louis, MO*
KUSA-TV	*Denver, CO*
Leader & Press	*newspaper, Springfield, Mo.*
Louis Harris & Assoc.	*research New York, NY; San Francisco, CA; Washington, DC; London; Paris*
New Mexican	*newspaper, Santa Fe, N.M.*
News Herald	*newspaper, Port Clinton, Ohio*
News Messenger	*newspaper, Fremont, Ohio*
News-Press	*newspaper, Ft. Myers, Fla.*

News	*newspaper, Springfield, Mo.*
News	*newspaper, Tarrytown, N.Y.*
News	*Pensacola, Fla.*
News	*newspaper, Wilmington, Del.*
News Star	*newspaper, Monroe, La.*
Norwich *Bulletin*	*newspaper, Norwich, CT*
Observer Dispatch	*newspaper, Utica, N.Y.*
Oregon Statesman	*newspaper, Salem, Ore.*
Pacific Daily News	*newspaper, Agana, Guam*
Palladium-Item	*newspaper, Richmond, Ind.*
Phoenix	*newspaper, Muskogee, Okla.*
Press Citizen	*newspaper, Iowa City, Iowa*
Press-Gazette	*newspaper, Green Bay, WI*
Press	*newspaper, Utica, N.Y.*
Press	*newspaper, Binghamton, N.Y.*
Public Opinion	*newspaper, Chambersburg, Pa.*
Record	*newspaper, Stockton, Calif.*
Register Star	*newspaper, Rockford, Ill.*
The Reporter	*newspaper, Lansdale, PA*
Reporter Dispatch	*newspaper, White Plains, N.Y.*
Saratogian	*newspaper, Saratoga, N.Y.*
Springfield Leader & Press	*newspaper, Springfield, Missouri*
Standard Star	*newspaper, New Rochelle, N.Y.*
Star-Bulletin	*newspaper, Honolulu, Hawaii*
Star Gazette	*newspaper, Elmira, N.Y.*
State Journal	*newspaper, Lansing, Mich.*
Sturgis *Journal*	*newspaper, Sturgis, MI*
Sun Bulletin	*newspaper, Binghamton, N.Y.*
Sun	*newspaper, San Bernardino, Calif.*
Tennessean	*newspaper, Nashville, Tenn.*
The Times	*newspaper, Gainesville, GA*
Times Delta	*newspaper, Visalia, Calif.*
Times Democrat	*newspaper, Muskogee, Okla.*
Times Herald	*newspaper, Port Huron, Mich.*
Times	*newspaper, St. Cloud, Minn.*
Times	*newspaper, Mamaroneck, N.Y.*
Times	*newspaper, El Paso, Texas*
Times	*newspaper, Shreveport, La.*

Times	*newspaper, Marietta, Ohio*
Times-Union	*newspaper, Rochester, NY*
Today	*newspaper, Cocoa, Fla.*
Today	*newspaper, Westchester, N.Y.*
Tribune	*newspaper, Fremont, Neb.*
Tribune	*newspaper, Oakland, Calif.*
USA TODAY	*newspaper, Washington, DC*
Valley News Dispatch	*newspaper, Tarentum, PA*
Virgin Islander	*magazine*
Wausau *Daily Herald*	*newspaper, Wausau, WI*
WCZY-AM/FM	*Detroit, Mich.*
WDAE-AM	*Tampa/St. Petersburg, FL*
WDOK-FM	*Cleveland, Ohio*
WGCI-AM	*Chicago, IL*
WGCI-FM	*Chicago, Ill.*
WIQI-FM	*Tampa/St. Petersburg, FL*
WLQV-AM	*Detroit, MI*
WLVI-TV	*Boston, MA*
World	*newspaper, Monroe, La.*
WTCN-TV	*Minneapolis-St. Paul, MN*
WWWE-AM	*Cleveland, Ohio*
WXIA-TV	*Atlanta, Ga.*

Garan Inc.

350 Fifth Ave.
New York, NY 10118
(212) 563-2000

Chief Executive Officer: Seymour Lichtenstein
1984 Annual Sales Volume: 177M
1984 Shares Outstanding: 3,283,100
Shareholders: 1,100
Exchange: AM
Symbol: GAN
Corporate History: The company was incorporated in 1957 as Myrna Mills Inc. It designs and makes men's, women's, and children's apparel under their own labels and private labels.
Brandnames of Products and Services:

Advantage	*women's sports wear*
Ban-Lon	*knit shirts*
Garan	*men's, women's, children's apparel*
Garan by Marita	*women's apparel*
Garanimals	*children's clothes*
The Garan Man	*menswear*

Garfinkle Brooks Brothers, Miller & Rhoads Inc.

1629 K St. NW
Washington, D.C. 20006
(202) 828-1800

Chief Executive Officer: D.R. Waters
Exchange: NY
Symbol: GBM
Corporate History: The company incorporated in 1939 as Julius Garfinkel & Co. and adopted its present title in 1967. It sells apparel and other merchandise through approximately 215 department and specialty stores.
Brandnames of Products and Services:

Ann Taylor	*women's apparel stores*
Brooks Brothers	*men's apparel store*
Catherine's Stout Shoppe	*women's apparel stores*
Garfinkel's	*department stores*
Harzfeld's	*department stores*
Miller & Rhoads	*department stores*
Miller's	*department stores*

Gaylords National Corp.

10 Enterprise Ave.
Secaucus, N.J. 07094
(201) 867-9300

Chief Executive Officer: J.A. Barrer
Exchange: AM
Symbol: GYL
Corporate History: The company, incorporated in 1933 as Gay Apparel Corp., operates discount department stores, catalog stores and other retail outlets in 14 states.
Brandnames of Products and Services:

Betty Gay	*women's apparel stores*
Gaylords	*department stores*
Towers	*jewelers, catalog showroom*

GenCorp

1 General St.
Akron, OH 44329
(216) 798-3000

Chief Executive Officer: M.G. O'Neil
1984 Annual Sales Volume: 2,727M
1984 Shares Outstanding: 21,465,518

Shareholders: 32,500
Exchange: NY
Symbol: GY

Corporate History: GenCorp emerged in 1984 as the new name for what was The General Tire & Rubber Company, founded in 1915. The restructured parent company now operates through its principal subsidiary companies: Aerojet General, a research and development unit important in the aerospace and defense industries; DiversiTech General, which is the new name for the company's former Chemical/Plastics/Industrial Products Group, a supplier of products to automotive, consumers, appliance, and other industries; General Tire, carrying on a manufacturing tradition which dates to the company's founding; and RKO General, well-known for its postition in the broadcasting and entertainment fields, and which is strongly involved in soft-drink bottling as well as motion picture production and hotel property development and management.

Brandnames of Products and Services:

Fashon/Beacon Hill	*wall coverings*
Frontier	*airline*
Frontier Horizon	*airline*
Gen Card	*in-house automotive credit card*
General Tire	*automotive products*
KHJ-TF	*Los Angeles*
Monterey Plaza	*hotel, Calfornia*
My Room	*juvenile wall coverings*
Penn	*tennis balls*
Westward Fools	*resort, Arizona*
WOR-TV	*Secaucus, NJ*

General Cinema Corp.

27 Boylston St.
Chestnut Hill, MA 02167
(617) 232-8200

Chief Executive Officer: R.A. Smith
1984 Annual Sales Volume: 916M
1984 Shares Outstanding: 37,701,000
Shareholders: 2,267
Exchange: NY
Symbol: GCN

Corporate History: The company was incorporated in 1950 as MidWest Drive-In Theatres. In 1960 the name was changed to General Drive-in Corp. and its present title was adopted in 1964. It is a major independent bottler of soft drinks and is the largest operator of multi-screen theaters in shopping centers in the nation. As of 1984 General Cinemas Corp. owned 1,040 theaters.

Brandnames of Products and Services:

General Cinemas	
WGRZ-TV	*Buffalo, NY*

General Electric Co.

3135 Easton Turnpike
Fairfield, CT 06431
(203) 373-2431

Chief Executive Officer: John F. Welch, Jr.
1984 Annual Sales Volume: 27,947M
1984 Shares Outstanding: 454,903,000
Shareholders: 511,000
Exchange: NY
Symbol: GE

Corporate History: The company traces its history back to 1878 when Edison Electric Light Company was founded to support Thomas Edison's work. It was incorporated in 1892 as General Electric. GE was in the vanguard of electric technology developing new products and diversifying. It used its dominance in the lightbulb market—at one time it controlled 85% of the market—to finance its growth in appliances. Today, General Electric Company is one of the largest and most diversified inudstrial corporations in the world with 15 major businesses in three groupings: core business (lighting, major appliances, motor, turbine, transportation, construction equipment); high-technology businesses (medical systems, aircraft engine, aerospace, materials and industrial electronics); and service businesses (financial, construction and engineering). The largest manufacturer of lighting products in the U.S., GE produced more than a billion light bulbs in 1984.

Brandnames of Products and Services:

GE	*appliances, light bulbs, home electronics*
General Electric	*financial services*
General Electric	*information services*
Hot Point	*appliances*
KCNC-TV	*Denver, Co*
Quik-Comm	*electronic mailbox system*

General Foods Corp.

250 North St.
White Plains, NY 10625
(914) 335-2500

Chief Executive Officer: J.L. Ferguson
1984 Annual Sales Volume: 9,000M

1984 Shares Outstanding: 49,000,000
Shareholders: 78,500
Exchange: NY
Symbol: GF
Corporate History: The company was incorporated in 1922 as Postum Cereal Co. and adopted its current name in 1929. It is one of the largest processors of packaged grocery products in the world. General Foods is the largest U.S.-based company operating solely in the food business. Worldwide, some 56,000 employees work at more than 100 locations in the United States and some 20 other countries. Seventy-five percent of its sales come from brands that hold the number-one position in their markets. More than 30 per cent of its sales come from businesses acquired during the last five years: Oscar Mayer processed meats, Entenmann's baked goods, Ronzoni pasta and Italian foods, and Oroweat specialty bread and rolls. In addition, the company has innovated frozen novelty products, sugar-free beverages and desserts, and other new products which help fulfill its mission of being the worlds's premier food and beverage company.
Brandnames of Products and Services:

Alpha-Bits	*cereal*
Baker's	*chocolate & coconut*
Birds Eye	*frozen foods*
Brim	*decaffeinated coffee*
Calumet Baking Powder	
Certo	*fruit pectin*
Claussen	*pickles*
Cool Whip	*whipped topping*
Country Kitchen Syrup	
Country Time Lemonade	
Crystal Light	*soft drink mix*
Dream Whip	*whipped topping*
D-Zerta	*gelatin dessert*
Entenmann's	*baked goods*
Fruit & Fibre	*cereal*
General Foods International Coffees	
Good Seasonings	*salad dressing mix*
Grape-Nuts	*cereal*
Honeycomb	*cereal*
Jell-O	*gelatin products*
Jell-O Pudding Pops	*dessert*
Kool-Aid	*soft dirnk*
Log Cabin Syrup	
Louis Rich	*turkey products*
Maxim	*freeze-dried coffee*
Maxwell House	*coffee*
Minute Rice	
Minute Tapioca	
Open Pit Barbeque	*sauce*
Oroweat	*bread & rolls*
Oscar Mayer	*processed meats*
Oven Fry	*coating mix*
Pebbles	*cereal*
Post	*cereals*
Post-Tens	*cereal*
Post Toasties	*cereal*
Postum	*cereal beverage*
Post 40% Bran	*cereal*
Rice Kringles	*cereal*
Ronzoni	*pasta & Italian specialties*
Sanka	*decaffeinated coffee*
Shake 'N Bake	*coating mix*
Stove Top	*stuffing mixes*
Sugar Crisp	*cereal*
Sure-Jell	*fruit pectin*
Swans Down Cake Flour	
Tang	*breakfast beverage*
Yuban	*coffee*

General Host Corp.

22 Gate House Rd.
Stamford, CT 06904
(203) 357-9900

Chief Executive Officer: Harris J. Ashton
1984 Annual Sales Volume: 563M
1984 Shares Outstanding: 18,895,000
Shareholders: 4,884
Exchange: NY
Symbol: GH
Corporate History: The company was incorporated in 1911 as General Baking Co., and its present title was adopted in 1967. The company is engaged in the production and sale of food, agricultural and salt products and operates a chain of nursery, craft and specialty food stores. In 1984 nursery and craft stores accounted for 36% of sales; specialty food stores 26%, frozen food products 23% and salt and agriculture products 15%. In 1984 the company acquired Flower Time Inc., a specialty retailer of indoor and outdoor plants and garden supplies sold through a chain of 20 stores in the greater New York metropolitan area.

Brandnames of Products and Services:

All American Gourmet Co.	*frozen foods*
Cudahy	*meat food products*
Flower Time	*chain of garden and craft stores*
Frank's Nursery & Crafts	*stores*
Hickory Farms of Ohio	*gourmet shops*
Hot Sam Stores	*pretzel stores*

General Housewares Corp.

P.O. Box 10265
Stamford, CT 06904-2265
(203) 325-4141

Chief Executive Officer: J.H. Muller, Jr.
1984 Annual Sales Volume: 84M
1984 Shares Outstanding: 2,331,679
Shareholders: 2,400
Exchange: NY
Symbol: GHW

Corporate History: General Housewares Corp., incorporated in 1967, is a manufacturer and marketer of home entertaining products in the cookware, tabletop giftware and specialty food product categories. The company manufactures 80% of the products of its twelve major lines, and markets it products to U.S. and Canadian general merchandise retailers.

Brandnames of Products and Services:

Boutique	*cookware*
Carousel	*giftware*
Chateau	*cookware*
Chocolate Almond	*cookware*
Classic	*cookware*
Classic American Foods	*cookware*
Classic Candles	*giftware*
Colonial candle of Cape Cod	*giftware*
Colonial Candles	*giftware*
Colonial Handipt	*giftware*
Columbian	*cookware*
Cordless	*giftware*
Country Collection	*cookware*
The Decorator Collection	*giftware*
Fabrique	*giftware*
Fancipans	*cookware*
Frontier Campware	*cookware*
giftware	
Good Cooking Equipment	*cookware*
Graniteware	*cookware*
Homemade	*cookware*
Leyse Professional	*cookware*
Leyson	*cookware*
Lo Temp	*cookware*
Magnalite	*cookware*
Magnalite Professional	*cookware*
Mom's	*cookware*
Oriental	*cookware*
PartyLine Gifts	*giftware*
Priscilla Ware	*cookware*
Renaissance Candles	*giftware*
Spectra	*cookware*
Sunshine Yellow	*cookware*
Textol	*giftware*
Toroware	*cookware*
Wagner Ware	*cookware*

General Mills Inc.

9200 Wayzata Blvd.
Minneapolis, MN 55440
(612) 540-2311

Chief Executive Officer: H.B. Atwater
1984 Annual Sales Volume: 5,601M
1984 Shares Outstanding: 46,900,000
Shareholders: 24,500
Exchange: NY
Symbol: GIS

Corporate History: General Mills was founded and incorporated in 1928 as a combination of several milling companies. Flour remained the basis of the business until after World War II, although the company did branch out into cereals—notably Wheaties. During the 1950s General Mills began to diversify. Beginning in 1961 it sold many of its acquisitions. A new wave of diversification began in 1966. The company bought small businesses in early stages of development and built them up. Between 1967 and 1969 General Mills acquired more than 40 businesses. Today the company is engaged in such varied activities as manufacturing toys and creating jewelry. It also is in the apparel industry, crafts and furniture. In 1984 half of the company's sales and earnings came from restaurants, toys, fashions and specialty retailing.

Brandnames of Products and Services:

Betty Crocker	*baking products*
Bisquick	*baking mix*
Blue Water	*seafood*
Body Buddies	*cereal*
Boo Berry	*cereal*
Buc Wheats	*cereal*
Care Bears	*toys*
Casa Gallardo	*Mexican restaurants*
Cheerios	*cereal*
Cinnamon Toast Crunch	*cereal*
Cocoa Puffs	*cereal*
Complete Pancake Mix	
Corn Total	*cereal*
Count Chocula	*cereal*
Country Corn flakes	*cereal*
Craft Master	*paint-by-numbers*
Darryl's	*restaurant*
Eddie Bauer	*sporting goods stores*
Family Pack/10 G's	*cereal*
Foot Joy	*golf footwear*
Franken Berry	*cereal*
Fruit Roll-Ups	*snack food*
Golden Grahams	*cereal*
Gold Medal Flour	*flour*
The Good Earth	*restaurants*
Gorton's	*seafood*
Hamburger Helper	*food mix*
Honey-Nut Cheerios	*cereal*
Izod	*apparel*
Kaboom	*cereal*
Kenner	*toys*
Kix	*cereal*
Lacoste	*apparel*
La Pina	*flour*
Lee Ward's Creative Crafts	*specialty stores*
Lionel Electric Trains	*toys*
Lucky Charms	*cereal*
Monet	*jewelry*
MPC Model Kits	*craft*
Nature Valley Granola	*cereal*
Nerf	*toy products*
New Bac-o's	*imitation bacon*
O-Cel-O	*sponges*
Parker Bros.	*games*
Pennsylvania House	*furniture*
Play Doh	*toys*
Potato Buds	*instant mashed potatoes*
Red Band	*flour*
Red Lobster Inns	*restaurants*
Ship 'n Shore	*women's apparel*
Smith's	*foods*
Star War I	*toys*
Stir n' Frost	*cake frosting mixes*
Strawberry Shortcake	*toys*
Super Moist	*cake mixes*
The Talbot's	*women's apparel*
Total	*cereal*
Wallpapers to Go	*home improvement stores*
We Are Sportswear	*specialty retailing*
Wheaties	*cereal*
Yoplait	*yogurt (importer)*
York Steak Houses	*restaurants*

General Motors Corp.

3044 W. Grand Blvd.
Detroit, Mich. 48202
(313) 556-5000

Chief Executive Officer:	Roger B. Smith
1984 Annual Sales Volume:	83,890M
1984 Shares Outstanding:	316,431,959
Shareholders:	943,831
Exchange:	NY
Symbol:	GM

Corporate History: General Motors was founded in 1908 by William Durrant to buy up stock in several existing car companies. Over the next two years it acquired two dozen other companies making cars, electric lamps and accessories. The company became the leading auto manufacturer in the nation during the 1930s through its policy of offering a wide variety of cars for every pocketbook and its emphasis on meeting consumer demands for comfort, power and style. It has held that place ever since. Today General Motors is a highly vertically-integrated business, consisting of the manufacture, assembly and sale of automobiles, trucks and buses and related parts and accessories classified as automotive products. Nonautomotive products of the corporation include diesel engines, diesel locomotives and other related products. Defense and space products of the corporation include turbine aircraft engines and components ordnance transmissions, inertial navigation, guidance and control systems and components, armored vehicles, as well as commercial products delivered for use by the military. Computer systems services include the design of large scale data processing systems and the operation of data centers and communications networks. Substantially all of General Motors' products are marketed through retail dealers and through distributors and jobbers in the United States and Canada and through distributors and dealers overseas. In 1984, there were approximately 11,500 General Motors motor vehicle dealers in the United States and Canada and approximately 5,400 outlets overseas. To assist in the merchandising of General Motors' products, General Motors Acceptance Corporation, a wholly-owned non-consolidated subsidiary, and its subsidiaries offer financial services and certain types of automobile insurance to dealers and customers.

Brandnames of Products and Services:

Buick	*automobiles*
Cadillac	*automobiles*
Chevrolet	*automobiles*
GMC	*compact van*
Oldsmobile	*automobiles*
Pontiac	*automobiles*
Saturn	*automobiles*

Genesco Inc.

Genesco Park
Nashville, TN 37202
(615) 367-7000

Chief Executive Officer: Richard W. Hanselman
1984 Annual Sales Volume: 604M
1984 Shares Outstanding: 15,044,934
Shareholders: 24,000
Exchange: NY
Symbol: GCO

Corporate History: Genesco was founded in 1924 as the Jarman Shoe Co. and incorporated the following year. Its name was changed to General Shoe Corp. in 1933 and shortened to Genesco in 1959. During the late 1930s the company developed a policy of aggressive acquisitions, first in the shoe industry and then in apparel. From 1956 to 1972 it acquired 95 companies, among them Bonwit Teller, I. Miller, Henri Bendel, and S.H. Kress. Genesco sold off companies and stores during the 1970s. Bonwit Teller, Kress and I. Miller were among those sold. Today Genesco is primarily a manufacturer and retailer of shoes and men's apparel. In fiscal 1984 footwear wholesale & manufacturing accounted for 33% of sales, footwear retailing 44% and men's apparel 23%.

Brandnames of Products and Services:

Aggies	*shoe stores*
Agnew	*shoe stores*
Anne Klein	*hosiery*
Bell Bros.	*shoe stores*
Big Val	*footwear*
Brittain's	*family shoe stores*
Camp	*hosiery*
Cedar Crest	*men's footwear*
Chaps by Ralph Lauren	*men's apparel*
Charm Step	*women's footwear*
Christian Dior	*hosiery*
Colours by Alexander Julian	*men's apparel*
Cover Girl	*women's shoe stores*
Dexter	*shoe stores*
Dominion	*footwear*
Donald Brooks	*men's apparel*
D'Orsay	*hosiery*
Easy Street	*women's footwear*
Factory to You	*shoe store*
Fantasy	*women's footwear*
Flagg Bros.	*shoe stores*
Foot Scene	*shoe stores*
Fortune	*men's footwear*
Fortune	*men's shoes*
Frank Bros.	*shoe stores*
Greif	*men's apparel*
Guarantee	*shoe stores*
Hardy	*shoe stores*
Innes Shoe Stores	*shoe stores*
Jarman	*men's footwear and shoe stores*
John Ritchie	*men's footwear*
Johnston & Murphy	*men's footwear and shoe stores*
Jordache	*hosiery*
Kilgour, French & Stanbury	*men's apparel*
Lanvin	*men's apparel*
Laredo	*men's footwear*
Mitre	*athletic footwear*
Oleg Cassini	*men's apparel*
Perry Ellis	*men's apparel*
Phoenix	*men's apparel*
Polo University	*men's apparel*
Rafael	*men's apparel*
Reward/Dexter	*shoe stores*
Sommer & Kaufman	*shoe stores*
Valmart	*shoe stores*
Vogue	*women's footwear*
Wrangler	*boots*

Georgia-Pacific Corp.

133 Peachtree Street, N.E.
Atlanta, GA 30303
(404) 521-4000

Chief Executive Officer: T. Marshall Hahn
1984 Annual Sales Volume: 6,682M
1984 Shares Outstanding: 103,000,000
Shareholders: 79,000
Exchange: NY
Symbol: GP
Corporate History: Georgia-Pacific was incorporated in 1927 as the Georgia-Hardwood Lumber Company and is a leading manufacturer of building products, pulp, paper and related chemicals, with more than 220 manufacturing facilities throughout the United States. Georgia-Pacific's building products division manufactures products including lumber, plywood, oriented strand board, waferboard, roofing felt, shingles, and gypsum wallboard. Georgia-Pacific is also one of the nation's largest suppliers of household paper products including paper toweling, napkins, and bath and facial tissue.
Brandnames of Products and Services:

Aqua Chem	*pool chemicals*
Cormatic	*soap, towel and toilet paper, and dispensers*
Coronet	*bath tissue, towels, napkins, facial tissue*
Delta	*toweling, napkins, toilet paper, facial tissue*
Georgia Pacific	*building products and pool maintenance equipment, consumer and commercial paper products*
Hudson	*toweling, napkins, toilet paper, facial tissue*
MD	*bath tissue*
Mr. Big	*toweling, napkins, toilet paper*

Gerber Products Co.

445 State St.
Fremont, Mich. 49412
(616) 928-2000

Chief Executive Officer: Carl G. Smith
1984 Annual Sales Volume: 805M
1984 Shares Outstanding: 13,640,586
Shareholders: 11,291
Exchange: NY
Symbol: GEB
Corporate History: The company was incorporated in 1901 as Fremont Canning Co., and its present title was adopted in 1941. It is a leading producer of baby foods and other baby care products, and holds 70% of the United States baby food market. Gerber was launched as a fruit and vegetable canner and first tried canning strained vegetables for children in 1928. Thirteen years later that became the company's sole enterprise. In 1967, the company began to diversify with term life insurance, offered to young parents recruited from Gerber's own mailing list. In 1983, it purchased Weather Tamer Inc., Skyland International Corp., Blue Arrow Inc., and Wooltex International. Weather Tamer produces a line of children's outerwear under the Weather Tamer brand, Skyland markets playwear and hosiery for children under the Buster Brown trademark, Blue arrow is a common motor carrier, Wooltex produces fabric wall hangings, crib items and other soft goods. In 1984, Gerber purchased Bates Nitewear Co., which produces pajamas and nightgowns for children.
Brandnames of Products and Services:

Babygro	*infant stretchwear*
Beginner Flakes	*dry baby food*
Bilt-Rite	*children's furniture*
Buster Brown	*apparel*
Century	*children's furniture*
Gerber	*baby clothes*
Gerber	*baby foods*
Gerber Children's Centers	*infant wear and furnishing stores*
Gerber Life Insurance	
Hankscraft	*humidifiers and nurses*
Nod-A-Way	*children's furniture*
NUK	*nipples*
Nursery Originals	*children's furniture*
Onesies	*apparel*
Reliance	*infant accessories*
Weather Tamer	*apparel*
Wooltex	*children's furniture*

Giant Food Inc.

6300 Sheriff Rd.
Landover, MD 20785
(301) 341-4100

Chief Executive Officer: I. Cohen
1984 Annual Sales Volume: 1,957M

1984 Shares Outstanding: 14,506,165
Shareholders: 5,400
Exchange: AM
Symbol: GFSA
Corporate History: The company, incorporated in 1935 as Giant Food Center, adopted its present title in 1957. In 1984, it operated 132 supermarkets including 1 gourmet store, 30 Pants Corral boutiques. Giant Food Inc. is the leading chain in the Washington, D.C. metropolitan area with about 40% of the market share. The company employs 19,000 people and operates stores, including 74 pharmacies, in Virginia, Maryland and the District of Columbia.
Brandnames of Products and Services:

Aunt Nellie's	*grocery store*
Dairy Kiss	*frozen foods*
Garden Kiss	*frozen foods*
Giant	*grocery store*
Giant Foods	*supermarkets*
Heidi	*bakery goods*
Kiss	*frozen foods*
Orchard Kiss	*frozen foods*
Pants Corral	*boutiques*
Renee	*Hosiery*

C. R. Gibson Co.

32 Knight St.
Norwalk, CT 06856
(203) 847-4543

Chief Executive Officer: Robert G. Bowman
1984 Annual Sales Volume: 28M
1984 Shares Outstanding: 1,597,971
Shareholders: NA
Exchange: OTC
Symbol: GIBS
Corporate History: The company, incorporated in 1969, produces a wide variety of gift and stationery items. The products are distributed through approximately 25,000 active accounts, most of which are retail outlets.
Brandnames of Products and Services:

C.R. Gibson	*gift and stationery items*

Gillette Co.

Prudential Tower Building
Boston, MA 02199
(617) 421-7000

Chief Executive Officer: C.M. Mockler, Jr.
1984 Annual Sales Volume: 2,288M
1984 Shares Outstanding: 30,822,171
Shareholders: 28,100
Exchange: NY
Symbol: GS
Corporate History: The Gillette Company, founded in 1901, is an international consumer products firm engaged in the development, manufacture, and sale of products for personal care or use. Major lines include blades and razors, toiletries and cosmetics, writing instruments and office products, and Braun electric shavers and small appliances. Manufacturing operations are conducted at 53 facilities in 24 countries and products are distrubted through wholesalers, retailers and agents in over 200 contries and territories. Gillette employs 31,400 persons, almost three-quarters of them outside the United States.
Brandnames of Products and Services:

Accu-point	*pens*
Adorn	*hair-care products*
Atra	*razor*
Atra Plus	*razors & cartridges*
Braun	*electric appliances*
Brush Plus	*shaving brush & cream*
Daisy	*women's disposable shavers*
Dry Idea	*deodorant*
Dry Look	*hair-grooming products*
Dupont	*cigarette lighters*
EarthBorn	*hair-care products*
Flair	*writing instruments*
Foamy	*shaving cream*
Foamy Gel	*shaving cream*
Gillette	*razors and blades*
Good News	*men's disposable shavers*
Jafra	*cosmetics*
Liquid Paper	*typewriter correction fluid*
Paper Mate	*writing instruments*
Right Guard	*deodorant*
Silkience	*hair conditioner*
Soft & Dri	*deodorants*
Tame	*creme rinse*
Techmatic	*razors*
Toni Home Permanents	*hair-care products*
Trac II	*razors*
White Rain	*hair care products*

Write Bros.	*pens*

Gino's Inc.

215 West Church Rd.
King of Prussia, Pa. 19406
(215) 768-4000

Chief Executive Officer:	L.C. Fischer
Exchange:	NY
Symbol:	GNO

Corporate History: The company, incorporated in 1960, operates fast-food restaurants in the mid-Atlantic states.

Brandnames of Products and Services:

Gino's	*restaurants*
Rustler Steak Houses	*restaurants*

Glenmore Distilleries Co.

Citizens Plaza
Louisville, KY 40202
(502) 589-0130

Chief Executive Officer:	James Thompson
1984 Annual Sales Volume:	196M
1984 Shares Outstanding:	2,049,497
Shareholders:	1,184
Exchange:	AM
Symbol:	GDSB

Corporate History: The company was established in 1875 and incorporated in 1943. It distills and bottles spirits and wines. Glenmore products are distributed in 50 states and 49 foreign countries.

Brandnames of Products and Services:

Amaretto di Saronno	*liqueur*
Balfour Cream	*sherry*
Corbett Canyon Vineyard	*wines*
Desmond & Duff 12-year-old	*scotch*
Expresso Coffee	*liqueur*
Felipe II Spanish	*brandy*
Gavilan	*tequila*
Glenmore	*gin and vodka*
Kentucky Tavern	*whiskey*
Mandarine Napoleon	*Liqueur*
Mr. Boston	*distilled spirits & bar guide*
Old Thompson	*whiskey*
Shadow Creek Sparkling	*wines*
Torre Dei Conti Asti Spumante	*wines*
Yellowstone	*whiskey*

Glosser Bros. Inc.

Franklin & Locust Sts.
Johnstown, PA 15901
(814) 536-6633

Chief Executive Officer:	L.J. Black
1984 Annual Sales Volume:	253M
1984 Shares Outstanding:	2,263,545
Shareholders:	2,000
Exchange:	AM
Symbol:	GEE

Corporate History: The company incorporated in 1946 to succeed a business founded in 1906. It operates combination department stores and supermarkets in Western Pennsylvania, Maryland and West Virginia.

Brandnames of Products and Services:

Dollar	*bargain stores*
Gee Bee Department Store	*and supermarkets*
Glosser Bros.	*department stores*
Warehouse	*outlet stores*

Godfrey Co.

1200 W. Sunset Dr.
Waukesha, WI 53187
(414) 542-9311

Chief Executive Officer:	Robert F. Norris
1984 Annual Sales Volume:	534M
1984 Shares Outstanding:	2,414,897
Shareholders:	2,028
Exchange:	OTC
Symbol:	GDFY

Corporate History: The company, incorporated in 1889 as E.R. Godfrey & Sons Co., distributes grocery and related products through a chain of 84 Sentry supermarkets and three Sun Foods Super Warehouse stores. The company operates 42 of the Sentry stores and 42 are operated by independent retailers render agreements with the company. The company also supplies independent grocers with goods and services through its distribution centers.

Brandnames of Products and Services:

Crestwood Bakery	*baked goods*
Jay's	*liquor store*
Jim Handy	*Hardware store*
Red & White	*food products*
Sentry	*food and home products*
Sentry Foods	*supermarkets and drug stores*
Sun	*food products*
Sun Foods	*warehouse store*
Sunrise	*canned food products*

Goldblatt Brothers Inc.

1615 West Chicago Ave.
Chicago, IL 60622
(312) 421-5300

Chief Executive Officer: William Hellman
1984 Annual Sales Volume: 62M
1984 Shares Outstanding: 5,950,254
Shareholders: 3,335
Exchange: MID
Symbol: NA

Corporate History: The company, incorporated in 1928, operates more than 30 department stores, furniture outlets and home center stores in the Midwest. In 1984, it acquired a majority interest in Milgram. Kagan Corporation, a retail shoe company, which operates 105 shoe stores.

Brandnames of Products and Services:

Barker Bros.	*home furnishings*
Capezio	*shoes*
Colby's	*home furnishings*
Florsheim	*shoes*
Freeman	*shoes*
Goldblatt's	*department stores*
Home Centers	*home improvement stores*
Huffman-Koos	*home furnishings*
Naturalizer	*shoes*
Red Cross	*shoes*

Golden Enterprises Inc.

2101 Magnolia Ave. South
Suite 212
Birmingham, AL 35205
(205) 326-6101

Chief Executive Officer: Sloan Y. Bashinsky Sr
1984 Annual Sales Volume: 99M
1984 Shares Outstanding: 7,321,686
Shareholders: 1,600
Exchange: OTC
Symbol: GLDC

Corporate History: The company incorporated in 1967 as Golden Flake Inc. to succeed a business founded in 1946 as Magic City Food Products. Its present title was adopted in 1977. The company makes a variety of snack food products marketed in the South and manufactures and distributes bolts and screws for wholesale and industrial use and operates an advertising agency.

Brandnames of Products and Services:

Golden Flake	*snack food products*

Golden Nugget Inc.

129 E. Fremont St.
Las Vegas, NV 89101
(702) 385-7111

Chief Executive Officer: Stephen A. Wynn
1984 Annual Sales Volume: 385M
1984 Shares Outstanding: 32,997,348
Shareholders: 17,861
Exchange: NY
Symbol: GNGP

Corporate History: The company, incorporated in 1949, operates two casinos and hotels in Las Vegas, Nevada and one in Atlantic City, New Jersey. The company also operates a fleet of intercity buses in the northeastern U.S. partly as an adjunct to its Atlantic City casino-hotel operation.

Brandnames of Products and Services:

Golden Nugget	*bus line*
Golden Nugget Casino-Hotels	

Golden West Homes

1308 E. Wakeham Ave.
Santa Ana, CA 92705
(714) 835-4200

Chief Executive Officer: Harry Karsten, Jr.
1984 Annual Sales Volume: 72M
1984 Shares Outstanding: 3,374,640
Shareholders: 1,300
Exchange: AM
Symbol: GWH

Corporate History: The company incorporated in 1965 as Golden West Trailers Inc. and adopted its present title in 1977. It makes mobile homes. The firm has also begun developing mobile home communities with the purchase of land in Palm Desert, California.

Brandnames of Products and Services:

Aquarius	*mobile homes*
Calypso	*mobile homes*
Country Estate	*mobile homes*
Golden Mansion	*mobile homes*
Golden West	*mobile homes*
Key Biscayne	*mobile homes*
Key West	*mobile homes*
Kingston	*mobile homes*
Somerset	*mobile homes*
Sunnybrook	*mobile homes*
Villa West	*mobile homes*

B.F. Goodrich Co.

500 South Main St.
Akron, OH 44318
(216) 374-3985

Chief Executive Officer: John D. Ong
1984 Annual Sales Volume: 3,437M
1984 Shares Outstanding: 22,407,236
Shareholders: 20,721
Exchange: NY
Symbol: GR

Corporate History: Founded in 1870, B.F. Goodrich is the oldest of America's rubber companies. During its history the company was involved in a number of innovations. It was the first producer of auto tires, commercial tubeless tires and the first American firm to introduce the radial tire. Goodrich was also a pioneer in the manufacture of synthetic rubber during World War II. Today the company manufactures and sells a broad line of plastics, specialty chemicals, tires, industrial rubber goods and products for the construction, mining and aerospace and defense industries, which are distributed in over 100 countries throughout the world.

Brandnames of Products and Services:

B. F. Goodrich	*tires and rubber products*

Goodyear Tire & Rubber Co.

1144 E. Market St
Akron, OH 44316
(216) 796-2121

Chief Executive Officer: Robert E. Mercer
1984 Annual Sales Volume: 10,200M
1984 Shares Outstanding: 92,500,000
Shareholders: 75,619
Exchange: NY
Symbol: GT

Corporate History: The Goodyear Tire & Rubber Co., incorporated in 1898, is the world's largest tire and rubber company and leads the U.S. original equipment and replacement tire market. Tires account for 60% of its business. The company manufactures products in 57 plants in the U.S. and 45 plants in 27 other countries and operates 7 rubber plantations, a resort hotel and a government-owned uranium enrichment plant. Goodyear manufactures and sells a broad spectrum of metal, rubber and plastic products for the transportation industry and various industrial and consumer markets, synthetic rubber, chemical and numerous high technology products for aerospace, defense and nuclear energy applications. Goodyear operates more than 2,000 other facilities around the world for the distribution and sale of its products. Goodyear also engages in oil and gas transmission, exploration and production activities in 14 states, primarily through the Celeron group of companies acquired in 1983.

Brandnames of Products and Services:

Goodyear	*tires, rubber, automotive accessories*
Neolite Soles	*shoe products*

Gordon Jewelry Corp.

820 Fannin St.
Houston, TX 77002
(713) 222-8080

Chief Executive Officer: Daniel P. Gordon
1984 Annual Sales Volume: 506M
1984 Shares Outstanding: 11,765,301
Shareholders: 2,466
Exchange: NY
Symbol: GOR

Corporate History: The company was incorporated in 1957. It operates one of the larger retail jewelry chains in the United States through 660 stores in 44 states and Puerto Rico. The company's principal lines of business include contemporary jewelry stores, traditional jewelry stores and catalog-show-room stores. Operations of the company's leased fine jewelry departments were discontinued in 1984.

Brandnames of Products and Services:

Citizens	*catalog-showroom stores*
Daniel's	*jewelry stores*
D.P. Paul	*jewelry stores*
Feder's Jewelers	*jewelry stores*

General Products	*catalog-showroom stores*
Gordon's	*jewelry stores*
J. Herbert Hall	*jewelry stores*
Lawton Jewelers	*jewelry stores*
Leonard Krower & Son	*catalog showroom stores*
Linz Bros.	*jewelry stores*
Mermod, Jaccard & King	*jewelry stores*
Rost Jewelers	*jewelry stores*
Sweeny & Co. Jewelers	*jewelry stores*
United Jewelers & Distributors	*catalog showrooms*

Gould Inc.

10 Gould Center
Rolling Meadows, Ill. 60008
(312) 640-4000

Chief Executive Officer: W.T. Ylvisaker
Exchange: NY
Symbol: GLD

Corporate History: Gould was incorporated in 1928 as the successor to the National Lead Battery Co., which began making storage batteries in 1918. Today it makes electrical products for industry as well as batteries for the consumer market.

Brandnames of Products and Services:

Gould	*battery systems*

W.R. Grace & Co.

1114 Avenue of the Americas
New York, NY 10036-7794
(212) 819-5500

Chief Executive Officer: J. Peter Grace
1984 Annual Sales Volume: 6,728M
1984 Shares Outstanding: 49,502,157
Shareholders: 35,752
Exchange: NY
Symbol: GRA

Corporate History: The company was founded in 1854 and incorporated in 1899 as a small banking and shipping enterprise. Today it is a major international chemical concern with interests in natural resources and selective consumer products and services. In 1984 56% of the company's operating income came from the chemical division, 17% from natural resources, 20% from restaurants and retailing and 7% from general business. As of 1984 the Company operated 582 restaurants in 34 states and 653 retail units in 38 states. The retail units include 325 "do-it-yourself" home improvement centers, 115 sporting goods and sports apparel stores, 121 stores featuring leather outerware, 82 jewelry stores and 10 stores selling western apparel and accessories. Grace operates in 47 states and 42 foreign countries.

Brandnames of Products and Services:

Angels	*home improvement stores*
Baxter's	*restaurants*
Berman's	*Western leisure apparel*
Bristol Bar & Grill	*restaurants*
Carrows	*restaurants*
Cashways/Allwoods Building Centers	*home improvement stores*
Channel	*home center stores*
Coco's	*coffee shops*
Del Taco Mexican Cafe	*Mexican restaurants*
El Torito	*Mexican restaurants*
Gladstone's	*restaurants*
Handy City	*home improvement stores*
Handy Dan	*home improvement stores*
Herman's World of Sporting Goods	*sporting goods stores*
Houlihan's Old Place	*restaurants*
House Works!	*home improvement stores*
J.B. Robinson	*jewelers*
La Fiesta	*restaurants*
Ole's	*home improvement stores*
Orchard Supply Hardware	*hardware stores*
Plankhouse	*restaurants*
Que Pasa	*restaurants*
Reuben's	*restaurants*
Shepler's	*Western leisure apparel*
TJ Applebee's	*restaurants*
Total Sports	*discount sports apparel*
Warehouse Club	*discount store*

Grand Auto Inc.

7200 Edgewater Dr.
Oakland, CA 94621
(415) 568-6500

Chief Executive Officer: I.E. Krantzman
1984 Annual Sales Volume: 154M
1984 Shares Outstanding: 2,996,865
Shareholders: 527

Exchange: AM
Symbol: GAI
Corporate History: The company, founded in 1946, incorporated in 1953, is based in California. It is the largest automotive accessary retailer in the Western United States. It operates 85 retail automotive accessory stores in California and Nevada with retail/wholesale interests in the Pacific Northwest.
Brandnames of Products and Services:

Cordovan	*tires*
Grand Auto	*automotive accessary stores*
Grand Champion	*motor oil*
Grand Custom	*seat covers - paint*
Grand Prix	*batteries, oil & air filters*
Grand Security	*locks*
Medalist	*rebuilt parts*

Grand Central Inc.

2233 S. Third East
Salt Lake City, Utah 84115
(801) 486-7611

Chief Executive Officer: D.A. Mackey
Exchange: AM
Symbol: GC
Corporate History: The company, founded in 1928 and incorporated in 1968, is a Utah-based retail chain. It operates stores in six Western states.
Brandnames of Products and Services:

Grand Central	*department stores*

Gray Drug Stores Inc.

666 Euclid Ave.
Cleveland, Ohio 44114
(216) 696-2070

Chief Executive Officer: J.A. Weinberger
Exchange: NY
Symbol: GRY
Corporate History: The company incorporated in 1928 as Weinberger Drug Stores Inc. It operates drugstores in southeastern Florida and Ohio, and discount department stores primarily in the Midwest. In 1978 it began diversifying into the apparel field with its Fashion Fair boutiques. By the end of 1980 it had over 50 in selected states. Gray is phasing out its Scoops ice cream parlor chain. In fiscal 1980 drug outlets accounted for 42.3% of sales and discount department stores 57.7%.

Brandnames of Products and Services:

Drug Fair	*drugstores*
Fashionfair	*apparel boutiques*
Gray Drug	*stores*
Picture Plaza	*photofinishing stores*
Rink's	*discount department stores*
Scoops	*ice cream parlors*
Soup 'r Scoops	*restaurants*

Great Atlantic & Pacific Tea Co. Inc.

2 Paragon Drive
Montvale, NJ 07645
(201) 573-9700

Chief Executive Officer: James Wood
1984 Annual Sales Volume: 5,878M
1984 Shares Outstanding: 37,523,677
Shareholders: 24,746
Exchange: NY
Symbol: GAP
Corporate History: The company, incorporated in 1925, ranks seventh in volume of domestic sales among the retail food chains in the US. The company operates five types of retail outlets, namely, traditional A&P supermarkets (860 stores), Family Mart supermarket-drug combination stores (22 stores), Super Fresh Food Markets (57 stores), Super Plus Warehouse Stores (8 stores), and Kohl's Food Stores (75 stores). In 1984 the company acquired 18 supermarkets from Panty Pride Inc., located in Viriginia. The company also maintains facilities which support its retail operations, including distribution centers, four coffee roasting plants and three bakeries.
Brandnames of Products and Services:

Ann Page	*food products*
A & P	*supermarkets*
A & P	*food products*
Bokar	*coffee*
Eight O Clock	*coffee*
Family Mart	*food and drug stores*
Jane Parker	*bakery products*
Kohl's Food Stores	*supermarkets*
Marvel	*canned foods*
Plus Discount	*food stores and food products*
Super Fresh Food Markets	*supermarkets*
Super Plus Warehouse Stores	*discount supermarkets*

Great Northern Nekoosa Corp.

75 Prospect St.
Stamford, CT 06904
(203) 359-4000

Chief Executive Officer: William R. Laidig
1984 Annual Sales Volume: 1,873M
1984 Shares Outstanding: 25,043,190
Shareholders: 17,896
Exchange: NY
Symbol: GNN

Corporate History: The company was incorporated in 1898 as Northern Development Co. Its name was changed to Great Northern Paper Co. in 1899, and to its present title in 1970. GNN is a major producer of pulp and paper. Pulp and paper manufacture, paper distribution and envelope manufacturing accounted for about 95% of slaes in 1984. GNN is the world's largest producer of paper for the office copier. GNN is also in the lumber and plywood business, and owns 2.9 million acres of timberland.

Brandnames of Products and Services:

Mail-Well Envelope	*envelope*
Nekoosa Paper Products	*office supplies*
Northern Tissues	*bathroom tissue*
Wisco	*envelope*

Greenman Bros. Inc.

105 Price Parkway
Farmingdale, NY 11735
(516) 293-5300

Chief Executive Officer: Bernard Greenman
1984 Annual Sales Volume: 173M
1984 Shares Outstanding: 3,771,558
Shareholders: 793
Exchange: AM
Symbol: GMN

Corporate History: Incorporated in 1946, Greenman Bros. Inc. is engaged in wholesale and retail distribution of toys, games and related products such as hobby kits and juvenile furniture; houseware products consisting of cookware, kitchen gadgets and utensils, cleaning aids, household chemicals and garden supplies; and stationery products. The company conducts distribution operations from four distribution centers located in New York, Florida, New Jersey and Georgia. It is one the largest wholesale distributors of toys, games, housewares and stationery products in the eastern United States. It operates 78 toy stores. In 1984, toys, games and related products accounted for 69% of sales, housewares 28% and stationery products 3%.

Brandnames of Products and Services:

Playland	*toy stores*
Playworld	*toy stores*

Greyhound Corp.

Greyhound Tower
Phoenix, AZ 85077
(602) 248-4000

Chief Executive Officer: John W. Teets
1984 Annual Sales Volume: 2,500M
1984 Shares Outstanding: 48,000,000
Shareholders: 93,500
Exchange: NY
Symbol: G

Corporate History: Greyhound was founded in 1925 as a merger of several midwestern bus companies. It gradually expanded its operation until it controlled almost half of the nation's interstate bus routes. In 1962 it branched into leasing ships and airplanes. Several years later it acquired Armour. Today it is a conglomerate with interests in transportation, bus manufacturing, car rentals, the food service industry and consumer products. Greyhound is the second largest money order firm in the nation. The U.S. Postal Service is first.

Brandnames of Products and Services:

Appian Way	*pizza*
Armour-Dial	*household products*
Armour Handcrafts	
Armour Star	*processed meats*
Brewster Transportation	*tours and sightseeing, Canada*
Bruce	*floor-care products*
California Parlor Car Tours Co.	*tours and sightseeing*
Greyhound Bus Service	*bus service*
Greyhound Group Travel	*tours*
Manpower	*men's toiletries*
Parson's	*ammonia*
Tone	*soap*

Gross Telecasting Inc.

2820 E. Saginaw St.
Lansing, Mich. 48701
(517) 372-8282

Chief Executive Officer: J.H. Gross
Exchange: AM
Symbol: GGG
Corporate History: The company incorporated in 1937 as WJIM Inc. and adopted its present title in 1955. It owns and operates one radio and two television stations in the Midwest.
Brandnames of Products and Services:

WJIM-TV and AM/FM	*radio station, Lansing, Mich.*
WKBT-TV	*station, La Crosse, Wis.*

Grow Group Inc.

Pan Am Building
200 Park Ave.
New York, NY 10166
(212) 599-4400

Chief Executive Officer: Russell Banks
1984 Annual Sales Volume: 254M
1984 Shares Outstanding: 9,907,000
Shareholders: 7,421
Exchange: NY
Symbol: GRO
Corporate History: The company, incorporated in 1950 as Metropolitan Communication Corp., changed its name to Grow Chemical in 1964, and adopted its present title in 1979. It manufactures paints and coatings.
Brandnames of Products and Services:

Alumigrip	*urethane coating*
Ameritone	*paints*
Awlgrip	*urethane coating*
Boysen	*paints*
Cello	*floor care products*
Color Key	*color selection system*
Commander	*household cleaning products*
Devoe	*paints*
Gladiator	*household cleaning products*
Gold Label	*floor finish*
Koro-Seal	*paints*
Like Magic	*household cleaning products & plant insectides*
Mirrolac	*paints*
Pantaloon	*cleaning and floor polishes*
Plasolux	*paints and varnishes*
Regency House	*paints*
Speed Rex	*paints and varnishes*
Trewax	*floor care products*
Tru-Glaze	*paints*
Wonder-Tones	*paints*

Grumman Corp.

Bethpage, NY 11714
(516) 575-0574

Chief Executive Officer: John C. Bierwirth
1984 Annual Sales Volume: 2,558M
1984 Shares Outstanding: 28,669,950
Shareholders: 15,100
Exchange: NY
Symbol: GQ
Corporate History: Grumman Corp. was organized in 1929 under the name Grumman Aircraft Engineering Corp. The activities of the company fall into three industry segments: aerospace, including the design and production of military aircraft, space systems, and commercial aircraft components and subassemblies; information and financial services, including electronic data processing services, financing of affiliate and outside products, and real estate and insurance services; and commercial products, non-aerospace, including fabrication and sale of aluminum truck bodies, fire trucks, fiberglass yachts and aluminum boats.
Brandnames of Products and Services:

Grumman	*pleasure boats*

GTE Corp.

One Stamford Forum
Stamford, CT 06904
(203) 965-2000

Chief Executive Officer: Theodore F. Brophy
1984 Annual Sales Volume: 14,547M
1984 Shares Outstanding: 204,727,145
Shareholders: 459,000
Exchange: NY
Symbol: GTE
Corporate History: GTE has three core business: telecommunications, lighting products and precision

materials. In telecommunications, the corporation provides local telephone service in portions of 31 states, two Canadian provinces and the Dominican Republic. It also offers long-distance telephone service and worldwide data communications services. In addition, GTE has subsidiaries which offer financing and insurance services to GTE operating companies.

Brandnames of Products and Services:

GTE	*local telephone service, equipment*
Spacenet	*satellite communications*
Sprint	*long-distance telephone service*
Sylvania	*lighting products*
Telenet	*nationwide data communications network, including Telemail and TeleMessager*

Gulf Oil Corp.

Gulf Building
Pittsburgh, Pa. 15230
(412) 263-5000

Chief Executive Officer: J. McAfee
Exchange: NY
Symbol: GO

Corporate History: Gulf was founded in 1901 and taken over by the Mellon family in 1907. Beginning in the 1920s it began exploring for and exploiting Middle Eastern oil. It developed its major base in Kuwait during the 1940s. In the next two decades Gulf derived two-thirds of its profits from foreign oil, chiefly from Kuwait. Gulf's dependence on Middle Eastern oil made it susceptible to the international political turmoil of the 1970s. It was the hardest hit of the large companies by the 1973 oil embargo. In addition, Gulf was hurt by Kuwait's nationalization of its oil industry. The company is not an Aramco partner and thus pays more for oil than Exxon or Mobil. In an effort to offset this it has begun tapping oil in the Gulf of Mexico and the West. Today it gets 54% of its oil from the United States. It is the seventh largest crude oil producer in the United States and ranks as the nation's fifth largest producer of natural gas. It sells gasoline through 17,000 service stations in 29 states.

Brandnames of Products and Services:

Gulf Oil & Gas Products

Gulf + Western Industries Inc.

One Gulf + Western Plaza
New York, NY 10023-9960
(212) 333-7000

Chief Executive Officer: Martin S. Davis
1984 Annual Sales Volume: 4,200M
1984 Shares Outstanding: 70,039,367
Shareholders: 50,000
Exchange: NY
Symbol: GW

Corporate History: Gulf & Western was founded in 1958 by Charles Bluhdorn, an Austrian immigrant. Its initial business was manufacturing auto replacement parts. During the next 20 years it followed a policy of aggressive acquisitions, scooping up more than 100 companies. Today Gulf+Western Industries, Inc. provides a broad range of products and services, principally to consumers, through four groups: entertainment and communications, publishing and information resources, financial services, and consumer and industrial products. Among G+W's major operating units are Paramount Pictures (motion pictures and television production and distribution); Madison Square Garden (sports and entertainment); Simon & Schuster (publishing and information resources); Associates Corporation of North America (consumer and commercial finance); Kayser-Roth (apparel and hosiery); Simmons (bedding and home furnishings); A.P.S. (automotive parts distribution); and Gulf+Western Manufacturing (products for automotive, electrical/electronic and construction industries).

Brandnames of Products and Services:

ACC	*books - medical*
Albert van Luit	*apparel*
Alex	*books*
Appleton-Century-Crofts	*books - medical*
APS	*automotive parts distribution*
Archway	*publishing house*
Arco	*books*
Associates of N. America	*consumer financing*
Barrington Publications	*periodicals*
Bay Club	*sport apparel*
BBP	*information*
Beautyrest	*mattress*
BIG A	*automotive parts distribution*
Bloomcraft	*home furnishing fabrics*

Blue Book of Pension Funds	*books - information*
Bookthrift	*remainder publishing*
Bookware	*computerbooks*
BPC Design	*periodicals*
Brady	*books*
Brentwood Publishing Corp.	*periodicals*
Bureau of Business Practice	*information*
Catalina	*apparel*
Champion	*men's apparel*
Cole of California	*apparel*
Comfort Stride by No Nonsense	*hosiery*
Companion Guides	*travel publications*
Cornerstone Library	*publishing house*
Deltak	*information & training*
Easy to Be Me	*hosiery*
EEE - Eastern Economy Editions	*international books*
ERC - Executive Reports	*information*
Erisa Benefit Funds	*books - information*
Esquire	*hosiery*
Excello	*men's apparel*
Famous Music Corp.	*publishing house*
Fireside	*publishing house*
Flotation	*water beds*
Frommer-Pasmantier	*publishing house*
Going Places	*apparel*
Greeff	*fabrics*
Her Majesty	*children's apparel*
Hide-a-Bed	*sofas*
IBD - International Book Distributors	*international books*
IBP - Institute for Business Planning	*information*
Insight Guides	*travel publications*
International Bureau of Software Test	*software testing*
Interwoven	*socks*
Jiffies	*slippers*
J.K. Lasser	*tax publications*
John Newcombe	*sports apparel*
John Weitz	*men's shirts*
Julian Messner	*publishing house*
Katzenbach & Warren	*wall coverings*
Kayser Roth	*women's apparel*
Korg	*musical instruments*
Leg Looks	*hosiery*
Linden Press	*publishing house*
Little Simon	*children's publications*
Long Shadow Books	*trade paperbacks*
Madison Square Garden	*New York, N.Y.*
Miss Universe-pageants	
Mojud	*women's apparel*
Monarch	*publishing house*
MSG	*cable broadcasting*
Nazareth	*sleepwear*
New World Dictionaries	*reference publications*
New York Knickerbockers	*basketball team*
New York Rangers	*hockey team*
No Nonsense	*panty hose*
NYIF • New York Institute of Finance	*seminars & training*
Pacers	*apparel*
Pandora	*women's apparel*
Paramount Pictures & TV entertainment	
Parker	*books*
PC Apprentice	*computerbooks & software*
PHalarope Books	*nature books*
PHA - Prentice-Hall of America	*international books*
PHB - Editora Prentice-Hall do Brasil	*international books*
PHH - Prentice-Hall Hispanoamericana	*international books*
PHINet	*information*
P-H Information Services Division	*books - information*
PHI - Prentice-Hall International	*international books*
Pocket Books	*publishing house*
Poseidon	*publishing house*
Prentice-Hall	*books, software, information*
Prentice-Hall Media	*books, audio/visual*
Reston	*books*
Reward Books	*books*

RSI Logo - Resource Systems International	*information, training*
Sandcastle	*apparel*
Selig	*home furnishing*
Simmons	*matresses and furniture*
Simon & Schuster	*publishing house*
Sock Sense	*men's hosiery*
Software Tenforty	*tax preparation*
A Spectrum Book	*books*
Star Trek	*specialty retailing*
Steeple Books	*religious books*
Summit	*publishing house*
Supp-Hose	*hosiery*
Thonet	*home furnishing*
Touchstone	*publishing house*
Treehouse Press	*children's books*
Ultra Sense by No Nonsense	
Vest Pocket Guides	*how-to-books*
Wallaby	*publishing house*
Wanderer Books	*publishing house*
Washington Square Press	*publishing house*

Hammermill Paper Co.

1540 East Lake Rd
Erie, PA 16533
(814) 456-8811

Chief Executive Officer: Albert F. Duval
1984 Annual Sales Volume: 1,855M
1984 Shares Outstanding: 14,009,550
Shareholders: 6,801
Exchange: NY
Symbol: HML

Corporate History: The company was incorporated in 1916 to succeed to the business of a company of the same name founded in Erie, Pennsylvania in 1898. The company makes fine writing papers; engages in the manufacture and sale of industrial and packaging papers; converts paper into envelopes and other products; and produces hardwood and softwood lumber. As of 1984, Hammermill had 33 manufacturing or processing locations and 96 distribution facilities withing the United States.

Brandnames of Products and Services:

Beckett Cover	*office paper supplies*
Buckeye Cover	*office paper supplies*
Hammermill Bond and Copier	*office paper supplies*
Hammermill Paper Products	*office paper supplies*
Strathmore Bond	*office paper supplies*

Hampton Industries Inc.

501 E. Caswell St.
P.O. Box 614
Kinston, NC 28502-0614
(919) 527-8011

Chief Executive Officer: David Fuchs
1984 Annual Sales Volume: 163M
1984 Shares Outstanding: 2,790,555
Shareholders: 601
Exchange: AS
Symbol: HAI

Corporate History: Hampton, a North Carolina corporation, is the successor of several predecessor corporations, the first of which was in corporated in 1925 in the state of New York under the name of Hampton Shirt Co. It adopted its present name in 1973. The company is engaged in the manufacture and selling of wearing apparel.

Brandnames of Products and Services:

Hampton Girl	*wearing apparel*
J.G. Hook for Boys	*boys wearing apparel*
J.G. Hook for Girls	*girls wearing apparel*
McGregor for Boys	*boys' shirts*
Sasson	*women's shirts*
Shirt Street	*women's shirts*

Hannaford Bros. Co.

145 Pleasant Hill Rd.
Scarborough, ME 04074
(207) 883-2911

Chief Executive Officer: James L. Moody, Jr.
1984 Annual Sales Volume: 707M
1984 Shares Outstanding: 5,366,814
Shareholders: 2,000
Exchange: AM
Symbol: HRD

Corporate History: The company is Northern New England's largest food retailer. Incorporated in 1902, it operates supermarkets and drug stores. In 1984 the company operated 68 supermarkets, 30 drug stores and 6 separate pharmacies within supermarkets in Maine, New Hampshire and Vermont. The company also makes wholesale sales to 28 other supermarkets.

Brandnames of Products and Services:

Bonnie Maid	*food products*
Martin's	*supermarkets*
Sampson's	*supermarkets*
Shop N Save	*supermarkets*
Sun Foods	*supermarkets*
Wellby Super Drugstores	

Harcourt Brace Jovanovich Inc.

Orlando, FL 32887
(305) 345-2000

Chief Executive Officer: William Jovanovich
1984 Annual Sales Volume: 713M
1984 Shares Outstanding: 9,825,859
Shareholders: 2,036
Exchange: NY
Symbol: ABJ
Corporate History: The company was founded in 1919 as Harcourt Brace & Co. It has published such distinguished authors as John Maynard Keynes, Sinclair Lewis and Carl Sandburg. Since 1960, it been publicly held. HBJ publishes textbooks and other materials, including software, for elementary and secondary schools and colleges; business and professional periodicals; scientific and medical books and journals; and general fiction and non ficition. It owns two book clubs and two VHF television stations. Its wholly owned subsidiary, Sea World Inc., operates three marine parks in conjuction with marine research. HBJ also owns an insurance underwriting company and several insurance agencies. HBJ's management counseling firm provides individual services to corporate executives and staffs.
Brandnames of Products and Services:

Academic Press	*publishing house*
Automotive Retailer Publishing	*business publications*
Bay Area Review Courses	
Bookhill	*publishing house*
Bystream	*publishing house*
Coronado	*publishers*
Dansville Press	*publishing house*
Davidson Printing Co.	
Drake Beam Morin Inc.	*career guidance firms*
F.A. Owen	*publishing house*
Grune & Stratton	*publishing house*
Harcourt Brace Jovanovich	*bookstores*
Harvest/HBJ	*publishing house*
Harvest Life	*insurance*
History Book Club	
Instructor Book Club	
Joh M. Riehle & Co. Inc.	*insurance*
Johnson Reprint	*publishing house*
Knox, Lent & Tucker Inc.	*insurance*
Kurt & Helen Wolff Books	*publishing house*
Law & Business Inc.	*publishing house*
Legal Times of Washington	*weekly newspaper*
Nebraska Farmer Co.	*magazine publishers*
Pyramid	*publishing house*
Sea World	*marine parks*
Sea World of Florida	*recreational facility*
Voyager/HBJ	*publishing house*
WDIO-TV	*station, Duluth, Minn.*
WIRT-TV	*station, Hibbing, Minn.*
Young Parent Book Club	

Hardwicke Companies Inc.

9 W. 57th St.
New York, N.Y. 10019
(212) 759-4650

Chief Executive Officer: C.H. Stein
Exchange: OTC
Symbol: HAWK
Corporate History: The company incorporated in 1968 as Lord Hardwicke Ltd., and adopted its present title in 1970. It operates restaurants, tax duty-free stores, tourist amusement parks and hotels. Hardwicke owns 50.25% of Ritz Associates which is managing the construction and operation of the Ritz Hotel-Casino in Atlantic City, N.J. In 1979 retail stores provided 48.5% of sales, restaurants 21.7%, resorts 17.3% and animal parks 12.5%.
Brandnames of Products and Services:

Ammex	*tax and duty-free stores*
Hardwicke Pubs	

Maxwell's Plum	*restaurant, Ghirardelli Square, San Francisco*
Ritz, The	*Atlantic City, N.J.*
Safety Harbor Spa	*health spa, Florida*
Samurai	*Japanese style steak houses*
Tavern-on-the-Green	*restaurant, New York City, NY*

Harper & Row Publishers Inc.

10 E. 53rd St.
New York, NY 10022
(212) 207-7000

Chief Executive Officer: B. Thomas
1984 Annual Sales Volume: 214M
1984 Shares Outstanding: 3,081,899
Shareholders: 3,500
Exchange: NY
Symbol: HPR

Corporate History: Harper & Row dates to 1817 when the four Harper brothers established a small publishing house, Harper & Bros. By the mid-nineteenth century it was the largest publishing firm in the world. Today it is the fourth largest publisher in the United States and the third largest publisher of medical material. In recent years Harper & Row has branched out into films, tapes and records.

Brandnames of Products and Services:

Ballinger	*publishing house*
Barnes & Noble	*publishing house*
Basic Books	*publishing house*
Harper & Row	*publishing house*
Lippincott	*medical publishing house*
Perennial	*publishing house*
Torchbook	*publishing house*

Harte-Hanks Communications Inc.

901 N.E. Loop 410
San Antonio, Texas 78209
(512) 828-8361

Chief Executive Officer: R.G. Marbut
Exchange: NY
Symbol: HHN

Corporate History: The company incorporated in 1970 as Harte-Hanks Newspapers and adopted its present title in 1977. It publishes newspapers and owns and operates radio and television stations. Its dailies are the only ones of general circulation published in the communities it serves. Newspaper operations account for 58% of total revenues.

Brandnames of Products and Services:

Basin Week	*San Angelo, Texas*
Bert's Bargain Bonanza	*Gatlinburg, Tenn.*
Branzo's Valley Review	*Bryan College Staion, Texas*
Caller	*Corpus Christi, Texas*
Coronado Journal	*San Diego, Calif.*
Courier-Democrat	*Russelville, Ark.*
Daily Citizen	*Searcy, Ark.*
Daily Leader	*Stuttgart, Ark.*
Daily Mail	*Anderson, S.C.*
Daily Record & Advertiser	*Malvern, Ark.*
Democrat & Advertiser	*Greenwood, Ark.*
Eagle	*Bryan College Station, Texas*
Echo	*Hamiltion, Ohio and Cincinnati, Ohio*
Express Progress	*Paris, Ark.*
Express	*Charleston, Ark.*
Fashion Showcase	*Dallas, Texas*
Gatlinburg Press	*Gatlingurg, Tenn.*
Greenwave	*Greenville, Texas*
Herald Banner	*Greenville, Texas*
Herald Republic	*Yakima, Wash.*
Herald	*Big Spring, Texas*
Herald	*Denison, Texas*
Home Buyers Guide	*Anderson, N.C.*
Homeowner	*Anderson, S.C.*
Independent	*Anderson, S.C.*
Item & Advertiser	*Huntsville, Texas*
Journal & Advertiser	*Commerce, Texas*
Journal News	*Hamilton, Ohio*
KAYT-FM	*radio station Phoenix, Ariz.*
KEMS-TV	*San Antonio, Texas*
KMJK-FM	*radio station Portland, Ore.*
KOY-AM	*radio station Phoenix, Ariz.*
KULF-AM	*radio station Houston, Texas*
KYND-FM	*radio station, Houston, Texas*
KYNO-FM	*radio station Houston, Texas*
KYTV	*Springfield, Mo.*
La Jolla Light	*San Diego, Calif.*

Leader Publishing Co.	
Life News Publishing	
Marshall Publishing	
Media Journal	*Malvern, Ark.*
Mountain States Publishing Co.	
Mountain Visitor	*Gatlinburg, Tenn.*
News Herald	*Del Rio, Texas*
News Messenger	*Marshall, Texas*
News	*Paris, Texas*
North Texas Publishing Co.	
Oxford Shopping News	*Oxford, Ohio*
Paris News	*Paris, Texas*
Pennysaver Plus	*Corpus Christi, Texas*
Press	*Ypsilanti, Mich.*
Press	*Gatlinburg, Tenn.*
Pulse Journal	*Hamilton, Ohio*
Record News	*Wichita Falls, Texas*
Record Publishing Co.	
Record Times	*Wichita Falls, Texas*
Red River Valley Bargain Bulletin	*Paris, Texas*
Reminder Publishing	
Reporter News	*Abilene, Texas*
Review	*Cooper, Texas*
San Diego (Calif.) Sentinel Publishing Co.	
San Francisco Progress	
Sentinel Publishers	
Sevier County News Record	*Sevierville, Tenn.*
Shopping Guide	*Anderson, N.C.*
South Middlesex Daily	*Framingham, Mass.*
Standard	*San Angelo, Texas*
Star News	*Framingham, Mass.*
Sunlight Shopper	*Corsicana, Texas*
Telesaver Publishers	
Times	*Wichita Falls, Texas*
Times	*Corpus Christi, Texas*
Times	*San Angelo, Texas*
Valley Scene	*Yakima, Wash.*
Valley View	*Yakima, Wash.*
Van/De Publishing Co.	
Walton Tribune	*Monroe, Calif.*
Weekly Light	*Corsicana, Texas*
WEZI-FM	*radio station Memphis, Tenn.*
WFMY-TV	*station Greensboro, N.C.*
White County Citizen	*Searcy, Ark.*
WLCY-AM	*radio station St. Petersburgh, Fla.*
WRBQ-FM	*radio station St. Petersburg, Fla.*
WRVA-AM	*radio station Richmond, Va.*
WRVQ-FM	*radio station Richmond, Va.*
WSGN-AM	*radio station Birmingham, Ala.*
WTLV-TV	*station Jacksonville, Fla.*

Hartfield Zody's Inc.

2525 Military Ave.
Los Angeles, Calif. 90064
(213) 477-0516

Chief Executive Officer: E.D. Solomon
Exchange: NY
Symbol: HRT

Corporate History: The company incorporated in 1945 as Hartfield Stores Inc. and adopted its present title in 1967. It manufactures apparel and operates a chain of approximately 60 clothing and shoe stores. In 1979-80 retailing accounted for 86% of sales and apparel manufacturing 14%.

Brandnames of Products and Services:

Gem	*discount department stores*
Hartfield	*apparel stores*
Hug-me-too	*apparel*
Jodette	*apparel*
Jody	*apparel*
Jody of California	*apparel*
Jody-Tootique	*apparel*
J-T	*women's apparel*
Just Tops	*apparel*
Karl's	*shoe stores*
Shoe Stop	*shoe stores*
Zodeems	*discount apparel store*
Zody's	*department store*

Hartmarx Corp.

101 North Wacker Dr.
Chicago, IL 60606
(312) 372-6300

Chief Executive Officer: Richard P. Hamilton
1984 Annual Sales Volume: 1,071M
1984 Shares Outstanding: 12,409,000
Shareholders: 9,500
Exchange: NY
Symbol: HMX

Corporate History: Hart Schaffner & Marx was founded in 1872 as a clothing store in Chicago. The company designs, manufactures and sells men's and women;s apparel. In 1984 the company operated 453 apparel stores in the U.S.: 257 specialty stores (of which 43 are wholly men's stores, 185 are men's stores which include a women's department, and 29 women's stores). In addition, the company operated 196 outlet-type stores. In 1983 the company effected a reorganization through which Hart Schaffner & Marx became a wholly-owned subsidiary of Hartmarx Corp. During 1984 the restructuring was completed as all other operating companies became direct subsidiaries of Hartmarx Corporation.

Brandnames of Products and Services:

Allyn St. George	*apparel stores*
Arthur Frank	*apparel stores*
Austin Reed for Women	*apparel*
Austin Reed of Regent Street	*apparel*
Austin Reed Sportswear	*apparel*
Baskin	*apparel stores*
Blackburns	*apparel stores*
Capper & Capper	*apparel stores*
Chas. A. Stevens	*apparel stores*
Christian Dior Grand Luxe	*apparel*
Christian Dior Monsieur	*apparel*
Country Miss	*women's apparel and stores*
Country Suburbans	*apparel*
deJongs	*apparel stores*
Fashionaire	*apparel*
Field Brothers	*apparel stores*
F.R. Tripler & Co.	*apparel stores*
Gleneagles	*apparel*
Graham & Gunn Ltd.	*apparel*
Great Western	*apparel*
Handmacher	*women's apparel*
Hart Schaffner & Marx	*apparel*
Hastings	*apparel stores*
Henry Grenthel	*apparel*
Hickey Freeman	*apparel*
Jack Henry Stores	*apparel stores*
Jack Nicklaus	*apparel*
Jaeger	*apparel*
Jas K. Wilson/ Washer Bros.	*apparel stores*
Jaymar	*apparel*
Jaymar	*apparel stores*
Jaymar/Sansabelt Shops	*apparel stores*
Jaymar Sport	*apparel*
Johnny Carson	*apparel*
J.O. Jones	*apparel stores*
J.P. Allen	*women's specialty stores*
Kleinhans	*apparel stores*
Klopfenstein's	*apparel stores*
Kucharo's	*apparel stores*
Kuppenheimer	*outlet store*
Lang Vicary	*apparel stores*
Leopold, Price & Rolle	*apparel stores*
Levy Wolf	*apparel stores*
Liemandt	*apparel stores*
Littler	*apparel stores*
Loro Piana	*apparel*
Man Store	*apparel stores*
Merritt Schaefer & Brown	*apparel stores*
Morris Levy	*apparel stores*
Nino Cerruti	*apparel*
Nino Cerruti	*apparel stores*
Old Mill	*outlet store*
Peer Gordon	*apparel store*
Pierre Cardin	*apparel*
Porter's Stevens	*apparel stores*
Racquet	*apparel*
Ray Beers	*apparel stores*
Ridingate	*apparel stores*
R.J. Boggs	*apparel stores*
Roots	*apparel store*
Sansabelt	*apparel*
Shulman's	*apparel stores*
Silverwoods	*apparel stores*
Sterling & Hunt	*apparel*
Walkers	*apparel stores*
Wallachs	*apparel stores*
Walter Holmes-Society Brand	*apparel*

Walter Morton	*apparel stores*
Weathervane	*apparel*
Wicks & Greenman	*apparel stores*
Wolf Bros.	*apparel stores*
Wolff's	*apparel stores*
Zachry	*apparel stores*

Hasbro Bradley, Inc.

1027 Newport Ave.
Pawtucket, RI 02861
(401) 726-4100

Chief Executive Officer: Stephen D. Hassenfeld
1984 Annual Sales Volume: 719M
1984 Shares Outstanding: 23,154,129
Shareholders: 3,241
Exchange: AM
Symbol: HAS
Corporate History: Incorporated in 1926, Hasbro makes toys, games and pre-school educational products. In 1977 it acquired Aviva Toy Co., providing it with a line of products built around the *Peanuts* cartoon characters. In 1984 the company acquired the Milton Bradley Company, a leading producer of board games and puzzles incorporated in 1894, and the company's name was changed to Hasbro Bradley, Inc.
Brandnames of Products and Services:

Aviva	*Toys*
Battleship	*board game*
Big Ben Puzzles	*puzzles*
Candy Land	*board game*
Challenge Yahtzee	*game*
Chutes and Ladders	*board game*
Connect Four	*board game*
Design Toys	*toys*
Dragonmaster	*board game*
Fresh 'n Fancy	*children's cosmetics*
game	
The Game of Life	*board game*
GI Joe	*toys*
Glenco Infants Items	*specialty items - infants*
Glo Worm	*toys*
Hangman	*game*
Hasbro	*toys*
Lite Brite	*number painting sets*
Mickey Mouse Talking Phone	*toy phone*
Milton Bradley	*board games*
Mr. Potato Head	*toys*
My Little Pony	*toys*
Numbers Up	*game*
Operation	*board game*
Playskool Toys	*toys for toddlers*
Romper Room	*toys*
Stay Alive	*game*
Stratego	*board game*
Tommee Tippee Playskool	*toys for toddlers*
TransFormers	*toys*
Twister	*game*
Word Yahtzee	*game*
Wuzzles	*toys*
Yahtzee	*game*

Health-Mor Inc.

151 East Twenty-Second St.
Lombard, IL 60148
(312) 953-9770

Chief Executive Officer: John M. Licht
1984 Annual Sales Volume: 14M
1984 Shares Outstanding: 1,760,488
Shareholders: 570
Exchange: AM
Symbol: HMI
Corporate History: Originally formed in 1928, the company was reorganized in 1968 as Health-Mor Inc. Although the main business of the company remains the manufacture and sale of vacuum cleaners, the company now also manufactures metal formed tubing, specialty machinery and plumbing supplies through its subsidiaries.
Brandnames of Products and Services:

Filter Queen	*vacuum cleaners*
HMI Credit Corp.	*financial services*
Princess	*vacuum cleaners*

Heck's Inc.

HUB Industrial Park, McJunkin Rd.
Nitro, WV 25143
(304) 755-8331

Chief Executive Officer: Russell L. Isaacs
1984 Annual Sales Volume: 465M
1984 Shares Outstanding: 8,862,898
Shareholders: 6,500

Exchange: NY
Symbol: HEX
Corporate History: The company incorporated in 1959 as Tri-State Distributors Inc. and acquired its present name in 1963. It operates 126 discount department stores and three warehouse distribution centers in a nine-state area.
Brandnames of Products and Services:

Heck's	*discount department store*

G. Heileman Brewing Co. Inc.

100 Harborview Plaza
La Crosse, WI 54601
(608) 785-1000

Chief Executive Officer: R.G. Cleary
1984 Annual Sales Volume: 1,171M
1984 Shares Outstanding: 26,850,402
Shareholders: 17,011
Exchange: NY
Symbol: GHB
Corporate History: The company was incorporated in 1918 as Manitowoc Breweries Co. and changed its name to Kingsbury Breweries in 1933. Its present title was adopted in 1962. In 1970 Heileman expanded out of brewing with the acquisition of several bakeries. It also began to manufacture precision metal parts for jet engines in 1967. In 1984, brewing accounted for 90% of sales, baking 9% and other sales including metal products, 1%.
Brandnames of Products and Services:

Altes	*beer*
Black Label L.A.	*beer*
Blatz	*beer*
Blatz L.A.	
Blatz Light	*beer*
Blatz Light Cream Ale	
Blitz	*beer*
Burgermeister	*beer*
Carling Black Label	*beer*
Carling Black Label Light	*beer*
Carling Red Cap	*beer*
Colt 45, Malt Liquor	
Drewrys	*beer*
Ege Kvist	*bake shop products*
Erickson	*bakeries*
Fall City	
Gardner's	*bakery products*
Grain Belt	*beer*
Heidelberg	*beer*
Henry Weinhard	*beer*
Holsum Bread	
Kingsbury	*beer*
Kingsbury Near Beer	
Lone Star	*beer*
Lone Star Light	*beer*
Malt Duck, Apple & Grape	*malt liquors*
Mickey's Malt	*malt liquor*
National Bohemian	*beer*
National Premium	*beer*
Old Style	*beer*
Old Style L.A.	*beer*
Old Style Light	*beer*
Pfeiffer	*beer*
Rainier	*beer*
Rainier Light	*beer*
Red, White & Blue	*beer*
Red, White & Blue Light	*beer*
Schmidt	
Schmidt	*beer*
Schmidt Light	*beer*
Special Export	*beer*
Stag	*beer*
Sterling	*beer*
Sunbeam	*bread*
Tuborg	*beer*
Wiedemann	*beer*
Zing (Near Beer)	

H.J. Heinz Co.

P.O. Box 57
Pittsburgh, PA 15230
(412) 237-5757

Chief Executive Officer: Dr. A.J.F. O'Reilly
1984 Annual Sales Volume: 3,954M
1984 Shares Outstanding: 69,831,277
Shareholders: 17,800
Exchange: NY
Symbol: HNZ
Corporate History: Heinz traces its history to 1869 when H.J. Heinz, the son of German immigrants, established a business selling food in bottles. During the late 19th century Heinz became one of the nation's leading firms, ranked number one in production of pickles, vinegar and ketchup. Today it is number four in the food industry, outranked by Beatrice, Kraft and Gen-

eral Foods, in that order. Heinz was the first American company to build a strong business overseas. International business represents 35% of its sales. It was also the first large food company to take a major position in the weight-control market. In 1970 Heinz entered the high fructose (corn-based sugar) market which has already replaced a substantial portion of the sugar market. Heinz has the capacity to supply 10% of the high fructose demand. Heinz is the largest frozen food company in the United States.

Brandnames of Products and Services:

9 Lives	*cat food*
Amore	*cat food*
Chico-San	*rice cakes*
Heinz	*baby foods, soup, ketchup, pasta, vinegar, etc.*
Jerky	*dog treats*
Meaty Bone	*dog food*
Ore-Ida	*frozen foods*
Star-Kist	*tunafish*
Steakumm	*frozen meats*
Weight Watchers	*foods and publications*

Helene Curtis Industries Inc.

325 N. Wells St.
Chicago, IL 60610
(312) 661-0222

Chief Executive Officer:	Gerold Gidwitz
1984 Annual Sales Volume:	330M
1984 Shares Outstanding:	3,935,050
Shareholders:	2,546
Exchange:	NY
Symbol:	HC

Corporate History: Helene Curtis was incorporated in 1928 as National Mineral Co. In 1945, the name was changed to National Industries, and in 1946 the present title was adopted. The company makes and sells packaged toilet goods, hair care products, cosmetics and beauty salon supplies. In fiscal 1984 beauty and hair care products accounted for 88.2% of sales and automotive sealants and adhesives accounted for 11.8%.

Brandnames of Products and Services:

Atune	*hair care products*
Enden	*shampoos*
Everynight	*hair care product*
Finesse	*hair care products*
Great Curl	*curling iron*
The Great One	*hair care appliances*
Moisture Quotient (M2)	
Quantum	*hair care products*
Spray Net	*hair spray*
Suave	*hair products*
Tender Touch	*bath oils*
Uniperm	*permanent wave*

Hershey Foods Corp.

100 Mansion Rd. East
Hershey, PA 17033
(717) 534-4000

Chief Executive Officer:	Richard Zimmerman
1984 Annual Sales Volume:	1,893M
1984 Shares Outstanding:	31,337
Shareholders:	16,729
Exchange:	NY
Symbol:	HSY

Corporate History: The Hershey Chocolate Company was founded in 1905 by Milton Snavely Hershey who built his chocolate factory in Derry Church, PA (renamed "Hershey" in 1906). It was decided to mass produce a single product which could be sold at a low price rather than continue a wide variety of chocolate novelties. Success was immediate and sales reached $5 million by 1911. In 1918, the business was donated to a trust for the Milton Hershey School for orphaned children, which had been established by Mr. and Mrs. Hershey nine years earlier. The school owned a 100% interest in the company until 1927, when approximately 20% of the stock was sold to the public. In the same year, Hershey Chocolate Company was incorporated. Up until this time, the administration of the company, the town and the school were intermingled. All was reorganized, with the Chocolate Corporation acquiring all chocolate properties; the Hershey Estates (now HERCO Inc.) administering the various businesses and public services of the town; and the Hershey Trust Company continuing to oversee the funds of the Milton Hershey School. Acquisitions in the 1970's included Y & S Candies, Inc.; Procino-Rossi and Skinner pasta manufacturing companies; and Friendly Ice Cream Corporation. In November, 1984, the corporation purchased American Beauty Macaroni, and named its pasta division The Hershey Pasta Group.

Brandnames of Products and Services:

American Beauty	*pasta*
Bassetts	*candy*
Big Block	*chocolate bar*
Clamboat	*clam platter*
Cory	*coffee brewing apparatus*
Cory-Lite	*coffee*

Delmonico	*pasta*
Familiar	*margarine*
Fishamajig	*fish sandwich*
Fribble	*ice-milk drink*
Friendly	*ice cream*
Friendly	*ice cream restaurants*
Friendly Frank	*frankfurter sandwich*
Friendly's Big Beef	*hamburger sandwich*
Golden Almond	*chocolate bar*
Hershey Baking Products	*and candy items*
Hershey's Kisses	*chocolates*
Kit Kat	*candy bar*
Krackel	*candy bar*
Light 'N Fluffy	*noodles*
Marabou	*candy*
Mini Chips	*semi-sweet chocolates*
Mr. Goodbar	*candy bar*
New Trail	*granola snack bar*
Nibs	*candy*
Office Spring	*rental services*
P & R	*pasta*
Perfection In The Cup	*electric beverage brewers*
Petybon	*pasta, biscuits*
Racing Wheels	*macaroni*
Ready Brew	*electric beverage brewers*
Reese's Peanut Butter Cups	*candy*
Reese's Pieces	*candy*
Rolo	*candy*
San Giorgio	*pasta*
Skinner Pasta	*products*
Skor	*toffee candy bar*
Special Dark	*sweet chocolate bar*
Twizzlers	*candy*
Whatchamacallit	*candy*
Y & S	*candy*

Heublein Inc.

Munson Rd.
Farmington, Conn. 06032
(203) 677-4061

Chief Executive Officer: W.B. Waldron
Exchange: NY
Symbol: HBL

Corporate History: Heublein goes back to a restaurant and hotel business founded in 1862. In the 1890s the company began making prepared cocktails which it sold first to hotels and then to consumers. It nearly failed during the Great Depression but survived on the profits of A-1 Steak Sauce. Heublein bought the rights to Smirnoff vodka in 1939 and after World War II started a major marketing campaign that helped make vodka one of the most popular alcoholic beverages in America. Its four brands account for 33% of the vodka consumed nationally. In 1969 Heublein diversified into wines with the acquisition of United Vintners. In 1971 the company bought Kentucky Fried Chicken, but initially did not do well with the chain. It seems to have overcome its difficulties with both acquisitions.

Brandnames of Products and Services:

Annie Green Springs Wine	
Arrow Cordials	
Bahia Liqueur	
Black & White Scotch	*whiskey*
Black Velvet	*Canadian whiskey*
Boggs	*cranberry liquer*
Cappela	*wines and brandies*
Club	*cocktails*
Colony	*wines*
Don Q	*imported rum*
Escoffier	*sauces*
Gambarelli & Davito	*wines*
Grey Poupon	*Dijon mustard*
Hartley	*brandies*
Harts Rolls	
Heublein	*cocktails*
H. Salt Esq.	*seafood restaurants*
Hungarian Tokay & Table Wines	
Inglenook	*wines*
Irish Mist	*liqueur*
Italian Swiss Colony	*wines*
Jacques Bonet	*wines*
Jose Cuervo Tequila	
Kentucky Fried Chicken	
Kiku Masamune	*Japanese sake*
Lejon	*wines*
Malcolm Hereford's Cows	*spirits*
Milshire	*gins*
Mission Bell	*wine*
Ortega	*Mexican food*
Ostrova	*vodka*
Petri	*wines*
Popov	*vodka*

Regina Wine Vinegar	
Relska	*vodka*
Sangrole	*wines*
Smirnoff	*vodka*
Snap-E-Tom	*tomato cocktail*
Tipo	*wines and brandies*
T.J. Swann	*wines*
Tullamore Dew	*Irish whiskies*
United Vintners	
Yukon Jack Canadian	*liqueur*
Zantigo Mexican American Restaurants	

Higbee Co.

100 Public Sq.
Cleveland, Ohio 44113
(216) 579-2580

Chief Executive Officer: R.R. Broadbent
Exchange: OTC
Symbol: HIGB
Corporate History: The company, incorporated in 1913, is a Cleveland-based operator of department stores and women's shoe stores.
Brandnames of Products and Services:

Higbee	*department stores*
Red Cross Shoes	*shoe stores*

Hillenbrand Industries Inc.

Highway 46
Batesville, IN 47006
(812) 934-7000

Chief Executive Officer: D.A. Hillenbrand
1984 Annual Sales Volume: 485M
1984 Shares Outstanding: 19,437,478
Shareholders: 5,000
Exchange: NY
Symbol: HB
Corporate History: Hillenbrand Industries was formed in the late 1800s. The company became a publicly held corporation in 1971 and owns all of the stock of four major operating companies: American Tourister, Inc. manufactures and sells luggage and attache cases; Batesville Casket Company Inc., now in its 101st year, makes metal and hardwood burial caskets; Hill-Rom Company, Inc, a hospital equipment manufacturer since 1929, specializes in making adjustable hospital beds, furniture for patient rooms and architectural systems; Medeco Security Locks, Inc. manufactures high-security locks for business, industry, and residential use. Hillenbrand Industries and its subsidiaries operate plants in six different states and Canada, and employ approximately 5,900 workers.
Brandnames of Products and Services:

American	*luggage*
American Tourister	*luggage*
Associates	*luggage*
Batesville	*caskets*
Beautiful on the Outside, American Tourister on the Inside	*luggage*
Bodyguard	*high security locks*
Business Equipment	*luggage*
Business Equipment by American Tourister	*luggage*
Canaveral	*luggage*
Chemgard	*caskets*
Classic Gold	*caskets*
Cross Country	*luggage*
Dependables	*luggage*
Escort	*luggage*
Euroline	*high security locks*
Free Wheelers	*luggage*
Frequent Flyer	*luggage*
Gorilla Bags	*luggage*
Le Mans	*luggage*
Living Memorial	*memorial tree plantings*
Medeco	*high security locks*
Monogard	*caskets*
Monoseal	*caskets*
Monte Carlo	*luggage*
Monterey	*luggage*
New Dimensions	*luggage*
Omega	*caskets*
Rally	*luggage*
Reliables	*luggage*
ResQ	*luggage repair & replacement services*
Saronno	*luggage*
Soft Riders	*luggage*
SoftTech	*luggage*
Space Makers	*luggage*
Spectrum	*luggage*
Styltex	*luggage*

Sureglide	*luggage*
Tourister	*luggage*
Triumph	*luggage*
Verona	*luggage*
Vilon	*luggage*
Vytex	*luggage*
Walking Wardrobe	*luggage*

Hitachi Ltd.

50 Prospect Avenue
Tarrytown, NY 10591-4698
(914) 332-5800

Chief Executive Officer: H. Yoshiyama
1984 Annual Sales Volume: 19,400M
1984 Shares Outstanding: 2,802,228,743
Shareholders: 239,776
Exchange: NY
Symbol: HIT
Corporate History: Hitachi was founded in 1910 and incorporated in 1920. It is Japan's largest general manufacturer of electronics and electrical equipment and one of the world's major suppliers. Manufacturing operations are conducted all over the world. Hitachi's growth is centered in heavy electrical equipment and consumer products. In the 1980s, the company will focus on electronics and energy.
Brandnames of Products and Services:

Hitachi	*electronic equipment*

HMW Industries, Inc.

High Ridge Park
Stamford, Conn. 06905
(203) 329-8414

Chief Executive Officer: J.W. Robbins
Exchange: NY
Symbol: HMW
Corporate History: Incorporated in 1982, HMW Industries Inc. produces silver flatware for the consumer market. It also manufactures furniture and electronic audio equipment.
Brandnames of Products and Services:

Handi-man	*fasteners (hardware)*
Wallace Silversmiths	*products*

Holiday Inns Inc.

3742 Lamar Avenue
Memphis, TN 38195
(901) 362-4001

Chief Executive Officer: Michael D. Rose
1984 Annual Sales Volume: 1,760M
1984 Shares Outstanding: 36,487,000
Shareholders: 24,620
Exchange: NY
Symbol: HIA
Corporate History: The company incorporated in 1954 as Holiday Inns of America Inc. and adopted its present title in 1969. It is the largest hotel and gaming business in the world. In 1984 hotel operations accounted for 57% of sales, gaming 37%, restaurants 6%
Brandnames of Products and Services:

Embassy Suites	*hotels*
Hampton Inns	*hotels*
Harrah's	*hotel/casino/resorts*
Holiday Inn Crowne Plaza	*hotels*
Holiday Inns - hotels	
Perkins Restaurant	*restaurants*
Residence Inns	*hotels*

Holly Sugar Corp.

P.O. Box 1052
Colorado Springs, CO 80901
(303) 471-0123

Chief Executive Officer: John L. Bushnell
1984 Annual Sales Volume: 269M
1984 Shares Outstanding: 1,114,253
Shareholders: 939
Exchange: NY
Symbol: HLY
Corporate History: Holly Sugar Corp., incorporated in 1916, is a manufacturer of beet sugar from sugar-beets at seven beet sugar factories located in the States of Montana, Texas, Wyoming and California.
Brandnames of Products and Services:

Holly	*sugar*

Honeywell Inc.

Honeywell Plaza
Minneapolis, MN 55408
(612) 870-5200

Chief Executive Officer: E.W. Spencer
1984 Annual Sales Volume: 6,074 M
1984 Shares Outstanding: 46,900,000
Shareholders: 46,500
Exchange: NY
Symbol: HON
Corporate History: Honeywell was founded in 1885 as a maker of temperature control systems, "damper flappers" for coal furnaces. It continues to produce environmental control items. During World War II it diversified into military equipment, making precision optics. Today, Honeywell is an international corporation that develops and applies high-technology systems and services to conserve energy, improve productivity, and meet defense needs.
Brandnames of Products and Services:

Honeywell	*office equipment and electrical products*

Hon Industries Inc.

414 E. Third St.
Muscatine, IA 52761
(319) 264-7400

Chief Executive Officer: S.M. Howe
1984 Annual Sales Volume: 397M
1984 Shares Outstanding: 10,959,442
Shareholders: 3,555
Exchange: OTC
Symbol: HONI
Corporate History: Hon Industries Inc. is the parent corporation of six companies. Incorporated in 1944 as The Home-O-Nize Co. the name was changed to Hon Industries Inc. 1968. The Hon Company is the original operating company and its largest division. It manufactures wood and metal office furniture.
Brandnames of Products and Services:

Corry Jamestown	*furniture*
Heatilator	*prefabricated fireplaces*
Holga	*office furniture*
Hon	*office furniture*
Prime-Mover	*material-handling equipment*
Rishel	*contract wood office funiture*

Hook Drugs Inc.

2800 Enterprise St.
P.O. Box 26285
Indianapolis, Ind. 46226
(317) 353-1451

Chief Executive Officer: N.P. Reeves
Exchange: OTC
Symbol: HOOK
Corporate History: Hook, incorporated in 1930, operates the largest retail drugstore chain in Indiana. In 1979 it expanded into the convenience-food market.
Brandnames of Products and Services:

Hook Drugstores
Quik-Way Convenient Food Stores

Hoover Co.

101 Maple St., East
North Canton, OH 44720
(216) 499-9200

Chief Executive Officer: Merle R. Rawson
1984 Annual Sales Volume: 683M
1984 Shares Outstanding: 12,382,838
Shareholders: 6,495
Exchange: OTC
Symbol: HOOV
Corporate History: Hoover, incorporated in 1922 makes and sells and services vacuum cleaners and accessories, electric floor polishers and other floor care appliances, as well as laundry equipment, dishwashers, refrigeration and small household appliances. Hoover products are sold through more than 100,000 retail outlets.
Brandnames of Products and Services:

Hoover	*home appliances*

George A. Hormel & Co.

501-16th Ave. NE
P.O. Box 800
Austin, MN 55912
(507) 437-5611

Chief Executive Officer: I.J. Holton
1984 Annual Sales Volume: 1,454M
1984 Shares Outstanding: 9,606,516

Shareholders: 5,000
Exchange: AM
Symbol: HRL
Corporate History: Hormel, founded in 1891, is one of the few remaining independent meat packers in the United States. It is mainly involved in pork processing. Spam, one of its products, is the world's largest-selling brand of canned meat.
Brandnames of Products and Services:

Black Label	*food products*
Curemaster	*food products*
Cure 81	*food products*
DiLusso	*food products*
Dinty Moore	*food products*
Frank N Stuff	*food products*
Great Beginnings	*food products*
Hormel	*meat products and prepared foods*
Light & Lean	*food products*
Little Sizzlers	*food products*
Mary Kitchen	*food products*
Old Smokehouse	*food products*
Range Brand	*food products*
Spam	*meat products*
Wranglers	*food products*

Host International Inc.

Pico Blvd. & 34th St.
Santa Monica, Calif. 90406
(213) 450-7566

Chief Executive Officer: H.E. Varner
Exchange: NY
Symbol: HII
Corporate History: The company was incorporated in 1914 as the Interstate Co., succeeding Interstate News Co. It adopted its present title in 1968. It is engaged primarily in the sale of food, beverages and merchandise to the traveling public. In 1980 airport operations accounted for 67% of sales, merchandise shops 14% and specialty restaurants 19%.
Brandnames of Products and Services:

Barley Mow	*restaurant*
Casa Maria	*restaurant*
Charlie Brown's	*restaurant*
The Continental	*retail store*
Detroit Metropolitan Airport Hotel	
Franciscan Gift Shop	*specialty store*
Franklin Stove	*restaurant*
Joshua Tree	*restaurant*
Marine Tobacco Co.	*tobacco store*
Phineas	*restaurant*
The Pier House Inn & Beach Club	*Key West, Florida*
Sacramento Metropolitan Airport Hotel	
Sparky's Virgin Island	*specialty store*
Tampa International Airport Hotel	
World Tobacco Co.	*tobacco store*

Houghton Mifflin Co.

One Beacon St.
Boston, MA 02108
(617) 725-5000

Chief Executive Officer: H.T. Miller
1984 Annual Sales Volume: 249M
1984 Shares Outstanding: 6,511,214
Shareholders: 3,264
Exchange: NY
Symbol: HTN
Corporate History: The company, founded in 1832 and incorporated in 1908, publishes educational texts, children's books, computer software, reference works, fiction and non-fiction in hard and soft cover editions. In 1984 textbooks and other educational materials accounted for 83% of sales.
Brandnames of Products and Services:

The Answer	*computer-based educational management system*
Clarion Books	*publishing house*
The Classroom Answer	*computer-based educational management program*
Dolphin Curricula	*computer-based education program*
GIS	*guidance information system*
Houghton Mifflin Software	*business & educational software*

Household International, Inc.

2700 Sanders Rd.
Prospect Heights, IL 60070
(312) 564-5000

Chief Executive Officer: Donald C. Clark
1984 Annual Sales Volume: 8,321,500,000
1984 Shares Outstanding: 59,300,000
Shareholders: 28,545
Exchange: NY
Symbol: HI

Corporate History: In 1981 Household International, Inc., became the holding company for the diversified interests of Household Finance Corporation. Household Finance Corporation, incorporated in 1925, traces its origins to 1878. In 1961 Household purchased Coast-to-Coast hard goods chain. In 1965, it acquired City Products Corporation (Ben Franklin, T.G.&Y.), now Household Merchandising. In 1968, it purchased King-Seeley Thermos Co. (King-Seeley, Scotsman, Structo, Thermos, Halsey Taylor, Almco, Albion). In 1969, Vons supermarket chain and National Car Rental (Lend Lease, Mud Cat) were acquired. In 1973, it purchased HFC Trust Limited. In 1977, Alexander Hamilton Life Insurance was acquired and HFC Leasing was formed. In 1981, it purchased Valley National Bank and Wallace Murray Corporation (Eljer, U.S. Brass, Simonds, Thorsen, Atrax/Newcarb, Schwitzer, Illinois Gear, Ohio Gear, Richmond Gear, Selkirk Metalbestos, GC Electronics). In 1982 Household Manufacturing was established to consolidate the management structures of King-Seeley Thermos Company and Wallace Murray Corporation. In 1984 Financial Services accounted for 56.2% of income, Merchandising 18.1%, Manufacturing 12.0% and Transportation 13.7%. Household Finance today provides its 2 million customers with a broad range of financial services including personal loans, real estate-secured loans, consumer banking, income tax services, consumer education, leveraged leasing and commercial financing. The product lines of Household Manufacturing include turbochargers, gears, plumbing fixtures, chimneys, cutting and hand tools, vacuumware, barbecue grills, commercial ice systems, water coolers, drinking fountains, and other consumer and industrial products.

Brandnames of Products and Services:

Alexander Hamilton	*ordinary life and credit insurance*
Ben Franklin	*franchised variety stores*
Coast-to-Coast	*franchised hardware stores*
HFC Income Tax Service	*income tax service*
Household	*Finance Corp.-consumer finance*
Household Bank	*consumer banking*
Lend Lease	*car leasing, truck rental and leasing*
Money Management Institute	*consumer education*
National Car Rental	*car rental*
Scotsman	*automatic ice machines*
Structo	*barbecue grills*
TG & Y	*general merchandise stores*
Thermos	*vacuumware, plastic insulated products*
Thorson	*non-powered hand tools*
U.S. Brass	*faucets, plumbing system*
Von's	*supermarkets*

House of Fabrics Inc.

13400 Riverside Dr.
Sherman Oaks, CA 91423
(213) 995-7000

Chief Executive Officer: D.I. Sofro
1984 Annual Sales Volume: 278M
1984 Shares Outstanding: 6,632,000
Shareholders: 2,400
Exchange: NY
Symbol: HF

Corporate History: The company, incorporated in 1946, is the nation's leading chain of company-owned and operated retail fabrics, crafts and sewing machines stores with 740 currently in operation in 47 states. The stores west of the Rocky Mountains use the name House of Fabrics and most of the stores in the other states use the name So-Fro Fabrics. The company operates 672 regular fabric stores, all of which have fabrics, notions and crafts departments, 570 of these have sewing machine departments. The company is the largest retailer of Singer Sewing Machines; it also markets its own brand sewing machine So-Fro by Singer. The company also operates 42 craft-only stores under the name Craft Showcase.

Brandnames of Products and Services:

Craft Showcase	*craft stores*
House of Fabrics	*fabric stores*
So-Fro by Singer	*sewing machines*
So-Fro Fabrics	*fabric stores*

House of Ronnie Inc.

One Penn Plaza
New York, N.Y. 10001
(212) 564-0900

Chief Executive Officer: Irving Paparo
Exchange: AM
Symbol: HRO
Corporate History: The company, incorporated in 1962, designs and makes popular-priced undergarments, sportswear and nightwear for young girls.
Brandnames of Products and Services:

Denise	*girls' lingerie*
House of Ronnie	*girls' apparel*
Miss Ronnie	*girls' apparel*
Ronnie Jana	*girls' apparel*
Ronnie Togs	*girls' apparel*

House of Vision Inc.

137 N. Wabash Ave.
Chicago, Ill. 60602
(312) 346-0755

Chief Executive Officer: R.C. Aversano
Exchange: AM
Symbol: HOV
Corporate History: The company, incorporated in 1924, is one of the largest independent eyewear retailers in the United States.
Brandnames of Products and Services:

House of Vision	*eyewear stores*

Huffy Corp.

7701 Byers Rd.
Miamisburg, OH 45342
(513) 866-6251

Chief Executive Officer: Harry A. Shaw III
1984 Annual Sales Volume: 273M
1984 Shares Outstanding: 5,334,542
Shareholders: 3,465
Exchange: NY
Symbol: HUF
Corporate History: Huffy was incorporated in 1928 as Huffman Mfg. Co. and in 1977 changed its name to Huffy Corp. It is the largest manufacturer of bicycles in the United States with 25% to 30% of the market. The company also makes other recreational products, including basketball, fishing and marine equipment, and physical fitness products.
Brandnames of Products and Services:

Gerry	*infant carriers, strollers, and juvenile products*
Huffy	*sports equipment*
Huffy Bicycle	
Raleigh	*Bicycles*

I.C. Industries Inc.

One Illinois Center
111 East Wacker Dr.
Chicago, IL 60601
(312) 565-3000

Chief Executive Officer: William B. Johnson
1984 Annual Sales Volume: 4,234M
1984 Shares Outstanding: 48,386,556
Shareholders: 38,585
Exchange: NY
Symbol: ICX
Corporate History: I.C. Industries was founded in 1851 as the Illinois Central Railroad, a line carrying freight and passengers north and south along the Mississippi River. For more than 100 years the company was engaged solely in transportation, but during the 1960s, branched out first into the manufacture of heavy industrial products such as brake linings for cars and hydraulic systems for airplanes, and then into consumer goods, such as car mufflers and food products. In 1984, Industries acquired the Pneumo Corp. Pneumo is engaged in the design and manufacture of landing gear and flight controls for military and commercial aircraft, and in food and drug retailing and wholesaling.
Brandnames of Products and Services:

Aunt Fanny	*bakery goods*
Bubble Up	*carbonated beverage*
Dad's Root Beer	
Downy Flake	*frozen foods*
Midas Muffler Shop	
Mussleman's	*fruit products*
Old El Paso	*Mexican foods*
Orleans	*oysters*
Pepsi-Cola General Bottlers	
Pet Inc.	*food products*
Pet-Ritz	*frozen foods*
Sego	*diet foods*
Whitman's	*chocolates and confections*

Ideal Toy Corp.

184-10 Jamaica Ave.
New York, N.Y. 11423
(212) 454-5000

Chief Executive Officer: L.A. Weintraub
Exchange: NY
Symbol: ID
Corporate History: The company, incorporated in 1972, makes recreational products including dolls, toys, action games, racing sets, camping gear and apparel. Ideal has traditionally been a company that introduced new heavily advertised toys annually. However it found that without a line of long-term sellers this practice was not profitable. The company has decided to focus on lower-priced merchandise rather than pouring research and marketing dollars into high-priced electronic games and dolls.
Brandnames of Products and Services:

Ideal	*toys*

Idle Wild Foods Inc.

Worcester Plaza
446 Main St.
Worcester, Mass. 01608
(617) 757-7761

Chief Executive Officer: M.H. Jacobson
Exchange: OTC
Corporate History: The company was established in 1949 and incorporated in 1973. It is a holding concern engaged in meat and food processing.
Brandnames of Products and Services:

Idle Wild Farm	*turkeys*

Insilco Corp.

1000 Research Pkwy.
Meriden, CT 06450
(203) 634-2000

Chief Executive Officer: Donald J. Harper
1984 Annual Sales Volume: 787M
1984 Shares Outstanding: 17,052,347
Shareholders: 21,300
Exchange: NY
Symbol: INR
Corporate History: Insilco Corporation is a diversified manufacturer and supplier of products for the electronics/communications, metal parts, housing, paint and publishing/office products markets. The company was incorporated in New Jersey in 1898 and became a Connecticut corporation in 1946. During its first 60 years, the company was engaged principally in the manufacture and sale of sterling silver, silverplate, stainless steel and pewter tableware products. During the 1950's, management noted changing market trends and commenced a major diversification program. During the past five years, the company has acquired Basic Industries (1981), Signal Transformer Co., Inc. (1983) and Thermal Components, Inc. (1984). In 1982, the company announced that it planned to sell the International Silver Company because it did not meet the company's criteria for growth of return on investment. Substantially all of the assets of International were sold in 1983. The holloware manufacturing operation of International was discontinued in 1981. Three other businesses owned by the company, McDonald Products Corp., MRM Industries Inc. and City Machine Tool & Die Co. Inc., were sold in 1982, 1983 and 1984, respectively.
Brandnames of Products and Services:

BPS Paints	
Enterprise Paints	
Magic Color Paint	
Mary Carter Paint	
McDonald Designs	*desk-top accessories*
Miles Do-It-Yourself Homebuilding	
Nation Wide Homes	*modular homes*
Red Devil Paints	
Rolodex	*rotary card files*
Sinclair	*paints and wall coverings*
Taylor Publishing	*yearbooks*

Integrity Entertainment Corp.

14100 So. Kingsley Dr.
Gardena, Calif. 90249
(213) 538-2314

Chief Executive Officer: L.C. Hartstone
Exchange: OTC
Symbol: INTG
Corporate History: The company, incorporated in 1970, operates stores specializing in phonographic items.
Brandnames of Products and Services:

Big Bens	*record and tape stores*
Wherehouse	*record and tape stores*

Interco Inc.

Ten Broadway
St. Louis, MO 63102
(314) 231-1100

Chief Executive Officer: Harvey Saligman
1984 Annual Sales Volume: 2,626M
1984 Shares Outstanding: 14,122,065
Shareholders: 11,500
Exchange: NY
Symbol: ISS

Corporate History: The company was incorporated in 1921 as the International Shoe Co., the successor to a corporation of the same name organized in 1911. At the same time, it took over Roberts, Johnson and Rand Shoe Co., formed in 1898, and Peters Shoe Co. founded in 1836. Its three principal areas of business are: wearing apparel, general retail merchandising and footwear manufacturing and retailing. The original business of the company was making shoes, but now almost half its earnings are derived from apparel and retail chains.

Brandnames of Products and Services:

Abe Schrader Corp	*women's apparel*
Allyn St. George	*men's apparel*
Ambassador	*men's footwear*
Big Yank	*men's apparel*
Biltwell	*men's apparel*
Broyhill	*furniture*
Campus	*apparel*
Campusport	*men's apparel*
Central Hardware Home Improvement Stores	
Cherokee	*men's apparel*
Clipper Mist	*apparel*
College Town	*apparel*
Cowden	*men's apparel*
Crawdad's	*women's footwear*
Devon	*apparel*
Di Vina	*women's footwear*
Donegal	*men's apparel*
Don Robbie	*men's apparel*
Duane's	*shoe stores*
Esprit by Campus	*apparel*
Ethan Allen	*furniture*
Ethan Allen Inn	*motor hotel, Danbury, Conn.*
Fine's	*men's shops*
Florsheim	*footwear and stores*
Florsheim Thayer McNeil	*stores*
Fog	*men's apparel*
Golde's	*department store*
Grizzlies	*footwear*
Hirsch Value Center	*general merchandise center*
Hy-Test	*footwear*
Idaho	*department store*
Idlers	*footwear*
It's Pure Gould	*apparel*
Janus	*women's apparel*
Jeans Galore	*department store*
John Alexander	*men's apparel*
Julius Marlow	*men's footwear*
Lady Devon	*apparel*
London Fog	*apparel*
London Towne	*apparel store*
Maincoats	*apparel*
Miller Taylor	*shoe stores*
Miss Wonderful	*footwear*
Outdoors Unlimited	*apparel*
Panther	*women's apparel*
Personality	*women's footwear*
Petite Concept	*women's apparel*
P.N. Hirsch Store	*general merchandise store*
Pro-Action by Campus	*men's apparel*
Queen Casuals	*apparel*
Rand	*men's footwear*
Rejoice	*apparel*
Royal Imperial	*footwear*
Rugged Country	*men's apparel*
Sky City Discount	*general merchandise store*
Standard Sportswear	*apparel store*
Startown	*men's apparel*
Studio One by Campus	*men's apparel*
Stuffed Shirt	*apparel*
Tailor's Bench	*men's apparel*
Thayer McNeil	*footwear stores*
Thomas Wallace	*women's footwear*
Thompson Boland & Lee	*apparel store*
Tour de France	*men's apparel*
United Shirt Store	*men's apparel store*
Weeds	*footwear*
Winning Edge	*women's apparel*
Winthrop	*men's footwear*
Worthmore	*men's footwear*

International Business Machines Corp.

Old Orchard Road
Armonk, N.Y. 10504
(914) 765-1900

Chief Executive Officer: John F. Akers
1984 Annual Sales Volume: 45,937M
1984 Shares Outstanding: 611,426,324
Shareholders: 792,506
Exchange: NY
Symbol: IBM

Corporate History: IBM began in 1911 as the Computing-Tabulating-Recording Co., a corporation composed of three companies that manufactured tabulating machines, scales and time recorders. Today, IBM is the largest manufacturer of data processing equipment and systems in the information-handling field. More than 95% of IBM's operations are in the industry segment encompassing information-handling systems, equipment and services to solve the increasingly complex problems of business, government, science, space exploration, defense, education, medicine and many other areas of human activity. IBM's products include information processing products and systems, program products, telecommunications systems, information distributors, office systems, typewriters, copiers, educational and testing materials, and related supplies and services.

Brandnames of Products and Services:

IBM	*products*
IBM Product Centers	*office equipment stores*

International Multifoods Corp.

Multifoods Tower
Box 2942
Minneapolis, MN 55402
(612) 340-3300

Chief Executive Officer: Andre Gillet
1984 Annual Sales Volume: 1,067M
1984 Shares Outstanding: 8,126,745
Shareholders: 6,220
Exchange: NY
Symbol: IMC

Corporate History: International Multifoods Corporation is a broadly based food manufacturing, processing and marketing company. The company operates in four industry segments: Consumer - retail grocery and food store products, fish, specialty meats, and cheese shops; Industrial - food products sold to industrial and commercial users, and grain merchandising; Agriculture - animal feed and health products, veterinary supplies, retail feed stores, seed operations, and pet food; and Away-From-Home Eating - franchising operations (primarily Mister Donut) and operation of high quality seafood and other restaurants.

Brandnames of Products and Services:

Adams	*peanut butter & nut snacks*
Boston Sea Party	*seafood restaurants*
Deli Gourmet	*specialty meats*
Kaukauna Klub	*cheese*
Kretschmer	*wheat germ & granola*
La Crosta	*pizza crust mix*
Mister Donut	*coffee and donut shops*
Morey's	*smoked & frozen fish*
Reuben	*specialty meats*
Robin Hood	*flour and mixes*
Sherwood Forest	*wild bird food*
Smoke Craft	*beef jerky and meat snacks*
Sun Country	*granola cereals*
Trail Blazer	*specialty meats*

International Paper Co.

220 E. 42nd St.
New York, N.Y. 10017
(212) 490-6000

Chief Executive Officer: E.A. Gee
Exchange: NY
Symbol: IP

Corporate History: The company, which began in 1898 and incorporated in 1941, is the largest papermaking organization in the world. Approximately 40% of its business is in packaging materials.

Brandnames of Products and Services:

Long-Bell Cabinets

International Seaway Trading Corp.

1382 W. 9th St.
Cleveland, Ohio 44113
(216) 696-7800

Chief Executive Officer: Harvey K. Gerdy
1984 Annual Sales Volume: 21M
1984 Shares Outstanding: 656,000
Shareholders: 401
Exchange: AM
Symbol: INS

Corporate History: The company, incorporated in 1960, is America's leading importer of fabric, vinyl, rubber and leather footwear, which it distributes throughout the United States and Canada. All the company's merchandise is imported from the Orient.

Brandnames of Products and Services:

AAU	*(Amateur Athletic Union) sports shoes*
Lasco	*shoes*
Surfboards	*shoes*
Windy Hill	*shoes*

Iroquois Brands Ltd.

41 W. Putnam Ave.
Greenwich, CT 06836-2000
(203) 622-9000

Chief Executive Officer:	Terence J. Fox
1984 Annual Sales Volume:	144M
1984 Shares Outstanding:	1,140,048
Shareholders:	1,914
Exchange:	AM
Symbol:	IBL

Corporate History: The company, incorporated in 1967, produces, imports and distributes specialty foods, beverages and nutritional products.

Brandnames of Products and Services:

Basic Organics	*vitamins*
Black Horse Ale	
Cara Coa	*carob drinks and candy products*
Champale Sparkling Wines	
Coolage	*malt beverage*
El Molino Mills	*food products*
G.B. Raffetto	*condiments*
Giroux	*grenadine and lime juice*
Javin	*Indian condiments*
La Sauce	*cooking and baking sauces*
Magic Mountain Herb Tea	
Major Grey's Chutney	
Metbrau	*nonalcoholic beer*
Mi-Lem	*lemon mix beverage*
Mr Marinade	*marinade products*
Natura Brands	*health food and vitamins*
Origin	*natural food supplements and vitamins*
Radiance	*natural food supplements and vitamins*
Raffetto	*specialty foods*
Romanoff	*caviar*
Sauce Maison	*food products*
Schiff Bro.	*food products*
Texas Best	*barbecue sauce and Bloody Mary mix*
Wuppermann	*lime and grenadine*
Yoo-Hoo	*milk-based noncarbonated beverages*

ITT Corp.

320 Park Ave.
New York, NY 10022
(212) 752-6000

Chief Executive Officer:	Rand V. Araskog
1984 Annual Sales Volume:	12,701M
1984 Shares Outstanding:	139,749,859
Shareholders:	127,000
Exchange:	NY
Symbol:	ITT

Corporate History: ITT was founded in 1920 by Sosthenes Behn as an international telephone system similar to AT&T's domestic configuration. Behn began in the Caribbean and by World War II had a firm hold in Europe as well. During the 1920s AT&T and ITT signed a secret agreement not to encroach on each other's territory. Under the direction of Harold Geneen during the 1950s and 1960s the company began a policy of aggressive acquisition, buying more than 275 companies. ITT's principal operations, either direct or through subsidiaries, are in telecommunications equipment, defense and space, automotive, connectors, components and semiconductors, industrial products, communications operations and information services, hotels and community development, insurance operations, financial services and natural resources.

Brandnames of Products and Services:

Burpee	*seeds*
Consumer Financial Corp.	*financial services*
Hartford Fire & Insurance Co.	
Pro Turf	*fertilizer*
Scotts	*lawn care products*
Sheraton	*hotels*
Turf Builder	*fertilizer*

Jaclyn, Inc.

635-59th St.
West New York, NJ 07093
(201) 868-9400

Chief Executive Officer: A. Ginsburg
1984 Annual Sales Volume: 49M
1984 Shares Outstanding: 1,767,274
Shareholders: 1,498
Exchange: AM
Symbol: JLN
Corporate History: Jaclyn, incorporated in 1968, is one of the largest producers of women's handbags in the country.
Brandnames of Products and Services:

Bonnie	*handbags*
Empress	*handbags*
Jaclyn	*handbags*
Tammy Brooke	*handbags*

Jamesway Corp.

40 Hartz Way
Secaucus, NJ 07094
(201) 330-6000

Chief Executive Officer: Herbert Fisher
1984 Annual Sales Volume: 475M
1984 Shares Outstanding: 6,778,797
Shareholders: 2,593
Exchange: NY
Symbol: JMY
Corporate History: The company, incorporated in 1966, operates a chain of 83 discount department stores, primarily in Pennsylvania, New York and New Jersey. Jamesway opened seven stores during 1984.
Brandnames of Products and Services:

Jamesway	*discount department stores*

Jefferson-Pilot Corp.

101 N. Elm St.
P.O. Box 21008
Greensboro, NC 27420
(919) 378-2011

Chief Executive Officer: W.R. Soles
1984 Annual Sales Volume: 9,047M
1984 Shares Outstanding: 31,795,402
Shareholders: 11,722
Exchange: NY
Symbol: JP
Corporate History: Jefferson-Pilot Corp., incorporated in 1968, is a holding company whose subsidiaries provide a variety of insurance, financial, and communications products and services. The corporation's two principal subsidiaries, Jefferson Standard Life and Pilot Life, began operations in 1907 and 1903, respectively, and today operate in 34 states, the District of Columbia, Puerto Rico and the Virgin Islands. The life insurance subsidiaries offer a complete line of life insurance, health insurance, annuity and pension products. Other financial subsidiaries of Jefferson-Pilot provide fire and casualty insurance, title insurance and mutual fund sales and management services. Jefferson-Pilot's Communications subsidiaries own and operate television stations and radio stations.
Brandnames of Products and Services:

KIMN-AM	*Denver, Colo.*
KSON AM&FM	*San Diego, CA*
KYGO-FM	*Denver, Colo.*
WBCY-FM	*Charlott, N.C.*
WBIG-AM	*Greensboro, N.C.*
WBT-AM	*Charlotte, N.C.*
WBTV-TV	*Charlotte, N.C.*
WGBS-AM	*Miami, Fla.*
WLYF-FM	*Miami, Fla.*
WQXI-AM-FM	*Atlanta, Ga.*
WWBT-TV	*Richmond, Va.*

Jerrico Inc.

101 Jerrico Dr., P.O. Box 11988
Lexington, KY 40579
(606) 268-5211

Chief Executive Officer: John E. Tobe
1984 Annual Sales Volume: 496M
1984 Shares Outstanding: 15,725,000
Shareholders: 3,400
Exchange: OTC
Symbol: JERR
Corporate History: Jerrico began in 1929 with a 5¢ hamburger stand in Kentucky called "White Tavern." The company was incorporated in 1946, and opened its first Jerry's Sandwich Shop. Today Jerrico operates and franchises more than 1,350 Long John Silver's Seafood Shoppes, mostly in the Midwest, South and Southwest, and a smaller chain of coffee shops and family restaurants. In fiscal 1984 restaurants provided 80% of the company's revenues.

Brandnames of Products and Services:

Gentry Inn	*Jackson, Tenn.*
Jerry's	*coffee shops*
Long John Silver's Sea Food Shoppes	*fast-food restaurants*

Jewel Companies Inc.

O'Hare Plaza
5725 N. East River Rd.
Chicago, Ill. 60631
(312) 693-6000

Chief Executive Officer: R.G. Cline
Exchange: NY
Symbol: JWL
Corporate History: The company was founded in 1899 and incorporated in 1916 as Jewel Tea Co. It adopted its present title in 1966. It operates more than 400 food stores in the Midwest. Jewel has signed on as a supermarket consultant to Japan's third largest grocery chain. In 1980 Jewel acquired Sav-On Drugs, operator of 140 super drugstores in California. In fiscal 1980, supermarket sales provided 74.9% of sales, and general merchandise stores and other sectors the remainder.
Brandnames of Products and Services:

Belmont	*foods*
Big E	*food stores*
Bluebrook	*food products*
Brigham's	*ice cream/candy parlors*
Buttrey	*food stores*
Chef Cut	*foods*
Chef Kitchen	*foods*
Cherry Valley	*canned foods*
Crackin' Good	*foods*
Dew Kist	*foods*
Eisner	*food stores*
Farm Stand	*foods*
Fashion Tone	*diet foods*
Grill Great	*foods*
Instant Maid	*foods*
JEB's	*foods*
Jewel	*food stores*
Jewel Maid	*foods*
Jewel T	*discount grocery stores*
Launder Maid	*foods*
Mary Dunbar	*food products*
Natural Harvest	*foods*
Old Bohemia	*foods*
Osco	*drugstores*
Royal Jewel	*foods*
Sable Soft	*foods*
Star	*food products*
Star	*supermarkets*
Taper	*foods*
University	*foods*
Velvetouch	*foods*
White Hen Pantry	*convenience food stores*
Yummy	*food products*

Jhirmack Enterprises Inc.

4350 Caterpillar Dr.
P.O. Drawer 4307
Redding, Calif. 96001
(916) 246-2100

Chief Executive Officer: Irene Redding
Exchange: OTC
Corporate History: The company, incorporated in 1968, makes ph-balanced hair care products.
Brandnames of Products and Services:

Algele	*hair care products*
EFA	*shampoo*
Gelave	*shampoo*
Jhirmack	*personal care products*
Moisturphlex	*hair conditioner*
NCA	*hair conditioiner*
Nutri-Pak	*hair conditioner*
PHinale	*hair conditioner*
Sean	*men's soap and fragrance*

Jim Walter Corp.

P.O. Box 22601
Tampa, Fla. 33622
(813) 871-4811

Chief Executive Officer: Joe B. Cordell
1984 Annual Sales Volume: 2,287M
1984 Shares Outstanding: 21,746,000
Shareholders: 25,500
Exchange: NY
Symbol: JWC
Corporate History: Jim Walter, incorporated in 1955, is one of the nation's 200 largest industrial companies, offering a diversified line of products and services for residential and non-residential construction, renovation/remodeling, water and waste water transmission, homebuilding, industrial and consumer markets on a worldwide basis. In addition, the company has major interests in the development of various natural resources, including coal, oil and gas, marble, granite, limestone and gypsum. Other business areas are produc-

tion of coke and industrial chemicals, distribution of quality printing papers, retail and wholesale jewelry operations, and insurance agency services.

Brandnames of Products and Services:

Best Insurors Insurance Agency	
Celotex	*building products*
Crusader	*paper products*
Jimco Stone Centers	*marble products*
Lorch Jewelry Stores	
Stenocraft	*paper products*
Supreme	*paper products*

Johnson & Johnson

One Johnson & Johnson Plaza
New Brunswick, NJ 08933
(201) 524-0400

Chief Executive Officer: J.E. Burke
1984 Annual Sales Volume: 6,125M
1984 Shares Outstanding: 187,400,000
Shareholders: 538,000
Exchange: NY
Symbol: JNJ

Corporate History: Johnson & Johnson, which began operations in 1886, was a pioneer in making antiseptic and sterile surgical dressings. In 1920 it developed the Band-Aid brand adhesive bandage. Today it is the world's foremost manufacturer of surgical dressings and related items. It has diversified into a variety of health and personal care products for both professionals and consumers. During the 1970s it introduced Tylenol, originally a prescription pain killer, which competed with Bayer Aspirin. Today it is the number one dollar producer in drugstores. However, battered by stiff competition from Procter & Gamble and Kimberly-Clark, the company got out of the disposable diaper market. In 1984 consumer products provided 42% of sales, professional goods 33%, pharmaceuticals 21% and industrial 4%.

Brandnames of Products and Services:

Assure	*panty liners*
Band-Aid	*bandage products*
Carefree	*panty shields*
CoEts	*cosmetic squares*
Delfen	*contraceptive*
Fenjala	*bath and soap products*
Iolab	*intraocular lenses*
Johnson & Johnson	*baby products*
Johnson's Dental Floss	*dental care product*
Micatin	*antifungal cream*
Modess	*sanitary napkins*
O.B.	*tampon*
Ortho-Novum	*contraceptive (oral)*
Purpose	*soap, shampoo and dry skin cream*
Reach	*toothbrush*
Retin A	*acne treatment*
Shower-to-Shower	*body powder*
Sine-Aid	*sinus reliever*
Stayfree	*sanitary napkins*
Steri-Pad	*sterile pads*
Sufenta	*analgesic/anesthetic*
Sundown	*sunscreen*
Sure & Natural Maxishields	*sanitary napkins*
Tylenol	*analgesic*

Johnson Products Co. Inc.

8522 South Lafayette Ave.
Chicago, IL 60620
(312) 483-4100

Chief Executive Officer: George E. Johnson
1984 Annual Sales Volume: 42M
1984 Shares Outstanding: 3,984,582
Shareholders: 1,686
Exchange: AMEX
Symbol: JPC

Corporate History: Johnson Products Co., Inc. headquartered in Chicago, was formed in 1954. It manufacturers and markets personal care products for the retail and professional markets in the U.S. and overseas. Its main product lines include hair relaxers, conditioners, dressings, shampoos and cosmetics. The company also operates 12 schools for beauticians in the midwest and south.

Brandnames of Products and Services:

Afro Sheen	*hair care products*
Bantu	*hair care products*
Classy Curl	*hair care products*
Debbie Howell Cosmetics	*cosmetics, make-up direct mail*
Gentle Treatment	*hair care products*
Moisture Formula	*cosmetics*

Ultra Precise Beauty Boutique	*hair care, make-up*
Ultra Sheen	*hair care, make-up*
Ultra Sheen's Precise	*hair care products*
Ultra Star	*hair care products*
Ultra Wave	*hair care products*

Jonathan Logan Inc.

50 Terminal Rd.
Secaucus, N.J. 07094
(212) 840-9400

Chief Executive Officer: R.J. Schwartz
Exchange: NY
Symbol: JOL
Corporate History: The company, incorporated in 1954, makes men's and women's apparel. It also produces footwear, swimwear and rainwear.
Brandnames of Products and Services:

Act III	*women's sportswear*
Alice Stuart	*blouses*
Amy Adams	*women's half-size apparel*
Butte Knit	*ladies' apparel*
Etienne Aigner	*leather products (imported)*
Gloria Vanderbilt for Jonathan Logan	*sport dresses*
Harbor Master	*men's outerwear*
Imerman	*children's sleepwear*
Jonathan Logan	*women's apparel*
Knit Studios	*women's apparel outlets*
Kollection	*women's apparel*
Misty Harbor	*women's outerwear*
Modern Junior	*women's sportswear*
R & K Originals	*dresses*
Rose Marie Reid	*swimwear*
Trebor	*underwear and knit tops*
Venice Industries	*knit dresses*
The Villager	*women's sportswear*

Jostens Inc.

5501 Norman Center Drive
Minneapolis, MN 55437
(612) 830-3300

Chief Executive Officer: H.W. Lurton
1984 Annual Sales Volume: 486M
1984 Shares Outstanding: 21,583
Shareholders: 4,800
Exchange: NY
Symbol: JOS
Corporate History: The company, incorporated in 1906, makes class rings, graduation announcements, diplomas, caps and gowns, athletic and academic awards and trophies, photography packages, loose-leaf binders, custom imprinted sports and casual wear, and specialized jewelry and awards for business. The company also operates a network of business and trade schools across the U.S. In 1984, Jostens acquired Hazel, Inc. of Washington, Mo., a manufacturer of leather & vinyl products.
Brandnames of Products and Services:

Artex	*apparel*
Cardinal	*business products*
Hazel	*leather and vinyl products*
Jostens	*school memorabilia*
Microsystem80	*computer software*
System80	*audio-visual units*
Ufonic	*computer voice synthesizer*

Justin Industries Inc.

2821 W. 7th St.
P.O. Box 425
Ft. Worth, TX 76101
(817) 336-5125

Chief Executive Officer: J.S. Justin, Jr.
1984 Annual Sales Volume: 284M
1984 Shares Outstanding: 5,900,000
Shareholders: 4,000
Exchange: OTC
Symbol: JSTN
Corporate History: Justin incorporated in 1916 as Acme Brick Co., successor to Acme Press Brick Co. The name was changed to First Worth Corp. in 1968 and to its current title in 1972. The company makes building products for the wholesale market and western, work, and safety footwear. It is one of the largest producers of quality Western boots in the United States. Its ceramic cooling tower company markets the only permanent cooling towers utilizing ceramic fill material encased either in concrete or fiberglass shells. Its featherlite companies manufacture concrete building components including block and precast and prestressed structural and architectural members. Justin also owns Northland Press, a publisher of books on Western Americana.
Brandnames of Products and Services:

Acme	*bricks*
Chippewa	*boots*

Featherlite	*building materials*
Justin Boots	
Nocona	*boots*
Northland Press	*publishing house*
Pathfinder	*boots*
Thermalite	*ceramic tile fill*

Kaman Corp.

Blue Hills Ave.
Bloomfield, CT 06002
(203) 243-8311

Chief Executive Officer: C.H. Kaman
1984 Annual Sales Volume: 538M
1984 Shares Outstanding: 7,113,000
Shareholders: 5,582
Exchange: OTC
Symbol: KAMNA
Corporate History: Kaman Corp. incorporated in 1945. Through internal diversification and acquisitions, it has expanded from a pioneering helicopter company into a supplier of aviation services and a manufacturer of musical instruments.
Brandnames of Products and Services:

Ovation	*guitars*

Kapok Corp.

923 McMullen Booth Rd.
Clearwater, FL 33519
(813) 726-4734

Chief Executive Officer: Aaron R. Fodiman
1984 Annual Sales Volume: 24M
1984 Shares Outstanding: 2,442,700
Shareholders: NA
Exchange: AM
Symbol: KPK
Corporate History: The company operates five restaurants; four are located in Florida, one in Maryland. In addition, the company is engaged in the production and sale of steel and pipe products. The company also is involved in the exploration and production of gas and oil in Texas and New Mexico. In 1983 the company acquired Elmont Steel.
Brandnames of Products and Services:

Kapok Tree Restaurants	*Clearwater, Ft. Lauderdale, Madeira Beach, Florida*
Peter Pan Restaurant	*Urbana, Maryland*
Savoy Restaurant	*Clearwater, Florida*

Katy Industries, Inc.

853 Dundee Ave.
Elgin, IL 60120
(312) 379-1121

Chief Executive Officer: Wallace E. Carroll
1984 Annual Sales Volume: 432M
1984 Shares Outstanding: 6,164,619
Shareholders: 5,078
Exchange: NY
Symbol: KT
Corporate History: Katy Industries Inc., incorporated in 1967, carries on business through six principal operation groups: consumer products; industrial machinery, equipment and products; electrical equipment and products; oil field and other services; transportation; and financial services. In 1983 the company acquired International Silver and combined it with its own company, Wallace Silversmiths, to form Wallace International Silversmiths.
Brandnames of Products and Services:

Beachport Spas	*recreational equipment*
Bee Gee Shrimp	*shrimp*
Delico	*cheese*
Ecru	*jewelry*
Elgin	*watches*
Glit	*scouring pads*
Hallmark Jewelry	*jewelry*
Hermann Loewenstein	*leather products*
International	*silver, holloware*
Kolb-Lena Cheese	*cheese*
Lake Valley Broadcasters	*broadcasting*
Missouri-Kansas-Texas Railroad	*railroad*
Moldan	*scouring pads*
Sahlman Seafoods	*seafoods*
Wallace	*silver, holloware*

Kay Corp.

320 King St.
Alexandria, VA 22314
(703) 683-3800

Chief Executive Officer: Anthonie C. Van Ekris
1984 Annual Sales Volume: 828M
1984 Shares Outstanding: 3,726,997
Shareholders: 1,800
Exchange: AM
Symbol: KAY
Corporate History: The company incorporated in 1953 as Kay Jewelry Stores and changed its name to the present title in 1972. The company is engaged, through its wholly-owned subsidiary, Balfour, Maclaine International Ltd., in importing and exporting a wide variety of goods and commodities, and through its wholly-owned subsidiary, Kay Jewelers, Inc., in operating fine jewelry stores and leased fine jewelry departments in department stores. It is a major importer of green coffee and seafood, as well as crude rubber, an exporter of rice, and a worldwide distributor of tea. It operates 15 jewelry stores under the name Black, Starr and Frost, 275 jewelry stores under the name Kay Jewelers, and 48 leased jewelry departments in department stores.
Brandnames of Products and Services:

Black, Starr & Frost	*jewelry stores*
Kay Jewelers	*jewelry stores*

KDI Corp.

5721 Dragon Way
Cincinnati, OH 45227
(513) 272-1421

Chief Executive Officer: L.W. Matthey
1984 Annual Sales Volume: 235M
1984 Shares Outstanding: 8,581,650
Shareholders: 7,342
Exchange: NY
Symbol: KDI
Corporate History: The company was incorporated in 1952 as Kraus Automatic Machines Corp. The present name was adopted in 1956. KDI is a diversified company. It manufactures electrical and electronic components, swimming pools, devices for the defense industry (such as fuses and grenade components), thermoplastic components, and other products. It also distributes such diverse items as organic chemicals and motion pictures.
Brandnames of Products and Services:

Sylvan	*swimming pools*

Keller Industries Inc.

18000 State Rd. Nine
Miami, Fla. 33162
(305) 651-7100

Chief Executive Officer: H.A. Keller
Exchange: NY
Symbol: KEL
Corporate History: The company was incorporated in 1951 as Jalousie & Window Engineering Inc. It changed its name to Air Control Products in 1955, and to its current name in 1965. The company makes household products. In 1979 aluminum products amounted for 48% of sales and furniture, ladders and carpeting the remainder.
Brandnames of Products and Services:

American Carpet Mills	*carpets*
Keller	*patio furniture, storm windows and doors*
Keller Carpets	

Kellogg Co.

P.O. Box 3423
Battle Creek, MI 49016-3423
(616) 966-2000

Chief Executive Officer: W.E. La Mothe
1984 Annual Sales Volume: $2,602 M
1984 Shares Outstanding: 74,690,000
Shareholders: 22,340
Exchange: NY
Symbol: K
Corporate History: Kellogg Company was founded in 1906 by Will Keith Kellogg, who had helped to develop new food products at the Battle Creek Sanitarium, where his brother was chief surgeon. The firm adopted its present title in 1922. Kellogg is ranked number one in the breakfast cereal market with 42% of the total. Its cereals are sold in 22 countries as well as the United States. Approximately one-third of its business is done abroad. In recent years the company has branched out into other food products but does not diversify through acquisitions.
Brandnames of Products and Services:

Dutch Maid	*pancake batter*

Eggo	*frozen waffles*
Hostess	*non-dairy creamer, batters, and whipped toppings*
Junket	*dessert*
Kellogg	*cereals*
LeGout	*canned soups, soup bases, gravies, gravy bases, vegetables, relish*
Mrs. Smith's Pies	
Pop Tarts	*toaster pastries*
Salada	*tea and dessert products*
Whitney's	*yogurt*

Kellwood Co.

600 Kellwood Parkway
St. Louis, Mo. 63017
(314) 576-3100

Chief Executive Officer: F.W. Wenzel
Exchange: NY
Symbol: KWD
Corporate History: The company, incorporated in 1961, makes apparel, curtains, bed coverings and coordinateddraperies as well as camping and hiking equipment. It also operates Ashley's outlet stores, which offer irregular and surplus merchanidse. Approximately 69% of its products are made for Sears, Roebuck & Co. In 1979 and 1980 apparel accounted for 69% of sales with outlet stores, home furnishings and recreational products making up the remainder.
Brandnames of Products and Services:

Asley's Retail Outlets	
Denver Jeans	*apparel*
Finesse	*home products*
Finesse	*hosiery*
Kellwood Fashions	*apparel*
Kellwood Kasuals	*apparel*
Kelty Pack	*recreational products*
Kicks	*apparel*
Kingswell Kasuals	*apparel*
Master Jac	*apparel*
Mountain Grown	*apparel*
Name Droppers	*hosiery*
NFL	*apparel*
Northfield	*apparel*
Sir Jac	*apparel*
Sun Brite	*apparel*
Van Raalte	*hosiery*
Visions	*home furnishing products*
Weatherrogue	*apparel*
Wenzel	*recreational products*

Kennington Ltd. Inc.

3209 Humboldt St.
Los Angeles, CA 90031
(213) 225-1655

Chief Executive Officer: L.J. Condon
1984 Annual Sales Volume: 36M
1984 Shares Outstanding: 5,687,838
Shareholders: 560
Exchange: OTC
Symbol: KENN
Corporate History: Incorporated in 1962, Kennington produces men's and boys' apparel.
Brandnames of Products and Services:

Alfie	*men's apparel*
Chemise by Kennington	*men's shirts*
Colore	*men's apparel*
Impulse	*men's apparel*
Kennington	*men's shirts*
Kennington for Boys	*boy's apparel*
Sagamore Hotel	*Lake George, NY*
Winner Wear	*active wear*

Kenwin Shops Inc.

505 Eighth Ave.
New York, NY 10018
(212) 695-1850

Chief Executive Officer: Irwin Moskowitz
1984 Annual Sales Volume: 29M
1984 Shares Outstanding: 464,212
Shareholders: 398
Exchange: AM
Symbol: KWN
Corporate History: The company, incorporated in 1946, operates 229 ladies' and children's apparel stores located in Georgia, Alabama, Mississippi, Tennessee, South Carolina, Louisiana, Texas, Arkansas, Florida and Oklahoma.
Brandnames of Products and Services:

Blends 'n Trends	*ladies' and children's apparel stores*
Dixie	*ladies' and children's apparel stores*

Kenwin	*ladies' and children's apparel stores*
Peyton	*ladies' and children's apparel stores*
Smart & Thrifty	*ladies' and children's apparel stores*
Suzanne	*ladies' and children's apparel stores*

Kidde Inc.

Park 80 West - Plaza Two
Saddle Brook, NJ 07662
(201) 368-9000

Chief Executive Officer: F.R. Sullivan
1984 Annual Sales Volume: 2,312M
1984 Shares Outstanding: 20,513,530
Shareholders: 13,163
Exchange: NY
Symbol: KDE

Corporate History: Kidde, founded in 1900 was originally known for manufacturing fire protection equipment. Today the company is a multi-billion dollar conglomerate that provides safety and security services and manufactures industrial and commercial equipment as well as household and recreational products. Almost half its sales are from consumer and recreation products. Approximately one quarter of the sales come from safety, security and protection services. Consumer and recreational products are the fastest growing segment of the company.

Brandnames of Products and Services:

Bear	*archery equipment*
Ertl	*replica toys*
Farberware	*cooking appliances*
Jacuzzi	*whirlpool baths & spas*
Kidde	*fire extinguishers*
Nissen	*gymnasium equipment*
P.G.A.	*(Professional Golfers' Association) golfing equipment*
Progress	*lighting*
Rexair Rainbow	*vacuum cleaners*
Spartus	*clocks*
Tucker	*plastic containers & housewares*
Universal	*gymnasium equipment*
Valley	*pool tables*
Vanity Fair	*toys*
Waltham	*clocks*

Kimball International Inc.

1600 Royal St.
Jasper, IN 47546
(812) 482-1600

Chief Executive Officer: T.L. Habig
1984 Annual Sales Volume: 320M
1984 Shares Outstanding: 5,658,000
Shareholders: 1,988
Exchange: OTC
Symbol: KBALB

Corporate History: Kimball International, incorporated in 1939, is one of the largest domestic manufacturers of office furniture, pianos, organs, and cabinets for television and stereo units. In addition, it makes reproductions of Victorian and French furniture, as well as home furniture under a private label. Its products also include electronic assemblies, molded polyurethane, carbide cutting tools, and processed wood materials such as dimension lumber, veneer, plywood, and banded flakeboard. In fiscal 1984, furniture and cabinets accounted for 64% of sales, pianos and organs 25%, and processed wood materials 9%. The company was originally called Midwest Manufacturing Company. Upon reorganization in 1950, it was renamed the Jasper Corporation and became Kimball International in 1974. The company entered the piano and organ business in 1959 by acquiring the W.W. Kimball Company. In 1969, through another acquisition, it added reproductions of period furniture to its products. The company moved into wood office furniture production in 1970. The company expanded its office furniture involvement in 1980 with the acquisition of the Artec line of office furniture systems. Kimball is the nation's largest independent manufacturer of cabinets for the television industry. Its customers over three decades have included all leading TV makers.

Brandnames of Products and Services:

Artec	*office furniture*
Bosendorfer	*pianos*
Conn	*pianos and organs*
Kimball	*pianos, office furniture, & electronic organs*
Krakauer	*pianos*
National	*office furniture*
Whitmore	*pianos*
Whitney	*pianos*
Woodlor	*molded polyurethane products*

Kimberly-Clark Corp.

401 North Lake Street
Neenah, WI 54956
(414) 721-2000

Chief Executive Officer: D.E. Smith
1984 Annual Sales Volume: 3,616M
1984 Shares Outstanding: 45,707,251
Shareholders: 20,548
Exchange: NY
Symbol: KMB

Corporate History: Kimberly-Clark Corporation, incorporated in 1928, its consolidated subsidiaries and equity companies are engaged in a single, worldwide business employing advanced technologies in absorbency, fiber-forming, and other fields. THe corporation produces and markets a wide range of products (most of which are made from natural and synthetic fibers) for personal care, health care, and other uses in the home, business and industry. The corporation also produces and markets specialty papers for specialized applications, as well as traditional paper and related products for newspaper publishing and other communication needs. Products for home use are sold directly to supermarkets, mass merchandisers, drugstores, home health care stores, variety stores, department stores, and other retail outlets as well as to wholesalers, brokers, and distributors.

Brandnames of Products and Services:

Anyday	*panty liners*
Avert	*facial tissue*
Ballet	*paper products*
bathroom tissues	
Boutique	*facial tissue*
Brevia	*feminine hygiene*
Casuals	*facial tissue*
Cellucotton	*beauty coil*
Classic	*writing paper*
Clout	*wiping product*
Crew	*wiping product*
Dawn	*bathroom tissue*
Dayfresh	*panty liners*
Delsey	*bathroom tissue*
Depend	*incontinence products*
Evolution	*nonwoven fabrics*
Fems	*feminine hygiene*
Futura	*feminine hygiene*
Hi-Dri	*paper products*
Huggies	*disposable diapers*
Kaydry	*wiping product*
Kimbies	*disposable diapers*
Kimguard	*sterile wrap & disposable workwear*
Kimtex	*wiping product*
Kimtowels	*wiping product*
Kimwipes	*wiping product*
Kleen Bebe	*disposable diapers*
Kleenex	*paper products & disposable diapers*
Kleenguard	*disposable garments*
Kleenups	*wiping product*
Kotex	*feminine hygiene*
Liberte	*feminine hygiene*
Lightdays	*panty liners*
Lithowipe	*wiping product*
Little Travelers	*facial tissue*
Lys	*facial tissue*
Man Size	*facial tissue*
New Freedom	*sanitary napkin*
Popee	*bathroom tissue*
Regio	*bathroom tissue*
Scribe	*school papers*
Security	*feminine hygiene*
Snuggems	*disposable diapers*
Softique	*facial tissue*
Spuncare	*disposable garments and bed linens*
Teri	*towels*
Tiss	*facial tissues*
Tough Cat	*automotive cleaning and care products*
Vogue	*facial tissue*
Wondersoft	*paper products*

Kleinerts Inc.

Whitemarsh Plaza, 15 East Ridge Pike
Conshohocken, PA 19428
(215) 828-7261

Chief Executive Officer: Jack Brier
1984 Annual Sales Volume: 40M
1984 Shares Outstanding: 1,599,744
Shareholders: 700
Exchange: OTC
Symbol: KLRT

Corporate History: The company was founded and incorporated in 1907 as I.B. Kleinert Rubber Co., and adopted its present title in 1969. The company is engaged primarily in the manufacture and sale of infants' and children's apparel and knitting and dyeing fabric for its own use and for sale to others. It is also involved in the personal apparel business.

Brandnames of Products and Services:

Kleinerts	*dress shields, swim caps and infant wear*
Teddy Bear	*infant wear*

K Mart Corp.

3100 West Big Beaver Rd.
Troy, MI 48084
(313) 643-1000

Chief Executive Officer: Bernard M. Fauber
1984 Annual Sales Volume: 21,096M
1984 Shares Outstanding: 125,063,839
Shareholders: 93,221
Exchange: NY
Symbol: KG

Corporate History: K Mart Corp. incorporated in 1916 as Kresge (S.S.) Co. By 1929 it had a chain of approximately 600 variety stores throughout the country. The company was a pioneer in the discount department store, called K Mart, opening the first outlet in 1962. In response to the concept's success the company was renamed K Mart in 1977. Today K Mart is the world's second-largest retailing chain. The company's principal business is general-merchandise retailing. The company operates a total of 2,400 general merchandise and 1,120 specialty retail stores in the United States, Canada and Puerto Rico. In 1984 K Mart stores accounted for more than 95% of the company's sales. The company also operates a chain of cafeterias in the southwestern, midwestern and western United States; a chain of apparel stores, and the nation's largest bookstore chain, Walden Books. Its most recent acquisitions are Builders Square (formerly Home Centers of America) and Pay Less Drug Stores Northwest.

Brandnames of Products and Services:

Bishop Buffets	*cafeterias*
Builders Square	*home improvement stores*
Designer Depot	*discount apparel stores*
Furr's	*cafeterias*
Jupiter	*discount stores*
K Mart	*general merchandise stores*
Kresge	*variety stores*
Pay Less Drug Stores	*drug stores*
Walden Book Company	*book stores*

Knight-Ridder Newspapers Inc.

One Herald Plaza
Miami, FL 33101
(305) 376-3800

Chief Executive Officer: Alvan H. Chapman
1984 Annual Sales Volume: 1,665M
1984 Shares Outstanding: 65,238,254
Shareholders: 8,769
Exchange: NY
Symbol: KRN

Corporate History: The company was formed in 1974 as a merger of two newspaper chains, Knight and Ridder. The action created one of the largest newspaper chains in the nation. Among the papers it publishes are three of the largest in the nation, the Detroit (Mich.) *Free Press,* Miami, (Fla.) *Herald* and Philadelphia (Pa.) *Inquirer.* The company also engages in television broadcasting, cable television operations, business news and information services, newsprint production, videotex operations, specialized mobile radio services and book publishing.

Brandnames of Products and Services:

American-News	*newspaper, Aberdeen, S.D.*
Beacon Journal	*newspaper, Akron, Ohio*
Daily Camera	*newspaper, Boulder, Colo.*
Daily News	*newspaper, Philadelphia, Pa.*
Daily Times	*State Slope, PA*
Democrat	*newspaper, Tallahassee, Fla.*
Dispatch	*St. Paul, MN*
Dispatch	*newspaper, St. Paul, Minn.*
Eagle-Beacon	*Wichita, KS*
Eagle	*newspaper, Wichita, Kan.*
Enquirer	*newspaper, Columbus, Ohio*
Free Press	*newspaper, Detroit, Mich.*
Herald	*Grand Forks, ND*
Herald	*Duluth, MN*
Herald	*Bradenton, FL*
Herald	*Miami, FL*
HP Books	*publishing company*
Inquirer	*Philadelphia, PA*
Journal of Commerce	*newspaper, New York, NY*
Ledger	*newspaper, Columbus, Ohio*
Lexington Herald-Leader	*newspaper, Lexington, Ky.*
Mercury News	*newspaper, San Jose, Calif.*
News	*newspaper, Macon, Ga.*
News	*Charlotte, N.C.*

News	*newspaper, Boca Raton, Fla.*
News	*newspaper, San Jose, Calif.*
News Sentinel	*newspaper, Fort Wayne, Indiana*
News-Tribune	*newspaper, Duluth, Minn.*
Observer	*newspaper, Charlotte, N.C.*
Pioneer Press	*newspaper, St. Paul, Minn.*
Post-Tribune	*newspaper, Gary, Ind.*
Press-Telegram	*newspaper, Long Beach, Calif.*
Star-News	*newspaper, Pasadena, Calif.*
Telegraph and News	*newspaper, Macon, Ga.*
Times	*newspaper, Seattle, Wash.*
Union Bulletin	*newspaper, Walla Walla, Wash.*
Union-Recorder	*Milledgeville, GA*
WJRT-TV	*Flint, Mich.*
WKRN-TV	*Nashville, TN*
WPRI-TV	*Providence, R.I.*
WTEN-TV	*Albany, N.Y.*
WTKR-TV	*Norfolk, VA*

Knudsen Corp.

231 E. 23rd St.
Los Angeles, Calif. 90011
(213) 747-6471

Chief Executive Officer: J.R. Vaughan
Exchange: OTC
Symbol: KNUD
Corporate History: The company began in 1914 as Knudsen's Laboratory and in 1919 became Knudsen Creamery Company of California. It adopted current title in 1968. It processes and distributes dairy products mainly in California and Southern Nevada.
Brandnames of Products and Services:

- 50-50 Bar
- Big Stick
- Choco Crunch
- Dari Valley
- Dreamsicle
- Drumstick
- Eskimo Pie
- Fudgesicle
- Health Bar
- Hoagy's Corner Deli
- Knudsen
- Malt Cup
- Nice 'n' Lite
- Partytime
- Popsicle
- Pushups
- Rich & Natural
- Scoopable
- Sidewalk Sundae

Kroehler Manufacturing Co.

222 E. Fifth Ave.
Naperville, Ill. 60540
(312) 420-6789

Chief Executive Officer: W.T. Welsh
Exchange: NY
Symbol: KFM
Corporate History: Kroehler Mfg. was founded in 1915 as a consolidation of four furniture makers. Today it makes popular-priced furniture.
Brandnames of Products and Services:

- Kroehler
- Kroehler Citation

The Kroger Co.

1014 Vine St.
Cincinnati, OH 45201
(513) 762-4000

Chief Executive Officer: Lyle Everingham
1984 Annual Sales Volume: 15,900M
1984 Shares Outstanding: 45,080,783
Shareholders: 45,428
Exchange: NY
Symbol: KR
Corporate History: The company was founded in 1883 in Cincinnati, Ohio, incorporated in 1902 as The Kroger Grocery & Baking Co., and adopted its present title in 1946. It operates a chain of food and drugstores in the South, Midwest, and West. Kroger is the fourth largest retailing concern and second largest food store chain in the nation. In 1980 its supermarket business accounted for more than 90% of sales. The company operates 1,318 supermarkets, 618 drugstores, 443 convenience stores, and 41 manufacturing plants in 31 states.
Brandnames of Products and Services:

Barney's	*discount grocery store, Cleveland*
Bilo Stores	*"no-frills" grocery stores*

City Market	*supermarkets*
Dillons Food Stores	*supermarkets*
Fry's Food Stores	*supermarkets*
Gasen	*drugstores*
Gerbes Supermarkets	*supermarkets*
King Soopers	*supermarkets*
Kroger Food Stores	*supermarkets*
Kroger Sav-On	*food and drug stores*
Kwik Shop	*convenience stores*
Lo-Buy	*discount grocery store, Youngstown*
Quik Stop Markets	*convenience stores*
Sav-Mor	*supermarkets*
SupeRx	*drug stores*
Time Saver	*convenience stores*
Tom Thumb Food Stores	*convenience stores*

K-Tel International

11311 K-Tel Dr.
Minnetonka, Minn. 55343
(612) 932-4000

Chief Executive Officer: Philip Kives
Exchange: AM
Symbol: KTL
Corporate History: The company incorporated in 1968 as Imperial Products Inc. and adopted its present title in 1971. It markets records and toys.
Brandnames of Products and Services:

Castle Rock	*toys*
K-Tel	*records*

Kuhn's-Big K Stores Corp.

245 Great Circle Rd.
Nashville, Tenn. 37228
(615) 259-2002

Chief Executive Officer: J.W. Kuhn
Exchange: AM
Symbol: KBK
Corporate History: The company, incorporated in 1946, is one of the leading retail chains in the Southeast with 116 outlets.
Brandnames of Products and Services:

Bargain Center	*discount department stores*
Big K/Edwards	*discount department stores*
Edward Variety	*variety stores*
Kuhn's Variety	*variety stores*

La Maur Inc.

5601 E. River Rd.
Minneapolis, MN 55432
(612) 571-1234

Chief Executive Officer: R.G. Spiegel
1984 Annual Sales Volume: 117M
1984 Shares Outstanding: 5,900,000
Shareholders: 2,000
Exchange: NY
Symbol: LMR
Corporate History: The company, incorporated in 1936, makes hair preparations and other personal grooming products.
Brandnames of Products and Services:

24 Hour	*deodorant*
Apple Pectin	*hair care product*
Beautifax	*hair care product*
Body Plus	*hair care product*
Fem Mist	*feminine hygiene product*
Ion	*hair care product*
La Maur	*hair care product*
Musk Dusk	*deodorant*
Namel Dry	*fingernail care products*
Natural Man	*hair care product*
New Era	*hair care product*
Nucleic A	*hair care product*
Perma Soft	*hair care product*
Style	*hair care products*
Vita E	*hair care product*

Lancaster Colony Corp.

37 W. Broad St.
Columbus, OH 43215
(614) 224-7141

Chief Executive Officer: J.B. Gerlach
1984 Annual Sales Volume: 418M
1984 Shares Outstanding: 8,094,000
Shareholders: 3,500
Exchange: OTC
Symbol: LANC
Corporate History: The company, incorporated in Delaware in 1961, manufactures a wide range of glass and pottery, cookware and food products, as well as automotive floor mats and mud flaps.

Brandnames of Products and Services:

August Barr	*athletic equipment*
Barr	*athletic equipment*
Bartlett-Collins	*glassware*
Candle-Lite	*candles*
Chef de Cuisine	*cookware*
Colony	*candles and glassware*
Enterprise Aluminum	*cookware*
Fostoria Glass	*glassware*
George A. Reach	*children's play balls*
Glass Shop	*glassware*
Heirloom	*cookware*
Indiana Glass	*glassware*
Loma-Rubber Queen	*plastic housewares*
Mountain Top	*frozen pies*
Nelson-McCoy	*potteryware*
New York Frozen Foods	*bread*
Pfeiffer Foods	*salad dressings*
Royal Chef	*cookware*
Rubber Queen	*auto accessories*
Squeeze	*children's play balls*
T. Mazetti	*salad dressings and condiments*

Lance Inc.

8600 South Blvd.
P.O. Box 32368
Charlotte, NC 28232
(704) 554-1421

Chief Executive Officer:	A.F. Sloan
1984 Annual Sales Volume:	337M
1984 Shares Outstanding:	12,480,149
Shareholders:	4,440
Exchange:	OTC
Symbol:	LNCE

Corporate History: Lance was founded in 1926. The company manufactures and sells food and related products, principally snack foods and other bakery products, through its operations and the operations of its three subsidiaries, Midwest Biscuit Co., Tri-Plas Inc. and Nutrition-Pak Corp., in 35 states and the District of Columbia. A significant portion of sales is made through vending machines.

Brandnames of Products and Services:

Big Town	*snack food product*
Choc-o-Lunch	*snack food product*
Gold-n-Chees	*snack food product*
Hancock's	*old-fashioned country ham*
Lance	*snack food products*
Lanchee	*snack food product*
Nekot	*snack food product*
Rye-Chee	*snack food product*
Toastchee	*snack food product*
Van-o-Lunch	*snack food product*
Vista	*cookies and crackers*

Lane Bryant Inc.

1501 Broadway
New York, N.Y. 10036
(212) 930-9200

Chief Executive Officer:	Arthur Malsin
Exchange:	NY
Symbol:	LNY

Corporate History: Lane Bryant, incorporated in 1920, operates apparel stores catering to the larger woman. As of 1980 it owned 236 stores: 192 Lane Bryant stores in 33 states, 19 Coward shoe stores in five Eastern states, and 25 Smart Size women's apparel shops in five states. At one time Lane Bryant also operated a chain of 17 Town & Country discount department stores, but discontinued it in 1977 as other large retailers moved toward outlet and discount stores.

Brandnames of Products and Services:

Beeline Inc.	*party goods*
Coward	*shoe stores*
Extra Special	*women's apparel store, Chicago, Ill.*
Farr's	*shoe stores*
Lane Bryant	*apparel stores*
Newman Benton	*apparel stores*
Smart Size	*women's apparel stores*

Laneco Inc.

1720 Butler St.
Easton, Pa. 18042
(215) 253-7155

Chief Executive Officer:	R.A. Bartolacci
Exchange:	AM
Symbol:	LNO

Corporate History: Laneco Inc., incorporated in 1971, operates supermarkets, department stores and combination stores in Pennsylvania and New Jersey. In 1980 Laneco agreed to a takeover by a group of investors led by Oppenheimer & Co. The price was $14 million ($13 a share). In fiscal 1980 supermarkets provided four-fifths of sales and department stores almost 20%.

Brandnames of Products and Services:

Food Lane	*supermarkets*
Lane	*discount department stores*
Laneco Stores & Discount Department Stores	
Lane Country	*food products*

Lane Co. Inc.

Franklin Ave.
Altavista, VA 24517
(804) 369-5641

Chief Executive Officer:	B.B. Lane
1984 Annual Sales Volume:	285M
1984 Shares Outstanding:	5,230,000
Shareholders:	1,000
Exchange:	OTC
Symbol:	LANE

Corporate History: The company incorporated in 1912 as the Standard Red Cedar Chest Co. and adopted its present title in 1922. It makes wood and upholstered products in the medium to medium-high price range; it is particularly well-known for its cedar chests. Lane's output is distributed nationally to more than 15,000 retail accounts.

Brandnames of Products and Services:

Action	*recliners*
Hickory	*furniture*
HTB	*furniture*
James River Collection	*furniture*
Lane	*furniture*
Lane Love Chests	*furniture*
Pearson	*upholstery*
Venture	*furniture*

La-Z Boy Chair Co.

1284 N. Telegraph Rd.
Monroe, MI 48161
(313) 242-1444

Chief Executive Officer:	C.T. Knabusch
1984 Annual Sales Volume:	156M
1984 Shares Outstanding:	4,639,884
Shareholders:	2,971
Exchange:	OTC
Symbol:	LAZB

Corporate History: La-Z-Boy incorporated in 1941, makes medium-priced upholstered chairs and convertible sofabeds.

Brandnames of Products and Services:

La-Z-Boy	*chairs*
La-Z-Lounger	*chairs*
La-Z-Rocker	*swivel rocker*
Reclina-Rocker	*reclining chair*
Reclina-Way	*wall recliner*
Signature II	*sofas and sofa beds*
Sofette	*reclining loveseat*

LD Brinkman Corp.

2123 Sidney Baker St.
Kerrville, TX 78028
(512) 896-5111

Chief Executive Officer:	L.D. Brinkman
1984 Annual Sales Volume:	287M
1984 Shares Outstanding:	6,122,721
Shareholders:	2,200
Exchange:	OTC
Symbol:	LDBC

Corporate History: LD Brinkman Corp. was reincorporated in 1983, changing its name from LDB Corp. The company was first incorporated in 1934. It is a leading carpet distributor which has diversified into the operation and franchising of pizza restaurants and the manufacture of mobile and modular homes.

Brandnames of Products and Services:

Gatti's	*pizza restaurants*
Lanchart	*mobile and modular homes*

Lear Siegler, Inc.

2850 Ocean Park Blvd.
Santa Monica, CA 90405
(213) 452-5444

Chief Executive Officer:	Robert T. Campion
1984 Annual Sales Volume:	1,942M
1984 Shares Outstanding:	18,351,842
Shareholders:	14,223
Exchange:	NY
Symbol:	LSI

Corporate History: Lear Siegler, Inc. founded in 1954, is a diversified company with operations in three major business segments: aerospace/technolgy, automotive and commercial/industrial. LSI produces Piper aircraft, boats for the recreational market, furniture components and housewares, heating and air conditioning units. In 1984 Lear Siegler acquired the Bangor Punta Corp., a diversified holding company.

Brandnames of Products and Services:

Cal	*sailboats*
Jeanneau	*pleasure boats*
Lear Siegler	*machine tools & office furniture*
O'Day	*sailboats*
Piper	*single & twin engine planes*
Prindle	*catamaran-pleasure boats*
Smith & Wesson	*hand guns*
Starcraft	*sailboats*

Lee Enterprises Inc.

130 East Second St.
Davenport, IA 52801
(319) 383-2202

Chief Executive Officer:	Lloyd G. Schermer
1984 Annual Sales Volume:	190M
1984 Shares Outstanding:	13,410,708
Shareholders:	3,600
Exchange:	NY
Symbol:	LEE

Corporate History: The Lee company, founded in 1890 and incorporated in 1950, is a diversified media company. It publishes daily newspapers in Illinois, Iowa, Minnesota, Montana, Nebraska, North Dakota, Oregon and Wisconsin; operates television stations in Hawaii, Illinois/Missouri, Oregon and West Virginia; owns directly or indirectly four radio stations in Illinois and Nebraska; participates in cable television services in Iowa and Wisconsin; and serves the graphic arts industry through NAPP System (USA) Inc., a joint venture of Lee and Nippon Paint Co., Ltd., Osaka, Japan, NAPP is the world's leading producer of photosensitive polymer printing plates for newspapers.

Brandnames of Products and Services:

Courier	*newspaper, Ottumwa, Iowa*
Gazette	*newspaper, Billings, Mont.*
Gazette-Times	*newspaper, Corvallis, Ore.*
Globe-Gazette	*newspaper, Mason City, Iowa*
Herald-Review	*newspaper, Decatur, Ill.*
Independent Record	*newspaper, Helena, Mont.*
Journal	*newspaper, Muscatine, Iowa*
Journal-Times	*newspaper, Racine, Wis.*
KFAB-AM	*radio station, Omaha, Neb.*
KGMB-TV	*station, Honolulu*
KGOR-FM	*radio station, Omaha, Neb.*
KHQA-TV	*station, Hannibal, Mo.*
KOIN-TV	*station, Portland, Ore.*
Missoulian	*newspaper, Missoula, Mont.*
Montana Standard	*newspaper, Butte*
Quad-City Times	*Davenport, IA*
Southern Illinoisan	*newspaper, Carbondale*
Star-Courier	*newspaper, Kewanee, Ill.*
Star	*newspaper, Lincoln, Neb.*
Tribune	*newspaper, La Crosse, Wis.*
Tribune	*newspaper, Bismarck, N.D.*
Winona Daily News	*Winona, MN*
Wisconsin State Journal	*newspaper, Madison*
WQCY-FM	*radio station, Quincy, Ill.*
WSAZ-TV	*radio station, Huntington/ Charleston, W. Va.*
WTAD-AM	*radio station, Quincy, Ill.*

Lehigh Valley Industries Inc.

200 East 42nd St.
New York, NY 10017
(212) 867-0300

Chief Executive Officer:	Jeffery K. Endervelt
1984 Annual Sales Volume:	21M
1984 Shares Outstanding:	7,918,425
Shareholders:	10,346
Exchange:	NY
Symbol:	LEH

Corporate History: Lehigh Valley Industries incorporated in 1928 while acquiring control of the Lehigh Valley Coal Sales Co. It adopted its present title in 1958. The company and its subsidiaries manufacture and sell dredging equipment and precision machined castings, electrical products and women's fashion footwear.

Brandnames of Products and Services:

Adores	*women's shoes*
Dori	*shoes*
Geppetto	*women's shoes*
Nolan Miller's Dynasty Collection	*women's shoes*
Umberto Bellini	*womens' shoes*

Lenox Inc.

Old Princeton Pike
Lawrenceville, N.J. 08648
(609) 896-2800

Chief Executive Officer: J.S. Chamberlin
Exchange: NY
Symbol: LNX
Corporate History: The company incorporated in 1889 as Ceramic Art Co. and adopted its present name in 1906. It makes casual dinnerware, fine china and giftware. In 1979, Lenox acquired A.H. Bond Co., a supplier of quality diamond engagement rings.
Brandnames of Products and Services:

Keepsake	*engagement rings*
Lenox	*china, crystal, jewelry*
Oxford	*bone china*
Temper-Ware	*cooking ware*

Leslie Fay Inc.

1400 Broadway
New York, N.Y. 10018
(212) 221-4000

Chief Executive Officer: J.J. Pomerantz
Exchange: NY
Symbol: LES
Corporate History: The company, last incorporated in 1959, makes women's sportswear. In 1980 the company agreed to sell out to a company to be formed by Wertheim & Co., an investment house, and W.J. Thomas, Jr., a private investor. The company's prospects are apparently good because it is in one of the fastest growing segments of the apparel industry.
Brandnames of Products and Services:

Andrea Gayle	*women's apparel*
Breckenridge	*women's apparel*
Fay's Closet	*junior sportswear*
Jeans by Kasper	
Kasper for Joan Leslie	*women's apparel*
Knitivo	*women's sportswear*
Leslie Fay	*women's apparel*
Leslie Fay Petite	*women's apparel*
Leslie J	*women's apparel*
Leslie Pomer	*women's apparel*
Ltd.	*women's apparel*
Outlander	*women's apparel*
Personal	*women's sportswear*
Personal Property	*intimate apparel*
Sasson's	*women's sportswear*
Sport	*women's apparel*

Levi Strauss & Co.

1155 Battery St.
San Francisco, CA 94111
(415) 544-6000

Chief Executive Officer: Robert D. Haas
1984 Annual Sales Volume: 2,514M
1984 Shares Outstanding: 36,930,955
Shareholders: 26,912
Exchange: NY
Symbol: LVI
Corporate History: The company was founded in 1850 by Levi Strauss who made canvas pants for California's gold miners. During the 1870s it developed the classic jean. Today, it designs, manufactures and markets a diversified line of apparel for men, women and children including jeans, slacks, shirts, jackets, skirts and hats. Most of the company's products are marketed under the Levi's® trademark and are sold in the United States and in numerous foreign countries.
Brandnames of Products and Services:

Action Casuals	*apparel*
Alias	*apparel*
Bend Over Pants	*women's apparel*
CMA	*apparel*
David Hunter	*men's dress apparel*
Dobbs	*hats*
Fashion Jeans	
Five-O-One	*jeans*
Frank Shorter Running Gear	*apparel*
Hardwear	*jeans*
Koret-City Blues	*women's apparel*
Koret of North America	*apparel*
Kover Alls	*workwear*
Levis	*apparel*
Levis for Feet	*footwear*
Oxxford Clothes	*men's apparel*
Perry Ellis America	*apparel*
Resistol Hats	*apparel*
Ski Levis	*skiwear*
Sutter Creek	*apparel*
Tourage SSE	*apparel*
Two Horse Brand	*men's apparel*

The Limited Inc.

One Limited Parkway
Columbus, OH 43230
(614) 475-4000

Chief Executive Officer: Leslie H. Wexner
1984 Annual Sales Volume: 1,343M
1984 Shares Outstanding: 59,370,146
Shareholders: 7,400
Exchange: NY
Symbol: LTD

Corporate History: The Limited Inc., a Delaware corporation, is the successor, through a reincorporation effected in 1982, to The Limited Stores Inc. The company engages in the purchase, distribution, and sale of women's apparel. Its retail activities are conducted under various tradenames through retail stores mail order operations. Merchandise is targeted to appeal to customers in specialty markets who have distinctive consumer characteristics, and includes regular and special sized fashion apparel available at various price levels. Merchandise includes coats, dresses, skirts, pants, sweaters, lingerie and accessories. During 1982 the company completed three acquisitions through which it increased its penetration in specialty markets. It acquired Lane Bryant Inc., Victoria's Secret Inc., and Roaman's Inc. In 1984 the company operated 1,412 retail outlets and six nationally distributed mail order catalogues.

Brandnames of Products and Services:

BryLane	*mail order catalogues*
Lane Bryant	*women's apparel stores, mail order catalogues*
Limited Express	*women's apparel stores, mail order catalogues*
Limited Stores	*apparel stores*
Nancy's Choice	*mail order catalogues*
Roaman's	*mail order catalogues*
Sizes Unlimited	*discount apparel stores*
Sue Brett	*mail order catalogue*
Tall Collection	*mail order catalogue*
Victoria's Secret	*mail order catalogue, womens' lingerie stores*

LIN Broadcasting Corp.

1370 Avenue of the Americas
New York, NY 10019
(212) 765-1902

Chief Executive Officer: Donald A. Pels
1984 Annual Sales Volume: 149M
1984 Shares Outstanding: 21,411,400
Shareholders: 2,400
Exchange: OTC
Symbol: LINB

Corporate History: The company, incorporated in 1961, is a communications corporation engaged in commercial broadcasting, specialty publishing, and telecommunications activities (Radio Common Carrier). In 1984 approximately 83% of the company's revenue was from television, 10% from radio, 7% from Radio Common Carrier and Specialty Publishing.

Brandnames of Products and Services:

GuestInformant	*hotel magazine*
KILT-AM/FM	*radio station, Houston, TX*
KTVV-TV	*Austin, TX*
KXAS-TV	*Ft. Worth/Dallas TX*
Leisureguides	*hotel magazine*
WAND-TV	*Springfield, Decatur, IL*
WANE-TV	*Fort Wayne, IN*
WAVY-TV	*Norfolk/Portsmouth, VA*
WBBF-AM	*radio station, Rochester, NY*
WEMP-AM	*radio station, Milwaukee, WI*
WFIL-AM	*radio station, Philadelphia, PA*
WIL-AM/FM	*radio station, St. Louis, MO*
WISH-TV	*Indianapolis, IN*
WMJQ-FM	*radio station, Rochester, NY*
WNYT-FM	*radio station, Milwaukee, WI*
WOTV-TV	*Grand Rapids, Kalamazoo, Battle Greek, MI*
WUSL-FM	*radio station, Philadelphia, PA*

Lionel Corp.

441 Lexington Ave.
New York, NY 10017
(212) 818-0630

Chief Executive Officer: Michael J. Vastola
1984 Annual Sales Volume: 358M
1984 Shares Outstanding: 7,104,955
Shareholders: 9,850
Exchange: PAC
Symbol: QLIO

Corporate History: The company was founded in 1901 by Joshua Lionel Cowen and conducted from 1906 to 1918 by Lionel Mfg. Co., a New Jersey corporation. It was incorporated in 1918. Lionel is primarily engaged in the specialty retailing of toys and leisure products and the manufacture and sale of electronics components. The company is no longer engaged in manufacturing model electric trains and other toys which at one time constituted a major portion of its business. In 1982 Lionel and two of its wholly-owned subsidiaries Lionel Leisure and Consolidated Toy Co. filed voluntary petitions under Chapter 11 of the Bankruptcy Code. Because of the Chapter 11 reorganization, the company's future course is unsettled.

Brandnames of Products and Services:

Fun City	*toy stores, Texas*
Lionel Kiddie City	*toy stores*
Lionel Playworld	*toy stores*
Lionel Toy Warehouse	*toy stores*
Playtown	*toy stores*
Toytown	*toy stores*

Litton Industries Inc.

360 North Crescent Dr.
Beverly Hills, CA 90210
(213) 859-5000

Chief Executive Officer: Fred W. Green
1984 Annual Sales Volume: 4,606M
1984 Shares Outstanding: 41,791,090
Shareholders: 87,800
Exchange: NY
Symbol: LIT

Corporate History: Litton is a technology-based company applying advanced electronics products and services to business opportunities in defense, industrial automation and geophysical markets. Research and product engineering emphasis is on developing advanced products which the company manufactures and supplies worldwide to commercial, industrial and government customers.

Brandnames of Products and Services:

American Book	*publishing house*
Crystal	*data analysis system*
Delmar	*publishing house*
Eldorado Tool	*metalworking tools*
Hudson	*publishing house*
Litton	*publishing house*
McCormick-Mathers	*educational publishing house*
New Britain Tool	*handtools*
Next	*magazine*
Van Nostrand Reinhold	*publishing house*

Lloyd's Electronics Inc.

180 Raritan Center Pkwy.
Edison, N.J. 08817
(201) 225-2030

Chief Executive Officer: A. Zagha
Exchange: AM
Symbol: LYD

Corporate History: Incorporated in 1968, Lloyd's is a designer-importer of audio products and calculators.

Brandnames of Products and Services:

Lloyd's	*portable audio equipment*
Monteverdi	*audio equipment and calculators*

Loctite Corp.

705 North Mountain Rd.
Newington, CT 06111
(203) 278-1280

Chief Executive Officer: Ken Butterworth
1984 Annual Sales Volume: 242M
1984 Shares Outstanding: 9,100,000
Shareholders: 2200
Exchange: NY
Symbol: LOC

Corporate History: Loctite, incorporated in 1953, makes chemical sealants, adhesives and auto care products.

Brandnames of Products and Services:

Duro	*household do-it-yourself products*
Loctite	*adhesive*
Permatex	*auto maintenance chemicals*

Loews Corp.

666 Fifth Ave.
New York, NY 10103
(212) 841-1000

Chief Executive Officer: Laurence A. Tisch
1984 Annual Sales Volume: 5,603M
1984 Shares Outstanding: 81,503,169
Shareholders: 5,650
Exchange: NY

Symbol: LTR

Corporate History: Loews was founded in 1946 as a hotel chain. Over the years it diversified until today it is a holding company with interests in tobacco, motion picture theaters, insurance, financial services and assets management, and hotel ownership and management and watches. Most of its profits come from insurance 66% of sales, and tobacco, 25% of sales. The company presently operates 14 hotels and motor hotels and 215 motion picture theaters.

Brandnames of Products and Services:

Anatole	*hotel, Dallas, Texas*
Bagpipe	*chewing tobacco*
Beech-Nut	*chewing tobacco*
Between-the-Acts	*little cigars*
Big Red	*chewing tobacco*
Bulova	*watches*
CNA Financial Corp.	*insurance*
Erik	*cigars*
Glenpointe	*hotel, Teaneck, New Jersey*
Golden Lights	*cigarettes*
Harbour Cove	*hotel, Paradise Island, Bahamas*
Havana Blossom	*chewing tobacco*
Howard Johnson	*motor lodge, New York, New York*
Kent	*cigarettes*
La Napoule	*hotel, La Napoule, France*
Le Concorde	*hotel, Quebec City, Canada*
L'Enfant Plaza	*hotel Washington, D.C.*
Loews Theatres	
Madison	*little cigars*
Max	*cigarettes*
Monte Carlo Hotel	*Monaco*
Newport	*cigarettes*
Old Gold	*cigarettes*
Omega	*little cigars*
Paradise Valley	*Resort-hotel, Paradise Valley*
Ramada Inn	*New York*
Regency	*hotel, New York, N.Y.*
Spring	*cigarettes*
Summit Hotel	*New York, N.Y.*
Triumph cigarettes	
True cigarettes	
Ventana Canyon	*Resort-hotel Tuscon, Arizona*
Westbury Hotel	*Toronto*

Lowe's Companies Inc.

State Highway 268 East
Box 1111
No. Wilkesboro, NC 28656-0001
(919) 651-4000

Chief Executive Officer:	Leonard G. Herring
1984 Annual Sales Volume:	1,689M
1984 Shares Outstanding:	36,248,475
Shareholders:	6,372
Exchange:	NY
Symbol:	LOW

Corporate History: The company was founded in 1945 and incorporated in 1952 as Lowe's North Wilkesboro Hardware Inc. Its present name was adopted in 1961. The firm is a retail-wholesale distributor of building materials, hardware, kitchen and home laundry products, and house and yard products. It has 248 lumber and building materials stores in 19 states, located principally in the South Atlantic and South Central regions of the United States.

Brandnames of Products and Services:

Lowe's	*general merchandise stores*

Lorimar

3970 Overland Ave.
Culver City, CA 90230
(213) 202-2000

Chief Executive Officer:	Merv Adelson
1984 Annual Sales Volume:	263M
1984 Shares Outstanding:	7,593,355
Exchange:	AM
Symbol:	LRM

Corporate History: Lorimar is engaged in the development, acquisition, production and distribution of television series, made-for-television movies and mini-series produced for network and/or pay television and of feature films. In 1983, Lorimar completed the acquisition of K&E, an advertising agency which plans, creates and places advertising on behalf of its clients in various media.

Brandnames of Products and Services:

Dallas	*tv series*
Eight is Enough	*syndicated tv series*
Falcon Crest	*tv series*
Knots Landing	*tv series*
Rowan and Martin's Laugh-In	*syndicated tv series*
The Waltons	*syndicated tv series*

M. Lowenstein Corp.

1430 Broadway
New York, N.Y. 10018
(212) 930-5000

Chief Executive Officer:	R. Bendheim
1984 Annual Sales Volume:	640M
1984 Shares Outstanding:	4,164,273
Shareholders:	1,600
Exchange:	NY
Symbol:	LST

Corporate History: M. Lowenstein manufactures a broad range of fabrics and consumer textile products. As a printer of fabrics, Lowenstein produces both printed and solid color fabrics which are sold to manufacturers of apparel and home furnishings, to industrial and utility users, and to the home sewing market. The company's consumer textile products include sheets, pillowcases, bedspreads, comforters, and curtains. Lowenstein has 16 plants in the southeastern United States; its subsidiary Clark-Schwebel Fiber Glass Corp. has 3 plants in this country, a subsidiary in Belgium, and an affiliate in Japan for the manufacture of fiber glass fabrics. The company has close to 9,000 employees. It was incorporated in 1918 as a successor to a textile firm founded in 1889.

Brandnames of Products and Services:

Pacific	*fabrics and home furnishings*
Pacific Silver Care	*home furnishings*
Wamsutta	*fabrics and home furnishings*

Luby's Cafeterias, Inc.

P.O. Box 33069
2211 N.E. Loop 410
San Antonio, TXs 78265
(512) 654-9000

Chief Executive Officer:	John Lahourcade
1984 Annual Sales Volume:	200M
1984 Shares Outstanding:	12,147,914
Shareholders:	3,000
Exchange:	NY
Symbol:	LUB

Corporate History: The company, incoporated in 1959, operates cafeterias located in suburban Texas shopping areas.

Brandnames of Products and Services:

Luby's	*cafeterias*

Lucky Stores Inc.

6300 Clark Ave.
P.O. Box BB
Dublin, CA 94568
(415) 833-6000

Chief Executive Officer:	S. Donley Ritchey
1984 Annual Sales Volume:	9,237M
1984 Shares Outstanding:	50,912,416
Shareholders:	33,391
Exchange:	NY
Symbol:	LKS

Corporate History: The company was founded in 1931 as a combination of six food stores in the San Francisco area. Today the company operates a total of 1,395 stores, primarily in the West, Midwest and South. The principal business of the company is the retail sale of food and non-food items. The company also operates processing facilities for certain food products and other household products which supply many of its stores.

Brandnames of Products and Services:

Checker Auto Parts Stores	
Dorman's Auto Centers	
Eagle Discount Centers	*supermarkets*
Food Basket	*supermarkets*
Fred Gang's	*restaurant*
Gemco	*membership department stores*
Hancock	*fabric stores and warehouses*
Harvest Day	*food products*
Its-A-Dilly	*women's specialty stores*
Kash N' Karry	*supermarket*
Kragen Auto Supply Store	
Lady Lee	*food products*
L & G Sporting Goods	*stores*
Lucky	*supermarkets*
Mays	*drugstore*
Memco	*membership department stores*
Pic-A-Dilly	*women's discount apparel stores*
Sirloin Stockade	*restaurant*
Stacy	*drugstores*
Yellow Front	*department stores*

Macmillan Inc.

866 Third Ave.
New York, NY 10022
(212) 935-2000

Chief Executive Officer: E.P. Evans
1984 Annual Sales Volume: 530M
1984 Shares Outstanding: 9,441,000
Shareholders: 7,000
Exchange: NY
Symbol: MLL
Corporate History: Macmillan was incorporated in 1920 and its present title was adopted in 1973. In 1979 a new management team, under the direction of Edward P. Evans, began to restructure the company. The reorganization was completed in 1981 and the company is now focused on three core business segments - educational publishing, instruction, and information services.
Brandnames of Products and Services:

Agnew Tech-Tran	*technical commercial translation service*
Associated Music Publisher	
Bennett Publishing	*vocational publisher*
Benziger	*religious and educational publishing house*
Berlitz	*language schools and publishing house*
Bradbury Press	*juvenile publisher*
Business Mailers	*professional mailing list*
Cassell	*publishing house*
Collamore Press	*medical books imprint*
Collier Macmillan	*publishing house*
Co-Op Mailings	*direct-response advertiser*
Dellen Publishing	*college text publisher*
Four Winds Press	*juvenile imprint*
The Free Press	*publishing house*
Glencoe	*publishing house*
Gumps	*specialty store*
Harper & Row School Division	*school textbook*
Katherine Gibbs School	*secretarial school*
Maclean Hunter	*vocational publisher*
Macmillan	*publishing house and book clubs*
Macmillan Prof. Journals	*health-care journals*
McKnight Publishing	*vocational publisher*
National Register Publishing	*information & directory publisher*
PennWell Publishing Co.	*college textbook publisher*
Pitman Learning	*vocational publisher*
Schirmer	*music store, New York, NY*
Schirmer	*publishing house*
Scribner Book Company	*publishing house*
Standard Rate and Data Service	*advertising rate reference works*
The Stone School	*executive secretarial school*
United Electronics Institute	*vocational training*
Washington Business School	*executive secretarial school*
The Zehring Company	*financial directory publisher*

R.H. Macy & Co. Inc.

151 W. 34th St.
New York, N.Y. 10001
(212) 695-4400

Chief Executive Officer: E.S. Finkelstein
Exchange: NY
Symbol: MZ
Corporate History: Macy's was established in 1858 by Roland Husland Macy, who had failed six times before to found a retail store. In 1883 the store was passed to Lazarus Strauss, whose family continued to control it until 1968. The family expanded Macy's into a chain which now included 83 stores in 10 states. Today Macy's operates the world's largest retail department store business.
Brandnames of Products and Services:

Bamberger's	*department stores*
Davison's	*department stores*
Lasalle's	*department stores*
Macy's	*department stores*

Magic Chef Inc.

740 King Edward Ave.
Cleveland, TN 37311
(615) 472-3371

Chief Executive Officer: S.B. Rymer Jr.
1984 Annual Sales Volume: 1,054M
1984 Shares Outstanding: 9,762,172
Shareholders: 5,634
Exchange: NY
Symbol: MGC
Corporate History: Magic Chef began as Dixie Foundry Company in 1916 in Cleveland, Tennessee. The company was founded by S.B. Rymer, Sr., and its first products were cast-iron skillets, sugar pots and tea kettles. In 1921, the company began making coal and wood cookstoves. In 1924 coal and wood heaters were added and in 1928, gas ranges were added. Magic Chef, Inc. is now one of the nation's larger manufacturers of major home appliances, small kitchen and portable appliances, and is prominent in the home air conditioning/heating industry, and in soft-drink vending equipment. Magic Chef, Inc. has increased sales over five times in the past 10 years, making it one of the fastest growing companies in the major home appliance industry. The company now has 16 manufacturing plants and 10 major distribution centers, located in 15 states; over 11,500 persons are employed.
Brandnames of Products and Services:

Admiral	*appliances*
Air Ease	*heating and air conditioning*
Armstrong	*heating and air conditioning*
Dixie	*appliances*
Edison	*heaters, fans & humidifiers*
Gaffers & Sattler	*gas and electric ranges*
Ingraham	*clocks*
Johnson	*heating and air conditioning*
Magic Chef	*appliances, heating & air conditioning*
Norge	*appliances*
Toastmaster	*appliances*
Williams	*heating and air conditioning*

Malone & Hyde Inc.

1991 Corporate Ave.
Memphis, Tenn. 38132
(901) 345-4200

Chief Executive Officer: J.R. Hyde
Exchange: NY
Symbol: MHI
Corporate History: The company, incorporated in 1911, engages in wholesale food distribution and operates supermarkets and retail drugstores. It is the largest food wholesaler in the South.
Brandnames of Products and Services:

Auto Shack	*auto accessory stores*
Consumer's Pharmacy	*drugstores*
Cooper-Martin	*supermarkets*
Fairway	*supermarkets*
Giant Foods of America	*supermarkets*
Hyde Park	*supermarkets*
Payrite	*drugstores*
Petty's	*drugstores*
Pic-Pac Supermarkets	
Quality Trading Stamps	
Raleigh Foods	*supermarkets*
Sommers	*drug stores*
Sunset Sport Center	*sporting goods stores*
Super D.	*drugstores*
Sureway Food Stores	

Manhattan Industries Inc.

1271 Avenue of the Americas
New York, NY 10020
(212) 265-3700

Chief Executive Officer: Laurence C. Leeds, Jr.
1984 Annual Sales Volume: 433M
1984 Shares Outstanding: 4,649,144
Shareholders: 2,564
Exchange: NY
Symbol: MHT
Corporate History: Manhattan Industries, incorporated in 1912, engages in three principal businesses. First, the company designs and markets, at wholesale, a wide range of men's, women's and children's apparel and accessories, under designer trademarks and other

nationally recognized brand names. Second, the company licenses or sub-licenses to others certain trademarks relating to apparel and accessories and, under contracts, shares in the net royalties earned through the licensing to others of designs and trademarks of Perry Ellis, one of the company's employee designers. Third, the company operates 41 retail specialty stores and 51 factory outlet stores in various parts of the United States.

Brandnames of Products and Services:

Amanda	*women's apparel*
Anne Klein	*women's apparel*
Anne Klein for New Aspect	*blouses*
Bayard Sport	*apparel*
Berkley Cravats	
Bronzini	*men's neckwear*
Etro	*men's neckware*
Frost Bros.	*apparel stores*
Glen York	*blouses*
Halston V & VI	*apparel*
Harness House	*men's accessories*
Henry Grethel	*apparel, accessories*
The Hub	*apparel stores*
John Henry	*apparel*
Jordache	*children's swimwear*
Lady Manhattan	*blouses*
Liberty of London	*accessories*
Liquidity by Alice Blaine	*women's wear*
Lucinda Rhodes	*women's wear*
Manhattan	*men's shirts*
Manhattan Factory Outlet	*apparel stores*
Mike Volbracht Sport	*women's sportswear*
Pelican	*children's apparel and swimwear*
Perry Ellis	*sportswear*
Peter Ashley	*scarves, accessories*
Portfolio by Perry Ellis	*apparel*
SAV	*women's wear*
Vera	*women's sportswear and table linens*
Voll/Bracht	*women's wear*
Yves Saint Laurent	*accessories*

Marantz Inc.

20525 Nordhoff St.
Chatsworth, CA 91311
(818) 998-9333

Chief Executive Officer:	Joseph S. Tushinsky
1984 Annual Sales Volume:	44M
1984 Shares Outstanding:	2,308,263
Shareholders:	1,885
Exchange:	NY
Symbol:	MTZ

Corporate History: The company was organized in 1954 under the name Superscope Inc. In 1984 the name was changed to Marantz Co. Inc. The company is primarily engaged in the marketing, distribution and sale of consumer audio electronic products designed for home entertainment.

Brandnames of Products and Services:

Marantz	*audio products*
Pianocorder	*electonic pianos*
Rentabeta	*video players*
Superscope	*audio products*
Tele-story	*casettes & books for children*

Marcade Group, Inc.

21 Caven Point Ave.
Jersey City, NJ 07305
(201) 433-0100

Chief Executive Officer:	Herbert I. Wexler
1984 Annual Sales Volume:	140M
1984 Shares Outstanding:	9,538,365
Shareholders:	6,000
Exchange:	NY
Symbol:	MAR

Corporate History: The Marcade Group Inc., incorporated in 1947, was called Unishops Inc. until 1981. It manufactures women's apparel such as blouses, sweaters, pants, shorts, dresses and pants sets through its wholly owned subsidiary Marlene Industries Corp. Since 1981 the company has disposed of its discount department store chain and its men's and boys' and shoes licensed operations. In 1984 Youth Centre, its children's specialty store chain, and Central Textile, a linen and domestics licensed operation, were sold.

Brandnames of Products and Services:

Daniel Hechter	*apparel*
Marlene	*apparel*

Marion Laboratories Inc.

9221 Ward Pkwy.
Kansas City, MO 64114
(816) 966-5000

Chief Executive Officer:	Fred W. Lyons, Jr.
1984 Annual Sales Volume:	226M
1984 Shares Outstanding:	18,554,726
Shareholders:	7,474
Exchange:	NY
Symbol:	MKC

Corporate History: The company, incorporated in 1952, develops, manufactures and sells pharmaceuticals as well as products for hospital and laboratory use.

Brandnames of Products and Services:

Ambenyl-D	*cough medicine*
Debrox	*ear wax softener*
Gaviscon	*antacid*
Gly-Oxide	*antiseptic*
Os-Cal	*calcium supplements*
Pretts	*diet product*
Protect	*toothpaste*
Silvadene	*burn medicine*
Stair-Glide	
Throat Discs	

Marriott Corp.

Marriott Dr.
Washington, D.C. 20058
(301) 897-9000

Chief Executive Officer:	J.W. Marriott, Jr.
1984 Annual Sales Volume:	3,524,937,000
1984 Shares Outstanding:	25,761,000
Shareholders:	28,033
Exchange:	NY
Symbol:	MHS

Corporate History: Marriott began in 1927 with the opening of the Hot Shoppe, a Mexican restaurant in Washington, D.C. Today feeding people is still one of the company's major activities. It is the largest independent supplier of meals and snacks served aboard airplanes. It also owns several chains of restaurants and caters meals to corporations and universities. In addition, Marriott operates or franchises 142 hotels and resorts. Lately it has moved toward managing hotels rather than owning them. The hotel business provided nearly 50% of its sales in 1984.

Brandnames of Products and Services:

Big Boy Jrs.	*restaurants*
Big Boy Restaurants	*restaurants*
Courtyard by Marriott	*moderately priced hotels*
Farrell's	*ice cream parlors*
Marriott Hotels & Resorts	*luxury hotels & resorts*
Monarch at Sea Pines	*vacation ownership resorts*
Roy Rogers	*restaurants*
Sun Line Cruise Ships	

Marshall Field & Co.

25 E. Washington St.
Chicago, Ill. 60690
(312) 236-7272

Chief Executive Officer:	A.R. Arena
Exchange:	NY
Symbol:	MF

Corporate History: The company incorporated in 1901. It is a leading department store chain which obtains one-half of its sales from the Chicago division. It is developing a growing position in the Pacific Northwest and the South.

Brandnames of Products and Services:

Breuners	*home furnishing stores*
The Crescent	*department stores*
Frederick & Nelson	*department stores*
Halle's	*department stores*
J.B. Ivey	*department stores*
Marshall Field	*department stores*
"The Union"	*department stores*

Marsh Supermarkets Inc.

P.O. Box 155 Depot St.
Yorktown, IN 47396
(317) 759-8101

Chief Executive Officer:	Don E. Marsh
1984 Annual Sales Volume:	605M
1984 Shares Outstanding:	3,737,029
Shareholders:	2,950
Exchange:	OTC
Symbol:	MARS

Corporate History: The company incorporated in 1952 as March Foodliners and adopted its present title in 1960. It is principally involved in the retail food business through 148 supermarkets, 142 convenience stores and four fresh produce markets. Marsh also operates nine drugstores in supermarket-drug combination units and, in addition, operates a greenhouse business which supplies the majority of potted plants sold in the floral departments of its supermarkets. Marsh does business in the midwest.

Brandnames of Products and Services:

Farmers' Market	*convenience food stores*
Foxfires	*family restaurants*
Marsh	*drug stores*
Tote 'N Save	*grocery stores*
Village Pantry	*convenience food markets*

Maryland Cup Corp.

10100 Reisterstown Rd.
Owings Mills, Md. 21117
(301) 363-1111

Chief Executive Officer: H. Shapiro
Exchange: NY
Symbol: MDC
Corporate History: Incorporated in 1926, the company makes paper cups and containers, paper and plastic drinking straws, ice cream and ice cream cones.

Brandnames of Products and Services:

Choco	*ice cream cones*
Copley Square	*plastic cups*
Eat-it-All	*ice cream cones*
Flex-Straws	
Guildware	*plastic cups*
Honey-Roll	*ice cream*
Maryland	*paper cups*
Silent Service	*plastic cups*
Sweetheart	*paper cups*
Ten-T	*ice cream cups*

Masco Corp.

21001 Van Born Rd.
Taylor, MI 48180
(313) 274-7400

Chief Executive Officer: Alex Manoogian
1984 Annual Sales Volume: 1,120M
1984 Shares Outstanding: 57,978,601
Shareholders: 5,800
Exchange: NY
Symbol: MAS
Corporate History: The company, incorporated in 1929, is a manufacturer of building and home improvement products, including faucets, plumbing fittings, bath and shower units, builders' hardware, steel measuring tapes, venting and ventilating equipment, insulation products and water pumps, as well as other products for the home and family, including recreational accessories and metal office products. In 1984 Masco Corp. transferred its products for industry line of business (consisting of custom engineered components, principally for the transportation industry and specialty products) to Masco Industries which then became a separate publicly owned company. Masco Corp. retains approximately 50% of Masco Industries' common stock.

Brandnames of Products and Services:

Auto-Flo	*humidifier air treatment*
Delta	*faucets*
Deltex	*faucets*
Deltique	*faucets*
Epic	*faucets*
Fulton	*recreational boating winches and equipment*
Peerless	*water filters*
Reese	*trailer hitches*
Rupert	*recreational vehicle highway reflectors, accessories*

C.H. Masland & Sons

70 Carlisle Springs Rd.
Carlisle, PA 17013
(717) 249-1866

Chief Executive Officer: B.C. Gardner
1984 Annual Sales Volume: 189M
1984 Shares Outstanding: 1,547,000
Shareholders: 1,122
Exchange: AM
Symbol: MLD
Corporate History: The company, incorporated in 1907, makes carpets used in homes, commercial and institutional buildings and interior trim parts and materials for automobiles.

Brandnames of Products and Services:

Allibar	*carpets*
Amphora	*carpets*
Amphora Stripe 1	*carpets*
Amphora Stripe 2	*carpets*
Amphora Stripe 3	*carpets*
Blue Chip	*carpets*
Bouquet	*carpets*
Brandon Street	*carpets*
Brigitte	*carpets*

Carte Blanche	*carpets*
Catalyst	*carpets*
Celtic Classics	*carpets*
Crossroads	*carpets*
Dunharrow	*carpets*
Hawthorne	*carpets*
High Time	*carpets*
Hopi	*carpets*
Italia	*carpets*
Jomon	*carpets*
King Arthur	*carpets*
Lady Luck	*carpets*
La Parade	*carpets*
Lochmoor	*carpets*
Mariarden	*carpets*
Maricopa	*carpets*
Mojave Motif Collection	*carpets*
Myriad	*carpets*
Palestra	*carpets*
Pastille	*carpets*
Pavonine	*carpets*
Pima	*carpets*
Puritan	*carpets*
Rare Find	*carpets*
Ravenwood	*carpets*
Rhianna	*carpets*
Sequence	*carpets*
Seurat	*carpets*
Shazam!	*carpets*
Sherbet	*carpets*
Shire Town	*carpets*
Stanza 30	*carpets*
Stanza 40	*carpets*
Telfair	*carpets*
Towne House	*carpets*
Weather Vane	*carpets*
Woodridge	*carpets*

Masonite Corp.

29 N. Wacker Dr.
Chicago, Ill. 60606
(312) 372-5642

Chief Executive Officer: R.N. Rasmus
Exchange: NY
Symbol: MNC
Corporate History: The company was incorporated in 1925 as Mason Fibre Co., and adopted its present title in 1928. It is the largest producer of hardboard in the world.

Brandnames of Products and Services:

Masonite	*interior paneling and exterior sliding*

Masters Inc.

725 Summa Ave.
Westbury, N.Y. 11590
(516) 997-8000

Chief Executive Officer: J. Biblowitz
Exchange: AM
Symbol: MSR
Corporate History: The company, incorporated in 1937, operates retail discount stores and retail leased and specialty departments.

Brandnames of Products and Services:

Lady Rose	*apparel stores*
Masters	*general merchandise discount stores*
Susan Terry	*apparel stores*
Urdang's	*apparel stores*
Village Casuals	*apparel stores*

Matsushita Electric Industrial Co. Ltd.

1006, Oaza Kadoma, Kadoma City
Osaka Osaka, Japan

Chief Executive Officer: Masaharu Matsushita
1984 Annual Sales Volume: 19,347M
1984 Shares Outstanding: 4,780,120
Shareholders: 199 (U.S. shareholders, 4.6% of common stock)
Exchange: NY
Symbol: MC
Corporate History: Matsushita Electric Industrial Co., Ltd. was founded in 1918 by Konosuke Matsushita and incorporated under the laws of Japan in 1935. The company expanded rapidly after World War II as it met the demand for consumer electric and electronic products such as washing machines, black-and-white television receivers and refrigerators. In the 1960's and 70's the company expanded its product range to include color television receivers, hi-fi components, air conditioners, microwave ovens, industrial equipment, communication and measuring equipment, and video tape recorders. The company is the largest manufacturer of consumer electric and electronic products in Japan and one of the world's largest producers in these fields. It operates 47 production facilities in 27 countries and 36 sales companies in 28 countries outside Japan. Matsu-

shita leads the world in production of home-use video cassette tape recorders and VCR cameras. In 1984 VCR's represented 28% of total sales.

Brandnames of Products and Services:

JVC	*home electronics*
Matsushita	*appliances, home electronic products*
National	*home electronics*
Panasonic	*home electronics*
Quasar	*home electronics*
Technics	*home electronics*
Victor	*home electronics*

Mattel Inc.

5150 Rosecrans Ave.
Hawthorne, CA 90250
(213) 644-0411

Chief Executive Officer:	A.S. Spear
1984 Annual Sales Volume:	881M
1984 Shares Outstanding:	29,216,000
Shareholders:	22,651
Exchange:	NY
Symbol:	MAT

Corporate History: Mattel, founded in 1945, is one of the nation's largest toy manufacturers with approximately 12% of the domestic market. It introduced such classic toys as the Barbie Doll, which since 1959 has sold more than 250,000,000 copies.

Brandnames of Products and Services:

Mattel	*toys*

May Department Stores Co.

611 Olive St.
St. Louis, MO 63101
(314) 342-6300

Chief Executive Officer:	David C. Farrell
1984 Annual Sales Volume:	4,744M
1984 Shares Outstanding:	43,026,428
Shareholders:	36,346
Exchange:	NY
Symbol:	MA

Corporate History: The May Department Stores Company is one of the nation's largest retail companies. Its three principal lines of retail business consist of 11 department store companies, quality discount stores and self-service family shoe stores. Through subsidiaries, the company is one of the largest national developers and operators of shopping centers. Approximately 75,000 people are employed in 42 states and in 12 offices overseas.

Brandnames of Products and Services:

Eagle Stamp Co.	*trading stamp co.*
Famous-Barr Co.	*department stores - St. Louis, Mo.*
G. Fox & Co.	*department stores, Hartford, Conn.*
Hecht's	*department stores, Washington-Baltimore, Md.*
Kaufmann's	*department stores - Pittsburgh*
May Centers, Inc.	*shopping centers*
May Co., California	*department stores - Los Angeles*
May Co., Cleveland	*department stores - Cleveland, Ohio*
May-Cohens	*department stores - Jacksonville, Fla.*
May D&F	*department stores - Denver*
Meier & Frank	*department stores - Portland, Ore.*
O'Neil's	*department stores - Akron, Ohio*
Payless Shoe Source (Volume Shoe Corp.)	*shoe stores*
Strouss	*department store, Youngstown, Ohio*
Venture	*discount stores*
Volume Shoe Corp.	*shoe stores*

Mayflower Corp.

9998 N. Michigan Rd.
Carmel, IN 46032
(317) 875-1000

Chief Executive Officer:	John B. Smith
1984 Annual Sales Volume:	481M
1984 Shares Outstanding:	5,177,144
Shareholders:	1,409
Exchange:	AM
Symbol:	MFL

Corporate History: Incorporated in 1973, Mayflower is a holding company whose business is divided into three segments: truck transportation services, other products and services and bus services and sales. The truck transportation services segment, primarily through Aero

Mayflower, is engaged in the truck transportation of household goods and other products in interstate commerce and, to a limited extent, in intrastate and international commerce. The other products and services segment is engaged in the wholesale distribution and retail sale of appliances and home entertainment products. The bus services and sales segment is engaged in contract school bus transportation and school bus sales.

Brandnames of Products and Services:

ADI Appliances	*appliances and home electronics*
The Entertainment Station	*home electronics retailer*
Gentry Insurance	*insurance*
Mayflower	*movers*
Rover of Indiana	*financial services*

J.W. Mays Inc.

510 Fulton St.
Brooklyn, NY 11201
(718) 624-7400

Chief Executive Officer:	Max L. Shulman
1984 Annual Sales Volume:	85M
1984 Shares Outstanding:	2,178,297
Shareholders:	5,000
Exchange:	NY
Symbol:	MJW

Corporate History: The company incorporated in 1927 as May's Furs & Ready-to-Wear Inc. and adopted its present title in 1946. It operates four department stores in the greater New York City area.

Brandnames of Products and Services:

Mays	*department stores*

Maytag Co.

Newton, IA 50208
(515) 792-7000

Chief Executive Officer:	D.J. Krumm
1984 Annual Sales Volume:	643M
1984 Shares Outstanding:	13,629,467
Shareholders:	16,241
Exchange:	NY
Symbol:	MYG

Corporate History: The company was founded in 1893 and incorporated in 1925. It makes such household and commercial appliances as laundry equipment, dishwashers and food disposals.

Brandnames of Products and Services:

Hardwick Stove Co.	*ranges, microwave ovens, washers, dryers, dishwashers, ranges, microwave ovens, food waste disposers, wall ovens and cooktops*
Jenn-Air	*electric grill-ranger and cooktops, microwave ovens, wall ovens, dishwashers, food waste disposers*
Maytag	*home appliances*

MCA Inc.

100 Universal City Plaza
Universal City, CA 91608
(818) 985-4321

Chief Executive Officer:	Lew R. Wasserman
1984 Annual Sales Volume:	1,651M
1984 Shares Outstanding:	47,811,588
Shareholders:	6,700
Exchange:	NY
Symbol:	MCA

Corporate History: MCA, often called the General Motors of the entertainment industry, was founded in 1924 and last incorporated in 1958. Initially a talent agency controlling such stars as Jimmy Stewart and Ronald Reagan, it is now engaged in television, motion picture and record production and distribution, publishing and real estate development among other things. It also owns savings and loan associations, computer services and tourist attractions. MCA is currently moving into the video disc field in partnership with IBM.

Brandnames of Products and Services:

ABC	*records and tapes*
Berkeley	*publishing house*
BJ	*publishing house*
Columbia Savings & Loan Association	
Coral	*records and tapes*
Coward-McCann & Geoghegan Inc.	*publishing house*
G.P. Putnam's Sons	*publishing house*
Jove	*publishing house*

Landmark Services	*tour of Federal Mall and Arlington National Cemetery in Washington, D.C.*
MCA	*TV programs*
MCA Home Video	*markets video casettes & video discs*
MCA Records	*manufactures and markets records and tapes*
Mount Vernon	*food and merchandising concessions*
Pioneer Savings & Loan	
The Runner	*magazine*
Spencer Gifts	*gift stores and mail order magazine*
Universal	*TV programs and motion pictures*
Universal Amphetheatre	*arena theatre*
Universal Studio Tours	
Womphopper's Wagon Works	*restaurant*
Yosemite National Park & Curry Co.	*visitor services (lodging, food, etc.)*

McCormick & Co. Inc.

11350 McCormick Rd.
Hunt Valley, MD 21031
(301) 667-7301

Chief Executive Officer: H.K. Wells
1984 Annual Sales Volume: 788M
1984 Shares Outstanding: 12,398,000
Shareholders: 7,991
Exchange: OTC
Symbol: MCCRK
Corporate History: Founded in 1889 and incorporated in 1915, McCormick & Company, Inc., is a diversified specialty food company in marketing, manufacturing, and distribution of seasoning, flavoring, and food products to the food industry—retail outlets, food service, and food processors. A packaging group markets and manufactures plastic bottles and tubes to food, personal care, and other industries. McCormick's products are processed at 58 facilities throughout the world and are sold in 84 countries. Real estate is another significant business. Subsidiaries develop, own, and manage industrial, office, and business properties, and provide design/build services.

Brandnames of Products and Services:

5th Season	*spices*
Bag'N Season Seasoning	*seasoning blends for meats*
Baker's Vanilla	*extract*
Baking Magic	*extracts*
Banquet Tea	*tea*
Bon Appetit	*seasoning blend*
Burst O Lemon	*lemon crystals*
Cake-Mate	*cake decorating products*
Gilroy Foods	*garlic*
Golden West	*frozen poultry & finished vegetable products*
Li'l Sauces	*seasoning*
McCormick	*spices, condiments and flavorings*
Salad Supreme	*seasoning*
Salad Toppins	*seasoning*
Schilling	*spices*
Seas-oleums	*seasoning*
Season-All	*seasoning*
Tea House Tea	*tea*
Tio Sancho	*Mexican-style dinners*
TV Time	*popcorn*

McDonald's Corp.

McDonald's Plaza
2111 Enco Drive
Oak Brook, IL 60521
(312) 887-3200

Chief Executive Officer: Fred L. Turner
1984 Annual Sales Volume: 10,007M
1984 Shares Outstanding: 85,859,050
Shareholders: 29,200
Exchange: NY
Symbol: MCD
Corporate History: McDonald's was founded in 1955 by Ray Kroc, a salesman, who received the franchise for his first hamburger stand from Maurice and Richard McDonald. Kroc developed the means for mass producing his product uniformly in great numbers. Over the years he built the business by expanding company-owned restaurants and granting franchises. Today most McDonald's are franchised. McDonald's now has 8,300 restaurants located in 35 countries and territories worldwide. The company packages a limited menu of quickly-prepared, moderately-priced foods, including hamburgers—the "Big Mac" and the "Quarter

Pounder"—french fried potatoes, "Chicken McNuggets," fish sandwiches, shakes, soft drinks.

Brandnames of Products and Services:

McDonald's	*self-service Restaurants*

McGraw Edison Co.

333 West River Rd.
Elgin, Ill. 60120
(312) 888-6800

Chief Executive Officer: E.J. Williams
Exchange: NY
Symbol: MGR

Corporate History: McGraw Edison was incorporated in 1926 as McGraw Electric Co. In addition to home electrical appliances, the company and its subsidiaries make products used in the transmission, utilization and control of electrical power.

Brandnames of Products and Services:

Comfort Sensor	*heaters*
Edison	*fans, heaters, power tools*
Ingraham	*clocks and timers*
Modern Maid	*kitchen appliances*
Shopmate	*home appliances and tools*
Speed Queen	*kitchen appliances*
Toastmaster	*kitchen appliances*
Village Blacksmith	*tools, lawn and garden implements*

McGraw-Hill Inc.

1221 Avenue of the Americas
New York, NY 10020
(212) 512-2000

Chief Executive Officer: Joseph L. Dionne
1984 Annual Sales Volume: 1,402,000
1984 Shares Outstanding: 50,410
Shareholders: 8,726
Exchange: NY
Symbol: MHP

Corporate History: McGraw-Hill is one of the world's leading corporations in information and communication. Through five operating companies, McGraw-Hill provides information in virtuallly every medium: magazines, newsletters and newswires; books, learning systems and training programs; software, on-line data bases and real-time electronic feed; film, videotape and audio cassettes; information systems, and broadcasting. McGraw-Hill's beginnings date to 1888 when James H. McGraw purchased the American Journal of Railway Appliances. The McGraw Publishing Co. was incorporated in 1899 and the Hill Publishing Company in 1902. In 1917 the two consolidated as McGraw-Hill Publishing Co. The present name-McGraw-Hill, Inc.-was adopted Jan. 1, 1964.

Brandnames of Products and Services:

Aardvark	*computer software*
American Machinist	*magazine*
Architectural Record	*magazine*
Aviation Week	*magazine*
Business Week	*magazine*
Byte	*magazine*
Chemical Engineering	*magazine*
Chemical Week	*magazine*
Coal Age	*magazine*
Data Communications	*magazine*
Data Resources	*economic services & econometric modeling*
Electrical Construction & Maintenance	*magazine*
Electronics Week	*magazine*
EMIS	*electronic markets & infor systems*
Engineering News Record	*magazine*
Graduating Engineer	*magazine*
International Management	*magazine*
KERO-TV	*Bakersfield, Calif.*
KGTV-TV	*San Diego, Calif.*
KMGH-TV	*Denver, Colo.*
McGraw Hill	*publishing house*
Metals Week	*newsletter*
Modern Plastics	*magazine*
Nucleonics Week	*newsletter*
Osborne Books	*computer books*
The Physician & Sports Medicine	*magazine*
Popular Computing	*magazine*
Postgraduate Medicine	*magazine*
Power	*magazine*
Schaum	*paperback publishing house*
Standard & Poors	*financial services*
Textile World	*magazine*
WRTV-TV	*Indianapolis, Ind.*

McKesson Corp.

Crocker Plaza
One Post St.
San Francisco, CA 94104
(415) 983-8300

Chief Executive Officer: Neil Harlan
1984 Annual Sales Volume: 5,000M
1984 Shares Outstanding: 17,000,000
Shareholders: 32,000
Exchange: NY
Symbol: MCK

Corporate History: McKesson is the nation's leading distributor of health and beauty aid products to drugstores, food stores and mass merchandisers. In 1985, McKesson's Drug & Health Care Group accounted for about 68% of the company's $5 billion in revenue. McKesson is also the nation's leading distributor of bottled drinking water and chemicals and makes and distributes Armor All Protectant, the number-one selling product in the automotive after-market. The company is the largest wholesaler of wine and spirits in the U.S. and also imports and markets certain alcoholic beverages including beer. This Beverage Group includes the bottled water business and is the second largest operating group representing about 21% of the company's sales. Within the past three years, McKesson has extended its distribution activities into such areas as office supplies, veterinary supplies, first aid supplies and safety equipment for business and industry, service merchandising of health and beauty aids to supermarkets and computer systems and services for drugstores, florists and other markets.

Brandnames of Products and Services:

Alhambra	*bottled drinking water*
Aqua-Vend	*bottled drinking water*
Armor All	*protectant*
Crystal	*bottled drinking water*
Hi Lights	*costume jewelry*
Rosegarden	*wine*
Sparklett's	*bottled drinking water*
Valu-Rite	*drug stores*

MCO Holdings, Inc.

10880 Wilshire Blvd.
Los Angeles, CA 90024
(213) 474-6264

Chief Executive Officer: Charles E. Hurwitz
1984 Annual Sales Volume: 184M
1984 Shares Outstanding: 6,149,296
Shareholders: 10,357
Exchange: AM
Symbol: MCO

Corporate History: Incorporated in 1963 and reorganized in 1980, MCO Holdings Inc. is engaged in the business of real estate development, oil and gas exploration and development, geothermal operations, and gas transmission and processing.

Brandnames of Products and Services:

Fountain Hills	*real estate development*
Holiday Island	*real estate development*
Lake Havasu City	*real estate development*
Pueblo West	*real estate development*
Spring Creek	*real estate development*
West Cliff	*real estate development*

Medalist Industries Inc.

735 N. 5th St.
Milwaukee, Wisc. 53203
(414) 241-8500

Chief Executive Officer: N.J. Fischer
Exchange: AM
Symbol: MDI

Corporate History: The company was incorporated in 1954 as J.M. Nash Co. Inc. and adopted its present title in 1968. It makes athletic uniforms, protective gear and gymnasium equipment. In 1980 Medalist acquired West Coast Supply Co., a Los Angeles-based distributor of bicycles and accessories.

Brandnames of Products and Services:

Cut 'n Jump	*sport accessories*
Gladiator	*athletic uniforms and equipment*
Medalist Ripon	*hosiery*
Pride	*athletic uniforms and equipment*
R C Sunlight	*roller skates*
Ripon	*sport socks*
Sand Knit	*athletic uniforms and equipment*
Ski Skin	*ski apparel*

Media General Inc.

333 E. Grace St.
Richmond, VA 23219
(803) 649-6000

Chief Executive Officer: James S. Evans
1984 Annual Sales Volume: 584M
1984 Shares Outstanding: 6,965,281
Shareholders: 2,298
Exchange: AM
Symbol: MEG.

Corporate History: Media General, incorporated in 1969, is engaged in newspaper publishing and broadcasting activities; it also manufactures newsprint.

Brandnames of Products and Services:

Beacon Press	*publisher*
Cablevision, TV	*Fredericksburg, VA*
Cliggott Publishing Co.	*publisher*
Golden West Publishing	*newpaper Mission Viejo, CA*
Highlander Publications	*newspaper, Hacienda Heights, CA*
Media General Cable-Cable TV	*Chantilly, VA*
Piedmont Publishing publisher	
Richmond Newspapers	*Richmond, VA*
Technical Information	*distribution service*
The Tribune	*newspaper Tampa, FL*
WCBD-TV	*Charleston, SC*
WJKS-TV	*Jacksonville, FL*
WXFL-TV	*Tampa, FL*

Medivix Inc.

209 West Central Street
Natick, MA 01760
(617) 655-4776

Chief Executive Officer: Michael Koll-Nescher
1984 Annual Sales Volume: 139.7M
1984 Shares Outstanding: 12,511,148
Shareholders: 1,760
Exchange: OTC
Symbol: DMJR

Corporate History: Medivix Inc. is a Delaware corporation organized in 1982. The company is engaged in the marketing of health care products manufactured by others. It has concentrated its efforts to date in the field of diabetes treatment.

Brandnames of Products and Services:

Diatron Easytest	*blood glucose monitoring system*
Excel	*diet supplement*
Illusions	*sugarless candies*
Medix Insulin Infusion Pump	*portable infusion pump*

Mego International Inc.

41 Madison Ave.
New York, N.Y. 10010
(212) 532-6333

Chief Executive Officer: M.B. Abrams
Exchange: AM
Symbol: MGO

Corporate History: The company, incorporated in 1969, makes toys. Most items are manufactured in Hong Kong.

Brandnames of Products and Services:

Mego	*toys and games*

Melville Corp.

3000 Westchester Ave.
PO Box 677
Harrison, NY 10528
(914) 253-8000

Chief Executive Officer: Francis C. Rooney, Jr.
1984 Annual Sales Volume: 4,424M
1984 Shares Outstanding: 52,921,486
Shareholders: 10,500
Exchange: NY
Symbol: MES

Corporate History: Melville was incorporated in 1914 as Melville Shoe Corp. and adopted its present name in 1976. It makes clothing and footwear for the entire family. It is one of the largest specialty retailers in the country. The company operates 5,911 retail stores and leased departments throughout the United States and Puerto Rico in four major product areas: footwear, apparel, drugs and toys. The company also owns the CVS (Consumer Value Stores) chain of discount drugstores.

Brandnames of Products and Services:

Chess King	*men's apparel stores*
Consumer Value Stores	*drugstores health and beauty aid stores*
Foxmoor	*women's apparel stores*
Kay-Bee	*specialty stores, offering toys and games*
K-Mart	*shoe stores*
Linens 'n Things	*discount linens, towels, and household items*
Marshalls	*family discount apparel stores*
Melville	*footwear*
Open Country	*shoe stores*
Thom McAn	*shoe stores*
Wilsons	*leather apparel and accessories*

MEM Co.

Union St. Extension
Northvale, N.J. 07647
(201) 767-0100

Chief Executive Officer: S.H. Mayer
Exchange: AM
Symbol: MEM

Corporate History: The company was founded in 1883 in Vienna and incorporated in the United States. It makes and sells toiletries and personal care products. In 1979 toiletries accounted for 79.8% of sales.

Brandnames of Products and Services:

Acqua di Selva	*toiletry products*
Blondit	*hair lightening products*
Caring	*women's toiletries*
Embracing	*women's cologne*
English Leather	*men's toiletries*
John Weitz	*men's fragrance*
Musk	*men's and women's toiletries*
Racquet Club	*men's toiletries*
Sharing	*women's cologne*
Timberline	*men's toiletries*
Tinkerbell	*children's cosmetics*
Vintage Bubble Bath	
Wind Drift	*men's toiletries*

Mercantile Stores Co. Inc.

1100 North Market St.
Wilmington, DE 19801
(302) 575-1816

Chief Executive Officer: L.F. Winbigler
1984 Annual Sales Volume: 1,707M
1984 Shares Outstanding: 14,738,294
Shareholders: 6,803
Exchange: NY
Symbol: MST

Corporate History: The company, incorporated in 1919, operates 80 department stores. The stores operate under 13 different chain names. In addition, the company operates 22 free standing beauty salons and maintains a partnership position in five shopping center ventures.

Brandnames of Products and Services:

Bacon's	*department stores*
Castner-Knott	*department stores*
de Lendrecie's	*department stores*
Gayfers	*department stores*
Glass Block	*department stores*
Hennessy's	*department stores*
J.B. White's	*department stores*
Jones Store	*department stores*
Joslins	*department stores*
Lion	*department stores*
McAlpin's	*department stores*
Right House	*department stores*
Roots	*department stores*

Meredith Corp.

1716 Locust St.
Des Moines, Iowa 50336
(515) 284-9011

Chief Executive Officer: R.A. Burnett
Exchange: NY
Symbol: MDP

Corporate History: The company incorporated in 1905 as Successful Farming Publishing Co. The name was changed to Meredith Publishing Co. in 1925 and to its present title in 1967. It publishes magazines, newspapers, and books, owns radio and television stations and operates a real estate firm.

Brandnames of Products and Services:

Apartment Life	*magazine*

Better Homes & Gardens Insurance Agency	
Better Homes & Gardens Real Estate	
Better Homes & Gardens	*magazine and books*
Campbell Press	*newspaper, San Jose, Calif.*
City Press	*weekly newspaper, Los Angeles*
Cupertino Courier	*newspaper, SanJose, Calif.*
East San Jose Sun	*weekly newspaper, San Jose, Calif.*
Independent	*weekly newspaper, Hollywood, Calif.*
KCEZ-FM	*radio station, Kansas City, Mo.*
KCMO-TV & AM	*radio station, Kansas City, Mo.*
KPCH-FM	*radio station, Atlanta, Ga.*
KPHO-TV	*station, Phoenix, Ariz.*
Los Feliz Hills News	*weekly newspaper, Los Angeles, Calif.*
Milpitas Post	*weekly newspaper, Milpitas, Calif.*
Mountain View Sun	*newspaper, Mountain View, Calif.*
North Sun	*newspaper, San Jose, Calif.*
Northwest Leader	*weekly newspaper, Los Angeles, Calif.*
Parkside Journal	*weekly newspaper, Los Angeles, Calif.*
Sail	*magazine*
Saratoga News	*newspaper, Santa Clara, Calif.*
Scribe	*weekly newspaper, Sunnyvale, Calif.*
South San Jose Sun	*newspaper, San Jose, Calif.*
Successful Farming	*magazine*
Sun	*weekly newspaper, San Jose, Calif.*
Sun	*newspaper, Santa Clara, Calif.*
Times Observer	*weekly newspaper, Los Gatos, Calif.*
Town Crier	*weekly newspaper, Los Altos, Calif.*
Westlake Post	*newspaper, Los Angeles, Calif.*
WGST-AM	*radio station, Atlanta, Ga.*
Wilshire Independent	*newspaper, Los Angeles, Calif.*
Wilshire Press	*newspaper, Los Angeles, Calif.*
WNEM-TV	*station, Bay City-Saginaw-Flint, Mich.*
WOLF-TV	*station, Orlando, Fla. 40% owned*
WOW-AM	*radio station, Omaha, Neb.*
WPGH-TV	*station, Pittsburgh, Pa.*
WTVH-TV	*station, Syracuse, N.Y.*

Metro-Goldwyn-Mayer Film Co.

10202 W. Washington Blvd.
Culver City, Calif. 90230
(213) 836-3000

Chief Executive Officer: F.E. Rosenfelt
Exchange: NY
Symbol: MGM
Corporate History: Metro-Goldwyn-Mayer was founded in 1924 as the merger of three companies. During the 1930s and 1940s it was one of the greatest film production studios in America. Its stars, directors, executives and motion pictures were world-renowned. Metro declined during the 1950s as television took center-stage. In the 1960s, the company diversified into hotels and casinos. In 1980 it split into the Metro-Goldwyn-Mayer Film Co. and MGM Grand Hotels. As of May, 1981 an agreement was reached for Metro-Goldwyn-Mayer Film Company to acquire United Artists from Trans America.
Brandnames of Products and Services:

Metro-Goldwyn-Mayer Productions

Metromedia Inc.

One Harmon Plaza
Secaucus, N.J. 07094
(201) 348-3244

Chief Executive Officer: J.W. Kluge
Exchange: NY
Symbol: MET
Corporate History: Metromedia was incorporated in 1955 as Dumont Broadcasting Corp. Its name was changed to Metropolitan Broadcasting Corp. in 1958

and to the present name in 1961. The company engages in radio and television broadcasting and publishing and entertainment activities.

Brandnames of Products and Services:

Cole	*publications*
Figi's	*mail marketer gift items*
Foster & Kleiser	*advertising*
Harlem Globetrotters	
Ice Capades	
KJR-AM	*radio station, Seattle*
KLAC	*radio station Los Angeles, Calif.*
KMBC-TV	*Kansas City, Mo.*
KMET-FM	*radio station, Los Angeles, Calif.*
KRIV-TV	*Houston, Texas*
KRLD-AM	*radio station, Dallas-Fort Worth, Texas*
KSAN-FM	*radio station, San Francisco-Oakland, Calif.*
KTTV-TV	*Los Angeles, Calif.*
WASH-FM	*radio station, Washington, D.C.*
WCBM-AM	*radio station, Baltimore, Md.*
WIP-AM	*radio station, Philadelphia, Pa.*
WMET-FM	*radio station, Chicago, Ill.*
WMMR-FM	*radio station, Philadelphia, Pa.*
WNEW-AM/FM	*radio station, New York, N.Y.*
WNEW-TV	*New York, N.Y.*
WOMO-FM	*radio station, Detroit, Mich.*
WSB-AM	*radio station, Atlanta, Ga.*
WTCN-TV	*station, Minneapolis-St. Paul, Minn.*
WTTG-TV	*Washington, D.C.*
WXIX-TV	*Cincinnati, Ohio*

MGM Grand Hotels, Inc.

3645 Las Vegas Blvd., South
Las Vegas, NV 89109
(702) 739-4111

Chief Executive Officer:	Alvin Benedict
1984 Annual Sales Volume:	333M
1984 Shares Outstanding:	31,817,522
Shareholders:	12,000
Exchange:	NY
Symbol:	MGM

Corporate History: MGM Grand Hotels was formerly part of Metro-Goldwyn-Mayer Inc. It was spun off in 1980. The company operates two major hotel-casino complexes in Las Vegas and Reno, Nev.

Brandnames of Products and Services:

MGM Grand Hotels

MGM/UA Entertainment Co.

10202 W. Washington Blvd.
Culver City, CA 90230
(213) 558-5000

Chief Executive Officer:	Frank Rothman
1984 Annual Sales Volume:	706.9M
1984 Shares Outstanding:	49,663,968
Shareholders:	17,006
Exchange:	NY
Symbol:	MGM

Corporate History: MGM/UA was incorporated under the laws of Delaware in 1980. It is the successor to Metro-Goldwyn-Mayer Inc., which was founded in 1924 as the merger of three companies, became one of the greatest film production studios in America, and declined during the 1950s as television took center-stage. In the 1960s, the company diversified into hotels and casinos, and in 1980, split into Metro-Goldwyn-Mayer and MGM Grand Hotels. It subsequently acquired United Artists from Trans America. In 1982, MGM/UA licensed to MGM/UA Home Entertainment Group exclusive worldwide rights to its filmed entertainment library for a term of 40 years. The latter includes home video and pay television markets. MGM/UA's operations include the financing, production, and world distribution of motion pictures and television series and the operation of a film processing laboratory.

Brandnames of Products and Services:

MGM/UA

Michigan General Corp.

1555 Valwood Pkwy., Suite ▪150
P.O. Box 115026
Carrollton, TX 75011-5026
(214) 247-3800

Chief Executive Officer:	John R. Boudreau
1984 Annual Sales Volume:	449M

1984 Shares Outstanding: 11,338,408
Shareholders: 3,403
Exchange: AM
Symbol: MGL
Corporate History: Michigan General Corporation is a retailer of homebuilding products through its Diamond Lumber homebuilding supply centers and clothing through its Savannah Wholesale Company, doing business as Allied Department Stores. It also is engaged in the manufacture and sale of windows and doors through Krestmark, and provides high technology engineering services through its Applied Consulting and Technical Services, Inc. subsidiary.
Brandnames of Products and Services:

Allied Department Stores	*department stores*
Diamond Lumber, Inc	*retail homebuilding products*
Krestmark	*doors & windows*
LFD	*furniture stores*

Mickelberry Corp.

405 Park Ave.
New York, N.Y. 10022
(212) 834-0303

Chief Executive Officer: J.C. Marlas
Exchange: AM
Symbol: MBC
Corporate History: The company incorporated in 1926 as Mickelberry's Food Products Inc. and adopted its present title in 1973. It is a meat processing and communications service company. In 1979 printing accounted for 45% of sales, processed meat 30% and advertising 25%. The company is interested in acquisitions in the printing, advertising, home furnishings and machine tool industries.
Brandnames of Products and Services:

Mickelberry	*meats*

Herman Miller Inc.

8500 Byron Rd.
Zeeland, MI 49464
(616) 772-3300

Chief Executive Officer: Max De Pree
1984 Annual Sales Volume: 403M
1984 Shares Outstanding: 24,55,557
Shareholders: 6,000
Exchange: OTC
Symbol: MLHR
Corporate History: Miller, incorporated in 1970, is a reorganization of a company formed in 1905. The company's principal business consists of the research, design, development, manufacture and sale of furniture systems, products and related services. Most of these systems and products are coordinated in design so they may be used together and interchangeably.
Brandnames of Products and Services:

Action Office	*office furniture*
Co-Struc	*office furniture*
Equa	*chairs*
Ergon	*chairs*
Ethospace	*office furniture*
Herman Miller	*furniture*

Miller-Wohl Co. Inc.

915 Secaucus Rd.
Secaucus, N.J. 07094
(212) 564-2800

Chief Executive Officer: Heinz Eppler
Exchange: NY
Symbol: MLW
Corporate History: The company, incorporated in 1932, operates retail stores in the Midwest and South, catering to the 17 to 30 age group.
Brandnames of Products and Services:

Jean Nicole	*women's apparel stores*
Lizzie B	*women's apparel stores*
Miller-Wohl	*women's apparel stores*
Three Sisters	*women's apparel stores*

Milton Bradley Co.

1500 Main St.
Springfield, Mass. 01115
(413) 525-6411

Chief Executive Officer: J.J. Shea, Jr.
Exchange: NY
Symbol: MB
Corporate History: The Milton Bradley Co., incorporated in 1884, is one of the largest manufacturers of toys and games in the United States. It has a strong product line of board games, puzzles, preschool toys and electronic games. In 1979 toys accounted for 95.5% of its sales. The company, through its foreign subsidiaries,

makes and sells games in eight European countries. In 1979 foreign operations provided 28% of sales.

Brandnames of Products and Services:

Milton Bradley
Toys
Playskool
Educational Toys

Minnesota Mining and Manufacturing Co. (3M)

3M Center
St. Paul, MN 55144
(612) 733-1110

Chief Executive Officer: Lewis W. Lehr
1984 Annual Sales Volume: 7,705M
1984 Shares Outstanding: 116,122,681
Shareholders: 112,432
Exchange: NY
Symbol: MMM

Corporate History: The company was founded in 1902 to mine corundum. It failed in its mining enterprise but succeeded as a manufacturer of sandpaper. In the 1920s it began manufacturing other products and in 1925 developed masking tape. The company expanded tremendously during the 1940s, 1950s and 1920s. by developing a wide variety of business products, adhesives, electrical and health care products. Today, the company, known as "3M," is organized into four business sectors: industrial and consumer, electronic and information technologies, life sciences, and graphic technologies. 3M does business in more than 100 countries.

Brandnames of Products and Services:

3M	*video cassettes, copying machines & supplies*
3M	*photographic film*
Buf-Puf	*facial sponges, pads*
Light Water	*fire-fighting agent*
Post-It	*stationery*
Scotch	*adhesive tapes*
Scotchban	*paper products*
Scotch-Brite	*abrasive cleaners*
Scotchguard	*fabric protector*

Minnetonka Inc.

Jonathan Industrial Park
Chaska, MN 55318
(612) 448-4181

Chief Executive Officer: Robert R. Taylor
1984 Annual Sales Volume: 88M
1984 Shares Outstanding: 8,369,271
Shareholders: 3,800
Exchange: OTC
Symbol: MINL

Corporate History: Minnetonka incorporated in 1964 as Village Bath Products Inc. and adopted its present name in 1977. It makes bath and gift products.

Brandnames of Products and Services:

Calvin Klein	*fragrance and cosmetics*
Check Up	*toothpaste*
Claire Burke	*potpourri*
Country Diary	*bath products & provisions*
Derma Scrub	*medical products*
Institute Swiss	*personal care products*
L'Homme	*men's fragrance & toiletries*
Obsession	*fragrance*
Roger & Gallet	*soaps & toiletries*
SoftSoap	*cream soap*
Village	*bath products and toiletries*

Minstar Inc.

1215 Marshall St. N.E.
Minneapolis, MN 55413
(612) 379-1800

Chief Executive Officer: Irwin L. Jacobs
1984 Annual Sales Volume: 598M
1984 Shares Outstanding: 10,853,317
Shareholders: 3,500
Exchange: OTC
Symbol: MNST

Corporate History: Minstar, Inc. (formerly Arctic Enterprises, Inc.) was incorporated in 1962. The company is engaged in three principal lines of business: transportation and storage, pleasure boat manufacturing and other manufacturing. In 1984 the company acquired Aegis Corp., a company engaged in the manufacture and sale of pleasure boats, tread rubber and natural gas and seismic compressor units.

Brandnames of Products and Services:

Bekins	*moving and storage*
Californian	*pleasure boats*
Larson	*pleasure boats*

Lund	*pleasure boats*
Wellcraft	*pleasure boats*

Mirro Corp.

1512 Washington St.
Manitowoc, Wis. 54220
(414) 684-4421

Chief Executive Officer: C.W. Ziemer
Exchange: NY
Symbol: MIR
Corporate History: The company incorporated in 1909 as Aluminum Goods Mfg. Co. It is one of the world's largest manufacturers of aluminum cooking utensils and small appliances.
Brandnames of Products and Services:

Cruisers	*boats*
Electric Works	*small appliances*
Kitchen Pride	*bakeware*
Leggacy	*cookware*
Mirro	*cookware and campware*
Mirro-Craft	*aluminum boats*
Rally	*boats*
Silverstone	*cookware*
"The Bakery"	*teflon bakeware*

Mobil Corp.

150 E. 42nd St.
New York, NY 10017-5666
(212) 883-4242

Chief Executive Officer: Rawleigh Warner, Jr.
1984 Annual Sales Volume: 60,474M
1984 Shares Outstanding: 407,808,677
Shareholders: 207,815
Exchange: NY
Symbol: MOB
Corporate History: Mobil was incorporated in 1882 as Standard Oil Co. of New York. Its name was changed to Socony Vacuum Corp. and to Socony Mobil Oil Co. in 1955. It adopted its present name in 1976. The company began refining and selling gasoline in the Northeast, which remains its major base of operations. In the early years of the century, one of its primary markets was China. Today Mobil sells gas through retailers in more than 100 countries. Traditionally, the company has been heavily reliant on crude from the politically volatile Middle East. In recent years, it has stepped up exploration in the North Sea, off the coast of the Atlantic and in the Western United States. The company's acquisition of Montgomery Ward in 1974 at the height of the oil crisis drew criticism from consumers and other oil companies who opposed using profits from expensive oil to acquire other businesses. Mobil is also involved in chemicals and, paperboard packaging. It has embarked on a number of joint projects in Saudi Arabia, including a refinery and petro chemical complex. In 1984 the company acquired Superior Oil, an independent oil and gas exploration and producing company.
Brandnames of Products and Services:

Guestware	*dishes*
Hefty	*trashbags*
Jefferson Ward	*discount stores*
Mobil	*automotive products*
Mobil Service Stations	
Montgomery Ward	*stores and catalog*

Modern Merchandising Inc.

5101 Shady Oak Rd.
Minnetonka, Minn. 55343
(612) 932-1616

Chief Executive Officer: Harold Roitenberg
Exchange: NY
Symbol: MOM
Corporate History: The company, incorporated in 1968, operates catalog showrooms. The showrooms sell a broad range of nationally advertised name-brand merchandise.
Brandnames of Products and Services:

Dolgin	*catalog showrooms*
Great Western	*catalog showrooms*
Jofco	*catalog showrooms*
La Belle's	*catalog showrooms*
Leeds	*catalog showrooms*
Miller Sales	*catalog showrooms*
Rogers	*catalog showrooms*
Standard Sales	*catalog showrooms*

Mohasco Corp.

57 Lyon St.
Amsterdam, N.Y. 12010
(518) 841-2211

Chief Executive Officer: Herbert J. Broner
1984 Annual Sales Volume: 716M
1984 Shares Outstanding: 6,739,437

Shareholders: 5,322
Exchange: NY
Symbol: MOH
Corporate History: The company incorporated in 1873 as Alexander Smith & Sons Carpet Co. Its name was changed to Alexander Smith Inc. in 1951 and to Mohasco Industries in 1955. The present name was adopted in 1974. It is a leading producer and distributor of carpets, furniture and other products for homes and public facilities. Mohasco also manufactures, distributes and rents interior furnishings.
Brandnames of Products and Services:

Alexander Smith	*carpets*
Avon	*furniture*
Barcalounger	*furniture*
Chromcraft	*furniture*
Firth	*carpets*
furniture rental	
Futorian	*furniture*
Mohawk	*carpets*
Monarch	*furniture*
Peters-Revington	*furniture*
Stratford	*furniture*
Stratolounger	*furniture*
Super Sagless	*furniture*
Trend Line	*furniture*

Mohawk Rubber Co.

50 Executive Pkwy.
Hudson, Ohio 44236
(216) 653-3111

Chief Executive Officer: H.M. Fawcett
Exchange: NY
Symbol: MWK
Corporate History: The company, incorporated in 1913, makes tires sold in the replacement market. It also manufactures rubber products for footwear, sporting goods and appliances. In 1979 the company produced about 3.2% of all tires sold in the United States replacement market. Sixty-nine per cent of the tires manufactured were sold to customers who market under their own private labels with Sears, Roebuck & Co. accounting for 13% of the total sales.
Brandnames of Products and Services:

Mohawk	*tires*

Monsanto Co.

800 N. Lindbergh Blvd.
St. Louis, Mo. 63166
(314) 694-1000

Chief Executive Officer: J.W. Hanley
Exchange: NY
Symbol: MTC
Corporate History: Monsanto was founded by John Francisco Queeny in 1901 to manufacture saccharin. It expanded gradually into a wide range of chemical products and today is one of the most important producers of basic chemicals in the nation. Very few of Monsanto's products are destined for the consumer; in fact, the company has been known to develop consumer goods and then sell the rights to produce them to another manufacturer. Monsanto has 98 plants in 20 countries and the United States. Foreign sales account for one-third of its business. The company is a leading producer of agricultural products, ranking third in the world behind Bayer and Ciba-Geigy. In 1980 these accounted for 60% of the company's profits.
Brandnames of Products and Services:

Astro Turf	*artificial ground cover*

Morrison Inc.

4721 Morrison Dr.
P.O. Box 160266
Mobile, AL 36625
(205) 344-3000

Chief Executive Officer: E.E. Bishop
1984 Annual Sales Volume: 471M
1984 Shares Outstanding: 15,706,303
Shareholders: 10,000
Exchange: OTC
Symbol: MORR
Corporate History: Incorporated in 1954, Morrison operates cafeterias throughout the South.
Brandnames of Products and Services:

L&N Seafood Grills	*specialty restaurant*
Morrison's	*cafeterias*
Ruby Tuesday's	*specialty restaurant*
Silver Spoon	*specialty restaurant*

Morse Shoe Inc.

555 Turnpike St.
Canton, MA 02021
(617) 828-9300

Chief Executive Officer: Manuel Rosenberg
1984 Annual Sales Volume: 527M
1984 Shares Outstanding: 5,434,266
Shareholders: 1,609
Exchange: NY
Symbol: MRS
Corporate History: The company, incorporated in 1961, is a retailer of popular priced family footwear through its own stores, and footwear departments operated by Morse, in leading self service discount and promotional department store chains. In 1984 the company operated 1,307 stores and departments in 36 states, the District of Columbia and all 10 Canadian provinces.
Brandnames of Products and Services:

Belle Amie	*footwear*
Country Boots	*footwear*
Fayva	*shoe stores*
Morse	*shoe stores*
Nurse-Mates	*footwear*
Olympian	*footwear*
Outdoor Boots	*footwear*
Pro-Champs	*footwear*
Soft Spot	*footwear*
Stormers	*footwear*
Upstage	*shoe stores*

Morton Shoe Companies Inc.

Boston Harbor Industrial Park
647 Summer St.
Boston, Mass. 02210
(617) 269-6100

Chief Executive Officer: M.I. Narva
Exchange: AM
Symbol: MOS
Corporate History: Incorporated in 1930, Morton retails popular-priced shoes.
Brandnames of Products and Services:

Celebres	*footwear*
Flites	*footwear*
Hampshire	*vinyl boots, air mattresses, wet-weather clothing*
Streetcars	*footwear*
Tagway	*shoe stores*
Wildwoods	*footwear*

Morton-Thiokol, Inc.

110 N. Wacker Dr.
Chicago, IL 60606
(312) 621-5200

Chief Executive Officer: Charles Locke
1984 Annual Sales Volume: 2,002M
1984 Shares Outstanding: 51,116,411
Shareholders: 14,330
Exchange: NY
Symbol: MTI
Corporate History: The company incorporated in 1969 and changed its name to Morton Thiokol in 1982. It is a manufacturer and marketer of high-technology propulsion systems, specialty chemicals, and salt.
Brandnames of Products and Services:

Morton	*salt*
Morton Lite Salt Mixture	*salt*
Morton Salt Substitute	*salt substitute*
Mortons Nature's Seanonings	*salt substitute*
Windsor	*salt*
Windsor Coarse Pickling Salt	*salt*

Mott's Supermarkets Inc.

59 Leggett St.
East Hartford, CT 06108
(203) 289-3301

Chief Executive Officer: Joseph P. Mott
1984 Annual Sales Volume: 298M
1984 Shares Outstanding: 2,786,224
Shareholders: 1,159
Exchange: AM
Symbol: MSM
Corporate History: The company incorporated in 1948 as Washington Market Inc. and adopted its present title in 1953. It presently operates 23 supermarkets under the name "Shop-Rite Super Markets" and one supermarket under the name "Price-Rite Super Market." The company presently operates in Connecticut and western Massachusetts.
Brandnames of Products and Services:

Price Rite	*supermarkets*

Shop-Rite	*supermarkets, drug and liquor stores*

Movie Star Inc.

392 Fifth Ave.
New York, NY 10018
(212) 563-3000

Chief Executive Officer: Irwin Goldberger
1984 Annual Sales Volume: 76M
1984 Shares Outstanding: 834,600
Shareholders: 421
Exchange: AM
Symbol: MVS
Corporate History: The company, incorporated in 1946, makes women's and men's, children's apparel. It is one of the country's largest and most diversified manufacturers in the loungewear and lingerie industry.
Brandnames of Products and Services:

Cinema Etoile	*lingerie*
Cine Star	*lingerie*
Movie Star	*lingerie and loungewear*

MTV Networks Inc.

75 Rockefeller Plaza
New York, NY 10019-6908
(212) 484-8680

Chief Executive Officer: David H. Horowitz
1984 Annual Sales Volume: 109.5M
1984 Shares Outstanding: 10,125,000
Shareholders: 1,400
Exchange: OTC
Symbol: MTVN
Corporate History: MTV Networks Inc. was incorporated in 1981. It owns and operates three channels of television programming, MTV: Music Television, Nickelodeon, and VH-1/Video Hits One, which it distributes via satellite throughout the United States primarily to cable television operators who in turn distribute the programming to viewers. In 1984, MTV reached 25 million households, Nickelodeon, 24 million households, and VH-1, 3 million households.
Brandnames of Products and Services:

MTV: Music Television	*cable TV service*
Nickelodeon	*cable TV service*
VH-1/Video Hits One	*cable TV service*

Multimedia Inc.

305 S. Main St.
PO Box 1688
Greenville, SC 29602
(803) 298-4374

Chief Executive Officer: Walter E. Bartlett
1984 Annual Sales Volume: 304M
1984 Shares Outstanding: 16,656,000
Shareholders: 2,231
Exchange: OTC
Symbol: MMED
Corporate History: Multimedia Inc. is a diversified communications media company with most of its holdings located in the Sunbelt. The company was incorporated in South Carolina in 1968, although its forerunning companies dated back to 1888, with origins in newspaper publishing. Since then, Multimedia has expanded its interests into radio and television stations, cable systems, and television production and syndicaition. In addition, the company has more than 100 cable franchises in 4 states. Among its better-known ventures in television programming are *Donahue, Sally Jessy Raphael, America Comes Alive, Music City USA, Pop Goes the Country,* and *Young People's Specials.* The firm's strong, steady performance attracted several attempted buyouts during 1984 by other prominent companies.
Brandnames of Products and Services:

Advertiser	*newspaper, Montgomery, Ala.*
Alabama Journal	*newspaper, Montgomery, Ala.*
The Ashland City Times	*non-daily newspaper, Ashland City, TN*
Baxter Bulletin	*weekly newspaper, Mountain Home, Ark.*
Citizen	*newspaper, Asheville, N.C.*
Citizen-Times	*newspaper, Asheville, N.C.*
Dickson Herald	*Tenn.*
Gallatin Examiner-News	*Tenn.*
KEEL-AM	*Shreveport, La.*
KMBQ-FM	*Shreveport, La.*
KSDK-TV	*St. Louis, Mo.*
Leaf Chronicle	*newspaper, Clarksville, Tenn.*
Moultrie Weekly Observer	*Ga.*

Multimedia Cablevision	*cable franchises, Wichita, KS*
Multimedia Entertainment	*music and entertainment, New York, NY*
Music City News	*Nashville, Tenn.*
News-Chief	*newspaper, Winter Haven, Fla.*
News	*newspaper, Greenville, S.C.*
Piedmont	*newspaper, Greenville, S.C.*
Point Pleasant Register	*W. Va.*
Progress	*weekly newspaper, Prattville, Ala.*
Record	*weekly newspaper, Nashville, Tenn.*
Sentinel	*newspaper, Pomery-Middleport, Ohio*
Star-News	*weekly newspaper, Hendersonville, Tenn.*
Star	*weekly newspaper, Auburndale, Fla.*
The Staunton Leader	*newspaper, Staunton, VA*
Stewart-Houston Times	*newspaper, Tenn.*
Times	*newspaper, Asheville, N.C.*
Times-Sentinel	*Sunday newspaper, Pomeroy-Middleport, Ohio*
Tribune	*newspaper, Gallipolis, Ohio*
WAKY-AM	*Louisville, Ky.*
WBIR-TV	*Knoxville, TN*
WEZW-FM	*Milwaukee-Wauwatosa, Wis.*
WFBC-AM/FM	*Greenville, S.C.*
WLWT-TV	*Cincinnati, Ohio*
WMAZ-TV & AM	*Macon, Ga.*
WVEZ-FM	*Louisville, Ky.*
WWNC-AM	*Asheville, N.C.*
WZTV	*Nashville, Tenn.*

Munford Inc.

1860-74 Peachtree Rd. N.W.
Atlanta, GA 30309
(404) 352-6641

Chief Executive Officer: Dillard Munford
1984 Annual Sales Volume: 424M
1984 Shares Outstanding: 4,095,139
Shareholders: 4,500
Exchange: NY
Symbol: MFD

Corporate History: Munford incorporated in 1924 and adopted its present title in 1971. It operates drive-in convenience food stores, mostly in the South, and also controls a chain of home-furnishing stores. In 1984 it had approximately 850 Majik Markets in 14 states and approximately 280 World Bazaar stores in 28 states, 90 of which were franchises.

Brandnames of Products and Services:

Craft Bazaar	*craft products stores*
Curious Cargo	*imported gift and household items stores*
Majik Market	*convenience food markets*
Michigan Markets	*convenience food markets*
World Bazaar	*imported gift and household items stores*

Munsingwear Inc.

724 N. First St.
Minneapolis, MN 55401
(612) 340-4700

Chief Executive Officer: George K. Hansen
1984 Annual Sales Volume: 93M
1984 Shares Outstanding: 1,266,772
Shareholders: 2,950
Exchange: NY
Symbol: MUN

Corporate History: Munsingwear Inc., organized in 1886 and incorporated in 1923, is a manufacturer of men's and boys' sportswear, of men's sleepwear and underwear, and of women's lingerie, robes, sleepwear, brassieres and girdles. Manufacturing activities include knitting, processing, cutting and sewing. The company's products are designed, produced and distributed directly to retailers located throughout the United States and approximately 30 other countries. Such retailers include major department, specialty and company-operated outlet stores. The outlet stores principally market overstocked, irregular and end-of-season goods.

Brandnames of Products and Services:

Banlon	*apparel*
Grand Slam	*golf shirts*
Munsingwear	*men's apparel*
Penguin	*apparel*
Vassarette	*women's intimate apparel*

G.C. Murphy Co.

531 Fifth Ave.
McKeesport, PA 15132
(412) 675-2000

Chief Executive Officer: C.H. Lytle
1984 Annual Sales Volume: 913M
1984 Shares Outstanding: 4,100,000
Exchange: NY
Symbol: MPH
Corporate History: The year 1906 marked the beginning of G. C. Murphy Company's history when the original 5¢-10¢ Murphy stores were opened. In 1911, J.S. Mack and W. C. Shaw purchased controlling interest in the 10-store George C. Murphy organization. G. C. Murphy stores and Murphy's Marts are located in 19 states and the District of Columbia, princiaplly in the Mid-East, North Central and Gulf Coast regions of the United States. Restaurants, cafeterias or snack bars are operated in 178 of the company's marts and larger conventional stores. As of the end of fiscal 1984, the company had 26 Bargain Worlds in operation, designed to sell irregulars and close-out merchandise. These locations are operated on a "no frills" basis. Sales for the year ended January 31, 1985 were generated from 383 stores.
Brandnames of Products and Services:

Bargain World	*department stores*
Big Murph	*men's & boy's apparel stores*
Murphy's	*general merchandise stores*
Murphy's	*general merchandise stores*
Pelham	*men's & boy's apparel stores*

Murray Ohio Manufacturing Co.

Franklin Rd.
Brentwood, TN 37027
(615) 373-6500

Chief Executive Officer: J.N. Anderson
1984 Annual Sales Volume: 384M
1984 Shares Outstanding: 3,889,345
Shareholders: 4,813
Exchange: NYSE
Symbol: MYO
Corporate History: Incorporated in 1919, the company is a leading domestic manufacturer of bicycles and lawn mowers.
Brandnames of Products and Services:

Murray	*lawn and sports equipment*

Nabisco Brands Inc.

Nabisco Brands Plaza
Parsippany, NJ 07054
(201) 898-7100

Chief Executive Officer: F. Ross Johnson
1984 Annual Sales Volume: 6,253M
1984 Shares Outstanding: 57,790,791
Shareholders: 80,750
Exchange: NY
Symbol: NB
Corporate History: Nabisco Brands Inc. was incorporated in 1981 when Standard Brands Incorporated and Nabisco, Inc., were combined. Nabisco Brands Inc., together with its domestic, Canadian and other international subsidiaries, is a major manufacturer, processor and distributor of packaged food and related products in the United States, Canada and abroad. The company is a leading producer of cookies and crackers and offers consumers many of the leading brands in margarines, yeast, nut products, snack products, hot and cold breakfast cereals, desserts, confectionery products and pet foods. It is also a supplier of food ingredients and imported beers. Of the company's total sales volumes, 41% was derived from sales of cookies and crackers in 1984; and 13% from sales of confectionery products.
Brandnames of Products and Services:

Almost Home	*cookies*
Baby Ruth	
Barnum's Animals	
Better Cheddars	
Bisco	
Blue Bonnet	
Bonkers!	
Breath Savers	
Bubble Yum	
Butcher Bones	
Butterfingers	
Cameo	
Care*Free	
Charleston Chew!	
Cheese Nips	
Chicken In A Biskit	
Chips Ahoy!	
Chuckles	
Cream of Rice	
Cream of Wheat	

Dromedary
Easy Cheese
Escort
Fig Newtons
Fleischmann's
Fleishmann's Egg
Beaters
Foster's
Heyday
Home Hearth
Honey Maid
I Screams
Junior Mints
Life Savers
Lorna Doone
Mallomars
Merckens
Milk-Bone *(dog biscuits)*
Mister Salty
Moosehead *beer*
Nabisco
Nilla
Nutter Butter
Oreo
Oysterettes
Party Grahams
Pearson
Pinwheels
Planters
Premium
Ritz
Royal
Social Tea
Spoon Size
Sugar Daddy
Team
Toasted Wheat &
Raisins
Triscuit
Uneeda
Waverly
Wheatsworth
Wheat Thins

Nashua Corp.

44 Franklin St.
Nashua, NH 03061
(603) 880-2323

Chief Executive Officer: Charles E. Clough
1984 Annual Sales Volume: 592M
1984 Shares Outstanding: 4,721,266
Shareholders: 2,552
Exchange: NY
Symbol: NSH
Corporate History: The company, incorporated in 1957, provides products and services in four business segments: office systems and supplies, coated products and supplies, computer products, and photo finishing. Most of the product lines relate to discrete particle technology. Nashua products are sold internationally by wholly-owned foreign subsidiaries and more than 90 distributors. Foreign sales and export sales from the United States totaled $252.4 million and represented 43 percent of the company's total sales in fiscal 1984.
Brandnames of Products and Services:

Nashua	*office equipment*
Ricoh	*paper copiers*

National Convenience Stores

3200 Travis St.
Houston, Texas 77006
(713) 529-5711

Chief Executive Officer: V.H. Van Horn
Exchange: AM
Symbol: NCV
Corporate History: National incorporated in 1959 as U-Tote-M of San Antonio, Texas. Its name was changed from National Drive-In Grocery Corp. to its present title in 1968. The company operates and franchises others to operate approximately 800 retail convenience stores.
Brandnames of Products and Services:

Jay's	*coin-operated laundromats*
Shop-n-Go	*convenience stores*
Stop-n-Go	*convenience stores*
Super Drug	*convenience stores*
Super Quik	*convenience stores*
Tex Super Duper Markets	

National Distillers & Chemical Corp.

99 Park Ave.
New York, NY 10016
(212) 949-5000

Chief Executive Officer: D.C. Bell
1984 Annual Sales Volume: 2,157M
1984 Shares Outstanding: 30,144,978

Shareholders: 63,000
Exchange: NY
Symbol: DR
Corporate History: The company, incorporated in 1924, is one of the four largest distillers in the United States. It has important stakes in metals, petrochemicals, and genetic engineering.
Brandnames of Products and Services:

Adriatica	*wine*
Alberta Springs	*Canadian whisky*
Almaden	*wines and sherry*
Bellows	*borubon, vodka, gin & scotch*
Bellows	*vodka*
Bellows Partners	*blended whiskey*
Bellows reserve	*blended whiskey*
Boissiere	*vermouth*
Bond & Lillard	*bourbon*
Bourbon de Luxe	*bourbon*
Bourbon de Luxe	*blended whiskey*
Brigadier	*gin*
Canada House	*Canadian whisky*
Century Club	*bourbon*
Charles Lefrance	*wines*
Choice	*blended whiskey*
CocoRibe	*rum specialty*
Commemorativo	*tequila*
Crab Orchard	*blended whiskey*
DeKruper	*cordials, liquers, brandies*
DeKruyper Geneva	*gin*
Gilbey's	*gin, vodka & rum*
Grande Marque Red and Grande Marque White	*bordeaux*
Henry Baron	*brandy*
Hepok Mostar	*wine*
Hermitage	*bourbon*
Hill and Hill	*bourbon*
Hill and Hill	*blended whiskey*
Hornitos	*tequila bourbon*
Indiana Insurance Company	
Kamchatka	*vodka*
Keller Geister	*wine*
Kentucky Colonel	*bourbon*
Kentucky Silk	*bourbon specialty*
King George IV	*scotch*
Le Domaine	*wines*
Mount Vernon	*blended whiskey*
Navip	*slivovitz*
Old Crow	*bourbon*
Old Dover	*bourbon*
Old Grand-Dad	*bourbon*
Old Log Cabin	*blended whiskey*
Old Overholt	*rye*
Old Taylor	*bourbon*
PM	*blended whiskey*
Ron Merito	*rum*
Sauza Silver and Sauza Gold	*tequila*
Suburban Propane Gas Corp	
Sunny Brook	*blended whiskey*
Sunny Brook	*bourbon*
Talisker 12	*scotch*
Tres Generacianoes	*tequila*
Vat 69 Gold and Traditional	*scotch bourbon*
Windsor Supreme	*whisky*

National Education Corp.

1300 Bristol St. North
Newport Beach, CA 92660
(715) 955-9400

Chief Executive Officer: H. David Bright
1984 Annual Sales Volume: 174M
1984 Shares Outstanding: 9,616,895
Shareholders: 2,371
Exchange: NY
Symbol: NEC
Corporate History: National Education Corporation is a "human resource" development company with worldwide operations in vocational training and United States operations in educational publishing. It operates 43 technical and business schools in 20 states. The company was originally incorporated in California in 1954 and reincorporated in Delaware in 1972.
Brandnames of Products and Services:

Action Code	*videodisc training system*
Allentown Business School	*school, Allentown, Pa.*
Anthony Schools	*real estate schools*
Brown Institute	*communications schools*
Bryman Schools	*medical and dental assisting schools*
Center for Degree Studies	*home-study schools*
Health Care Services	*provides health care personnel*
International Correspondence Schools	*home-study schools*

Kansas City Business College	*school, Kansas City, Mo.*
North American Correspondence Schools	*home-study schools*
RETS	*electronics schools*
Sawyer Schools	*secretarial schools*
Spartan School of Aeronautics	*school Tulsa, Okla.*
Steck-Vaughn	*publishing*
Thompson Insitute	*business/secretarial schools*
Vale Technical Institute	*automotive school Pa.*

National Lampoon Inc.

635 Madison Ave.
New York, NY 10022
(212) 688-4070

Chief Executive Officer: Matty Simmons
1984 Annual Sales Volume: 9.4M
1984 Shares Outstanding: 1,537,926
Shareholders: 672
Exchange: OTC
Symbol: NLPI

Corporate History: The company is engaged in the publishing and entertainment business. It is the publisher of *National Lampoon*, a monthly magazine of contemporary humor and satire, first published in 1970, and *Heavy Metal*, a monthly magazine of adult illustrated fantasy and science fiction first published in 1977. The company also creates and develops motion picture, television and related projects under the National Lampoon and Heavy Metal names.

Brandnames of Products and Services:

Heavy Metal	*magazine*
National Lampoon	*magazine*

National Patent Development Corp.

375 Park Ave.
New York, NY 10152
(212) 826-8500

Chief Executive Officer: Jerome I. Feldman
1984 Annual Sales Volume: 128M
1984 Shares Outstanding: 10,886,745
Shareholders: 8,133
Exchange: AM
Symbol: NPD

Corporate History: National Patent Development Corp., incorporated in 1959, has three main business segments. The ophthalmic products group manufactures and sells soft contact lenses and accessories. The medical and health care group manufactures and sells first aid products, surgical dressings and other hospital and medical products. The consumer products group distributes paint, paint specialties and garden supplies.

Brandnames of Products and Services:

Hydron	*medical supplies*
Leuen	*paint, paint specialties, garden supplies*
Zero	*contact lens*

National Presto Industries Inc.

3925 North Hastings Way
Eau Claire, WI 54703
(715) 839-2121

Chief Executive Officer: Melvin S. Cohen
1984 Annual Sales Volume: 89M
1984 Shares Outstanding: 7,371,490
Shareholders: 2,068
Exchange: NY
Symbol: NPK

Corporate History: The company incorporated in 1905 as Northwestern Steel & Iron Works. Later its name was changed to National Pressure Cooker Co. It adopted its current name in 1953. The company manufactures and distributes electrical appliances and housewares, including private label products and premium sales products. Among the electric appliances are deep fryers, griddles, fry pans, skillets, pressure cookers, dutch ovens, food slicers, portable range.

Brandnames of Products and Services:

Presto	*pressure cookers and cooking accessories*

National Service Industries Inc.

1180 Peachtree St. NE
Atlanta, GA 30309
(404) 892-2400

Chief Executive Officer: Erwin Zaban
1984 Annual Sales Volume: 1,073M
1984 Shares Outstanding: 24,639,676
Shareholders: 8,513
Exchange: NY
Symbol: NAS

Corporate History: The company, incorporated in 1928 as National Linen Service Corp., adopted its present title in 1964. It rents out bed and table linens, towels, uniforms and furniture. The company also manufactures chemical products, business and specialty evelopes, men's apparel, products for the construction industry, and lighting equipment. In addition, the company offers marketing services for the carpet industry.

Brandnames of Products and Services:

Certified Leasing	*furniture*
Jordache Bigandtall Men's Sportswear	*mens' apparel*
Jordache Contemporary Mens' Sportswear	*men's apparel*
Jordache Young Men's Sportswear	*men's apparel*
Kudos	*men's apparel*
Yukon Trail	*men's apparel*

National Silver Industries Inc.

241 Fifth Ave.
New York, N.Y. 10016
(212) 689-7300

Chief Executive Officer: M. Bernstein
Exchange: AM
Symbol: NSL

Corporate History: The company, incorporated in 1969, is a leading distributor of housewares, kitchenware, ceramics and glassware. It also designs and manufactures silverplated holloware.

Brandnames of Products and Services:

F.B. Rogers	*silverplated holloware; copper and brass items*
National Silver Company	*ceramics, flatware and mugs*

National Tea Co.

9701 W. Higgins Rd.
Rosemont, Ill. 60018
(312) 693-5100

Chief Executive Officer: V.W. Schulz
Exchange: NY
Symbol: NTY

Corporate History: The company, incorporated in 1902, operates a chain of supermarkets in the Midwest and Southcentral part of the United States. It is 84% owned by Loblaw Cos. Ltd. & George Weston.

Brandnames of Products and Services:

Applebaum's	*food markets*
National	*supermarkets*
National Food	*products*

Nature's Bounty, Inc.

90 Orville Dr.
Bohemia, NY 11716
(516) 567-9500

Chief Executive Officer: Arthur Rudolph
1984 Annual Sales Volume: 36M
1984 Shares Outstanding: 3,653,075
Shareholders: 2,000
Exchange: OTC
Symbol: NBTY

Corporate History: Founded in 1971, Nature's Bounty manufactures and sells a wide range of vitamins and health care products. 90% of the products sold by the company are manufactured by Starlen Labs, a division of the company. The company's products are sold through kiosk stores located in shopping centers, direct mail order, and catalogue mailings to the customers of companies such as Spiegel, Lane Bryant, Montgomery Ward and Sears Roebuck. It operates 72 Vitamin World discount vitamin stores in 72 shopping malls in 15 states.

Brandnames of Products and Services:

Arco	*vitamins*
Doctors' Pride	*vitamins*
Good 'N Natural	*vitamins*
Natural Wealth	*vitamins*
Nature's Bounty	*vitamin vitamin stores*
Puritan's Pride	*mail order vitamins*
Vitamin World	*vitamins & kiosk stores*

Nature's Sunshine Products, Inc.

1655 North Main
Spanish Fork, UT 84660
(801) 798-9861

Chief Executive Officer: Kerry O. Asay
1984 Annual Sales Volume: 33M
1984 Shares Outstanding: 1,847,120
Shareholders: 373
Exchange: OTC
Symbol: AMTC

Corporate History: Nature's Sunshine Products, Inc. was incorporated in 1976 under the name of Amtec Industries Inc. It changed its name to Nature's Sunshine

Products Inc. in 1982. The company is engaged in the sale of health related nutritional and personal care products. Its products are sold directly to consumers by an independent sales force throughout the United States, Canada, Australia and New Zealand.

Brandnames of Products and Services:

En. R. Gizer	*exercise trampoline*
Nature's Spring	*water purifier*
Nature's Sunshine	*vitamins, personal care products.*
Sunshine Slender	*weight loss food*
Tiarra	*personal care products*

NCR Corp.

1700 South Patterson Blvd.
Dayton, OH 45479
(513) 445-5000

Chief Executive Officer:	C.E. Exley Jr.
1984 Annual Sales Volume:	4,074M
1984 Shares Outstanding:	99,636,968
Shareholders:	30,326
Exchange:	NY
Symbol:	NCR

Corporate History: NCR traces its history back to 1882 when a small factory was established to produce "thief catchers" or cash registers as they came to be known. The registers were first produced to insure honesty among sales personnel. Through aggressive marketing, the company captured 90% of the cash register market in 1910. However, it stagnated following the death of its founder, John Henry Patterson, in 1922 and little was done to keep it abreast of technological innovation or maintain profits. This changed in 1972 when William Anderson became the president. He pushed NCR to the forefront of the electronic business equipment industry. Today it ranks second in the computer industry behind IBM. NCR was one of the first companies to establish a business relationship with the People's Republic of China.

Brandnames of Products and Services:

NCR	*business machines and computers*
NCR Tower	*small main frame computer*
NCR Worksaver	*Office automation system*
NCR 32	*32-bit micro processor*

Nestle-LeMur Co.

529 Fifth Ave.
New York, N.Y. 10017
(212) 867-8900

Chief Executive Officer:	J.S. Lindemann
Exchange:	AM
Symbol:	NMR

Corporate History: The company incorporated in 1928 as a consolidation of the C. Nestle Co. and the LeMur Co. It makes personal grooming products. In 1979 foreign operations provided 10.2% of the sales.

Brandnames of Products and Services:

Beautyskin	*baby care products*
Djerkiss	*women's toiletries*
Egyptian Henna	*hair care product*
Le Mur	*(black) hair care products*
Lov'me	*women's toiletries*
Lucien Lelong	*women's toiletries*
Marchand	*toiletries*
Mavis	*women's toiletries*
Nestle	*hair care products*
Pinaud	*men's toiletries*
Seaforth	*men's toiletries*
Yu	*after-shave lotions*

Neutrogena Corporation

5755 W. 96th Street
Los Angeles, CA 90045
(213) 776-5223

Chief Executive Officer:	Lloyd E. Cotsen
1984 Annual Sales Volume:	59M
1984 Shares Outstanding:	5,992,488
Shareholders:	552
Exchange:	OTC
Symbol:	NGNA

Corporate History: The company, incorporated in 1962, makes premium priced skin care products. It wants to keep marketing costs low and make its presence known in luxury hotels and the medical profession. It would like to see pharmaceuticals play a major role in Neutrogena's growth. Noxell owns 13% of Neutrogena and would like to acquire the rest of the company. Neutrogena soap accounts for 62% of company sales.

Brandnames of Products and Services:

Melanex® Topical Solution	*skin care products*
Neutrogena	*skin care products*

Neutrogena Origine Suisse System™	*skin care products*
Norwegian Formula Hand Cream	*skin care products*
Rainbath	*bath oil*
T/Derm® Tar Emollient	*skin care products*
T/Gel® Therapeutic Shampoo	*shampoo*

Newell Companies Inc.

29 E. Stephenson St.
Freeport, IL 61032
(815) 235-4171

Chief Executive Officer: Daniel C. Ferguson
1984 Annual Sales Volume: 308M
1984 Shares Outstanding: 8,601,049
Shareholders: 2,157
Exchange: NY
Symbol: NWL

Corporate History: The company, last incorporated in 1970, manufactures drapery hardware, painting accessories and a variety of other products for home maintenance and improvement. It also produces art needlework and sewing notions.

Brandnames of Products and Services:

Baker	*paint brushes*
Boye	*sewing and knitting notions*
Brearley	*bathroom scales*
Bulldog	*hardware*
Chief Kitchen Tools	*aluminum utensils and plastic kitchen tools*
Classic Chiefware	*aluminum cooking and baking utensils*
Clean Stroke	*paint products; brushes, rollers, trays*
Comet	*aluminum cooking and baking utensils*
Counselor	*bath scales*
Creative Bakeware	*aluminum cooking and baking utensils*
Creative Cookware	*aluminum cooking and baking utensils*
Crochemaster	*needlework and craft products*
Debut	*aluminum cooking and baking utensils*
Designers Guild	*drapery and hardware accessories*
Diana	*sewing and knitting accessories*
Dorfile	*shelving and accessories*
Earth Grown	*aluminum cooking and baking utensils*
Easy Shelf	*wallhung shelving system components*
Ebonware	*aluminum cooking and baking utensils*
Edgecraft	*shelving and accessories*
Escort Kitchen Tools	*aluminum cooking and baking utensils and plastic kitchen tools*
Esprit de Cuisine	*aluminum cooking and baking utensils*
EZ Paintr	*paints and accessories*
EZ Roller	*paint products; brushes, rollers, trays*
Foley Foodmill	*aluminum cooking and baking utensils and plastic kitchen tools*
Foley VIII Cookware	*aluminum cooking and baking utensils and plastic kitchen tools*
The Great Cooks Collection	*aluminum cooking and baking utensils*
Handi-Man	*hardware*
Hoop-De-Doo	*needlework and craft products*
Jordan	*hardware*
Knitmaster	*needlework and craft products*
Magic Fit	*drapery hardware and accessories*
Masterbilt	*aluminum cooking and baking utensils*
Masterset	*aluminum cooking and baking utensils*
Mirra Cote	*hardware*
Mirro	*aluminum cooking and baking utensils*
Needlemaster	*needlework and craft products*
Newell	*drapery hardware and hardware accessories*
Panther	*brazing torches*
Protouch	*paint products, brushes, rollers, trays*

Regalwood	*shelving and accessories*
Space Arranger	*wall hung shelving system components*
Strips & Clips	*wall hung shelving system components*
Ventaire	*wall hung shelving system components*
Wilshire	*lighting fixtures*
Windsor Kitchen Tools	*aluminum cooking and baking utensils and plastic kitchen tools*
Worthmore	*aluminum cooking and baking utensils*

New York Times Co.

229 W. 43rd St.
New York, NY 10036
(212) 556-1234

Chief Executive Officer:	A.O. Sulzberger
1984 Annual Sales Volume:	1,200M
1984 Shares Outstanding:	39,971,947
Shareholders:	9,850
Exchange:	AMEX
Symbol:	NYT

Corporate History: *The New York Times* was founded in 1851. It remained a small paper unable to compete with more sensational journals of the time until bought by Adolph Ochs in 1896. Under his direction it became profitable and built a reputation for excellence that has made it the "newspaper of record." In the 1960s the paper ran into financial trouble as its readership moved to the suburbs and its labor costs rose. Union strength delayed technological innovations and management could not develop an effective marketing program. During the 1970s the company modernized and began diversifying. Today it is a communications conglomerate that owns radio stations, magazines, television, cable and news services as well as 33 other newspapers. About 17% of its revenues now come from such magazines as *Family Circle.* The company also owns significant equity interests in three Canadian and one U.S. paper-mill.

Brandnames of Products and Services:

Banner-Independent	*newspaper, Booneville, MS*
Clairborne Progress	*newspaper, Tazewell, Tenn*
Comet	*newspaper, Thibodaux, La.*
Commercial	*newspaper, Leesburg, Fla.*
Cruising World	*magazine, Newport, R.I.*
Daily Corinthian	*newspaper, Corinth, Miss.*
Daily Courier	*newspaper, Hanna, La.*
Daily Enterprise	*newspaper, Harlan, Ky*
Daily News	*newspaper, Middlesboro, KY*
Daily World	*newspaper, Opelousas, La.*
Dispatch	*newspaper, Lexington, N.C.*
Family Circle	*magazine*
Golf Digest	*magazine*
Golf World	*magazine, London, England*
Herald-Journal	*newspaper, Spartanburg, S.C.*
Herald-Tribune	*newspaper, Sarasota, Fla*
KFSM-TV	*Fort Smith, Ark.*
Ledger	*newspaper, Lakeland, Fla.*
Messenger	*newspaper, Madisonville, Ky.*
News-Leader	*weekly newspaper, Fernandina Beach, Fla.*
News	*weekly newspaper, Sebring, Fla.*
News	*newspaper, Palatka, Fla.*
News	*newspaper, Tuscaloosa, Ala*
News-Topic	*newspaper, Lenoir, N.C.*
New York Times Index	
New York Times News Service	
New York Times	*newspaper*
Press-Democrat	*newspaper, Santa Rosa, Cal.*
Reporter	*newspaper, Lake City, Fla.*
Star-Banner	*newspaper, Ocala, Fla.*
Star-News	*newspaper, Wilmington, N.C.*
State Gazette	*newspaper, Dyersburg, Tenn*
Sun	*weekly newspaper, Avon Park, Fla.*
Sun	*newspaper, Gainesville, Fla.*
Tennis Magazine	
Times Daily	*newspaper, Florence, Ala*
Times-News	*newspaper, Hendersonville, N.C.*
Times	*newspaper, Gadsden, Ala*
Tribune	*newspaper, Healdsburg, Cal*
WHNT-TV	*Huntsville, Ala.*
WQAD-TV	*Moline, Illinois*
WQXR-AM/FM	*NYC*
WREG-TV	*Memphis, Tenn.*
York County Coast Star	*Kennebunk, Ma.*

Nexus Industries Inc.

950 Third Ave.
New York, N.Y. 10022
(212) 421-6300

Chief Executive Officer: G.L. Cohen
Exchange: AM
Symbol: NEX
Corporate History: Nexus Industries incorporated in 1948 as Harvey's Apparel Shops and adopted its present name in 1975. The company sold its chain of unprofitable women's and children's apparel stores in 1978. It now only makes shirts and sweatshirts.
Brandnames of Products and Services:

Apparel Unlimited	*shirts*
Great American Factory	*shirts*
Premium	*shirts*
Shirt Shed	*shirts*
Top Half	*T-shirts*
Tropix Togs	*shirts*

S.E. Nichols Inc.

275 Seventh Ave.
New York, NY 10001
(212) 206-9400

Chief Executive Officer: Manfred Brecker
1984 Annual Sales Volume: 266M
1984 Shares Outstanding: 4,650,371
Shareholders: 1,200
Exchange: AM
Symbol: NCL
Corporate History: The company, incorporated in 1968, operates a chain of 44 discount department stores in the eastern United States. The stores are located primarily in smaller communities rather than in major metropolitan areas, where they serve as important retailing outlets. All the stores have garden and patio shops in season; 40 have automotive service centers; 22 have licensed pharmacies; 34 have home improvement centers.
Brandnames of Products and Services:

Nichols	*discount department stores*
Nichols Discount City	*discount department stores*

Nissan Motor Co., Ltd.

17-1 Ginza 6-chome, Chuo-Ku
Tokyo 104, Japan
(03) 543-5523

Chief Executive Officer: Takashi Ishihara
1984 Annual Sales Volume: 14,472M
1984 Shares Outstanding: 2,135,744,124
Shareholders: 64,248
Exchange: OTC
Symbol: NSAN
Corporate History: Nissan Motor Co., Ltd., was established in Japan in 1933. The company is the second-largest automobile manufacturer in Japan and one of the largest in the world. Automobile production includes passenger cars, busses, trucks, and related parts and accessories. The company has 24 assembly or manufacturing plants in 21 countries on six continents. Nissan also manufactures aerospace equipment, textile machinery, industrial machinery, and marine products.
Brandnames of Products and Services:

Atlas/Condor (Cabstar)	*trucks*
Bluebird	*passenger cars, vans*
Cedric	*passenger cars*
Datson	*passenger cars, trucks*
Laurel	*passenger cars*
March (Micra)	*passenger cars*
President	*passenger cars*
Pulsar	*vans*
Skyline	*passenger cars*
Sylvia	*passenger cars*

Noel Industries Inc.

350 Fifth Ave.
New York, N.Y. 10118
(212) 563-2700

Chief Executive Officer: Leon Ruchlamer
1984 Annual Sales Volume: 35M
1984 Shares Outstanding: 1,134,300
Shareholders: 503
Exchange: AM
Symbol: NOL
Corporate History: The company, incorporated in 1965, designs, markets and manufactures a complete line of quality fashion jeans for the entire family and girls' knit tops. These products are sold to department, chain and discount stores throughout the country. The company also manufactures and sells unbranded jeans

for the family, which are sold to chain and discount stores.

Brandnames of Products and Services:

Cheap Jeans	*jeans*
Green Apples	*children's jeans*
Joe Namath	*men's and boys jeans and slacks*
Live Ins	*junior, children's, men's jeans*
New Friends	*children's jeans*

Nordstrom Inc.

1501 Fifth Ave.
Seattle, WA 98101
(206) 628-2111

Chief Executive Officer:	John N. Nordstrom
1984 Annual Sales Volume:	983M
1984 Shares Outstanding:	18,595,602
Shareholders:	14,500
Exchange:	OTC
Symbol:	NOBE

Corporate History: The company, incorporated in 1946, as a successor to a retail shoe business started in 1901 is a specialty retailer selling a wide selection of apparel, shoes and accessories for women, men and children. It presently operates 30 large specialty stores and nine smaller specialty stores emphasizing younger fashions. The stores are located in Washington, Oregon, Alaska, California, Utah and Montana, Nordstrom also operates leased shoe departments in 10 department stores in Hawaii, one retail shoe store in Oregon and four clearance stores in Washington, Oregon and California.

Brandnames of Products and Services:

Nordstrom's	*apparel stores*
Place Two	*apparel stores*

Norlin Corporation

Westchester One
White Plains, N.Y. 10601
(914) 683-0001

Chief Executive Officer:	Norton Stevens
Exchange:	NY
Symbol:	NRL

Corporate History: The company incorporated in 1969 as ECL Industries Inc. and adopted its present title in 1970. Its predecessor originally had been incorporated in the Bahamas in 1937 as Ecuadorian Corp. It is one of the largest producer and distributor of musical instruments in the United States.

Brandnames of Products and Services:

Epiphone	*guitars and accessories*
Gibson	*guitars and accessories*
Lab Series	*amplifiers*
Lowrey	*pianos and organs*
Moog	*synthesizers*
Pearl	*drums*
Story & Clark	*pianos*

Norris Industries Inc.

One Golden Shore
Long Beach, Calif. 90802
(213) 435-6676

Chief Executive Officer:	H.J. Meany
Exchange:	NY
Symbol:	NRI

Corporate History: Norris Industries incorporated in 1940 as Norris Stamping & Manufacturing Co. Its name was changed in 1951 to Norris-Thermador Corp., and to the present title in 1966. The company makes building materials for both individual and industrial use.

Brandnames of Products and Services:

Artistic	*brass faucets*
Home Hardware	*cabinet hardware*
Price Pfister	*plumbing fixtures*
Thermador	*appliances*
Waste King	*appliances*
Weiser	*door locks*

North American Philips Corp.

100 E. 42nd St.
New York, NY 10017
(212) 697-3600

Chief Executive Officer:	Cees Bruynes
1984 Annual Sales Volume:	4,326M
1984 Shares Outstanding:	28,836,711
Shareholders:	7,965
Exchange:	NY
Symbol:	NPH

Corporate History: The company incorporated in 1959 as Consolidated Electronics Industries Corp. and adopted its present title in 1969. One of the 100 largest companies in the U.S., its principal products and services are as follows: electronic home entertainment products, lighting products (both consumer and industrial), personal care products, home appliances, brush products, furnishings, musical instruments, bus transportation, electrical and electro-mechanical products, electronic components and materials, medical systems, electronic instrumentation, cable television systems and business systems, government electronic products for submarine warfare, navigation signal processing equipment and military radio communications equipment. N.V. Philips, a Netherlands firm, supplies many innovative products to North American Philips and provides the company with access to a worldwide research and development capability.

Brandnames of Products and Services:

Anchor Brush	*cosmetic, health brushes*
Bach	*musical instruments*
Baker	*furniture*
Baker, Knapp & Tubbs	*furniture*
Buescher	*musical instruments*
Bundy	*musical instruments*
Cafe Duo	*coffee maker*
Carolina Coach	*bus coach*
Complexion Plus	*face scrubber*
Curly 2	*curling wand*
Dial-A-Brew	*drip filter coffee maker*
Genie	*remote control door opener*
Glaesel	*stringed instruments*
Gotcha	*hair dryer*
Ladybug	*razor*
Lady Schick	*shavers*
Ludwig	*percussion instruments*
Magnavision	*consumer electronics*
Magnavox	*electronic products*
Man Care Collection	*personal care products*
Nail Dazzler	*manicure appliance*
Networx	*computer accessories*
Norelco	*personal care products, appliances*
Palladian Collection	*furniture*
Philco	*home electronics*
Philips Lamps	*light bulbs*
Philips-MCA	*consumer electronics*
Philips PL	*fluorescent lights*
Satin Collection	*personal care products, appliances*
Schick	*shavers*
Selmer	*musical instruments*
Signet	*musical instruments*
Smokey	*smoke detector*
Statley Homes Collection	*furniture*
Sylvania	*home electronics*
Tenna-Rotor	*TV antenna rotator*
Travel Care Collection	*personal care products*
Westinghouse Lamps	*light bulbs*
Wire Tree Plus	*computer accessory*

Northwest Industries Inc.

6300 Sears Tower
Chicago, IL 60606
(312) 876-7000

Chief Executive Officer:	Ben W. Heineman
1984 Annual Sales Volume:	1,432M
1984 Shares Outstanding:	19,908,274
Shareholders:	13,800
Exchange:	NY
Symbol:	NWT

Corporate History: Northwest Industries, incorporated in 1967, is a management and holding company which, through its operating companies, manufactures and markets consumer soft goods, batteries, chemicals and electrical products. The markets of these operating companies are primarily domestic. The company's subsidiary Union Underwear is the largest manufacturer of men's and boys' underwear in the U.S. In 1984, Union Underwear had record sales and earnings as it sold nearly one-half billion garments and accounted for more than one-third of the total men's and boys' underwear market in the U.S.

Brandnames of Products and Services:

Acme	*boots*
B.V.D.	*men's underwear*
Dan Post	*boots*
Dingo	*boots*
Fruit of the Loom	*underwear and sports apparel*
Lucchese	*boots*
Polo	*Western boots*
Ralph Lauren	*Western boots*
Screen Star	*underwear*
Union Underwear	*underwear*

Norton Simon Inc.

277 Park Ave.
New York, N.Y. 10017
(212) 832-1000

Chief Executive Officer: D.J. Mahoney
Exchange: NY
Symbol: NSI
Corporate History: The company incorporated in 1968 as a consolidation of Canada Dry Corp., Hunt Foods & Industries and McCall Corp. In 1971, McCall Publishing house sold its cookbook club, trade book division and *Saturday Review* magazine. Its subsidiary, Avis, is the second largest firm in the American rental car business.
Brandnames of Products and Services:

Avis	*rental cars*
Barrelhead Root Beer	
Canada Dry	*beverages and mixes*
Geminesse	*cosmetics*
Halston	*cosmetics and fashions*
Hine	*cognac*
Hunt-Wesson	*food products*
Jean D'Albert	*cosmetics*
J. Hungerford Smith	*food toppings*
Khara	*perfume*
Manwich Sandwich Sauce	
Mary Quant	*cosmetics*
Max Factor	*cosmetics*
Maxi	*cosmetics*
McCall's	*sewing patterns*
Miners	*cosmetics*
Orange Spot	*soft drinks*
Orlane	*cosmetics*
Orville Redenbacker's	*popping corn*
Outdoor Girl	*cosmetics*
Parfumes Corday	
Pfeiffer	*salad dressings*
Prima Salsa	*spaghetti sauce*
Pure Magic	*cosmetics*
Puritan	*cooking oil*
Rebel Yell	*bourbon*
Reddi-Whip	*dessert topping*
"Show-Me"	*fashions*
Snack Pack	*puddings*
Stephen Burrows	*men's fragrance*
Sunlite	*sunflower oil*
Ultra-Lucent	*cosmetics*
Wesson	*cooking oil*

Noxell Corp.

11050 York Rd.
Hunt Valley, MD 21030
(301) 628-7300

Chief Executive Officer: G.L. Bunting, Jr.
1984 Annual Sales Volume: 350M
1984 Shares Outstanding: 1,945,008
Shareholders: 158
Exchange: OTC
Symbol: NOXLB
Corporate History: Noxell incorporated in 1917 as Noxzema Chemical Co. and adopted its present title in 1966. In 1984 cosmetics and toiletries accounted for 81% of consolidated net sales.
Brandnames of Products and Services:

Cover Girl	*cosmetics*
Lestoil	*household cleaner*
Noxzema	*skin and shaving products*
Rain-Tree	*skin-care products*
Wick Fowler's Famous 2-Alarm Chili	*food*

NVF Co.

6917 Collins Ave.
Miami Beach, FL 33141
(305) 866-7771

Chief Executive Officer: Victor Posner
1984 Annual Sales Volume: 1,276M
1984 Shares Outstanding: 55,765,722
Shareholders: 15,460
Exchange: NY
Symbol: NVF
Corporate History: The company incorporated in 1904 as the National Vulcanized Fibre Co. Its present title was adopted in 1965. NVF's principal business is the production and sale of basic steel mill products. NVF is also engaged in the manufacture and sale of vulcanized fibre and industrial laminated plastics and in the fabrication and sale of copper and brass products; in the manufacture and sale of welded stainless steel pipe and tubing and steel strapping; and in secondary lead refining. For the consumer, it manufactures a variety of tissue paper products; aluminum doors and windows; wood cabinets; housewares, containers and giftware made of plastic.

Brandnames of Products and Services:

Colortex	*paper products*
Evans	*wood cabinets*
Orchid	*paper products*
Riviera	*cabinets*

Oak Industries Inc.

16935 W. Bernardo Dr.
Rancho Bernardo, Calif. 92127
(714) 485-9300

Chief Executive Officer: E.A. Carter
Exchange: NY
Symbol: OAK
Corporate History: The company incorporated in 1960 under the name Oak Manufacturing Co. Its name was changed to Oak Electro/Netics Corp. in 1964 and to its present title in 1972. It is the world's leading provider of subscription television (STV) services.
Brandnames of Products and Services:

ON TV	*national subscription TV*

Oakwood Homes Corp.

2225 South Holden Road
P.O. Box 7386
Greensboro, NC 27417-0386
(919) 292-7061

Chief Executive Officer: Nicholas J. St. George
1984 Annual Sales Volume: 81M
1984 Shares Outstanding: 3,606,495
Shareholders: 1,387
Exchange: ASE
Symbol: OMH
Corporate History: The company, incorporated in 1971, designs and produces mobile homes. It operates three manufacturing plants in North Carolina. Homes manufactured by the company are sold at retail through 58 company-owned sales centers in North Carolina, Virginia, West Virginia, Tennessee, South Carolina, Florida and Georgia. The company retails homes purchased from other manufacturers through 10 company-owned sales centers in Texas and New Mexico and one in North Carolina. In addition the company is engaged in the development and management of mobile housing communities.
Brandnames of Products and Services:

Oakwood	*mobile homes*
Rich Craft	*mobile homes*
Richfield	*mobile homes*

Ogden Corp.

277 Park Ave.
New York, NY 10172
(212) 754-4000

Chief Executive Officer: Ralph E. Ablon
1984 Annual Sales Volume: 2,137M
1984 Shares Outstanding: 19,036,548
Shareholders: 13,600
Exchange: NY
Symbol: OG
Corporate History: Ogden Corp., incorporated in 1939, is a diversified company engaged in services, marine and modular construction, and products. Services include building and plant maintenance; aviation fueling and ground handling services; engineering, design, drafting and other technical services; contract food services; racetracks; food and housekeeping services to offshore drilling rigs; logistical support services to remote industrial campsites; security; and the design, construction, ownership, maintenance, and management of properties including refuse-fueled power plants. Marine and modular construction includes the design, construction and repair of vessels, offshore drilling structures and modular units. Products include the recovery, preparation and brokerage of ferrous materials for recycling; aluminum recycling; production of special-purpose railroad cars; fabrication of custom metal components; design and production of heat transfer equipment; production of machine tools; processing and marketing of branded specialty food products and, to a lesser extent, the production of private label fruits and vegetables. In 1982, Ogden acquired the Allied Maintenance Corp., which provides mechanical maintenance and housekeeping services for a variety of facilities, and the Atlantic Design Co., Inc., which provides technical services to industry.
Brandnames of Products and Services:

Fairmount Park	*race track, Collinsville, Ill.*
Hain	*health foods*
Hollywood	*health foods*
Las Palmas	*Mexican foods*
Montini	*tomato products*
Progresso	*Italian foods*
Ramirez & Feraud	*Mexican foods*
Waterford Park	*race track, Chester, W. Va.*
Wheeling Downs	*Race track, Wheeling, W. Va.*

Ohio Art Co.

P.O. Box 111
Bryan, OH 43506
(419) 636-3141

Chief Executive Officer: William C. Killgallon
1984 Annual Sales Volume: 34M
1984 Shares Outstanding: 636,523
Shareholders: 749
Exchange: AM
Symbol: OAR
Corporate History: The company, incorporated in 1930, makes children's toys and games.
Brandnames of Products and Services:

Emenee	*disco dance machine and toy musical instruments*
"Etch-A-Sketch"	*toy*
Lil'Sport	*preschool activity toys*
Ohio Art	*toys*

Olin Corp.

120 Long Ridge Rd.
Stamford, CT 06904
(203) 356-2000

Chief Executive Officer: John M. Henske
1984 Annual Sales Volume: 2,065M
1984 Shares Outstanding: 23,300,000
Shareholders: 24,400
Exchange: NY
Symbol: OLN
Corporate History: The company incorporated in 1892 as the Mathieson Alkali Works. Its name was changed to Mathieson Chemical Corp. in 1948 and to Olin Corp. in 1969. It is a diversified manufacturer of chemicals , paper and cellophane and metals for industrial use. In addition it supplies firearms, hunting equipment and skis to the consumer market.
Brandnames of Products and Services:

Double X	*ammunition*
Olin	*skis*
Silvertip	*ammunition*
Super-Max-22	*ammunition*
Weaver	*scopes, ammunition, traps*
Winchester	*firearms*

Olympia Brewing Co.

P.O. Box 947
Olympia, Wash. 98507
(206) 754-5000

Chief Executive Officer: L.F. Schmidt
Exchange: OTC
Symbol: OLYB
Corporate History: The company, incorporated in 1896, produces beer. It is the seventh largest producer of malt beverages in the nation.
Brandnames of Products and Services:

ABC Truck Rental	
Buckhorn	*beer*
Hamm's	*beer*
Lone Star	*beer*
Olympia	*beer*
Olympia Gold	*beer*

Oneida Ltd.

Oneida, NY 13421
(315) 361-3000

Chief Executive Officer: J.L. Marcellus, Jr.
1984 Annual Sales Volume: 275M
1984 Shares Outstanding: 6,522,000
Shareholders: 5,732
Exchange: NY
Symbol: OCZ
Corporate History: Oneida incorporated in 1880 as Oneida Community Ltd. and adopted its present title in 1935. The company is the nation's largest producer of stainless steel flatware. It also produces plated and sterling silver flatware and holloware products in a variety of metals. Oneida products are distributed through retail outlets, foodservice operations, and special sales customers who use the products as premiums, incentives, and business gifts. Its subsidiary companies include Buffalo China, the nation's largest producer of commercial chinaware and Camden Wire, a supplier of products for the transportation, electronics, energy, construction, and appliance industries.
Brandnames of Products and Services:

Buffalo	*china*
Community	*tableware*
Oneida	*tableware*

Orange-Co. Inc.

1301 Alternate Highway 27 South
Lake Hamilton, FL 33851
(813) 439-1585

Chief Executive Officer: S. Robert Davis
1984 Annual Sales Volume: 61M
1984 Shares Outstanding: 3,507,389
Shareholders: 2,100
Exchange: NY
Symbol: OJ
Corporate History: Orange-Co. last incorporated in 1969 as National Fast Food Corp., successor to a company founded and incorporated in 1968 as S. Robert Davis National Leasing Co. Its name was changed to N.F.F. Corp. in 1971 and to its present title in 1973. The firm is Florida's largest single packer of fresh citrus fruits. It also makes fresh and frozen citrus fruit juices. The company owns about 7,900 acres of land in Florida. It raises nine varieties of oranges, four varieties of grapefruit, three varieties of tangerines, and three varieties of tangelos (a hybrid grapefruit-tangerine).
Brandnames of Products and Services:

Natural Sun — *frozen orange juice*

Orion Pictures Corp.

711 Fifth Avenue
New York, NY 10022
(212) 758-5100

Chief Executive Officer: Eric Pleskow
1984 Annual Sales Volume: 223M
1984 Shares Outstanding: 9,432,591
Shareholders: 4,954
Exchange: NY
Symbol: OPC
Corporate History: The company, originally incorporated in 1952, changed its name from Filmways Inc. to Orion Pictures in 1982. The company is primarily engaged in the financing, production and distribution of motion pictures for the theatrical market, including distribution of motion pictures financed and produced by others. In addition, the company distributes motion pictures to the free television, cable and pay television markets and to the video cassette and video disc markets. It also finances, produces and distributes television programming.
Brandnames of Products and Services:

Cagney & Lacey — *television series*

Orion — *motion pictures, TV programs*

Oshman's Sporting Goods Inc.

2302 Maxwell Lane
Houston, TX 77023
(713) 928-3171

Chief Executive Officer: A.N. Lubetkin
1984 Annual Sales Volume: 304M
1984 Shares Outstanding: 6,406,000
Shareholders: 480
Exchange: OTC
Symbol: OSHM
Corporate History: The company incorporated in 1946 as Oshman Outdoor Store. It operates sporting goods stores.
Brandnames of Products and Services:

Abercrombie & Fitch — *sporting goods stores*

Oshman's — *sporting goods stores*

Outboard Marine Corp.

100 Sea Horse Dr.
Waukegan, IL 60085
(312) 689-6200

Chief Executive Officer: C.D. Strang
1984 Annual Sales Volume: 922M
1984 Shares Outstanding: 16,830,285
Shareholders: 8,234
Exchange: NY
Symbol: OM
Corporate History: The company incorporated in 1936 as Outboard Marine & Manufacturing Co., which originated in 1929 and included Johnson Motor Co., formed in 1921. In 1956 its name was changed to its present title. Today Outboard Marine Corporation has grown to a multi-national company. It is the world's largest producer of outboard motors—with manufacturing facilities in six countries and distribution in nearly every nation of the free world. OMC's Drive Systems unit markets OMC stern drives and OMC Sea Drive marine power systems. OMC Parts and Accessories manufactures and distributes parts and accessories through more than 5,000 retail marine dealers in the U.S. and through both company-owned and independent distributors throughout the world. In the non-marine area, OMC produces two lines of power mowers, Lawn-Boy and Ryan. It makes Cushman industrial vehi-

cles and Cushman and Ryan turf care equipment for the maintenance of large tracts of grass such as golf courses and parks.

Brandnames of Products and Services:

Cushman	*golf carts*
Evinrude	*outboard motors*
Johnson	*outboard motors*
Lawn-Boy	*mowers*
Ryan	*mowers*

Outlet Co.

176 Weybosset St.
Providence, R.I. 02902
(401) 331-8700

Chief Executive Officer: B.G. Sandlun
Exchange: NY
Symbol: OTU

Corporate History: Outlet incorporated in 1925 to acquire the department store business of J. Samuels & Brother Inc., which had been established in 1894. The company engaged in broadcasting and retailing operations. As of 1980 it operated four TV stations and 166 department and specialty stores, primarily in the East. In fiscal 1980 broadcasting accounted for 14.9% of sales and retailing operations 85.1%. The firm has decided to reduce its presence in the retail industry and concentrate on expanding in communications.

Brandnames of Products and Services:

Baker	*apparel stores*
Cherry & Webb	*apparel stores*
Denby's	*junior department stores*
Edward Malley	*department stores*
Flair	*apparel stores*
Hughes & Hatcher	*men's specialty stores*
Jacob Reed & Sons	*men's specialty stores*
KIAA-FM	*radio station, Los Angeles, Calif.*
KOVR-TV	*Stockton/Sacramento, Calif.*
KSAT-TV	*San Antonio, Tex.*
Outlet	*men's department stores*
Philipsborn	*apparel stores*
Small's	*men's apparel stores*
Touraine	*apparel store*
Warwick Shoe Company	
WCMH-TV	*Columbus, Ohio*
WDBO-TV and AM/FM	*radio station, Orlando, Fla.*
WIOQ-FM	*radio station, Philadelphia, Pa.*
WQRS-FM	*radio station, Detroit, Mich.*
WRLM-FM	*radio station, Taunton, Mass.*
WTOP-AM	*radio station, Washington D.C.*

Owens-Illinois, Inc.

One SeaGate
Toledo, OH 43666
(419) 247-5000

Chief Executive Officer: Robert J. Lanigan
1984 Annual Sales Volume: 3,500M
1984 Shares Outstanding: 28,705,195
Shareholders: 23,000
Exchange: NY
Symbol: OI

Corporate History: Owens-Illinois incorporated in 1907 as the Owens Bottle Machine Co. and adopted its present title in 1965. The company is one of the world's leading manufacturers of packaging products, including glass and plastic containers.

Brandnames of Products and Services:

L.E. Smith Glass	*handmade glass products*
Libbey	*stemware and decorative glassware*

Oxford Industries Inc.

222 Piedmont Ave. N.E.
Atlanta, GA 30308
(404) 659-2424

Chief Executive Officer: J.Hicks Lanier
1984 Annual Sales Volume: 577M
1984 Shares Outstanding: 11,075,948
Shareholders: 1,881
Exchange: NY
Symbol: OXM

Corporate History: The company incorporated in 1960 as Oxford Mfg. Co. and adopted its present title in 1967. It makes popular-priced apparel. In fiscal 1984 men's wear accounted for 62% of sales and women's wear 38%. J.C. Penney Co. and Sears Roebuck & Co. provided 21% and 11% of the sales respectively. At present, Oxford is broadening and strengthening its production base in the United States, Far East, and Latin America.

Brandnames of Products and Services:

Cobbies by Cos Cob	*women's apparel*
Cos Cob	*women's apparel*
Gil Truedsson	*men's and women's apparel*
Holbrook	*men's apparel*
"JBJ"	*men's apparel*
Jeffrey Banks	*men's and women's apparel*
Jhane Barnes	*men's and women's apparel*
John Henry	*boy's shirts*
Lanier	*men's apparel*
Lee Wright	*men's and women's apparel*
Manchester	*men's and boys' shirts*
McGregor	*men's apparel*
Merona Sport	*men's, women's and children's sportswear*
Oleg Cassini	*men's apparel*
OSA	*men's apparel*
Oscar de la Renta	*men's apparel*
Polo by Ralph Lauren	*boys' apparel*
Ralph Lauren	*for girls*
Ramar	*boys' apparel*
Robert Stock	*men's apparel*

Pabst Brewing Co.

917 W. Juneau Ave.
Milwaukee, Wis. 53201
(414) 347-7300

Chief Executive Officer: F.C. DeGuire
Exchange: OTC
Symbol: PABT

Corporate History: The company was founded in 1844 by Jacob Best and was originally incorporated as Phillip Best Brewing Co. In 1889 the name was changed to Pabst Brewing Co. Pabst is the fourth largest brewer in the United States.

Brandnames of Products and Services:

Andeker	*spirits*
Big Cat	*malt liquor*
Blitz Weinhard	*spirits*
Burgermeister	*beer*
Eastside	*beer*
Henry Weinhard Private Reserve	*beer*
Olde English 800	*malt liquor*
Pabst Blue Ribbon	*beer*
Pabst Extra Light East Side	
Red White & Blue Beer	
Select	*spirits*

Pacific Gamble Robinson Co.

10829 N.E. 68th St.
Kirkland, WA 98033
(206) 828-6200

Chief Executive Officer: Douglas S. Gamble
1984 Annual Sales Volume: 842M
1984 Shares Outstanding: 1,985,615
Shareholders: 5,960
Exchange: OTC
Symbol: PGAM

Corporate History: The company incorporated in 1931 as the successor to a wholesale fruit and vegetable business formed in 1890. Today it is divided into wholesale and retail divisions. The wholesale division distributes fresh fruit and vegetables, refrigerated and frozen foods, and groceries; it operates 64 branch warehouses in 17 midwest and northwestern states along with North Carolina and the Canadian provinces of British Columbia and Ontario. The retail division operates 88 retail food stores in Washington and Oregon.

Brandnames of Products and Services:

Family Market	*supermarkets*
Prairie Market	*supermarkets*
Snoboy	*food products*
Standby	*canned foods*
Tradewell	*supermarkets*

Palm Beach Inc.

400 Pike St.
Cincinnati, OH 45202
(513) 241-4260

Chief Executive Officer: E.L. Ward
1984 Annual Sales Volume: 459M
1984 Shares Outstanding: 3,720,765
Shareholders: 4,800
Exchange: NY
Symbol: PMB

Corporate History: Incorporated in 1931, the company initially manufactured a single item—men's suits. In the 1960s it began to market regular weight as well as lightweight suits, sportcoats, and slacks. Between 1968 and 1979 major acquisitions included Austin-Hill Ltd., Calvin Clothing Co., Craig Craely, Evan-Picone, Seinsheimer, Eagle Shirtmakers, Gant, and Haspel. Today the company is evenly balanced between men's and women's wear in volume and profits. Palm Beach's formal wear division is located in Chicago, and carries on a wholesale-retail business throughout the country.

Brandnames of Products and Services:

Adler	*pants*
Austin Hill	*women's apparel*
Calvin	*clothes*
Classic Woman	*women's apparel*
Country Set	*women's apparel*
Craig Craely	*dresses*
Dione	*women's apparel*
Dudley Casuals	*women's apparel*
Eagle Shirts	*men's apparel*
Epic	*missy dresses*
Evan Picone	*women's apparel, men's apparel, hosiery*
Fitzgerald	*men's apparel*
Gant	*shirts, pants, jackets*
Haspel	*men's and women's suits*
Hunter Haig	*men's apparel*
John Weitz	*men's apparel*
Joseph Picone	*women's apparel*
Miss Austin	*women's apparel*
Palm Beach	*suits*
Pierre Cardin	*jeans, shirts, formal apparel*
Polo for Boys by Ralph Lauren	*designer boys' apparel*
Royal Palm Beach	*men's apparel*
Seinsheimer	*men's apparel*
Solo	*women's apparel*
Sports Ralley	*sportswear*
Turnbury	*men's apparel and ladies apparel*
TWCC	*(Today's Woman Clothing Co.) women's clothing*
Varsity Town	*men's apparel*

Pan Am Corp.

Pan Am Bldg.
200 Park Ave.
New York, N.Y. 10166
(212) 880-1234

Chief Executive Officer:	C. Edward Acker
1984 Annual Sales Volume:	3,685M
1984 Shares Outstanding:	103,319,405
Shareholders:	123,500
Exchange:	NY
Symbol:	PN

Corporate History: Pan Am was incorporated in 1927. Under the direction of Juan Trippe, it grew from a small mail carrier to the nation's first international airline. Today it flies to 89 cities in 47 countries. For years it flew principally foreign routes. In 1979 it merged with National Airlines to give the company domestic coverage as well. In 1984, Pan Am Corp. became the publicly held parent of Pan American World Airways Inc., the airline, and of Pan Am World Services, a contract services company.

Brandnames of Products and Services:

Pan American Airlines

Pantry Pride, Inc.

6500 North Andrews Ave.
Fort Lauderdale, FL 33309
(305) 771-8300

Chief Executive Officer:	Grant C. Gentry
1984 Annual Sales Volume:	770M
1984 Shares Outstanding:	37,781,761
Shareholders:	19,700
Exchange:	NY
Symbol:	PPR

Corporate History: Pantry Pride, Inc., incorporated in 1935, operates food stores in the southeastern U.S. In 1984 the company operated a chain of 94 Pantry Pride supermarkets and a chain of six Sun Food Stores. In that year, the company acquired Devon Stores, Inc. a national chain of 71 specialty retail stores in 22 states selling merchandise primarily to military personnel.

Brandnames of Products and Services:

Devon	*specialty retailing*
Pantry Pride	*supermarkets*
Sun Foods	*supermarkets*

Papercraft Corp.

Papercraft Park
Pittsburgh, PA 15238
(412) 362-8000

Chief Executive Officer:	Marshall P. Katz
1984 Annual Sales Volume:	178M
1984 Shares Outstanding:	11,624,112
Shareholders:	7,500
Exchange:	NY
Symbol:	PCT

Corporate History: The company, incorporated in 1945, makes gift wrapping papers, household cleaning products, shoe and foot care accessories, and tapes and adhesive. In 1981 it acquired American Technical Industries, a major producer of artificial Christmas trees and subcomponents for computers, sorters, and parts for the U.S. Postal Service.

Brandnames of Products and Services:

American	*artificial Christmas trees and wreaths, ornaments*
Cabbage Patch Kids	*giftwrap products*
Calico Goose	*kitchen textiles*
Care Bears	*kitchen textiles*
Esquire	*shoe care products*
Gourmet Gallery	*kitchen textiles*
Greenhouse	*kitchen textiles*
He-Man and the Masters of the Universe	*giftwrap products*
Kiss the Cook	*kitchen textiles*
Knomark	*fabric softener*
Le Page's	*adhesives*
Modern Ortho	*foot care products*
Mountain King	*artificial Christmas trees*
Santa Claus, The Movie	*giftwrap products*
Sunshine Fresh	*fabric softener*
Tintex	*dyes*
Ty-D-Bol	*toilet bowl cleaner*

Parker Pen Co.

One Parker Place
Janesville, WI 53545
(608) 755-7000

Chief Executive Officer: Mitchell S. Fromstein
1984 Annual Sales Volume: 709M
1984 Shares Outstanding: 17,107,908
Shareholders: 4,600
Exchange: NY
Symbol: PKR
Corporate History: The company, incorporated in 1892, is a leading manufacturer of writing instruments. Through Manpower, Inc. it also operates the world's largest temporary help employment agency.

Brandnames of Products and Services:

Eversharp	*writing instruments*
Fox Point	*sportswear*
Manpower	*temporary job placement*
Parker	*writing instruments*
Super Quink	*ink*

Pat Fashions Industries Inc.

1370 Broadway
New York, N.Y. 10018
(212) 695-3510

Chief Executive Officer: S. Cooper
Exchange: AM
Symbol: PI
Corporate History: The company, incorporated in 1966, is an apparel manufacturer and importer.

Brandnames of Products and Services:

Pat Fashions	*women's apparel*

Payless Cashways Inc.

2301 Main
P.O. Box 466
Kansas City, MO 64141-0466
(816) 234-6000

Chief Executive Officer: David Stanley
1984 Annual Sales Volume: 1,176M
1984 Shares Outstanding: 32,333,004
Shareholders: 4,027
Exchange: NY
Symbol: PCI
Corporate History: The company, incorporated in 1968, operates a chain of building materials stores serving the home improvement and company needs of the serious stores in and tradesman. The company operates 157 retail facilities in 17 states. In 1984 the company acquired Prime Home Improvement Centers Inc., Hugh M Wood Brothers Lumber Co., and Somerville Lumber and Supply Co.

Brandnames of Products and Services:

Furrow	*building materials stores*
Hugh M Woods	*building materials stores*
Lumberjack	*building materials stores*
Payless Cashways	*building materials stores*
Somerville Lumber	*building materials stores*

Pay Less Drug Stores Northwest Inc.

9275 S.W. Peyton Lane
Wilsonville, Ore. 97070
(503) 682-4100

Chief Executive Officer: E.B. Hart
Exchange: NY
Symbol: PAY

Corporate History: The company, incorporated in 1967, operates drugstores. Traditionally it has expanded by acquiring marginally profitable chains and making them a success. In 1980 it significantly expanded its operations by acquiring Pay Less Drug Stores, a barely profitable chain not related to it. Prior to its acquisition Pay Less. Drug Stores Northwest operated 90 drugstores. Today it operates 150.

Brandnames of Products and Services:

House of Value	*drugstores*
Payless	*personal health and beauty care products*
Pay Less Drug	*drugstores*
Tested	*personal health and beauty care products*
Value Giant	*drugstores*

Pay 'n Save Corp.

1511 Sixth Ave.
Seattle, Wash. 98101
(206) 447-6019

Chief Executive Officer: M. Lamont Bean
Exchange: OTC
Symbol: PAYN

Corporate History: Pay 'n Save incorporated in 1905 as Ernst Hardware Co. and adopted its present name in 1960 upon merger with Pay 'n Save Drugs Inc. It operates drugstores and sporting goods stores in the Western United States.

Brandnames of Products and Services:

Bi-Mart	*drugstores*
Ernst-Malmo	*do-it-yourself home centers*
Lamonts	*department stores*
Pay 'n Save	*drugstores*
Sportwest	*sporting goods and apparel stores*
Von Tobel's	*do-it-yourself home centers*
Yard Birds	*home improvement store*

Peavey Co.

730 2nd Ave.
Minneapolis, Minn. 55402
(612) 370-7500

Chief Executive Officer: G.K. Gosko
Exchange: NY
Symbol: PV

Corporate History: The company was founded in 1874 and incorporated in 1922. It manufactures flour-based food products and operates general merchandise, building supply and specialty stores.

Brandnames of Products and Services:

Brownberry Ovens	*bread, stuffing mixes and croutons*
Fish	*building supply center*
High Altitude Hungarian	*baking mixes*
Home Brands	*condiments*
King Midas	*baking mixes*
Northwest Fabrics	*fabric stores*
Occident	*baking mixes*
Peavey Marts	*general merchandise stores*
Peavey/ Thunderbird	*building supply center*
S & S	*general merchandise stores*
Steamex	*carpet cleaning products*
Wheelers	*general merchandise stores*

J.C. Penney Co., Inc.

1301 Avenue of the Americas
New York, NY 10019
(212) 957-4321

Chief Executive Officer: William R. Howell
1984 Annual Sales Volume: 13,451M
1984 Shares Outstanding: 74,384,882
Shareholders: 70,000
Exchange: NY
Symbol: JCP

Corporate History: The company can trace its history back to 1902 when J.C. Penney established a drygoods store in Kemmerer, Wyo. Over the years the company grew phenomenally. In 1914 it had 48 retail stores and 1941, 1,600. Today it has more than 2,000 stores throughout the United States and in Puerto Rico and Belgium as well. During these years the company expanded from selling clothes to a full range of personal and household items. It also diversified into insurance, banking and drugstores. In 1984, its catalog operations accounted for $1.9 billion of its total sales.

Brandnames of Products and Services:

J.C. Penney	*department stores and mail order merchandise*
Thrift Drugstores	

Penn Traffic Co.

319-347 Washington St.
Johnstown, PA 15901
(814) 536-4411

Chief Executive Officer: Guido Malacarme
1984 Annual Sales Volume: 560M
1984 Shares Outstanding: 2,063,524
Shareholders: 2,600
Exchange: AM
Symbol: PNF

Corporate History: Incorporated in 1903, the Penn Traffic Co. was the successor to a retail business which can be traced to 1854. From 1854 until 1962, the company operated a single department store in Johnstown, Pennsylvania. In 1962, the company merged with S.V. Corp. (now known as Riverside Markets). In 1968, the company merged with the Johnstown Sanitary Dairy Company. In 1979, the Company merged with Quality Markets, Inc. In 1982, the Company sold substantially all of the inventory, fixed assets and store facility leases of its department store division. Today the company principally operates supermarkets and a dairy business. There are 33 Riverside and eight Quality supermarkets in Pennsylvania and 15 Quality supermarkets in New York.

Brandnames of Products and Services:

Perky	*dairy food products*
Quality	*supermarkets*
Riverside	*supermarkets*
Sani-Dairy	*food products*

Pennwalt Corp.

Three Parkway
Philadelphia, Pa. 19102
(215) 587-7000

Chief Executive Officer: Edwin E. Tuttle
1984 Annual Sales Volume: 1,047M
1984 Shares Outstanding: 12,810,075
Shareholders: 11,795
Exchange: NY
Symbol: PSM

Corporate History: The company, incorporated in 1850 as Pennsylvania Salt Mfg. Co., adopted its present title in 1969. It makes several thousand chemical, health and specialized equipment products which are distributed world-wide.

Brandnames of Products and Services:

Allerest	*decongestant*
Caldecort	*dermatitis ointment*
Caldesene	*for treatment of diaper rash*
Cold Factor 12	*decongestant*
Cruex	*medicated body powder*
Desenex	*foot care products*
Fresh	*deodorant*
Sinarest	*decongestant*
Ting	*foot care products*

Pennzoil Co.

Pennzoil Place
Houston, Texas 77001
(713) 236-7878

Chief Executive Officer: J.H. Liedtke
Exchange: NY
Symbol: PZL

Corporate History: Pennzoil, incorporated in 1889, explores for, produces and processes, refines and markets oil and gas. Drilling is conducted in most of the major oil and gas producing areas in the United States, Canada, Netherlands, North Sea, Brazil, Australia and People's Republic of China. Its motor oils and lubricants are marketed in all 50 states as well as abroad. Through its Duval subsidiary, the company mines copper sulfur and potash. Substantially all its mining operations are in the United States.

Brandnames of Products and Services:

Pennzoil	*motor oil*
Wolf's Head	*auto lubricant*

Penobscot Shoe Co.

North Main St.
Old Town, ME 04468
(207) 827-4431

Chief Executive Officer: Irving Kagan
1984 Annual Sales Volume: 13M
1984 Shares Outstanding: 691,704
Shareholders: 426
Exchange: AM
Symbol: PSO

Corporate History: The company incorporated in 1935 as Philco Shoe Corp. and adopted its present name in 1943. It makes casual and leisure time footwear. Products are sold under its own brandname as well as private labels to approximately 1,300 retailers at 3,100 locations throughout the United States.

Brandnames of Products and Services:

Old Maine Trotters	*shoes*

Peoples Drug Stores Inc.

6315 Bren Mar Drive
Alexandria, Va. 22312
(703) 750-6100

Chief Executive Officer: S.W. Fantle
Exchange: NY
Symbol: PDG
Corporate History: The company, incorporated in 1928, operated a chain of 480 stores in 13 states. In 1979 it acquired Haag Drug Co. Inc. and B.H. Krueger, Inc. The latter was a manufacturer of private label cosmetic and beauty aids.
Brandnames of Products and Services:

Haag	*drugstores*
Health Mart	*drugstores*
Lane	*drugstores*
Lee	*drugstores*
Peoples	*drugstores*
Reed	*drugstores*

Pep Boys - Manny, Moe & Jack

3111 West Allegheny Ave.
Philadelphia, PA 19132
(215) 229-9000

Chief Executive Officer: Benjamin Strauss
1984 Annual Sales Volume: 352M
1984 Shares Outstanding: 7,843,722
Shareholders: 1,329
Exchange: NY
Symbol: PBY
Corporate History: Pep Boys incorporated in 1925 as Pep Auto Supply Co. and in 1928 adopted its present title. It operates a chain of retail stores which sells automotive services and products and household products. Its 135 stores are located in: Arizona, 13; California, 71; Delaware, 4; District of Columbia, 2; Maryland, 7; Nevada, 4; New Jersey, 9; Pennsylvania, 23; Virginia, 2.
Brandnames of Products and Services:

Cadet	*car batteries*
Check	*shock and brake fluid*
Cornell	*tires*
Dekent	*lubricants*
Du Bois	*automotive spray Enamels*
Kent	*transmission fluid*
Lloyd	*automotive products*
Mystee-Moly	*automotive additive*
Pep Boys	*automotive product stores*
Varsity	*spray automotive paints*

PepsiCo Inc.

Purchase, NY 10577
(914) 253-2000

Chief Executive Officer: Donald M. Kendall
1984 Annual Sales Volume: 7,699M
1984 Shares Outstanding: 94,041,911
Shareholders: 66,000
Exchange: NY
Symbol: PEP
Corporate History: The company, incorporated in 1919 as Loft Inc., changed its name to Pepsi-Cola Co. in 1941 and adopted its present title in 1965 with the merger of Frito-Lay, Inc. It is a leading distributor and producer of beverage concentrates and soft drinks. Pepsi Cola is the second largest selling soft drink in the United States. (Coca-Cola is first.) The company's other major businesses are food products, food service (fastfood restaurants), and sporting goods. PepsiCo operates worldwide.
Brandnames of Products and Services:

Aspen	*apple drink*
Baken-ets	*snacks*
Biddles Rice Chips	*snack food*
Chee-Tos	*cheese-flavored snacks*
Diet Pepsi	*beverage*
Diet Pepsi Free	*soft drink*
Diet Slice	*soft drink*
Doritos	*convenience and snack foods*
Fantastix	*snacks*
Frito-Lay	*convenience and snack foods*
Fritos	*dip mixes*
Funyuns	*onion-flavored snacks*
Grandma's	*cookies*
La Petite Boulangerie	*bakeries*
Lay's	*potato chips*
Lee Way Motor Freight	
Mirinda	*soft drink*
Mountain Dew	*beverage*
Munchos	*snack foods*

North American Van Lines	
O'Grady's	*potato chips*
On-Tap	*root beer*
Patio	*beverage*
Pepsi Cola	*beverage*
Pepsi Free	*soft drink*
Pepsi Light	*soft drink*
Pizza Hut	*restaurants*
Rold Gold	*pretzels*
Ruffles	*potato chips*
Sabritos	*potato chips*
Slice	*soft drink*
Taco Bell	*restaurants*
Teem	*beverage*
Tiffles	*corn chips*
Tostitos	*tortilla chips*
Wilson	*sporting goods*

Petrie Stores Corp.

70 Enterprise Ave.
Secaucus, NJ 07094
(201) 866-3600

Chief Executive Officer: Milton Petrie
1984 Annual Sales Volume: 955M
1984 Shares Outstanding: 21,266,752
Shareholders: 2,198
Exchange: NY
Symbol: PST

Corporate History: The company was founded in 1927 and incorporated in 1932. In 1984, it acquired the Miller-Wohl Co., a chain of some 400 women's specialty stores. All together, it operates 1,362 women's specialty stores throughout the United States.

Brandnames of Products and Services:

David's	*apparel stores*
Diana Marco	*women's apparel stores*
Franklins	*women's apparel stores*
G & G Shops	*apparel stores*
Hartfields	*women's apparel stores*
Jean Nicole	*women's apparel stores*
Marianne	*women's apparel stores*
Petrie Stores	*women's apparel stores*
Rave	*women's apparel stores*
Stuarts	*women's apparel stores*
Three Sisters	*women's apparel stores*
Whitney	*women's apparel stores*
Winkelman's	*women's apparel stores*

Pfizer Inc.

235 E. 42nd St.
New York, N.Y. 10017
(212) 573-2323

Chief Executive Officer: E.T. Pratt, Jr.
1984 Annual Sales Volume: 3,855M
1984 Shares Outstanding: 167,300,000
Shareholders: 59,000
Exchange: NY
Symbol: PFE

Corporate History: The company was founded in 1849 and incorporated in 1924 as Chas. Pfizer & Co., a chemical manufacturer. During the 1920s it entered the drug market primarily as a producer of vitamins and by the end of World War II also was producing half of the world's penicillin. The company today is a multinational producer and distributor of drugs and health care, chemical agricultural materials, science, and consumer products. Pfizer seriously entered the drug market in the 1950s by aggressively promoting its products to doctors at a time when such promotion was unconventional. Today it holds a leading position in the market for antibiotics. In the 1980s Pfizer hopes to become the top company in the drug industry. The company gets approximately 44% of its sales from foreign markets.

Brandnames of Products and Services:

Air Spun	*cosmetics*
Barbasol	*shaving products*
Ben Gay	*personal care products*
Coty	*fragrances and cosmetics*
Desitin	*ointment*
Equasion	*cosmetics*
Hai-Karate	*men's fragrances*
Leeming/Pacquin	*skin care products*
Pacquin	*hand cream*
Rheaban	*personal care products*
Roman Brio	*men's fragrances*
Visine	*eye drops*

Philip Morris Inc.

120 Park Ave.
New York, NY 10017
(212) 880-5000

Chief Executive Officer: Hamish Maxwell
1984 Annual Sales Volume: 10,137M
1984 Shares Outstanding: 120,923,245
Shareholders: 30,408

Exchange: NY
Symbol: MO
Corporate History: Philip Morris, incorporated in 1919, makes cigarettes and beer. With R.J. Reynolds it accounts for 64% of all cigarette sales in the U.S. Philip Morris has 31% of the total market; its Marlboro brand is the world's largest-selling cigarette. Traditionally, the company has used the tremendous profits from its cigarette business to expand into other areas, particularly beer and soft drinks. When the company took over Miller brewing in 1970, Miller was seventh among American brewers; now it is second. Philip Morris also engages in land development in Southern California. An industrial division manufactures and sells tissue products, specialty papers, packaging materials, and specialized labels.
Brandnames of Products and Services:

Aliso Viejo	*real estate*
Benson & Hedges	*cigarettes*
Cambridge	*cigarettes*
Highlands Ranch	*real estate*
Like	*beverage*
Lite	*beer*
Lowenbrau	*beer*
Marlboro	*cigarettes*
Meister Brau	*beer*
Merit	*cigarettes*
Miller High Life	*beer*
Milwaukee's Best	*beer*
Mission Viejo	*real estate*
Parliament	*cigarettes*
Philip Morris	*cigarettes*
Players	*cigarettes*
Saratoga	*cigarettes*
Seven Up	*beverages*
Virginia Slims	*cigarettes*

Philips Industries Inc.

4801 Springfield St.
Dayton, OH 45401
(513) 253-7171

Chief Executive Officer: J. Philips
1984 Annual Sales Volume: 463M
1984 Shares Outstanding: 12,861,000
Shareholders: 4774
Exchange: NY
Symbol: PHL
Corporate History: The company, incorporated in 1957 as Jalousies of Ohio Co., adopted its present title in 1961. It manufactures components for all segments of the building industry, residential (both on-site and in-factory), industrial and commercial as well as some products for markets outside the building industry such as agricultural irrigation, chemical processing, utility trailers and electronic equipment.
Brandnames of Products and Services:

Conaire	*humidifiers*
Lasco	*showers and tubs*
Lau & Conaire	*blowers and fans*
Malta	*wood windows and patio doors*

Phillips Petroleum Co.

Phillips Building
Bartlesville, OK 74004
(918) 661-6600

Chief Executive Officer: C.J. Silas
1984 Annual Sales Volume: 15,537M
1984 Shares Outstanding: 154,082,000
Shareholders: 113,400
Exchange: NY
Symbol: P
Corporate History: Phillips, incorporated in 1917, is the 11th largest oil company in the United States. It also is a major chemical manufacturer, largely of olefins, cyclics, petrochemicals, plastics and carbon black. Phillips 34 state market area is primarily in the Midwest where it has more than 10,500 Phillips 66 gas stations. Despite the number of stations, the company has only 4% of the gasoline market. Phillips is regarded as having an extremely advantageous position in the industry. It drilled the first successful oil wells in the North Sea. And although slightly less than half its production comes from foreign sources, the majority of this is from areas unaffected by political turmoil.
Brandnames of Products and Services:

Phillips	*automotive products and fuel*
Trop-Artic	*motor oil*

Phillips-Van Heusen Corp.

1290 Avenue of the Americas
New York, NY 10104
(212) 541-5200

Chief Executive Officer: Lawrence S. Phillips
1984 Annual Sales Volume: 506M
1984 Shares Outstanding: 6,082,711
Shareholders: 2,838

Exchange: NY
Symbol: PVH
Corporate History: The company incorporated in 1918 as Phillips-Jones Corp., successor to a business begun in 1859, and adopted its present name in 1957. The company makes medium-priced men's and boy's apparel and operates 107 retail stores. As of 1980 it began marketing a collection of women's apparel.
Brandnames of Products and Services:

417	*men's apparel*
Alan Flusser	*apparel*
Allyn St. George	*men & women's apparel*
Baracuta	*men's apparel*
Blake's	*apparel stores*
Cacharel	*women's apparel*
Cotton 100	*men's apparel*
Country Britches	*men's and boys' apparel*
Cricketeer	*men's and women's apparel*
Etienne Aigner	*apparel*
Geoffrey Beene	*men's apparel*
Halston	*apparel*
Hamburger's	*apparel stores*
Harris & Frank	*apparel stores*
Hennessey	*apparel*
Hennessey	*men's apparel*
Juster's	*apparel stores*
Kennedy's	*apparel stores*
McGregor	*apparel*
PGA Tour	*apparel*
Players	*Apparel*
PVH Outlet Stores	*discount outlet stores*
Super Silk	*men's apparel*
Titus McDuff	*men's apparel*
Van Heusen	*men's apparel, women's apparel*
VH	*apparel*
Windbreaker	*boy's and men's apparel*

Piccadilly Cafeterias, Inc.

P.O. Box 2467
Baton Rouge, LA 70821
(504) 293-9440

Chief Executive Officer: James C. Malmberg
1984 Annual Sales Volume: 174M
1984 Shares Outstanding: 6,046,447
Shareholders: 1,228
Exchange: OTC
Symbol: PICC
Corporate History: Piccadilly Cafeterias, founded in 1940, is one of the largest and most successful cafeteria chains in the nation with locations in 13 southern and southwestern states. Approximately 50 million customers, nearly one-fourth the nation's population, will walk through the service lines of the cafeterias in 1985. The company has enjoyed a rich and colorful history and was invoked in Louisiana governor Earl Long's campaign slogan, "I got fat eating at the Piccadilly!"
Brandnames of Products and Services:

Piccadilly	*cafeterias*

Pic 'N' Save Corp.

P.O. Box 58667
Los Angeles, CA 90058
(213) 537-9220

Chief Executive Officer: Arthur Frankel
1984 Annual Sales Volume: 235M
1984 Shares Outstanding: 26,314,915
Shareholders: 1,507
Exchange: OTC
Symbol: PICN
Corporate History: The company, founded in 1950 and last incorporated in 1971, operates a chain of stores in the Southwest, specializing in the sale of new "close-out" merchandise. In 1984 Pic 'N' Save operated 90 stores in seven southwestern states.
Brandnames of Products and Services:

Pic 'N' Save	*"close out" stores*

Pillsbury Co.

200 South Sixth St.
Minneapolis, MN 55402
(612) 330-4966

Chief Executive Officer: John M. Stafford
1984 Annual Sales Volume: 4,170M
1984 Shares Outstanding: 43,500,000
Shareholders: 20,000
Exchange: NY
Symbol: PSY
Corporate History: Pillsbury was founded in 1869 as a flour milling company. Today it encompasses two major sectors: The Restaurant Group (42.4% of the company's 1984 sales includes the Burger King hamburger chain and S & A Restaurant Corp., manager of the Steak and Ale, Bennigan's and JJ. Muggs restaurant businesses. *The Foods Group* (57%.6% of sales) consists of Consumer Foods and Agri-Products. Consumer Foods includes an array of dry grocery, refrigerated, frozen and canned products sold primarily through supermarkets, both domestically and internationally. The

company's leading brand names include Pillsbury, Green Giant, Haagen-Dazs, Totino's and VandeKamp's. Agri-Products includes flour and rice milling, bakery mixes and grain and feed ingredient merchandising, as well as supporting storage, distribution and transportation systems.

Brandnames of Products and Services:

Apollo	*Greek pastry products*
Azteca	*frozen Mexican food*
Ballard	*dough*
Bennigan's	*restaurant*
Burger King	*restaurants*
Clark	*food products*
Farina	*hot cereal*
Figurines	*diet meals*
Food Sticks	*snack food*
Fox Deluxe	*pizza*
Green Giant	*canned and frozen foods*
Haagen-Dazs	*ice cream*
Hungry Jack	*pancake mixes*
Kounty Kist	*canned foods*
Le Sueur	*canned foods*
Niblets	*canned foods*
Pillsbury	*baking and bakery products*
Pillsbury Best	*food products*
Poppin Fresh Doughboy	*dough*
Sedutto	*ice cream*
Sprinkle Sweet	*sweetener*
Steak & Ale	*restaurants*
Sweet 10	*food sweetner*
Totino's	*frozen pizza*

Pitney-Bowes Inc.

Walter H. Wheeler Jr. Dr.
Stamford, CT 069260-0700
(203) 356-5000

Chief Executive Officer:	George B. Harvey
1984 Annual Sales Volume:	1,732M
1984 Shares Outstanding:	36,520,312
Shareholders:	18,427
Exchange:	NY
Symbol:	PBI

Corporate History: The company incorporated in 1920 as Pitney-Bowes Postage Meter Co., a consolidation of Universal Stamping Machine and American Postage Meter Co. Its present name was adopted in 1979. It makes business equipment. In 1984 mailing business equipment accounted for 54% of sales, copier products 11%, dictating systems 11% and business supplies and services 23%. It is the world's largest manufacturer of postal meters. Beginning in 1981 the company, along with Dodwell & Co. Ltd. of England, began marketing PBI business products in Japan.

Brandnames of Products and Services:

Ansafone	*answering machine*
Dict Alert	*office equipment*
Dicta Mate	
Dictaphone	*office equipment*
Drawing Board	*office supplies*
Grayarc	*office supplies*
Miniwriter	*office equipment*
Pathfinder	*Labeler*
Pitney-Bowes	*business machines, postage meters*
Veritrac	*office equipment*

Playboy Enterprises Inc.

919 N. Michigan Ave.
Chicago, IL 60611
(312) 751-8000

Chief Executive Officer:	H.M. Hefner
1984 Annual Sales Volume:	187M
1984 Shares Outstanding:	9,405,684
Shareholders:	27,395
Exchange:	NY
Symbol:	PLA

Corporate History: Founded in 1953, Playboy was incorporated in 1964 and was made public in 1972. Playboy Enterprises, Inc. is a media and marketing company that publishes consumer magazines, produces video programming for pay-television, and merchandises the Playboy name and trademarks through product and magazine licensing, direct marketing, and a worldwide chain of Playboy Clubs. The company hails a new business in video and cable.

Brandnames of Products and Services:

Games	*magazine*
licensed goods bearing company symbol &/or name	
Playboy	*clubs*
The Playboy Channel	*cable tv service*
Playboy Home Video	*discs and cassettes*
Playboy	*magazine*

Plenum Publishing Corp.

233 Spring St.
New York, NY 10013
(212) 620-8000

Chief Executive Officer:	Martin E. Tash
1984 Annual Sales Volume:	36M
1984 Shares Outstanding:	2,297,656
Shareholders:	977
Exchange:	OTC
Symbol:	PLEN

Corporate History: Plenum Publishing Corp. publishes and distributes advanced scientific and technical material. The company's principal markets are public and private libraries, technically oriented corporations, research organizations and individual scientists, engineers, research workers, doctors and graduate students. Marketing is done by direct mail and by advertising in scientific publications, including its own journals. The company's DaCapo Press publishes reprints of books in music, dance, visual arts, and the social sciences—most of which have been long out of print.

Brandnames of Products and Services:

Career Placement Registry, Inc.	*information system*
Consultants Bureau	*publisher*
DaCapo Press	*publisher*
IFI/Plenum Data	*publisher*
Plenum Press	*publisher*

Polaroid Corp.

549 Technology Sq.
Cambridge, MA 02139
(617) 577-2000

Chief Executive Officer:	William McCune, Jr.
1984 Annual Sales Volume:	1,272M
1984 Shares Outstanding:	30,959,175
Shareholders:	26,697
Exchange:	NY
Symbol:	PRD

Corporate History: Polaroid Corp. was founded in 1937 by Edwin Land who had discovered a method for polarizing light, reducing glare. The company's first product was sunglasses. It was extremely profitable during World War II because of the military demand for the glasses but the company nearly collapsed after the war when demand slackened dramatically. In 1948 Land introduced the first instant camera, saving the company and creating a revolution in the consumer photography market. The company designs, manufactures and markets a variety of products primarily in instant image recording fields. These include instant photographic cameras and films, magnetic media, light polarizing filters and lenses, and diversified chemical, optical and commercial products.

Brandnames of Products and Services:

Polaroid	*film, cameras and accessories, video cassettes*

Ponderosa Inc.

P.O. Box 578
Dayton, OH 45501
(513) 890-6400

Chief Executive Officer:	Gerald S. Office Jr.
1984 Annual Sales Volume:	418M
1984 Shares Outstanding:	9,669,490
Shareholders:	3,844
Exchange:	NY
Symbol:	PON

Corporate History: The company was incorporated in 1968 under the name Ponderosa Systems Inc. In 1982 the name was changed to Ponderosa Inc. The company operates and franchises restaurants both in the U.S. and abroad. In 1984 the company operated 433 steakhouses in the U.S. and two steak & salad restaurants in England. The company franchises 188 steakhouses in the U.S. and abroad. It also operates 19 mexican restaurants and franchises one mexican restaurants.

Brandnames of Products and Services:

Ponderosa Steak House	*restaurants*
Steak & Salad	*restaurants*

Post Corp.

306 W. Washington St.
P.O. Box 59
Appleton, Wis. 54911
(414) 733-4411

Chief Executive Officer:	V.I. Mirahan
Exchange:	AM
Symbol:	POS

Corporate History: The company, incorporated in 1898 is involved in publishing and broadcasting. It derives nearly two-thirds of its profits from broadcasting.

Brandnames of Products and Services:

Daily Transcript	*newspaper, Dedham, Mass.*

Herald	*weekly newspaper, Collinsville, Ill.*
KBIZ-AM	*radio station, Ottumwa, Iowa*
KTVO-TV	*La. and Mo.*
News-Banner	*weekly newspaper, Wadsworth, Ohio*
News	*newspaper, West Bend, Wis.*
News-Tribune	*newspaper, Waltham, Mass.*
Post-Crescent	*newspaper, Appleton, Wis.*
Post Newspapers	*suburban Milwaukee, Wis.*
Post Productions	*TV and film production*
Press-Record	*weekly newspaper, Granite City, Ill.*
Sun Newspapers	*suburban Cleveland, Ohio*
Transcript	*newspapers, suburban Boston, Mass.*
Twin City News-Record	*newspaper, Neenah-Menasha, Wis.*
WAXX-AM	*radio station, Eau Claire, Wis.*
WEAU-TV	*Eau Claire, Wis.*
WLUC-TV	*Marquette, Miss.*
WLUK-TV	*Greenbay, Wis.*
WOKR-TV	*Rochester, N.Y.*

Pratt & Lambert, Inc.

75 Tonawanda St.
Buffalo, NY 14207
(716) 873-6000

Chief Executive Officer: Raymond D. Stevens, Jr.
1984 Annual Sales Volume: 173M
1984 Shares Outstanding: 1,905,892
Shareholders: 2,289
Exchange: AM
Symbol: PM
Corporate History: Pratt & Lambert, Inc. founded in 1849, develops, produces, and sells architectural finishes, industrial coatings, and adhesives.
Brandnames of Products and Services:

Accolade	*paint*
The Paint Place	*paint stores*
Pierce & Stevens	*adhesives*
Pratt & Lambert	*paints*
Ten Year	*paint*

Prentice-Hall Inc.

Route 9W
Englewood Cliffs, N.J. 07632
(201) 592-2000

Chief Executive Officer: F.J. Dunnigan
Exchange: ASE
Symbol: PTN
Corporate History: Prentice Hall, founded in 1913 and incorporated in 1929, is one of the country's largest publishers of college texts. It also is a major publisher of elementary, secondary and vocational school books. In 1979 textbooks and other educational materials accounted for approximately 45.1% of sales, business and professional subscription products 26.1% and business and professional books 16.2%.
Brandnames of Products and Services:

Arco	*publishing house*
Prentice-Hall	*publishing house*
Spectrum Books	*publishing house*

Procter & Gamble Co.

301 E. 6th St.
Cincinnati, Ohio 45202
(513) 562-1100

Chief Executive Officer: Owen B. Butler
1984 Annual Sales Volume: 13,125M
1984 Shares Outstanding: 167,047,272
Shareholders: 100,585
Exchange: NY
Symbol: PG
Corporate History: Proctor & Gamble was incorporated in 1905 and was the out growth of a company founded in 1837 as a soap and candle business. The company remained primarily a soap manufacturer for almost 100 years. During the 1940s it introduced detergent to the American market and in the 1950s branched out into foods with the acquisition of Duncan Hines and paper products with the acquisition of Charmin Paper Mills. In 1965 it expanded into personal care products with Scope. In 1983 the company introduced Citrus Hill orange juice, already a national brand. The company's growth in the pharmaceutical business was achieved through the 1984 acquisition of Norwich Eaton Pharmaceuticals. Today it is one of the largest manufacturers of household and personal care products and foods in the nation. It ranks among the first in the detergent, toothpaste, shampoo and deoderant markets. Procter & Gamble is also one of the nation's largest advertisers.

Brandnames of Products and Services:

Always	*maxi pads and pantyliners*
Attends	*incontinent briefs*
Banner	*toilet tissue*
Biz	*detergent*
Bold 3	*detergent*
Bounce	*fabric softener*
Bounty	*paper towels*
Camay	*soap*
Cascade	*detergent*
Charmin	*toilet tissue*
Cheer	*detergent*
Chloraseptic	*sore throat spray*
Citrus Hill	*orange juice*
Coast	*soap*
Comet	*cleaning product*
Crest	*toothpaste*
Crisco	*shortening and oil*
Dash	*detergent*
Dawn	*detergent*
Downy	*fabric softener*
Dreft	*detergent*
Duncan Hines	*baking products*
Encaprin	*arthritis pain reliever*
Era	*detergent*
Folger's	*coffee*
Gain	*detergent*
Gleem	*toothpaste*
Head & Chest	*cold medicine*
Head & Shoulders	*shampoo*
High Point	*coffee*
Hires	*soft drinks*
Ivory	*shampoo and conditioner*
Ivory	*soap*
Ivory Liquid	*detergent*
Ivory Snow	*detergent*
Jif	*peanut butter*
Joy	*detergent*
Lava	*soap*
Lilt	*home permanent*
Luvs	*diapers*
Mr. Clean	*cleaning product*
Norwich	*aspirin*
Orange Crush	*beverage*
Oxydol	*detergent*
Pampers	*diapers*
Pepto Bismol	*indigestion medicine*
Pert	*shampoo*
Prell	*shampoo*
Pringle's	*potato chips*
Puffs	*tissue*
Puritan	*oil*
Safeguard	*soap and deodorant*
Scope	*mouthwash*
Secret	*deodorant*
Solo	*detergent*
Spic & Span	*cleaning product*
Sure	*deodorant*
Tender Leaf	*tea bags*
Tide	*detergent*
Top Job	*cleaning product*
White Cloud	*toilet tissue*
Wondra	*hand lotion*
Zest	*soap*

Pro Group Inc.

99 Tremont St.
Chattanooga, TN 37405
(615) 267-5631

Chief Executive Officer:	John M. Tucker
1984 Annual Sales Volume:	25M
1984 Shares Outstanding:	2,572,889
Shareholders:	4,000
Exchange:	OTC
Symbol:	PRGR

Corporate History: The company incorporated in 1931 as Professional Golf Co. and adopted its present name in 1975. It makes golf equipment, accessories and apparel.

Brandnames of Products and Services:

Arnold Palmer	*golf accessories*
Duckster	*nylon jackets*
First Flight	*golf clubs*
Hendel	*golf and sports apparel*
Hotze	*golf bags*
James H. McClory	*golf equipment*
Jimmy McClory's Golf Shop	*catalog of golf equipment*
Peerless	*golf clubs*
Standard	*golf clubs*
Tony Trabert	*sport products*

Purex Industries, Inc.

5101 Clark Ave.
Lakewood, Calif. 90712
(213) 634-3300

Chief Executive Officer:	W.R. Tincher
Exchange:	NY
Symbol:	PRX

Corporate History: The company incorporated in 1927 as Purex Chemical Corp., and adopted its present name in 1973. It markets grocery products.

Brandnames of Products and Services:

Ayds	*diet product*
Bo-Peep	*ammonia*
Brillo	*soap pads*
Cameo	*cleaner*
Cuticura	*skin care product*
Doan's Pills	*drugs and toiletries*
Ellio's	*pizza*
Fels-Naptha	*soap*
Ferry-Morse	*vegetable and flower seed packets*
Gentle Fels	*dishwashing liquid*
Hi-Lex-Liquid	*bleach*
Kurly Kate	*cleaning aids*
La France	*whitener-brightener*
Old Dutch	*cleanser*
Purex	*cleaning products*
Sweet-Heart	*soap*
Trend	*detergent*

Puritan Fashions Corp.

1400 Broadway
New York, N.Y. 10018
(212) 575-0800

Chief Executive Officer: C. Rosen
Exchange: NY
Symbol: PFC

Corporate History: The company incorporated in 1958 as a wholly-owned subsidiary of Reliance Mfg. Co. and adopted its present title in 1961. The company makes popular-priced and designer women's apparel, as well as men's, women's and children's jeans. Its entry into the designer apparel market has greatly helped sales.

Brandnames of Products and Services:

Calvin Klein	*jeans*
Diane Von Furstenberg	*women's apparel*
Diane Young	*women's apparel*
Domani	*apparel*
Forever Young	*apparel*
Gale Gould	*sportswear*
Gloria Swanson	*apparel*
Gurian	*apparel*
Happenstance	*apparel*
Just Young	*women's apparel*
Penny Young	*women's apparel*
Philip Gurian	*apparel*
Puritan Dress	*women's apparel*
Saybrook	*apparel*
Verona Knits	*apparel*

Quaker Oats Co.

Merchandise Mart Plaza
Chicago, Ill. 60654
(312) 222-7111

Chief Executive Officer:	William D. Smithburg
1984 Annual Sales Volume:	3,344M
1984 Shares Outstanding:	19,849,197
Shareholders:	26,785
Exchange:	NY
Symbol:	OAT

Corporate History: Quaker Oats traces its history back to 1891 when seven of the nation's largest millers organized the American Cereal Co. It reincorporated in 1901, adopting its present name. The company holds over 50% of the hot cereal market; its largest selling product remains oatmeal. During the 1920s the company became involved in chemical production to make use of the waste products of milling. Forty years later Quaker diversified into toys, restaurants, crafts and ethnic foods. In 1984, the company acquired Stokely-Van Camp Inc. Its operating strategies are achieve profitable, better-than-average real volume growth in worldwide grocery and toy businesses; improve profitability of low-return businesses or divest; establish a meaningful position in specialty retailing businesses which will enhance overall corporate growth.

Brandnames of Products and Services:

100% Natural	*cereal*
Aunt Jemima	*pancake and waffle mixes and syrups*
Bran & Raisin Instant Oatmeal	
Brookstone	*mail order catalog*
Burry's	*cookies*
Cap'n Crunch	*cereal*
Celeste	*frozen pizza*
Cinnamon Life	*cereal*
Corn Bran	*cereal*
Engine House Pizza	*restaurants*
Euphrates	*crackers*
Eyelab	*eyewear*
Fisher Price Toys	
Fixler Brothers	*needlecraft stores*
Flako	*pie crust*
Fudgetown	*food products*
Gatorade	*beverage*

Gaucho	*food products*
Granola Dipps	*snack bars*
Halfsies	*cereal*
Herrschners	*mail order yarn and crafts*
Jos. A. Bank	*mail order clothing*
Ken-L Ration	*pet food*
Kibbles 'n Bits	*pet food*
Life	*cereal*
Magic Pan Creperies	*restaurants*
Mr. T	*cereal*
Needle Queen	*needlecraft products*
The Proud Popover	*restaurants*
Puffed Rice	*cereal*
Puffed Wheat	*cereal*
Puss 'n Boots	*cat food*
Quaker	*cereals and other products*
Scooter Pie	*snack food*
Snausages	*dog food*
Tender Chunks	*pet food*
Van Camp's	*pork and beans*
Wolf Brand	*chili products and grains*
Wonder Art	*needlecraft products*

Quaker State Oil Refining Corp.

255 Elm St.
Oil City, PA 16301
(814) 676-7676

Chief Executive Officer: Q.E. Wood
1984 Annual Sales Volume: 925M
1984 Shares Outstanding: 21,770,000
Shareholders: 15,000
Exchange: NY
Symbol: KSF

Corporate History: Quaker State's primary business is marketing consumer automotive products. Quaker State motor oil is the nation's number one selling brand. The company, incorporated in 1931, also markets anti-freeze, rustproofing products, filters, batteries, car chemicals and tires. A major subsidiary, Heritage Insurance Group, sells credit/life, credit/accident and automobile maintenance insurance primarily through car dealers. Another subsidiary, Truck-Lite Company, manufactures and markets truck, trailer and automobile lighting equipment. As by-products of its lubricant refineries, Quaker State produces and wholesales fuels and waxes. In non-automotive markets, Quaker State produces crude oil and natural gas and through a subsidiary, Valley Camp Coal Company, steam coal in Pennsylvania, West Virginia and Utah. Valley Camp Inc. operates an iron ore and potash dock in Thunder Bay, Ontario, and a small chemical company near Toronto. Great Lakes Coal and Dock Company, another subsidiary, operates a coal and other bulk materials transfer facility and dock in St. Paul, Minnesota.

Brandnames of Products and Services:

Chain & Bar Lubricant	*lubricating oils for chain saws and parts*
COMP & Design	*customized oil maintenance program*
DeLuxe	*motor oil*
Duplex	*lubricating oils and greases*
Gold Seal	*lubricating oils*
Penn Seal	*motor oil, kerosene, gasoline and illuminating oil*
Q	*tires*
Q/S	*tires and batteries*
Quadrolube	*lubricating oils and greases*
Quaker Koat	*undercoater and sound deadener*
Quaker State	*automotive products*
Quaker State	*automotive products*
Quaker State ATA	*automotive transmission additive*
Quaker State ATF	*transmission fluid*
Quaker State Carsaver Undercoating	*automotive undercoating*
Quaker State FLM	*automatic transmission fluid*
Quaker State Metal-Gard Undercoating	*automotive undercoating*
Quaker State Q	*automobile oil filters*
Quaker State SDA	*motor oil*
Quaker State VCC	*valve and cylinder cleaner*
Quality	*oils and greases*
Sterling	*illuminating oils, lubricating oils, lubricating greases, gasoline, kerosene and crude petroleum*
Super Blend	*motor oil*
Superflex	*petroleum waxes and blends*

Quality Mills, Inc.

U.S. Highway 52 South
Mount Airy, NC 27030
(919) 789-6161

Chief Executive Officer: John E. Woltz
1984 Annual Sales Volume: 49M

1984 Shares Outstanding: 1,298,378
Shareholders: 500
Exchange: OTC
Symbol: QLTY
Corporate History: Quality Mills, Inc. manufactures and markets knit wearing apparel consisting of men's, ladies' and children's knit sportswear and playwear. The company also manufactures and markets a variety of knit fabrics to the apparel trade.
Brandnames of Products and Services:

Cross Creek	*men's & women's apparel*
Quality Mills	*knit apparel*
Toddly Winks	*children's apparel*
Tweens	*pre-teens apparel*

Questar Corp.

180 East First South St.
Salt Lake City, UT 84147
(801) 534-5000

Chief Executive Officer: R.D. Cash
1984 Annual Sales Volume: 687M
1984 Shares Outstanding: 18,060,013
Shareholders: 11,081
Exchange: NY
Symbol: STR
Corporate History: Questar Corp. was organized in 1984. In the same year, it bacame the parent of Mountain Fuel Supply Co. Questar is engaged in the exploration, production, gathering, transmission, storage and distribution of natural gas and in the production of liquid hydrocarbons. The company also manufactures and markets brick and related building materials; conducts business development and energy research activities; and owns and manages real estate.
Brandnames of Products and Services:

Interstate Brick	*brick, tile, building materials*
Mountain Fuel	*natural gas distributor*
Questar Development	*real estate*

Questor Corp.

One John Goerlich Sq.
Toledo, Ohio 43691
(419) 259-3461

Chief Executive Officer: P.M. Grieve
Exchange: NY
Symbol: IQ
Corporate History: Questor incorporated in 1923 as Dunhill Internaitonal Inc. to gain a controlling interest in the various Dunhill companies of Europe. The company adopted its present title in 1968. It acquired Lullabye Furniture Co. and Baby Line Furniture Co. in 1970 for $8 million. In 1979 automotive products for the replacement market accounted for 43% of sales, recreation products 35%, juvenile products 15% and home environmental items 7%.
Brandnames of Products and Services:

Ajust-A-Rail	*ornamental wrought iron*
Baby Line	*juvenile furniture*
Caber	*recreational and athletic products*
Classic	*ornamental wrought iron*
Evenflo	*infant feeding products*
Infantseat	*juvenile recliner*
Kantwet	*children's apparel*
Leslie-Locke	*decorative shutters, ornamental wrought iron*
Lullabye	*juvenile furniture*
Snauwaert	*recreational and athletic products*
Spalding	*recreational and athletic products*
Style-A-Rail	*ornamental wrought iron*
Toss'ems	*toy*
Versa	*ornamental wrought iron*

Ralston Purina Co.

Checkerboard Square
St. Louis, MO 63164
(314) 982-1000

Chief Executive Officer: William P. Stiritz
1984 Annual Sales Volume: 4,980M
1984 Shares Outstanding: 83,511,625
Shareholders: 38,538
Exchange: NY
Symbol: RAL
Corporate History: The company was founded and incorporated in 1894 as a supplier of animal feed. Today it ranks number one in production of feed for livestock, poultry and pets. It is the largest wholesale baker of fresh bakery products in the United States. Other grocery products include cereals and canned tuna. It is also a major producer of isolated soy protein. In addition, the company operates a chain of 788 fast-service restaurants. In fiscal 1984 agricultural products accounted for 45% of sales, grocery products 38% and restaurants and other units 17%.

Brandnames of Products and Services:

Alley Cat	*cat food*
Beefsteak	*rye bread*
Bonz	*pet food*
Bremmer's Biscuits	
Butcher's Blend	*pet food*
Chex	*cereals*
Chicken-of-the-Sea	*tuna*
Chow	*pet food*
Chuck Wagon	*pet food*
Cookie Crisp	*cereals*
Country Stand	*produce*
Cracker Jack	*cereal*
Crispy Oatmeal	*cereal*
Deco-Plants	*home party plan*
Dry Kitten Chow	*pet food*
Field 'n Farm	*pet food*
Fit & Trim	*pet food*
Good Mews	*pet food*
Happy Cat	*cat food*
Hero	*dog food*
Home Pride	*bread*
Hostess	*cakes and pies*
Jack-in-the-Box	*restaurants*
Keystone	*resort, Denver, Colo.*
Lovin Spoonfuls	*pet food*
Meow Mix	*pet food*
Moist & Chunky	*pet food*
Purina	*pet food*
Rainbow Brite	*cereal*
Ralston	*cereals*
Ralston Purina	*food products*
RyKrisp	*crackers*
Sea Dog	*dog food*
Twinkies	*cakes*
Van Camps	*seafood products*
Whisker Lickins	*pet food*
Wonder	*breads*

Ramada Inns Inc.

3838 E. Van Buren St.
Phoenix, AZ 85008
(602) 273-4000

Chief Executive Officer: Richard Snell
1984 Annual Sales Volume: 600M
1984 Shares Outstanding: 37,207,932
Shareholders: 44,801
Exchange: NY
Symbol: RAM

Corporate History: The company, last incorporated in 1961, operates hotels, resorts and casino hotels. As of 1984, the company owned 46 hotels in 28 states, nine hotels in Europe and four in Canada. In addition, there are 509 hotels operated under lease arrangements.

Brandnames of Products and Services:

Ramada Hotels	
Ramada Inns	
Ramada Renaissance Hotels	
Tropicana Hotel & Country Club	*Las Vegas, NV*
Tropicana Hotel and Casino	*Atlantic City, NJ*

Rangaire Corp.

501 South Wilhite St. (P.O. Box 177)
Cleburne, TX 76031
(214) 477-2161

Chief Executive Officer: J.M. Hill
1984 Annual Sales Volume: 72M
1984 Shares Outstanding: 3,824,316
Shareholders: 1,544
Exchange: OTC
Symbol: RANG

Corporate History: Rangaire, incorporated in 1950, manufactures kitchen appliances and equipment, mines & processes limestone into quicklime & hydrated lime, and is a major general contractor in the Dallas-Ft. Worth area.

Brandnames of Products and Services:

Frost Queen	*freezers*
Gro Master	*fluorescent lighting*
Magnawave™	*induction cooktop*
Rangaire	*lighting fixtures, induction cooktop, range hoods, freezers, refrigerators*
Rangaire	*kitchen ranges*
Ranger	*freezers*
Vistalite	*lighting fixtures*

Raytheon Co.

141 Spring St.
Lexington, MA 02173
(617) 862-6600

Chief Executive Officer: T.L. Phillips
1984 Annual Sales Volume: 5,996M
1984 Shares Outstanding: 84,354,000

Shareholders: 27,800
Exchange: NY
Symbol: RTN
Corporate History: The company incorporated in 1928 as Raytheon Mfg. Co. and adopted its present title in 1959. It produces household appliances, electronic systems for government, industrial and commercial use, aircraft and heavy construction equipment. It also publishes textbooks.
Brandnames of Products and Services:

Amana	*household appliances*
Beech	*aircraft*
Caloric	*household appliances*
D.C. Heath & Co.	*educational publishing house*
Glenwood	*household appliance*
Modern Maid	*household appliances*
Radarange	*household appliance*
Speed Queen	*household appliances*

RB Industries Inc.

1801 Century Park East, Suite 2101
Los Angeles, CA 90067
(213) 553-3655

Chief Executive Officer: Joseph Sinay
1984 Annual Sales Volume: 134M
1984 Shares Outstanding: 3,398,662
Shareholders: 932
Exchange: NY
Symbol: RBI
Corporate History: Incorporated in 1956, RB Industries operates a chain of 63 furniture stores in the West. In 1984, the company acquired the rights to use the name "W & J Sloane;" it presently operates five W & J Sloane stores.
Brandnames of Products and Services:

RB Furniture	*furniture stores*
W & J Sloane	*furniture stores*

RCA Corp.

30 Rockefeller Plaza
New York, NY 10020
(212) 621-6000

Chief Executive Officer: Robert R. Frederick
1984 Annual Sales Volume: 10,112M
1984 Shares Outstanding: 82,084,018
Shareholders: 183,569
Exchange: NY
Symbol: RCA
Corporate History: RCA incorporated in 1919 as Radio Corporation of America. That same year it acquired Marconi Wireless Telegraph Co. of America, which owned all commercial radio communication facilities within the United States. Under the direction of David Sarnoff, it became a leader in broadcasting. The company developed the first television set in 1939 and began marketing TV sets commercially after World War II. During the 1950s it also became an important defense contractor. Today it is a giant conglomerate with interests in communications and broadcasting, publishing, food production, household furnishings and insurance, among others. Most of the company's sales come from its electronic equipment and its television network.
Brandnames of Products and Services:

Buzza	*greeting cards*
Coronet	*carpets*
Gibson	*greeting cards*
Hertz	*car rental*
KNAI-FM	*radio station, San Francisco, Calif.*
KNBC-TV	*station, Los Angeles, Calif.*
KNBR	*radio station, San Francisco, Calif.*
National Broadcasting Co.	
Pleasant Thoughts	*greeting cards*
RCA	*televisions, radios, records, VCR's, related products*
Success	*greeting cards*
WKYC-TV	*station, Cleveland, Ohio*
WKYS-FM	*radio station, Washington, D.C.*
WMAZ-TV & AM	*radio station, Chicago, Ill.*
WNBC-TV & AM	*radio station, New York, N.Y.*
WNIS-FM	*radio station, Chicago, Ill.*
WNWS-FM	*radio station, New York, N.Y.*
WRC-TV & AM	*radio station, Washington, D.C.*

Redken Laboratories Inc.

6625 Variel Ave.
Canoga Park, Calif. 91303
(818) 992-2700

Chief Executive Officer: J.E. Meehan
1984 Annual Sales Volume: 101M
1984 Shares Outstanding: 2,710,000
Shareholders: 5,000
Exchange: OTC
Symbol: RDKN

Corporate History: The company, incorporated in 1960, manufactures hair and skin conditioning products sold exclusively through beauty salons and barber styling establishments. Redken products are used and sold by cosmetologists and barbers in some 20 countries around the world.

Brandnames of Products and Services:

Clinical Response	*skin care*
Moisture Renewal	*skin care lotion*
Paula Kent	*fragances*
PH Plus	*skin care products*
Pique	*women's fragrance*
Redken	*hair care products*
Redken/Lapinal	*hair care products*
RK for Men	*hair care products*
Styling Research	*hand-held electrical hair styling appliances*

Redman Industries Inc.

2550 Walnut Hill Lane
Dallas, TX 75229-5672
(214) 353-3600

Chief Executive Officer: James Redman
1984 Annual Sales Volume: 345M
1984 Shares Outstanding: 9,752,034
Shareholders: 10,000
Exchange: NY
Symbol: RE

Corporate History: Redman Industries, Inc., founded in 1937 and incorporated in 1960, is one of the largest mobile housing producers in the United States and is a major producer of both mobile housing and general aluminum and wooden building products. Through its largest subsidiary, Redman Homes, Inc., the Company manufactures quality affordable homes. Redman Homes currently operates 19 manufacturing facilities in 13 states. The Company conducts its building products business through its subsidiary, Redman Building Products, Inc. The Company markets nationally such shelter-related products as a full line of aluminum windows, doors and storm products, as well as extruded aluminum and vinyl. Wooden building components, such as roof and floor trusses, wall panels and complete framing systems. Redman Building Products currently operates 10 manufacturing facilities in 5 states with 9 distribution centers located in major metropolitan areas.

Brandnames of Products and Services:

Boanza	*mobile homes*
Eaton Park	*mobile homes*
Flamingo	*mobile homes*
Kirkwood	*mobile homes*
New Moon	*mobile homes*
Redman	*aluminum window and door products*
Sheraton	*mobile homes*
Walden	*mobile homes*

Reeves Brothers Inc.

1271 Avenue of the Americas
New York, N.Y. 10020
(212) 397-5700

Chief Executive Officer: J.D. Moore
Exchange: NY
Symbol: RVS

Corporate History: Incorporated in 1922, the company manufactures textiles. In fiscal 1980 consumer products accounted for 24.5% of sales with the remainder in industrial apparel, textiles and industrial coated fabrics.

Brandnames of Products and Services:

Cinderella	*underwear and T-shirts*
Comfy Home Furnishings	*ready-made slip covers*

Resorts International Inc.

915 N.E. 125th St.
North Miami, FL 33161
(305) 891-2500

Chief Executive Officer: James M. Crosby
1984 Annual Sales Volume: 463M
1984 Shares Outstanding: 6,555,908
Shareholders: 8,966
Exchange: AM
Symbol: RTA

Corporate History: Incorporated in 1958, the Company is engaged in the ownership and operation of casino gambling, resort and hotel facilities in Atlantic City, New Jersey and Paradise Island, the Bahamas. The

Company also provides consultative management security services, operates an amphibious airline between South Florida and the Bahamas and a helicopter airline between New York City and Atlantic City.

Brandnames of Products and Services:

Casino Hotel	*casino gambling resort & hotel - Atlantic City, NJ*
Chalk's International Airline	*amphibious airline*
Intertel	*security service*
Ocean Club	*resort & hotel - Paradise Island - Bahamas*
Paradise Beach Inn	*resort & hotel - Paradise Island - Bahamas*
Paradise Island Casino	*casino resort & hotel - Paradise Island - Bahamas*
Resorts International Airlines (RIA)	*amphibious airline*

Restaurant Associates Industries, Inc.

1540 Broadway
New York, N.Y. 10036
(212) 997-1400

Chief Executive Officer: M. Brody
Exchange: AM
Symbol: RA

Corporate History: The company, incorporated in 1968, operates food establishments, newstands and tobacco shops. It runs specialty restaurants in the New York City area and elsewhere in the East and 120 newstands, mostly in the New York area. In 1979 food services accounted for 73% at sales and restaurants and tobacco shops 27%.

Brandnames of Products and Services:

Adam & Eve	*coffee shop, New York, N.Y.*
Brasserie	*restaurant, New York, N.Y.*
Charlie Brown's	*restaurant, New York, N.Y.*
Coffee Cafe	*New York, N.Y.*
Crafts Inn	*restaurant, Mass.*
Dockside Terrace	*restaurant, Miami, Fla.*
Everglades Park Motel	*Fla.*
Hungry Charlie's	*coffee shop, Syracuse, N.Y.*
Jake's	*Restaurant, Conn.*
John Peel	*restaurant, Long Island, N.Y.*
Jolly Trolley	*steakhouses, New Jersey*
Mamma Leone's	*restaurant, New York, N.Y.*
Nassau Inn	*lodging Princeton, N.J.*
Palmer Square	*restaurant, N.J.*
P.J. Barnum's	*restaurant, New York, N.Y.*
Promenade Cafe	*New York, N.Y.*
Publick House	*lodging, Sturbridge, Mass.*
Reflections on the Bay	*restaurant, Miami, Fla.*
Seymour's	*steakhouses, New Jersey*
Trattoria	*restaurant, New York, N.Y.*
What's Your Beefs	*steakhouse, New Jersey*
Zum Zum	*coffee shops*

Restec Systems, Inc.

1317 East Broad St.
Columbus, OH 43205
(614) 258-3191

Chief Executive Officer: David A. Winters
1984 Annual Sales Volume: 3M
1984 Shares Outstanding: 1,792,914
Shareholders: 700
Exchange: OTC
Symbol: RTEC

Corporate History: The company, incorporated in 1983, operates fast food restaurants in southern Ohio.

Brandnames of Products and Services:

Rax	*restaurants*

Revco D.S. Inc.

1925 Enterprise Pkwy.
Twinsburg, OH 44087
(216) 425-9811

Chief Executive Officer: Sidney Dworkin
1984 Annual Sales Volume: 2,228M
1984 Shares Outstanding: 36,593,102
Shareholders: 6,500
Exchange: NY
Symbol: RDS

Corporate History: Revco was incorporated in 1956, and through its subsidiaries, operates principally in the specialty retail industry. In 1984, the company operated 1,793 drugstores located in 28 states. The company has opened or acquired 672 drugstores in the last five years. In 1981, the company acquired the 146 drugstore Skillern Drug Division of Zale Corp. The company merged with Odd Lot Trading Inc. in 1984. Odd Lot operates as a retailer and wholesaler of close-out merchandise.

Including the stores formerly operated by Revco and Odd Lot on a joint venture basis, there were 111 Odd Lot stores located in seven states.

Brandnames of Products and Services:

Odd Lot Trading	*close-out merchandise*
Revco	*discount drug stores*
Revco	*health and beauty products*

Revere Copper & Brass Inc.

605 Third Avenue
New York, NY 10016
(212) 578-1500

Chief Executive Officer: Hugh H. Williamson III
1984 Annual Sales Volume: 601M
1984 Shares Outstanding: 5,712,922
Shareholders: 3,350
Exchange: NY
Symbol: RVB

Corporate History: Incorporated in 1928 as General Brass Corp., the company changed its name the same year to Republic Brass Corp., and adopted its present title in 1929. The company formed in 1928 by the consolidation of six copper fabricating companies, one of which was founded in 1801 by Paul Revere. In 1982, the company filed voluntary petitions in the United States Bankruptcy Court for the Southern District of New York for reorganization under Chapter 11 of the Bankruptcy Code under which cases are pending. The principal business of the company is the production and sale of nonferrous metal products in the following business segments: (1) primary aluminum, (2) fabricated aluminum, (3) fabricated copper and brass, (4) metal stampings and (5) other products include copper, zinc and magnesium engravers' plates, lead and tin foil and data based management systems. The principal markets for the company's copper and brass mill products are transportation, building and construction, electrical, capital goods and consumer durable goods. The principal markets for fabricated aluminum products are transportation, building and construction, consumer durable goods and packaging. Primary aluminum is also used in the company's own fabricating operations. Virtually all of the company's products are sold directly by the company to the using industries and through independent general product distributors; copper and brass mill products are also sold through specialty distributors. Utensil products are sold to department stores, independent housewares and hardware distributors, chains, premium firms and catalog houses.

Brandnames of Products and Services:

Revere Ware	*kitchen utensils and specialty cookware*

Revlon Inc.

767 Fifth Ave.
New York, NY 10153
(212) 572-5000

Chief Executive Officer: M.C. Bergerac
1984 Annual Sales Volume: 2,399M
1984 Shares Outstanding: 38,228,197
Shareholders: 14,200
Exchange: NY
Symbol: REV

Corporate History: The company, sometimes called the "General Motors of beauty" was founded in 1933 as Revlon Nail Enamel Corp. The name changed to Revlon Products Corp. in 1939 and to its present title in 1955. Under the direction of Charles Revson, Revlon expanded first into the lipstick and general cosmetic business and then into pharmaceuticals, proprietary drugs and optical products. Today Revlon is an international company engaged in the health care and beauty products businesses. Revlon's health care business consists of the manufacture and distribution of vision care products, ethical pharmaceutical products, proprietary and certain other health care products (principally fine chemicals and industrial analytical and hospital information systems), and medical diagnostic systems and related reagents. In the United States, it also operates clinical diagnostic and research laboratories. Revlon's beauty products business consists of the manufacture and distribution of cosmetics and fragrances (including face and eye makeup, lipsticks, haircolor and nail products and perfumes, colognes and other fragrance products) and beauty care and treatment products (including shampoos, conditioners and other hair care products, cleansing and moisturizing creams and lotions, antiperspirants, nail care and other beauty implements and professional beauty products and equipment).

Brandnames of Products and Services:

Advanced Formula	*cosmetics*
Andiamo	*fragrance*
Aquamarine	*hair care products*
Barnes-Hind	*contact lens products*
Bill Blass for Women	*fragrance*
Blush-On	*cosmetics*
Brace	*denture adhesive*
Braggi	*men's fragrance*

Calcimax	*calcium supplement*
Cerissa	*fragrance*
Charlie	*fragrance*
Chaz	*men's fragrance*
Ciara	*fragrance*
Clean & Clear	*skin care products*
Coburn	*optical products*
Collegev Complex	*skin care product*
Colorsilk	*cosmetics*
Colourscents	*fragrances*
Comfort Drops	*optical products*
Continuous Curve	*contact lens*
Cream of Nature	*hair care products*
Custom Eyes	*cosmetics*
Di Borghese	*cosmetics*
Ecco	*cosmetics*
Eppy	*optical products*
Esoterica	*skin treatment*
Eterna 27	*cosmetics*
Etherea	*cosmetics*
Fanci-Full	*hair care products*
Fiamma	*cosmetics*
Fleurs de Jontue	*fragrance*
Flex	*cosmetics and hair care products*
Formula 2	*cosmetics*
Hair's Daily Requirement	*hair care products*
Hi & Dri	*deodorants*
Hydra-Mat	*optical products*
Hydro-Minerali	*skin care products*
Intimate	*cosmetics*
Jontue	*fragrance*
Liquiprin	*analgesic*
Lumina	*cosmetics*
Milk Plus 6	*cosmetics*
Miss Balmain	*cosmetics*
Mitchum	*antiperspirant*
Monsieur Balmain	*men's fragrance*
Moon Drops	*cosmetics*
Natural Honey	*skin care products*
Natural Wonder	*cosmetics*
Natural Wonder Super Nails	*nail care products*
Nature's Remedy	*laxative*
Norell	*cosmetics*
NoSalt	*salt substitute*
One Solution	*optical products*
Orafix	*denture adhesive*
Oxy	*acne products*
Perfumatics 2000	*fragrance*
Polished Amber	*cosmetics*
Pretty Feet & Hands	*rough skin remover*
Princess Marcella Borghese	*cosmetics*
Realistic	*hair care products*
Revlon	*cosmetics*
Rocket	*optical products*
Roux	*hair color*
Scoundrel	*fragrance*
Skin Balancing Makeup	*cosmetics*
Soft Mate	*optical products*
Soquette	*optical products*
Terme de Montecatini	*skin care products*
Titan	*optical products*
Tums	*antacid*
Ultima II	*cosmetics*

R.J. Reynolds

Reynolds Blvd.
Winston-Salem, N.C. 27102
(919) 748-4000

Chief Executive Officer: J.P. Sticht
Exchange: NY
Symbol: RJR

Corporate History: The company, founded in 1875 and last incorporated in 1970, is one of the nation's largest manufacturers of cigarettes with 33% to the American market. For years its Camel brand was the most popular in the United States; in the 1920s almost half of the nation's smokers used that brand. In 1955 the company introduced the first filter cigarette—Winston. Lately, it has diversified into such fields as transportation, food and beverage products. It owns the largest vegetable and fruit packer in the United States (Del Monte) and sells more oriental food (Chung King) than any other vendor. Although almost one-half of its sales are outside the tobacco area, cigarettes account for 80% of its total profits.

Brandnames of Products and Services:

Apple	*tobacco products*
Apple Sun Cured	*tobacco products*
Brer Rabbit	*molasses*
Brown's Mule	*tobacco products*
Camel	*cigarettes*
Carter Hall	*tobacco products*
Chun King	*oriental food products*
College Inn	*food products*
Coronation	*specialty foods*

Davis	*baking powder*
Days Work	*tobacco products*
Del Monte	*food products*
Doral	*cigarettes*
George Washington	*tobacco products*
Granny Goose	*potato chips*
Hawaiian Punch	*fruit drinks*
Madeira	*tobacco products*
Milk-Mate	*chocolate-flavored milk enricher*
More	*cigarettes*
My T Fine	*pudding*
Now	*cigarettes*
Our Advertiser	*tobacco products*
Patio	*Mexican foods*
Prince Albert	*tobacco products*
Real	*cigarettes*
Reynolds' Natural Leaf	*tobacco products*
Salem	*cigarettes*
Sunkist	*products*
Swing	*beverage mix*
Tempo	*cigarettes*
Top	*tobacco products*
Vantage	*tobacco products*
Vermont Maid	*maple syrup*
Winchester	*little cigars*
Winston	*cigarettes*
Work Horse	*tobacco products*

Reynolds Metals Co.

6601 West Broad St.
Richmond, VA 23261
(804) 281-2000

Chief Executive Officer: D.P. Reynolds
1984 Annual Sales Volume: 3,728M
1984 Shares Outstanding: 21,557,739
Shareholders: 22,000
Exchange: NY
Symbol: RLM

Corporate History: Reynolds Metals Company was founded by R.S. Reynolds, Sr. in Louisville, Ky. in 1919. Originally called the U.S. Foil Company, the company began as a producer of lead and tin foil for cigarette packaging. Today, Reynolds is a major worldwide, vertically integrated aluminun manufacturer and the second-largest aluminum company in the U.S. Reynolds produces alumina; primary and reclaimed aluminum; aluminum sheet, plate and extrusions, and hundreds of finished products such as aluminum cans, flexible packaging, Reynolds Wrap household aluminum foil and other consumer products; building products; solar hot water heating systems, and electrical wire and cable.

Brandnames of Products and Services:

Diamond Foil	*aluminum foil*
Flex-Can Retortable Pouch	*food pouch*
Reynolds Freezer Paper	*freezer paper*
Reynolds Oven Cooking Bags	*oven cooking bags*
Reynolds Plastic Wrap	*plastic wrap*
Reynolds Redi-Pan Aluminum Foilware	*aluminum containers*
Reynolds Wrap Household Aluminum Foil	*aluminum foil*

Richardson-Vicks Inc.

10 Westport Rd.
Wilton, Conn. 06897
(203) 834-5000

Chief Executive Officer: Smith Richardson Jr.
1984 Annual Sales Volume: 1,280M
1984 Shares Outstanding: 23,285,145
Shareholders: 8,390
Exchange: NY
Symbol: RXM

Corporate History: The company was founded in 1828 and last incorporated in 1933 as Vick Chemical Inc. It adopted its present name in 1981. Its first product was Vicks VapoRub, designed to aid cold sufferers. During the 1930s it expanded the line to include nose drops and cough drops. Today the company is engaged primarily in the development, manufacturing and marketing of personal care products, including toiletries and hair care products, and health care products, including proprietary medicines. It also manufactures and sells laboratory and bulk chemicals, diagnostic instruments and reagents, wood care products, nutrition products and other products. The company's products are marketed in more than 100 countries.

Brandnames of Products and Services:

Bacimycin	*ointment*
Benzodent	*denture products*
Cepacol	*throat lozenges and mouthwash*
Clearasil	*skin medications*
Complete	*denture cleanser*

Demure	*douche*
Denquil	*toothpaste for sensitive teeth*
Fasteeth	*denture adhesive*
Fixodent	*denture adhesive*
Formby's	*wood care products*
Formula 44	*cough medicine*
Homer Formby's	*wood stain and finishes*
Kleenite	*denture product*
Kolantyl	*antacid*
Mill Creek	*hair and skin care products*
NyQuil	*cold medicine*
Oil of Olay	*skin moisturizers*
Oracin	*throat lozenges*
Percogesic	*analgesic tablets*
Plus	*health food products*
Saxon	*aftershave skin conditioner*
Sinex Tigers Milk	*nutritional supplement*
Tempo	*soft antacid tablets*
Thompson's Water Seal and Seal Stain	*waterproofing compounds*
Tiger's Milk	*nutrition boosters and nutrition care products*
Topex	*acne cleansing product*
Tri-Flow	*specialty lubricant*
Vaporub	*cough drops*
Va-tra-nol	*cough drops*
Vicks	*products*
Vidal Sassoon	*shampoos and hair products*

Richton Int'l Corp.

1345 Avenue of the Americas
New York, NY 10105
(212) 765-6480

Chief Executive Officer: Franc M. Ricciardi
1984 Annual Sales Volume: 35M
1984 Shares Outstanding: 1,826,373
Shareholders: 1,086
Exchange: OTC
Symbol: RIHL

Corporate History: Richton International Corp. is engaged in the design, manufacture and marketing of fashion jewelry and personal leather accessory products. In 1984 the company sold Richton Sportswear, Aspen Skiwear and Richton Headwear.

Brandnames of Products and Services:

Bond Street Ltd.	*accessories*
Coro	*jewelry*
Corocraft	*jewelry*
Dicini	*jewelry*
Marvella	*jewelry*
Oscar de la Renta	*accessories*
Pavanne	*jewelry*
Richton International Limited	*jewelry*
Vendome	*jewelry*

Riegel Textile Corp.

Green Gate Park, Suite 800
25 Woods Lake Rd.
Greenville, SC 29607
(803) 242-6050

Chief Executive Officer: R.E. Coleman
1984 Annual Sales Volume: 429M
1984 Shares Outstanding: 3,762,738
Shareholders: 2,764
Exchange: NY
Symbol: RTX

Corporate History: Riegel, incorporated in 1946, is a completely integrated textile manufacturing and selling organization. During the past five years the company and its subsidiaries have been engaged primarily in the manufacture and sale of textile mill products made primarily from cotton and synthetic fibers and in the manufacture and sale of convenience products made from wood pulp. Consumer products include infants clothing, accessories, disposable diapers and kitchen accessories. The company also manufactures apparel and upholstery fabrics for sale to garment and furniture manufacturers.

Brandnames of Products and Services:

Babycare	*knitwear and accessories*
Baby Comfort	*baby products*
Cabbage Patch Kids	*disposable diapers*
Homecare	*kitchen accessories*
Kitchen Mates	*kitchen accessories*
Mason	*athletic wear*
Nitey Nite	*baby products*
Rainbow Kitchen Center	*kitchen accessories*
Teddy Time	*cribs and infant products*

Rite Aid Corp.

Trindle Rd. and Railroad Ave.
Shiremanstown, PA 17011
(717) 761-2633

Chief Executive Officer: Alex Grass
1984 Annual Sales Volume: 1,223M
1984 Shares Outstanding: 41,252,882
Shareholders: 9,000
Exchange: NY
Symbol: RAD
Corporate History: The company was incorporated in 1968. Today it operates 1154 discount drugstores in 19 states. The company has three other divisions: Rack Rite Distributors, a rack jobber that supplies non-food products primarily to food markets; Sera-Tec Biologicals, a plasma and plasma products concern with nine plasmapheresis centers in the eastern United States; and a specialty retailing division encompassing Circus World Toys Stores, Inc., with 179 toy stores in regional malls, ADAP, Inc., a chain of 36 discount automotive parts outlets and Heaven, a small group of contemporary variety stores. In addition, Rite Aid holds a 46.8% interest in Super Rite Foods, Inc., a distributor of wholesale grocery products and a 28.2% stake in Superdrug Stores P.L.C., which owns a chain of health and beauty aid stores in Great Britain.
Brandnames of Products and Services:

ADAP Inc	*automotive supply chain*
Circus World Toy Stores	*toystore chain*
Heaven	*contemporary variety store chain*
Rite Aid	*health and beauty stores and products*

Rival Manufacturing Co.

36th St. & Bennington Ave.
Kansas City, MO 64129
(816) 861-1000

Chief Executive Officer: I.H. Miller
1984 Annual Sales Volume: 111M
1984 Shares Outstanding: 6,278,829
Shareholders: 3,688
Exchange: OTC
Symbol: RIVL
Corporate History: The company, incorporated in 1963, makes and sells portable household appliances. These include can openers, electric space heaters, ultrasonic humidifiers, food slicers, mixers, wafflers, and ice crushers.
Brandnames of Products and Services:

Corona	*ultrasonic humidifiers*
Rival	*kitchen appliances and accessories*
Titan	*heaters and humidifiers*

A.H. Robins Co. Inc

1407 Cummings Dr.
Richmond, VA 23220
(804) 257-2000

Chief Executive Officer: E. Claiborne Robins Jr.
1984 Annual Sales Volume: 632M
1984 Shares Outstanding: 25,037
Shareholders: 6,952
Exchange: NY
Symbol: RAH
Corporate History: A. H. Robins has been in continuous operation since 1866—the year Albert Hartley Robins opened a small apothecary and manufacturing chemist's shop in downtown Richmond, Virginia. Under the guidance of four generations of the Robins family, it has become a diversified multinational corporation doing business in more than 100 countries. The Company engages primarily in the manufacture and marketing of ethical pharmaceuticals and consumer products consisting principally of pharmaceuticals marketed directly to consumers, pet care products, health and beauty aids and perfumes. Nearly 350 scientists, physicians, and technicians are engaged in research and development activities. Research is conducted in the Company's principal product areas and in such fields as the central nervous system and cardiovascular, inflammatory, gastrointestinal and rheumatic diseases. R&D activity also extends to medical instrumentation, animal health and consumer products.
Brandnames of Products and Services:

Allbee	*vitamins*
Caron	*perfumes*
ChapStick	*lip balm*
Dimacol	*cold and cough capsules*
Dimatane	*antihistamine*
Dimetapp	*antihistamine/decongestant*
Dopram	*respiratory stimulant*
Micro-K Extencaps	*potassium supplement*
Phenaphen	*analgesic*
Robaxin	*muscle relaxant*
Robitussin	*cough syrups*

Sergeant's	*pet care products*
Z-BEC	*vitamins*

Ronco Teleproducts Inc.

1200 Arthur Ave.
Elk Grove Village, Ill. 60007
(312) 640-0700

Chief Executive Officer: R.M. Popeil
Exchange: AM
Symbol: RTI
Corporate History: The company, last incorporated in 1969, markets housewares and hardware, hobbycrafts, personal care, and entertainment products. It generally utilizes intensive spot television advertising.
Brandnames of Products and Services:

Auto Cup	*coffee in a cup*
Battery Tester	
Cellutrol	*soap massage*
Electric Egg Scrambler	
Food Dehydrator	
Miracle Broom	
Miracle Sander	
Mr. Dentist	*teeth care product*
Record Vacuum	*record cleaner*
Roller-Measure	*measuring devise*
Smokeless Ashtray	

Ronson Corp.

One Ronson Rd.
Bridgewater, NJ 08807
(201) 526-5900

Chief Executive Officer: Louis V. Aronson II
1984 Annual Sales Volume: 30M
1984 Shares Outstanding: 4,412,575
Shareholders: 9,770
Exchange: NY
Symbol: RON
Corporate History: The company incorporated in 1928 as Art Metal Works Inc. and adopted its present title in 1954. The company is principally engaged in the business of manufacturing, servicing and distributing in four areas: consumer products; rare earth and metal alloys; areospace, hydraulic and pneumatic components; helicopter and airplane operations and service.
Brandnames of Products and Services:

Kleenol	*spot remover*
Multi-Fill	*butane gas injector*
Multi-Lube	*penetrant spray lubricant*
Ronsonol	*lighter-fluids and flints and wicks for lighters*

Roper Corp.

1905 W. Court St.
Kankakee, IL 60901
(815) 937-6000

Chief Executive Officer: R.E. Cook
1984 Annual Sales Volume: 572M
1984 Shares Outstanding: 6,383,248
Shareholders: 2,005
Exchange: NY
Symbol: ROP
Corporate History: The company was founded in 1926 as Central Oil & Gas Co., changed its name to Florence Stove Co. in 1923 and to Geo. D. Roper Corp. in 1958. It adopted its current name in 1963. Roper makes kitchen appliances, outdoor power equipment and coated metal products. It is one of Sears, Roebuck & Co.'s major suppliers. In fiscal 1984, Sears accounted for 72% of Roper's net sales. Outdoor power equipment contributed 54% of the company's sales, with kitchen appliances and coated metal products making up the remainder.
Brandnames of Products and Services:

Craftsman	*lawn equipment*
Eastern	*lawn utility buildings*
IBG	*greenhouses*
Kenmore	*kitchen ovens and ranges*
Roper	*power lawn mowers and household appliances*
Rotary	*lawn mowers*

Rorer Group Inc.

500 Virginia Dr.
Ft. Washington, PA 19034
(215) 628-6541

Chief Executive Officer: John W. Eckman
1984 Annual Sales Volume: 522M
1984 Shares Outstanding: 21,374,727
Shareholders: 7,477
Exchange: NY
Symbol: ROR
Corporate History: Pharmacist William H. Rorer founded the company in 1910. Rorer Group Inc. was incorporated in 1968 under the name Rorer-Amchem

Inc. as a holding company for two major subsidiaries, William H. Rorer Inc. and Amchem Inc. In 1977, the name of the company was changed to Rorer Group Inc. The company is now engaged solely in the manufacture and sale of health care products. The business is divided into two major groups of products, pharmaceutical and surgical. The company markets its products in the United States and more than 70 foreign countries. In 1984, the company acquired the Pharbil Group, pharmaceutical firms in Belgium and the Netherlands.

Brandnames of Products and Services:

Ascriptin	*aspirin with maalox*
Ascription A/D	*pain reliever and anti-inflammatory*
Benzagel	*acne medication*
Camalox	*antacid*
Comfortine	*baby ointment*
Emetrol	*nausea medication*
Fedahist	*sinus medication*
Fermalox	*iron supplement*
Fomac Foam	*acne cleansing scrub*
Hytone	*acne medication*
Jeri	*bath lotion*
Maalox	*antacid*
Maalox Plus	*antacid*
Maalox Theraputic Concentrate	*antacid*
Nitrol	*angina treatment*
Parepectolin	*antidiarrheal drug product*
Perdiem	*laxative*
Shepard's	*hand cream*
Slo-bid	*asthma and emphysema medication*
Slo Phyllin	*asthma and allergy medication*
Vanoxide	*acne lotion*
Vetar	*shampoo*

Royal Crown Companies Inc.

41 Perimeter Center East, N.E.
Atlanta, Ga. 30346
(404) 394-6120

Chief Executive Officer:	D.A. McMahon
Exchange:	NY
Symbol:	RCC

Corporate History: The company was founded in 1905 and incorporated in 1928 as Nehi Corp. Its name was changed to Royal Crown Cola in 1959 and the present title adopted in 1978. The company which is the 5th largest factor in soft drink industry, makes soft drink beverages and concentrates. It also produces home decorative accessories, and operates a fast-food restaurant chain. In 1980 soft drinks accounted for half of the company's sales with the remainder evenly distributed between, home decorating products, citrus juices, and fast-food operations.

Brandnames of Products and Services:

Adams	*citrus juices*
Arby's Roast Beef	*restaurants*
Athens	*furniture*
Couroc	*serving trays*
Diet Rite Cola	*carbonated*
Frederick Cooper	*lamps*
Hoyne	*mirror tiles*
National	*home accessories*
Nehi	*carbonated beverages and beverage flavorings*
Par-T-Pak	*beverages*
RC Cola	*carbonated beverage*
RC-100	*sugar free cola*
Texsun	*citrus juices*
Tyndale	*home accessories*

Rubbermaid Inc.

1147 Akron Rd.
Wooster, Ohio 44691
(216) 264-6464

Chief Executive Officer:	S.C. Gault
1984 Annual Sales Volume:	566.4M
1984 Shares Outstanding:	16,941,232
Shareholders:	4,400
Exchange:	NY
Symbol:	RBD

Corporate History: The company incorporated in 1920 as Wooster Rubber Co. and adopted its present title in 1957. It makes and distributes rubber and plastic products for the home. Products are sold in retail stores and through the party plan to consumers. Over the years, the company has expanded its product line from the original housewares offerings into other markets such as the home horticulture, decorative coverings, microwave cookware, food service, health care, sanitary maintenance, office, and industrial markets. In 1984, it acquired Little Tikes, Inc. a manufacturer and marketer of high quality plastic toys for infants and preschool cildren.

Brandnames of Products and Services:

Con-Tact	*self-adhesive decorative coverings*
Cookables	*microwave cookware*
Heatables	*cookware*

Little Tikes	*toys*
Rubbermaid	*household products and kitchen accessories*
Servin' Saver	*food storage containers*
Smooth 'n Easy	*shelf liner*

Russell Corp.

P.O. Box 272
Alexander City, AL 35010
(205) 234-4251

Chief Executive Officer: Eugene C. Gwaltney
1984 Annual Sales Volume: 353M
1984 Shares Outstanding: 19,747,292
Shareholders: 11,500
Exchange: AMEX
Symbol: RML
Corporate History: The company incorporated in 1902 as Russell Mfg. Co. and adopted its present name in 1973. It makes athletic clothing, sportswear, knit apparel and woven fabrics. In 1984 approximately 85% of sales were from apparel, 15% from woven fabrics.
Brandnames of Products and Services:

Russell	*custom sports attire*
Sportswear	*sports apparel*

Russell Stover Candies Inc.

1104 Baltimore Ave.
Kansas City, Mo. 64105
(816) 842-9240

Chief Executive Officer: L.L. Ward
Exchange: OTC
Symbol: RUSS
Corporate History: The company incorporated in 1960 as Ward-Muffin Corp. and adopted its present name in the same year. It is one of the nation's biggest candy companies.
Brandnames of Products and Services:

Mrs. Stover's	*candies*
Russell Stover	*candies*

Russ Togs Inc.

1411 Broadway
New York, NY 10018
(212) 354-0700

Chief Executive Officer: Eli L. Rousso
1984 Annual Sales Volume: 251M
1984 Shares Outstanding: 5,121,000
Shareholders: 3,700
Exchange: NY
Symbol: RTS
Corporate History: The company, incorporated in 1946, makes and sells sportswear and dresses for ladies, misses, children, pre-teens and juniors, as well as shirts, sweaters and active sportswear for men and boys. They are sold by department stores, chain stores and specialty shops throughout the United States.
Brandnames of Products and Services:

Brut	*apparel*
Christie Brinkley	*women's apparel*
Composites	*apparel*
Crazy Horse	*women's apparel*
Crazy Horse Girl	*girl's apparel*
Crazy Horse Teen	*girl's apparel*
Kelli Kaye	*women's dresses*
Lady Laura	*half-size dresses*
Monika Tilley for Christie Brinkley	*swim and beachwear*
Ms. Russ	*women's apparel*
New Attitude	*apparel*
R & M Kaufman	*women's apparel*
Rawlings	*apparel*
Russ	*missy sportswear*
Russ Girl	*children's sportswear*
Russie	*apparel*
Russ Petites	*women's apparel*
Russ Teen	*girl's apparel*
Russ Togs	*apparel*
Sutton	*shirts*
Toni Petite	*women's apparel*
Toni Todd	*women's dresses*
Ursula Gogel	*women's apparel*
Vicky Vaughn	*junior dresses*

Rusty Pelican Restaurants, Inc.

2862 McGaw Ave.
Irvine, CA 92714
(714) 660-9011

Chief Executive Officer: Louis A. Siracusa
1984 Annual Sales Volume: 36M
1984 Shares Outstanding: 2,275,400
Shareholders: 334
Exchange: OTC
Symbol: RSTY
Corporate History: Founded in 1965 as Ancient Mariner restaurants, Rusty Pelican Restaurants became a public corporation in 1983. It operates a chain of 19 seafood restaurants in seven states — Arizona, California, Illinois, Missouri, Oregon, Texas, Washington.
Brandnames of Products and Services:

Rusty Pelican Restaurants	*seafood restaurants*

Safeway Stores Inc.

4th & Jackson Sts
Oakland, CA 94660
(415) 891-3000

Chief Executive Officer: Peter A. Magowan
1984 Annual Sales Volume: 19,642M
1984 Shares Outstanding: 59,931,664
Shareholders: 47,053
Exchange: NY
Symbol: SA
Corporate History: Safeway was incorporated in 1926. The original company was established in Los Angeles in 1915 with four stores. Today it operates 2,571 supermarkets, including 100 "Food Barn" warehouse type food stores and 98"Liquor Barn" discount liquor stores. The "Liquor Barn" stores are located in California and Arizona. Overall stores locations are as follows: 2,012 in the United States, 291 in Canada, 110 in the United Kingdom, 123 in Australia, and 35 in West Germany. In support of its retail operations the company operates 95 manufacturing and processing facilities, including 21 fluid milk plants, 17 bakeries, 17 ice cream plants, 5 soft drink bottling plants, 5 meat processing plants, 5 egg candling plants, 4 fruit and vegetable processing plants, 2 jam and jelly plants, 2 household chemicals plants and 17 other manufacturing and processing plants. At year-end 1984 there were also 363 full-service pharmacies in Safeway Supermarkets.

Brandnames of Products and Services:

Airway	*instant coffee*
Amigo Hermanos	*wines*
Band Box	*ice cream products*
Barossa Valley	*wines*
Bel-Air	*fruit bars*
Best Buy	*cheese products*
Blossom Time	*food products*
Bowling Green	*bourbon*
Breeze	*cheese products*
Brocade	*air fresheners and disinfectants*
Brown Derby	*beer*
Busy Baker	*cookies and crackers*
Canadian Hill	*whiskey*
Candi Cane	*sugar*
Canterbury	*tea*
Captain's Choice	*seafood products*
Coldbrook	*margarine*
Cotillion	*ice cream products*
Country Pure peanut butter and condiments	
Covered Wagon	*pancake mix and cornmeal*
Cragmont	*soft drinks*
Crown Colony	*spices and extracts*
Dairy Glen	*butter*
Dairyland	*milk products*
Dalewood	*margarine*
Dom Brau	*beer*
Dorothy Duncan	*cake*
Edwards	*coffee*
El Grande	*flour*
Empress	*condiments*
Enchanted Isle	*canned fruit*
Evergreen	*brooms*
Fidelis	*brandy*
Fluf-Puft	*marshmallows*
Frydenlund	*beer*
Gardenside	*canned fruit and vegetables*
Highway	*canned fruits and vegetables*
Jell-Well	*pie fillings and puddings*
Joyett	*imitation ice cream products*
Karl Manheim	*wine*
Kat Nip	*pet food*
Kavlana	*vodka*
Kitchen Craft	*paper products*
Lalani	*drinks*
La Mesa	*wine*
Lucerne	*dairy products*
Maison Blanc	*sparkling wine*
Marigold	*household paper products*

McNairs	*Scotch*
Melrose	*cookies and crackers*
Mountain Castle	*wine*
Mrs. Wright's	*bakery products*
Nob Hill	*coffee*
Nu-Made	*convenience foods*
Old Calhoun	*bourbon*
Ovenjoy	*bakery products*
Pack Train	*syrup*
Padre	*beer*
Par	*cleaning products*
Parade	*cleaning products*
Par No Phosphate Detergent	
Party Pride	*ice cream products and snack food*
Penedro Rose Wine	
Peralta	*wine*
Piedmont	*condiments*
Pooch	*dry pet food*
Prince Paul	*canned fish*
Rock Brook	*bourbon*
Royal Satin	*shortening*
Safeway	*grocery products*
Scotch Treat	*frozen vegetables and fruit*
Sea Trader	*canned fish*
Shady Lane	*butter*
Shasta	*beverages*
Skylark	*breads and rolls*
Sleepy Hollow	*syrup*
Smok-A-Roma	*meat products*
Snow Star	*ice cream products*
Snowy Peak	*soft drinks*
Stantons	*gin*
St. Elmo	*rum*
Sterling	*lunch meats*
Sunnybank	*margarine*
Su-Purb	*spray cleaner and detergent*
Tartan Royal	*Scotch*
Toranto	*olive oil*
Town House	*canned foods*
Trophy	*charcoal briquets*
Trophy	*frozen and canned foods*
Truly Fine	*toilet tissue*
Velkay	*shortening*
Verdi	*Italian dry salami*
Westag	*vanilla*
White Magic	*cleaning products*
Yamato	*wines and sake*

Saga Corp.

One Saga Lane
Menlo Park, Calif. 94025
(415) 854-5150

Chief Executive Officer:	CA Lynch
1984 Annual Sales Volume:	1,130M
1984 Shares Outstanding:	12,956
Shareholders:	3,328
Exchange:	NY
Symbol:	SGA

Corporate History: Saga Corporation owns and operates four restaurant businesses, owns and franchises three fast-service restaurant chains, and provides contract foodservice management to corporations, colleges and hospitals throughout the United States and Canada. Saga began as a partnership in education contract foodservice between Harry W. Anderson, W.P. Laughlin and William P. Scandling. The three, seniors at Hobart College in Geneva, N.Y., took over the college's unprofitable dining hall and served their first meal in 1948. Saga was incorporated in 1949, and over the years it expanded its educational foodservice operations across the country. In 1962, corporate headquarters were moved from New York to California. Saga established a division to provide contract foodservice in the health-care industry in 1963. The company made its initial public offering of stock in 1968. In 1969, Saga entered the corporate foodservice market by acquiring Harding-Williams Corporation, and it acquired two California pizza companies to form Straw Hat Pizza. In 1971, Saga acquired the Velvet Turtle restaurant chain, and the next year it purchased Stuart Anderson's Black Angus restaurants. In 1983, Saga established a division to operate restaurants and foodservice in hotels. That same year it acquired Grandy's. The next year Saga purchased Spectrum Foods Inc. of San Francisco, which operates eight specialty restaurants in California.

Brandnames of Products and Services:

Grandy's	*restaurants*
Spoons	*restaurants*
Straw Hat Pizza	*restaurants*
Stuart Anderson's Black Angus/ Cattle Company	*restaurants*
The Velvet Turtle	*restaurants*

Salant Corp.

330 Fifth Ave.
New York, N.Y. 10001
(212) 971-9600

Chief Executive Officer: G.H. Herman
Exchange: NY
Symbol: SLT
Corporate History: The company incorporated in 1919 as Salant & Salant Inc. and adopted its present title in 1971. It makes men's, women's and children's apparel.
Brandnames of Products and Services:

Funny Girl	*junior and misses jeans*
Lady Thomson	*apparel*
Mr. Leggs	*junior and misses jeans*
Thomson	*slacks*

Savannah Foods & Industries Inc.

P.O. Box 339
Savannah, GA 31402
(912) 234-1261

Chief Executive Officer: W.W. Sprague
1984 Annual Sales Volume: 591M
1984 Shares Outstanding: 3,378,351
Shareholders: 2,768
Exchange: OTC
Symbol: SVAN
Corporate History: The company was founded in 1916 and last incorporated in 1969 as Savannah Industries. It adopted its present name in 1970 upon merger with the Savannah Sugar Refining Corp. Savannah makes sugar and pet food products. During 1984 the company acquired Michigan Sugar Company which is now a wholly owned subsidiary.
Brandnames of Products and Services:

Bonnie	*pet food*
Dixie Crystals	*sugar*
Everglades	*sugar*
Golden Choice	*pet food*
Pard	*pet food*
Splash	*pet food*
Sportmix	*pet food*
Wells	*pet food*

Savin Corp.

9 West Broad St.
Stamford, CT 06904-2270
(203) 967-5000

Chief Executive Officer: E. Paul Charlap
1984 Annual Sales Volume: 278M
1984 Shares Outstanding: 19,784,450
Shareholders: 8,839
Exchange: NY
Symbol: SVB
Corporate History: The company, organized in 1978, is the successor by merger to Savin Business Machines Corp. organized in 1959. The company markets office equipment, consisting primarily of plain paper copiers and related supplies. These copiers are designed for low and mid-volume users and are manufactured for the company by Ricoh Company, Ltd., a Japanese corporation. The company is currently conducting field and reliability testing on a new high-volume liquid ink copier/duplicator which it plans to manufacture and assemble in its own facilities.
Brandnames of Products and Services:

Savin	*business copying machines*

Saxon Industries Inc.

1230 Avenue of the Americas
New York, N.Y. 10020
(212) 246-9500

Chief Executive Officer: S. Lurie
Exchange: NY
Symbol: SXP
Corporate History: The company was incorporated in 1924 as Saxon Paper Corp., and adopted its present name in 1975. In 1979, 75% of its sales came from paper and paper products; the remainder from business and specialty products.
Brandnames of Products and Services:

Fonda	*paper tableware*
Hoyle	*playing cards and calendars*
Royalcraft	*home paper products (doilies, placemats, shelf lining)*
Saxon	*photocopiers*
Stancraft	*playing cards, games, clocks, gifts, calendars*

F. & M. Schaefer Corp.

3 Park Ave.
New York, N.Y. 10016
(212) 561-6600

Chief Executive Officer: W.J. Schoen
Exchange: NY
Corporate History: The company was founded in 1842 and incorporated in 1878. This regional brewer, whose market is primarily in the East, is the eleventh largest in the United States. Recently, Schaefer's profits have been declining, and in 1980 Stroh Brewery Co., a privately held Detroit brewer, proposed acquiring the remaining common shares.
Brandnames of Products and Services:

Gunther	*beer*
Piels	*beer*
Schaefer	*beer*
Schaefer Bock Beer	
Schaefer Cream Ale	

Schering-Plough Corp.

One Giralda Farms
Madison, NJ 07940-1000
(201) 822-7000

Chief Executive Officer: Robert P. Luciano
1984 Annual Sales Volume: 1,874M
1984 Shares Outstanding: 50,600,000
Shareholders: 31,200
Exchange: NY
Symbol: SGP
Corporate History: Schering-Plough Corporation was formed in 1971 by the merger of Schering Corporation U.S.A., an international research-based pharmaceutical company founded in the United States in 1929, and Plough, Inc., a major mass merchandiser of widely known consumer products, begun in 1902. Today, Schering-Plough is a worldwide company primarily engaged in the discovery, development, manufacturing and marketing of pharmaceutical and consumer products. Pharmaceuticals include prescription and over-the-counter drugs, animal health and vision care products promoted to the medical and allied professions. The consumer products group consists of proprietary medicines, toiletries, cosmetics and foot care products marketed directly to the public. In consumer products, Maybelline is the leading cosmetics line in the U.S. in both unit and dollar volume. Its sun care products, led by the Coppertone brand, account for over half of the U.S. market. In 1984, ethical pharmaceutical products accounted for 56% of sales and consumer products 44%. Foreign operations comprised 43% of sales.
Brandnames of Products and Services:

A & D	*ointment*
Afrin	*nasal spray*
Aftute	*antifungal cream*
Artra	*skin cream*
Aspergum	*chewing gum and aspirin*
Brush 'n Blush	*cosmetics*
Chlor-Trimeton	*cold allergy medicine*
Cod Liver Oil	
Coppertone	*suntan lotion*
Coricidin	*cold relief medicine*
Correctol	*laxative*
Cushion Grip	*denture adhesive*
Di-Gel	*antacid*
Drixoral	*cold preparation*
Duration	*nasal decongestant*
Emko	*contraceptive foam*
Feen-A-Mint	*laxative*
Fresh & Lovely	*cosmetics*
Gloss-8	*cream*
Maybelline	*cosmetics*
Mexsana	*medicated powder*
Moisture Whip	*cosmetics*
Moroline	*petroleum jelly*
Musterole	*cream*
Nail Color	*cosmetics*
OP	*tanning lotion*
Paas	*Easter egg coloring kit*
PAAS	*Easter basket stuffers*
PAAS	*Halloween make-up*
Pro-Comfort	*sports medicine products*
Quick Tan (Q.T.)	*tanning lotion*
Ril-Sweet	*liquid sweetener*
Saraka	*laxative*
Sardo	*bath oil*
Sardoettes	*bath oil*
Scholl	*foot care products and sandals*
Shade	*sunscreen*
Showtime	*cosmetics*
Smooth Touch	*dipilatory*
Solarcaine	*sunburn spray*
St. Joseph	*children's medications*
Sudden Tan	*tanning lotion*
Sulfur-8	*shampoo*
Tinactin	*athlete's foot medication*
Tropical Blend	*tanning lotion*
Zemo	*ointment*

Joseph Schlitz Brewing Co.

235 W. Galenast
Milwaukee, Wisc. 53212
(414) 224-5000

Chief Executive Officer: F.J. Sellinger
Exchange: NY
Symbol: SLZ
Corporate History: Schlitz was founded in 1849 and incorporated in 1920. The company produces beer, and for a time during the 1950's, was the nation's number one brewer. Now it is in third place, behind Budweiser and Miller. The company also is involved in promoting wine consumption and is beginning a major distribution of white wines and wines in a can.
Brandnames of Products and Services:

Erlanger	*beer*
Geyser Peak	*wine*
Old Milwaukee	*beer*
Primo	*beer*
Schlitz	*beer*
Schlitz Light	*beer*
Schlitz Malt Liquor	
Tribute	*light beer*

Scholastic Inc.

730 Broadway
New York, NY 10003
(212) 505-3000

Chief Executive Officer: Richard Robinson
1984 Annual Sales Volume: $157.5M
1984 Shares Outstanding: 1,753,749
Shareholders: 812
Exchange: OTC
Symbol: SCHL
Corporate History: Scholastic Inc. was founded in 1920. Scholastic is principally engaged in the development of innovative learning materials in a variety of media that supplement the formal textbook and teaching materials used by schools. The company publishes three broad categories of educational materials - magazines, books and computer software. These products are distributed through schools, through trade distribution channels for retail sale and by direct mail to the home. Scholastic's wholly owned foreign subsidiaries publish children's books, periodicals, and supplementary text materials, which are distributed through schools, trade distribution channels, and by mail to the home in Australia, Canada, New Zealand and the United Kingdom. The company's wholly owned subsidiary, Scholastic Productions, Inc., is engaged in the production and distribution of family-oriented domestic and international broadcast and cable television programming.
Brandnames of Products and Services:

Bank Street Writer	*word processing program*
Blue Ribbon	*books*
Coach	*magazines*
Electronic Learning	*magazines*
Family Computing	*magazines*
Forecast	*magazines*
Get Along Gang	*books*
K-Power	*magazine*
Microzine	*children's magazine on a disk*
Reader's Choice Catalog	*children's books*
Teaching and Computers	*magazine*

Abe Schrader Corp.

530 Seventh Ave.
New York, N.Y. 10001
(212) 840-7733

Chief Executive Officer: M.J. Schrader
Exchange: AM
Symbol: AMS
Corporate History: Incorporated in 1968, Schrader makes various types of women's medium to higher priced apparel.
Brandnames of Products and Services:

Abe Schrader	*women's apparel*
Schrader Sport	*women's apparel*
Stephen Casuals	*women's apparel*
Trigere Sport	*coats*

SCM Corp.

299 Park Ave.
New York, NY 10171-0161
(212) 752-2700

Chief Executive Officer: Paul H. Elicker
1984 Annual Sales Volume: 1,963M
1984 Shares Outstanding: 9,834,856
Shareholders: 24,900
Exchange: NY
Symbol: SCM
Corporate History: The company was incorporated in 1924 as L.C. Smith & Bros. Typewriter Co., succeeding a company organized in 1803. Its name was changed to

Smith-Corona Inc. in 1953, to Smith-Corona Marchant Inc. in 1958 and to its present title in 1962. Today the operations of SCM Corporation are grouped into five segments: chemicals, coatings and resins, paper products, foods and typewriters. In 1984 chemicals accounted for approximately 18.4% of sales; coatings and resins, 33.4%; food, 20%; paper 17.9% and typewriters, 10.1%. The company bolstered its titanium dioxide business with the acquisition of a titanium dioxide plant at Ashtabula, Ohio.

Brandnames of Products and Services:

Cris & Pitt's	*condiments*
Durkee	*condiments*
Frank's	*condiments*
Glidden	*coatings and paints*
Lecroy	*condiments*
Mister Mustard	*condiment*
M.W. Smith Lumber Co.	*wholesale and retail lumber*
O & C	*condiments*
SCM	*supplies for office copiers*
Smith-Corona	*typewriters and ribbon cartridges*
Snow Crest	*foods, frozen foods*
Spred	*paints and coatings*
Spred Satin	*paints and coatings*

SCOA Industries Inc.

33 N. High St.
Columbus, OH 43215
(614) 221-7262

Chief Executive Officer:	H.H. Schiff
1984 Annual Sales Volume:	1,424M
1984 Shares Outstanding:	17,111,128
Shareholders:	5,015
Exchange:	NY
Symbol:	SOA

Corporate History: The company, last incorporated in 1969, is engaged in general merchandising and footwear retailing. Hills Department Stores, operator of 123 discount department stores in the mid-central states, is the company's largest division, accounting for most of the company's sales.

Brandnames of Products and Services:

By-Way Shoe Stores	*shoe stores*
Dry Goods	*off-price apparel stores*
GallenKamp	*shoe stores*
Hills	*discount department stores*
Scats	*athletic shoes*

Scot Lad Foods Inc.

One Scot Lad Lane
Lansing, Ill. 60438
(312) 895-2300

Chief Executive Officer:	J.J. Lickteig
Exchange:	NY
Symbol:	SLF

Corporate History: The company incorporated in 1961 as Roy Miner Corp. and adopted its present title the same year. It engages in the processing and wholesale and retail distribution of food and non-food products. Its operations are primarily in the Midwest.

Brandnames of Products and Services:

Bonnie	*bakery products*
Queen of Scot	*food products*
Scot Farms	*food products*
Scot Lad	*food products*
Scott	*drugstores*

Scott & Fetzer Co.

28800 Clemens Rd.
Westlake, OH 44145
(216) 892-3000

Chief Executive Officer:	Ralph Schey
1984 Annual Sales Volume:	695M
1984 Shares Outstanding:	6,640,106
Shareholders:	4,718
Exchange:	NY
Symbol:	SFZ

Corporate History: The company was founded in 1914, incorporated in 1917 as Scott & Fetzer Machine Co. and adopted its present title in 1919. It makes cleaning systems, household products and educational items.

Brandnames of Products and Services:

Childcraft	*children's publishing house*
Jason	*scissors*
Kirby	*vacuum cleaners*
Quikcut	*cutlery*
Science Year	*publications*
United Consumer	*financial services*
Wayne	*home equipment*
World Book	*encyclopedias and dictionaries*
Year Book	*publications*

Scott Paper Co.

Scott Plaza
Philadelphia, PA 19113
(215) 522-5000

Chief Executive Officer: Philip E. Lippincott
1984 Annual Sales Volume: 2,847M
1984 Shares Outstanding: 48,251,082
Shareholders: 55,900
Exchange: NY
Symbol: SPP

Corporate History: Scott Paper Co. incorporated in 1922 as a consolidation of Scott Paper Co. and Chester Paper Co. It makes a variety of packaged paper products. The company's consolidated operations are in the paper, pulp and forest products business and are reported in three segments: (1) sanitary paper products, which includes a broad range of trademarked sanitary paper products, as well as nonwoven products and personal cleansing products and systems; (2) printing and publishing papers, which includes printing, publishing and specialty papers; and (3) pulp, forest products and minerals, which includes pulp and forest products sold to unaffiliated customers, and the Company's mineral activities. Scott is a leader in sanitary tissue paper products with 16% of the worldwide market.

Brandnames of Products and Services:

American	*placemats, tray covers*
Andrex	*toilet tissue*
Baby Fresh Wipes	*child care products*
Confidents	*sanitary napkins*
Cottonelle	*toilet tissue*
Cut Rite	*wax paper*
Family Scott	*household paper products*
Fiesta	*paper towels*
Job Squad	*paper towels*
Lady Scott	*toilet tissue*
Paper Fresh	*wipes*
Purex	*toilet tissue*
Scott	*household paper products*
Scott Family	*napkins*
Scotties	*household paper products*
ScotTissue	*toilet tissue*
ScotTowels	*paper towels*
ScotTowels Junior	*paper towels*
Soft 'n Pretty	*toilet tissue*
Soft Weve	*toilet tissue*
Viva	*paper towels, napkins*
Waldorf	*toilet tissue*
Wash A-bye Baby	*child care products*

Scovill Inc.

500 Chase Pkwy.
Waterbury, CT 06708
(203) 757-6061

Chief Executive Officer: William F. Andrews
1984 Annual Sales Volume: 825M
1984 Shares Outstanding: 12,280,818
Shareholders: 9,577
Exchange: NY
Symbol: SCO

Corporate History: Scovill was founded during the 19th century as a button manufacturer and producer of brass for notions. It was incorporated in 1881 as the successor to a business which had been in operation since 1802. During the 1960s Scovill began diversifying. Today the company manufactures built-in housing products, kitchen electrical appliances, sewing notions, hardware, pneumatic control products and automotive parts.

Brandnames of Products and Services:

Ajax	*cabinet hardware*
Artolier	*lighting fixtures*
Clinton	*sewing notions*
Dominion	*electric housewares*
Dritz	*sewing notions*
Gripper	*snap fasteners*
Hall Mack	*bathroom accessories*
Hamilton Beach	*electric housewares*
Hero	*knitting needles*
Lightcraft	*lighting fixtures*
Markel	*electric heaters*
Mirage	*zippers and sewing notions*
Norton	*locks*
NuTone	*household appliances*
Nyguard	*sewing notions*
Scovill	*sewing notions*
Sportsmap	*snap fasteners*
Staylastic/Smith	*tapes and sewing accessories*
Sterling	*lighting fixtures*
Whippersnap	*snap fasteners*
Yale	*locks*

Seagram Co. Ltd.

1430 Peel St.
Montreal, Quebec Canada H3A 1S9
(514) 849-5271

Chief Executive Officer: Edgar M. Bronfman
1984 Annual Sales Volume: 2,821M

1984 Shares Outstanding: 90,896,522
Shareholders: 14,350
Exchange: NY
Symbol: VO

Corporate History: The company was incorporated in 1928 as a holding company to acquire the stocks of Distillers Corp. Ltd. and Joseph E. Seagram & Sons Ltd. Its name was changed from Distillers Corp. Seagrams Ltd. to Seagram Co. Ltd. in 1975. The firm is the world's largest producer and vendor of distilled spirits and wines with affiliates in 27 countries. It produces or markets 190 brands of distilled spirits and 600 brands of wines, champagnes, sherries and port. Following the 1980 sale of the company's United States oil and gas properties, Seagram obtained 20.2% of the outstanding shares of the E.I. Dupont de Nemours and Company. Further acquisition of common shares of DuPont has brought Seagram's percentage to 22.5%. Recent acquisitions include the distribution network of Matheus M[illegible]uer in Germany and the retail chains of Gough Brothers and Oddbins in the United Kingdom.

Brandnames of Products and Services:

100 Pipers	*Scotch*
Adam's Antique Canadian Whiskies	*whiskey*
Barton & Guestier (B & G)	*wines*
Benchmark	*bourbon*
Bersano	*spirits*
Boodles	*gins*
Burnett's	*vodka*
Cacique	*rum*
Calvert Extra	*whiskey*
Captain Morgan	*rum*
Carstairs	*bourbon*
Chateau de La Chaize	*wines*
Chivas Regal	*Scotch*
Christian Brothers	*wines and brandies*
Crown Royal Canadian	*whiskey*
Crown Russe	*vodka*
Four Roses	*whiskey*
Frank Schoonmaker	*spirits*
Glen Grant Single Malt	
Glenlivet	*Scotch*
Gold Seal	*wines and brandies*
Grauado	*rum*
Harwood Canadian	*whiskey*
James Fox	*Canadian whiskey*
Jameson	*Irish whiskey*
Kaiser	*wines*
Kessler	*whiskey*
Kijafa	*wines*
Leroux	*brandies and liqueurs*
Lochan Ora	*liqueur*
Logan Deluxe	*whiskey*
Lord Calvert	*Canadian whiskey*
Mattingly & Moore	*bourbon*
Mumm	*champagne*
Myers	*Jamaican rum*
Nectarose	*wines*
Nikolai	*vodka*
Olmeca	*tequilla*
Palo Viejo	*Puerto Rican rum*
Party Tyme	*bar products*
Pasha	*liqueur*
Passport	*Scotch*
Paul Masson	*wine and brandies*
Premium	*bourbon*
Queen Anne	*Scotch*
Ricasoli	*spirits*
Ronrico	*rum*
Royal Salute 21	*Scotch*
Sandeman Ports and Sherries	*Port, sherry*
Seagram's V.O.	*Canadian whiskey*
Seagram's 7 Crown	*whiskey*
Something Special	*Scotch*
Vandermint	*liqueur*
White Horse	*whiskey*
Wolfschmidt	*vodka*

G.D. Searle & Co.

P.O. Box 1045
Skokie, IL 60076
(312) 982-7000

Chief Executive Officer: Donald Rumsfeld
1984 Annual Sales Volume: 1,246M
1984 Shares Outstanding: 49,600,000
Shareholders: 18,300
Exchange: NY
Symbol: SRL

Corporate History: The corporation now known as G.D. Searle and Co., was initially established in Omaha, Nebraska in 1888. Searle is a research-based company which markets products in 126 countries. The company has 26 manufacturing operations in 14 countries. Products include prescription pharmaceuticals and NutraSweet and consumer products. NutraSweet is

Searle's brandname for the low-calorie sweetener aspartame.

Brandnames of Products and Services:

Dramamine	*motion sickness drug*
Equal	*low calorie tabletop sweetener*
Icy Hot	*pain-relieving ointment*
Metamucil	*laxative*
NutraSweet	*low-calorie sweetening ingredient*

Sears, Roebuck & Co.

Sears Tower
Chicago, IL 60684
(312) 875-2500

Chief Executive Officer:	Edward R. Telling
1984 Annual Sales Volume:	38,828M
1984 Shares Outstanding:	361,895,969
Shareholders:	340,831
Exchange:	NY
Symbol:	S

Corporate History: Sears was founded in 1886 as the R.W. Sears Watch Co., a retailer of timepieces. It gradually expanded first into jewelry and then into general mail order merchandising. Most of its customers were located in the rural Midwest. Today the company is the nation's largest retailer of general merchandise with 798 stores in all 50 states. A large portion of Sears' business comes from Allstate, the nation's second largest insurer of homes and cars; the company also operates the Dean Witter Financial Services Group and the Caldwell Banker Real Estate Group. Sears has substantial investment in numerous companies that supply its goods. The stores carry only their own brands, which Sears buys from 12,000 suppliers.

Brandnames of Products and Services:

Allstate	*insurance*
Caldwell Banker Real Estate Group	
Cling Alon	*leotards*
Courier	*luggage*
Craftsmen	*tools*
Dashmate	*car radio*
Dean Witter Financial Services Group	
Die Hard	*batteries*
Easy Living	*paint*
Endurables	*hosiery*
Forecast	*luggage*
Free Spirit	*bicycles*
Heat Screen	*firescreen*
Hillary	*outdoor equipment*
Homart	*furnaces*
Junior Bazaar	*junior clothing*
Kenmore	*home appliances*
Muzzler	*mufflers*
Pak-A-Potti	*portable toilets*
Ready Stick	*floor tiles*
Sears, Roebuck	*department stores*
Thumsup	*jeans*
Toughskins	*jeans*
Video Arcade	*video games*
Weatherbeater	*paint*
Winnie-the-Pooh	*children's apparel*

Seaway Food Town Inc.

1020 Ford St.
Maumee, OH 43537
(419) 893-9401

Chief Executive Officer:	Wallace D. Iott
1984 Annual Sales Volume:	468M
1984 Shares Outstanding:	1,944,849
Shareholders:	1,199
Exchange:	OTC
Symbol:	SEWY

Corporate History: The company, incorporated in 1957, operates a chain of 73 supermarkets in Ohio and Michigan.

Brandnames of Products and Services:

Food Town	*supermarkets*
Kash 'n Karry	*supermarkets*

Seligman & Latz Inc.

1133 Avenue of the Americas
New York, NY 10036
(212) 382-7400

Chief Executive Officer:	J.S. Kubie
1984 Annual Sales Volume:	342M
1984 Shares Outstanding:	2,177,624
Shareholders:	1,279
Exchange:	NY
Symbol:	SAL

Corporate History: The company, a successor to a business founded in 1911, leases and operates beauty salons and fine jewelry departments in department and specialty stores belonging to more than 100 leading department and specialty store organizations.

Brandnames of Products and Services:

Adrien Arpel	*cosmetics*
Directories	*hair care products and shampoos*
SLJ	*watches*

Service Merchandise Co. Inc.

P.O. Box 24600
Nashville, TN 37202
(615) 366-3300

Chief Executive Officer: Raymond Zimmerman
1984 Annual Sales Volume: 1,657M
1984 Shares Outstanding: 33,229,178
Shareholders: 6,199
Exchange: OTC
Symbol: SMCH
Corporate History: The company, incorporated in 1970, is a catalog showroom merchandising firm. Today the company operates a total of 183 catalog showrooms in 35 states. The company sells jewelry, diamonds, and nationally advertised brand-name hardgoods merchandise which include housewares, small appliances, silverware, luggage, cameras, radios, televisions, home electronics, toys, sporting goods and home and garden equipment.
Brandnames of Products and Services:
Service Merchandise Catalog Showrooms

SFN Co.

1900 East Lake Ave.
Glenview, Ill. 60025
(312) 729-3000

Chief Executive Officer: G.R. Hjalmarson
Exchange: NY
Symbol: SFZ
Corporate History: SFN incorporated in 1969 as Delaware Scott Foresman & Co. It publishes textbooks as well as fiction and nonfiction trade books. The company has just entered two new areas, electronic publishing and direct mail of special instructional materials.
Brandnames of Products and Services:

Fleming H. Revell	*publishing house*
Lothrop, Lee & Shepard	*publishing house*
Southwestern	*publishing house*
University Park Press	*publishing house*
William Morrow & Co.	*publishing house*

Shaklee Corp.

444 Market St.
San Francisco, CA 94111
(415) 954-3000

Chief Executive Officer: J.G. Shansby
1984 Annual Sales Volume: 459M
1984 Shares Outstanding: 12,872,000
Shareholders: 13,200
Exchange: NY
Symbol: SHC
Corporate History: The company, incorporated in 1962, is a manufacturer and distributor of cosmetics, nutritional supplements and household items through direct-selling. Nutritional supplements and foods comprise 75% of its sales.
Brandnames of Products and Services:

Alfalfa Tabs	*nutritional product*
Apricot Hand & Body Lotion	*personal care product*
Arrange® Hair Spray	*personal care product*
At Ease® Scouring Cleaner	*household product*
Basic-D® Automatic Dishwashing Concentrate	*household product*
Basic-H® Concentrated Organic Cleaner	*household product*
Basic-H® Concentrated Soil Conditioner	*household product*
Basic-I® Industrial Cleaner	*household product*
Basic-L® Laundry Concentrate	*household product*
Basic Skin Care Trios	*personal care product*
Bath Essence Bubble Bath	*personal care product*
B-Complex	*nutritional product*
Calcium Magnesium	*nutritional product*

Chewable Multivitamin and Multimineral Supplement	*nutritional product*
Deodorant Cream	*personal care product*
Desert Wind® Roll-On Deodorant	*personal care product*
Energy Bars	*nutritional product*
EPA	*nutritional product*
Fiber Wafers	*nutritional product*
Foot Cream	*personal care product*
Healthy 'n Light Entrees	*nutritional product*
Herb-Lax® Laxative	*nutritional product*
household product	
Instant Protein® Drink Mix	*nutritional product*
Iron plus Vitamin C	*nutritional product*
Lady Shaklee Body Creme	*personal care product*
Lecithin	*nutritional product*
Liquid-L® Laundry Concentrate	*household product*
Liqui-Lea® Multivitamin with Iron Supplement	*nutritional product*
Meadow Blend® Soap-Free Cleansing Bar	*personal care product*
Meadow Blend® Soap-Free Liquid Cleanser	*personal care product*
Nature-Bright Concentrated Laundry Brightener	*household product*
New Concept® Organic Dentifrice	*personal care product*
Pro-Lecin® Nibblers	*nutritional product*
Proteinized Shampoo	*personal care product*
Rainsilk™ Hair Care Products	*personal care product*
Satin Sheen® Dishwashing Liquid	*household product*
Shaklee Classics Beauty Products	*personal care product*
Shaklee Naturals Skin Care and Hair Care Products	*personal care product*
Shaklee Slim Plan Cream of Chicken-Flavored Soup	*nutritional product*
Shaklee Slim Plan Drink Mix	*nutritional product*
Softer Than Soft® Concentrated Fabric Conditioner	*household product*
Special Skin Care Products	*personal care product*
Tioga® Men's Cologne	*personal care product*
Tioga® Men's Skin Conditioner	*personal care product*
Vita-Cal® Vitamin and Mineral Supplement	*nutritional product*
Vita-C® Vitamin C Supplement	*nutritional product*
Vita-E® Vitamin E Supplement	*nutritional product*
Vita-Lea® for Children	*nutritional product*
Vita-Lea® Multivitamin and Multimineral Supplement	*nutritional product*
Zinc	*nutritional product*

Shaw Industries Inc.

616 E. Walnut Ave.
P.O. Box Drawer 2128
Dalton, GA 30722-2128
(404) 278-3812

Chief Executive Officer: R.E. Shaw
1984 Annual Sales Volume: 454M
1984 Shares Outstanding: 8,734,774
Shareholders: 1,507
Exchange: NY
Symbol: SHX

Corporate History: The company incorporated in 1967 as Philadelphia Holding Co. Inc., a successor to a company that had been in the business since 1846. Its present title was adopted in 1971. The company makes carpets for residential and commercial use, mostly in the medium-to higher-priced range.

Brandnames of Products and Services:

Magee	*carpets*

Philadelphia	*carpets*
Sabre	*carpets*

Shell Oil Co.

One Shell Plaza
P.O. Box 2463
Houston, TX 77001
(713) 241-6161

Chief Executive Officer: J.F. Bookout
1984 Annual Sales Volume: 20,701M
1984 Shares Outstanding: 309,215,000
Shareholders: 21,000
Exchange: NY
Symbol: SUO

Corporate History: Shell Oil Company is an integrated oil and petrochemical company operating primarily in the United States. Based on sales revenue, it is among the 20 largest corporations in the United States. Shell Oil grew out of two small companies, both organized by the Royal Dutch/Shell Group of Companies in 1912 — the American Gasoline Company, a West Coast gasoline marketer, and Roxana Petroleum Company, Midwest producer of crude oil. The company was incorporated in Delaware in 1922 as Shell Union Oil Company, but its name was changed some years later to Shell Oil Company. Shell opened its first U.S. refinery in 1915. A research organization, Shell Development Company, was set up in 1928. A year later, the company entered the petrochemical business with the creation of Shell Chemical Company. Shell Oil's activities can be roughly divided into two areas — exploration and production of oil, natural gas, and coal and the manufacture and distribution of oil and chemical products. It explores for and produces oil and gas principally in the United States, although its subsidiaries are exploring in 13 foreign countries and have production in four. Shell Oil is the largest crude oil producer in the Gulf of Mexico on a cumulative basis through 1984. It is also among the U.S. leaders in producing oil by supplemental methods such as steam injection and waterflooding, and has major projects underway to recover more oil through carbon dioxide injection. The company has interests in other energy sources. They include coal in Wyoming, Ohio, Montana, Indiana and Illinois; lignite in Texas and Arkansas; and tar sands in Alberta, Canada. A Shell subsidiary is involved in a joint venture developing photovoltaic cells for converting sunlight into electricity. The company also is active in research in coal gasification and biotechnology. Shell Oil refines, transports, and sells in the U.S. oil products used in transportation, home heating and industry. It is among the nation's leading gasoline and commercial jet fuel marketers. As a manufacturer of chemicals, Shell Oil ranks first among U.S. oil companies, with chemical products sales among the top 10 in the U.S. chemical industry as a whole.

Brandnames of Products and Services:

Shell	*automotive products & gasoline stations*

Shelter Resources Corp.

24200 Chagrin Blvd.
Beachwood, Ohio 44122
(216) 831-0076

Chief Executive Officer: J.P. Maloney
Exchange: AM
Symbol: SHL

Corporate History: The company incorporated in 1970 as Electronic Capital Corp., successor to a company of the same name incorporated in 1959. Its present title also was adopted in 1970. The firm makes factory-built homes sold through approximately 650 independent dealers in the South and West. In 1980 it began diversifying by acquiring Cole Consumer Products, a manufacturer of keys, letters and numbers for signs.

Brandnames of Products and Services:

Cape Town	*mobile homes*
Citation	*mobile homes*
Colony	*mobile homes*
Country Roads	*mobile homes*
Crimson	*mobile homes*
English Squire	*mobile homes*
Flamenco	*mobile homes*
Gettysburgh	*mobile homes*
Glenwood	*mobile homes*
Hermitage	*mobile homes*
Marietta	*mobile homes*
Marlin	*mobile homes*
Monaco	*mobile homes*
Montego	*mobile homes*
Monterey	*mobile homes*
Parkwood	*mobile homes*
The Residential	*mobile homes*
Royal Cambridge	*mobile homes*
Royal Chateau	*mobile homes*
Royal English	*mobile homes*
Royal Lancer	*mobile homes*
Royal Monarch	*mobile homes*
Salem	*mobile homes*
Sheridan	*mobile homes*
Sherwood	*mobile homes*

Shiloh	*mobile homes*
Sunburst	*mobile homes*
Sunridge	*mobile homes*
Villager	*mobile homes*
Winston II	*mobile homes*
Woodridge	*mobile homes*

Sherwin-Williams Co.

101 Prospect Ave., N.W.
Cleveland, OH 44115
(216) 566-2000

Chief Executive Officer: J.G. Breen
1984 Annual Sales Volume: 2,075M
1984 Shares Outstanding: 23,295,807
Shareholders: 9,777
Exchange: NY
Symbol: SHW

Corporate History: Sherwin-Williams's business is the manufacturing, selling, and distribution of coatings and related products. The company also sells prescription, health and beauty aids, cosmetics, and general merchandise through the Gray Drug and Drugfair chains in 10 states. Sherwin-Williams architectural coatings, industrial finishes and associated supplies are sold through company-operated paint and wallcovering stores in 48 states. The company also produces coatings for original equipment manufacturers in a number of industries and special-purpose coatings for the automotive aftermarket, and industrial maintenance and traffic paint markets.

Brandnames of Products and Services:

Sherwin-Williams	*paint stores*

Shoney's South Inc.

2158 Union Ave.
Memphis, TN 38104
(901) 725-6400

Chief Executive Officer: James H. Prentiss
1984 Annual Sales Volume: 169M
1984 Shares Outstanding: 5,616,133
Shareholders: 1,321
Exchange: OTC
Symbol: SHNS

Corporate History: The company, incorporated in 1968, is primarily engaged in the business of operating and developing moderately priced restaurants. The company currently owns and operates 205 restaurants and is the franchisor of 26 restaurants, located in Illinois, Missouri, North Carolina, South Carolina, Alabama, Tennessee, Kentucky, Louisiana, Mississippi, Arkansas, Georgia and Texas. Each of the company's restaurants features food items which are freshly prepared at each restaurant, in contrast to being prepared and prepackaged at a commissary.

Brandnames of Products and Services:

Captain D's	*restaurants*
Danvers	*restaurants*
Hungry Fisherman	*restaurants*
J.P. Seafield's	*restaurants*
Shoney's	*restaurants*
Willie Moffatt's	*restaurants*

Shopwell Inc.

400 Walnut Ave.
Bronx, NY 10454
(212) 759-3400

Chief Executive Officer: Martin Rosengarten
1984 Annual Sales Volume: 557M
1984 Shares Outstanding: 1,662,175
Shareholders: 2,324
Exchange: AM
Symbol: SH

Corporate History: The company incorporated in 1952 as Daitch Crystal Dairies Inc. Its present title was adopted in 1973. The company operates a chain of retail food stores which as of 1984 included 57 supermarkets. Stores are located in New York and Connecticut. The company also sells products at wholesale.

Brandnames of Products and Services:

Daitch	*dairy products*
Food Emporium	*food products and supermarkets*
Shopwell	*food products and supermarkets*
Value Center	*supermarkets*

Signal Companies Inc.

11255 North Jorrey Pines Rd.
La Jolla, CA 92037
(619) 457-3555

Chief Executive Officer: Forrest N. Shumway
1984 Annual Sales Volume: 6,005M
1984 Shares Outstanding: 109,360,442
Shareholders: 98,700
Exchange: NY

Symbol: SGN

Corporate History: The company was incorporated in 1928 to take over Signal Gasoline Co. Inc. and Signal Gasoline Corp. In 1968, its name was changed from Signal Oil & Gas Co. to its present title. Signal Companies Inc. is a diversified, technologically based corporation whose activities are conducted in four major industry segments: aerospace, electronics and instrumentation; process technologies and services; engineering and construction services; and other operations.

Brandnames of Products and Services:

Ampex	*electronic products*
Frye Copysystems	*printing products*
Fryemaric	*printing products*
Impact	*printing products*
Signal Capitol	*financial services*
Signal Landmark Properties	*land development, real estate*

Silvercrest Industries Inc.

299 N. Smith Ave.
Corona, CA 91720
(714) 734-6610

Chief Executive Officer: Howard Sherman
1984 Annual Sales Volume: 61M
1984 Shares Outstanding: 2,088,134
Shareholders: 619
Exchange: AM
Symbol: SLV

Corporate History: Incorporated in 1969, Silvercrest Industries Inc. designs and makes mobile homes. In addition, the company markets its products directly to developers who place such products in mobile home or planned subdivisions. In the latter instance, the developer sells the home and land as one complete unit to the retail customer. Of the five western states in which the company operates, California, Washington, Oregon and Nevada accounted for 63%, 14%, 9% and 6% respectively, of the company's sales in 1984. The company's four manufacturing facilities are located in Southern California (2), Northern California and Central Oregon. The company has been engaged since 1978 in the development of Lake Mountain Estates, an 88-acre home subdivision overlooking Lake Mead in Boulder City, Nevada, which consists of 335 terraced-view lots.

Brandnames of Products and Services:

Buckingham	*mobile homes*
Cottage	*mobile homes*
Edinborough	*mobile homes*
Howard Manor	*mobile homes*
Kingsbrook	*mobile homes*
Sherwood Manor	*mobile homes*
Silvercrest	*mobile homes*
Silverwood	*mobile homes*
Starcrest	*mobile homes*
Supreme	*mobile homes*

Simco Stores, Inc.

385 Gerard Avenue
Bronx, NY 10451
(212) 292-7777

Chief Executive Officer: Joseph C. Warner
1984 Annual Sales Volume: 9M
1984 Shares Outstanding: 1,253,649
Shareholders: 570
Exchange: AM
Symbol: SSM

Corporate History: Simco, formed in 1934 and publicly owned since 1968, operates a chain of 25 shoe stores located in three states, with the concentration in the New York metropolitan area. The fashion shoe stores offer popularly-priced footwear, handbags, hosiery, and related accessories for women and teen-aged girls.

Brandnames of Products and Services:

Lauren Evan	*shoes*
Simco	*shoes and accessories*

Singer Co.

8 Stamford Forum
Stamford, CT 06904-2151
(203) 356-4200

Chief Executive Officer: J.B. Flavin
1984 Annual Sales Volume: 2,519M
1984 Shares Outstanding: 17,141,977
Shareholders: 25,857
Exchange: NY
Symbol: SMF

Corporate History: Singer Co. was founded in 1851 and incorporated in 1873 as Singer Mfg. Co. Today the company develops and produces high-technology electronic systems for government and industry, and manufactures or markets sewing and consumer durable products in the United States and more than 100 other nations. The company is divided into three groups. Government products represents 47% of the company's total revenues. Approximately three-quarters of the group's sales are made under U.S. government prime contracts and sub-contracts. It is among the top 40 prime contractors to the U.S. Department of Defense and supplies high-technology systems to NASA, foreign governments, and commercial/industrial customers. The North American consumer products group contributed 30% of total company revenues in 1984. Motor products and furniture sales to Sears, Roebuck and Co. were approximately 11% of total company revenues in 1984. Singer is one of the leading U.S. manufacturers of portable electric power tools, such as drills, saws, and routers. It has supplied these products to Sears, its sole domestic customer. Singer is a leading distributor of sewing products in North America. These products are sold largely under two types of dealership arrangements: regional and national fabric store chains and independent sewing machine stores. During 1984, more than 600 outlets were added to this network, bringing the total number of dealers in North America to approximately 3,300. Finally, the international group contributed 23% of total company revenues. The group's sewing machine factories and assembly plants are strategically located to serve its worldwide markets. The major facilities are in Campinas, Brazil; Taichung, Taiwan; Monza, Italy; and Utsunomiya, Japan (a 50-percent-owned affiliate). These factories manufacture sewing machines both for export and sale to domestic customers.

Brandnames of Products and Services:

Caramate	*sound/slide projectors*
Craftsman	*power tools*
Manor House	*furniture*
Singer	*sewing machines, sewing products*

Skyline Corp.

2520 Bypass Road
Elkhart, IN 46514
(219) 294-6521

Chief Executive Officer:	Arthur J. Decio
1984 Annual Sales Volume:	384M
1984 Shares Outstanding:	9,283,305
Shareholders:	5,297
Exchange:	NY
Symbol:	SKY

Corporate History: Skyline, incorporated in 1959, as successor to a business founded in 1951, designs, manufactures, and distributes manufactured housing (mobile homes) and recreational vehicles (travel trailers, mini-motor homes, fifth wheels and van conversions). In fiscal year 1984, 66% of sales were from manufactured homes and 34% recreational vehicles. Principal markets for manufactured homes are the suburban and rural areas of the United States.

Brandnames of Products and Services:

Aljo/Aly	*recreational vehicles*
Aljo/Aly Alliance	*recreational vehicles*
Aljo Aries	*recreational vehicles*
Austen	*mini-motor homes*
Crestwood	*recreational vehicles*
Jamee	*mini-motor homes*
Kensington	*recreational vehicles*
Key Largo	*recreational vehicles*
Layton	*recreational vehicles*
Layton Celebrity	*recreational vehicles*
Layton Funtime	*recreational vehicles*
Lindy	*mini-motor homes*
Nomad Century	*recreational vehicles*
Nomad Weekender	*recreational vehicles*
Scottsdale	*recreational vehicles*
Skyline Vans	*van conversions*
Tahoe	*recreational vehicles*

SmithKline Beckman Corp.

One Franklin Plaza
Philadelphia, PA 19101
(215) 751-4000

Chief Executive Officer:	Henry Wendt
1984 Annual Sales Volume:	2,949M
1984 Shares Outstanding:	80,800,000
Shareholders:	29,000
Exchange:	NY
Symbol:	SKB

Corporate History: SmithKline Beckman is a technology-intensive health-care company which markets a broad line of prescription and proprietary products for human and animal health care, as well as diagnostic and analytical products worldwide. The company incorporated in 1929 as Smith Kline & French Laboratories, makers of prescription drugs. It became SmithKline Corporation in 1973 and adopted its present title in 1982 when SmithKline merged with Beckman Instruments. The company entered the eye and skin care business in 1979-80 with the acquisitions of Humphrey Instruments and Allergan Pharmaceuticals, Inc. It folded its cosmetics operations (Love) in 1979 and sold its industrial products business in 1984.

Brandnames of Products and Services:

00550	*LC-65*
Acnomel	*acne cream*
ARM	*allergy medicine*

Benzedrex	*nasal decongestant*
Blink 'n Clean	*contact lens care product*
Clean 'n Soak	*contact lens care product*
Congestac	*congestion relief medicine*
Contac	*cold/cough medicines*
Contac Jr.	*cold medicine for children*
Danex	*dandruff shampoo*
Ecotrin	*safety coated aspirin*
Fast Aid	*skin anesthetic*
Feasol	*iron supplement*
Feosol Plus	*iron/vitamin supplement*
Hydrocare Cleaning/ Disinfecting Solution	*contact lens care product*
Hydrocare Saline Solution	*contact lens care product*
Lacri-Lube	*lubricating eye ointment*
Lens Clear	*contact lens care product*
Lens Plus	*contact lens care product*
Lens Rins	*contact lens care product*
Lens Wet	*contact lens care product*
Liquifilm Forte	*artificial tears*
Liquifilm Tears	*artificial tears*
Liquifilm Wetting Solution	*contact lens care product*
Ornacol	*cough/cold medicine*
Ornex	*decongestant/analgesic*
Prefrin	*eye drops*
Sine Off	*sinus medicines*
Soakare	*contact lens care product*
Soflens	*enzymatic contact lens cleaner*
Sorbicare	*contact lens care product*
Tears Plus	*artificial tears*
Teldrin	*antihistamine*
Total	*contact lens care product*
Troph-Iron	*vitamin/iron supplement*
Trophite	*vitamin supplement*
Vanseb	*dandruff shampoo*
Wet 'n' Soak	*contact lens care product*

J.M. Smucker Co.

Strawberry Lane
Orrville, OH 44667
(216) 682-0015

Chief Executive Officer: Paul H. Smucker
1984 Annual Sales Volume: 215M
1984 Shares Outstanding: 3,708,022
Shareholders: 3,518
Exchange: NY
Symbol: SJM
Corporate History: The company was founded in 1897 and incorporated in 1921. It makes food products, including preserves and jellies, ice cream toppings, juice concentrates, pancake syrup, pickles, peanut butter and relishes. Its products are sold throughout the United States, principally to wholesale grocers, cooperative buying groups, and retailers. In 1984 the company acquired Knudsen & Sons Inc., a manufacturer of fruit & vegetable juices and juice blends.
Brandnames of Products and Services:

Dickinson's	*condiments*
Nice & Natural	*health foods*
Recharge	*juice*
R.W. Knudsen Family	*condiments, juicies*
Smucker's	*condiments*

Sonoma Vineyards

11455 Old Redwood Hwy.
Healdsburg, Calif. 95448
(707) 433-6511

Chief Executive Officer: K.J. Kwit
Exchange: OTC
Symbol: SNMAC
Corporate History: Sonoma, incorporated in 1964, chiefly produces bottled wine. The company sells about half of its volume via mail. It is the largest mail-order vendor of wine in the United States.
Brandnames of Products and Services:

Pacific Freight Supply	*mailorder hand and machine tools*
Sonoma Vineyards	*wine*
Windsor Vineyards	*wine*

Sony Corp.

7-35 Kitashinagawa 6-Chome, Shinagawa-Ku, Tokyo, 141 Japan
U.S. Office: 9 W. 57th St.
New York, N.Y. 10019
(212) 371-5800

Chief Executive Officer: Akio Morita
1984 Annual Sales Volume: 5,149M
1984 Shares Outstanding: 230,924,000
Shareholders: 56,842

Exchange: NY
Symbol: SNE
Corporate History: The company incorporated in 1946 as Tokyo Telecommunications Engineering Corp., and adopted its present title in 1958. Sony is engaged in the development, manufacture and sale of electronic equipment, instruments and devices. It manufactures a wide variety of consumer electronic equipment.
Brandnames of Products and Services:

Betamax	*videotape recorder*
Currentron	*video tape recorders and cassettes*
Dynamicron	*video tape cassettes*
Express Commander	*remote control for TV receivers*
Sony	*electronics*
Trinitron	*TV receivers*
Walkman	*personal portable stereos*

Soundesign Corp.

34 Exchange Place
Jersey City, N.J. 07302
(201) 434-1050

Chief Executive Officer: S.E. Ashkenazi
Exchange: AM
Symbol: SON
Corporate History: The company, incorporated in 1964, designs, makes, imports and distributes stereo systems, consoles, portable radios and related products. In 1979 stereo systems accounted for more than half of its sales.
Brandnames of Products and Services:

Acoustic Dynamics	*audio equipment*
Realtone	*audio equipment*
Soundesign	*audio equipment*
Tanglewood	*audio equipment*

Southland Corp.

2828 N. Haskell Ave.
Dallas, TX 75204
(214) 828-7011

Chief Executive Officer: J.P. Thompson
1984 Annual Sales Volume: 12,100M
1984 Shares Outstanding: 46,972,000
Shareholders: 8,927
Exchange: NY
Symbol: SLC
Corporate History: Southland, incorporated in 1961, is the country's largest operator and franchisor of convenience food stores. The company also operates other retail stroes. In 1985 it had 7,500 convenience stores operating in 42 states. Southland brought the convenience store to Japan, and today its area licensee runs more than 2,000 7-Eleven stores in that country.
Brandnames of Products and Services:

7-Eleven	*food stores and food products*
Adohr Farms	*dairy products*
Bancroft	*dairy products*
Barricini	*supermarkets*
Big Deal	*dairy products*
Big Wheel	*dairy products*
Briggs	*grocery items*
Cabell's	*dairy products*
Candy Stores	
Charles & Co.	*gourmet shops*
Chief Auto Parts	*automotive store*
Cooper Farms	*grocery items*
Embassy	*dairy products*
Gram Daddy	*dairy products*
Gristede's	*supermarkets*
Harbison's	*dairy products*
Horten's	*dairy products*
Hudgins	*truck rental*
Knowltown	*dairy products*
Landshire	*food products*
Lilly	*ice cream*
Midwest Farms	*dairy products*
Reddy Ice	*food products*
Slurpee	*soft drink*
Southland	*food centers*
Specialty Foods	*dairy products*
Velda Farms	*dairy products*
Wanzer's	*dairy products*

Specialty Restaurants Corp.

2977 Redondo Ave.
Long Beach, Calif. 90806
(213) 426-0451

Chief Executive Officer: D.C. Tallichet
Corporate History: The company, incorporated in 1968, is engaged in the restaurant business throughout the United States. It operates 47 restaurants which offer moderately priced meals. It is not engaged in franchise operations and has granted no licenses. In fiscal 1980 restaurants provided 97.4% of sales.

Brandnames of Products and Services:

91st Bomb Group	*restaurant, Tenn.*
94th Aero Squadron	*restaurants, Calif., Colo., Pa., Wis.*
Baby Doe's Matchless Mine	*restaurants, Tex., Ala., Colo., Mo.*
Boatyard Village & Trail	*shopping area, Oakland, Calif.*
Boundary Oak	*restaurant, Calif.*
Castaway	*restaurants, Calif.*
Chili Pepper	*restaurant, Colo.*
Crabcooker	*restaurant*
Crawdaddy's	*restaurant, Fla.*
His Lordship's	*restaurant, Calif.*
Jack London Village	*shopping area, Oakland, Calif.*
Jamoke Landing	*restaurant*
Luminarias	*restaurants, Calif.*
Mary's Gate Village	*shopping area, Long Beach, Calif.*
Moshulu	*restaurant, Pa.*
Normandy Beach	*restaurant, Fla.*
Odyssey	*restaurant, Calif.*
Orange Hill	*restaurant, Calif.*
Pieces of Eight	*restaurant, Calif., Colo.*
Ports O' Call	*restaurant, Calif.*
Proud Bird	*restaurant, Calif.*
Queen Mary	*restaurant*
Reef	*restaurant, Calif.*
Rusty Pelican	*restaurant, Fla.*
Shanghai Red's	*restaurant, Tex.*
Sophie's	*restaurant*
Sunbird	*restaurant, Colo.*
Yankee Whaler	*restaurant, Calif.*

Spencer Companies Inc.

450 Summer St.
Boston, Mass. 02210
(617) 542-8120

Chief Executive Officer: C.Charles Marran
1984 Annual Sales Volume: 101M
1984 Shares Outstanding: 1,800,000
Shareholders: 3,000
Exchange: AM
Symbol: SPN

Corporate History: Spencer incorporated in 1928 as Spencer Chain Stores Inc., and adopted its present title in 1970. Spencer is engaged in the manufacture and sale of footwear and ladies apparel. The company operates 214 shoe stores and shoe departments. It also operates a chain of 32 ladies apparel stores. In 1984 the company acquired Fashion World, a 15-unit apparel chain, situated primarily in Massachusetts.

Brandnames of Products and Services:

Fashion Gallery	*ladies apparel stores*
Goldtred	*shoes*
Happy Legs	*junior apparel*
Marrantino	*shoes*
Ranchos	*shoes*
Super Sole	*shoes*
Sybil	*women's apparel*
Topnicks	*shoes*
Ultra Image	*blouses*

Sperry Corp.

1290 Avenue of the Americas
New York, NY 10104
(212) 484-4444

Chief Executive Officer: Gerald G. Probst
1984 Annual Sales Volume: 5,200M
1984 Shares Outstanding: 54,347,911
Shareholders: 70,913
Exchange: NY
Symbol: SY

Corporate History: Sperry Corporation is a key supplier of electronic systems, including the computers, terminals, software and services that make up integrated information systems, defense and aerospace systems and equipment. Under the Sperry New Holland name, the company is also a leading producer of specialized farm equipment. Electronic systems represents more than 85% of Sperry's revenues.

Brandnames of Products and Services:

New Holland	*farm equipment*
Sperry	*computers, electronic data processors*
Univac	*computers, electronic data processors*

Springs Industries, Inc.

205 North White St.
P.O. Box 70
Ft. Mill, SC 29715
(803) 547-2901

Chief Executive Officer: Walter Y. Elisha
1984 Annual Sales Volume: 945M
1984 Shares Outstanding: 8,884,000
Shareholders: 3,500
Exchange: NY
Symbol: SMI

Corporate History: The company was founded 1887 as Fort Mill Manufacturing Company. Later, the company was known as The Springs Cotton Mills and the Springs Mills. The present name, Springs Industries, was adopted in 1982. Springs is a major manufacturer of finished fabrics and home furnishings. The company's Finished Farics Group sells fabrics to apparel manufacturers, fabric stores, specialty manufacturers, the couture market, and producers of decorative home furnishings. The Home Furnishings Group sells such diverse products as sheets, pillowcases, quilted bedspreads, comforters, draperies, bed accessories, towels, tufted area and scatter rungs, window shades, blinds, drapery rods and hardware, and decorative fringe. Springs has 16,600 employees in 31 states, Canada, Mexico and the United Kingdom. There are 25 manufacturing plants, 24 sales and administrative offices, and 16 distribution centers.

Brandnames of Products and Services:

Bestpleat	*pleater tapes*
Custom Designs	*waterbed liners*
Graber	*window decorating products*
Morgan Jones	*sheets, pillowcases, bedspreads, comforters*
Pequot	*sheets, pillowcases, bedspreads, comforter*
Radiance	*sheets, pillowcases, bedspreads, comforters*
Skinner	*fabrics*
So Soft Pom Poms	*pom poms*
Springmaid	*sheets, pillowcases, bedspreads, comforters, bed accessories, and fabric for apparel*
SpringsPerformance	*standard and waterbed liners*
Ultrasuede Brand Fabric	*fabric*

Squibb Corp.

Route 206 & Province Line Rd.
Princeton, NJ 08540
(609) 921-4000

Chief Executive Officer: Richard M. Furland
1984 Annual Sales Volume: 1,886M
1984 Shares Outstanding: 53,737,000
Shareholders: 45,000
Exchange: NY
Symbol: SQB

Corporate History: Squibb was founded in 1858 as a drug manufacturer. Its first product was chloroform. The company's three main industry segments are: pharmaceuticals (cardiovascular, anti-infective, anti-inflammatory and psychotropic agents; insulins; vaccines; and vitamins) medical products (companies in this group include Advanced Technology Laboratories Inc ▪ultrasound imaging products▪ ConvaTec ▪wound management and incontinenece produces▪, Edward Weck & Co., Inc. ▪medical instruments, lasers, and sterilization monitoring systems▪, and Argon Medicl Corp. ▪guide wires for catheters, surgical drapes and customized surgical packs▪); and personal care products (Charles of the Ritz Croup & Ltd). In 1984 pharmaceuticals represented 58% of sales, medical products 21% of sales, and personal care products 21% of sales.

Brandnames of Products and Services:

Age Zone Controller	*cosmetics*
Alexandra	*fragrance*
Alexandra de Markoff	*cosmetics*
Aromance	*fragrance*
Aromance 2001 Disk Player	*perfume diffuser*
Aston	*men's fragrance*
Auraseva	*cosmetics*
Bain de Soleil	*suntan lotion*
Charivari	*fragrance*
Charles of the Ritz	*cosmetics*
Countess Isserlyn	*cosmetics*
Country Cordovans	*cosmetics*
Enjoli	*fragrances*
Enjoli Midnight	*fragrance*
Forever Krystle	*fragrance*
Fresh Music	*fragrance*
Gianni Versace	*fragrance*
Gianni Versace Pour L'Homme	*fragrance*
Golden Bounty	*vitamins*

Jean Nate	*personal care products*
Kouros	*fragrance*
Liqui Creame	*lipstick*
Opium	*fragrance*
Pine Bros.	*cough drops*
Pour Homme	*fragrance*
Power Glow	*cosmetics*
Revenescence	*cosmetics*
Rive Gauche	*fragrance*
Soft Glow	*cosmetics*
Spec-T	*cough and cold products*
Sweeta	*noncaloric sweetener*
Theragran	*vitamins*
Vigran	*vitamins*
Y	*men's fragrance*
YSL	*fragrance*
Yves Saint Laurent	*cosmetic products*

A.E. Staley Manufacturing Co.

2200 Eldorado St.
Decatur, IL 62525
(217) 423-4411

Chief Executive Officer: Donald E. Nordlund
1984 Annual Sales Volume: 2,140M
1984 Shares Outstanding: 27,869,000
Shareholders: 8,997
Exchange: NY
Symbol: STA

Corporate History: The company was founded in 1898 as a producer of cornstarch. Parenthetically, it was also the original bankroller of the Chicago Bears baseball team. Today the company develops processes and sells a wide line of food ingredients. It is the nation's second largest refiner of corn (after CPC International) and a major processor of soybeans. The major cola companies decision in 1980 to use high fructose corn syrup instead of sugar in their colas has been a boon for big corn-sweetner producers like Staley. During 1984, Staley acquired CFS Continental Inc. A leading full-line supplier to the foodservice industry. In addition to corn refining and soybean milling, Staley is active in grain merchandising and financial and commidity futures trading.

Brandnames of Products and Services:

Cream	*cornstarch*
Diaper Sweet	*laundry aid*
Gregg's Gold-n-Soft	*margarine*
Rain Drops	*water conditioner*
Re-Mi Foods	*food products*
Sno-Bol	*bathroom cleaner*
Sta-Flo	*laundry starches*
Staley	*pancake syrup*
Sta-Puf	*laundry softener*
Wagner	*fruit drinks*

Standard Brands Inc.

625 Madison Ave.
New York, N.Y. 10022
(212) 759-4400

Chief Executive Officer: F.R. Johnson
Exchange: NY
Symbol: SB

Corporate History: Standard Brands, founded and incorporated in 1929, is a major food processor whose roots can be traced back a century to three companies: a distiller, a baking powder manufacturer and a coffee and tea merchant. Today it sells a wide variety of consumer products—groceries, pet foods, candies, wine, beer and liquor. In 1980 it acquired all of American Distilling Co.'s alcoholic beverages. More than 33% of the company's sales are foreign. Standard Brands is particularly strong in Canada. The company has not marketed a successful new product since 1972, when it brought out Egg Beaters. In the spring of 1981, Nabisco Inc. and Standard Brands Inc. agreed to merge into a company called Nabisco Brands Inc. Based on 1980 results, the new company would have had revenues of $5.59 billion, making it the fourth largest food manufacturer in the U.S.

Brandnames of Products and Services:

American	*vodka*
B & B	*imported liqueur*
Baby Ruth	*candy bar*
Blue Bonnett	*margarine*
Bourbon Supreme	
Burton's	*gin*
Butterfinger	*candy bar*
Cafe Lolita	*liqueur*
Canadian Ltd.	*whiskey*
Chase & Sanborn	*coffee*
Cherry Elsinore	*wine*
Churchill	*whiskey*
Coconut Grove	*candy*
Comandon	*imported cognac*
Curtiss	*candy*
Droste	*Dutch chocolates*
Duval	*imported vermouth*
Egg Beaters	*egg substitute*
El Toro	*tequilla*
Erza Brooks	*bourbon*
Fleischmann's	*margarine*

Fleischmann's	*whiskey, gin and vodka*
Fleischmann's	*yeast*
Foster's Lager	*Australian beer (importer)*
Garnier	*cordial*
Grenadier	*ceramics*
Guckenheimer	*whiskey*
Inver House	*whiskey and Scotch*
King James	*Scotch*
Laphroaig	*Scotch*
La Tolteca	*Scotch*
Light Tasty Spread	*margarine*
Lolita	*cordials*
Melville	*candy*
Metaxa 5-Star & 7-Star	*brandies*
No-Bake Cheese Cake	
Paso Fino Rum Liqueur	
Pearson	*candies*
Pinata	*Mexican foods*
Planters	*nuts and candy*
Reggie	*candy*
Robertson's Oporto Port	*wine*
Royal	*gelatins and puddings*
Royal Dragon	*frozen Chinese Food*
Semkov	*vodka*
Soft	*diet margarine*
Southern Bell	*nuts*
Southern Host	*liqueur*
Souverain	*wine*
Stillbrook	*bourbon*
Tender Leaf Tea	
Tvarscki	*vodka*
Wayne Bun	*candy bar*
Weibel	*wines*
William Alsatian	*wines*
Williams & Humbert	*wine*

Standard Register Co.

626 Albany St.
Dayton, OH 45401
(513) 443-1000

Chief Executive Officer: John K. Darragh
1984 Annual Sales Volume: 413M
1984 Shares Outstanding: 5,423,779
Shareholders: 2,920
Exchange: OTC
Symbol: SREG
Corporate History: The company, incorporated in 1912, is one of the world's largest designers and manufacturers of business forms and systems. When Standard Register was founded, its only products were two innovations — pinfeed autographic registers and marginally punched continous forms. Now, a broad line of business forms of all kinds and constructions, including pressure sensitive lables, as well as an extensive offering of forms handling and data systems equipment, make the company a full line supplier to the paperwork systems needs of commerce, industry, institutions and governments. the design and production of business forms constitute the major activities of the company. Two recent changes are noteworthy: in 1983 the company purchased the Rein Co., and in the same year a new subsidiary was formed, Stanfast Inc. Standard Register markets it products nationally by means of a direct selling organization established in sales offices located in all 50 states.
Brandnames of Products and Services:

Form-A-Label	*business forms*
Stanbond	*business forms*
Standard Register	*business forms*
Stanset	*business forms*
Stanwid	*business forms*
Zipset	*business forms*

Standex International Corp.

Manor Pkwy.
Salem, N.H. 03079
(603) 893-9701

Chief Executive Officer: D.E. Hogan
Exchange: NY
Symbol: SXI
Corporate History: The company incorporated in 1955 as Standard Publishing Co. and changed its name to Standard International Corp. in 1958. It adopted its present title in 1973. It is a diversified manufacturing and marketing corporation with sales in four areas: institutional products, consumer graphics and industrial and electronic goods. In 1980 consumer products accounted for 24% of sales and graphics 21%.
Brandnames of Products and Services:

Berean	*religious bookstores*
Club Aluminum	*cookware*
Dresher	*brass bedroom furniture and accessories*
Frank Lewis Grapefruit Club	*mail order gift packages*

Pilgrim	*furniture stores*
Pilgrim House	*furniture*
Standard	*religious and educational publishing house*
Yield House	*Colonial-style home accessories*

Stanhome, Inc.

333 Western Ave.
Westfield, MA 01085
(413) 562-3631

Chief Executive Officer: H.L. Tower
1984 Annual Sales Volume: 333M
1984 Shares Outstanding: 5,211,000
Shareholders: 3,538
Exchange: OTC
Symbol: STHMK

Corporate History: Stanhome Inc., incorporated in 1931, is a worldwide marketer in design giftware and specialty industrial markets. These businesses are supported by a well-developed, international service network. The company's multinational direct sales subsidiaries provide health, home and personal care products and career opportunities worldwide. The Enesco subsidiary distributes family giftware and collectibles to domestic and international markets. The industrial division furnishes custom cleaning systems and products to specialty industrial markets.

Brandnames of Products and Services:

Aquilaun	*laundry soap*
Country Calico Mice	*giftware*
Country Cousins	*giftware*
Dear God Kids	*giftware*
Garfield	*giftware*
Gradu-Weight	*meal replacement food*
Growing Up	*giftware*
Miss Piggy	*giftware*
Muppet Babies	*giftware*
Poppyseed Collection	*giftware*
Precious Moments	*giftware*
Selectives	*nutritional supplements*
Semplice	*skin care products*
Stan-Homme	*men's toiletries*
Stanley Hostess Party Plan	
Stanley U-Install	*garage door opener*
Strawberry Shortcake	*giftware*
Treasured Memories	*giftware*
Try-It	*household cleaner*

Stanley Works

1000 Stanley Dr.
P.O. Box 7000
New Britain, CT 06050
(203) 225-5111

Chief Executive Officer: Donald W. Davis
1984 Annual Sales Volume: 1,158M
1984 Shares Outstanding: 27,877,000
Shareholders: 23,238
Exchange: NY
Symbol: SWK

Corporate History: The company, founded in 1843 and incorporated in 1852, is a worldwide marketer and manufacturer of consumer, builders and industrial products, including tools for professionals and do-it-yourselfers. Stanley also makes hardware and complementary products for the home, the factory and the building industry.

Brandnames of Products and Services:

Dura-Glide	*sliding door*
Hot Shot	*hardware*
Life Span	*hardware*
Magic-Door	*doors*
Pipe Line	*plumbing products*
Powerlock	*hardware*
Stanley	*tools*
Stan-Ray	*motion sensors*
Swivel-Lock	*utility knife*
U-install	*garage door openers*

Stanwood Corp.

4819 Park Rd.
Charlotte, NC 28220
(704) 527-5270

Chief Executive Officer: Thomas N. Roboz
1984 Annual Sales Volume: 115M
1984 Shares Outstanding: 1,532,935
Shareholders: 6,024
Exchange: AM
Symbol: SNW

Corporate History: The company incorporated in 1936 as Rufus D. Wilson Inc. Its name was changed to Chadbourn Hosiery in 1944 and to its present name in 1975. The firm is engaged in the manufacture and sale of apparel. In 1984 knitwear and underwear accounted for approximately 62% of total sales. Work and leisure wear accounted for approximately 38% of total sales. Approximately 33% of sales are made to the major chain stores in the United States under their brand names. The company's remaining sales are made through wholesalers, major department stores and retailers.

Brandnames of Products and Services:

Carwood	*men's and boys' apparel*
Flirt	*men's and boys' apparel*
Health Knit	*men's and boys' apparel*
Olevia St	*men's and boys' apparel*
Pony	*men's and boys' apparel*
Quail Hollow	*men's and boys' apparel*
Rosario	*men's and boys' apparel*
Stallion	*men's and boys' apparel*

Sterling Drug Inc.

90 Park Avenue
New York, N.Y. 10016
(212) 907-2000

Chief Executive Officer: John M. Pietruski
1984 Annual Sales Volume: 1,858M
1984 Shares Outstanding: 60,238,496
Shareholders: 38,657
Exchange: NY
Symbol: STY

Corporate History: Sterling Drug Inc., founded in 1901 in Wheeling, West Virginia as The Neuralgyline Company, is a diversified pharmaceuticals company with worldwide operations. Sterling's businesses include the development, manufacturing and marketing of prescription pharmaceuticals, over-the-counter medicines, household and industrial cleaners and disinfectants, cosmetics and toiletries, insecticides and rodenticides, and specialty chemicals and pigments.

Brandnames of Products and Services:

6-12 Plus	*insect repellent*
Bayer	*aspirin*
Beacon	*floor wax*
Breacol	*cough medication*
Bronkaid	*bronchial medication*
Campho-Phenique	*antiseptic*
Crepe de Chine	*fragrances*
d-Con	*insecticides and rodenticides*
Diaparene	*baby products*
Dorothy Gray	*cosmetics*
Energine	*cleaning fluid*
Fergon	*iron tablets*
Haley's M-O	*laxative*
Ironized Yeast	*tablets*
Love My Carpet	*rug and room deodorizer*
Lysol	*household cleaner and deodorizer*
Measurin	*pain reliever*
Midol	*pain reliever*
Minwax	*wood finishing products*
Mop & Glow	*floor cleaner*
Mucilose	*antacid and laxative*
Neo-Synephrine	*nasal decongestants*
NTZ	*nasal spray*
Ogilvie	*hair-care products*
Panadol	*non-aspirin pain reliver*
Phillips' Milk of Magnesia	*laxative*
PhisoAc Cream	*acne product*
PhisoDan	*shampoo*
PhisoDerm	*skin cleanser*
Pontocaine	*ointment*
Rid-X	*septic tank and cesspool cleaner*
Stri-Dex	*acne product*
Tussy	*deodorant*
Vanquish	*pain reliever*
Wet Ones	*moist towelettes*
Wingel	*antacid*

Sterling Stores Co. Inc.

6500 Forbing Rd.
P.O. Box 2301
Little Rock, Ark. 72203
(501) 568-1371

Chief Executive Officer: Dave Grundfest
Exchange: OTC
Symbol: STRS

Corporate History: The company, incorporated in 1931, operates a chain of 100 discount department stores in six South Central states.

Brandnames of Products and Services:

Magic Mart	*discount department stores*
Sterling	*discount department stores*

Sterndent Corp.

1455 East Putnam Ave.
Old Greenwich, Conn. 06870
(203) 637-5461

Chief Executive Officer: G.R. Knight
Exchange: NY
Symbol: SDT
Corporate History: The company incorporated in 1965 as Stern Metals Corp. and adopted its present title in 1972. It is engaged in precious metal operations, which in 1979 accounted for 67.3% of sales. It also sells dental equipment (24.4% of sales) and optical products (8.3%).
Brandnames of Products and Services:

Bill Blass	*eye-glass frames*
Givenchy	*eye-glass frames*
Universal	*eye-glass frames*

J.P. Stevens & Co. Inc.

1185 Avenue of the Americas
New York, NY 10036
(212) 930-2000

Chief Executive Officer: Whitney Stevens
1984 Annual Sales Volume: 2,144M
1984 Shares Outstanding: 17,486,260
Shareholders: 12,300
Exchange: NY
Symbol: STN
Corporate History: The company, founded in 1813 and incorporated in 1923, is a diversified manufacturer of almost every textile product. It is the second largest publicly-owned textile company in the Unites States. Stevens is also one of the nation's leading commercial printers. The company is a major printer of mail order catalogs and among the largest printers of telephone directories, Yellow Pages, and special-interest magazines. The company is also engaged in aircraft sales and maintenance and the production of certain elastomeric and plastic products. During 1984, the company entered into an agreement with Roger LaViale Ltd. of New York to style and sell a line of menswear worsted suiting fabrics under the LaViale name. The company acquired Stevcoknit, Inc., knitters of cotton and cotton-blend sportswear and outerwear fabrics and Gav-Tred Mills, Inc., bath rug manufacturers, in 1983. The company also acquired, in 1983, exclusive licensing rights in connection with the marketing of home furnishings designed by Gloria Vanderbilt. During 1982, the company signed an agreement with Ralph Lauren providing exclusive licensing rights for the marketing of a home furnishings collection designed by Lauren.
Brandnames of Products and Services:

Beauti-Blend	*linens*
Beauticale	*linens*
Big Mama	*hosiery*
Contender	*carpets*
Embracable	*towels, bathroom accessories*
Fine Arts	*towels and linens*
Finesse	*hosiery*
Fortsmann	*blankets*
Gloria Vanderbilt Collection	*home furnishings*
Gulistan	*carpets*
Merryweather	*carpets*
Pinehurst	*carpets*
Roger LaViale	*fabrics*
Simtex	*table linens*
Spirit	*hosiery*
Tastemaker	*kitchen and bedroom accessories*
Utica	*sheets, towels, bedroom accessories*

Stokely-Van Camp Inc.

941 N. Meridian St.
Indianapolis, Ind. 46206
(317) 631-2551

Chief Executive Officer: A.J. Stokely
Exchange: NY
Symbol: SVC
Corporate History: The company incorporated in 1936 as Stokely Bros. & Co. and adopted its present name in 1944. It processes a broad range of food products, and is one of the largest producers of pork and beans in the United States.
Brandnames of Products and Services:

Beanee Weenee	*food products*
Betty Zane	*popcorn*
Dixie	*margarines*
Gatorade Thirst Quencher	*beverage*
Kingstaste	*food products*
Kuner's	*canned foods*
PictSweet	*frozen foods*
Pomona Sunshine	*food products*
Popeye	*popcorn*
Stokely's Finest	*canned and frozen food products*

Sunshine	*food products*
Van Camp's	*food products*

Stop & Shop Companies Inc.

P.O. Box 369
Boston, MA 02101
(617) 770-8000

Chief Executive Officer: Avram J. Goldberg
1984 Annual Sales Volume: 3,247M
1984 Shares Outstanding: 13,757,245
Shareholders: 6,201
Exchange: NY
Symbol: SHP
Corporate History: Stop and Shop was founded in 1914 as a chain of food stores and incorporated in 1925 as Economy Grocery Stores Corp. The company adopted its present title in 1970. It is a diversified retailer, operating a total of 386 department stores, drug stores, supermarkets and tobacco shops in Maryland, New England, New Jersey, New York, Pennsylvania and Virginia. The company entered the discount department store business with its purchase of Bradless in 1961, and in 1968 further diversified into the super discount drug store business with the formation of Medi Mart. In 1969, the company acquired the Charles B. Perkins Tobacco Shops which now include Hallmark Card and Gift Shops and Perkins/Hallmark combination stores. The comany also operates the Stop & Shop Manufacturing company, which includes a bakery, carbonated beverage plant, comissary, dairy, seafood processing plant, household chemical plant, photo finishing plant and recycling center.
Brandnames of Products and Services:

Almy's	*department stores*
Bradlees	*discount department stores*
Charles B. Perkins	*tobacco shops*
Medi Mart	*drugstores*
Stop & Shop	*supermarkets*
Stop & Shop	*food products*

Storer Broadcasting Co.

12000 Biscayne Blvd.
Miami, FL 33181
(305) 899-1000

Chief Executive Officer: P. Storer
1984 Annual Sales Volume: 537M
1984 Shares Outstanding: 16,400,000
Shareholders: 6,000
Exchange: NY
Symbol: SCI
Corporate History: The company incorporated in 1927 as the Fort Industry Co. and acquired its first radio station in 1928. In the 1940s, it entered the television industry, becoming the first independent broadcaster to build three TV stations. Stores entered the cable television industry in 1963, and accellerated its expansive cable system franchise and acquisition program 1978-83, concurrent with the advent of satellite and broadband communications technology. Its radio stations were sold to help finance the effort. The company currently owns and operates seven television stations and is the country's fifth-largest cable operation, serving 1.5 million subscribers in 18 states.
Brandnames of Products and Services:

CATV	*cable TV*
KCST-TV	*San Diego, Calif.*
WAGA-TV	*Atlanta, Ga.*
WITI-TV	*Milwaukee, Wis.*
WJBK-TV	*Detroit, Mich.*
WJKW-TV	*Cleveland, Ohio*
WSBK-TV	*Boston, Mass.*
WTVG-TV	*Toledo, Ohio*

Strawbridge & Clothier

801 Market St.
Philadelphia, PA 19105
(215) 629-6000

Chief Executive Officer: Francis R. Strawbridge III
1984 Annual Sales Volume: 631M
1984 Shares Outstanding: 3,873,312
Shareholders: 3,668
Exchange: OTC
Symbol: STRW
Corporate History: The company, incorporated in 1922, operates general merchandise stores comprised of its main department store at its original location in downtown Philadelphia, 11 suburban branch department stores and its 19 self-service Clover stores. Its principal market is Philadelphia, the surrounding Delaware Valley area of Pennsylvania, New Jersey and Delaware, and the Lehigh Valley area of Pennsylvania.
Brandnames of Products and Services:

Clover	*department stores*
Strawbridge & Clothier	*department stores*

Stride Rite Corp.

Five Cambride Center
Cambridge, MA 02142
(617) 419-8800

Chief Executive Officer: Arnold Hiatt
1984 Annual Sales Volume: 290M
1984 Shares Outstanding: 7,495,000
Shareholders: 3,300
Exchange: NY
Symbol: SRR

Corporate History: The company incorporated in 1919 as Green Shoe Mfg., and adopted its present title in 1972. Stride Rite is one of the largest manufacturers and retailers of children's footwear in the United States and is a major producer of adult work and outdoor recreational shoes and boots. Recently, it acquired the footwear division of Uniroyal.

Brandnames of Products and Services:

Grasshoppers	*sport shoes*
Herman	*shoes*
Herman Survivors	*out door wear*
"John Muir Collection"	*recreational boots*
Keds	*sport shoes*
Knockarounds	*sport shoes*
Pro Keds	*atheletic footwear*
Royal Red Ball	*sport shoes*
Sperry Topsider	*sport shoes*
Stride Rite	*childrens shoes*
Stride Rite Booteries	*sport shoes*
Weber	*shoes*
Zips	*children's shoes*

Sunbeam Corp.

5400 W. Roosevelt Rd.
Chicago, Ill. 60650
(312) 854-3500

Chief Executive Officer: R.P. Gwinn
Exchange: NY
Symbol: SMB

Corporate History: Sunbeam traces its history to the 1880s when Chicago Flexible Shaft Co. was incorporated as a manufacturer of industrial equipment. In 1910 the company made its first consumer product—an electric iron—in an effort to escape the seasonal cycle of much of its industrial merchandise. It began calling its appliances Sunbeam in the 1920s and in 1946 adopted "Sunbeam" as part of its name. Sunbeam has been an innovator in the consumer appliance industry, pioneering such appliances as electric frying pans, egg cookers and portable hair driers. Four-fifths of its sales come from consumer products. It sells almost as many of these household goods overseas as it does in the United States.

Brandnames of Products and Services:

Aircap	*lawn mowers*
Bennett-Ireland	*fireplace enclosures*
Hanson	*household scales*
Hurst	*automobile accessories*
Le Chef	*food appliances*
Mixmaster	*food appliances*
Neosho	*barbecue grills*
Northern	*electric blankets*
Oster	*food appliances*
Springfield	*thermometers*
Sunbeam	*food appliances*

Supermarkets General Corp.

301 Blair Rd.
Woodbridge, NJ 07095
(201) 499-3000

Chief Executive Officer: Leonard Lieberman
1984 Annual Sales Volume: 4,347M
1984 Shares Outstanding: 17,806,907
Shareholders: 3,449
Exchange: NY
Symbol: SGL

Corporate History: Supermarket General Corp. originated in Shop-Rite, a small grocers' cooperative formed to permit it to compete against the major retail food chains. In 1966 the two largest members of the group broke off and incorporated as Supermarkets General Corp. Two years later the company opened the Pathmark chain, which sells products, particularly its private labels, at low prices. Today it is one of the major chains in the Mid-Atlantic states. The company is primarily engaged in the operation of 227 supermarkets and drug stores, located principally in densely populated suburban and urban residential areas in New Jersey, New York, Massachusetts, Pennsylvania, Delaware, Connecticut, New Hampshire and Maryland. It also operates nine L'il Peach convenience food stores and has granted franchises for 50 others in Massachusetts. The company's other retail units include 41 Rickel home improvement centers and 29 department and specialty stores, which operate under the names Howland-Steinbach and Hochschild-Kohn. Rickel's trading area is the New Jersey, New York, eastern Pennsylvania, Connecticut, Maryland and Delaware markets. The department stores operate under the Howland name in New York, Connecticut, Massachusetts and New Hampshire, the Steinbach name in New Jersey and the Hochschild-Kohn name in greater Baltimore, Maryland. The general merchandise businesses are for the most part situated in well-populated suburban areas.

Brandnames of Products and Services:

Heartland	*supermarkets and drug stores*
Hochschild-Kohn	*fashion department and specialty stores*
Howland	*department store and specialty stores*
L'il Peach	*convenience food stores*
Pathmark	*supermarkets and drug stores*
Pharmacity	*drug stores*
Purity Supreme	*supermarkets*
Rickel Home Centers	*general merchandise stores*
Steinbach	*department store and specialty stores*

Super Valu Stores Inc.

11840 Valley View Road
Eden Prairie, MN 55344
(612) 828-4000

Chief Executive Officer:	Michael W. Wright
1984 Annual Sales Volume:	5,900M
1984 Shares Outstanding:	36,943,000
Shareholders:	7,137
Exchange:	NY
Symbol:	SVU

Corporate History: The company incorporated in 1925 as Winston & Newell Co. and adopted its present title in 1954. It is the nation's largest wholesale distributor of groceries and non-food items to retail food stores with outlets in 29 states in the Central, Southeast, Southwest and Eastern United States. Its food business accounts for 85% of sales. The company is concentrating on expansion of warehousing facilities and development of food and general merchandise stores.

Brandnames of Products and Services:

Cub Foods	*warehouse markets*
Mr. Quik	*food convenience stores*
ShopKo	*discount department stores*
Sunflower	*supermarkets*
Super Valu	*supermarkets*

Swank Inc.

6 Hazel St.
Attleboro, Mass. 02703
(617) 222-3400

Chief Executive Officer:	M. Tulin
Exchange:	NY
Symbol:	SNK

Corporate History: Swank, incoporated in 1936, makes men's and ladies' fahion accessories. It entered the women's fragrance market in 1980.

Brandnames of Products and Services:

Biagi	*women's jewelry*
Flora Danica	*fragrance*
Jade East	*fragrance*
Pierre Cardin	*men's and women's fragrances*
Prince Gardner	*men's fashion accessories*
Princess Gardner	*women's fashion accessories*
Royal Copenhagen	*men's fragrances*
Swank	*men's jewelry, fashion accessories*
Wedgwood	*men's jewelry*

Taft Broadcasting Co.

1718 Young St.
Cincinnati, OH 45210
(513) 721-1414

Chief Executive Officer:	Charles S. Mechem Jr.
1984 Annual Sales Volume:	375M
1984 Shares Outstanding:	9,012,303
Shareholders:	10,535
Exchange:	NY
Symbol:	TFB

Corporate History: Taft was incorporated in 1959. The company and its subsidiary corporations are principally engaged in televsion and radio braodcasting, televsion and motion picture production, distribution of programming to television networks and stations, amusement park operations and cable television operations.

Brandnames of Products and Services:

Canada's Wonderland	*amusement part*
Coney Island	*amusement park, Cincinnati Ohio*
KEX-AM	*Portland, Ore.*
KKRZ-FM	*Portland, Ore.*

KYYS-FM	*radio station, Kansas City, Mo.*
WBRC-TV	*Birmingham, Ala.*
WCIX-TV	*Miami, Fla*
WDAF-TV & AM	*radio station, Kansas City, Mo.*
WDCA-TV	*station, Washington D.C.*
WDVE-FM	*radio station, Pittsburgh, Pa.*
WGR-AM and FM	*radio stations, Buffalo, N.Y.*
WGR-FM	*radio station, Buffalo, N.Y.*
WKRC-TV & AM	*radio station, Cincinnati, Ohio*
WKRQ-FM	*radio station, Cincinnati, Ohio*
WLVQ-FM	*radio station, Columbus, Ohio*
WSUN-AM	*radio station, Tampa/St. Petersburg, Fla.*
WTAF-TV	*station, Philadelphia, Pa.*
WTVN-TV & AM	*radio station, Columbus, Ohio*
WYNF-FM	*radio station, Tampa/St. Petersburg, Fla.*

Talley Industries Inc.

2702 North 44th St.
Phoenix, AZ 85008
(602) 957-7711

Chief Executive Officer: William H. Mallender
1984 Annual Sales Volume: 306M
1984 Shares Outstanding: 5,925,275
Shareholders: 4,578
Exchange: NY
Symbol: TAL
Corporate History: Talley Industries is a diversified manufacturer and supplier of high performance aerospace and industrial products and services. The company also manufactures and markets stainless steel bar and rod products; produces and markets timepieces and other timekeeping instrumentation; markets popularly priced men's and women's apparel; and invests in and develops real estate. In fiscal 1984 aerospace and industrial products accounted for 49% of sales, timepieces and housewares 20%, apparel 15% and real estate 16%.
Brandnames of Products and Services:

Adorence	*apparel*
Andrew St. John	*men's apparel*
Andriano	*apparel*
Bay Trading Co.	*apparel*
Big Ben	*clocks*
Botany	*men's apparel*
Botany 500	*men's apparel*
Ecologizer	*air and water purification system*
McGregor	*women's apparel*
Measure Up	*apparel*
Seth Thomas	*clocks and housewares*
Westclox	*clocks*

Tambrands Inc.

10 Delaware Drive
Lake Success, NY 11042
(516) 437-8800

Chief Executive Officer: E.H. Shutt
1984 Annual Sales Volume: 390M
1984 Shares Outstanding: 11,072,248
Shareholders: 6,178
Exchange: NY
Symbol: TMB
Corporate History: The company was organized in 1936. It has wholly-owned subsidiaries operating in Canada, the United Kingdom, Ireland, South Africa and France, and equity investments in companies operating in Spain and Mexico. The company and its subsidiaries are engaged in the manufacture and sale of menstrual protection products and other personal care products in various countries around the world.
Brandnames of Products and Services:

Maxithins	*sanitary pads & panty shields*
Petal Soft	*tampons*
Tampax	*tampons*

Tandy Brands Inc.

500 Bailey
Fort Worth, TX 76107
(817) 334-8200

Chief Executive Officer: Carson R. Thompson
1984 Annual Sales Volume: 61.6M
1984 Shares Outstanding: 2,322,000
Shareholders: 4,000
Exchange: AM
Symbol: TAB
Corporate History: Tandy Brands, Inc. was incorporated in 1975, a Delaware corporation, to operate the leather manufacturing segment of Tandy Corporation. Beginning with a small chain of "western style" stores

at the time of the spin-off from Tandy Corporation, the company has developed a specialty retailing segment by acquiring two other specialty retailers. The company currently operates with two segments; i.e., leather manufacturing and specialty retailing. The leather manufacturing segment includes T.A.B. Accessories and Tex Tan Western Leather. These divisions comprise the men's finished leather goods and accessories and most of the saddlery and riding equipment product classes. The specialty retailing segment also includes Grate Home & Fireplace Centers, a retailer of fireplaces and related accessories, and The Bombay Company, a retail chain selling antique reproductions. Men's leather accessories are sold under the *Hickok* and *Tex Tan* trademarks. Leather accessories are also marketed under the names of Don Loper, Hush Puppies and London Fog. These are staple and fashion lines and are sold through major department stores and men's furnishing stores in the continental United States, and in foreign countries through direct sales to distributors and through licensing agreements. Saddlery and riding equipmentare sold under the *Tex Tan Western* and the Hereford Brand trademarks. Boots are sold under the *Bona Allen* name. Sales are made in all 50 states through sales to independent dealers. The items sold consist of saddles, boots, holsters, belts, buckles, billfolds and sundry gift-accessory items. Sales are primarily to Western outfitters, ranch supply and outdoor stores, with distribution largely in the western states.

Brandnames of Products and Services:

Bombay Company	*antique reproduction*
Bona Allen	*boots*
Don Loper	*leather accessories*
Grate Home and Fireplace Centers	*fireplaces*
Hickok	*leather accessories*
Hush Puppies	*leather accessories*
London Fog	*leather accessories*
T.A.B. Accessories	*men's and boys' accessories*
Tex Tan Western	*leather goods*

Tandy Corp.

1800 One Tandy Center
Fort Worth, Texas 76102
(817) 390-3700

Chief Executive Officer:	P.R. North
Exchange:	NY
Symbol:	TAN

Corporate History: Tandy Corp. was founded in 1899 as American Hide & Leather Co. Its name was changed to General American Industries in 1956 and to its current title in 1960. Tandy was founded as a leather store and expanded into a chain of hobby and craft stores. In 1963 it acquired the nearly bankrupt Radio Shack chain of electronic equipment stores. During the next decade Radio Shack grew tremendously until it now consists of 7,000 stores. Its nearest competitor is only one-eighth its size. During the late 1970s CB radios were its biggest selling item. Now home computers are one of its most popular products. The company pioneered marketing small computer to individuals. Tandy spunoff its leathergoods and crafts businesses. Today it is exclusively in electronics. Sales and earnings have doubled since 1976.

Brandnames of Products and Services:

Archer	*electronic equipment*
Micronta	*electronic equipment*
Patrolman	*electronic equipment*
Radio Shack	*electronic products and stores*
Radio Shack Computer Centers	*computer stores*
Realistic	*electronic equipment*
Science Fair	*electronic equipment*

Tandycrafts Inc.

2727 W. Seventh St.
Fort Worth, TX 76107
(817) 870-0361

Chief Executive Officer:	Kenneth L. Gregson
1984 Annual Sales Volume:	67M
1984 Shares Outstanding:	2,355,661
Shareholders:	4,991
Exchange:	NY
Symbol:	TAC

Corporate History: Initially a wholly owned subsidiary of Tandy Corp., Tandycrafts Inc. incorporated in 1975. It makes materials, kits and equipment for leatherwork and operates specialty retail stores.

Brandnames of Products and Services:

Magee	*picture frames*
Tandy Leather Stores	*leather-working equipment stores*
Tandy Tool Stores	*tool stores*

Tasty Baking Co.

2801 Hunting Park Ave.
Philadelphia, PA 19129
(215) 221-8500

Chief Executive Officer:	N.G. Harris
1984 Annual Sales Volume:	222M
1984 Shares Outstanding:	2,749,600
Shareholders:	4,836
Exchange:	AS
Symbol:	TBC

Corporate History: The company was incorporated in 1914, it went public in 1962. Current product development activities at Tastykake include a donut line, brownies, and soft and chewy cookies.

Brandnames of Products and Services:

Buckeye	*cookies, potato chips, snack foods, diet candies and cookies, beverage mixes, pretzels & spices*
Creamies	*cream filled cake*
Juniors	*sponge cake*
Kandy Kakes	*enrobed choc. covered cakes*
Krimpets	*sponge cake with butterscotch icing or jelly filling.*
Tastykake	*cookies, pies, cakes, pretzels, donuts*
Tempty	*cream filled cupcake*

Technicolor Inc.

2049 Century Park East
Los Angeles, Calif. 90067
(213) 553-5200

Chief Executive Officer:	M. Kamerman
Exchange:	NY
Symbol:	TK

Corporate History: The company, incorporated in 1922, is mainly engaged in film processing and related services, including development of motion picture film and processing videotape.

Brandnames of Products and Services:

Technicolor	*film processing*

Tech/Ops Inc.

One Beacon St.
Boston, Mass. 02108
(617) 523-2030

Chief Executive Officer:	M.G. Schorr
Exchange:	AM
Symbol:	TO

Corporate History: Incorporated in 1951, Tech/Ops is a diversified company with interests in construction and broadcasting. It also manufactures high-technology products for industry. In fiscal 1980 technological products accounted for 87% of sales and broadcasting 13%.

Brandnames of Products and Services:

WFOG-AM/FM	*radio station, Suffolk/ Norfolk, Va.*
WJYE-FM	*radio station, Buffalo, N.Y.*
WLKW-AM/FM	*radio station, Providence, R.I.*

Teledyne Inc.

1901 Ave of the Stars
Los Angeles, CA 90067
(213) 277-3311

Chief Executive Officer:	Henry E. Singleton
1984 Annual Sales Volume:	3,494M
1984 Shares Outstanding:	11,709,478
Shareholders:	21,000
Exchange:	NY
Symbol:	TDY

Corporate History: Teledyne, incorporated in 1960, is largely engaged in the manufacture of heavy equipment. The company's major business segments include aviation and electronic products, industrial products, specialty metal products and consumer products. Teledyne also owns several companies which engage in the insurance and finance business.

Brandnames of Products and Services:

AR	*speakers and turntables*
Fireside Thrift	*consumer finance operations*
Home Entertainment	*stores*
Instapure	*water filter*
Olson	*stereo and video equipment*
Shower Massage	*showerheads*
Super Saver	*showerheads*
Teledyne	*stereo and video equipment*
Unicoa Corp.	*insurance*

Water Pik	*dental product*

Telex Corp.

P.O. Box 1526
Tulsa, OK 74101
(918) 627-2333

Chief Executive Officer: Stephen J. Jatras
1984 Annual Sales Volume: 325M
1984 Shares Outstanding: 14,424,194
Shareholders: 10,354
Exchange: NY
Symbol: TC

Corporate History: Incorporated in 1963, Telex is comprised of two subsidiaries. It's major subsidiary is Telex Computer Products, Inc. (ICP) is a worldwide designer, manufacturer and marketer of terminals, printers, controllers, intelligent workstations, and OEM tape storage products. Through its acquisition of Raytheon Data Systems, Telex has become the leading supplier of computer terminal systems to the airline industry, in addition to being the largest independent supplier of IBM compatible terminals. Telex's other subsidiary is Telex Communications, Inc. (TCI) which manufactures tape recorders, tape drives and players, headphones and headsets, microphones, hearing aids, visual audio equipment, and antennas for marine and amateur radios and for military and commercial communications.

Brandnames of Products and Services:

Magnecord	*tape recorders*
Telex	*tape recorders*
Viking	*tape recorders*

Telstar, Corp.

1900 Avenue of the Stars
Los Angeles, CA 90067
(213) 556-5650

Chief Executive Officer: Gerald A. Bartell
1984 Annual Sales Volume: 9M
1984 Shares Outstanding: 95,529,581
Shareholders: 5,600
Exchange: OTC
Symbol: TSTR

Corporate History: Telstar Corp. was founded in 1981 to deliver television programming by satellite. The company has utilization rights to four AT&T satellite channels ("transponders"). Telstar offers both "free-to-guest" and "pay-per-use" services to hotel and motel customers. Telstar was a founder of the cable televison channel Country Music Television. In 1984 Telstar exchanged its 46% ownership of CMT for 49.5% of CMT's parent company Music Village Productions.

Brandnames of Products and Services:

Country Music Television	*pay television*
ESPN	*pay television*
Playboy Channel	*pay television*
Showtime/The Movie Channel	*pay television*

Temtex Industries Inc.

1601 LBJ Freeway Suite 605
Dallas, TX 75234
(214) 484-1845

Chief Executive Officer: James E. Upfield
1984 Annual Sales Volume: 33M
1984 Shares Outstanding: 1648,765
Shareholders: 520
Exchange: OTC
Symbol: TMTX

Corporate History: The company incorporated in 1969 as a real estate developer. In 1970 it began manufacturing products for the home. Today, the company manufacturers factory built wood-burning fireplaces in its Nashville, Tennessee, and Perris, California plants. The fireplaces are distributed nationally under the Temco label and are used in both new residential construction and modernization and remodeling projects. Texas Clay Industries, a division of Temex, produces high quality face brick for use in residential and commercial structures. The brick is distributed in Texas and the four-state surrounding area. In addition the company fabricates specialized military products for the United States and other governments.

Brandnames of Products and Services:

Amberlight	*patio grills*
Design-Tex	*heat shields for fireplaces*
Temco	*built-in metal fireplaces and floor furnaces*
Texas Clay	*brick face*

Tenneco Inc.

P.O. Box 2511
Houston, TX 77001
(713) 757-2131

Chief Executive Officer: J.L. Ketelsen
1984 Annual Sales Volume: 14,779
1984 Shares Outstanding: 118,158,756
Shareholders: 231,608
Exchange: NY
Symbol: TGT

Corporate History: The company was founded in 1943 and incorporated in 1947 as Texas Gas Transmission Co. It adopted its present title in 1966. Tenneco, one of the 25 largest industrial companies in the United States, is involved in such varied businesses as developing natural gas and oil, building nuclear submarines, manufacturing shock absorbers and providing life insurnace. During its comparatively short history it expanded aggressively through acquisition. In fewer than 30 years it acquired more than 100 companies here and abroad. Approximately 75% of Tenneco's profits come from energy, primarily the production of gas and oil. Most of its reserves are in the Gulf states but it is also drilling in Canada, Africa and the North Sea. The greatest portion of its market is in the Northeast. New York, Pennsylvania, and Massachusetts receive 50% of their natural gas supplies from Tenneco. In an effort to enter areas less regulated than energy, Tenneco has branched into agriculture, ship building and plastics.

Brandnames of Products and Services:

Case International	*agricultural equipment*
Direct	*gasoline*
House of Almonds	*mail-order food*
Monroe	*shock absorbers*
Philadelphia Life	*insurance*
Southwestern General Life Ins.	*insurance*
Southwestern Life Insurance	*insurance*
Speedy Muffler King - auto park	
Sun Giant	*fruits and nuts*
Tenneco	*gasoline*
U Fill'em	*gasoline*
Walker	*exhaust systems*

Texaco Inc.

2000 Westchester Ave.
White Plains, NY 10650
(914) 253-4000

Chief Executive Officer: John K. McKinley
1984 Annual Sales Volume: 47,334M
1984 Shares Outstanding: 237,768,316
Shareholders: 415,000
Exchange: NY
Symbol: TX

Corporate History: The company, founded in 1902 and incorporated in 1926. Its name was changed in 1941 to the Texas Co. and in 1959 to Texaco Inc. The company is engaged in the worldwide exploration for and production, transportation, refining, and marketing of crude oil and its products including petrochemicals. In 1984 the company acquired the Getty Oil Co.

Brandnames of Products and Services:

Havoline	*motor oil*
Texaco	*automotive stations and products*

Texas Instruments Inc.

P.O. Box 225474
Dallas, TX 75265
(214) 995-2011

Chief Executive Officer: J. Fred Bucy
1984 Annual Sales Volume: 5,741M
1984 Shares Outstanding: 24,210
Shareholders: 30,701
Exchange: NY
Symbol: TXN

Corporate History: Texa Instruments is a multinational, diversified, technology-based company with more than 50 manufacturing plants in 18 countries. The company was founded in 1930 to provide contract geophysical services to the petroleum industry, exploiting its technological innovation, the reflection seismograph. TI continues as a world leader in this field through its subsiiary, Geophysical Service Inc., but in 1946 addedi electronic systems manufacturing and entered a new era of dynamic growth. Now, Texas Instruments is engaged in the development, manufacture and sale of a variety of products in the electrical and electronics industries for industrial, consumer and government markets. These products consist of components (semiconductors, such as integrated circuits, and electrical and electronic control devices); digital products (such as minicomputers, data terminals, electronic calculators, and learning aids); and government electronics (such as radar, infrared surveillance systems and missile guidance and control systems). The company also produces metallurgical materials (primarily clad metals) for use in a variety of applications, such as automotive equipment, and provides services, primarily through the electronic collection and processing of seismic data in connection with petroleum exploration.

Brandnames of Products and Services:

Texas Instruments	*calculators, computers and watches*

Textron Inc.

40 Westminster St.
Providence, RI 02903
(401) 421-2800

Chief Executive Officer:	B.F. Dolan
1984 Annual Sales Volume:	3,221M
1984 Shares Outstanding:	36,469,000
Shareholders:	49,000
Exchange:	NY
Symbol:	TXT

Corporate History: The company was founded in 1928 as Franklin Rayon Corp. During the 1950s, under the direction of Royal Little who developed the idea of a conglomerate, it began diversifying. Today it is involved in aerospace, industrial and metal production as well as the manufacture of consumer goods. In the mid-1970s its Bell Helicopter susidiary grew so fast that by 1978 it contributed nearly one-third of the company's sales. In February 1985 Textron completed the acquisition of AVCO Corporation, a diversified company with operations in financial services, propulsion systems, aerospace technology and management services. AVCO's 1984 sales were $2.9 billion. Shortly, thereafter Textron announced that it is seeking buyers for its Spencer Kellogg specialty resins division and its Bell Helicopter Textron subsidiary to reduce the debt incurred in the AVCO purchase.

Brandnames of Products and Services:

At-A-Glance	*appointment books*
Berkshire	*paper*
Bostitch	*staples*
British Sterling	*men's toiletries*
Duo-Tang	*report covers, folders*
Eaton	*stationery*
Elizabeth Arden	*eyeglass frames*
E-Z-Go	*golf carts*
Gorham	*silver*
Homelite	*saws, stringtrimmers*
Jacobson	*lawn mowers*
Sheaffer	*writing instruments*
Shuron	*eyeglass frames*
Speidel	*watchbands and men's toiletries*
Valentine Sands	*greeting cards, gift wrap*

TFI Companies Inc.

10960 Wilshire Blvd.
Los Angeles, Calif. 90024
(213) 478-0188

Chief Executive Officer:	G. Chase
Exchange:	AM
Symbol:	TFI

Corporate History: The company incorporated in 1960 as Tastee Freez Industries Inc. Its present title was adopted in 1969. Initially it developed a chain of soft ice cream drive-ins. Today it grants franchises to and supplies a chain of fast-food outlets.

Brandnames of Products and Services:

Bar M	*smoked meats*
Big T	*family restaurants*

Thomas Industries Inc.

207 E. Broadway
Louisville, KY 40202
(502) 582-3771

Chief Executive Officer:	T.R. Fuller
1984 Annual Sales Volume:	292M
1984 Shares Outstanding:	8,478,071
Shareholders:	4,000
Exchange:	NY
Symbol:	TII

Corporate History: The company incorporated in 1928 as Electric Sprayit Co. It adopted its present title in 1953 when it acquired Moe Light Inc. which was organized in Wisconsin in 1929. The company makes lighting fixtures, decorative home accessories, hardware, and tools.

Brandnames of Products and Services:

Benjamin	*commercial/industrial lighting fixtures and signals*
Builders Brass	*architectural hardware & door controls*
C & M	*lighting fixtures*

Capri	*recessed and track lighting fixtures*
Contempra	*barbecue equipment*
Gardco	*architectural lighting fixtures*
Harris & Mallow	*clocks, weather instruments*
Jetline	*blower, vacuum & CO_2 powered equipment*
Lennon	*wall paper*
Oliver-MacLeod	*chimneys and zero clearance fireplace*
Portland Willamette	*fireplace accessories*
Pouliot	*artificial/preserved floral arrangements*
Sprayit	*paint spray equipment*
Starlight	*lighting and household accessories*
Thomas	*paint brushes, rollers and pads*
Thomas	*lamps*
Thomas	*lighting and household accessories*

Thorn Apple Valley, Inc.

18700 West Ten Mile Road
Southfield, MI 48075
(313) 552-0700

Chief Executive Officer: Henry S. Dorfman
1984 Annual Sales Volume: 664M
1984 Shares Outstanding: 3,582,530
Shareholders: 1,063
Exchange: OTC
Symbol: TAVI
Corporate History: The company, originally incorporated in 1959, engages in the slaughtering and butchering of hogs, the sale of prime cuts of pork and pork by-products, and in the sale of processed meat products such as frankfurters, sausages, bologna, luncheon meats, bacon and smoked hams. In 1984 fresh pork & pork by-products accounted for 48% of sales and processed meat products for 52% of sales. In 1984 the company changed its name from Frederick & Herrud, Inc. to Thorn Apple Valley Inc.
Brandnames of Products and Services:

Bar-H	*pork products, processed meats*
Beefeater	*pork products, processed meats*
Herrud	*pork products, processed meats*
Hickory Host	*pork products, processed meats*
Holly Ridge Farm	*pork products, processed meats*
Olde Virginie	*pork products, processed meats*
Royal Crown	*pork products, processed meats*
Thorn Apple Valley	*pork products, processed meats*

Thorofare Markets Inc.

650 N. Meridian Rd.
P.O. Box 120
Youngstown, Ohio 44501
(216) 792-9051

Chief Executive Officer: W.L. Reiff
Exchange: AM
Symbol: TMI
Corporate History: The company incorporated in 1922 as U.S. Stores and adopted its current name in 1949. It operates a chain of supermarkets in the Midwest.
Brandnames of Products and Services:

First Stop	*supermarkets*
Penny Fare	*supermarkets*
Thorofare	*supermarkets*

Thrifty Corp.

3424 Wilshire Blvd
Los Angeles, CA 90010
(213) 251-6000

Chief Executive Officer: Leonard H. Strauss
1984 Annual Sales Volume: 1,299M
1984 Shares Outstanding: 19,966,009
Shareholders: 7,800
Exchange: NY
Symbol: TFD
Corporate History: The company, founded in 1929 and incorporated in 1935, is engaged in the drug and discount chain store business. The company operates 542 drug and discount stores; 455 of the stores are located in California, the rest in Arizona, Idaho, Nevada, New Mexico, Oregon, Utah, Washington and Wyoming. The company also operates 71 sporting goods stores, 171 discount bookstores, 43 discount au-

tomotive part and accessories stores and an importing business.

Brandnames of Products and Services:

Big 5	*sporting good store chain*
Crown Bookstores	*bookstore chain*
Giant T	*discount drug store chain*
Thrifty	*discount drugstore chain*
Trak Auto West	*discount automotive parts and accessories chain*

Time Inc.

Time & Life Bldg., Rockefeller Center
New York, NY 10020
(212) 586-1212

Chief Executive Officer: J. Richard Munro
1984 Annual Sales Volume: 3,067M
1984 Shares Outstanding: 60,785,303
Shareholders: 18,174
Exchange: NY
Symbol: TL

Corporate History: The company was incorporated in 1922 by Henry Luce a dominant figure in publishing who developed the first modern news magazine. Today Time Inc. is a major information and entertainment company in the print and video fields. It is the largest magazine publishing company in the world, with seven magazines that had a combined circulation of 15.8 million copies at the end of1984. The company is also a leading publisher of trade, text, and professional books and the largest marketer of book series sold by direct mail. Time Inc. also operates Selling Areas-Marketing, Inc., the second largest marketing information service. In the video field, Time Inc.'s Home Box Office is the largest pay-TV programming service in the U.S., and a companion service, Cinemax, ranks third. The company's American Television and Communications Corp. is the second largest cable television system operating company.

Brandnames of Products and Services:

Book of the Month Club	
Cinemax	*pay TV*
Discover	*magazine*
Fortune	*magazine*
HBO	*pay television service*
Life	*Magazine*
Little Brown & Co.	*publishing house*
Money	*magazine*
New York Graphic Society	*publishing*
Oxmoor House	*how-to books*
People	*magazine*
Sports Illustrated	*magazine*
Time-Life	*book series, films, TV*
Time	*magazine*

Times Mirror Co.

Times Mirror Sq.
Los Angeles, CA 90053
(213) 972-3700

Chief Executive Officer: R.F. Erburu
1984 Annual Sales Volume: 2,771M
1984 Shares Outstanding: 68,722,653
Shareholders: 5,131
Exchange: NY
Symbol: TMC

Corporate History: The company incorporated in 1884, succeeding *Los Angeles Times,* founded in 1881, and *Times Mirror Press,* started in 1873. Newspapers bring in almost half of its revenues, books about 9% and paper and wood products approximately 14%. The company is expanding in the fields of broadcasting, cable television and electronic publishing. The *Los Angeles Times,* a subsidiary, is the second largest metropolitan newspaper in the U.S. in terms of daily circulation.

Brandnames of Products and Services:

The Advocate	*newspaper, Stamford, Conn.*
C.V. Mosby	*publishing*
Golf	*magazine*
Graphic Controls Corporation	*recording charts and marking systems*
Harry N. Abrams Co.	*publishing*
The Hartford Courant	*newspaper, Hartford, Conn.*
The H.M. Gousha Company	*road map and automotive services and maintenance guide publisher*
Jeppesen Sanderson	*aviation information and training programs*
KDFW-TV	*Dallas/Ft. Worth, Texas*
KTBC-TV	*Austin, Texas*
KTVI-TV	*St. Louis, Mo.*

Los Angeles Times	*newspaper, Los Angeles, Calif.*
Matthew Bender	*legal publishing house*
Newsday	*newspaper, Long Island, N.Y.*
Outdoor Life	*magazine*
Popular Science	*magazine*
Post	*newspaper, Denver, Colo.*
Publishers Paper Co.	*newsprint and forest products*
Ski	*magazine*
Sporting Goods Dealer	*magazine*
Sporting News	*magazine*
Time	*newspaper, Greenwich, Conn.*
Times-Herald	*newspaper, Dallas, Texas*
Times Mirror Cable Television	*cable television systems*
Times Mirror Press	*printing house*
WETM-TV	*Elmira, N.Y.*
WHTM-TV	*Harrisburg, Penn.*
WSTM-TV	*Syracuse, N.Y.*
WVTM-TV	*Birmingham, Ala.*
Year Book Medical	*publishing*

Tonka Corp.

6000 Clearwater Drive
Minnetonka, MN 55343
(612) 475-9500

Chief Executive Officer: S.G. Shank
1984 Annual Sales Volume: 139M
1984 Shares Outstanding: 2.1M
Shareholders: 1,490
Exchange: NY
Symbol: TKA
Corporate History: The company, incorporated in 1946, is a leading toy manufacturer, known for its lines of metal toy trucks.
Brandnames of Products and Services:

C.L.A.W.	*battery-powered toy vehicles*
Clutch Poppers	*toy vehicles*
C.R.A.B.	*battery-powered toy vehicles*
Fast Traks	*toy vehicles*
GoBots	*male action toys*
Mighty Cycles	*ride-on/3-wheel cycles*
Mighty Robots	*male action toys*
Mightys	*toy trucks*
Mighty Tonka	*toy trucks*
Powersuits	*male action toys*
Puzzler	*male action toys*
Regular Tonka	*toy trucks*
Star Fairies	*fantasy dolls and animals*
Tiny Mightys	*toy trucks*
Tiny Tonka	*toy trucks*
T-N-T's	*toy racing cars*
Tonka	*toys*

Tony Lama Co. Inc.

1137 Tony Lama St.
El Paso, Texas 79915
(915) 778-8311

Chief Executive Officer: R.E. Souder
Exchange: OTC
Symbol: TLAM
Corporate History: Incorporated in 1946, Tony Lama is one of the leading producers of handcrafted, Western-style boots and accessories in the nation.
Brandnames of Products and Services:

Tony Lama	*Western apparel and stores*

Tootsie Roll Industries Inc.

7401 S. Cicero Ave.
Chicago, IL 60629
(312) 838-3400

Chief Executive Officer: M.J. Gordon
1984 Annual Sales Volume: 93M
1984 Shares Outstanding: 2,732,081
Shareholders: 3,733
Exchange: NY
Symbol: TR
Corporate History: The company incorporated in 1919 as the Sweets Co. of America. It adopted its present title in 1966. Throughout its history it has remained a candy company and has never attempted to diversify. The company has plants located in Illinois and Mexico.
Brandnames of Products and Services:

Bonomo Turkish Taffy	*candy*
Mason	*candy*
Tootsie	*candy*
Tootsie Roll	*candy*

Topps Chewing Gum Inc.

254 36th St.
Brooklyn, N.Y. 11232
(212) 768-8900

Chief Executive Officer: A.T. Shorin
Exchange: AM
Symbol: TCG
Corporate History: The company, incorporated in 1947, makes bubble gum and novelty candy.
Brandnames of Products and Services:

Bazooka	*bubble gum*
Big Buddy	*bubble gum*
Blockbusters	*bubble gum*
Gold Rush	*bubble gum*
Jewel	*candy*
Pop Bottles	*candy*
Pop the Juicy	*bubble gum*
Ring	*bubble gum*
Smooth n' Juicy	*gum*
Super Bazooka	*bubble gum*

Toro Co.

8111 Lyndale Ave. South
Bloomington, MN 55420
(612) 888-8801

Chief Executive Officer: Kendrick B. Melrose
1984 Annual Sales Volume: 280M
1984 Shares Outstanding: 6,699,702
Shareholders: 4,136
Exchange: NY
Symbol: TTC
Corporate History: The company, founded in 1914 and incorporated in 1935 as Toro Manufacturing Co. of Minnesota, makes consumer lawn equipment, snow removal equipment, professional turf equipment and turf irrigation equipment.
Brandnames of Products and Services:

Toro	*power tools, power mowers, snow removal equipment, irrigation equipment*

Towle Manufacturing Co.

144 Addison St.
Boston, MA 02128
(617) 569-7600

Chief Executive Officer: Leonard Florence
1984 Annual Sales Volume: 265M
1984 Shares Outstanding: 4,830,440
Shareholders: 2,377
Exchange: NY
Symbol: TOW
Corporate History: Towle, incorporated in 1880, is engaged in the manufacture and distribution of giftware, predominantly tableware products. The principal tableware products consist of sterling silver flatware and holloware with which its name has long been identified, silverplated, pewter, brass and chrome holloware, stainless steel and silverplated flatware, crystal, ceramic, porcelain and bone china giftware, cutlery, candles and ice buckets. Its other products include Christmas ornaments, cloth silverpouches, artificial flowers, fashion jewelry and class rings. In fiscal 1984 sterling products accounted for 7.7% of sales, silverplated products 27.4%, crystal products 10.6%, stainless steel products 11.5% and other items 42.8%.
Brandnames of Products and Services:

Arabia	*tableware*
Carvel Hall	*cutlery*
A Christmas Place	*ornaments*
Drulane	*tableware*
F.B. Rogers	*silver*
Gailstyn-Sulton	*enamel cookware*
Gallway Irish	*crystal*
Georgian House	*stainless steel flatware*
Gloria Vanderbilt	*giftware*
Gold Lance	*jewelry-school rings*
Irvinware	*housewares*
Javit	*crytal*
Lauffer	*stainless steel flatware*
Leonard	*silver products*
National	*silver*
Old Harbor	*candles*
Oxford Hall	*stainless steel flatware*
P.M.C. (Sheffield)	*giftware*
Poole-Silversmiths	*cutlery*
Seiden	*brass giftware*
Shelton Ware	*ice buckets*
Sigma Gifthouse	*gift store*
Supreme	*stainless steel flatware*
Tiffin	*crystal*
Towle	*sterling and stainless flatware, giftware*

Val St Lambert	*crystal*
Westfield Design	*brass housewares*
William Adams	*giftware*

Toys "R" Us Inc.

395 West Passaic St.
Rochelle Park, NJ 07662
(201) 845-5033

Chief Executive Officer:	Charles Lazarus
1984 Annual Sales Volume:	1,702M
1984 Shares Outstanding:	81,712,750
Shareholders:	9,600
Exchange:	NY
Symbol:	TOY

Corporate History: The company incorporated in 1928 as Interstate Department Stores, consolidating 22 companies that operated 23 stores. It adopted its present title in 1978. It is the largest toy specialty retail chain in the United States. In 1984 the company operated 203 toy stores in 28 states. The stores sell children's and adult toys, games, bicycle and wheel goods, sporting goods, electronic and video games, home computers, small pools, records, books, infant and juvenile furniture, infant's and children's clothing. In the past few years, the company has concentrated on expansion of the toy market from more traditional age groups to include teenagers and adults. It also operates four toy stores in Canada and one in Singapore.

Brandnames of Products and Services:

Interstate	*department stores*
Kids "R" Us	*children's apparel stores*
Toys "R" Us	*toy stores*

Transamerica Corp.

600 Montgomery St.
San Francisco, CA 94111
(415) 983-4000

Chief Executive Officer:	James R. Harvey
1984 Annual Sales Volume:	5,399M
1984 Shares Outstanding:	65,400,935
Shareholders:	106,900
Exchange:	NY
Symbol:	TA

Corporate History: Transamerica, incorporated in 1928, is a diversified company engaged through subsidiaries in insurance, finance, manufacturing and transportation. Transamerica's insurance services include life insurance, insurance brokerage, and property and casualty insurance. Finance services include consumer lending and title operations. Transportation services include equipment leasing, air travel, and car and truck rental. In 1984 insurance provided 66% of the company's profits, transportation 16%, finance 9%, manufacturing 7% and the remaining 2% of profits came from real estate and leasing.

Brandnames of Products and Services:

American Life Insurance Co. of New York	
Budget Rent-a-Car Corp.	*car & truck rentals*
Countrywide Life Insurance Co.	
Crown Valley Insurance	
Fred S. James & Co. Inc.	*insurance brokerage*
Lyon	*moving and storage*
The Money Stores	*consumer loans*
Occidental Life Insurance Co.	
Pacific Finance Loans consumer loans	
Transamerica Accidental Life Insurance Co.	
Transamerica Airlines	*charter airlines*
Transamerica Financial Corp.	
Transamerica Insurance Co.	
Transamerica Life Insurance & Annuity Co.	
Transamerica Title Insurance Co.	
Trans International Airlines	*charter airlines*
Wolverine	*insurance*

Trans-Lux Corp.

110 Richards Avenue
Norwalk, CT 06854
(203) 853-4321

Chief Executive Officer:	Richard Brandt
1984 Annual Sales Volume:	29.5M

1984 Shares Outstanding: 1,594,827
Shareholders: 1,425
Exchange: AM
Symbol: TLX
Corporate History: Trans-Lux Corp. was founded in 1920. The company operates 26 motion picture theaters in three states. It also operates two multi-media presentations, "The New York Experience" and "The South Street Venture," in New York City. In addition, Trans-Lux produces, leases, sells and maintains electronic teleprinters which are used primarily as terminal equipment on the Telex, TWX, and DDD networks and produces equipment and LED displays for the dissemination of stock and commodity markets' quotations, financial and other news.
Brandnames of Products and Services:

"The New York Experience"	*multi-media presentation*
"The South Street Venture"	*multi-media presentation*
Trans-Lux	*motion picture theaters*

Trans World Airlines Inc.

605 Third Ave.
New York, NY 10158
(212) 692-3000

Chief Executive Officer: C.E. Meyer, Jr.
1984 Annual Sales Volume: 3,657M
1984 Shares Outstanding: 32,791,713
Shareholders: 21,347
Exchange: NY
Symbol: TWA
Corporate History: Trans World Airlines Inc. is one of the largest U.S. airlines serving major metropolitan centers in the U.S., Europe, the Mediterranean Area, the Arabian Gulf and India. TWA's principal U.S. routes serve more than 60 major cities. TWA carries more passengers in scheduled service between the U.S. and Europe than any other airline. Prior to 1983 TWA was a wholly-owned subsidiary of Trans World Corp. In 1983 six million shares of TWA common stock were sold to the public. Remaining shares were distributed as a dividend to Transworld stockholders and as a result TWA was established as a separate publicly owned company in 1984.
Brandnames of Products and Services:

TWA	*airline*

Transworld Corp.

605 Third Ave.
New York, NY 10158
(212) 972-4700

Chief Executive Officer: L. Edwin Smart
1984 Annual Sales Volume: 2,002M
1984 Shares Outstanding: 35,600,934
Shareholders: 22,800
Exchange: NY
Symbol: TW
Corporate History: The company was organized in 1928 by a group of private investors and incorporated in 1934 as Transcontinental & Western Air Inc. Its present name was adopted in 1979. Transworld Corp. is a diversified consumer services company operating wholly-owned subsidiaries in three principal segments —food services, hotel services and real estate services. As of 1984, TWA Airlines ceased to be a subsidiary of Transworld Corp. and became a company in its own right.
Brandnames of Products and Services:

Canteen	*food serviceand vending machines*
Cenguard Insurance	
Century 21	*real estate offices*
Drake Hotel Chicago	
Dunhill Personal	*placement services*
Hardee's	*fast-food restaurants*
Hilton International Hotels	
Quincy's Family Steak House	*restaurants*
Vista International	*hotels*

Triangle Pacific Corp.

16803 Dallas Pkwy.
P.O. Box 660100
Dallas, TX 75266-0100
(214) 931-3000

Chief Executive Officer: Abraham Meltzer
1984 Annual Sales Volume: 271M
1984 Shares Outstanding: 4,135,014
Shareholders: 1,465
Exchange: NY
Symbol: TPC

Corporate History: The company incorporated in 1943 as Triangle Lumber Corp. and adopted its present title in 1973. Today the company is the nation's largest manufacturer of kitchen and bathroom cabinets and hardwood flooring.

Brandnames of Products and Services:

Beauty Queen	*metal cabinets*
Bruce	*do-it-yourself hardwood floors*
Classic Bath	*wood cabinets*
Del Mar	*wood cabinets*
IXL	*wood cabinets*
Mutschler	*wood cabinets*
Tri Pac	*wood cabinets*

Tultex Corp.

P.O. Box 5191
Martinville, VA 24115
(703) 632-2961

Chief Executive Officer:	W.F. Franck
1984 Annual Sales Volume:	286M
1984 Shares Outstanding:	9,003,676
Shareholders:	2,275
Exchange:	AM
Symbol:	TTX

Corporate History: The company incorporated in 1937 as Sale Knitting Co. and in 1971 changed its name to Tully Corp. of Virginia. It adopted its present title in 1976. The company makes fleeced and laminated knit sportswear. Principal apparel customers include discount and chain stores and mailorder houses. In fiscal 1984 apparel accounted for approximately 84.1% of sales and yarn products 10.6%.

Brandnames of Products and Services:

Discus	*family apparel*
Tultex	*family apparel*

Twin Fair Inc.

One Twin Fair Corporate Center
Box 861
Buffalo, N.Y. 14240
(716) 828-1000

Chief Executive Officer:	H.A. Egan
Exchange:	AM
Symbol:	TWN

Corporate History: The company, incorporated in 1915, operates discount department stores in the East.

Brandnames of Products and Services:

Hens & Kelly	*department stores*
Twin Fair	*discount department stores*

Tyson Foods Inc.

2210 W. Oaklawn Dr.
Springdale, AR 72764
(501) 756-4000

Chief Executive Officer:	Don Tyson
1984 Annual Sales Volume:	750M
1984 Shares Outstanding:	7,809,024
Shareholders:	3,284
Exchange:	OTC
Symbol:	TYSN

Corporate History: The company was founded in 1935 and incorporated in 1947 as Tyson Feed & Hatchery. It adopted its present name in 1962. The company produces, markets and distributes a variety of fresh and frozen packages of poultry and poultry products, live pork and chips, tortillas and other Mexican food products. Its integrated operations consist of breeding and rearing chickens, cornish game hens and hogs; feed milling; processing; pre-packaging; pre-cooking; further processing; and marketing of these food products. Products are sold to major national and independent grocery chains, regional food distributors, military operations and national retail fast food franchisers. In 1983, the company acquired Mexican Original Products Inc.

Brandnames of Products and Services:

Mexican Original	*Mexican food products*
Tyson	*poultry products*

UAL Inc.

1200 Algonquin Rd.
P.O. Box 66919
Chicago, IL 60666
(312) 952-4000

Chief Executive Officer:	Richard J. Ferris
1984 Annual Sales Volume:	6,968M
1984 Shares Outstanding:	34,794,059
Shareholders:	26,736
Exchange:	NY
Symbol:	UAL

Corporate History: UAL Corp., incorporated in 1968, is a major force in the travel, leisure and insurance businesses. One of its major components, United Airlines, was formed out of an amalgam of aviation companies in the late 1920s and 1930s. Today it is the largest carrier in the United States and the world's largest investor-owned airline in terms of passenger revenues. United serves 159 cities in all 50 states, the District of Columbia; the Bahamas; Alberta, British Columbia and Ontario, Canada; Mexico; Hong Kong and Japan. United accounted for approximately 89% of UAL's consolidated operating revenues in 1984. The company's Westin Hotels operates or is affiliated with 51 hotels in the United States, Canada, Mexico and other countries.

Brandnames of Products and Services:

Alameda Hotel	*Mexico City*
Alaska Prince Hotel	*Tokyo*
The Arizona Biltmore Hotel Phoenix	
Bayshore Inn	*Vancouver*
Bellevue Staford Hotel	*Philadelphia*
Benson Hotel	*Portland*
Bonaventure Hotel	*Montreal, Los Angeles*
Calgary Inn	*Calgary*
Camino Real Hotel Cancun, Guadalajara, Mazatlan, Mexico City, Puerto Vallarta, Saltillo, San Salvador	
Carlton Hotel	*Johannesburg*
Carlton House Hotel	*Pittsburg*
Century Plaza Hotel	*Los Angeles*
Chosun	*Seoul*
Continental Plaza Hotel	*Chicago*
Copley Place	*Boston*
Crown Center Hotel	*Kansas City*
Detroit Plaza Hotel	
Dusit Thani Hotel	*Bangkok*
Edmonton Plaza Hotel	
Galleria	*Dallas*
Galleria Plaza Hotel	*Houston*
Hotel Scandinavia	*Copenhagaen, Oslo*
Hotel Toronto	
Houston Oaks Hotel	
Ilikai Hotel	*Honolulu*
Las Brisas	*Acapulco*
Las Brisas Hotel	*Acapulco*
Mauna Kea Beach Hotel	*Kona, Hawaii*
Mayflower Hotel	*Washington, D.C.*
Michigan Inn Hotel	*Detroit*
Miyako Hotel	*Kyoto, San Francisco*
Olympic Hotel	*Seattle*
Peachtree Plaza Hotel	*Atlanta*
Philippine Plaza Hotel	*Manila*
Plaza Hotel	*New York, N.Y.*
Shangri-La Hotel	*Hong Kong*
South Coast Plaza Hotel	*Calif.*
Space Needle	*restaurant, Seattle, Wash.*
St. Francis Hotel	*San Francisco, Calif.*
Takanawa Prince Hotel	*Tokyo*
Tokyo Prince Hotel	*Tokyo*
United Airlines	
Utah	*Salt Lake City*
Wailea Beach Hotel	*Hawaii*
Washington Plaza Hotel	*Seattle, Wash.*
Wentworth Hotel	*Sydney*
Westin Hotels	
William Penn	*Pittsburgh*
William Plaza Hotel	*Tulsa, Okla.*

Unimax Group Inc.

425 Park Ave.
New York, N.Y. 10022
(212) 755-8800

Chief Executive Officer: T. Scheinman
Exchange: AM
Symbol: UMX
Corporate History: The company, incorporated in 1968, is a diversified manufacturer of electronic components and also operates jewelry stores.

Brandnames of Products and Services:

Arnold's	*jewelry stores*
Barry's	*jewelry stores*
Gold Art Creations	*jewelry stores*
Hirsch & Son	*jewelry stores*
Le Roys	*jewelry stores*
Ringmakers	*jewelry stores*
Ships Bell	*jewelry stores*

Union Carbide Corp.

39 Old Ridgebury Rd.
Dunbury, CT 06817-0001
(203) 794-2000

Chief Executive Officer: Warren M. Anderson
1984 Annual Sales Volume: 9,508M
1984 Shares Outstanding: 70,486,670
Shareholders: 108,954
Exchange: NY
Symbol: UK

Corporate History: Union Carbide, founded in 1886 incorporated in 1917, is one of the largest industrial companies in the United States and the world. International operations contributed nearly a third of total sales in 1984. The company is active in five industry segments: petrochemicals; industrial gases; metals and carbon products; consumer products; and technology, services and specialty products.

Brandnames of Products and Services:

Energizer	*batteries*
Glad	*plastic wrap, disposer bags*
Prestone II	*antifreeze*
Simoniz	*car wax*

Union Corp.

Jones St.
Verona, PA 15147
(412) 362-1700

Chief Executive Officer: Robert H. Sabel
1984 Annual Sales Volume: 139M
1984 Shares Outstanding: 6,972,328
Shareholders: 6,303
Exchange: NY
Symbol: UCO

Corporate History: The company incorporated in 1938 as Super Electric Products Corp. It changed its name to Union Spring & Mfg. Co. in 1952 and adopted its present title in 1966. It is a diversified company engaged principally in supplying industrial equipment and components and raw materials to the transportation, capital goods, defense and other industries. The company also operates a national collection agency.

Brandnames of Products and Services:

Capital Credit	*collection agency*

Uniroyal Inc.

Middlebury, CT 06749
(203) 573-2000

Chief Executive Officer: J.P. Flannery
1984 Annual Sales Volume: 2,209M
1984 Shares Outstanding: 33,900,000
Shareholders: 39,440
Exchange: NY
Symbol: R

Corporate History: The company incorporated in 1892 as United States Rubber Co. and adopted its present title in 1967. It makes a diversified line of plastic, rubber and chemical products. Tires account for nearly one-half of its sales, with chemicals currently at 30% of sales. Seventy percent of its tires go to General Motors.

Brandnames of Products and Services:

Arrest	*fungicide*
Comite	*miticide*
Dimilin	*insecticide*
Dyanap	*herbicide*
Fisk	*tires*
Fleetmaster	*tires*
Laredo	*tires*
Naugahyde	*coated fabric*
Rallye 340 & 280	*tires*
Royal Seal	*tires*
Steeler	*tires*
Steelmaster	*tires*
Tiger Pan	*tires*
Uniroyal	*tires*
Vitavax	*systemic fungicide*

Unishops Inc.

21 Caven Point Ave.
Jersey City, N.J.
(201) 433-0100

Chief Executive Officer: H.I. Wexler
Exchange: OTC
Symbol: UNSS

Corporate History: The company incorporated in 1947 as Uniroy of Hempstead. The name was changed to United Church Shops in 1953 and to its present title in 1962. The company operates discount and general merchandise stores in New England and the Midwest. In 1979 it acquired Marlene Industries, a major private label manufacturer of apparel in the medium to low-price range. In fiscal 1980 retail discounting accounted for approximately 66.5% of sales, specialty stores 6.6% and manufacturing 17%.

Brandnames of Products and Services:

Chaps	*apparel/stores*
Clarkin's	*discount department stores*
Paul-Marshal	*baskets*
Perry's	*shoe stores*
Youth Centre	*young adult apparel stores*

United Brands Co.

1271 Avenue of the Americas
New York, NY 10020
(212) 307-2000

Chief Executive Officer: Seymour Milstein
1984 Annual Sales Volume: 3,306M
1984 Shares Outstanding: 12,957,000
Shareholders: 13,672
Exchange: NY
Symbol: UB

Corporate History: The company incorporated in 1899 as United Fruit Co. and adopted its present title in 1970. United Brands is one of the world's leading producers, processors and distributors of food products. Bananas and related products include the production and sale of bananas, palm oil and processed bananas, and the wholesale distribution in Europe of bananas and other fresh fruits and vegetables. Meat operations involve the slaughtering of livestock and processing and distribution of fresh, frozen and processed meat (pork, beef and lamb), including sausage, frankfurters, bacon, canned hams and luncheon meats. Other food products include the production and marketing of margarine and shortening, and the importing and distribution of specialty food products. Diversified operations include the production and sale of plastic products and animal feeds, and the operation of an international telecommunications carrier.

Brandnames of Products and Services:

Austrian Alps	*food products*
Bob Ostrow	*meat products*
Brander	*food products*
Chico	*bananas*
Chiquita	*bananas*
Clover	*food products*
Corona	*food products*
Cremelado	*food products*
Danish Crown	*food products*
E-Z Cut	*meat products*
Fyffes	*bananas*
Golden Smoked	*meat products*
Green Tree	*food products*
Hunter	*meat products*
John Morrell	*meat products*
Krey	*meat products*
Nathan Famous	*meat products*
Numar	*food products*
Parafan	*food products*
Partridge	*meat products*
Peyton's	*meat products*
Queen Kristina	*food products*
Rodeo	*meat products*
Scott Petersen	*meat products*
Table Trim	*meat products*
Tobin's First Prize	*meat products*
Tom Sawyer	*meat products*
Weight Watchers	*meat products*

United Foods, Inc.

100 Dawson Ave.
Bells, TN 38006-0119
(901) 663-2341

Chief Executive Officer: James I. Tankersley
1984 Annual Sales Volume: 176MM
1984 Shares Outstanding: 13,838,428
Shareholders: 8,200
Exchange: AM
Symbol: UFD

Corporate History: The company incorporated in 1956 as United Industries, and adopted its current name in 1961. It is engaged in the processing and sale of frozen vegetables and prepared entrees The company also transports general commodites in all states except Alaska and Hawaii.

Brandnames of Products and Services:

Dulany	*frozen vegetables*
Everfresh	*frozen vegetables*
Freezer Queen	*frozen vegetables*
Pictsweet	*frozen vegetables*
Prime Froz'n	*frozen vegetables*
Soup Ladle	*frozen vegetables*
Stokey	*frozen vegetables*
Tennessee	*frozen vegetables*
Winter Garden	*frozen vegetables*

United Merchants and Manufacturers Inc.

1407 Broadway
New York, NY 10018
(212) 930-3900

Chief Executive Officer: Uzi Ruskin
1984 Annual Sales Volume: 563M
1984 Shares Outstanding: 8,807,949
Shareholders: 10,168
Exchange: NY
Symbol: UMM

Corporate History: United Merchants and Manufacturers Inc incorporated in 1928, engages in the design and distribution of apparel and accessories and the manufacture and distribution of textiles and related products. It also produces fiberglass for industrial and other applications. The company's operations are primarily located in the United States and South America. In 1984, the company acquired Jonathan Logan Inc. which designs and distributes apparel and accessories, principally for women.

Brandnames of Products and Services:

Act III	*apparel*
ActionScene	*apparel*
Alice Stuart	*apparel*
Ameritex	*fabric manufacturing*
Bill Blass	*apparel (license)*
Chase	*curtains*
Citation	*costume jewelry*
Cohama Riverdale	*decorative fabrics*
Con-Tact	*adhesive paper products and shelving*
Encore	*costume jewelry*
Etienne Aigner	*shoes, leather accessories, apparel*
Givenchy	*costume jewelry*
Kwik-Kover	*household paper products and shelving*
Lisner	*costume jewelry*
Misty Harbor	*apparel*
R & K Originals	*apparel*
Richelieu	*costume jewelry*
Roomaker	*shower curtains*
Rose Marie Reed	*apparel*
Seneca Textiles	*bedding, draperies, home furnishings*
Sudamatex	*fabric manufacturing*
Villager	*apparel*

United States Industries Inc.

250 Park Avenue
New York, N.Y. 10017
(212) 697-4141

Chief Executive Officer: Gordan A. Walker
Exchange: NY
Symbol: USI

Corporate History: The company, incorporated in 1951 as Pressed Steel Car Corp., adopted its present title in 1954. It manufactures varied products including wearing apparel, household items and boats. In 1979 consumer sales accounted for only 29.3% of sales, with industrial products and building and furnishings making up the remainder.

Brandnames of Products and Services:

Durango	*boots*
Erik Andrews	*men's apparel*
European Health Spas	
Fairmont	*men's shirts*
Fiberform	*boats*
Givenchy Sport	*apparel*
Jack La Lane	*health spas*
Jevco	*kitchen accessories, household products*
Oomphies	*women's footwear*
Poly Flinders	*children's apparel*
Ruffies & Tuffies	*plastic refuse bags*
Seaway	*camping and sporting goods equipment*
Talbott Knits	*apparel*
Teters	*floral products*
Young Squire	*men's apparel*

United States Shoe Corp.

One Eastwood Dr.
Cincinnati, OH 45227
(513) 527-7000

Chief Executive Officer: P.G. Barach
1984 Annual Sales Volume: 1,717M
1984 Shares Outstanding: 21,905,000
Shareholders: 5,668
Exchange: NY
Symbol: USR

Corporate History: U. S. Shoe is a significant factor in specialty retailing and the company has representation in regional shopping malls. The company has increased its strong value retailing participation in women's apparel, bed, bath, housewares and gift stores and apparel superstores. The type of retailing location used in these operations provides the company the ability to grow by using neighborhood shopping locations in addition to regional enclosed shopping centers. U. S. Shoe also competes in non-store retailing focusing on children's toys. U. S. Shoe manufactures, imports, wholesales and retails footwear for men and women. The company is a quality footwear supplier to department stores, specialty stores and shoe stores.

Brandnames of Products and Services:

Amalfi	*women's shoes*
Arpeggios	*women's shoes*
August Max	*women's apparel stores*
Bandolino	*women's shoes*
The Banister Shoe Co	*family shoe stores*
Bill Blass	*men's boots*
Brandstand	*Family shoe stores*
Capezio/Q	*shoes and shoe boutiques*
Career Image	*women's apparel stores*
Caren Charles	*women's apparel stores*
Casual Corner	*women's apparel specialty stores*
Cincinnati Shoe Co	*shoe stores & leased Depts.*
Cobbie Cuddlers	*women's shoes*
Cobbies	*shoes*
Crackers	*childrens apparel stores*
David Eving	*women's shoes*
El Dorado	*men's boots*
Evan-Picone for Women	*shoes*
Freeman	*shoes and shoe stores*
French Shriner for Men	*shoes*
Front Row	*men's, womens, childrens apparel & shoes*
Garolini	*women's shoes*
Giggletree	*direct mail catalog*
Hahn	*shoe stores*
Hilliary Jaymes	*women's apparel stores*
Home Front	*linens & houseware stores*
J Chigholm	*men's boots*
Joyce	*shoes*
J. Riggings	*men's apparel stores*
Just for Kids	*direct mail catalog*
Kenny Rogers	*men's boots*
Liz Claiborne	*women's shoes*
Members Only	*men's shoes*
Mushrooms	*women's shoes*
Outrigger	*men's apparel stores*
Pappagallo	*shoes and boutiques*
Petite Sophisticate	*women's apparel stores*
Precision Lenscrafters	*Eye wear stores*
Proving Ground	*men's apparel stores*
Red Cross	*shoes and shoe stores*
Selby	*shoes and shoe stores*
Socialites	*shoes*
Stuart Brooks	
Texas Boots	*shoes*
T.H. Mandy	*women's apparel stores*
VPS'N Downs	*womens' apparel stores*
V.S. Kids	*children's apparel stores*

United States Tobacco Co.

100 W. Putnam Ave.
Greenwich, CT 06830
(203) 661-1100

Chief Executive Officer:	Louis F. Bantle
1984 Annual Sales Volume:	444M
1984 Shares Outstanding:	27,782,417
Shareholders:	10,967
Exchange:	NY
Symbol:	UBO

Corporate History: The company incorporated in 1911 as Weyman-Bruton Co. and adopted its present title in 1922. It makes a variety of tobacco products, smokers accessories, wine, writing instruments and operates two televisions stations. The company also owns and operates certain agricultural properties. Smokeless tobacco will remain the core of the business in the future.

Brandnames of Products and Services:

Amphora	*tobacco products*
Argosy Black	*tobacco products*
Blend Eleven	*tobacco products*
Bond Street	*tobacco products*
Borkum Riff	*tobacco products*
Briggs	*tobacco products*
Bruton	*tobacco products*
Cadillac	*pet food*
CC	*tobacco products*
Cedar King	*pencils*
Charley	*pens*
Copenhagen	*tobacco products*
Devoe	*tobacco products*
Dills	*pipe cleaners*
Don Thomas	*cigars*
Dr. Grabow	*pipes*
Drum	*tobacco products*
Field & Stream	*tobacco products*
Frieder	*tobacco products*

Happy Days	*tobacco products*
Happy Jim	*tobacco products*
Honor Roll	*pencils*
House of Windsor	*cigars*
Key	*tobacco products*
Mapleton	*tobacco products*
Mark IV	*cigars*
Mastercraft	*pipes*
Model	*tobacco products*
Mustang	*pens*
Perfecs Garcia	*tobacco products*
Red Seal	*tobacco products*
Revelation	*tobacco products*
Right Cut	*tobacco products*
Rooster	*tobacco products*
Seal	*tobacco products*
Skoal	*tobacco products*
Smokemaster	*pipes*
Standard	*tobacco products*
Ste. Michelle	*wines*
Union Leader	*tobacco products*
WB Cut	*tobacco products*
Wolf Bros.	*cigars*
WPBN-TV	*Traverse City, MI*
WTOM-TV	*Chaboygan, MI*
Zig Zag	*cigarette papers*

Universal Cigar Corp.

660 Madison Ave.
New York, N.Y. 10021
(212) 753-5700

Chief Executive Officer: E. Gropper
Exchange: AM
Symbol: UCG
Corporate History: The company, incorporated in 1922, manufactures cigars.
Brandnames of Products and Services:

7-20-4	*cigars*
Blackstone	*cigars*
Dexter	*cigars*
El Trelles	*cigars*
Haddon Hall	*cigars*
La Primadora	*cigars*
Optimo	*cigars*
Santa Fe	*cigars*

Universal Foods Corp.

433 E. Michigan St.
Milwaukee, WI 53202
(414) 271-6755

Chief Executive Officer: J.L. Murray
1984 Annual Sales Volume: 430MM
1984 Shares Outstanding: 7,100,000
Shareholders: 4,482
Exchange: NY
Symbol: UFC
Corporate History: Universal foods, incorporated in 1882 as the Meadow Springs Distillery, is a national manufacturer and marketer of specialized food ingredients and selected retail food items. These include the world's most diversified line of yeast products, a complete line of Italian-style, imported and substitute cheeses; deydrated vegetables and seasonings; food colors and flavors, and imported gourmet foods. These items are sold to other food processors for inclusion in their products, to food service parties (schools, hospitals, restaurants) and to the consumer through retail distribution. In 1984 the cheese Division accounted for 32% of revenues; the fermentation Division, 32%; the import Division, 22%; The Dehydrated Seasonings Division, 10%; and the food color and flavor Division, 4%.
Brandnames of Products and Services:

Amore	*gourmet foods*
Bonavita	*food items*
Fancifood	*gourmet items*
Ile de France	*cheese*
Pizza Pal	*cheese*
Red Seal	*food colors*
Red Star	*yeast*
Spectracoat	*food colors*
Stella	*cheese*
Uni-Chef	*cheese*

Unocal Corp.

1201 West Fifth St.
Los Angeles, CA 90017
(213) 977-7600

Chief Executive Officer: Fred L. Hartley
1984 Annual Sales Volume: 11,538MM
1984 Shares Outstanding: 173,900,781
Shareholders: 82,673
Exchange: NY
Symbol: UCL
Corporate History: The company incorporated in 1890 to unify the interests of Hardison & Stewart Oil Co., Sespe Oil Co. and Torrey Canon Oil Co. of California. It engages in the worldwide exploration, production, purchase and sales of crude oil and natural gas. This predominantly domestic integrated oil company has major refining and marketing interests on the West

Coast and in the Midwest. It has important crude oil production facilities outside the United States. The firm also is engaged in chemical and mineral mining and manufacturing. In 1983 Union Oil Co of California became a wholly-owned subsidiary of Unocal, Inc. The company holds about 3.2 million yet to be explored acres in 29 states. Its products are distributed in 46 states.

Brandnames of Products and Services:

Union 76	*automotive stations and products*

URS Corporation

155 Bovet Rd.
San Mateo, Calif. 94402
(415) 574-5000

Chief Executive Officer: A.H. Stromberg
Exchange: AM
Symbol: URS

Corporate History: The company incorporated in 1957 as Broadview Research Corp. In 1962 its name was changed to United Research Services Inc. and in 1964 to URS Corp. It designs projects and systems in the energy, health care, transportation and water resources fields. In fiscal 1979 the U.S. government provided 6% of sales, state and local governments, 34%, and commercial and industrial customers, 60%.

Brandnames of Products and Services:

Evelyn Wood Reading Dynamics	*speed-reading program*

U.S. Air Group Inc.

1911 Jefferson Davis Highway
Arlington, VA 22202
(703) 892-7224

Chief Executive Officer: Edwin I. Colodny
1984 Annual Sales Volume: 1,629M
1984 Shares Outstanding: 26,698,316
Shareholders: 15,826
Exchange: NYSE
Symbol: U

Corporate History: US Air Group, a holding company, is organized under the laws of the State of Delaware, as its wholly owned operating subsidiary, US Air Inc. The company also owns US Air Finance N.V., a Netherlands Antilles finance subsidiary. US Air, originally organized in 1937, became a subsidiary of the company in 1983. USAir, which carried approximately 17.3 million passengers in 1984, is one of 11 carriers which were classified by the Civil Aeronautics Board as "major" airlines in 1984. The airline provides regularly scheduled air service through 70 airports to 95 cities in the United States and Canada. A substantial portion of USAir's revenue passenger miles ("RPMs") is flown in competitive markets within the northeastern and midwestern regions of the United States. In recent years its route system has been expanded to include many new competitive points in the southern and western regions of the country. USAir's primary connecting hub is Pittsburgh, Pennsylvania. As of 1985, USAir's operating fleet of 133 jet aircraft consisted of 14 Boeing 727-200 aircraft, 4 Boeing 737-300 aircraft, 23 Boeing 737-200 aircraft, 71 Douglas DC-9-30 aircraft and 21 British Aerospace BAC 1-11 aircraft.

Brandnames of Products and Services:

US Air

USG Corp.

101 S. Wacker Dr.
Chicago, IL 60606
(312) 321-4000

Chief Executive Officer: Edward W. Duffy
1984 Annual Sales Volume: 2,319M
1984 Shares Outstanding: 16,587,039
Shareholders: 17,516
Exchange: NY
Symbol: USG

Corporate History: The United States Gypsum Co. was incorporated in 1901. In 1984, it acquired the Masonite Corp., a leading manufacturer of hardboard products, furniture components, and commercial interiors. USG Corporation was incorporated in 1984. Also in 1984, the United States Gypsum Co. became a wholly-owned subsidiary of USG Corp. USG's businesses are divided into five segments: gypsum products, wood fiber products, metal products, refractory products and other products.

Brandnames of Products and Services:

Arc-Hard	*brick*
Arcustone	*ceiling product*
Auratone	*ceiling product*
Castlegate	*textured door*
Colonist	*door facings*
Durock	*tile backer board*
Flame Test	*siding*
Franklin Fiber	*gypsum filler*
Greenal-Go	*brick*
Grip Street	*safety grating*

Jambseal	*sealer*
Kinkead	*shower enclosures*
Lo-Abrade GR	*brick material*
Structodek	*roofing underlay*
Structo-Tex	*ceilings - mobile homes*
Thermafiber	*insulation*
Ultrawall	*partitions*
USG Ready-Mixed Plus 3	*joint compound*
Woodfield	*interior paneling*
Woodruf	*roofing*

Valmac Industries Inc.

855 Ridge Lake Blvd.
Suite 101
Memphis, TN 38119
(901) 685-8251

Chief Executive Officer: Shelby D. Massey
1984 Annual Sales Volume: 276M
1984 Shares Outstanding: 2,329,000
Shareholders: 803
Exchange: AM
Symbol: VMI

Corporate History: The company incorporated in 1970 as a wholly-owned subsidiary of Arkansas Valley Industries. In 1983 Boss Brothers Enterprises Inc. acquired approximately 80.5% of the company's common stock. Today the company is engaged in agribussiness serving national and international markets. The company's business is divided into two division. The first division, Tastybird Foods, is engaged in poultry production. It operates feed mills, hatcheries and processing plants in Arkansas and Texas. Customers include wholesale distributors, government agencies, super market chains, fast food outlets and institutional food establishments. The second division, Geo. St. McFadden & Bro. has been prominent in international cotton merchandising for more than 120 years. The division has offices and representatives in 13 U.S. cities and 34 foreign countries. They also operates cottong gins—six in Brazil, 4 in Mexico and one in Australia.

Brandnames of Products and Services:

Janet Davis	*poultry*
Tasty Bird	*poultry*
Willow Brook Farms	*poultry*

Valspar Corp.

1101 Third St South
Minneapolis, MN 55415
(612) 332-7371

Chief Executive Officer: C. Angus Wurtele
1984 Annual Sales Volume: 224M
1984 Shares Outstanding: 5,883,806
Shareholders: 1,919
Exchange: AM
Symbol: VAL

Corporate History: The company, founded in 1806 and incorporated in 1934, makes consumer and industrial coating products. It ranks among the five largest U.S. firms in the paint and coatings industry. It has 20 manufacturing plants plus warehouse facilities located throughout the U.S. and in Canada.

Brandnames of Products and Services:

Colony	*paints and coatings*
Elliott	*paints and coatings*
Masury	*paints and coatings*
Minnesota	*paints and coatings*
Valspar	*paints and coatings*

Vermont American Corp.

100 E. Liberty St.
Louisville, KY 40202
(502) 587-6851

Chief Executive Officer: Robert I. Baker
1984 Annual Sales Volume: 226M
1984 Shares Outstanding: 7,884,000
Shareholders: 2,258
Exchange: AM
Symbol: VACA

Corporate History: The company incorporated in 1948 and changed its name in 1966 from LBT Corp. to the present title. Vermont American Corporation manufactures and markets a variety of cutting tools, power tool accessories, hand tools, garden tools and fastening tool components for industrial and consumer use. Many of the Corporation's products are used in conjunction with "power packs". Some are used directly by hand such as taps, dies, thread gages, hand and mitre saws, lathe chisels, pruning saws, and screwdrivers. Garden tools include products such as water nozzles, oscillating and impulse sprinklers, garden sprayers and hose repair products. Power tool accessories used with routers, radial and table saws, planers and jointers and drill presses have been developed and have expanded Vermont American's product line.

Brandnames of Products and Services:

Atkinson	*tool boxes*
Deluxe	*cutting tools*
Gilmour	*garden tools Water bearing & spraying products*
Lineberry	*cutting tools*
Magna	*screwdriver bits, nut setters & sockets*
Marshall	*precision ground tool steel & drill rod*
McCrary	*cutting tools*
Multi-Metals	*tungsten carbide tools bits & blanks*
Snap-Cut	*lawn & garden tools & power tools accessories*
Valued	*cutting tools hand tools & power tool accessories*
Vermont American	*tools, cutting & hand; tool boxes; power tool accessories*
Vermont Tap & Die	*precision industrial cutting tools*

VF Corp.

1047 North Park Rd
Wyomissing, PA 19610
(215) 378-1151

Chief Executive Officer:	Lawrence R. Pugh
1984 Annual Sales Volume:	1,167M
1984 Shares Outstanding:	30,940,738
Shareholders:	9,518
Exchange:	NY
Symbol:	VFC

Corporate History: The company incorporated in 1899 as Vanity Fair Mills Inc. and adopted its present title in 1969. It designs, markets and manufactures apparel principally through three wholly-owned subsidiaries. It produces women's intimate apparel, jeanswear and casual apparel, and activewear. In 1984, VF Corp. acquired two privately-held companies: Modern Globe, Inc. and Troutmen Industries Inc., both North Carolina manufacturers.

Brandnames of Products and Services:

Bassett-Walker	*activewear*
Briarcreek	*mens slacks, casual wear*
BW	*active wear*
Gad-about	*active wear*
Lee	*Western apparel*
Lee Riders	*jeanswear, casual apparel*
Lollipop	*intimate apparel*
Modern Globe	*intimate apparel*
Ms. Lee	*jeanswear, casual apparel for women*
Skeets	*men's & boy's casual wear*
Statler	*men's & boy's casual wear*
Troutman	*casual wear for men & boys*
Vanity Fair	*intimate apparel*

Viacom International Inc.

1211 Avenue of the Americas
New York, NY 10036
(212) 575-5175

Chief Executive Officer:	Terrence A. Elkes
1984 Annual Sales Volume:	320M
1984 Shares Outstanding:	13,621,632
Shareholders:	19,680
Exchange:	NY
Symbol:	VIA

Corporate History: Viacom, incorporated in 1970, is a diversified communications and entertainment company. It operates cable television systems serving nearly 800,000 subscribers in the U.S.; provides satellite entertainment services for pay television to more than 8.5 million subscribers; owns four television and seven radio stations; develops and produces programming for all media; distributes television programs, motion pictures and television commercials to networks and stations worldwide.

Brandnames of Products and Services:

KIKK-AM/FM	*radio station, Houston, TX*
KSLA-TV	*Shreveport, LA*
Lifetime	*cable television*
Showtime/The Movie Channel	*pay television*
WHEC-TV	*Rochester, NY*
WLAK-FM	*radio station, Chicago, IL*
WLTW-FM	*radio station, New York, NY*
WMZQ-AM/FM	*radio station, Washington, D.C.*
WNYT-TV	*Albany, NY*
WRVR-FM	*radio station, Memphis, TN*
WVIT-TV	*New Britain, CT*

Vicorp Restaurants Inc.

400 West 48 Avenue
Denver, CO 80216
(303) 296-2121

Chief Executive Officer: Gordon H. Miles
1984 Annual Sales Volume: 242M
1984 Shares Outstanding: 6,656,148
Shareholders: 442
Exchange: OTC
Symbol: VRES

Corporate History: Vicorp Restaurants Inc. was incorporated in 1959. It operates restaurants in two principal divisions — the family restaurant group and the specialty restaurant group. Vicorp owns and operates 377 restaurants in 19 states, including 291 family restaurants and 86 specialty restaurants. The family restaurants consist of 77 Village Inn units, 60 Bakers Square units and 154 units acquired from Sambo's Restaurants Inc. The specialty restaurant group offers four concepts: beef or seafood dinnerhouses, a more casual dining experience called Carlos Murphy's, and a gourmet food boutique called Piret's. As a corollary to its restaurant operations, the Company operates Vicom Production and Distribution Company, Inc., a bakery production and food distribution system.

Brandnames of Products and Services:

Bakers Square	*restaurants*
Carlos Murphy's	*restaurants*
Monterey Whaling Co.	*restaurants*
Piret's	*gourmet foods*
Village Inn	*restaurants*

Victoria Station Inc.

Wood Island
Larkspur, CA 94939
(415) 461-4550

Chief Executive Officer: Richard A. Niglio
1984 Annual Sales Volume: 101M
1984 Shares Outstanding: 3,532,000
Shareholders: 1,500
Exchange: OTC
Symbol: VSTA

Corporate History: Incorporated in 1969, Victoria Station operates a chain of 91 full or self-service restaurants. The restaurants are located in most major metropolitan areas.

Brandnames of Products and Services:

	Bonkers
Quinn's Mill	*restaurants, Atlanta, GA, Portland, Ore.*
Victoria Station	*restaurants*

Victory Markets, Inc.

54 E. Main St.
Norwich, NY 13815
(607) 335-4711

Chief Executive Officer: Darryl R. Gregson
1984 Annual Sales Volume: 361M
1984 Shares Outstanding: 1,675,910
Shareholders: 1,600
Exchange: OTC
Symbol: VMKT

Corporate History: The company incorporated in 1908 as Dunne (W.H.) Co., and adopted its present name in 1959. It markets food products, and operates 85 supermarkets and four self-service gasoline stations in central and northern New York and northern Pennsylvania. The company also serves as a wholesales for the Chicago Market chain and independent grocers in the central New York area

Brandnames of Products and Services:

Food King	*food stores*
Great American Food Stores	*supermarkets*
Topco	*food products*
Top Frost	*frozen foods*
U Pump'em	*self-service gasoline stations*
Victory	*supermarkets*
Village Market	*food stores*

Vintage Enterprises, Inc.

3825 Northeast Expressway
Atlanta, GA 30340
(404) 458-3144

Chief Executive Officer: Thomas S. Cheek
1984 Annual Sales Volume: 48M
1984 Shares Outstanding: 1,900,510
Shareholders: 611
Exchange: AMEX
Symbol: VIN

Corporate History: Incorporated in 1958, Vintage Enterprises is a manufacturer and retailer of mobile homes.

Brandnames of Products and Services:

Colonial	*mobile homes*

Volume Merchandising Inc.

75 Ninth Ave.
New York, N.Y. 10011
(212) 924-6585

Chief Executive Officer: P. Wise
Exchange: AM
Symbol: VLM
Corporate History: The company, incorporated in 1949, operates family apparel stores throughout the United States.
Brandnames of Products and Services:

Aaronson's Brothers Stores	*family apparel stores*
Allegany Mall	*family apparel stores*
Betty Gay	*family apparel stores*
Beverly Shop	*family apparel stores*
Cal-Fed	*family apparel stores*
Charles	*family apparel stores*
Charm Shops	*family apparel stores*
Fashion Complex	*family apparel stores*
Garlind	*family apparel stores*
Granson	*family apparel stores*
Gray's	*family apparel stores*
Joy Shop	*family apparel stores*
Kelly's Corner	*family apparel stores*
La Moda	*family apparel stores*
Pam's for Fashion	*family apparel stores*
Primera	*family apparel stores*
Sanborns	*family apparel stores*
Stelens	*family apparel stores*
Thrifty Shop	*family apparel stores*
Tops	*family apparel stores*
Wise Fashion	*family apparel stores*

Volunteer Capital Corp.

Two Maryland Farms (Suite 100)
P.O. Box 184
Brentwood, Tenn. 37027
(615) 373-5700

Chief Executive Officer: M.V. Hussung
Exchange: OTC
Symbol: VLCC
Corporate History: The company, incorporated in 1971, operates a chain of fast-food restaurants.

Brandnames of Products and Services:

Mrs. Winner's Fried Chicken	*fast-food outlets*

Vornado, Inc.

174 Passaic St.
Garfield, N.J. 07026
(201) 773-4000

Chief Executive Officer: F. Zissu
Exchange: NY
Symbol: VNO
Corporate History: Vornado, incorporated in 1965, operates general merchandise stores and catalog showrooms.
Brandnames of Products and Services:

Sutton Place	*catalog showrooms*
Two Guys	*general merchandise discount stores*

Walgreen Co.

200 Wilmot Rd.
Deerfield, IL 60015
(312) 940-2500

Chief Executive Officer: C.R. Walgreen III
1984 Annual Sales Volume: 2,745M
1984 Shares Outstanding: 30,690,998,000
Shareholders: 15,100
Exchange: NY
Symbol: WAG
Corporate History: The company incorporated in 1907 as C.R. Walgreen & Co., succeeding a business founded in 1901. It adopted its present title in 1961. Walgreen, a diversified merchandiser of consumer products, operates the nation's oldest and largest retail drug chain. It is centered in the Midwest. The firm manufactures more than 400 Walgreen products, including cosmetics, drugs and household goods. In addition it runs about 200 restaurants, most in conjunction with its drugstores.
Brandnames of Products and Services:

Briar Gate	*cafeterias*
Humpty Dumpty's	*fast-food restaurants*
Robin Hood	*restaurants*
Wag's	*coffee shops*
Walgreen	*drugstores and products*

Hiram Walker Resources Ltd.

1 First Canadian Place
Toronto, Ontario Canada M5X 1O5
(416) 864-3300

Chief Executive Officer: A.E. Downing
1984 Annual Sales Volume: 3,676M
1984 Shares Outstanding: 72,180,245
Shareholders: 51,984
Exchange: NY
Symbol: WCH
Corporate History: The company was founded in 1848 and grew through the merger with Hiram Walker-Gooderham and Worts. It is a major distiller of alcoholic beverages. It also operates Home Oil Co. Ltd., a major presence in the oil and gas industry in Canada with additional investments in the United States, the North Sea, Indonesia and Australia. Another unit of the firm is the Consumers' Gas Co. Ltd., a gas distribution utility.
Brandnames of Products and Services:

Ambassador Deluxe	*Scotch whiskey*
Ballantine	*Scotch whiskey, gin*
Barclay's Gold Label	*Canadian whiskey*
Barclay's Rare Old Gin	
Corby's Reserve	*whiskey*
Courvoisier	*cognac*
Gooderham Bonded Stock	*Canadian whiskey*
Government House	*rum*
Grand MacNish	*Scotch whiskey*
Hiram Walker	*liqueurs and cordials*
Hiram Walker Crystal	*vodka*
Hiram Walker Crystal Gin	
Hiram Walker Special Canadian	*Canadian whiskey*
Hiram Walker Special Old Canadian	*Canadian whiskey*
Imperial	*Canadian whiskey*
Imperial	*whiskey*
Kahlua	*Liqueurs*
Lauder's	*Scotch whiskey*
Maraca	*rum*
Old Smuggler	*Scotch whiskey*
Royal Canadian	*Canadian whiskey*
Salignac	*cognac*
Skol	*vodka*
Ten High	*bourbon*
Walker's Deluxe	*bourbon*

Wal-Mart Stores Inc.

702 S.W. Eighth St.
P.O. Box 116
Bentonville, AZ 72712
(501) 273-4000

Chief Executive Officer: Sam M. Walton
1984 Annual Sales Volume: 6,401M
1984 Shares Outstanding: 140,222,373
Shareholders: 375
Exchange: NY
Symbol: WMT
Corporate History: The company incorporated in 1969, succeeding a business founded in 1945. It operates approximately 750 discount department stores in twenty states.
Brandnames of Products and Services:

Helen's	*arts & crafts stores*
Sam's Wholesale Clubs	*membership wholesale stores*
Wal-Mart	*discount department stores*

Walt Disney Productions

500 South Buena Vista St.
Burbank, CA 91521
(818) 840-1000

Chief Executive Officer: Michael D. Eisner
1984 Annual Sales Volume: 1,656M
1984 Shares Outstanding: 33,752,000
Shareholders: 62,000
Exchange: NY
Symbol: DIS
Corporate History: Walt Disney Productions incorporated in 1938. Under the direction of Walt Disney the company was in the forefront of film animation, and its cartoons and cartoon characters captured the imagination of the world. In the 1950s it branched out into television and created the longest running TV show, *The wonderful World of Disney.* In recent years Disney has built a recreational empire that includes Disney World, Disneyland, EPCOT Center (a permanent world's fair for adults in Orlando, Florida) and Tokyo Disneyland. At present Walt Disney Productions is a diversified international company engaged in family en-

tertainment and community development with operations in four business segments: entertainment and recreation, filmed entertainment, community development and consumer products.

Brandnames of Products and Services:

The Addison, Boca Raton, Florida	*luxury condominium*
Arvida Corp.	*real estate development*
Arvida Executive Center, Boca Raton, Florida	*planned community*
Arvida Financial Services	*financial services*
Arvida Park of Commerce, Boca Raton, Florida	*planned community*
Arvida Realty Sales	*real estate brokerage*
Boca West, Boca Raton, Florida	*planned community*
Buena Vista Distribution Co.	*records, film, television distribution*
Chimney Lakes, Atlanta, Georgia	*planned community*
Chimney Springs, Atlanta Georgia	*planned community*
Cocoplum, Coral Gables, Florida	*planned community*
Coto de Caza, California	*planned community*
Country Walk, Miami, Florida	*planned community*
The Crossings, Miami, Florida	*planned community*
The Disney Channel	*pay TV service*
Disney Development Co.	*real estate*
Disneyland Park, Anaheim, California	*amusement theme park*
Epcot Center, Orlando, Florida	*adult theme park*
Lakes of the Meadow, Florida	*planned community*
Longboat Key Club, Florida	*planned community*
Magic Kingdom, Orlando, Florida	*theme park*
Millpond, Boca Raton, Florida	*planned community*
The Moors, Miami Lakes, Florida	*planned community*
Paseos, Boca Raton, Florida	*planned community*
Sabal Chase, Miami, Florida	*planned community*
Sawgrass, Jacksonville, Florida	*planned community*
Timber Creek, Boca Raton, Florida	*planned community*
Touchstone Films	*theatrical motion pictures*
Town Center	*planned community*
Town Place, Boca Raton, Florida	*planned community*
Walt Disney Pictures	*theatrical motion pictures*
Walt Disney Travel Co.	
Walt Disney World Complex, Orlando, Florida	*theme parks, hotels, recreation facilities, transportation*
Weston, Fort Lauderdale, Florida	*planned community*
Willow Springs, Atlanta, Georgia	*planned community*
Wonderland Music Co.	

Wang Laboratories, Inc.

One Industrial Avenue
Lowell, MA 01851
(617) 459-5000

Chief Executive Officer:	An Wang
1984 Annual Sales Volume:	2,184M
1984 Shares Outstanding:	138,655,729
Shareholders:	44,662
Exchange:	AM
Symbol:	WANB WANC

Corporate History: Wang Laboratories, Inc. designs, manufactures, and markets computer systems and provides related products and services, primarily for the worldwide office automation marketplace. These systems perform word and data processing, and some perform audio processing or image processing functions. All of the company's products can be incorporated into an office network that provides extensive communications capabilities among interconnected systems. The company's products and services enable people to manage and communicate information more effectively.

Brandnames of Products and Services:

Wang	*personal & office computers*

Ward Foods Inc.

2 Penn Plaza
New York, N.Y. 10001
(212) 564-1010

Chief Executive Officer: J.A. Marshall
Exchange: NY
Symbol: WD

Corporate History: The company incorporated in 1912 as Ward Baking Co. and adopted its current name in 1964. It processes a variety of food goods including meat and seafoods, candy and desserts; fresh baked goods and snacks.

Brandnames of Products and Services:

Bit-O-Honey	*candy*
Buttermaid	*baked goods*
Champion	*baked goods*
Chunky	*candy*
Dainty Maid	*baked goods*
Farm Crest	*baked goods*
Goobers	*candy*
Honey Crust	*baked goods*
Ivory Club	*seafood*
Johnston's	*pie crusts*
Jumbolina	*seafood*
Kitchens of the Oceans	*seafood*
La Crosse	*rolled oats*
Mr. Big	*baked goods*
Mr. Continental	*seafoods*
Nosy Club	*seafoods*
Oh Henry	*candy*
Pacific Club	*seafoods*
Plymouth Rock	*processed meats*
Poseidon	*seafood products*
Quinlan	*pretzels*
Raisinettes	*candy*
Ready Crust	*pie crusts*
Simple Simon	*frozen pies*
Sno Caps	*candy*
Superior	*potato chips*
Supper Club	*seafoods*
Tip Top	*bread*
Ward Bros.	*baked goods*

Warnaco Inc.

350 Lafayette St.
Bridgeport, CT 06601
(203) 579-8272

Chief Executive Officer: Robert J. Matura
1984 Annual Sales Volume: 561M
1984 Shares Outstanding: 10,154,936
Shareholders: 5,400
Exchange: NY
Symbol: WRC

Corporate History: The company was founded in 1874 and reincorporated in 1961. It changed its name from Warner Brothers Co. to Warnaco in 1968. The firm makes men's dress and sport shirts, sweaters, neckwear, accessories and jewelry, sportswear, skiwear, swimwear, and women's sportswear, activewear, skiwear, swimwear, knitwear, and intimate apparel.

Brandnames of Products and Services:

Albert Nipon	*men's apparel and accessories*
Chaps by Ralph Lauren	*men's dress, sport shirts, neckwear, sportswear*
Christian Dior	*men's dress shirts*
Dior	*men's shirts and ties*
Geoffrey Beene	*women's sportswear*
Hathaway	*men's apparel*
Jack Nicklaus	*men's golf shirts & sportswear*
Olga	*women's intimate apparel & daywear*
Pringle of Scotland	*men's, women's sweaters & knitwear*
Puritan	*men's apparel*
Rosanna	*women's apparel*
Spalding	*active sportswear*
Speedo	*racing and fashion swimwear*
Thane	*men's apparel*
Warner's	*women's intimate apparel*
White Stag	*women's apparel*

Warner Communications Inc.

75 Rockefeller Plaza
New York, NY 10019
(212) 484-8000

Chief Executive Officer: S.J. Ross
1984 Annual Sales Volume: 2,000M
1984 Shares Outstanding: 60,800,000
Shareholders: 80,000
Exchange: NY
Symbol: WCI
Corporate History: Warner Communications Inc. is engaged in the communications and entertainment business through operations in filmed entertainment, recorded music and music publishing, publishing and related distribution, and broadcast and cable television (50%-owned Warner Amex Cable Communications, 33%-owned MTV Networks Inc., 40.5%-owned Showtime/The Movie Channel Inc. and 42.5%-owned BHC, Inc.) and the 26%-owned Hasbro Bradley, Inc. In 1984, WCI reported income from continuing operations of $13.1 million, but had a net loss of $586.1 million or $9.73 per share. The net loss resulted primarily from substantial operatings losses at Atari during the year and writedowns of discontinued operations, which included Atari.
Brandnames of Products and Services:

Asylum	*records*
Atco	*records*
Atlantic	*records*
Chaps	*men's fragrances*
Cotillion	*records*
DC	*comics*
Elektra	*records*
Knickerbocker	*toys*
Ladd	*films*
Mad	*magazine*
Malibu Grand Prix	*mini-amusement center*
Nonesuch	*records*
Polo	*men fragrance*
Reprise	*records and music publishing house*
Tuxedo	*women's fragrance*
Warner Books	*publishing house*
Warner Bros.	*TV programs, films and records*

Warner-Lambert Co.

201 Tabor Rd.
Morris Plains, NJ 07950
(201) 540-2000

Chief Executive Officer: Ward S. Hagan
1984 Annual Sales Volume: 3,167M
1984 Shares Outstanding: 78,859,676
Shareholders: 62,000
Exchange: NY
Symbol: WLA
Corporate History: The company incorporated in 1920 as William R. Warner & Co. It became Warner-Lambert Pharmaceutical Company in 1955 and Warner-Lambert Co. in 1970. It makes a diversified line of health care products and specialty foods. The company's health care business, which accounts for nearly three-fourths of its sales, provides a broad range of prescription pharmaceuticals, intravenous infision systems, diagnostic and surgical products, scientific instruments, non-prescription pharmaceuticals and personal care products. Additional company products includ chewing gums and breath mints as well as shaving and pet care products. The company enploys approximately 41,000 employees, operates more than 100 production facilities and maintains 17 major research laboratories in more than 130 countries.
Brandnames of Products and Services:

Adams	*sour ball/gum*
Agoral	*laxative*
Anusol	*hemorrhoidal suppositories*
Aosoft	*soft contact lens*
Benylin	*cough syrup*
Benylin DM	*cough syrup*
Bromo Seltzer	*antacid*
Bubblicious	*gum*
Caladryl	*calamine lotion*
Certs	*breath mints*
Chewels	*gum*
Chiclets	*gum*
Clorets	*breath mints*
Cool Ray	*sunglasses*
Dentyne	*gum*
Dynamints	*breath freshener*
Efferdent	*denture cleanser*
Effergrip	*denture adhesive*
Entenmann	*baked goods*
e.p.t.	*home pregnancy test*
e.t.p. Plus	*pregnancy test*
Freshen-up	*gum*
Gelusil	*antacid*
Good 'n Fruity	*candy*

Good 'n Plenty	*candy*
Halls	*cough drops*
Lavocol	*health care products*
Listerex	*medicated cream*
Listerine	*mouthwash*
Listermint	*mouthwash*
Lubriderm	*medicated cream*
Mediquell	*cough syrup*
Myadec	*vitamins*
Personal Touch	*razors and blades*
Plus Platinum	*razors blades*
Remgel	*antacid*
Rolaids	*antacid*
Rothschilds	*candy*
Saf-Tip	*personal care products*
Schick	*personal care products and appliances*
Schick-Super II	*razors and blades*
Sinutab	*sinus relief medicine*
Soft	*contact lens*
Spring	*gum*
Super Chromium	*razor blades*
Symptom	*cold and allergic relief*
Teltra	*pet products*
Trident	*gum*
Tucks	*personal care product*
Ultrex	*razors and blades*

Washington Post Co.

1150 15th St. NW
Washington, D.C. 20071
(202) 223-6000

Chief Executive Officer: Katharine Graham
1984 Annual Sales Volume: 984M
1984 Shares Outstanding: 14,050,000
Shareholders: 1,975
Exchange: AM
Symbol: WPOB
Corporate History: The *Washington Post* began in 1877 as a penny paper and today is the nation's 5th largest daily by circulation. As in the case of the *New York Times* and *Times Mirror* in Los Angeles, the company grew into a communications corporation to secure the survival of its flagship newspaper. In 1984 newspaper publishing and related operations provided 52% of sales, magazine publishing 34% and broadcasting 14%.
Brandnames of Products and Services:

Herald	*newspaper, Everett, Wash.*
Newsweek	*magazine and books*
The Washington Post National Weekly Edition	*weekly tabloid*
Washington Post	*newspaper, Washington, D.C.*
WDIV-TV	*Detroit, Mich.*
WFSB-TV	*Hartford, Conn.*
WJXT-TV	*Jacksonville, Fla.*
WPLG-TV	*Miami, Fla.*

Wayne-Gossard Corp.

701 Market St., Suite 922
Chattanooga, TN 37402
(615) 756-8146

Chief Executive Officer: Robert B. Colbert Jr.
1984 Annual Sales Volume: 83M
1984 Shares Outstanding: 1,354,191
Shareholders: 1,336
Exchange: NY
Symbol: WKT
Corporate History: The company incorporated in 1891 as Wayne Knitting Mills and adopted its present name in 1967 upon merger with H.W. Gossard Co. It makes women's, men's, children's and infants' apparel and accessories. In 1984 underwear, sportswear and knitwear provided 82% of sales; sweaters, knitshirts and women's knit apparel 15%; other 3%. all the company's manufacturing facilities are located in the U.S. and substantially all of its sales are domentic.
Brandnames of Products and Services:

Gossard-Artemis	*lingerie*
Heritage	*men's and boys' sweaters and shirts, women's knit apparel*
Joan Vass U.S.A.	*women's knit apparel*
Signal	*men's, women's boy's, girl's and juveniles sportswear*
Tijuca by Laura Pearson U.S.A.	*women's fashion apparel*

WD-40 Co.

1061 Cudahy Place
San Diego, CA 92110
(619) 275-1400

Chief Executive Officer: J.S. Barry
1984 Annual Sales Volume: 57MM
1984 Shares Outstanding: 7,494,921

Shareholders: 2,012
Exchange: OTC
Symbol: WDFC
Corporate History: The company, incorporated in 1953, as Rocket Chemical Co., manufactures only one product—WD-40, a lubricant, rust preventative and moisture displacer. It changed its name to WD-40 in 1970.
Brandnames of Products and Services:

WD-40	*lubricant*

Del E. Webb Corp.

3800 N. Central Ave.
Phoenix, AZ 85012
(602) 264-8011

Chief Executive Officer: Robert K. Swanson
1984 Annual Sales Volume: 479M
1984 Shares Outstanding: 7,764,472
Shareholders: 6,721
Exchange: NY
Symbol: WBB
Corporate History: Del E. Webb Corp. was incorporated as Del E. Webb Construction Co. in 1946, succeeding a general construction business begun by the firm's founder, the Del E. Webb, in 1928. In 1960, the Phoenix-based company changed its name to Del E. Webb Corp. A diversified company, Del E. Webb Corp. is engaged in the management and development of leisure and real estate operations.
Brandnames of Products and Services:

Bullfrog	*resort and marina, Utah*
The Claridge Casino/Hotel	*Atlantic City, N.J.*
Dangling Rope Marina	*Utah*
Del Webb's High Sierra Casino/Hotel	*South Lake Tahoe, Nevada*
Hall's Crossing	*resort and marina, Utah*
Hite Marina	*Utah*
Mint Casino Hotel	*Las Vegas, Nev.*
Nevada Club Casino/Hotel	*Nev.*
Wahweap Lodge and Marina	*Pager, Ariz.*

Weisfield's, Inc.

800 South Michigan St.
Seattle, WA 98108
(206) 767-5011

Chief Executive Officer: Herman Blumenthal
1984 Annual Sales Volume: 45M
1984 Shares Outstanding: 1,299,674
Shareholders: 612
Exchange: OTC
Symbol: WEIS
Corporate History: The company, founded in 1917 and last incorporated in 1930, operates a chain of 79 jewelry stores in the Western States of Arizona, California, Colorado, Nevada, Oregon and Washington.
Brandnames of Products and Services:

Weisfield's Jewelry	*stores*

Weis Markets Inc.

1000 S. Second St.
Sunbury, PA 17801
(717) 286-4571

Chief Executive Officer: Sigfried Weis
1984 Annual Sales Volume: 958M
1984 Shares Outstanding: 20,563,970
Shareholders: 3,372
Exchange: NY
Symbol: WEIS
Corporate History: Incorporated in 1924, Weiss Markets operates 119 supermarkets and eight restaurants in Pennsylvania, Maryland, New York and West Virginia. The company also operates Weiss Food Service, which distributes groceries and frozen food to restaurants and institutions.
Brandnames of Products and Services:

Amity House	*restaurants*
Big Top	*canned foods*
Dutch Valley	*snack foods*
Weis	*markets and canned foods*

Wellco Enterprises Inc.

Waynesville, N.C. 28786
(704) 456-3545

Chief Executive Officer: Rolf Kaufman
Exchange: AM
Symbol: WLC

Corporate History: Wellco Enterprises incorporated in 1941 as Wellco Shoe Corp. and adopted its present name in 1967. It makes casual and leisure footwear.

Brandnames of Products and Services:

Foamtread	*slippers*
Hi-Pals	*boys' and men's boots*
Lady Wellco Magic Band	*casual shoes*
Wellco	*slippers*

Wendy's International Inc.

4288 W. Dublin-Granville Rd.
P.O. Box 256
Dublin, OH 43017
(614) 764-3100

Chief Executive Officer:	R.L. Barney
1984 Annual Sales Volume:	2,400M
1984 Shares Outstanding:	55,000,000
Shareholders:	31,225
Exchange:	NY
Symbol:	WEN

Corporate History: The company, incorporated in 1969, owns and offers franchises for Wendy's Old-Fashioned Hamburgers Restaurants fast-service restaurant chain. As of Decembe, 1984, there were 1,057 company-owned restaurants and 1,867 franchise-owned restuarants nationally and internationally.

Brandnames of Products and Services:

Garden Spot	*salad bar*
Wendy's Old-Fashioned Hamburgers	*restaurants*

Westinghouse Electric Corp.

Westinghouse Building
Gateway Center, Box 2278
Pittsburgh, PA 15222
(412) 642-3800

Chief Executive Officer:	B.D. Danforth
1984 Annual Sales Volume:	10,265M
1984 Shares Outstanding:	177,301,873
Shareholders:	140,799
Exchange:	NY
Symbol:	WX

Corporate History: Westinghouse, founded and incorporated in 1886, is a major supplier of electronic and electrical equipment and services for electrical utility, industrial and construction market applications, and of electric systems for defense. Its businesses also include; broadcasting and cable televsion operations, community development, bottling and distribution of beverage products, transport refrigeration, and financing services.

Brandnames of Products and Services:

Atmos	*clocks*
CATV	*cable television system*
Jubilee	*watch*
KDKA-TV & AM	*Pittsburgh, Pa.*
KFWB-AM	*Los Angeles, Calif.*
KJQY-FM	*San Diego, Calif.*
KOAX-FM	*Dallas/Ft. Worth, Texas*
KODA-FM	*Houston, Texas*
KOSI-FM	*Denver, Colo.*
KPIX-TV	*San Francisco, Calif.*
KQXT-FM	*San Antonio, Tex.*
KYW-TV & AM	*Philadelphia, Pa.*
Longines-Wittnauer	*watches and clocks*
Polara	*watches*
WBZ-TV, AM/FM	*Boston, Mass.*
WIND-AM	*Chicago, Ill.*
WINS-AM	*New York, N.Y.*
Wittnauer	*watch and clocks*
WJZ-TV	*Baltimore, Md.*

West Point-Pepperell Inc.

400 W. Tenth St.
West Point, GA 31833
(404) 645-4000

Chief Executive Officer:	Joseph L. Lanier, Jr.
1984 Annual Sales Volume:	1,333M
1984 Shares Outstanding:	10,315,248
Shareholders:	11,300
Exchange:	NY
Symbol:	WPM

Corporate History: The company, incorporated in 1955 as West Point Manufacturing Co., produces household fabric. It adopted its present name in 1965. Today the company manufactures and sells a wide variety of textiles for the apparel, household and industrial markets. Its manufacturing plants are located in Alabama, Georgia, Florida, Maine, North Carolina, South Carolina, Texas, Virginia and Costa Rica. Household fabrics which include bed and bath products and carpets and rugs comprise 58% of sales; apparel fabrics 28% and industrial fabrics 14%.

Brandnames of Products and Services:

Alamac	*knitted fabrics*
Cabin Craft	*carpets*

Carlin	*towels and sheets*
Duplexx	*woven and knitted goods*
Georgian	*carpets*
Grifftex	*carpets*
Lady Pepperell	*towels and sheets*
Luxor	*towels*
Martex	*towels and sheets*
Pepperell	*carpets*
Vellux	*towels, sheets, blankets*
Walter	*carpets*

Westvaco Corp.

299 Park Ave.
New York, NY 10071
(212) 688-5000

Chief Executive Officer: David L. Luke III
1984 Annual Sales Volume: 1,766M
1984 Shares Outstanding: 28,550,673
Shareholders: 16,480
Exchange: NY
Symbol: W

Corporate History: The company incorporated in 1899 as West Virginia Pulp & Paper Co. and adopted its present title in 1969. It is a leading producer of paper and paperboard in the U.S. It converts paper into a variety of end-products, manufactures a variety of specialty chemicals, produces lumber, sells timber from its timberlands, and is engaged in land development and coal mining.

Brandnames of Products and Services:

Edgemate	*panel edging*
Reed	*paper partygoods*
Reply	*envelopes*
SelecTone	*envelopes*

Wetterau, Inc.

8920 Pershall Rd.
Hazelwood, MO 63042
(314) 524-5000

Chief Executive Officer: Ted C. Wetterau
1984 Annual Sales Volume: 2,684M
1984 Shares Outstanding: 10,575,500
Shareholders: 6,080
Exchange: OCT
Symbol: WETT

Corporate History: The company, incorporated in 1961, is principally engaged in the sale and distribution of food and nonfood products to independently owned and operated supermarkets and local and regional chain stores in various parts of the United States. Its activities also include company owned and operated retail food and general merchandise operations as well as providing various ancillary services, including financial, construction, advertising, printing, insurance, and promotional services to retail grocers. Westerau's 13 food distribution centers serve rearly 1,700 IGA, Foodland, Red & White, Bi-Rite and others retailers in 22 states.

Brandnames of Products and Services:

Brights	*department store*
Carriage Drugs	*drug stores*
Food Lane	*supermarkets*
Just Be Natural	*health food stores*
Lane	*department stores*
Laneco	*combination stores*
Milgram	*supermarkets*
Save Mart	*warehouse stores*
Shop'N Save	*supermarkets*
Toy City	*toy "supermarkets"*

Weyenberg Shoe Manufacturing Co.

234 E. Reservoir Ave.
P.O. Box 1188
Milwaukee, WI 53201
(414) 374-8900

Chief Executive Officer: Thomas W. Florsheim
1984 Annual Sales Volume: 108M
1984 Shares Outstanding: 576,005
Shareholders: 1,080
Exchange: OTC
Symbol: WEYS

Corporate History: Incorporated in 1906, the company makes and distributes men's shoes. The company sells to more than 8,000 retail shoe dealers throughout the United States, and operates 67 shoe stores and 80 leased shoe departments in men's clothing and department stores.

Brandnames of Products and Services:

Adler Shoe Shops	*shoe stores*
Morgan-Hayes of Houston	*shoe stores*
Nunn-Bush	*shoe stores & shoes*
Stacy Adams	*shoe stores & shoes*
Standard Shoes	*shoe stores*
Weyenberg	*shoes*
Weyenberg Massagic	*shoes*

Wherehouse Entertainment, Inc.

14100 South Kingsley Dr.
Gardena, CA 90249
(213) 538-2314

Chief Executive Officer: Louis A. Kwiker
1984 Annual Sales Volume: 106M
1984 Shares Outstanding: 3,919,343
Shareholders: 870
Exchange: AM
Symbol: WEI
Corporate History: Wherehouse Entertainment, Inc., founded in California in 1970 as a record retailer, is a specialty retailer of home entertainment products consisting of prerecorded music, video movies and music and blank audio and video tape. As of 1984, all 130 of the company's stores sold prerecorded music consisting of records and cassettes, blank audio and video cassettes. In addition, 84 stores sold and rented prerecorded video cassettes and 106 sold computer software, consisting primarily of entertainment, educational and personal productivity programs for use on personal and home computers.
Brandnames of Products and Services:
Wherehouse Entertainment — *video stores*

Whirlpool Corp.

2000 US 33 North
Benton Harbor, MI 49022
(616) 926-5000

Chief Executive Officer: Jack D. Sparks
1984 Annual Sales Volume: 3,137M
1984 Shares Outstanding: 36,617
Shareholders: 8,912
Exchange: NY
Symbol: WHR
Corporate History: Whirlpool Corporation started in 1911 as the Upton Machine Company. Lou and Fred Upton formed the business to make electrically-powered wringer washers. In 1929 Upton Machine merged with the Nineteen Hundred Company of Binghamton, New York, and the new company was named the Nineteen Hundred Corporation. In 1950, the company changed its name to Whirlpool Corporation. In 1955, Whirlpoo Corporation, Seeger Refrigerator Company, and the Estate range and air conditioning divisions of the Radio Corporation of America were merged into the Whirlpool-Seeger Corporation. In 1957, the company changed its name back to Whirlpool Corporation. By this time it was manufacturing a full line of major home appliances. Heil-Quaker Corporation is a wholly-owned subsidiary producing heating and cooling equipment. Whirlpool Acceptance Corporation, the company's wholly-owned finance subsidiary, is located next to the corporate headquarters in Benton Harbor. Whirlpool has a majority interest in the Canadian appliance manufacturer, Inglis, Ltd. It holds significant minority positions in three Brazilian appliance companies. A wholly-owned subsidiary, Whirlpool Trading Co., Inc., was formed in 1984 to consolidate many of the company's international activities. Whirlpool is number one in the domestic home appliance business followed by General Electric and White Consolidated. Its principal customer is Sears, Roebuck & Co. Which accounted for 41% of its sales in 1984.
Brandnames of Products and Services:
Heil — *air conditioners and heating appliances*
Whirlpool — *household appliances*

White Consolidated Industries Inc.

11770 Berea Rd.
Cleveland, OH 44111
(216) 252-3700

Chief Executive Officer: Roy H. Holdt
1984 Annual Sales Volume: 1,906M
1984 Shares Outstanding: 15,758,000
Shareholders: 13,974
Exchange: NY
Symbol: WSW
Corporate History: The company was founded in 1876 and incorporated in 1926 as White Sewing Machine Corp. Its present title was adopted in 1964. White makes major household appliances under its brandnames as well as under private labels for such retailers as Sears, Roebuck & Co. and Montgomery Ward. It also manufactures industrial machinery and equipment, principally machine tools, highway construction equipment, valves, controls, commercial air conditioning, heating and refrigeration products.
Brandnames of Products and Services:
Bendix — *laundry appliances*
Cold Guard — *freezers*
Crosley — *freezers*
Domestic — *sewing appliances*
Elna — *sewing appliances*
Frigidaire — *household appliances*
Gibson — *household appliances*
Hilton — *sewing appliances*

Kelvinator	*household appliances*
Leonard	*kitchen appliances*
Philco	*household appliances*
Roy	*household appliances*
Universal	*sewing appliances*
Vesta	*kitchen appliances*
White	*sewing appliances*
White Westinghouse	*household appliances*

Whittaker Corp.

10880 Wilshire Blvd.
Los Angeles, CA 90024
(213) 475-9411

Chief Executive Officer:	J.F. Alibrandi
1984 Annual Sales Volume:	1,437M
1984 Shares Outstanding:	13,800,000
Shareholders:	17,000
Exchange:	NY
Symbol:	WKR

Corporate History: The company incorporated in 1947 as Telecomputing Corp. and adopted its present title in 1964. It manufactures chemical, technical and metal products for industry and distributes medical supplies. In 1984 life sciences accounted for 50% of sales, metals 19%, technology 16%, and marine and chemical products 15%.

Brandnames of Products and Services:

Bertram	*pleasure boats*
Riva	*pleasure boats*
Trojan	*pleasure boats*

Wickes Corp.

110 West A St.
San Diego, Calif. 92101
(714) 238-0304

Chief Executive Officer:	E.L. McNeely
Exchange:	NY
Symbol:	WIX

Corporate History: Wickes pioneered in the development of home improvement "supermarkets," introducing the first store in 1954. During the 1960s it extended its supermarket concept to furniture retailing. The company is also involved in agriculture and lumber production as well as manufacturing furniture and home building products.

Brandnames of Products and Services:

Blazer Financial Services	
Builder's Emporium	*retail do-it-yourself home improvement stores*
Double Up	*women's sportswear stores*
Fabs Fashion Fabrics	*fabric stores*
Gamble Alden Life Insurance Co.	
Gamble Department Stores	
House of Fabrics	*fabrics*
Howard's Brandiscount	*general merchandise stores*
J.M. McDonald's	*junior department stores*
John Alden Life Insurance Co.	
Leath	*home furnishing stores*
MacGregor	*golf clubs*
Maxwell	*home furnishing stores*
Rasco	*variety stores*
Red Owl	*food and drugstores*
Roshek's Department Store	*department stores*
Sarco	*discount stores*
Snyder	*drugstores*
Toy World	*toy stores*
Wickes	*lumber and furniture stores*
Woman's World	*apparel stores*
Yorktowne	*cabinets*

John Wiley & Sons, Inc.

605 Third Ave.
New York, NY 10158
(212) 850-6000

Chief Executive Officer:	Andrew H. Neilly, Jr.
1984 Annual Sales Volume:	185M
1984 Shares Outstanding:	4,278,618
Shareholders:	869
Exchange:	OTC
Symbol:	WILL

Corporate History: John Wiley & Sons, Inc., founded in 1904, is engaged in the business of developing and marketing educational and professional materials including college textbooks, technical, scientific, business and medical publications (including journals), data base and software products, and learning programs for industry.

Brandnames of Products and Services:

John Wiley	*publisher textbooks, educational materials*
Wiley Learning Technologies	*publisher-training programs*
Wilson Learning Corp.	*publisher-training programs*

Wilson Brothers

6917 Collins Ave.
Miami Beach, FL 33141
(305) 866-7771

Chief Executive Officer: Victor Posner
1984 Annual Sales Volume: 67M
1984 Shares Outstanding: 3,321,039
Shareholders: 3,669
Exchange: AMEX
Symbol: WLB
Corporate History: Incorporated in 1898, the company makes quality men's shirts, women's shirts and decorative glass.
Brandnames of Products and Services:

ENRO	*men's shirts*
Foxcraft	*women's shirts*
Houze	*glass*
Hunter Hill	*men's shirts*
Keystone Ridgeway	*giftware and ceramic gift items*

Winkelman Stores Inc.

25 Parsons St.
Detroit, Mich. 48201
(313) 833-6900

Chief Executive Officer: S.J. Winkelman
Exchange: AM
Symbol: WNK
Corporate History: Winkelman Stores, incorporated in 1928, operates 82 women's apparel stores in the Midwest.
Brandnames of Products and Services:

Thal's	*ladies' apparel stores*
Today	*ladies' apparel stores*
Winkelman	*ladies' apparel stores*

Winn-Dixie Stores Inc.

5050 Edgewood Ct.
Jacksonville, FL 32205
(904) 783-5000

Chief Executive Officer: A. Dano Davis
1984 Annual Sales Volume: 7,302M
1984 Shares Outstanding: 40,968,000
Shareholders: 47,800
Exchange: NY
Symbol: WIN
Corporate History: The company, founded in 1925, operates approximately 1,260 food stores across the sunbelt in 13 states. In addition to retailing, it operates 27 manufacturing or processing plants.
Brandnames of Products and Services:

Buddies	*supermarkets*
Deep South	*foods*
Dixie Darling Bakers	*foods*
Foodway	*supermarkets*
Grackin' Good Bakers	*foods*
Kimball	*supermarkets*
Sunbelt	*foods*
Superbrano	*dairy products*
Winn-Dixie	*supermarkets*

Winnebago Industries Inc.

P.O. Box 152
Forest City, IO 50436
(515) 582-3535

Chief Executive Officer: Ronald E. Haugen
1984 Annual Sales Volume: 411M
1984 Shares Outstanding: 25,397,000
Shareholders: 30,300
Exchange: NY
Symbol: WGO
Corporate History: The company was founded in 1957 in Forest City, Iowa, as a branch factory of Modernistic Industries, a California travel trailer company. In 1961, the company moved into larger facilities in Forest City; and changed its name to Winnebago Industries, Inc. Winnebago Industries currently produces motor homes, vans and van conversions and licenses its name on outdoor clothing and camping equipment.
Brandnames of Products and Services:

Itasca	*mobile homes, recreational vehicles, cars, trucks*

Winnebago	*stoves*
Winnebago	*jugs*
Winnebago	*soft sided bags*
Winnebago	*rugged and casual footwear*
Winnebago	*sail boats*
Winnebago	*physical fitness equipment*
Winnebago	*bycycles*
Winnebago	*shirts*
Winnebago	*add-a-rooms*
Winnebago	*propane lanterns*
Winnebago	*gloves*
Winnebago	*screen houses*
Winnebago	*mobile homes, recreational vehicles, cars, trucks*
Winnebago	*hats and scarves*
Winnebago	*outerwear*
Winnebago	*sweaters*
Winnebago	*sleeping bags*
Winnebago	*chemical toilets*
Winnebago	*pants*
Winnebago	*coolers*
Winnebago	*flotation equipment*
Winnebago	*bass boats*
Winnebago	*bike assessories*
Winnebago	*tents*
Winnebago	*air mattresses*
Winnebago	*canoes*

Winter, Jack Inc.

8100 North Teutonia Ave.
Milwaukee, WI 53209
(414) 357-4840

Chief Executive Officer: Jack A. Winter
1984 Annual Sales Volume: 48M
1984 Shares Outstanding: 3,645,445
Shareholders: 1,796
Exchange: NY
Symbol: JWI
Corporate History: The company, incorporated in 1936, makes and sells women's apparel to more than 5,500 department, specialty and outlet stores.
Brandnames of Products and Services:

Clothesworks	*women's apparel*
Jacksport	*women's apparel*
Jack Winter	*women's apparel*

Witco Chemical Corp.

520 Madison Ave.
New York, NY 10022-4236
(212) 605-3800

Chief Executive Officer: William Wishnick
1984 Shares Outstanding: 14,648,203
Shareholders: 6,174
Exchange: NY
Symbol: WIT
Corporate History: The company incorporated in 1956 as Witco Chemical Co. and adopted its present title in 1968. It manufactures a wide range of specialty chemicals and petroleum products and engineered materials for industrial and consumer uses. In 1984 the company acquired Continental Carbon Co., a producer of carbon black sold primarily to the rubber industry for the manufacture of tires.
Brandnames of Products and Services:

Amalie	*motor oil*
Kendall	*motor oil*
LubriMatic	*lubricators, lubricant equipment*
Superior	*lubricators, lubricant equipment*

Wolf, Howard B. Inc.

3809 Parry Ave.
Dallas, TX 75226
(214) 823-9941

Chief Executive Officer: H.B. Wolf
1984 Annual Sales Volume: 9M
1984 Shares Outstanding: 1,081,191
Shareholders: 523
Exchange: AM
Symbol: HBW
Corporate History: The company, incorporated in 1952 as Texas Dress Corp., designs and manufactures women's sportswear and dresses.
Brandnames of Products and Services:

Ernesto W.	*women's apparel*
Howard Wolf	*women's apparel*
Pret-a-Porte	*women's apparel*

Wolverine World Wide Inc.

9341 Courtland Dr.
Rockford, MI 49351
(616) 874-8448

Chief Executive Officer: Thomas D. Gleason
1984 Annual Sales Volume: 379M
1984 Shares Outstanding: 7,172,377
Shareholders: 5,183
Exchange: NY
Symbol: WWW

Corporate History: The company, originally founded in 1883 and last incorporated in 1969, began in the shoe tanning business. Today the company is principally engaged in the manufacture and sale of footwear, primarily casual shoes, slippers, moccasins, woman's dress shoes, boots, athletic shoes, and work shoes. The company is the largest domestic tanner of pigskin. Pigskin is used in a significant portion of shoes manufactured and sold by the company, and is also sold to other domestic and foreign manufacturers of shoes and other products and to the company's foreign trademark licensees. In addition to its wholesale activities the company operates about 190 retail shoe stores and leased shoe departments.

Brandnames of Products and Services:

Bates Floataways	*footwear*
Bates Floaters	*footwear*
Brooks	*footwear*
Coleman	*footwear*
Harbor Town by Hush Puppies	*footwear*
Hush Puppies	*footwear and shoe stores*
Kaepa	*footwear*
The Linen Locker	*towels, linen stores*
Little Red Shoe House	*shoe stores*
Quoddy	*footwear*
Reed St. James	*footwear*
Sioux Mox	*moccasins*
Town & Country	*footwear*
Tru-Stitch	*slippers and moccasins*
Viner	*footwear*
Wimzees	*footwear*
Wolverine	*footwear*

Wometco Enterprises Inc.

306 N. Miami Ave.
Miami, Fla. 33128
(305) 374-6262

Chief Executive Officer: M. Wolfson
Exchange: NY
Symbol: WOM

Corporate History: The company incorporated in 1925 as Wolfon-Meyer Theatre Enterprises Inc. and adopted its present title in 1959. It owns and operates television stations and motion picture theatres as well as bottles and distributes soft drink beverages under franchise agreement. In 1979 soft drink operators accounted for 34% of sales, vending 26%, boroadcasting and cable television 26% and entertainment 14%.

Brandnames of Products and Services:

CATV	*systems*
Circus Tower	*tourist attraction, Orlando, Fla.*
Conch Tour Train	*tourist attraction, Key West, Fla.*
KVOS-TV	*station Bellingham, Wash.*
Miami Seaquarium	*tourist attraction, Miami, Fla.*
WLOS-TV & FM	*radio station, N.C. and S.C.*
Wometco	*home theatre box office*
WSNL-TV	*station Smithtown, N.Y.*
WTVJ-TV	*station, Miami, Fla.*
WWHT-TV	*station, Newark, N.J.*
WZZM-TV	*station, Grand Rapids/ Kalamazoo, Mich.*

Woodstream Corp.

69 N. Locust St.
Lititz, PA 17543
(717) 626-2125

Chief Executive Officer: R.G. Woolworth
1984 Annual Sales Volume: 44M
1984 Shares Outstanding: 939,879
Shareholders: 1,250
Exchange: AM
Symbol: WOD

Corporate History: The company is one of North America's leading manufacturers of outdoor sports equipment. It is also the world's foremost supplier of traps for rodent and pest control. The company's products, manufactured and distributed in five plants in the

United States and Canada, are sold by a marketing network of distributors and retailers. There are approximately 650 employees in five divisions, a wholly-owned subsidiary, and at corporate headquarters.

Brandnames of Products and Services:

Conibear	*wildlife traps*
Fenwick	*fishing rods, reels and tackle boses*
Havahart	*live animal cage traps and pet supplies*
Holdfast	*rodent traps*
Newhouse	*wildlive traps*
Northwoods	*wildlife traps*
Old Pal	*fishing equipment*
Oneida	*wildlife traps*
Trump	*molded fiber floral containers*
Victor	*pest control traps*

Woodward & Lothrop Inc.

11th & F Sts. NW
Washington, D.C. 20013
(202) 347-5300

Chief Executive Officer: E.K. Hoffman
Exchange: OTC
Symbol: WOOD

Corporate History: The company, incorporated in 1955, operates 14 department stores in the East. In terms of net profit sales, it is one of the most profitable department store operations in the United States.

Brandnames of Products and Services:

Woodward & Lothrop	*department stores*

F.W. Woolworth Co.

233 Broadway
New York, NY 10279
(212) 553-2000

Chief Executive Officer: John W. Lynn
1984 Annual Sales Volume: 5,737M
1984 Shares Outstanding: 31,504,829
Shareholders: 60,821
Exchange: NY
Symbol: Z

Corporate History: Woolworth traces its history back to 1879 when Frank Woolworth opened his first 5¢ store. Shortly thereafter, he added 10¢ goods and changed the name to Woolworth's 5 and 10 Cent Store. By the time Woolworth died in 1919 he had more than 1,000 variety stores in the United States and Great Britain. Today Woolworth's sells a broad range of general merchandise, apparel, footwear and accessories through more than 5,500 stores in the U.S., Puerto Rico, U.S. Virgin Islands, Canada, Germany and Australia. The company has a 49% interest in Woolworth Mexicana, S.A. de C.V. which operates 26 stores in Mexico. The company also operates 10 factories which manufacture footwear and three factories which manufacture men's wear.

Brandnames of Products and Services:

Activeworld	*apparel*
Anderson-Little	*men's and boys' clothing*
Athletic Shoe Factory	*shoes*
Foot Locker	*athletic shoe stores*
Fredelle	*apparel*
Frugal Frank's	*apparel*
Harvest House	*restaurants*
J. Brannam	*brand-name general merchandise outlets*
Kids Mart	*apparel*
Kinney	*shoe stores*
Krone Mode	*apparel*
Lady Foot Locker	*shoes*
Lewis	*apparel*
Little Folk Shop	*apparel*
Live Wire	*apparel*
Randy River	*apparel*
Richman Brothers	*apparel*
Sacaldi	*apparel*
Susie's	*women's shoe stores*
Woolco	*discount department stores*
Woolworth	*variety stores*

Wrather Corp.

270 North Cannon Dr.
Beverly Hills, CA 90210
(213) 278-8521

Chief Executive Officer: Christopher Wrather
1984 Annual Sales Volume: 111M
1984 Shares Outstanding: 7,001,617
Shareholders: 683
Exchange: AM
Symbol: WCO

Corporate History: The company incorporated in 1956 as Wrather Instrument Corp. That same year it changed its name to Lassie Programs Inc. The present title was adopted in 1961. It owns and distributes TV film episodes. It has interests in oil and gas properties in Louisiana and Texas. In addition, the company owns and operates hotels and attractions in California. It is also engaged in the development, construction and sale of a number of residential real estate projects in the west.

Brandnames of Products and Services:

Disneyland Hotel & Convention Center	*Anaheim, Calif.*
Lassie	*television series*
Lone Ranger	*television series*
Queen Mary/ Spruce Goose	*hotel, banquet facility Long Beach, Calif*
Sergeant Preston of the Yukon	*television series*
Skippy, The Bush Kangroo	*television series*

Barry Wright Corp.

One Newton Executive Park
Newton Lower Falls, MA 02162
(617) 965-5800

Chief Executive Officer:	Ralph Z. Sorenson
1984 Annual Sales Volume:	202M
1984 Shares Outstanding:	9,041,434
Shareholders:	5,016
Exchange:	NY
Symbol:	BAR

Corporate History: Incorporated in 1934 as Wright Line Inc., Barry Wright Corp. is a diversified industrial company with two industry segments. Wright Line Inc. specializes in products and systems for organizing, filing, accessing and protecting diversified information media. The industrial and Aero products group provides engineered components and systems to control vibration and other dynamic forces and specialized products which improve the efficiency of industrial equipment and flexible automation systems.

Brandnames of Products and Services:

Docu-Mate	*office furniture*
Optimedia	*office furniture*
PC Work Center	*office furniture*
Wright Line Direct	*mail order catalogue*

William Wrigley Jr. Co.

410 N. Michigan Ave.
Chicago, IL 60611
(312) 644-2121

Chief Executive Officer:	William Wrigley
1984 Annual Sales Volume:	591M
1984 Shares Outstanding:	7,038,752
Shareholders:	8,748
Exchange:	NY
Symbol:	WWY

Corporate History: From 1891 to 1903, the company was operated as a proprietorship until its incorporation in Illinois as Wm. Wrigley, Jr. & Co. in December, 1903. It was last incorporated in 1927. Throughout its history, the company has concentrated on one principal line of business: the manufacturing and marketing of quality chewing gum products, which constitute more than 90% of consolidated worldwide sales and revenues.

Brandnames of Products and Services:

Big Red	*gum*
Doublemint	*gum*
Extra	*sugarless gum*
Freedent	*gum*
Hubba Bubba Bubble Gum	*bubble gum*
Juicy Fruit	*gum*
Wrigley's Spearmint	*gum*

Wurlitzer Co.

403 E. Gurler Rd.
DeKalb, IL 60115
(815) 756-2771

Chief Executive Officer:	G.B. Howell
1984 Annual Sales Volume:	63M
1984 Shares Outstanding:	1,786,000
Shareholders:	2,000
Exchange:	NY
Symbol:	WUR

Corporate History: The company incorporated in 1890 as the Rudolph Wurlitzer Co. and adopted its present title in 1957. It is one of the oldest and largest producers of pianos, organs and educational musical instruments in the nation.

Brandnames of Products and Services:

Wurlitzer	*pianos and organs*

Wynn's International, Inc.

2600 Nutwood Ave.
Fullerton, CA 92631
(714) 992-2000

Chief Executive Officer: J.F. Lillicrop
1984 Annual Sales Volume: 214M
1984 Shares Outstanding: 3,705,595
Shareholders: 826
Exchange: NY
Symbol: WN

Corporate History: The company, incorporated in 1973, originally manufactured automotive and petrochemical specialty products as well as sporting goods and recreational equipment. It also distributes hardware to retail dealers. In 1980 the company sold its recreation and sporting goods division. In 1982, the company sold its Cragar wheel business and in 1983, the company sold its Peat Manufacturing die casting business. In 1984, the company acquired substantially all of the assets of Star-Lite Industries, a manufacturer of automotive seat covers, seat cushions, floor mats, and accessories.

Brandnames of Products and Services:

Frostemp	*automobile air conditioners*
Starlite	*automotive seat covers, seat cushions*

Xcor International Inc.

505 International Blvd.
Great Neck, NY 11021
(516) 482-5254

Chief Executive Officer: Edward J. Flinn
1984 Annual Sales Volume: 11M
1984 Shares Outstanding: 3,513,311
Shareholders: 2,080
Exchange: OTC
Symbol: XCORA

Corporate History: The company incorporated in 1971 as Seeburg Industries Inc., a manufacturer of pinball machines. It adopted its present title in 1977. Today it makes musical instruments, hearing aids and audiometers. It spunoff Williams Electronics, which makes pinball machines, in 1981. The musical instruments are manufactured and distributed by the company's French subsidiary throughout Europe and the Far East. In 1984 hearing aids accounted for 64% of sales, audiometers 11% and musical instruments 16%.

Brandnames of Products and Services:

Benge	*trumpets*
Cleveland	*musical instruments*
De Ford	*flutes and piccolos*
Excella	*musical instruments*
Front Row	*theatre, Cleveland, Ohio*
Lemaire	*clarinets*
Malerne	*musical instruments*
Manhasset	*music stands distributor*
Marigaux	*musical instruments*
Qualitone	*hearing aids and accessories*
Strasser	*clarinets*
Tempo	*musical instruments*

Xerox Corp.

P.O. Box 1600
Stamford, CT 06904
(203) 329-8711

Chief Executive Officer: D.T. Kearns
1984 Annual Sales Volume: 8,971M
1984 Shares Outstanding: 95,700,000
Shareholders: 104,000
Exchange: NY
Symbol: XRX

Corporate History: The company was founded and incorporated in 1906 as the Haloid Co., a maker of photographic paper. In 1947 it bought the rights to develop an "electrophotography" machine and in 1959 introduced the commercial photocopier. Xerox became the success story of the 1960s and 1970s. In the 15 years between 1959 and 1974 profits rose from $2 million to $331 million. Today three-quarters of the company's revenues come from the sale and lease of Xerox equipment. In 1984 international operations accounted for 36% of revenues. Because of increased competition, in the photocopy field, Xerox has diversified into publishing, the manufacture of office equipment, and financial services.

Brandnames of Products and Services:

Cheshire	*mailing label equipment*
Diablo	*computer printer*
Ginn	*textbooks publisher*
Telecopier	*facsimile transceiver*
Versatec	*plotters*
Weekly Reader	*classroom periodicals*
Xerox	*office equipment*

Zale Corp.

901 West Walnut Hill Lane
Irving, TX 75038-1003
(214) 257-4000

Chief Executive Officer: Donald Zale
1984 Annual Sales Volume: 1,003M
1984 Shares Outstanding: 11,876,776
Shareholders: 7,836
Exchange: NY
Symbol: ZAL
Corporate History: The company incorporated in 1924 with one retail jewelry store in Wichita Falls, Texas. Today it operates the largest chain of retail jewelry stores in the United States and is the world's largest retailer of diamond jewelry merchandise. The company is involved internationally in the purchasing and wholesaling of diamonds and other precious gems and also operates its own diamond cutting and diamond jewelry manufacturing facilities. It has more than 1,500 retail outlets in 49 states and around the world.
Brandnames of Products and Services:

Aaron Rose	*jewelers*
Argenzio Bros.	*jewelers*
Bailey, Banks & Biddle	*jewelry store*
Bohm-Allen	*jewelry*
Boswells' of Vandevers	*jewelry store*
Brodnax Jewelers	
Corrigan	*jewelers*
Cowell & Hubbard	*retail jewelry*
Dobbins	*jewelry*
Granat Brothers	*jewelry*
Hausmann	*jewelers*
Henry's	*jewelers*
Hershberg's	*jewelers*
Hertzberg	*jewelers*
Hess & Culbertson	*jewelers*
Jaccard's	*jewelry retail*
Jacobs	*jewelers*
Jobe-Rose	*jewelers*
Koerber & Baber	*jewelers*
Levitts	*jewelers*
Litwin	*retail jewelry*
Max Davis	*jewelers*
McNeel's	*jewelers*
Mindlin	*jewelers*
Mission	*jewelers*
Morgan	*jewelers*
O.G. Wilson	*catalogue showrooms*
Pidgeon's	*jewelers*
Rider's	*jewelers*
Rogers	*jewelers*
Rosenfield	*jewelers*
Rosenzweig's	*jewelers*
Selco	*jewelers*
Slavick	*jewelers*
Stifft's	*jewelry*
Stowell	*jewelry*
Wagner's	*jewelry*
Willoughby & Taylor	*direct mail companies*
Wiss & Lambert	*jewelry*
Wolf	*jewelry*
Wright Kay	*jewelry*
Zell Bros.	*jewelry*

Zayre Corp.

770 Cochituate Rd.
Framingham, MA 01701
(617) 620-5000

Chief Executive Officer: Maurice Segall
1984 Annual Sales Volume: 2,614M
1984 Shares Outstanding: 19,784,944
Shareholders: 7,000
Exchange: NY
Symbol: ZY
Corporate History: The company, incorporated in 1962, operates 847 self-service discount department stores and off-price apparel specialty stores in 36 states. In addition, the company has introduced several wholesale warehouse outlets on a test basis.
Brandnames of Products and Services:

BJ's Wholesale Club	*warehouse outlets*
Chadwick's of Boston	*mail order catalogue*
Hit or Miss	*women's apparel stores*
T.J. Maxx	*family apparel stores*
Zayre	*discount department stores*

Zenith Electronics Corp.

1000 Milwaukee Ave.
Glenview, IL 60025
(312) 391-7000

Chief Executive Officer: Jerry K. Pearlman
1984 Annual Sales Volume: 1,716M
1984 Shares Outstanding: 22,144,058

Shareholders: 45,000
Exchange: NY
Symbol: ZE
Corporate History: The company, incorporated in 1958, is a leading manufacturer of television sets, radios, consoles, portable stereo and phonograph sets and video cassette recorders. Zenith remains (with RCA) a market leader in the color T.V. industry and is in a good position to tap the video revolution of the 1980s. A decade ago the company concentrated all its efforts on T.V. and radio products and now aims to be a leading full-line supplier for the emerging home electronic market.
Brandnames of Products and Services:

Heath	*do-it-yourself electronics*
Zenith	*electronic products*

Zimmer Corp.

5801 Congress Ave.
P.O. Box 3058
Boca Raton, FL. 33431
(305) 997-0700

Chief Executive Officer: P.H. Zimmer
1984 Annual Sales Volume: 153M
1984 Shares Outstanding: 4,654,000
Shareholders: 4,500
Exchange: AM
Symbol: ZIM
Corporate History: Zimmer incorporated in 1964 as Princess Homes Inc., as Zimmer Homes Corp. in 1968, and it's present title, Zimmer Corp. in 1982. It designs and manufactures recreational vehicles and mobile homes. In March 1984 Zimmer acquired Black Fin Yacht Corp., a Fort Lauderdale, FL, manufacturer of offshore sportfishing boats.
Brandnames of Products and Services:

Astron	*motor homes*
Black Fin	*yachts*
Duke	*mobile homes*
Mobile Traveler	*recreational vehicles*
MT	*recreational vehicles*
Nashua	*mobile homes*
Viscount	*motor homes*
Windsor	*mobile homes*
Windsor	*vans*
Zimmer	*vans*
Zimmer	*mobile homes*
Zimmer Cabriolet, Elegance Classic, Convertible	*motorcars*

Section III

Largest Foreign Consumer Companies Selling in the United States

Section III

Largest Foreign Consumer Companies Selling in the United States

Foreign Investor: **Agache-Willot Group (France)**

U.S. Company:	% Owned
Korvettes	100

Brandnames

Christian Dior apparel and accessories
Korvettes department stores
Ted Lapidus apparel stores

Foreign Investor: **Ahold N.V. (Netherlands)**

U.S. Company:	% Owned
Bi-Lo	100

Brandnames

Bi-Lo Markets

Foreign Investor: **B.A.T. Industries (United Kingdom)**

U.S. Company:	% Owned
Batus	100

Brandnames

Barclay cigarettes
Belair cigarettes
Brown and Williamson cigarettes
Eagle Star life insurance
Frederick and Nelson wearing apparel
Germaine Monteil creams and lotions
Gimbels department store
Iveys wearing apparel
Kohl supermarkets
Kool cigarettes
Marshall Field sundry goods
Raleigh cigarettes
Richland cigarettes
Saks Fifth Avenue department stores
St. James Court cigarettes
State Express cigarettes
Viceroy cirgarettes

Foreign Investor: **Bayer A.G. (Federal Republic of Germany)**

U.S. Companies:	% Owned
Cutter Laboratories	100
Miles Labs	100

Brandnames

Agfa film
Alka Seltzer
Ames Visidex II diabetes home tests
Bactine first aid antiseptic
Bugs Bunny vitamins
Cutter first aid kits and insect repellants
Flintstone vitamins
One-A-Day vitamins
Sencor weed killer
S.O.S. soap pads

Foreign Investor: **Beecham Ltd. (United Kingdom)**

U.S. Company:	% Owned
Beecham Inc.	100

Brandnames

Ace combs
Andron by Jovan cologne
Aqua Velva after shave lotion
Aquafresh toothpaste
BFI antiseptic powder
Black Label cologne
Brylcreem hair dressings
Calgon bath products
Cling Free fabric softener
Conti shampoo
Fruit Fresh preservative
Geritol liquid and tablet
Hold Cough suppressant
Jovan Musk toiletries
Kellogg's castor oil
Lancaster cosmetics and fragrances
Macleans toothpaste
Massengill feminine hygiene
N'ICE cough lozenges
Sominex 2 sleeping aid
ST37 antiseptic solution
Sucrets lozenges
Vitabath soap and bath additive
Yardley cologne

Foreign Investor: **Brenninkmeyer Family (Netherlands)**

U.S. Companies:	% Owned
Maurice's	100
Ohrbach's	100
The Lodge	100

Brandnames

The Lodge apparel stores

Maurice's apparel stores
Ohrbach's apparel stores

Foreign Investor: **Cadbury Schweppes Ltd. (United Kingdom)**

U.S. Company:	% Owned
Cadbury Schweppes U.S.A.	100

Brandnames

Cadbury candy bars
Grandma's molasses
Holland House cocktail mixes and cooking wines
Mott's apple juice, apple sauce
Peter Paul candy
Powerhouse candy
Rose's lime juice, lime and orange marmalades
Schweppes beverages
York mints

Foreign Investor: **Ciba-Geigy Ltd. (Switzerland)**

U.S. Company:	% Owned
Ciba-Geigy	100

Brandnames

Acutrim reducing pills
Airwick home cleaning products
Binaca breath freshener
Chore Boy scouring pads
Softcolors contact lens
Spectrum lawn care products

Foreign Investor: **Dalgety Ltd. (United Kingdom)**

U.S. Company:	% Owned
Modern Maid Food	100

Brandnames

Modern Maid food products

Foreign Investor: **Delhaize-Le Lion S.A. (Belgium)**

U.S. Companies:	% Owned
Alterman Foods	100
Food Town Stores	52

Brandnames

Alterman Foods
Food Town Stores
Lowe Supermarkets

Foreign Investor: **Dunlop Holdings Ltd. (United Kingdom)**

U.S. Company:	% Owned
Dunlop Tire & Rubber	100

Brandnames

Dunlop tires, tennis balls and other sporting goods
Slazenger sporting goods (tennis balls, racquets, golf balls)

Foreign Investor: **AB Electrolux (Sweden)**

U.S. Company: % Owned

Dometic Inc. 100

Brandnames

Emerson ceiling fan, air conditioner
Eureka vacuum cleaners
Facit small business machines
Quaker Maid kitchen cabinets
Tappan home appliances

Foreign Investor: **Franz Haniel & Cie (Germany)**

U.S. Company: % Owned

Scrivner 100

Brandnames

Best Yet food stores
Food World food stores
Sharps department store, Texas

Foreign Investor: **General Electric Ltd. (United Kingdom)**

U.S. Company: % Owned

A.B. Dick 100

Brandnames

A.B. Dick office equipment
Scriptomatic address labeler

Foreign Investor: **Generale Occidentale S.A. (France)**

U.S. Companies: % Owned

Big Star 100
Grand Union 100

Brandnames

Big Star supermarkets
Grand Union supermarkets

Foreign Investor: **George Weston Ltd. (Canada)**

U.S. Companies: % Owned

Interbake Foods 100
National Tea 84
Stroehmann Brothers 100

Brandnames

F.F.V. bakery goods
National T supermarkets
Stroehmann Brothers bakeries

Foreign Investor: **Grand Metropolitan (United Kingdom)**

U.S. Company:	% Owned
Liggett Group	89

Brandnames

Absolut vodka
Alamo dog food
Alpo dog food
Baileys Irish cream liqueur
Bombay gin
Dorado cigarettes
Eve cigarettes
Grand Marnier liqueur
Intercontinental hotels
J&B whiskey
L&M cigarettes
Red Man tobacco

Foreign Investor: **Imasco Ltd. (Canada)**

U.S. Companies:	% Owned
Hardee's Food Systems	47
Shoppers Drug Mart	100
Tinder Box International	100

Brandnames

Burger Chef restaurants
Hardee's drive in restaurants
Peoples drug stores
Shoppers Drug Mart
Tinder Box tobacco stores

Foreign Investor: **Imperial Group Ltd. (United Kingdom)**

U.S. Company:	% Owned
Howard Johnson	100

Brandnames

Ground Round restaurants
Howard Johnson hotels and restaurants
Lea and Perrins Worcestershire sauce
Red Coach grills

Foreign Investor: **IngC Olivetti and C SpA (Italy)**

U.S. Company:	% Owned
Olivetti Corp.	100

Brandnames

Olivetti business equipment
Underwood business equipment

Foreign Investor: **Nestle S.A. (Switzerland)**

U.S. Companies:	% Owned
Alcon Laboratories	100

Beech-Nut Nutrition Corp.	100
Hills Bros. Coffee Inc.	100
Libby, McNeill & Libby	100
Nestle Co.	100
Stouffer Corp.	100

Brandnames

Beech Nut baby foods
Carnation dog food, evaporated milk
Crosse and Blackwell food specialties
Deer Park sparkling water
Hills Bros. coffee
Libby's canned food products
Nescafe instant coffee
Nestea instant tea
Nestle chocolate bars
Stouffer frozen foods, restaurants, hotels, food vending machines
Sunrise instant coffee
Taster's Choice coffee

Foreign Investor: **Olsen, Lehmkuhl Families (Norway)**

U.S. Company:	% Owned
Timex	100

Brandname

Timex watches and clocks

Foreign Investor: **Reckitt & Colman Ltd. (United Kingdom)**

U.S. Company:	% Owned
Reckitt & Colman (NA)	100

Brandnames

Cattleman's barbecue sauce
French's spices, extracts, sauces, potatoes, foods, cake decorations
Widmer's wines

Foreign Investor: **Sandoz Ltd. (Switzerland)**

U.S. Company:	% Owned
Sandoz U.S.	100

Brandnames

Meritene vitamin supplement
Northrup King seeds
Ovaltine beverage mixes
Triaminic cough/cold preparation

Foreign Investor: **Seagram Co. Ltd (Canada)**

U.S. Company:	% Owned
Joseph E. Seagram & Sons	100

Brandnames

Boodles gin
Calvert whiskey
Chivas Regal scotch whiskey
Christian Brothers

Glenlivet scotch whiskey
Kessler whiskey
Mumms champagne and cognac
Nikolai vodka
Seagram's whiskey
Taylor wines
Tuaca liqueur
Wolfschmidt vodka

Foreign Investor: **Sony Corp (Japan) (See Domestic Section)**

U.S. Company:	% Owned
Sony Corp. of America	100

Foreign Investor: **Thomson Newspapers Ltd. (Canada)**

U.S. Company:	% Owned
Thomson Newspapers Inc.	100

Brandnames

Dothan (Ala.) Eagle (e-S)
Enterprise (Ala.) Ledger (e-S)
Opelika (Ala.) News (e-S)
Douglas (Ariz.) Dispatch (e)
Fayetteville (Ark.) Northwest Arkansas Times (e-S)
Barstow (Calif.) Desert Dispatch (e)
Eureka (Calif.) Times-Standard (e-S)
Oxnard (Calif.) Press-Courier (e-S)
West Covina (Calif.) San Gabriel Valley Daily Tribune (m-S)
Whittier (Calif.) Daily News (e-S)
Yreka (Calif.) Siskiyou Daily News (e)
Ansonia (Conn.) Evening Sentinel (e)
Key West (Fla.) Citizen (e-S)
Marianna (Fla.) Jackson County Floridan (e-S)
Orange Park (Fla.) Clay Today (e)
Punta Gorda (Fla.) Herald-News (e)
Americus (Ga.) Times-Reporter (e)
Cordele (Ga.) Dispatch (e)
Dalton (Ga.) Daily Citizen-News (e)
Griffin (Ga.) Daily News (e)
Thomasville (Ga.) Times-Enterprise (e)
Tifton (Ga.) Gazette (e)
Valdosta (Ga.) Daily Times (e-S)
Jacksonville (Ill.) Journal-Courier (m-e-S)
Mt. Vernon (Ill.) Register-News (e)
Kokomo (Ind.) Tribune (e-S)
New Albany (Ind.) Tribune (e), Ledger & Tribune (S)
Council Bluffs (Iowa) Nonpareil (e-S)
Oelwein (Iowa) Daily Register (e)
Atchinson (Kan.) Daily Globe (e-S)
Leavenworth (Kans.) Times (e-S)
Corbin (Ky.) Times-Tribune (e-S)
Lafayette (La.) Daily Advertiser (e-S)
Salisbury (Md.) Daily Times (e-S)
Fitchburg-Leominster (Mass.) Daily Sentinel and Enterprise (e)
Waltham (Mass.) News-Tribune (e)
Taunton (Mass.) Daily Gazette (e)

Adrian (Mich.) Daily Telegram (e)
Escanaba (Mich.) Daily Press (e)
Houghton (Mich.) Mining Gazette (e)
Iron Mountain (Mich.) Daily News (e)
Marquette (Mich.) Mining Journal (e)
Albert Lea (Minn.) Evening Tribune (e-S)
Austin (Minn.) Daily Herald (e)
Laurel (Miss.) Leader-Call (e)
Cape Girardeau (Mo.) Southeast Missourian (e-S)
Carthage (Mo.) Press (e)
Sikeston (Mo.) Daily Standard (e-S)
Portsmouth (N.H.) Herald (e-S)
Herkimer (N.Y.) Evening Telegram (e)
Newburgh (N.Y.) Evening News (e-S)
Oswego (N.Y.) Palladium-Times (e)
Florence (S.C.) Morning News (m-S)
Rocky Mount (N.C.) Evening Telegram (e-S)
Canton (O.) Repository (e-S)
Coshocton (O.) Tribune (e-S)
East Liverpool (O.) Evening Review (e)
Greenville (O.) Daily Advocate (e)
Lancaster (O.) Eagle-Gazette (e)
Marion (O.) Star (e-S)
Middletown (O.) Journal (e-S)
Newark (O.) Advocate (e-S)
Piqua (O.) Daily Call (e)
Portsmouth (O.) Times (e)
Salem (O.) News (e)
Steubenville (O.) Herald-Star (e-S)
Xenia (O.) Daily Gazette (e)
Zanesville (O.) Times Recorder (m-S)
Ada (Okla.) Evening News (e-S)
Altoona (Pa.) Mirror (e)
Connellsville (Pa.) Daily Courier (e)
Easton (Pa.) Express (e-S)
Greenville (Pa.) Record Argus (e)
Hanover (Pa.) Evening Sun (e)
Kittanning (Pa.) Leader-Times (e)
Lebanon (Pa.) News Pennsylvanian (e-S)
Lock Haven (Pa.) Express (e)
Meadville (Pa.) Tribune (m)
Monessen (Pa.) Valley Independent (e)
Mitchell (S.D.) Republic (e)
St. George (Ut.) Spectrum (e-S)
Petersburg (Va.) Progress-Index (e-S)
Fairmont (W.Va.) Times-West Virginian (m-S)
Weirton (W.Va.) Daily Times (e)
Appleton (Wis.) Post Crescent (e-S)
Fond du Lac (Wis.) Reporter (e-S)
Manitowoc (Wis.) Herald-Times-Reporter (e-S)
Waukesha (Wis.) Freeman (e)
Wisconsin Rapids (Wis.) Daily Tribune (e)

Foreign Investor: **Thorn EMI Ltd. (United Kingdom)**

U.S. Company:	% Owned
Capitol Ind-EMI	100

Brandnames

Capitol records and tapes

EMI America records
Thorn EMI records and tapes

Foreign Investor: **Unilever N.V. (Netherlands)**

U.S. Companies:	% Owned
Lever Bros.	100
Thomas J. Lipton	100

Brandnames

Aim toothpaste
All detergent
Caress soap
Close-Up toothpaste
Dove soap
Good Humor ice cream
Imperial margarine
Knox gelatine
Lawry's seasonings
Lipton tea and soups
Mrs. Butterworth's syrup
Spatini spaghetti sauce
Wish-Bone salad dressings
Wisk detergent

Foreign Investor: **United Biscuits Holdings Ltd. (United Kingdom)**

U.S. Companies:	% Owned
Keebler	100
Specialty Brands	90

Brandnames

Animal crackers
Bacon Toast crackers
Butter Flavored Thins cookies
Butter 100s cookies
Butter Pretzel Braids
Butter Pretzel Knots
Butter Pretzel Nibblers
C.C. Biggs cookies
Cheddars cracker
Chedo cracker
Cheese Shindigs cracker
Chocolate Chip 100s cookie
Chocolate Fudge Sandwich cookie
Cinnamon Crisp cookie
Cinnamon Sugar 100s cookie
Club Crackers
Coconut Chocolate Drops cookie
Danish Wedding cookie
Deluxe Grahams cracker
Double Nutty cookie
Elfwich cookie
Export Soda cracker
Fig Bars cookie
French Vanilla Creme cookie
Fudge Creme cookie
Fudge Marshmallow cookie
Fudge Nutty cookie
Fudge Sticks cookie
Fudge Stripes cookie

Ginger Snaps 100s cookie
Honey Grahams cracker
Ice Cream Cups cookie
Iced Animal 100s cookie
Iced Oatmeal cookie
Iced Oatmeal & Raisin cookie
Iced Raisin Bar cookie
Krisp Kreem coookie
Milk Lunch Biscuit
McDonaldland cookie
Nacho Cheese Snackfood
Old Fashion Oatmeal cookie
Old Fashion Sugar cookie
Onion Toast cookie
Opera Creme Sandwich cookie
Pecan Sandies cookie
Pitter Patter cookies
Pizza Shindigs cracker
Pumpernickel Toast cracker
Rich 'n Chips snackfood
Rye Toast
Savory Sesame cracker
Sea Toast cracker
Sesame Sticks snackfood
Sesame Toast cracker
Snax-Pax snackfood
Soup & Oyster cracker
Sour Creme & Onion Shindigs cracker
Spice Islands seasonings
Spiced Windmill cookies
Sugar Cones cookies
Town House cookies
Tuc Crackers
Vanilla Cremes cookies
Vanilla Wafers cookies
Waldorf Low Sodium cracker
Wheat Crisps cracker
Wheat Toast
Zesta Saltines
Zesta Unsalted Top cracker

Foreign Investor: **Wellcome Fdtn. (United Kingdom)**

U.S. Company:	% Owned
Burroughs Wellcome	100

Brandnames

Borofax ointment
Empirin analgesic
Emprazil cold product
Marezine motion sickness product
Neosporin burn and cut ointment
Polystorin ointment
Sudafed cough and cold products
Zincofax skin cream for diaper rash

Section IV

Index

A

B

C

D

E

F

G

H

I

J

K

L

M

N

O

P

Q

R

S

T

U

V

W

X

Y

Z

0

1

2

3

4

5

6

7

9